THE LETTERS

OF

LEWIS, RICHARD, WILLIAM and JOHN MORRIS,

of Anglesey,

(Morrisiaid Mon)

1728—1765.

Transcribed from the Originals and Edited by

JOHN H. DAVIES, M.A.

VOL. I.

ABERYSTWYTH:
Published privately by the Editor and printed for him by
Fox, Jones & Co., Kemp Hall, Oxford.
1907.

Three Hundred Copies of this Book
have been printed for Subscribers
on O.W. hand-made paper.

No ....

THIS BOOK

IS

Dedicated

TO

THE MEMORY OF

Sir Lewis Morris

of Penbryn, Carmarthen,

THE DISTINGUISHED DESCENDANT OF LEWIS MORRIS
(LLEWELYN DDU O FON).

Grawn gwin ac aeron a gaid
Ar bren ir o'r barwniaid;
Ysbys i dengys bob dyn,
O ba radd y bo'i wreiddyn.
O ffrwyth achos ffrith uchel
Y ceidw dâst y coed y dêl.

Pen. MSS. 110, f. 82.

ON FOUR PATRIOT BROTHERS.

PROŒMIUM

BY

SIR LEWIS MORRIS

Four patriot brothers of the Cymric race,
Of low estate, but sprung from gentle blood,
These letters hidden long, shall serve to trace
Their life-long love for Gwalia and her good.

All held their country dear, all prized as we
Her long heroic Past, her ancient tongue
That blossoms still, her strong sons' bravery,
Her songs, by lover and by warrior sung.

Here, through their own quaint use of either speech
We know them, now their native accents tell
Their story, now in nervous Saxon each
Brother to brother speaks, and both are well.

Here no unreal eulogy arrays
The dead in robes not theirs, nor partial hand
Conceals 'neath insincere or venal praise,
Foibles, it profits well to understand.

But each fraternal soul with loving care
Reveals itself; unchanged through time and change
And absence, still its inner thought lays bare
Nor thro' the estranging mists of years grows strange.

But frank and boyish still, can ne'er forget
'Mid service of the State and pride of place
The farm, the handicraft, and lingering yet—
The sire's shrewd wit, the mother's kindly grace.

Thus in close concord, lived they, till the call
Sounded too soon, which comes alike to all,
And severed here the gracious brotherhood
Knit fast by patriot aims and common blood.

* * * * * *

John, first, the bright young sailor comes, whose life
Perished 'neath Carthagena's frowning wall,
Falling in conquering Britain's world-wide strife,
As still, to-day, her youthful lives must fall.

A new, yet henceforth, a beloved name,
Frank, bold, warm-hearted, whom his mother's heart
Mourned long, who went too soon, may be, for fame
But not to have played, and well, his manly part.

Then gentle William, whose home-keeping thought
Strayed never far from Mona's wind-swept shore,
Whom Nature—herb, shell, flower, and fossil—taught
To reverence her Maker, more and more.

Nor loved these only, but to bring to light
The buried Cymric lore, his kindly hand
Sowed broadcast, not for lucre, oer the land
Treasures half-hidden, or forgotten quite.

Dear to his brethren, dear to Wales, to all
Who loved the unselfish care which freely gave
Rich store, which heard the buried ages call
And raised them from oblivion and the grave.

Then Richard, who 'mid London's emulous throng
Rose high, from "Môn the Mother," exiled far,
And served content, laborious years and long
Our thundering navies, waging ceaseless war.

Yet still remembered Gwalia and the debt
He owed her, and her sons, and willing lent
His scanty leisure hours, nor could forget
Those, who 'mid alien myriads, lonely, spent,

Pined for her, but with Lewis toiled to bind
A link of union, which renewed to-day
Knits Cymric lives together heart and mind
And cheers the exile's solitary way.

Who, when his life-long toil seemed now complete,
Gave all his native learning to make plain
In the old tongue the Word, to guide men's feet
On the strait Heavenward path, nor toiled in vain.

And Lewis, chief of all and noblest far
My dear sire's grandsire, whose protecting hand
Long saved Goronwy from himself, a star
Waking the brooding twilight of his land.

Who lived for her, yet loved his Britain well
Artificer, musician, scholar, bard,
Philosopher, antiquary, who men tell
With wonder, no achievement found too hard.

Wise, many-tongued, like his young kinsman great*
Who sang, how freemen best can build the State,
The blameless poet-jurist long at rest
Here, beneath Paul's high dome, there, with the Blest.

Who with skilled hand the Celtic roots laid bare
Where-from in name and speech our Gwalia grew,
The annals buried deep, the fancies fair,
The hoary faiths our dim forefathers knew.

Who framed the harp with fingers deft and strong
And drew his music from it, who could build
A bark and sail it forth, a seaman skilled,
Or pen an Ode and wing its words with song,

And traced the hidden secrets of the mine,
And mapped the treacherous shallows of the sea ;
Strong soul, of all these lavish gains of thine
Nought, but the gift of verse, descends to me !

But more than all the conquests of his brain ;
His generous hand I prize, his noble heart,
To which no struggling bard appealed in vain
For help or guidance in his sacred Art.

And yet the jealous schemers year by year
Assailed him, planned his fall, denied his skill,
With violence drove him forth in mortal fear
(Hard lot is his, who scales the Olympian Hill !)

* Sir William Jones, see Lord Teignmouth's Life.

To the cold Guelphic London, far away,
Sickening for home, to meet alone the hate
Of selfish men, the cruel law's delay
The jealousies of the intriguing Great.

And face them long, unfriended, unafraid
"The proud, hot Welshman" who the Crown's high trust
Never through all that weary strife betrayed,
But kept the scornful silence of the just.

Till at the last, when the long fight was done,
Broken in frame, although with victory won,
Leaving the Law's chicane, the knavish great,
He turned contented, though of poor estate,

To the scarred hill-side, and forsaken deep
Of lone Goginan, there he knew at length
The homely restful life, the new found strength
Of sitting still, the nights' untroubled sleep.

Tending his brood of childish lives, the wife
He loved so well, aiding his neighbours round
With simple leechcraft, rapt in dreams profound
Of science and the riddle of our life;

Now, like some fabled alchemist of old,
Armed with retort and crucible, the ore
Of his loved hills assayed, now mid the lore
Of Celtic annals delved and won their gold;

Now grappling with the Electric Mysteries
Now penning the swift Englyn or high Ode,
Watching contented, 'neath the autumnal skies
His ruddy orchards bear their yearly load.

As they bear still, and I, as doth indeed
How many a pilgrim from the Atlantic main!
Last Autumn, tasting, sowed a little seed
In memory of that precious heart and brain;

And him who to the last a patriot yet,
Through cares and painful age and limbs outworn,
Did never the old race and tongue forget,
Nor the lone, wind-swept isle, where he was born.

* * * * * *

Good brothers, Lewis, Richard, William, John,
The fire ye kindled burns unfailing on;
Dead nigh two ages, but remembered yet
May these your words, forbid men to forget!

I would ye might return to earth and view
By "dark Llewelyn's" grave, the stately shrine
The peasants reared, where, youths and maids combine
In emulous studies, part inspired by you.

I would ye might return awhile and know
The awakening of the subtle Cymric brain,
And see to what high fates your Wales doth grow,
And mark your brotherhood renewed again;

Four brothers of your blood, alike in name,*
All looking to the Wales that is to be,
And one who, of the patriot company
Of Pioneers, enjoying modest fame

At Penbryn,† like his ancestor, grows old,
Leaving the din, the dust, the soil of Town
And hastening, ere his heart and brain grow cold,
With these last strains his bardic lyre lays down.

Good brothers, worthy patriots, faithful, just!
I, who have lived my life and loved you long,
Bring this hereditary wreath of song
And lay it willing on your honoured dust!

And bless the pious hands which long time kept
These ancient records, while our Gwalia slept,
And murmur o'er each lone ancestral grave
O Dad yn dy dangnefedd, cadw ef!

LEWIS MORRIS, Penbryn.

* Lewis, William, John, Charles.

† In Carmarthenshire.

[Just as I was revising the last proofs of this volume there came the sad news of the death of Sir Lewis Morris. He had been for many years most anxious that the Letters should be published, and in many ways he helped to bring this about. He took an intense interest in every detail regarding his great ancestor and read the parts as they were published with the keenest avidity. He was also good enough to write the Poem, which will be found at the beginning of this volume, expressly for the book. It has a pathetic interest as it was probably the last poem he wrote. A few weeks ago I had the pleasure of accompanying him to Galltvadog, the secluded hill-side farm in Cardiganshire, where Lewis Morris lived from 1746 to 1757. We sat in the low, old-fashioned kitchen with its sturdy oak beams, and read over some of the letters written there by Lewis Morris one hundred and fifty years ago. Sir Lewis had long waited for an opportunity to visit the spot and it would be difficult to exaggerate the delight he took in examining the house and rambling about its grounds. His conversation that afternoon was full of interesting reminiscences of the distinguished persons he had met, and his kindly, childlike nature was seen at its best. I had dedicated the book to him, and I looked forward with pleasure to presenting him with the complete volume. Alas! this is now impossible.—J. H. D.]

INTRODUCTION.

THE four brothers, whose letters have been collected together in this work, were the sons of Morys ap Richard Morys, of Pentre Eirianell, in the parish of Penrhos Lligwy, Anglesey, and his wife Margaret, the daughter of Morys Owen of Bodafon y Glyn. On the father's side they were descended from the ancient family of Bulkeley, and on the mother's side they were connected with several old Carnarvonshire families. Morys ap Richard Morys or Morris Prichard, was a carpenter and cooper, and it appears that several members of the family had achieved a considerable reputation as skilful and ingenious craftsmen. His wife, Margaret Owen, was one of the daughters of a reputable farmer in the same district. For some reason or other, perhaps owing to the lowly circumstances of the young lover, Morris Owen, her father did not regard the courtship of the two young people with favour. At any rate Morris Prichard found it necessary to induce his Juliet to consent to a secret marriage, and the tradition goes that one night she escaped through the window of her father's abode at her lover's behest, and was hastily married to him on the spot by an unbenificed clergyman, who had been prevailed upon to become accomplice in the plot. After the ceremony had been performed the bride returned to the safe custody of her father's house, telling nobody of the incident. This occurred in the month of June, 1699.* But the secret could not be long kept. A few months later Margaret Morris had gone to the fair, known as Ffair Wyl Ifan, at

*The authority for this and the subsequent statement is to be found in the MS. notes of John William Prichard, Plasybrain, preserved in a copy of "Diddanwch Teuluaidd" at the Cardiff Free Library, and copied for me through the kind offices of Mr. Ballinger by Mr. J. Ifano Jones.

Bangor. Her husband did not accompany her but remained at his home Tyddyn Melus. Some time in the course of the afternoon a rumour reached Morris Prichard that the ferry boat at Menai Bridge had capsized, and that all the occupants had been drowned, with the sole exception of one woman. The young swain was beside himself with grief, and started off at once for the scene of the disaster, fearful lest his young wife should have been of the number drowned. However to his great joy, the first person he met as, spent and exhausted, he reached the shores of the Menai Straits, was his wife Margaret, who it appears had crossed by another boat. This incident had such an effect upon them, says the chronicler, that they there and then decided to face the bride's parents and declare their secret. So they returned to Bodafon y Glyn and were received with kindness and never did the bride's family express any grief or discontent at the marriage. This story, says J. W. Prichard, was related to him by his father, one Richard William of Plas Gronw, to whom it had been told by Morris Prichard himself. The three eldest sons of this romantic union were born at Tyddyn Melus in the parish of Llanfihangel Tre'r Beirdd, and they were all duly baptized in the parish church—Lewis on March 2nd, 1700-1; Richard on February the 7th, 1702-3; and William on May the 6th, 1705. As a lad Lewis showed signs of great ability, but owing to the straightened circunstances of his parents he got very little schooling, and whatever learning he had in subsequent years was picked up by self-application to his studies in his leisure time. The three brothers being much of an age played together, and together learnt the elements of their father's craft. William in one of his letters refers to the happy times when they ran about naked on the Dulas sands, and shared all spoils in common, and their affection for one another is evident throughout their correspondence in later years.

From a very early age they were imbued with a love for poetry and literature and entered with zest into the literary life of the island, such as it was. Among the Morris Manuscripts preserved at the British Museum is a large collection of songs and local ballads collected by Richard Morris when quite a youth,* and the Editor has

* Additional MSS. 14992.

in his possession an MS. of old Welsh Poetry copied by Lewis Morris in April, 1726.* In 1728 Lewis Morris was one of the chief protagonists in a kind of bardic duel between the poets of Carnarvonshire and Anglesey, and it was on this occasion that he proved his superiority over all his contemporaries in the mastery of the Welsh alliterative metres. On the 9th of July, 1729, Lewis was appointed to the post of waiter and searcher at the Customs at Beaumaris and Holyhead, a post which he held up to March 15th, 1743, when his brother-in-law, Owen Davies, superseded him. On March 29th, 1729, he married Elizabeth Griffiths of Tywridyn, Rhoscolyn, a young girl sixteen years old, and in her right became entitled to a small estate in the county.† By her he had three children, Lewis, Margaret and Elen. Lewis died young, but the two daughters are frequently referred to in the letters. In addition to his work as a Government official, it appears that he was in frequent request as a surveyor, and it was probably in this capacity that he became acquainted with Mr. Owen Meyrick, of Bodorgan, an acquaintance which proved of great assistance to him and his brothers in their efforts at self-advancement. In the year 1737 he was engaged by the Admiralty to make a survey of the coast of Wales, a work which he subsequently completed and published in the year 1748. For the purposes of this survey, he was granted the use of a well-equipped vessel, in which he made the complete tour of the coast. He was also employed by the Crown in 1744 to make a survey of the Manor of Perfedd in North Cardiganshire, and it was probably in this way that he became acquainted with the possibilities of the lead industry there, which eventually resulted in his being appointed in 1746, deputy steward of the Crown Manors in Cardiganshire.‡ Most of his poetry was written during the period he resided in Holyhead as a Customs House officer; for after he went to reside to Cardiganshire he had little or no leisure for creative literary work, though he compiled his dictionary of Celtic proper names at odd times during the last ten years of his life. In the year 1735, he set up a printing-press at Holyhead with the intention of printing selections from Welsh

*See Hist. MSS. Catalogue, vol. ii p. 903.
†*v.* page 90.
‡Cymmrodor xv. p. 5, 84.

literature; but the speculation was not successful, and after publishing two parts, of eight pages each, of his periodical he gave it up.* He next proposed, in April, 1736, to print by subscription a treatise called "Chwedlau Doethion Rhufain; or, The Tales of the Wise Men of Rome," but it does not appear that this treatise was ever published. His interest in Welsh literature never slackened, and to the end of his days he remained a patron of Welsh poets, and an ardent collector of manuscripts and books relating to the history and literature of the country. On the 20th October, 1749, he married Anne Lloyd of Penbryn as his second wife, and she became the mother of a numerous family of six sons and four daughters.

The story of his connection with the Cardiganshire Lead Mines has been admirably told by Mr. Lleufer Thomas in his article in the *Cymmrodor*, Vol. XV., which every reader of these Letters should consult. It will be convenient, however, to explain the nature of the troubles and difficulties which harassed him and made it necessary for him to remain in London for lengthy periods of time. Soon after Morris's appointment to the deputy stewardship of the Crown Manors in Cardiganshire, his superior, William Corbett, became engaged in litigation with Thomas Pryse, of Gogerddan. Corbett, together with one Charles Richards, (possibly of Penglais) had leased certain lands from the Crown for the purpose of sinking for lead, and the partners had been resisted by Thomas Pryse, probably on the ground that the land belonged to him. This was the first of a long series of law-suits in which Lewis Morris was engaged. Sometime in the year 1751 two workmen discovered rich deposits of lead ore at Esgair Mwyn†, a place situated in the parcel of Gwnnws, about halfway between Pontrhydfendigaid and Ysbytty Ystwyth, and not far from Crosswood, the seat of Lord Lisburne. In his capacity as Crown Steward, Morris let the mine for the term of one year, from July 1st, 1751, to three working miners (Evan Williams, John and David Morgan) at the rent of 10s. for every ton of ore raised. These men being

* This periodical, which is called "Tlysau yr Hen Oesoedd," was reproduced in facsimile by the late Mr. Isaac Foulkes of Liverpool.

† See pp. 214, 215.

ignorant and unable to carry the business through took Lewis Morris into partnership, but not until he had informed the Treasury of the transaction. The mine turned out to be exceptionally rich, so that the partners cleared (according to William Morris) about £4,000 in the first year. After the expiration of the year's lease, the Treasury appointed Morris, on July 15th 1752, Agent and Superintendent of the Esgair Mwyn mine ‡. The Crown warrant gave him "full power and authority by himself and his assistants and workmen to open and work and manage as well the said mines discovered [Esgair Mwyn] or to be discovered and belonging to His Majesty in the places aforesaid for His Majesty's use and best advantage during his pleasure." In pursuance of this authority Morris set about developing the mine with great energy. But the success of the mine awakened the greed of the adjacent gentry, and several of them, including Lord Lisburne and the Rev. William Powell of Nanteos, immediately began to contest the Crown's claims. Their first step was to gain posession of the mine itself, and this they duly proceeded to do, taking Lewis Morris prisoner and carrying him to Cardigan gaol (see page 223). The claimants being now in posession of the mine worked it for their own profit, but they were soon forced to deliver up posession to the Crown, pending the trial. In due course Lewis Morris was released from gaol, and was soon immersed in preparation for the trial. The legal proceedings, however, lasted a long time, and it was not until the 24th May, 1754 (fifteen months after the mine had been seized), that the Crown eventually established its claim. Lewis Morris wrote an account of the whole transaction in the form of a Scripture narrative, which he entitled "The First Book of the Chronicles of ye Mines." This narrative verges upon blasphemy in places, and is also too long for reproduction, but it appears from it that the Rev. William Powell of Nanteos, who had recently inherited the estate, was the chief instigator of the trouble. He induced Lord Lisburne to join with him in the proceedings, much to the latter's eventual discomfiture, for after the verdict had been given it turned out that Lord Lisburne was heavily in arrears to the Crown for Manorial rents. As a sample

Introduction contd.

‡ Addit. 15025, p. 150

Introduction contd.

of this production the following which describes the onslaught on the mine, will serve :—

CHAPTER 2.

When the morning was come the chief rulers took council how they might put the king's servant (i.e., Lewis Morris) to death. Then came Josiah from the king's servants, who also betrayed them unto Herber Mc Walter (Herbert Lloyd of Peterwell *) saying " Behold the king's servants are many in number like grass-hoppers on the face of the earth, and moreover they have weapons and cannons among them. Come therefore do wisely. Entice them out of their camp, encompass them on every side, and surprise them unawares, that you may by some means stop their thunder, for if they speak you will all perish." These sayings pleased them well and he passed through the Vale of Florida (Strata Florida) covered with brass from head to foot, and his spear was like a yard which three taylors could hardly lift, and he said in his heart, I defy the armies of any king living. And he met his army at Phebipolis or the Sun tavern at the ford, and encamped where they kept the market of oxen on the top of Pisgah (i.e. at Ffair Rhôs) over against ye king's servant, and his army consisted of horse and foot followed by women and baggage, and they had asses and mules in abundance to carry off the spoil. And he sent on the east side of them 151, on ye west 151, on ye north 151, and on ye south he sent 151, and they were in all 604, all men of valour that drew the sword.

CHAPTER 3.

And when the sun came over the valley of ye Caronian shepherds, so the king's servants saw the neighbouring hills covered with men in number like the sands of ye sea. And there were among them several of ye nation of the Torybites and of the nation of Jacobites that rode upon wild mountain horses with long tails and manes like lions. And Herber McWalter, Jones sad dog, the false prophet (probably George Jones of Rhoscellan), and Illtudus, the scribe,† were at the head of them with fire in their hands, ordering them in battle array. And the king's servants sent messengers unto them, to ask them saying, are your hearts set upon peace or war? And they answered and said, our forefathers have left us a law : "he that

* Sir Herbert Lloyd was the son of Walter Lloyd.

† One Illtud Evans was Mayor of Aberystwyth in 1753. He appears to have been a lawyer, see *Aberystwyth and its Court Leet*, by G. Eyre Evans, p. 12.

refuseth to give, compel him with a strong hand," and we have added thereto, "he that borrows let him never pay," and they said come out to us and we will treat of peace. And they enticed the king's servant (Lewis Morris) out of ye camp with fair words and then they said unto him, "Lo, the King hath given us a power to send thee to prison, and there thou must remain till thou payest fine and ransom." And they imprisoned the king's servant and took possession of the king's treasures and carried them to their own houses, and they rifled the king's houses and turned out his people, and spared neither young nor old nor the women in labour."*

Introduction contd.

Lewis Morris continues in the same strain to describe the subsequent proceedings. No doubt he relieved his feelings in this manner, and probably wrote it for the benefit of his brother Richard and his London friends.

For the rest of his life Morris was never quit of litigation, and his latter years were clouded by the need of providing for a young and numerous family. He also suffered from a complication of physical ailments, to which he finally succumbed on April 11th, 1765. A contemporary described him in the following terms:

*Through the kindness of my friend Mr. Richard Ellis, B.A., Welsh Librarian at the University College of Wales, I am able to re-produce the following letter, which throws considerable light on the personnel of the attacking party:—Cardigan, March 20th, 1753.—Dear Cozin ... Mr. Herbert Lloyd supported by the Deputy Sheriff and a rabble of about 200 people, who they were pleased to dub with the title of the Posse of the County, made lately a most audacious attack upon the King's Mines in this County:—he in conjunction with George Jones a crasey and unqualifyed Justice of our County under pretence of executing the Laws against forceible entrys, sent Mr. Lewis Morris, the King's chief agent, to this gaol, dispersed the under agents and miners, and put the rioters in possession. But these violent proceedings did not hold long. The agent was removed by Habeas Corpus and is gone from hence in his way for London. Aberystwyth is now filled with soldiers, and the Lieftenant and Custos Rotulorum of the county are ordered to attend to quarter the forces to make a proper inquiry into this proceeding and to report it to the Government. And it is to be hoped the rioters and their ringleaders will be rewarded according to their merits. Mr. Morris, when a prisoner here, informed me that when this bold attack was made there was about £8,000 worth of [ore] in the store houses and on the banks, and that the mine alone whillst it continues as it now is will produce to the King above £10,000 per annum clear profit. I own it is a valluable bone of contention, but peace and a competency is far more eligible in the oppinion of, dear sir, your most affectionate kinsman and humble servant, J—— Morgan.

Introduction contd.

"He was a strong and active man, of handsome mien, jovial and witty, and beloved wherever he went. It is a thousand to one that Wales will ever see his like again, particularly as to his general attainments and his genius in mechanics. He was a credit to Wales while he lived, and he deserves the praise of all who cherish her ancient tongue and honour the history of their ancestors."

It will be necessary to return to some other aspects of Lewis Morris's life in the preface to the second volume of this work, as we have only barely touched upon his connection with Welsh Literature, and the part he played as patron to those two ill-starred sons of Wales: Goronwy Owen and Ieuan Brydydd Hir.

RICHARD MORRIS, the second brother appears to have gone to London about the year 1721 or 1722.* The first letter from him in this work is dated from London, the 20th of March, 1728. He does not seem to have settled down in a regular situation for some years, but apparently lived a hand-to-mouth existence. By profession he was an accountant, and it was probably due to the ability he showed in dealing with the accounts of the estate of Lord Londonderry, who died in 1729, that he owed his berth in the Navy Office. It is difficult to piece together the few stray facts that we possess regarding his life in London prior to 1740. Like his brother Lewis, he was in his younger days a jovial, rollicking young fellow, fond of wine and song. Much of his poetry is still preserved in manuscript in the British Museum,† and it is from this volume that we glean the following facts.

It appears that Richard became surety for one John Wade, who subsequently failed or decamped. At any rate Richard's goods were sold, and as he had not sufficient to meet the creditors he was put into the Fleet Prison for debt, where he remained for a whole year. During this period he wrote a great deal of poetry, in which he bemoaned his sad estate, and some of this poetry is well worth preservation. The following englynion were written in 1737.

*This appears from a letter he wrote on the 15th June, 1771, to a Mrs. Penny, in which he states that he had been fifty years out of Wales. In a letter sent to Goronwy Owen about the same time, he says that he is in the 70th year of his age and the 50th year of his sojourn in London.

† Addit. MSS. 14929.

AR FY NGHYSTUDDIAU, &c., YNG NGHAERLUDD.

Tair ar ddeg, rhi' deg ar hugain—fy oed
Pan fu adwyth milain
I'm gorfod, syndod y sain
Uchel a chwerw fy ochain!

Yngharchar, mewn alar, yn wylo—bum
Beunydd yn penydio,
Flwyddyn yn erchyll floeddio
A'm càn oedd myned o'm cô'.

Blinwyd fi'n dost dair blynedd—yn Llundain
A llawnder anhunedd
Diolch, Amen, i'r Senedd
O mhoen a roddes i'm hêdd,

Tra'r wyf iach, bellach, heb ballu—gwiliaf
Bob gelyn, rwy'n credu;
Mae'n rhaid, o f'enaid am fu,
I Forys edifaru.

Ni chymraf, ni roddaf i'r un—o goel
Gwelaf fod yn wrthun;
Ni flina mhen am wenfun,
Y baw am dy gwmni bûn.

Felly yn dra hy, drwy hedd,—iawn allu
Enillaf anrhydedd:
A byw'n ddi rain heb gamwedd,
O hyd drwy'r byd, draw i'r bedd.

He also appears to have been unfortunate in his first marriage, though few particulars can be gleaned as to this. He eked out his livelihood by acting as interpreter in the Law Courts, and by supervising the printing of Welsh books in London. He also indexed the Welsh manuscripts of Moses Williams, which had been purchased by William Jones, the mathematician, and these indexes are still preserved in the Llanstephan collection.

In 1742, through the good offices of the Rev. Thomas Ellis, Vicar of Holyhead, he was recommended to the Bishop of Bangor as a person well-fitted to correct and revise the proofs of some Welsh pamphlets about to be printed in London.* In 1744 he was appointed to revise the edition of the Welsh Bible which was then being printed by the S.P.C.K.,† and this was the means of bringing him into considerable prominence. The Bible was issued in 1746, and a subsequent edition in 1752.‡

* See page 66, 67. † See page 80. ‡ See Bible in Wales, 1907, pp. 42-44.

Introduction contd.

He and his brother Lewis were the founders of the Honourable Society of Cymmrodorion in 1751, and through the means of the Society, and by their own personal efforts, they succeeded in interesting all classes of Welshmen in the history and literature of their native land. The letters bear eloquent testimony to the continual help and support they afforded to Welsh literati. Richard outlived all his brothers, dying in the year 1779. Lewis Morris wrote a long and interesting description of Richard in a letter to William, which will be found in the second volume, and this description though not altogether complimentary, gives us a very clear view of the essential kindliness of his character:

> Hwyl fab ei dad yw Rhisiart, nid da gantho ai cynghoro, ag etto fe wyr fod y cynghor yn dda, ag ai canlyn feallai, ond ei gael wrth siawns. Positive, precipitate, indefatigable, quick enough and ingenious, but too credulous. Loves his country to excess and for that reason his countrymen, who all impose upon him that he deals with, and he choses to deal with them because they are his countrymen. I would for my part sooner deal with a Turk or a Jew than with a London Welshman. He owns they are rogues, but like the hare, he loves to lie near the dog kennel. I am afraid that foolish meeting of Cymmrodorion will make an end of him, for he stays there till one, two, three or four in the morning, and sometimes comes as far as his door (or has done it), and there sleeps till the watch awake him. . . . . There is no Welshman in London hardly but what has been with their common father (the Llywydd)* borrowing money. I have endeavoured to banter him out of this folly and silly pride, (fe roe fenthyg i gnaf brwnt pan fyddai ei deulu ei hun mewn eisiau), and I believe he has refused some of them lately. He hath (or had) a notion that he had no occasion to hoard any money or goods for his children, for that after his death, some good people that had a value for him would take care of his family, as he has taken care to assist several helpless children.

This description was written by Lewis Morris in October, 1757, and it must be remembered that he was at the time harassed by law suits and financial troubles. Nevertheless, it is clear that the two brothers were the best of friends, though they did not always see eye to eye. It is a misfortune that nearly all the letters written

* Richard Morris was President of the Cymmrodorion.

by Richard Morris to his brothers have been lost or destroyed, and there only now remain about forty written by him between 1759 and 1763. Some of these are the most interesting letters in the whole series.

Introduction contd.

WILLIAM MORRIS, unlike his two brothers lived and died in Anglesey. He seems to have spent some considerable time in Liverpool when a young man and he also visited London, but for the last twenty years of his life he rarely stirred out of his native county. He was appointed Collector of the Customs at Holyhead on February 24th, 1736-7, and as time went on he obtained other small offices at the same port. In a letter written to Richard in April, 1741, he amusingly describes himself as deputy customer, collector, deputy comptroller, comptroller of the coal duties, deputy searcher, coast waiter and searcher, water bailiff, deputy vice-admiral, collector of the Skerry lights, surgeon, florist and botanist to the Garrison of Holyhead.†

William's life was uneventful; he experienced none of the vicissitudes of fortune which fell to the share of his brothers, nor did he rise to any distinction in the worlds of literature and affairs. Nevertheless in as far as his personal character is unfolded in the letters, William is perhaps the most interesting of the brothers. His letters have not the vivacity of those of his brother Lewis, nor the charm of John's, but they cover a very wide field of interest and are always eminently sane and natural. He contrives also to give us a complete picture of himself; we know him as he was with all his likes and dislikes, his virtues and his failings, his hobbies, his friends, his official duties, and his home. Both brothers look up to him with respect, and he is made the arbiter in their disputes. His letters abound in quaint turns and expressions of speech, and he is never happier than when he invents some pseudonym for himself as the finishing touch of a letter‡

† See page 50.

‡ The following are some of the names chosen: Gwilym Tew, Gwilym Hiraethog, Gwilym Gontrowliwr, Gwilym Fynglwyd, Gwilym Ddu o Fôn, Y Twrch Trwyth, Gwilym Ddu o Gybi, Gwilym Cybi, Gwilym Amhorys, Gwilym Rwydd-dew, Gwilym Lwyttu, Gwilym Fyngfrith, Gwilym o'r Dollfa, Gwilym Gregynwr, Y Cregynydd, Gwilym Rwyddfras, Gwilym y Garddwr, Gwilym Doll-goes neu Goes-dolly, Gwilym Ogloff, William y Trydydd, etc.

Like his brother Lewis he was a man of many accomplishments, a good musician, a surgeon, a fair linguist, a student of Welsh literature and antiquities, and an expert botanist and conchologist. He spent many years in making a Botanologium or Herbal, but this work seems now to have been lost. The Rev. Hugh Davies in his Welsh Botanology mentions a MS. by William Morris entitled "A Collection of Plants gathered in Anglesey," and it is not unlikely that Davies made extensive use of this MS. in the composition of his "Catalogue of the Native Plants of Anglesey." The Collections of Poetry made by William Morris have been preserved, and many of his MSS. are now in the British Museum. Amongst these is the "Delyn Ledr,"* a manuscript beautifully written by him on vellum. This was the MS. which Morris lent to Goronwy Owen, and failed for years to get back, until he purchased it from a pawnbroker in Liverpool.

By far the greatest number of the letters of the brothers still in existence were written by William Morris. This is due to the fact that Richard, to whom the letters were addressed, preserved them with jealous care and on his death bequeathed them to the Welsh School, whence they were transferred to the British Museum. Very few of the letters written by Richard have been discovered, but it is quite possible that they are still in existence. We know that William was as careful as Richard in keeping the letters, for those written to him by Lewis are now in the possession of Sir Lewis Morris, and it is unlikely that he destroyed those of his brother Richard. There should be six batches of correspondence, viz., letters written by Lewis to Richard, by Lewis to William; by Richard to Lewis, by Richard to William; and by William to Lewis and William to Richard. Of these the only ones which have survived in any quantity are those written by Lewis to Richard and William, Richard's letters to Lewis and William's letters to Richard.

JOHN MORRIS, the youngest of the brothers is little known to fame. A writer in the *Cambrian Register*, 1796, p. 232, gives the following account of him:—"John died mate of the *Torbay* man-of-war, in the expedition of 1740, against Carthagena, aged 34 years.

* Now Addit. MS. 14884.

He is said to have been the most promising genius of all the brothers; but of the three who enjoyed the common duration of life, Lewis had the credit of being the most vigorous character."

In preparing these letters for the press, it has been the Editor's aim to omit nothing, so that the writers might appear in their natural garb. It often happens, however, that the letters are torn or otherwise imperfect, and sometimes they are indistinct and difficult to read. A very few other omissions have been made where the writers offended against what are considered in this age to be the canons of good taste, but it is seldom that they require a surgical operation of this kind. The letters were transcribed by the Editor, Mr. T. Vaughan Roberts, B.Sc., Mr. E. A. Lewis, M.A., D.Sc., and the late Mr. T. Hamer Jones. The Editor and Mr. Vaughan Roberts have carefully collated all the proofs with the original letters, but they do not make a pretence of infallibility, and there are doubtless many errors of transcription still uncorrected.

It is hoped to complete the series of MORRIS LETTERS in another volume, to be followed by comprehensive indices and notes.

J. H. DAVIES.

THE MORRIS' LETTERS.

LONDON, 20th March, 1728.

Dear Brother,—Yours of 21st ultimo I received which I read with great pleasure and satisfaction. I observe thou art going the way of the world, if not gone already, and am in hopes things will answer thy expectation, so that thou'lt never need to wish thy head out of Cawell yr Ynfydion. If 'tis over, I pray God to bless you both, and I begg that my kind love be remembered to my new relation; I wish I had the honour of knowing her, but I hope in about a year's time I shall be at leisure and able to bear the expences of a journey to Anglesey, when I propose to myself a great deal of happiness in seeing all my friends and acquaintance, and who knows but I may carry down along with me a female friend as near related to you as the above is to me. I do really design to run the same hazard between this and Midsummer, and should have done it before now had not family sickness prevented it, but now the young chapp seems to be on ye mending hand. I've writ to cousin Jack and to brother William this day; also to Mr. Perocheon at Lisbon, Mr. Sidwell in Lincolnshire, John Prichard in Maryland, Mr. Dowe at Jamaica (where he went on a second expedition), also to Thomas Bryan at Llanerchymedd for Dick Morris of Hampstead. Believe me, I write so many letters R. to L.

R. to L. contd.

that it almost takes away half my time, being (besides what I do to my own friends) a secretary to near a score of my countrymen: a wondrous great man! and worthy of prodigious encouragement. I admire thy awen which is so ready to gingle rimes upon all occasions. Counsellor Lewis went from hence about a week ago, and I unfortunately happen'd to be so very busy that I had not time to send one letter by him, neither could I get the Grammar ready; but I've sent my cousin's Grammar, also several letters I received from Lisbon, Roderick, Sidwell, Maryland, Conway, etc. If ever thou goest to Flintshire I would have thee call on Mr. Connway of Sychdun, he would be extream glad to see thee, being a great lover of antiquities and the best good-natur'd man living. Perhaps he might get thee some surveying work if thou would accept of it, fail not in this if thou goest that way and give my humble service to him; I intend to write there very shortly. What made me send the above letters was chiefly that brother William may see Perocheon's when he comes to the country in Easter or Whitsuntide, which contain several mysteries in trade of great service to him; but pray let them be all returned when you have done with them. You see there a letter from R. Jones to whom the Cywydd belongs. There's a couple of sticks of red wax for thee in the parcell—shall take care to send the Grammar interleav'd per first opportunity. I wish thou would send the pedigree, etc., per Thos. Williams's return. Thou should not complain so much of trafferth now, for what wilt thou do when oblig'd to work the nights as well as days! O hard case! I understand Lord Bulkeley has drop'd the lawsuit about Mynydd y Twr. I hope what thou say'st about our sister's seeing her folly is true. I've writ her an out-of-the-way letter also, which I suppose she has received. I am surpriz'd I can hear nothing from Dr. Evans, and whether to impute it to his pride, neglegence or hurry of business I cannot tell. There's nothing done yet in the Custom House affair; but there are several scores turn'd out lately in this river, so that 'tis an easy matter with small interest to gett in here at present. As to what I mention'd about my going abroad, you must know I'm bound with Capt. Jones till next Christmas or Lady Day following, and after that he promises me a place of near £100 a year in this town, or a much more profitable one abroad; but I shall have time enough to consider of it between this and that time. Shall make it my business to inspect as much as I can into Mr. Edwards's business, which if I see to bear a good profit, perhaps in case the Widdow's affair answers, I shall enter in partners with him. But £100 a year profit is a fine thing! Do we run no risque of breaking, which is too common here now-a-days. Mr. Hughes, the orrange merchant, is broke, through the means of a rascally . . . [torn] who arrested him, and set all his creditors upon his back at once, so . . . [torn] after he paid him he was obliged to abscond to the verge of the Court, till his . . . [torn] are made up. I believe there will be a statute out against him this week. I've settled all his accounts for him and it appears he owes about £600, and has about £300 to pay a composition of 7s. 6d. or 10s. per pound—he had but £500 with his wife which was too much to lose, though 'twas reported she had above £1000 fortune. I'm heartily sorry for the poor good woman, and cannot imagine as yet what they'll do to live in the world after this misfortune; more per next. I believe we shall have a war after all, there seems no hopes of ye contrary. St. David's Day was observ'd here with great ceremony, the sermon was preach'd in English by Mr. John Morgan and they [sic] prayers in British by Mr. Phillips, at St. Clement's Danes, in the Strand; but the Prince was not there. The 12 stewards and the Society walk'd in procession to Merchant Taylor's Hall where they din'd, consisting of about a thousand people, Welsh and English, and made a handsome collection for the Charity Children descended from British parents which they keep. The stewards wore plumes of feathers in their hatts and underneath ye motto, *Ich Dien*, work'd in silver very pretty. I did not dine with them yt day because they had prick'd me down for a steward next year, and sent me a summons to meet them, but being unwilling to be about £10 out of pocket, I retir'd with about 12 countrymen into a private house, where we din'd and drank all the healths we could think on, and return'd home sober as judges. I could say more but must defer it to another opportunity.—*Thy Brother Brynaich*, *Rhist Morus*. R. to L. contd.

I've gott a place for John Price by the week at Mr. Edwards's, to look after the shop, go of errands, carry out, etc., and his wife

R. to L. contd. is to wash for us all in the house, upon which account they are to come and live near us. My last letter was little burnt, and the seal is Mr. Edwards's coat-of-arms.

N.B.—I've been this week past writing out Weston's book of shorthand, and design, if I can, to learn that incomparable piece of Art which has made so much noise in ye world.

Endorsed: To Mr Lewis Morris, Land Surveyor, at Penrhos Lligwy, near Llysdulas, in Anglesey, North Wales.

Copied by Mr. Richard Williams, F.R. Hist. S., Newtown, from the original in the possession of the late W. J. Kirkham.

GARTRE, ANGLESEY, 24th Feb., 1738.

L. to R. II. Mrawd Rhisiart yna,—Here is your letter of ye 24th of January before me. 'Roeddwn yn disgwyl bob dydd gael clywed gair neu ddau dy fod gwedi cael rhyw gymorth gan Mr. Meyrig: os meder, mi wn y gwna. Mi ddiolchais orau gallwn iddo yn fy llythyr diweddaf. "There's no pity but amongst ye poor," medd yr hen ddihareb, beth a dal ini gwyno i'n gilydd: nid oes ond cymryd y byd a geffir, ni wiw mynd i guro pobl oni chawn a geisiom. Dyma nhad, newydd mendio o glefyd mawr fu arno yn ddiweddar. Torrodd y postwm arno, a bu yn wan iawn. He hath an ulcer (abscess) in ye stomach, or ye colon, ag ni bydd holliach nes ymado o'r byd hwn. Mae mam yn rhesymol, ond ei bod yn heneiddio yn dost, ag yn fusgrell. Fy chwaer a'r teulu yn dda iawn, ninnau yma yn rhwydd iach. Ni chefais etto mo'r diben gida'm Harglwyddi o'r Amralti, na'm cyflog am yr haf diweddaf. Y post diweddaf ond un cefais lythyr oddiwrth fy anwyl a'm parchedig gyfaill, y Brawd Du o Nannau, yn dwedyd ei fod newydd ddyfod i Lundain i ymddangos yn y Senedd-dy. Os medr y gwr urddasol hwnnw gymmorth yn y byd iti i gael yn sgrifenydd i'r Seneddwyr, fei gwna. Ymofyn am William Vaughan, Esq., at ye coachmaker, in St. James's Street, ond ynghynta gwna ddau neu dri o englynion i ddywedyd iddo mae pererin wyd yn Llundain, gwedi dyfod o Wynedd er's —— mlynedd, heb chwimio erioed o honi, ag mae brawd wyd i Lewelyn Ddu o Fôn. Sign your name Richard Morris alias Rhisiart Amheurig Loywddu. Yr englynion a ganlyn a yrrais iddo y post diweddaf, being some remarks upon the button-hole, a riddle; yr hwn a yrassai imi yn ei lythyr. [Then follow the englynion.]

Hyn a 'sgrifenais yma, nid i fwrw meddyliau anuwiol yn y pen, ond i ddangos ychydig o dymmer dynion y byd. Mr. Selden's Speechman was in the right. He could not make ye Mayor a speech without the measure of his mouth, ag felly anodd ydyw gwneuthur englyn i ddyn heb gymeryd mesur ei geg. L. to R. contd.

This gentleman may be of infinite service to you while he is in town. Os oes llyfr cywydd genit, dos ag ef yno yr ail tro (nid y tro cyntaf). Gwych gan y gwr gael llith allan o lyfr cywydd.

Let me hear of your reception per first post. I suppose you need pay for no more letters. I can inclose them to him, and you may have franks. *Thy affectionate brother*, *L. M.*

Let me know what family Mr. Vaughan hath in town.

[HOLYHEAD], 24th Chwefr., 1738.

Cher Frere,—Mi faswn wedi sgrifennu attoch er's llawer dydd pe b'ase ffrank yw gael, a mawr oedd gennyf eich rhoddi mewn *4d* o gost heb ddim daioni yw yrry am danynt. Yr oeddwn yn gweled mai afraid oedd immi sgrifennu at Mr Brereton ynghylch y swydd hono, oblegit nid yw ef a Meurig ddim yn gyttun a'i gilydd, er pan dro'ed Mr H. Williams allan o Fôn, ag felly fo fuase Owain Amheurig ond odid yn ddigllon pei clywse'ch bod yn ammeu ei allu, &c. And indeed I can't well ask any favour of Mr Brereton since his giving me this bread has much more than compensated for what service I have or can do him. Ond gwyn ei fyd a allasai wneuthur i chwi ryw faint o lês. W. to R. III.

Daccw mrawd wedi gyrry i chwi yr holl *Ddomestick News*, dyma i chwi air neu ddau o *Foreign*. Cawsom lythyr oddiwrth mrawd Sion o Gibraltar, o'r 30 Rhagfyr, y pryd roedd newydd dirio yno. Nhw a gawsont wynt o'r *ffeinia* o Gaernarfon yno. Roedd y brawd yn erchi ei wasanaeth attoch.

Dyma heddyw lythyr arall oddiwrtho o Farseilles o'r 7 Chwefror. Yr oeddynt wedi bod yn Marselona. Dyma ddarn o'r bystol:—

> Hwyliasom o Gibraltar y 5 Ionawr. Ni fedrwn lai wrth amgylchu y mynydd na bonllefain y cyffelybiaeth hyn:
>
> Gibraltar un herr a haran,—Och rwyg!
> Cribog ymylog y man
> A'i chreigiau hyll anian
> A Boss mal mynydd Basan.

W. to R. contd.

Cael gwynt teg, a digon honaw hyd na ddaethom ymhlith yr ynysoedd Ivica, Majorca, etc., ymhle buom ddauddydd neu dri, a minnau yn tynny lluniau'r bryniau a'r trwynau, etc., ag yn gwneud ambell englyn fal hyn:

Heb wynt wâr helynt i'r hwyl—ar gefnfor
Gwag ynfyd yw'r gorchwyl
Hwyra daag hir yw disgwyl
A sala gwaith Sul a gwyl.

Mae'n dywedyd nad yw'r englynion yn tyfu mor rhywiogaidd ffordd honno ag ynhir Gwynedd. They have taken a fraight to sette thence to Roterdam. The ship is called the Mary of Leverpoole, Captain Carreg. Daccw Jack Prichard wedi mynd yn ei ol i Leverpoole, ag mae'n mynd, hyd rwyn deall yn Gadpen ar *West Indiaman* of 150 tons. Ces lythyr oddiwrtho'r dydd arall i ymgynghori ar y pwnc pwysfawr hwnnw. Y cefnder, Huw Evans, o'r Ffers, a fu farw yn diweddar. Mae bachgen a lodes o blant nghyfnither Elsbeth ar ei ol, rwyn meddwl ei fod yn o dacclus. Nid ai ddywedyd yn rhagor am y trô. Gadewch glywed 'ch hanes, a Duw a f'och plaid. *Eich brawd anwiw,*

William Morris.

LEVERPOOLE, 5th July, 1739.

L. to R. IV.

Dear Brother,—It is but a folly for me to acquaint you of my proceedings since I wrote you last, since (as I suppose) you've been inform'd of it from Anglesey, from whence after my arrival here I was acquainted that they had lately heard from you and that you was well, a bod y rhôd wedi troi, yr hyn oedd dda iawn gennyf glywed, a gobeitho na thru'n ol mwyach. I writt you from here before I went out last voyage, but never got an answer. I think it is now about sixteen months since I received your last, with Cywydd marwnad y frenhines, etc., which I answer'd in due time from Holyhead, and wrott you again from Porthdinlleyn when we were lading corn for Lizbon. I went to visit Monsr. Perocheon one Sunday (we being consign'd to him) but was not at home, so next day I went to ye Exchange and there I met with him. Invited me home to dine with him and a grand entertainment there was, he ask'd about you several times, and always call'd you his friend.

There were several gentlemen, masters of ships, etc. in company, so I could not for shame acquaint him of your circumstances at that time, but defer'd it, expecting to see him another time by himself, but never could have that happiness. I've been out seven months and a half this last trip and I promis'd myself all along, when I return'd, to take a jaunt to Anglesey, but here's the vessel that I belong to lading of salt for Dublin and they would feign have me to go with her thither, and by the time we return they'll have a cargo ready for us for the Streights again, which I should like very well if it should happen so; but there's no depending on our Owners, besides, as far as I can understand, this embargo reaches over them that are bound for Ireland as well as them to foreign parts, so I am of two minds whither to stay by y[e] vessel or go to Anglesey. I shall resolve this doubt soon. J. to R. contd.

Cefais lythyr o'r Pen Sanctaidd, un o Bentre'r Annell, un o Lundain, ag un oddiwrth Ddoctor Bifan, er pan ddaethym i dre, ag iach lawen y'nt oll. Mae'r Car Will Huws yn lysdi ai wraig ai ferch. Pan scrifenoch attaf llwybreiddiwch y llythyr iw adel yn ei dy ef, mal (os byddaf wedi mynd i bant) y gallo ef gymryd gofal am ei yrru immi. Rwy'n ofni fod ei weithiau yn mron mynd ir pwll, oblegyd nid oes yno fawr neb yn gweithio un amser, gresyn oedd. Mi glowaf fod llawer iawn o droeadau y Môn er pan fum i yno, mae arnaf gryn flys am roi tro yn eu plith unwaith etto, ag wedy'n canu'n iach dros dro.

I wish you would enquire what's become of Mr. Weston, him that was our chief mate in ye Harrington. If he's a Captain I I should like it in my heart to take another trip to India; however, I design to visit both Guinea, W. India, and North America before I leave off rambling, if God spares my life so long. In the mean-time I begg you would write to me per first post and let me know how things hath happened with you since I received your last, and how John Price, Ben Jones, Carn Mynawyd, etc., and all old acquaintances hath made it out since.

This minute dyma'r Car Will Huws wedi mynd o'n llong ni, yr hwn a ddywaid imi dderbyn eich llythyr er's dyddie, ond roedd arno ofn 'scrifennu attoch drachefn mal yr oedd arno o hyd er pan ddaeth oddiyna, a hyn a barodd imi eich gwneyd yn yspys o honaw,

J. to R. contd.

ar achos ydoedd hyn: h.y., Ei feistr Hopkins a scrifennodd atto ddwywaith, ychydig ar ol iddo ddyfod ir dre' yma, ai siarsio'n drwm na scrifenna atto chwi mwyach yn anad neb dan boen colli ei le, felly'r dyn ydoedd yn byw mewn ofn hyd yr amser heb wybod yr achos, weithiau'n meddwl mae o herwydd y trwblaethau a syrthiodd arnoch, weithiau eraill yn tybied mae ofni rydoedd ei feistr y datcuddiech ei gwaith nhw, neu'r cyffelyb; felly 'rydoedd y dyn yn anesmwyth ag heb feiddio datcuddio ei feddwl rhag ofn drwg, ond y rwan mae'r gwr yn dymuno arnoch scrifenu atto gynta' galloch ach meddwl or peth ag fe'ch ettyb gyda dychweliad y post, mi debygwn nad oes gan y gwr fawr fatter er digio ei feistr yn awr os gwel yn dda.

I am just now going to our Owners and to know their minds what they intend to do, if they don't give me sufficient wages, I shall make the best of my way to Sir Vôn; but, however, let me go to what sîr I will, if you direct for me as before, he'll take care to forward it to me if I be gone. Ni feddaf iw chwanegu ond brysiwch atteb hwn, ach llawn hanes, etc., minne yrraf i chwithe fy hanes inne, a byddwch wych, medd . . . *Ioan Amhorys.*

LEVERPOOLE, 22nd July, 1739.

J. to R. V.

Dear Brother,—Yours of the 12th came to hand, which I did not intend to answer till I came to Anglesey, where I design'd to set out for about this time, but that last Friday I unluckily strain'd my knee, and now I am forced to go with a stick, and obliged to stay till I get my passage with some vessel or other. I would have you know that I am a gentleman at large at present, having left the ship after I got her laden and rigg'd, it being too expensive for me to stay here all the time of the embargo, paying for my dieting and lodging, besides what I spend otherwise, and the Owners not allowing me a grain towards it; and that ye custom here.

Da iawn yw clywed eich bod cystal arnoch, ag mae nghobaith y dowch i fynu cystal cynt, er maint o drwblaethau a fu ich dilyn yn ddiweddar, drwy waith a chynorthwy rhai ewyllyswyr drwg maleisgar, a gobeitho mae er lles i chwi rhaglaw y digwyddodd yr unrhyw, os y chwi a wneiff wasanaethgarwch o honaw ag nid oes le ammeu na wnewch, a chwitheu ar byd och blaen, a chwedi cael penn y ffordd yn eich llaw. Diau nad oes un well gantho glywed eich bod yn mynd ymlaen mor odidawg, a Duw ach cynnorthwyo yn eich holl amcanion. J. to R. contd.

Cousin Will Hughes ask'd me whether you said anything about him, etc. I told him that you desir'd to be remember'd to him and his wife, so he desir'd me to give him directions to write to you, seems to be afraid that you've fall'n out with him, says he'll send you a letter soon, and some Neat's tongues, or something or other. A welwch chwi beth ydyw dyn pan fyddo'n dda arno, pawb a rydd iddo ; pan fo'n dlawd ai ben yn y dŵr, hwda di hwrdd iddo hyd na bo dan ddŵr. Dyna fal i mae'r byd yn mynd erioed hyd yn heddyw, mal y gwyddoch.

Received a letter from father of the same date with yours ; no news, but yt they were all well there and at the Head. Am danafi mi wneuthum esgus i ymadael ar llong gan ddweyd fy mod yn glaf, etc., ag nad oeddwn abl i gwplhau'r siwrnai, ond yr achos oedd fod y cyflog yn rhy fychan ar siwrnai gan fyrred (sef i Dduflun), na chwittia'r gost aros gyda'r llong, gan na buasai'r ffordd yn rhydd i fynd ir Mor Canoldir pan ddychwelsem o Dduflun. Mi af i Fôn i roi tro yn enw Duw dros bymthegnos neu dair wythnos, ag yno dychwelaf yma i fynd ir mor eilwaith. Ef a gynnygiodd Maer y Dre immi fynd yn *second mate* ar un o'i longau sydd yn mynd i *Guinea*, os byddaf yma erbyn iddi fynd i ffitio allan, ag a addawodd scrifenu attaf i Fôn pan fyddai arno fy eisiau. Mae'n anhawdd i ddynan diethr om bath i gael mynd yn forwyn bennaf, o eisiau *interest*, etc. It's certain that Guinea is the best place for a young fellow of my learning to go to out of this place, for if he lives, he's undoubtedly preferr'd ye next voyage if he keeps the same employ, for the captains and officers, etc., dies so often that there's continually new ones sent out, but never a chief mate hardly but what has been before upon the coast, so I am actually resolv'd to venture one trip, please God to give me health. If I die in the prosecution, God's will be done: I have neither wife (nor children to my knowledge) to cry after me, and if I don't go abroad now while I'm free I am sure I never shall if I alter my state, except it be through some other means more than ordinary that I should be obliged *perforce* to go. So much for that.

J. to R. contd.

They continue to beat up here for Volunteers for the land service, and they get a good many. But we have had no impress yet. I hope we shall hear soon of Admiral Haddock's sinking or taking some of the Spaniards. We hear they have taken several of our ships that were atrading in ye Bay of Honduras. Gresyn na cheid rhoi golchfa jawn iddynt unwaith, os happia, y daliant eu tafodau wedyn.

Pa Lyfr Navigation sydd newydd ei roi allan, a pha un sydd oreu o naddynt, rwy'n ffaelio taro wrth un etto wrth fy mhwrpas, although I have at present by me six or seven epitomes; still in my oppinion there may be better . . . [torn] consider [whether you] can get the above books, or if you have any of your own in these affairs you could spare, I should be very glad you'd send 'em directed to cousin W. Hughes, so as I could receive them before I go to sea. Nid o rann brolio na dadsio, I keep as regular a journal as any Captain that sails out of the town, and far preferable to many, who can hardly work a day's work, ay, some that does not know how to make a right-angled triangle gets to be captains of good ships here, as more than one or two of our dear countrymen hath, the more the shame for them that trusts their ships and cargoes with 'em. E ddaw haid i gwch Alis. Mae hi rwan yn pwyso tua'r gwaelod, ag mae'n anghenrhaid rhoi diben, er y medrwn scrifenu cymaint arall pei bae le, ni feddaf fymryn o newydd a roech yn eich llygad ond pâr o ddillad newydd (chwedl Dr. Bifan), a rheini rhaid imi wrthynt i fynd i Fôn onite hwy ddwedant fy mod yn gwarrior'r cwbl ir bol, ac yn gadel y cefn yn llwmm, a minne'n rhoi'r cyfan rhwng y cefn a llyfre ar cyffelyb, mal nad wyf ffyrling cyfoethogcach yn arian rwan na'r pryd cynta y deuais ir fangre, ond mawl i Dduw nid oes arnaf ddim eisiau etto, ag mae y rhann fwyaf o fy fentr y siwrnai ddiwaethaf gennyf heb eu gwerthu etto, gobeithio daw hynny a digon i mewn i brynnu fentr arall i fynd allan y siwrnai nesaf i ba le bynnag y bydd. Wala, dyna i chwi'r sut i mae gyda mi, bellach gadewch wybod pa drefn sydd arnoch chwithe'n trin y byd newydd, a pha helynt a fy arnoch er pan gefais eich llythyr er llynedd, a hyn a fydd cymeradwy jawn, a bid yn siwr o honoch fod eich llythyr cyn llawned a hwn, a llwybreiddiwch ef i Ddulas, ymha fan rwy'n gobeitho bod o hyn i ddiwedd yr wythnos nesaf, a llyma'r cwbl y pryd hyn gyda fy ngharedigol annerch attoch, ag at bob cyfaill cywir gonest a garo ddyn yn ei gefn. *Wyf hyd angau eich ffyddlon frawd, Ioan Amhorys.* J. to R. contd.

LEVERPOOLE, 19th October, 1739.

Dear Brother,—Yours of the 16th inst. (inclosed in cousin W. Hughes's) came to hand this day, and am glad to hear of your well-doing, ach bod hefyd wedi mynd i ymweled yr hen Whormby, gresyn na chawsach ei weled, for I am resolv'd now to be one amongst them i ladd Yspaengwyns. I might have berths enough here, ond rwan wedi lledfalchio, and I won't accept of every small offers. Pwy wyr nad eill eich geirie ddyfod i ben ryw dro os medr dyn ladd a llosgi digon or Spaeniaits gwaedlyd accw. I writt to brother Lewis last Sunday to desire him to send up for a furlough for me, to keep one from being press'd by ye way in going up, and to be put aboard of another ship. Here's some Cheesemen bound for London, and I may get my passage with one or other of them, if I do but get that thing in time before they sail, and perhaps shall get something in my way besides ye opportunity of getting my chest, bedding, and other things yn rhad ac yn ddidrwbl, I hope. Brother . . . writt about it, a gwych a fyddai pei bae genychwithe g . . . i fynd i ddweyd gair yn'r achos wrth yr hen Whormby, gwr mwyna yn y byd ydyw, medd y brawd L. Cousin W. Hughes could not think what to make of your letter, but I explain'd it as well as I could to him, and told him ye reason, as I thought. Mae bob amser yn hir groesawys imi, ond cythrael ydyw'r wraig weithiau. Y^e letter came to her hands first (he being at ye shop); she open'd it, and seeing Welsh and English mixt, thought it had been some other language, and was frightened out of her wits almost, sent ye girl to fetch him home, and said that there was a letter from his brother about some mischief or other. Roedd y wreigan ymron anhwylio. I call'd at ye Widdow Hamiltons and enquired about Mr. Boyd. He's left that service, and is gone to Maryland, in Mr. Goodwin's employ, of this town, and is to stay in ye country some time as his factor. I know the man by sight, he went out in ye Goodwin galley, one I. Owen, from Aberffraw, went chief mate in her. I have been here since J. to R. VI.

J. to R. contd.

last Wednesday was seven nights, yn byw ar fy nghost fy hun. Mae arnaf ofn na fydd genyf ffyrling i ymgroesi erbyn y delwyf yna, nid oedd dim cymmhorth i'w gael Ymôn. Mae'r hen bobl, Duw ai helpio, yn talu pob ceiniog a gaffont at ei gilydd i geisio yscafnhau peth ar y ddyled fawr sydd arnynt, ar swyddogion nis gwn i pa beth y maent yn ei wneud ai harian, ni chefais i gymaint ag a brynna i mi bâr o sgidiau prin er pan welsoch fi, ond a weithiais yn galed am dano, and being so long at home now, and last year ye same way, I've much to do to keep both ends together, but if I once get that berth that I expect, baw i wyr Lerpwl, ag felly byddwch wych. Os scrifenwch gyda dychweliad y post, siawns na ddaw o hyd imi yma, at Mr. J. Prichard's, merchant, etc. *Ioan Amhorys.*

LEVERPOOLE, 6th November, 1739.

J. to R. VII.

Dear Brother,—Yours of ye 23rd ult. I received, and would have answer'd it sooner but that I daily expected to hear from Mr. Whormby, yr hyn a gefais or diwedd, ag a attebais gyda dychweliad y post nos Wener diwaethaf. He tells me that he hath got a grant of a master's mate's berth for me aboard the *Torbay*, which is soon to be put in commission, and will send me a ticket from ye Captain, which he can't grant till this in commission, and advises me to stay here till then, which I believe will be my best way. Mae yma long caws yn llwytho i ddyfod yna (os ni byddaf barod i ddyfod fy hun), mi yrraf fy nghist am dillad gwelu, etc., gyda hi, ag ai directia i dŷ Ben Jones; mi scrifenaf atto pan fo'r llong yn barod i hwylio, ai henw, etc. We had ye war declar'd here against Spain ye day I received your letters, and next day came in a man-of-war's tender, and made a sad havoc here, but is now gone for Beumares, as some says, where there lies wind-bound several ships bound for this place, gwae Fôn ag Arfon. Received this day a letter from ye Head—all well at home. I [expect] a letter daily from father. Din'd this day with cousin W. Hughes. Both him and his wife desir'd to be remember'd to y^e, and I've forgot whether he told me he had wrote y^e, or whether he would write; however, it's no great matter. Pawb yn iach, cenwch. I should be very glad if you could get an opportunity i fynd i ymweled yr hen Whormby. He writt me a very kind letter, and says he, "When y^e^ *Torbay* is put in commission (which is soon expected), you shall be master's mate in her!" Dyna i chwi, hen gorph. Ie, ag os gwelach ef, diolch tippyn ir hen wr drostwyf, etc. We are here day and night killing Spaniards, and taking rich prizes, mal Mad Pirs Llwyd, Lligwy gynt, ar y traeth coch, ag ynte gartre. I have not a grain of news to send you, ond fy mod i gwedi blino yma yn diogi hyd yr amser, gwyn ei fyd na bawn yn cael rhan o ddal rhai or Spaeniaid accw, but I hope I shall be at 'em soon, ag yno, either a golden chain or a wooden leg. Should be glad to hear from you ere I leave this place. With service to all friends at London, if there be any, and love to yourself, is all at present. *From your loving brother in hast,* *John Morris.* J. to R. contd.

LEVERPOOLE, 27th November, 1739.

Dear Brother,—I writt you a good while ago to acquaint you of my receiving Mr. Whormby's letters, with a promise of a master's mate berth in the *Torbay*, for which I expected to have an answer before now. This comes to let you know that I've put aboard of the *Recovery*, Captain Cotes, potun ymenyn a chosyn wedi ei lapio i fynu mewn cwd lliain a chwart coppr, y cwbl wedi ei llwybreiddio fal y llythyr yma, a chwedi ei rhoi dan siars Mr. Eules, y forwyn, yr hwn a addawodd eu cludo yn rhad. Y menyn a'r caws a ddaeth o Fôn, a'r coppr a adewais yn angof heb ei yrru yn fy nghist, yr hon sydd wedi mynd ymaith ers dyddie yn y *John and Martha*, Captain Nevill, ynghyd am dillad gwelu am *guardvine*, gwedi eu llwybreiddio i dy Ben Jones. Mi scrifenais atto yn eu cylch ag i ddymuno arno gymryd gofal gyda hwynt, au ceisio i ryw dy i ryw le yn ddiogel hyd oni ddelwyf yna; rwyf agos a blino yn disgwyl yma hyd yr amser. Cefais lythyr or pen Sanctaidd heddyw—pawb yn iach yno ag yn Nulas. John Pritchard, o Maryland gynt, a gollodd ei long dydd arall ar *goast* y Werddon wrth ddyfod adre o Virginia. Efe ydoedd y meistr, ag i mae wedi briwo'n arw medd rhai. I desire of you to tell B. Jones (if you see him before the ship arrives with my things) that he'd take all ye care that ever he can not to tumble the chest or case, for fear of breaking ye bottles that there is in both, with some liquor in J. to R. VIII.

J. to R. contd. that may make us merry when we meet, but would make me full sad if the bottles were to break and ye liquor spillt about my books and cloaths, etc.; and I forgot to write to B. Jones about ye freight of them, though I don't think that Captain Nevill will take anything for the carriage of them, yet I imagine it would be proper to ask him what he demands, but never ask anybody but himself, I forgot to mention this in my letter to Ben. You have at the end of this, a line or two to Captain Cotes's mate, who'll deliver you the butter, etc. I've no news worth sending, therefore rhaid canu'n iach, a da fyddai cael clywed oddiwrthych os bydd modd cyn cychwyn, a gwybod a fuoch yn siarad byth ar hen Whormby, a dyna'r cwbl y tro yma, o rann rwy ar frys cynddeiriog a chenyf ddau lythyr etto i'w scrifenu. *Ioan Amhorys.*

P.S.—Received a letter this day also from cousin J. Salsb', who's well, and all our relations that way, and says he'll write to you soon.

LEVERPOOLE, 8th December [January], 1739-40.

J. to R. IX. Anwyl Frawd,—Scrifenais attoch er's talm byd mawr, ag at Ben Jones hefyd, a chyfri fy mod wedi gyrru fy nghist, dillad gwelu, etc., gyda'r *John and Martha*, Captain Nevill, a photun ymenyn a chosyn gyda'r *Recovery*, Captain Cotes, y rhai cyntaf gwedi eu llwybreiddio i dy Ben, ar diwaethaf i *Jack's coffee house*, ond ni chlywais byth air oddiwrth un o honoch, a minne yn y fann yma yn disgwyl (fal y llwynog wrth geilliau'r tarw gynt) am rywbeth nas gwn pa bryd y daw; ond dyma newydd wedi dyfod ir dre fod y *John and Martha* yn Hylelake, wedi troi'n ôl ar ol bod yn curo'r mor yn wreichion, a Duw wyr pa drefn sydd ar fy methau ynddi. Mae ei protecsiwn allan, a'r gwyr wedi diangc oll i lan, rhag ofn cael eu pressio gan wyr y *Bonetta* sloop sydd yn Heilac ar yr achos hwnnw, ag a ydis yn ei disgwyl ir afon er's dyddie oni bae erwined y rhew, yr hwn sydd mynd yn ol ag ymlaen gyda'r trai ar llanw mor erchyll nad eill neb wrthsefyll monaw. Cefais lythyre o Fôn yn ddiweddar; pawb yn jach, a'n rhieni (mawl i Dduw) yn cael eu hiechyd yn well nag ers blynyddoedd or blaen. Rwy'n gobeitho y caf ryw newydd or *Navy Office* ar fyr, ond mawr na bae gennych gyfleu i fynd at yr hen Whormby iw roi ar gof fy mod yn fyw, ag fy mod yma'n disgwyl hyd yr amser, gobeithio na ollwng monwyf yn angof. Ni feddaf i ddim chwaneg iw adrodd y tro yma, ond fy ngharedigol annerch attoch, a dymuno cael llythyr gynta galloch. J. to R. contd.

Yr hwn wyf eich ffyddlon frawd, *Ioan Amhorys.*

I've heard y^e^ *Recovery* is arriv'd at London long ago; there's a copper cann of mine with ye butter and cheese.

LEVERPOOLE, 19th January, 1739.

Anwyl Frawd,—Doe brydnhawn derbyniais ddau llythyr, un oddiwrth y brawd William, or 12th inst., ag arall oddiwrthych chwithe, a diau mae odiaeth oedd clywed eich geiriau'ch deuwedd, ag megys mêl ir gwefusau ydynt imi yn y fangre aniddan honn, y man nad oes gennyf na chyfaill na châr a eill gymorth im ddifyrru y tywydd rhewlyd anwydog yma. Cam gymeryd enw'r mis a wneuthym y tro diwaethaf. Mae'n dda genyf fod y menyn ar cosyn wedi dyfod yna, am fy mhethau fi mae'nt yn Heilac etto, ond mi yrrais at un o'r *pilots* yno i beri iddo ei ceisio ir lann au gyrru yma gan gynted ag y bo modd, oblegyd mae yma longau a phrotecsiwn ganthynt a fydd yn barod i hwylio ar fyrder, ag y gallaf yrru'r pethau gyda hwynt, a chael fy hunan hefyd pei meiddiwn. Aie dyna'r fath wr yw nghymydog Ben? Pei gwybuaswn oddiwrth y Turner hwnnw nid aethwn i falchio mor gwr arall. Mae'n dda gennyf fod y traed yn iachau, ach bod yn ymweled ar hen Whormby. I long to receive them good news he promises to send me; they need be good, for they be a confounded long while acoming. Mae hen ddihareb: "Ni bu erioed dda o hir aros." Da i gwnn na bu dda i mi eisioes mor aros yma er decpunt, heblaw colli cymaint or peth gwerthfawr hwnnw—Amser, a gorfod rhedeg mewn dyled gyda hynny; ond gobeitho y daw haid i gwch etto. I've nothing to say to Mr. Whormby, but that I've lost a deal of time and refus'd several mate's berths out of this place, both to Guinea, West Indies, and Virginia, etc., but it cannot be helpt now but by his endeavours, and other good friends, to get me a suitable berth that will balance these losses. You talk of your Llewelyn and Meirian! Ai D——l a gafodd wall ar y gwr bonheddig? Ymhle clywn i sôn J. to R. x.

J. to R. contd. am danynt? Nid oes bosibl eich bod yn briod, a chanthoch blant, etc., a minne heb glywed gair sôn erioed! Mae'n debyg mae wrth siawns y cawsoch hwynt (rwy'n gofyn nawdd fy chwaer-ynghyfraith os wy'n camdybio, ond ai fi wyr pwy yw hi?). Os felly, ni buasai waith o ddraen crîn pei'r aethai Farian gyda'u brawd. 'Ry'ch yn alaru ar ei ol mal Dafydd brophwyd gynt am ei fachgen. Duw r'o amunedd i chwi. I congratulate with you in the late honour you had, to get in company with such great and eminent personages, as you call them; but it should be more by accident than freewill that I should be in company with them had they serv'd me as they've done by you. But such things will happen sometimes against one's will, and when one is fall'n into bad bread (as sailors says), he must make the best of a bad market.

Mae'r cyfrifon yna'n hir greulon yn mynd i benn, yn siwr mae i chwi ryw daledigaeth dda am eich poen; gobeitho nad megys *iob* y cym'rasoch y gwaith, ag fod eich cyflog yn calyn yr amser. Am newyddion nid oes genyfi ond ychydig iawn. Y dydd ympryd a gweddi (sef y 9fed), a gadwyd yn y dre yma'n sanctaidd; ni wyddechi ragor rhyngtho ar Sul, yr Eglwysydd yn llawn o bob math ar Gristnogion, ni wnn i glywed erioed y cyfryw bregeth odiaethol ag a bregethwyd yn Eglwys St. George gan y Person Woolstenholm; rwy'n tybio na fedr un Esgob yn y deyrnas wneyd ei bath.

Mae'r rhew'n dal yma etto yn gethin a'r llonga'n methu chwimied gantho. Y brawd William a ddywaid i'n chwaer ddyfod ar ei gwelu'n ddiweddar, a geni iddi ddau feib, sef yr henwyd hwynt Iorwerth a Morys, a marw a orug y ddau, au claddu a wnaethpwyt yn'r un arch yn Eglwys Penrhôs. Fe gafodd eu mam amser go galed heb neb ond ein mam ninne, Duw ai helpo, i roddi help llaw iddi, yr hon drwy eistedd i fynu ag ymegnïo mwy nai gallu ai taflodd ei hunan i afiechyd, mal cynt gyda minne pan syrthiais ir badell ar brecci, nid hwyrach y caf well newydd y foru, os gwel Duw'n dda, rwy'n disgwyl atteb i lythyr a yrrais ers dyddie. Y Doctor Bevan a chantho eneth fechan. Mr. John Lewis, Llanfihangel, a chanddo un arall. Dic Wmffras, y Ffeiriad, a chantho ddau faib (yn lle'r ddau uchod fu farw) oi wraig, merch Sion Lewis or Gadlys. Y brawd Lewis wedi mynd tua Dulas i 'mweled ar cleifion, a dyna gymaint ag a gofiais o newyddion o Fôn. Ef a ddywaid hefyd fod 'nhad yn cael ei iechyd yn rhagorol, ai fod yn yfed cwrw'n odiaethol, yr hyn beth ni wnaeth yn fy nghoffadwriaeth i. Mae pobl yn meirw'n dre yma'n amlach nag y gwelais fi ermoed; 6 chynhebrwng yn Eglwys St. Peter ddoe, ag 8 heddyw, heblaw oedd yn y llaill. J. to R. contd.

20fed dydd.—Bellach gorphenaf eich epystol hwn gan ddwedyd imi dderbyn heddyw lythyr oddiwrth y brawd Lewis, o Ddulas, yr hwn a ddywaid imi'r drefn sydd ar y mam. She was taken ye 6th inst. with a violent nervous fever, which had like to carry her off, but by ye extraord'nary judgement of ye doctor in the distemper, through God he saved her life, though he was ill of ye fever ye same time. She hath past the crisis, and there's all ye good signs in ye world she'll do well. Duw ai cynhalio ag a wellhao arni. Myfi a gae'r golled fwya (pei gwelai Dduw'n dda ei chymryd atto) o honom i gyd. Brother Lewis had received a letter from Mr. Whormby, of ye 7th inst., which he sent me. His words are: "I would have answered yours, etc., but that I waited a proper opportunity of seeing Commissioner Purviss here at our general court of Saturday last. It was he who promised, and still promiseth, the *Torbay* for your brother, but I do not yet hear when she will be put in commission. I will therefore use my endeavours to get him another ship of the same rate, and if I succeed, will send for him up with ye Captain's ticket, to secure him from ye press which he may otherwise be in great danger of." A dyna eiriau'r hen wr, ag felly mae rhyw obaith, chwi welwch. Duw ddelo a newydd da. Roeddwn ar fedr ymweled y Car Will Huws heddyw, yr hwn a ddywaid i mi echdoe fod y wraig a'r plentyn yn glaf, ond yr oedd y tywydd mor ffyrnig mal p'rin y gallais fentrio ir deml. Roedd y brawd Lewis newydd gael llythyr oddiwrth Feurig, a da oedd gan yr hen wr glywed fy mod ar y tir y ddryghin ddiwaethaf. Nid wyfi'n deall un gair etto ynghylch y Llewelyn a Meirian yna; gadewch wybod mewn gwirionedd pa sut y mae'r byd yn bod. Ni fynnwn i na adwaenwn fy holl geraint yn enwedig rhai mor agos o waed. Ni feddaf y

J. to R. contd. tro yma iw chwanegu ond deisyf ar Dduw roddi llwyddiant ag iechyd i chwi, a blwyddyn newydd dda.—*Eich caredigawl frawd*,

Ioan Amhorys.

Scrifenwch gynta galloch, yma y byddafi.

The song referred to in the previous letter, "Ni buasai waeth o ddraen crin pe i'r aethai Feirian gyda'i brawd Llywelyn," is in Addit. 14929, f 90. It is called Marwnad Llewelyn, ar ddull cyffes ei dad; and consists of eight verses. Apparently it was composed by Lewis Morris. Two of the verses we give here:

Ow, Llewelyn, felyn fab, melyn fab moel ynfyd,
Paham y syrthiaist mewn un awr i lawr y gweryd?
Torraist galon Mammi bach yn iach am dŷ bychan;
Nid oes cysur yn y gaer ond dy chwaer Meirian.

Ow, Llewelyn, dordyn daer, clyw dy chwaer Meirian,
Neu glyw Dadi, Sol, La, Mi, dyma iti degan.
Unig iawn yw chwaeren bach ac afiach gan gafod,
Ni wiw morol ar d'ol di i chware Babïod.

PENTRE'RIANELL, February 7th, 1739.

W. to R. XI. Dear Brother,—Yours of the 26th ulto. to my father lies before me, but as he is at present indisposed, can give you no satisfactory answer relating to the kelp. As there is no stock of old in hand, it will require some time to contract for the quantity you mention'd, which, however, could not be ready till about August, and I much question whether there is a 100 tons a year burnt on this island. My father, please God he recovers his health, would be glad to serve the gentleman you mention, and would be as able to do it as anyone here. Our kelp in North Wales is good, strong kelp, but pretty full of stones, occasion'd by their burning on stone hearths. It stands here in about twenty-five shillings per ton, delivered on board at the sundry creeks where it is burnt, which are many, and where a large vessel can't come, so there would be an additional charge in bringing it together. The freight, I suppose, would be about twenty shillings per ton to London; but we have but few vessels of burthen in these parts. So much for kelp.

My mother has kept her bed for this month past, and is even now so weak that she can hardly sit up abed. She has had a nervous fever, which had like to have carried her off, but with severe blisters, etc., etc., she (I hope) is in a way of recovery. Sister (about the time mother fell ill) was brought to bed of twins, which died soon after, and she narrowly escaped, but now is pretty well recover'd. My father has been very much out of order for this week past, of some distemper in his head, which, by the assistance of Dr. Evans, is now somewhat better, though has not as yet been able to go out of doors, ac felly mae ymma'r methiantwch gerwina a welsochi erioed. Bu mrawd Lewis neu fi yma rhan fwya o'r amser; oni bae hynny, nis gwn i par sut a fase ymma. Roedd y doctor yn cadw ei welu pan oedd y mam waetha, mae o rwan . . . ceffyl. Rwdwy yn ofni mae digon o waith afae nhad yn . . . hwnnw, oblegyd ei fod yn fusgrell, ac heblaw hynny fe fydde raid cael llawer o arian ymlaen llaw, o ran pobyl dlodion yw'r llongwrs, a rhaid iddynt gael y rhan fwya o'r arian i brynny bwyd tra bont yn gweithio, ac hwyrach na thybia'r gwr yna ddim yn addas roi ei arian allan, medd hwnnw, a pha'r fodd y talae ef i nhad am ei drwbl. Considriwch ol a blaen, a gadewch glywed oddiwrthych yn dippyn mynychach. Aie fo aeth Llew. r'un ffordd ai gyfnither Margaret. Nefoedd ir eneidiau, chwedl pobl Môn.—*I am, your affectionate brother, William Morris.* W. to R. contd.

P.S.—I left all well at the Head yesterday.

NERPWL, 4ydd Mawrth, 1739. J. to R. XII.

Anwyl Frawd,—Wala ymhell bell (chwedl Bardd Cwsg) tu draw i Fôr Iwerddon y bythwyf, onid ydych yn hen anial wrthyfi, os hen y cyfrifir dyn a phlant ganthaw. Y grôg ir sawl a wyddei os Sion pwy ydoedd y ddau efaill pan sgrifenais attoch, er darfod imi glywed rhyw son Ymôn ynghylch rhywbeth tebyg i hynny; ond yn wir roeddwn wedi anghofio yn gwbl, ag mae'n edifar rwan genyf sôn am danynt pei bae fatter yn y peth, ag yn wir ni allasei Sion Llwyd, Pant Hywel, neud iddo roi gwell profiadau am y diniweidrwydd nag a roesoch chwithe. Fy mendith gyda'u mammau. Ni choeliai y priodafi fyth, ond digon o hyn.

Aie dyna fath wr y prifiodd Sion Prys? Ond chwi wnaethoch yn dda wneyd uniondeb rhwng y ddeu wr, i ddangos ych bod yn philosophydd, y medrech anghofio anghymwynasau, etc. Ag yn wir ni faswni byth yn meddwl y buasai Sion yn meddwl cymaint o ddrwg i chwi ag a wnaeth, a chan fwyned ag mor groesawys i byddai bob amser yn ymddangos pan fyddwn i yna, ond mi welaf nad oes ymddiried i blant y byd hwn : rhywogaeth gwiberod ydyw llawer iawn onaddynt. Rhoddwch hwynt yn eich bynwes a nhwy ach brathant yn eich calon.

J. to R. contd. I'm afraid father would not be able to go about to procure so much kelp for you as you talk of, having lately had a fit of sickness (which I suppose you've heard from Môn); although both he and mother are now pretty well recover'd as I understand by a letter from brother Owen* of the 27th ult. They've had a very hard time on't. God help them and praised be God that brothers were so nigh them, and good Dr. Evans, who hath saved their lives with God's assistance before this time. I would have answer'd yours of the 2nd and 9th ult. sooner but that I expected news from Môn, ag ar fy nghydwybod os meddaf rithyn, amgen na bod yr hen bobl a phawb or teulu'n rhesymol yn ol yr achos, a rhyw boblach ddieithr i chwi yn meirw ac yn priodi, etc., a bod yr hin yn gwellhau yno mal mewn manneu eraill. Am fy newyddion inne hwdiwch—Cefais lythyr o'wrth y car Salsbri dydd arall ac heb ronyn o newydd ond hanes yr *Election* a rhyw fregedd felly, ai fod wedi derbyn llythyr oddiwrthych chwithe, ond dim son ei fod yn cael gwraig.

Cefais echdoe ynghylch hanner dwsing o linelli o'r Pen Sanctaidd gyda'r hen Brins Llywelyn gynt, a dim ond dweyd fod pawb yn iach. Wel mewn difri rydwyf agos a gwallcofi orfod aros yn y fangre yma cyd, a ch'yd yn colli fy amser ag yn gwario cymaint o arian a feddwn, ag a fedrwn fenthygcio. Yn lletyfa mewn ty cwrw (Mrs. Partis at y[e] Scipio on y[e] Dock side) where I pay 3s. 6d. a week—victuals and lodgings, and obliged by the custom of the town to call for a pint of ale every dinner and supper, which amounts to six shillings within twopence every week, besides what I spend here and there when I meet with my countrymen (whom I can't shun for sake of news, etc.), and other acquaintances, which things will be very heavy upon me when I go away. Mae mor galed ar ein rhieni na fedraf yn fy myw ofyn iddynt ddim, a llyma fi wedi cael benthyg tri gini eisioes gan y brodyr swyddogion, ag ar fendi nis gwnni pa sut a fydd pan elwyf i fynd ymaith. Diammeu y bydd rhaid benthygca, ond nis gwn i gan bwy pei crogid fi. Nis gwn beth i ddywedyd bellach. Gadso gwir, Jno. Prichard, sail'd from here (after he had lost his ship on y[e] coast of Ireland) in a ship of Mr. Cunliffe's for Virginia; there to purchase her

* Owen Davies, brother-in-law to the writer.

cargo and lade her, and then to fall to and build a ship of above 400 tons for his master, and John to come master of her home. But I'd like to forget to tell you after they'd been a two days from here they were put back again, and he went now directly to Cheshire, and so to St. Asaph's to meet a girl from Holyhead, that had come there with Mr. Vickars, her brother-in-law, of purpose to be married. So at Llanraidr, Jack and she were join'd fast, stay'd with her one night, so parted—he here and she home again. So he got a fair wind again as soon as he came, and away he went and will not return in less than two years. Now I'm quite aground. No: Margaret Ligo, ye old landlady in this town, is dead. Mrs. Wright (alias Bulkely) is lately brought to bed of a son and heir. I've got my chest, etc., back again, but not without damage and charges too. I think to send them with a Welch sloop that's going to lade lead for London. But however, you shall hear when I send them. In the meantime I hope I shall hear from you whether my affairs goes on there, and if you've spoke to Mr. Whormby since. I wish now I had never thought of going into the King's Service, for I'm almost sure I could have done better out of this town, but it signifies nothing now, for if I dont go, I shall be lookt upon as the greatest liar in ye world. I've a black lad about 16 years old to sell for a friend, and I can't get any body to buy him. I wish I had him at London, I'd sell him under £30, ay, a little above £25. Now I must leave off, though I could say more now I begin to bring to mind. There's no embargo upon coasters, so I've a pacquet to send with these Welch men-of-war to Anglesey, so wishing us both good luck and a happy meeting, I rest your brawd ungalon, *Ioan Amhorys.* J. to R. contd.

CHATHAM, 4th April, 1740. J. to R. XIII.

Dear Brother,—Seeing this opportunity with one of my shipmates, I thought proper to send you a line. I writt you a letter yesterday before I left London, but forgot to put it in ye penny post. I could never hear anything of the sloop with my things, but have left directions with Mr. Turner how to send them to ye rendesvouz when they come. I forgot to get the copper pot, so I desire you'd send it to Mr. Turner and let him send it with the chest, etc. There's no freight to pay but what charges Mr. Turner will

J. to R. contd. be at in getting them down. I told him he should be paid by you, ag mi dalaf inneu pan welwyf chwi nesaf. Call at Williams's now and then to see if there be any letters for me. I believe I shan't be here long, for I understand the tender is ready, and we shall go directly for Dublin, where she is to deliver some goods, and then i'r fann a fynnom. Ni choeliai y scrifenai at neb ond hynny, ond os daw yna un llythyr imi o hyn i ddechre'r wythnos nesaf gyrrwch hwynt yma. Ni feddai iw chwanegu ond fy annerch at bob ffrind, ag wyf eich ffyddlon frawd, *Ioan Amhorys.*

L. to R. XIV.

HOLYHEAD, 10th April, 1740.

Dear Brother,—I received a letter, with newspapers, dated 29th March, for which I'm obliged, and as long as you have franks you'd do well to send us something every post. We take in no papers ourselves. The *Daily Gazeteer* comes to ye Post Office and two other places, but we hardly have a sight of even that. The *London Evening and Common Sense* we see once a week sometimes. The *St. James's Evening Post* I would choose to have. Could not you get it at second-hand from some coffee house? Mae'n rhy ddryd imi'r llaw gynta. I wrote to Mr. Whormby this day about the Skerries business. I wish I could get it. It would be at least twenty pound a year in my way. I wrote to him ye 6th March last a letter with a pilot's bill (to be received of ye Navy Office) in it, but never heard a syllable from him, nor have I, I think, since November last. You are also exceeding lazy. Why don't you tell me what reception you had with Mr. Vaughan, from whom I had not a syllable since he received my letter with my affidavit, to be delivered at the Admiralty. Yn enw Duw, beth ddarfu i'r bobl i gyd?

I sent you ye foregoing songs for your edification. The *marwnad* will come also to the tune of Morfa Rhuddlan, and is to be sung with an audible voice in all companies that love the game.

I suppose we are to expect brother John at ye Head soon. You mention y^{e} . . . and of ye tender; but he doth not himself in his last letter. I wish he may keep sober—dyna wendid y mab.

I wish you had let me know how Mr. Whormby is inclin'd, whether you think he is a hearty friend, whether now much entangled in business, or what may be ye reason of his not writing so often as usual. I have a suspicion that the old fox Nicholson doth me no good in London. I am glad Mr. Meyrick us'd you and brother John so well. He is a worthy good man to our family—let others say of him as they find him. I had lately a very kind letter from Mr. Lloyd, of Cardigan. Mi wneuthum iddo tipyn o gymwynas yn ddiweddar. Nid oes niwed er ei fod yn foneddigeiddlyd, mae ef er hynny yn wr digon mwyn. L. to R. contd.

I wrote to brother John to Chatham last post, which I hope will reach him. Mae pawb yn lled iach yn Mhentrerhianell. If you can give me a catalogue of ye Men of War, their force, etc., and where station'd, I shall be much oblig'd to you. Pray, is ye scheme of voluntary registring of seamen quite knock'd in ye head? Mr. Whormby would have got by it, if ye management had been left in ye Trinity House.

I shall expect to hear from you as soon as possible. Consider the life of man is not above two inches long, and most things here below are but vanity. Charity and honesty are the most lovely things I know.

Nicholson's nephew (James Brisco), now collector of Beaumares, is also at London. He is somewhat an honester man than ye old one. He is married to ye widdow of John Edmunds, ye heiress of John Prytherch, of Tregayan, and is now come to settle two of her children with their uncle, Doctor Henry Edmunds, the great antiquarian. I mention his character lest you should happen to fall into his company. Plant Alis i gyd oll.

Nid oes yma fawr le ond hynny, felly ffarwel rwan.

Dy frawd trafferthus, L. Morris.

FROM ON BOARD HIS MAJESTY'S SHIP TORBAY, AT CHATHAM, 16th April, 1740. J. to R. XV.

Anwyl Frawd,—Scrifenais attoch er's dyddiau byd mawr, ag yr oeddwn yn disgwyl atteb cyn hyn, a rhyw hanes o' nghist, etc., gan hynny, mae'n debyg i'r llythyr feddwi a cholli'r ffordd. Cefais lythyr o'r Pen Sanctaidd o'r 7fed presenol. Dim newydd yn y byd ond bod pawb yn iach, etc. Gresyn na yrrach y ffranciau immi mal y cawn sgrifenu'n rhad at boblach Cymru. Ef a gododd rhyw rwttws melldigedig drwy gefnau fy nwylo dydd arall, a chwyddo a orugasant yn ddirfawr, a chosi a dolur cethin o

J. to R. contd. naddynt. Gorfu arnaf waedu y Sadwrn diwaethaf yn un braich, a dydd Llun yn y llall, yr hyn am gwnaeth mor anwydog nad wyf abl i ddangos fy nhrwyn ar y deck etto. Yr wy'n gorwedd y nos yn hamocc y mate arall, a diau mae aniddan iawn ydyw bod fal hyn, heb na llyfr i'w ddarllain oriau segur, na dilledyn iw newid, ond gwisco dydd Sul beunydd. Gorfod benthygca pin ag inc a phapir, ag mewn ychydig eirie rwy wedi mynd yn benbrydd gynddeiriog o'r achos.

Dyma ni'n barod er's dyddiau i fynd i lawr i'r *Nore*, ond eisiau gwynt têg, a dyna'r peth sy'n cadw'r tender hefyd rhag dyfod oddiyna. Ond nis gwn i pa beth sy'n llestair fy nhist i, etc., rhag dyfod. Pan ddelo, na anghofiwch yrru y pot coppr imi hefyd. Os gorfydd arnaf fynd ymaith gyda'r tender cyn cael fy nghist, nis gwn yfi pa beth a ddaw o honwyf. Mi fyddaf yn noeth luman cyn dychwel i'r llong eilwaith, a minne mewn y fath anghaffael. Pa beth a wnaf, ah? Scrifenais atteb i'r brodur o'r Pen Sanctaidd y post diwaethaf. Gadewch glywed oddiwrthych gyda dychweliad y post, a *rhyw newydd* da i gysuro calon dromm, a chwi ryngwch fodd. *Eich brawd ffyddlonaf*, *Ioan Amhorys.*

Direct for J. M., mate on board His Majesty's ship, *Torbay*, at Mr. Large's, near the Dockyard . . .

Ni chefais i ffyrling arian gan Garreg gwedi'r cwbl, felly nis gwybod pa sut fydd talu ir câr Will Huws, sidanwr. Mae'n gwilydd noeth gerth. Gyrrwch imi hefyd hanes y Ffreinigwyr. Mae'r gair yma eu bod yn taro gyda'r Spaeniaid, etc., ag y bydd rhyfel bentan rhyngom ar fyr amser. Ni bu monwyf ar y lann etto ond y noswaith gynta ar ol dyfod yma. Bu agos imi a rhynnu wrth ddyfod yma. Buom noson ar y dŵr, a minne heb na bwyd na diod dros ugain awr. Dyna fyd caled, on'te? Mae gwell chwant i fwyd rwan na phan oeddwn yna, ag yn cael digon o waith gael llonaid bol bob pryd.

Brysiwch scrifenu rhag ofn i mi fynd i bant.

J. to R. XVI.

FROM ON BOARD THE TORBAY, AT BLACKSTAKES,
May 2nd, 1740.

Anwyl Frawd,—Mi gefais eich llythyr ar ffrancs, etc., ar fy nyfodiad ir llong, yr hyn ydoedd brydnawn echdoe, ag wele da ydoedd gan y cadpen fy nyfod oblegyd mae meistr y llong yn

Llundain er cyn immi fynd or llong, ag wmbwrdd o waith i edrych ar ol *honno*. Bwyd a diod yn yr *hold*, ag heb ond un mate i mewn. Ond pei dwedwn gyhyd a chywydd i chwi, mae nhw'n siared y byddwn yn hwylio oddiyma naill ai foru ai trennydd ir *Nore*. A pha hyd yr arhoswn yno nis gwyr neb. Mae fal y scrifenwch ir wlad i ddweyd fy hanes, fe allai na chaf gyfleu i yrru llythyr ir lan ennyd, bynnag pa'r fodd, sgrifenaf linell at nhad heno i ddweyd fy mod yn fyw, etc. Ni feddafi newydd yn y byd ond fy mod yn llawer gwell ar fiechyd nag oeddwn pan ddaethym yna, ag mae'r dwylo'n holliach. Ni chaf hamdden i chwanegu, ond fy nghorchymyn at bawb yna ag yn y wlad, a byddwch wych. J. to R. contd.

Wyf eich caredigol frawd, Ioan Amhorys.

Direct for me at the *Nore*, or elsewhere.

Rhag ofn na byddwn yno, send ye letters per one of the passage boats that comes to Sheerness. Either Franks at Irongate or Adams at Wapping New Stairs. Ond oedd gwall arnafi na buaswn yn cofio (hyd yr amser y bum yna) am brynu llyfr pappir gwyn i gadw journal un folio ag ynghylch 3 chweir neu 4 o bappir a chaead memrwn. Gwyn ei fyd na fedrach yrru imi un, mi dalwn i chwi yn onest am dano, neu os byddai'n beth mwy na 4 quire, goreu oll fyddai.

FROM ON BOARD HIS MAJESTY'S SHIP, TORBAY, J. to R.
AT BLACKSTAKES, May 18th, 1740. XVII.

Dear Brother,—I wonder I can't hear from you all this time, and I've writt you so long ago. I'm afraid you did not get the letter. I had enclos'd in it another to father (frank'd), which I desir'd you to send forward, but never heard of neither of them. I'm uneasy about this, and don't know how to write to father till I hear from you. In that letter I had desir'd you to send me per one of the Sheerness passage boats a book of four or five quires white paper, bound in parchment, and a quire of loose paper, for I am in great need thereof, having forgot to buy when I was at London. I suppose you've heard that Admiral Stuart hoisted his flag on board her last Sunday, and was saluted by all the ships in the place, the garrisons likewise, and ever since we have ye white flag the foretopmast head; and last Thursday *His Majesty* was . . . to put in Sheerness (wind-bound). The garrison saluted him with sixty-one guns, the ships with twenty-one, and we seventeen,

J. to R. contd.

because we were a flag-ship. The *King* had a flag at each mast-head, viz., the Standard of Great Britain at ye maintopmast head, the Anchor and Hope at ye foretopmast head, and ye Union Flag at ye mizentopmast head, besides an Ensign and Jack, and Sir Charles Wager has ye white flag at ye maintopmast head. Roedd yna orfoledd cethin, ag yma mae'r Brenin, etc., etto, ond fe ddygodd ddryghin arw gydag efo, ag i mae'n parhau etto. Ni chlywai sôn i ble y bydd raid ini fynd, ond mae'n siccr y bydd rhaid ini ddanfon yr Admiral i Bortsmouth, ymha fann y mae i'n gadael ag i hossio ei fflag yn y *Boyn*, llong 90 gwnn. I've no more to add at present, but desiring you would send ye above things per first opportunity, and I'll pay you as soon as I can, and call at Williams's to see if there be ere a letter for me. So expecting to hear from you soon, I rest, your loving brother, *John Morris.*

Direct for me aboard the ship at Blackstakes or elsewhere. It must be either frank'd or post paid, or else I shall never have it.

J. to R. XVIII.

FROM ON BOARD THE TORBAY, May 24th, 1740.

Dear Brother,—Seeing the opportunity, per Mr. Mathews (my brother's mate and messmate) thought proper to send you a line or two, though I should let it alone on account I never can hear from you (nor anybody else for that matter). This is either the third or fourth I writt you since I left London, and took care to put ye last in ye post office myself, so that I can't believe they all miscarried. The main purport of all the letters was to desire you'd send me per one of Sheerness passage boats a folio book of white paper, containing about four quires, and likewise a couple of quires loose writing paper. Now this is to desire once more that you would not fail sending them, and the price, and you shall be paid. We expect to sail to the Nore next Monday, and what time we shall stay there I cannot tell, but I believe it won't be long. The Admiral is to leave us soon, and to go aboard another ship. I've writt to Anglesey, Liverpoole, Creuddyn, and to all friends since I came down here, but can't get a line from anybody. Mr. Mathews will direct you how to send ye above to me. So with love to you and service to all friends, I rest, your loving brother,

John Morris.

Brys cethin.

FROM ON BOARD HIS MAJESTY'S SHIP, TORBAY, AT BLACKSTAKES, May 28th, 1740. J. to R. XIX.

Dear Brother,—Yours of ye 20th inst., with ye other letters and papers, I received last Sunday night; and writt to brother Lewis immediately about Ned Edwards. I told him that I thought it would be of no service to ye lad to come here except he had recommendations to some commission'd, or warrant officer, or another, if he expects to get any post; and told him that I did not know one office aboard the ship that he could execute. How should he when he has never been at sea in his lifetime, only in little boats about Holyhead Bay? Ag yn wir, rhyngo chwi a minne, ni waeth gan Sion am ei gwmni, for I'm sure I should always be plagued with him. I'd willingly do any service to the lad if he had any knowledge of the sea; but, as it is, one may as well take a prentice to teach him, as he that knows nothing. I'm in great want of the book and papers, but see nothing of its coming. I'm certain I have not forgot myself, and that I have sent a frankt letter to father, inclos'd in yours, but understand you have not received it. So the old people thinks I've forgot them. Shall write to-morrow, or next day, to brother Owen, in answer to this you sent me last. He sent me no news, only of Michael Huws, (Lligwy gynt's) being married again to another Sioned that I was to have, as I thought. Bendith ei mam gyda hi, a bendith fy mam inne hefyd. Aie mynd iw briodi mae'r brawd Lewys? Ni fedrai dyfeisio pwy eill y fenyw fod; tebyg mae gwawdio mae. Da os ceiff y *scent*. It's said with us that Admiral Balchen is at Plymouth, and has been there this three weeks. Ffei! ffei! we are going to lose our flag again. The Admiral is going on board the *Cambridge*, another 80-gun ship just ahead of us, and we expected to've struck the flag this day.

We've got our sailing orders this three days past, but the wind continues easterly here, so that there is no going out of this. I believe we shall make but a short stay at the Nore, having a pilot (from ye Nore to ye Downs) on board already, and another from here to the Nore, so I don't expect to hear from any of you any more till I get to Spithead; ay right, I writt you last Friday, per Mr. Mathews, my messmate, and hope he'll find you out, and then I

J. to R. contd. shall expect a line. I can't tell whether the tender will be sent down to Liverpoole or not, for we've had lately nigh two hundred and fifty men turn'd over to us from the *Edinburgh*, which lately came home. However, you'll know the first opportunity. I'm sorry you had not more franks, for the d——l a letter I shall ever get if it ben't either frankt or post-paid. I can't come and see you any more this time, therefore remember me to all friends and acquaintances, which is all at present from your loving brother,

John Morris.

P.S.—Onid af i Nerpwl, pa sut fydd gyrru gini melyn y lodes fain iw modryb, ah? Beth meddwch? Two months' advance, and ye bounty and conduct money will be paid at ye Nore, but am afraid I shall not come in for ye bounty money, for I expect they'll not pay it any officer; besides, I'm a day too late set down in ye check office, although by the ship's book I'm entitled to it. The Captain promised to rectify ye matter.

J. to R. XX.

CHATHAM, 2nd June, 1740.

Dear Brother,—I received yours of the 31st ult., and the other of brother Lewis inclosed. Rwyn credu fod y dyn yn ynfyd ynghylch ei frawd-ynghyfraith. Roedd heb dderbyn fy llythyr diweddaf, ond fe geiff yn hwnw gyflawn hanes o'meddwl i'n y mater. Mae'n gofyn fwy o gwestiwnau yn ei lythyr nag wyfi etto abl i atteb, megis dimensions y llong, examination y meistr, etc. Pa sut y gallai'r gwr feddwl y dylwni wybod y fath bethau mewn gan lleied amser. Mae gennyfi ddigon ar fy llaw i holi ac ymofyn ynghylch fy ngwasanaeth fy hunan dros ennyd fawr—Nid mewn diwrnod y gwnaed Rhufain. I'm sorry my messmate did not call again with you for the book, for I want it sadly; however, if this comes to your hand in time, you may send it safely to-morrow with Adams's passage boat, who'll set out from Iron Gate at high water, which will be about six a clock if this wind continues. He constantly calls aboard of us every time he comes here. You can give him orders where to deliver it at London when he comes back if we be gone, but I don't see any sign of it, for the wind continues against us still.

We've men enough now having had all ye men out of the *Edinburgh*, that lately came home from Lisbon, in number nigh

300. Let me know the price of the book and paper if you send any. I shall write to brother Lewis again when I first get time. I was sent up here this morning for some of our people that were at the hospital, but they are in a poor condition to go on board. Our ship is very sickly and has been for some time. My messmate is not come on board yet, I wonder what makes him stay. It's hard for me myself to act, having so many men to look after. The other mate that came down from the *Rondezvous* is a mere novice as yet, worse than I was at first. Yn rhodd byddwch cystal ar gair yn gyrru yr holl newyddion imi. Heddyw mae'n gorfod arnaf dorri gini melyn y lodes wirion yn ddrylliau mân, ond gobeithio y caf un arall yn ei le mewn ychydig amser. We are to receive the bounty, conduct, and advance money at the Nore if we stay there but a day or two. Have not time to enlarge but remembring me to all my friends, I rest your loving brother, J. to R. contd.

John Morris.

P.S. Mae'n ddrwg genyf glywed fod y brawd Lewys ar y ffordd i golli'r Sieris, a cholli'r holl gyflog am ei drafferth yn mesuro, hefyd gobeithio na ddigwydd felly. Pa fusnes sydd ganthaw gyda Mr. Llwyd?

From on Board His Majesty's Ship, Torbay, J. to R.

at Spithead, 21st June, 1740. XXI.

Dear Brother,—This comes to acquaint that we arriv'd here safe on Thursday last in the afternoon, having left the Downs on Wednesday night. I can't as yet send you any account upon what expedition we are to go, but depend upon it we shall go away in a short time for there's come on board of us already bedding for 90 marines, so is there on board of the ships here, being upwards of 20 sail of the line of battle, besides fireships, shore ships, hospital ships, etc. I writt you from ye Downs but have had no answer. Llyma gant o lythyrau i boblach eraill sy'n perthyn ir llong ond wenwyn un imi. Nis gwn y fi pa beth a wneir am arian i brynu llyfr a phapir, ni chawsom geiniog etto, na dim son pa bryd y cair. Let me hear from you as soon as possible, and let's have some news from Môn. I'll write there next post, but I am so fatigu'd and have been ever since I came from the Downs that I can

J. to R. contd. hardly lay pen to paper to write any body yet. Let's hear also how the war goes on for I believe that I shall hardly trouble myself to go ashore here for any news, having ond ychydig arian wedi eu gadel yn awr. I can't think of any more to say at present, but remember me to all friends in general.

Who am your loving brother, John Morris.

Call at Williams's to see if there be any letters for me.

J. to R. XXII

SPITHEAD, 3rd July, 1740.

Dear Brother,—I received yours of Midsummer's Day in due time, but had not an opportunity to answer it sooner, all of us being hurry'd out of our lives nearly, being in expectations of sailing every minute, though Duw wyr pa bryd yr awn oddiyma. Diolch yn fawr am y newyddion a gefais; fe fu'r llythyrau eraill yn hir gynddeiriog. Mi gefais lythyr arall oddiwrth y brawd Owen, a hanes fod fy narpar gwraig Ymôn (nid Sioned or Cei), gwedi cael gwr arall, a llawer o hanesion difyr. Ond ni welais hanes o Ned Edwards yn . . . etto. Mae'n debyg ei fod wedi ei bresio. Rwyn disgwyl beunydd atteb ir llythyrau a yrrais i Fôn. We are kept aboard so strictly that there is not one allow'd to go ashore for fear we should not be ready when we get our orders to sail. We expect the Duke of Cumberland on board of us to-morrow. General Wade and a great number of persons of distinction went past here this afternoon for the Isle of Wight, when Sir John Norris saluted them with seventeen guns. Our foretopsails have been loose this two days, and we expect to receive two months' advance to-morrow. I was flung out of the bounty money, and conduct money, too. Being a petty officer I can't get an opportunity to go and see Dick Owen, though he belongs to Sir John in the next ship. Gwych fal y passiodd Vernon y Spaengwn. Passiwn ninne'r Ffreinigwyr hyd na bont yn stics yn ei crwyn pan elom oddiyma. As for Will Roberts, that heiress was at Leverpoole when I left the place, and I had a deal of conversation with her; told me the whole affair between Will and she. Sion Williams, seler, Aberffraw (our uncle) marry'd her own aunt, and he's her guardian, and was along with her at same time. Will is a sad rake—spent all his wife's fortune and left her children to beg their bread. She was worth upwards of £300. Duw wnel i Mr. Meyrig brynu Llaniden. E fydd yn beth gwell ir hen bobl, a ninne hefyd. Ni feddafi ddim chwaneg o bapir, felly rhaid i chwi gymeryd hyn y tro yma, ag os caf gyfleu'n y byd, scrifenaf etto cyn hwylio. Yn y cyfamser, bydd wych, anerchwch at bawb yna. J. to R. contd.

Wyf, eich ffyddlon frawd, Ioan Amhorys.

St. Hellen's Road, 18th July 1740. J. to R. XXIII.

Dear Brother,—I writt you t'other day before we sailed from this place, at which time had not hardly leisure to turn myself round, and now I'm not much better, for here's the boat almost ready to go for Portsmouth, and I shan't have much time, only to acquaint that we sail'd from this place last Monday morning, in company with Sir John Norris, Admiral Cavendish, and Rear-Admiral Ogle, and their squadrons, consisting of nigh thirty sail of ships (fireships, etc., included), and yesterday, about three a.m., being very dark and blowing a very hard gale, and being about twelve leagues south-west-west from the hill of Portland, the Admiral (viz., Sir John) made a signal for all the fleet to bear away, the *Lyon*, a 70-gun ship having run'd foul of him and carried away his cut-water and all the head, spritsail, yard, etc., and lost herself her foremast by the board, and one man and her maintop gallant mast and spritsail, yard, etc., and we got in here yesterday p.m. This hath ruined our cruize, I'm afraid, for to-morrow the *Victory* is to be got into the harbour at Portsmouth, and Sir John is to hoist his flag on board the *Boyn*, but whether he'll continue there and go to sea in her, or stay till his own ship is repair'd, I can't determine, but it's everybody's oppinion that we shan't stay for the *Victory* to be refitted. Ned Edwards came here safe, but happen'd to be a day too late, for the Captain had given his weekly account to the Admiral that morning he came, or else he would have been enter'd a week sooner. I don't doubt but shall make something of the lad if we go a cruise. Writt to father and to the Head, a derbynais y llythyr digrifaf erioed oddiwrth fy nghariad y Môn heddyw, pei gwelach chwi dorrach ar eich traws o wir chwerthin, ffolineb mawr! Mae'n ddrwg gennyf drosti'n wirionedd. Deusyf atteb gyda dychweliad y post yw'r cwbl y tro yma oddiwrth eich caredicaf frawd, *Ioan Amhorys.*

Brys melldigedig bob amser.

I. to R.
XXIV.

On Board the Torbay, in Torbay, 14th August, 1740.

Dear Brother,—I writt you some time ago, but I've forgot when. However, this I remember, that I writt you from this place, but whether it was after our first putting in here, or the second, or both, I can't tell, and am at a loss to know. A stranger would take me by this to be a great wit, having such short memory, but as my ill-favoured stars would have it I am quite otherwise, for I'm very nigh depriv'd of the small stock I us'd to carry about me. We lie in such an out of the way part of the kingdom, and always in expectation of a shift of wind, that it would be next kin to madness to write any body for an answer, and I very seldom write twice to my good friends before I am answer'd, which custom hath made me forgetful of writing oftener; not so much for want of having you all in my mind, but of a line to freshen the memory and rub up new supplies in the brain, so to enable me to shake off with more vigour these lethargick fits and to endeavour to recover my almost senseless senses. If I have not inform'd you of our last cruize from this place, you've no doubt read of it in the public papers, and I can't tell you any more if I was to be made an Admiral for my pains; but here we are still, and like to be while this wind continues, but I hope it wont be long. I wish we may return from this cruize (if we are to return) before the heavy winter comes on, that brings cold piercing weather with it; or else that we may be order'd into some warmer climate to pass away the dark long tedious nights, and where we may divert and amuse our dull and heavy senses with something more pleasant than is to be found in these colder climes at that unseasonable season, and likewise refresh our wearied bodies with a coque of wine or a swingeing bowl of good punch, which necessaries (of all things most necessary to a seaman) we are debarr'd of and not allow'd to get upon any account: nothing allow'd to be brought on board of our ship but eatables—no manner of drinkables, even plain ale and cider is prohibited. Fish, we have plenty brought to us; some fresh meat now and then, and fruit, and some few kind good natur'd country lasses brings us a little fresh butter and milk when the weather permits. But what benefits all this without liquor? Good humming beer, or stiffning for a can of philip, or a bowl of good punch! We can't drink Saturday night's health after this rate. Strange doings! I know you'll expect news, but where should a body get any such thing on board a ship?—except one would believe our own news. We have daily a great many Pacquets coming in—one off the quarter-deck, another off the fore-castle, others off ye poop from the great cabin, gun-room, ward-room, ollop, steward-room, cockpit, and several other remote parts, and the only story that reigns at this time is that this fleet is to go acruising off the coast of Spain (*i.e.*, off of Feroll, Cadiz) etc., whilst our transports passes by with the marines from the Isle of Wight, and so on to ye West Indies. It's likely enough there may be something in it for all that. But another piece of news I have more, *viz.*: One of our people the other day was try'd by a Court Martial on board Sir John Norris for swimming away from the ship, and he was sentenc'd to receive one hundred lashes with a cat. Accordingly this forenoon the Admiral made a signal for all ships' boats in the Fleet to attend the prisoner, arm'd, etc. We had a pair of gallows erected in our longboat, and the prisoner was order'd into her and there bound to the gallows, where the Provost Martial of the Fleet read his orders and gave the prisoner twenty lashes. From hence they were tow'd on board the three Admirals, where he received twenty lashes on board each, attended by upwards of thirty boats, and then return'd on board here, and received twenty more, which made up the complement. **J. to R. contd.**

Sgrifenais dydd arall at Mr. Whormby lythyr mwyaf diolchgar ar a fedrwn ei lunio, ynghyd ag ychydig o'n hanes, etc. Ond odid digio wna'r hen gorph am scrifenu atto heb achos. Sgrifenais hefyd (rwy'n cofio) at nhad i'r Pen Sanctaidd, a rhyw leoedd eraill, nis gwnn pa fann, fe allai imi sgrifenu atto chwithe. Now I would have you to send me a line at a random per return of post, and let me know how affairs goes in Môn; a bydded oll yn Gymraeg rhag ddigwydd iddo fethu dyfod im llaw. If you see Mr. Meirig and Mr. Whormby remember me to them. Write as soon as possible to Môn, and let them know that we're here. If I had thought that we should have stayed here half this time I would have desir'd an answer in my last to you all.

J. to R. contd. Heddyw ydyw ffair Lanerchmedd, onid digrif fyddai fod yno gyda'r nos yn cofleidio Morfydd, ah! Gwraig gwr arall meddwch chwithe, wala, pwy eill help. Nis gwn fi amcan a dalodd neb y pedair gini etto ir sidanwr. Gobeitho mai do; a pha fodd yn rhodd yr hebrynga finne y gini ir lodes fain yna? Ni wiw disgwyl mynd i Nerpwl bellach rhawg byd. Dyma fi agos yn fy ngwelu ag yn gysgadur creulon. Felly, nos dda iwch. Anerchwch fi at yr holl ffyddlonieit, a byddwch wych. *Eich caredicaf frawd, Ioan Amhorys.*

Direct on board the ship in Torbay, Devonshire (or Devon).

J. to R. XXV.

ON BOARD THE TORBAY, IN TORBAY,

Saturday Night, 6th September, 1740.

Anwyl Frawd,—Scrifennais attoch yr wythnos ddiwaethaf a'n hanes, etc., hyd y pryd hynny, pan yr oeddwn yn disgwyl y cawswn lythyr oddiwrthych yn atteb i un a yrraswn or blaen oddi yma i ddeusyf cael clywed pa ddelw mae'n rhieni, etc., Ymôn, ond ni chlywais air etto. Pa'r un a wnaethoch chwi na nhwythau ai derbyn fy llythyrau ai peidio, yr hyn sydd yn fy ngwneyd yn amheuys na dderbyniasoch monynt; gan hynny os hwn a ddaw ich llaw, bydded yspys i chwi na chefais un llythyr o le'n y byd ar pan adawsom *Spitt head*, er imi scrifenu gryn haner cant at hwn ar llall. Hwyliasom oddiyma echdoe a daethom yn ol heddyw brydnhawn mewn dryghin hyll. Dyma'r pummed tro ini droi i mewn ir *Bay* hwn, ag rwy'n dybio nad oes lwcc ini gael or *Sianel* yma yleni gan wyntoedd a dryghinoedd, canys pan ddelom i mewn yma bydd y tywydd yn deg a rhywiog, a phan gynta yr elom allan ir mor nid oes iw gael ond y tywydd gwaethaf bwy gilydd. Ef a gafodd y llongau masnach oedd gyda'm ni fwy o golledion am hwyl-brennau, etc., y tro diwaethaf yma nag un amser or blaen. Duw au helpo oll, mae'n ddigon caled arnynt. Ni waeth tewi na siarad, os hwn a ddaw ich llaw gadewch glywed oddiwrthych ynghylch pawb gartre. Yr hwn gyda fy ngharedigol annerch attoch a phawb or ffyddlonieit yw'r cyfan y pryd hyn oddiwrth eich ffyddlon frawd, *Ioan Amhorys.*

Direct for J.M., mate of His Majesty's Ship *Torbay*, Devon. Ni thâl ddraen oni roddwch i ddyn ei deitlau, etc., a cheisiwch ei ffrancio neu dalwch y *postage.*

ON BOARD THE TORBAY, AT SPITHEAD, J. to R.
13th September, 1740, 8 p.m. XXVI.

Dear Brother,—I writt you I can't tell you how many letters from Torbay, and one or two from this place before we sailed from here the second time, but never did hear whether you received any of them or not, as I have likewise to father, to y[e] Head, and also to Mr. Whormby. We sail'd from Torbay yesterday p.m., with a short warning, for this place, a Duw a wyr pa beth yw'r achos. Nyni a ddaethom yma ynghylch 3 p.m. heddyw, ag aeth y Duc William ir lan yn union, ar hanes cyffredin trwy'r llong i gyd rwan ydyw ein bod ni i fynd gyda Sir Chaloner Ogle (yr hwn yw'n Amral ni) ir Gorllewinol India, a bod 32 llong rhyfel i gyd i fynd yno, a ydychwi yna yn clywed dim or fath chwedlau? Gobeithio nad gwir monynt, canys nid oes dim byw yn y llongau tri deck yma yn y gwledydd gwresog hynny, ond os ein tynged fydd i fynd yno, croeso iddi, ond bydded mewn llong lai; ag os yno'r awn, pa beth a wneir am arian i ffittio allan a dillad teneuon, etc? Rhaid gwneyd llythyr cymmun a gadel llythyr Attwrnai i ryw un neu gilydd yn y fangre anghysbell yma, ag os digwydd i ddyn fynd at ei deidiau cyn dychwel adre, yn iach ddisgwyl i neb oi berthynas ddim byth oddiwrtho. Maent yn dweyd na cheiff un dyn sydd yn y llynges fynd ir lann yma, nag un cwch chwaith, eithr cychod y *tenders* sydd i gario y llythyrau, etc., nol ag 'mlaen i gludo bwyd a diod ini a phob peth, ond ni wn i pa sutt fydd etto. Chwi gewch wybod mwy yn fy nesaf, ond cael clywed oddiwrthych ynghynta a gwybodaeth pa ddelw mae'n rhieni, etc., yr hyn sydd arnaf eisiau i glywed yn gethin. Ni chaf hamdden i chwanegu gan fy mod yn flin ag yn gysgadur, ag yn sgrifenu llinell neu ddwy adre hefyd, felly brysiwch scrifenu a byddwch wych.

Wyf eich ffyddlon frawd, Ioan Amhorys.

ON BOARD THE TORBAY, AT SPITHEAD, J. to R.
22nd September, 1740. XXVII.

Dear Brother,—Yours of the 13th inst. I received some three days ago, but as I had writt you since our arrival here I thought improper to write again 'till I got an answer, which I met with this day ashore, having gone to Portsmouth upon duty, and did not return on board 'till eight this night, very much fatigued. I'm

J. to R. contd.

sorry I should lose all them letters and newspapers, etc. I am glad to hear all are well at Môn, and that brother Lewis's affair at the Admiralty is likely to be brought to bear at last. Have not had one letter from any of 'em yet. Thanks for ye news. Digri ydoedd i fy hen gadpen baffio gwyr Angria. Pwy ydyw y ddynes honno mae'r brawd Lewis yn i ganlyn am dani? Digri hefyd i Fwclai Bawchwanen briodi'r ferch hynaf. Deg i un na bydd yn Arglwydd ar fyrder. Roeddwn yn tybio hyd yr amser fod gwraig or blaen gan Llwyd Mabwys. Ond gwych or difyrrwch a gewch yn y llûn rhyfel yna, eithr nid mor ddigri a difyr ag a gawn ni ar fyrder yn' llenwi'n poccedau a Spanish dollars pan elom ir West Indias draw, i bwy fan mae pawb agos yn dweyd yr awn yn siccr, ond Duw wyr pa le yr awn; ond hyn sydd siccr, ein bod yn cymryd bwyd, diod, a phob math ar stores i mewn i'n cynnal dros chwe mis. Eithr e ddywaid rhai nad awn oddiyma'r tymmor yma; ond gwaeth nar cwbl, dyma'r hen wr goreu'n y Llynges Freiniol yn myned oddiwrthym, sef ein parchedigcaf a'n bonheddigcaf Gadpen, yr hwn (o herwydd rhyw glwy'n ddilyn ers llawer dydd) nid yw abl i gymryd y fath fordaith yn llaw, ag felly yn myned tua thre at ei wraig, etc. I don't know whether it would not be best to write to Mr. Whormby for another recommendation to ye Captain that comes next. But who knows who or what he is? We can't have any intelligence as yet who is to come. A dyma'n Lifftenant Gwyddelig ni (sef y cyntaf) a minne wedi lled syrthio allan a'n gilydd, ag fe allai y rhydd hoel dan fy ngwadn ag am teifl o'm lle pan ymadawo Captain Parker a nyni; so that I don't know what's best to do, except I knew what captain is to come in his room. Diawl yn lle dyn yw'r Gwyddyl, ag nid oes un o'r isaf ir uchaf yn y llong ai câr, a phawb yn tyngu dial yn ei erbyn; ni feddaf fymryn chwaneg o newydd, ond darfod i Gafendish dynnu ei fflag i lawr dros y dydd a neithiwr ei rhoi i fynu drachefn. Llawer iawn o longau yma etto, Comadore Anson and his squadron sail'd, etc. All the Fleet sickly, which I believe in a great part is owing to our having so many soldiers on board. It's past ten o'clock, and I must go upon deck to watch at twelve, felly nos dawch, a brysiwch yrru imi dippyn chwaneg o newyddion, a gobeitho caf lythyr o Fôn y foru, neu drennydd or pellaf; ag erbyn y caffwyf eich nesaf, deg i un na fedraf roi gwell hanes o honom ein hunain. Yn y cyfamser should be glad if you'd either wait on, or send a penny post letter, to Mr. Whormby to acquaint him of the above, and desire to know his oppinion of the above case. I mention'd a word of it in mine to him from Torbay. I wish he may have receiv'd it. I would not go in the same ship with him (viz., Lieutenant) if I could help it without good recommendations to the Captain. Mr. Whormby can get Commissioner Purviss to do it at his request, or else have me remov'd into another ship which I would not like so well neither, though of two evils the least is best; but of this I must submit to higher powers. **J. to R. contd.**

24 die. Had not an opportunity to send this ashore yesterday, so I send it this morning per our boat, and I hope to have some news when she comes off again. Dim chwaneg o newydd, felly byddwch wych a gorchmynwch fi at bawb yna, a brysiwch scrifenu, etc. *Eich ffyddlon frawd, Ioan Amhorys.*

HOLYHEAD, 14th October, 1740. **W. to R. XXVIII.**

Dear Brother,—I received yours with the newspapers, and annext have sent you a catalogue of the plants, etc., growing in a small garden which is in partnership betwixt the Rev. Mr. Ellis, our curate, and myself. He is a gentleman that is pretty curious in those things, ond 'ch brawd Gwil ydyw'r meistr. The few roots we have was sent him from Oxford. We have our seeds from London and Dublin now and then, but I generally *cynhafa* 'em myself. If you have any seeds that are not mention'd in the catalogue we should be vastly proud if you would send us a few done up neatly in a frank. As for roots there is no getting of them without you could lite of some person a-coming to the country that would stow a few in his portmanteau. We have no room as yet to raise any trees or shrubs. I don't remember whether ever I told you that I've for upwards of three years been a-studying botany. Ag myn d——l, ni rown i mom llaw ar fy nghap i un gwr yn Ngwynedd na Deheubarth am adnabod llysiau a deiliach! I've made a catalogue in English, Welsh, and Latin of the plants, etc., growing in and about Holyhead, where we have a great many pretty rare ones, and likewise made a kind of a dry garden, or specimen of each plant. I've lately taken in

W. to R. contd. hand and finish'd (with a design of adding the same to Dr. Davies's Botanologium) a catalogue of all the plants (in Latin, Welsh, and English) out of Mr. Ray's Synopsis Stirpium Britanniciarum, Dilenius's Edition—gwaith pwysfawr oedd hwn. I intend to add the Exoticks os caf ennyd. And all for the good of the publick —chwedl y Mountibank am ei ffwgws. Maen debyg eich bod yn meddwl bellach fod 'ch brawd Gwilym yn hogyn o egotist, ag nid heb achos. Wala, wala, mae gwendid ar bawb weithiau. Pa beth a wneir am wraig ir Cardinal yn lle Bess? Par sut a fu ir ddau syrthio i'r afon? Nid wyf yn deall fod y brawd Ioan wedi mynd ymaith o Spithead etto. Pa beth ydyw'r achos? Mae nhw y ffordd yma yn bwrw'r bai ar ewyrth Rhobat. Gadewch glywed a y'ch yn gydnabyddus a dim botanists. Os y'ch mi yrraf gwestiwnau yw hatteb ganddynt ynghylch rhyw new plants. Pa beth a barodd i'r brawd Ioan adael ei will and powers of Attorney, Ymhortsmouth? Pa'r sut y mae'r llanc yn disgwyl y talwn ni pedair gini drosto fo ir sidanwr, ag ynteu yn gadael ei effects yn nwylo eraill pedae amgen na da?

Mi fum yngwylmabsant Penrhose lle y cyfarfum Joan Salsbri, etc. Roedd yn rhieni yn rhesymol ar relyw or teulu. Buom yn cwmnhieth gida'r hen gyfeillion fal arferol. Ni chwanegaf am y tro, namyn fy mod. *Eich caredigawl frawd, William Morris.*

A catalogue of plants, flowers, roots, seeds, etc., which are rais'd in the garden of the Rev. Thomas Ellis, A.M., and W. Morris, of Holyhead.

Adonis's Flowers.
Affrican Mary Gold.
French Mary Gold.
Double Corn do.
Alkakengi.
Athea.
Alexander.
Amaranthus, common.
Do. tricolor (no seed).
Androsanam Sponts.
Anemonies, various sorts.
Angelica.
Snap Dragon, one sort, Carnation colour.
Thorn Apple.
Columbine, common.
Aristolochia Rotund.
Aparabana.
Tripolium or Aster.
Avens, common.
Auricula's, very few.
Balm.
Balsam Apple, no seed.
Gostmary.
Scarlet Bean.
Black Helebore.
Orchis, no good ones.
Hyacynths, common spont.
Betony, Sponts.
Convolvulus, Blue (Major and Minor).
Bistort.

English Mercury Sponts.
Boor Cole.
Sea Cole, etc. Sponts.
Butcher's Broom.
Burnet.
Camomile.
Campanula, viz., Canterbury Bells,
Venus's Looking Glass.
Rose Campion.
Scarlet Lychnis.
Dwarf Lychnis.
Candy Tufft.
Carduus Benedict.
Chardoons.
Carnations.
Celandine.
Celery.
Tree Primrose or Onagra.
Clary.
Oculus Christi.
Perwinkle, common.
Maudlin.
Comffrey.
Conval Lillies, or the Lily of the Valley.
Coriander.
Great Corn Flag, redflower.
Large Peren. Sun Flower.
Sea Cudweed, Sponts.
Am. Cudweed, hir i hoedl.
Polyanthus, various sorts.
Geranium Columbinum.
Do. Moschat.
Indian Creeper, two sorts.
Garden do., two sorts.
Winter Creeper.
Common Garden Crocus, various sorts.
Ranunculus's, do.
Dragon.
Sweet Sultan, white and Carnation colour.
Dames Violet.
Day Lilly and Com. Lilly.
Larkspur, blue, white, and Carnation colour.
Dill.
Filipendula.
Dulcamara.
Endive.
Lathyrus, viz., Everlasting Pea, Sweet Scented Pea, etc.
Orpine, Spontans, here.
Feaverfew
Germander.
Stock Gilly Flower.
Ten Weeks Stock.
Dwarf Annual Stock.
Wall Flower.
Meadow Rue. two sorts, Sponts.
Golden Rod, Sponts. here.
Scorsonera.
Gromil, Sponts.
Holyhocks, various sorts.
French Honey Suckle.
Honesty or White Satin.
Horn'd Poppy Sponts.
Yellow Poppy of Wales do.
Horse Radish.
Vernal Starry Hyacynth of Wales, Sponts., very pretty.
Hyssop.
Jacob's Ladder.
Jerus. Sage.
Some few Jonquils.
Common Iris.
Bulbous do.
Lavender.
Do. Cotton.
Geum.
Lupins, white, yellow, and two sorts of blue.
Ladies' Mantle, Sponts.
Tree Mallow. do.
Marjoram, two.
Marvel of Peru, no seeds.
Double Mary Gold.
Muster Wort.
Melitot.
English Rhubarb.
Monks' Hood.
Motherwort.
Orach.
Peony.

W. to R. contd.

LIST OF PLANTS—*continued.*

Common Violet.
Viola Tricolour, Sponts.
Pelitory of the Wall, do.
Parsley.
Pinks.
Indian do.
Gentianella Palustris, or Pneumonanthe, very pretty, Sponts.
Rue.
Sage.
Sopewort.
Scabioris, sweet scented, no seed.
Bastard Sena.
Skirets.
Snow Drops, common.
Solomon's Seal.
Sweet William.
Curled Tansey.
Thrift, Sponts.
Thyme.
Tobacco.
Tulips, no great stock.
Rose, white and red.
Wingd Pease.
Common and Round Spinage.
Lettuce.
Radish, two sorts.
Cole Flowers.
Summer and Winter Savory.
Ladies' Laces.
Double Daises.
Great Valerian.
Double Primrose, or Paper Primrose, and the common sorts.
Dodons's Valerian.
Madder.
Borrage.
Double Rocket.

Nis gwn i na b'o rai orhain yn eisiau yn ein gardd ni o achos y rhew mawr, ond i maent yw cael yn y gymydogaeth pan fynnom. Chwi welwch nad oes gennyf fawr o flodau. Yr hâf sych ai pera' oni bae hynny baswn bûr gefnog, oblegid heuais gryn gant o rywogaethau, a ffaeliodd y gwraidd, etc., o eisiau lleithdra, etc.

L. to R. XXIX.

BEAUMARES, 16th October, 1740, 3 in ye afternoon.

Dear Brother,—Just now arrived here from Holyhead, upon an affair of my father's in ye County Court, and ye Postmaster just gives me leave to write two lines in my brother's letter. I wish you could let me hear about my affair if you hear anything of it. I suppose young Mr. Meyrick is come by this time to London. I have heard nothing from Mr. Whormby, nor Mr. Meyrick, nor anybody since I wrote to you. Never mind franks as to single letters. I shall be at home soon and write to you further, but I have hardly my senses about me now being in a hurry. Did you ever see my survey of Anglesey? It is with Mr. Meyrick, he got ye loan of it out of ye Admiralty. No news; all well in ye country.

Thy Loving Brother, Llewelyn.

On Board the Torbay, at Spithead, J. to R.
17th October, 1740. XXX

Dear Brother,—I receiv'd yours yesterday, with another enclos'd therein to Captain Gascoigne, for which I am very much oblig'd to Mr. Whormby, and desire that he may be acquainted thereof the first opportunity, and wish it might lie in my power to make him amends. I sent the letter into y[e] Captain in his cabin, but he did not say anything to me about it yet. We unmoor'd last Wednesday, and last night moor'd again, and this night the Captain says we must unmoor again in the morning. I am sadly tired, having been upon hard duty all this day, and am like to be so all this night, having three vessels alongside with beer and water which we must take all in this night. Rwyfi fal dyn oi gof. Am oblig'd to do everything myself, the rest of the mates being sick, and some ashore, ag os ni chaf air da y Cadpen rwan ni chaf byth; but to more of the purpose. I can't forgive myself (as I told you in my last) for signing that paper of pardon, and I don't know how to look any of you in the face hardly if I should live to come that way; but I would never have done it if it had not been for a young gentleman that was concern'd in the affair more than myself, who writt to y[e] Lieutenant to ask his pardon, etc., and the Lieutenant kept his letter, and he was afraid he might get a claw of him upon that account, and he told the Lieutenant that he would get the rest of us to sign along with him, or else mi dorraswn fy llaw ddeheu cyn y rhoeswn wrth y fath beth cywilyddus. Gwych fase pei gwelsech Lord Vere, canys roedd un o honom (sef hwnnw fu mewn heuyrn) yn anferth ffrind iddo, ag a sgrifenodd atto ynghylch y peth, a phei buasai i chwithe ddweyd iddo fy stori inne mi wrantaswn y Gwyddyl na ddaethai mwyach in trwblio ni, ond nid oes ammeu na chawn achos i achwyn arno etto. As for Mr. Whormby's saying he'll make me master, I'm afraid I shan't be entitled to it a long time, having not serv'd any considerable time in y[e] Navy, though there are some made that hath never been in the Navy. I should stand a better chance to be a lieuteuant if I had been long enough in y[e] Service, a Duw wyr mae llawer llai trwblaeth ydyw fod yn y swydd hono na bod yn feistr. I wish I had thought of it in my last to desire you to go to

J. to R. contd.

Mr. Secretary Corbett for recommendations, and I'm sure he'd not refuse Mr. Wright's accountant (his cousin, of Leverpoole), but Lord Vere would have been ye best. Os cewch gyfleu'n y byd siaradwch ag ef yn fy nghylch, oni wyddoch fod dwy long yn ei gweithio'n Nerpwl? Ond gwych fyddai gael mynd yn feistr ar un o honynt hwy, ah? A master of a 40-gun ship is a good birth, but enough of this. I've made neither will nor power to anybody yet, nor will not, for if I should want any money abroad ye Purser would supply me with what I should want. I shall make a will to be sure as soon as we go to sea, and shall keep it myself, but I can't believe we shall be long from home. It's now past one a Saturday morning, and at two I go to stow the hold. I've hardly my senses about me to write anything, and am afraid shan't get time to write my father, therefore I desire you'd write him to acquaint that we are just a-sailing except either the wind shifts, or a contradicting order comes, and that I bid them all adieu, hoping shall live to see 'em all well again, but if I get any opportunity shall write myself. Pwy dybygach sydd yn lieutenant ar ein sawdwyr ni ond Mr. John Bodvel, brawd Mr. Bodvel, o Fadryn. Mae efe a minne'n anferth ffrindie. Dwedwch i nhad ei fod yma, ag fy mod yn tybio y geill fod o wasanaeth imi. Mi wranta bydd yn dda gan deulu Llys Dulas glywed y newydd. Y tan a losco yr Arglwydd Cathcart; fe'n rhoes ni bod o un allan o'n cyfleusdra. Ni feddaf nag amser na phwyll i anghwanegu, felly ni fedraf mwy na gobeithio y cewch chwi a minne ein byd wrth ein bodd, ag ymgyfarfod dedwydd, ag felly, byddwch wych.

Wyf eich caredigcaf frawd, John Morris.

W. to R.

XXXI.

HOLYHEAD, 20th February, 1740.

Dear Brother,—All your letters to Brother Lewis came in due course to hand, and has been forwarded him at Aberffraw, where he has been about a month attending a ship loading of tobacco stranded near that capital. We are infinitely oblig'd to you for the papers and pamphlets. Chwedl chwitheu pa beth a wneir pan gyfodo'r Senedd? Yn wir hi fydd yn ddigon caled arnom am dipyn o newydd. Now to the affair in hand. What makes me put you to this charge, etc., is to know whether you'll undertake to procure the money hereafter mentioned. If so, you will be able to pay yourself. Dyma i chwi'r hanes. **W. to R. contd.**

One John Buttler, of this town, a batchelor died on board the Rochester Ship of Warr, and there was wages due to him as below. His mother hath administered, and is entitled to his effects. If you can take this affair in hand I shall send you a copy of the administration, which I presume will be sufficient authority (Qu: a power of attorney must be had), and you may satisfy yourself for your trouble what you may judge reasonable. If you can't spare time to attend the Pay Office I wish you would recommend some honest person that would transact this affair reasonably, or put the poor woman in a way how to come at the cash, which I believe would be very acceptable.

John Butler, pressed at Dublin, 11th January, 1739, died 20th June, 1740.

Wages due at 7s. 6d. per month ...	£6	9	4
Apparel sold at Mast for	2	2	0
Short Allowance Money	0	6	0
	8	17	4
He ow'd the Purser	0	3	2
	£8	14	2

Let me have a line per return of the post or as soon as you can. You can soon know if the vessel is paid, and what there is due to him on the books, and should likewise be glad to know what charges may attend the receiving of the money. It may be paid to the hands of Mr. Meyrick, and Mr. Evans, his steward, may pay it the widow. Gan nad oes gennym fawr o waith y Brenin yw wneuthur yr amser ymma or tymmor, mi gymerais yn llaw er's dyddiau sgrifennu mewn llyfr newydd tanlli gymaint o waith yr ardderchog fardd hwnnw, Dafydd ab Gwilym, ag a fedrwn ddyfod o hyd iddynt o dwll ag o drafais, ag wele fi wedi cynnull ir llyfr hwnnw well na 90 o gywyddau ag owdlau, er y 5ed Ionawr. Diolch am yr had a addawsoch, hi ddaw yn amser yw hau ar fyrder. Par fodd y gwneir iawn am y cymwynasau ymma, ah? Nid oeddwn i yn meddwl amgenach na roe fyrth Rhobat godwm ir mân gyfarthgwn rheini pan welai fo yn dda. Pam na adawant lonydd i'r gwr wneuthur ei orchwyl?

W. to M. contd. Roedd y teulu yn Nulas yn iach dydd arall. Mi gefais y pamphlet ynghylch Charity Schools, ac, yn wir, rhyfedd oedd weled bod cymaint yn ei haddysgu. A oes peth o rywogaeth Whitfield yn y Jones hwnnw? Yn rhodd gadewch gael tippyn o hanes a phar fodd y maent yn carrio'r gwaith ymlaen. Pan weloch Mr. Davies, Carn, a Mr. Price, dymuno ngwasanaeth attynt. Oes dim gwrageddos iddynt ettwa? Ni adwaenais i mo Sion Evan a'r Wyddeles yn iawn erioed. Dim colled fawr debygai. Ni bu mo honwyf Ymhenrhos er y Gwyl mabsant. Nid oes ymma geffyl a eill prin garrio Gwenhidyw chwaethach llwyth Cartwen o swyddog. Ni welwyd erioed fath brinder porthiant i anifeiliaid na mwy o grwyn ar baradwydd, y farchnad yn llawer drytach ar ydau nag yna. Dyma long o Lundain yn rhwym i Lerpwl ag yn gwerthu peth oi hŷd, sef haidd am 4s. y Winchester bushel, yw hau, y peth a brynwyd yna am 21s. y chwarter. Duw a ddel a llawnder. Da ydyw clywed fod Sir Chas. Ogle wedi cael i blith y Spaeniaid, gobeitho ei fod wedi rhoi iddyn nhw olchfa cyn hyn. Dymma'r cwbl sy gennyf yw adrodd am y tro. Mae'r eira wedi fferu ymysaidd i. *Dy frawd ungalon, Gwilym Morus.*

P.S.—Upon second thought I thought it the best way to send this under cover to Mr. Vychan, for I was not sure as to the directions to you.

W. to R.
XXXII.

Nos Wener, 13th March, 1740.

Dear Brother,—Dyma fi wedi derbyn eich dau lythyr, sef o'r 24ain Chwefror, ar 7fed o'r mis ymma, a chwedl yr hen ddynan hwnnw: da oedd ei cael, mi dynga' i chwi hynny. Can diolch am yr hadau gwerthfawr yma, mi debygwn mae math ar snap dragon yw un, a math or mithridate mustard (nid hwyrach mae Rose of Jerico) yw'r llall, pa un bynnag fo geir gwel'd ar fyrder. Mi roddais rai o honynt yn y ddaear heddyw ar y medr hwnnw. Maer tywydd ymma yn dra thêg, ond bod y nos yn llwydrewlyd, ni wnaeth hi ymma na gwynt na glaw i son am dano er y 26ain o Chwefror, tebygcach i Fehefin nag i Fawrth. A dedwydd iawn yw i bobl Fôn ar les ei hanifeiliaid sydd yn barawd i lewygu. Gresyn hefyd oedd farw yr Arglwydd Cathcart, ond rwy'n deall mae celwydd a ddywedasant ynghylch Gasgoigne a bod y gwr yn fyw iach y Nadolig. Gadael yn angof a wnaeth ymrawd Llewelyn ddywedyd i chwi yn un oi lythyrau fod O'Hara wedi tarrio ar ol y llong yn Lloegr. Cadpen Parker a ddywedodd innî, ag mae *incog* yr ydoedd rhag ofn cael drwg nes i ryw un gael pardwn iddo. Cymryd arno bod yn glâf, felly dyna Siontyn wedi cael gwared un gelyn. Aie fo gadd Siors y Doctor fyn'd yn ddarn o feddyg? Llanc cywraint ydoedd, ond bod cnicell ynddaw. Da iawn ydoedd gweled yn 'ch ail llythyr fod y Pendefig yna, sef Mr. Vaughan, yn dechreu troi ar mendio. Roedd ymrawd Llewelyn wedi clywed yn yr Aberffraw ei fod wedi marw, ag roedd mewn dychryn mawr. Gyrrais inneu ddyn yn ungwaith pan ge's eich llythyr yw lawenychu. Y mae ef byth yn garcharor yn y brif ddinas honno, ag nid oes dim gobaith rhyddhad am a glywaf i. The case was thus. A ship belonging to one Seel, of Leverpoole, laden with tobacco from Maryland, was drove ashore there by a violent gale of wind the 22nd January last, the men all saved. Every hogshead of the cargo was damag'd, but all or most of it brought ashore to highwater mark; the ship went to pieces, but the materials saved; brother at the head of about ten officers have been there ever since, watching said cargoe for it must be all burnt, and the King pays thirty shillings a hogshead premium for it. Now ye said cargo was insured in London, so the commissioners and insurers have not as yet agreed how and where it must be destroy'd, and I believe the officers are partly at a loss who shall be their paymasters. My brother is the whole manager of the affair and I believe wishes he had been excus'd the jobb. I was at the same place about three years agon upon much the same errand, on account of a ship of Mr. Cunliffe, of Leverpoole, but I was very handsomly rewarded. I don't know how these insurers will behave. Now I'm repeating histories pray let us have a little account of the affair betwixt O'Hara and brother Jack. We never heard one syllable of it. As for the copper ore vessel, she was a sloop from Wexford, in Ireland, of, and for, Leverpoole, and was driven into this bay 1st November, having split all their sailing, and the men being four in number had shut themselves up in the cabbin, and notwithstanding the vessel ran herself on a rock almost dry, they never came up till it was too late, for they all perished before our faces. My brother, as being deputy vice-

W. to R. contd.

W. to R. contd.

admiral, took care of what things there was saved, till a proper proof being made, Sir Arthur gave up his claim upon satisfying my brother and a small premium for himself. Diwedd.

Rwy'n gobeitho clywed oddiwrthych y foru ynghylch arrian Butler, a phwy a wyr na chawn i lythyr oddiwrth Sion Longwr? Ond y mae'r tawelwch mawr ymma yn cadw'r llongau allan heb yn ddiolch yn ei danheddau. Amser trafferthus ydoedd hi ar y *mates* yn *St. Kits* a *Dominico*, o ble-id ei swydd hwynt oedd gweled gosod y dwfr yn ei le, ag angori a diangori y llongau, etc., ag felly rwyn gobeitho nad rhaid gwanobeitho nad yw'r gwr yn jach lawen a chwedi bellach guro'r Spaeniaid, etc., hyd na bo'nt yn sienigl yn eu crwyn. Dyma fam Iorwerth a mam-ynghyfraith ein brawd Llewelyn yn glaf wan, a deg i un y daw drwyddi hi. Colled fawr ir ddwy lodesig yma, o ran prin y gwybuant erioed eisiau eu mam gan eu bod dan asgell yr hen nain. Duw a mendio arni hi. Amen.

Mae ymma glefydon mawr, sef y bloody flux, neu glwy'r gwaed mewn rhai mannau, ar cryd poeth yn arteithio teuluoedd. Dyma Mr. Edward Owen, o Benrhose, y cymydog goreu a feddan i yn y wlad ar drancedigaeth, a kind of galloping consumption, in all probability can't live not above two or three days. My brother and self will lose a sincere good friend in him. You may remember that I was with you when at London at his lodgings at the King and Pearl, in Tavistock Street. He was then a limner, and a second brother. Yn wir, colled fawr am ŵr mwyn diddanol, yr hwn ni edy mo'i fath oi ol ym Môn. Yn iach ganu 'Salmau yn beraidd ynghôr Cybi, ag ar air yn iach pob diddanwch a chymydogaeth dda, o hyn allan. Ce's lythyr ddoe oddiwrth Lywelyn, yn sponcio o wir lawenydd fod y Brawd Du o Nannau yn byw; had a letter the day before from Dulas, were all well. Laus Deo.

I think you mention'd something in a letter to brother some time agoe about Will Morus's (Caereinallt) sister, who, with her husband, kept the lights at Skerries. They are now in this parish, and I'm afraid very poor; the husband is a lusty fellow, but can't get any work. A friend of mine who called at the house where they are, the other day told me that the fellow was a-spinning at a wheel, anything to get a morsel of bread. It would be a deed of charity to relieve them.

If you receive Buttler's money I shall beg of you to procure me a few seeds to the tune of a couple of shillings or so. Our garden is but excessive small, and about a pennyworth or two of each sort would go a great way with us. I've sent you a catalogue; I don't think they are all to be had in shops, however, you may perhaps pick up a few of 'em. Felly nos dawch heno. Duw a roddo inni ymgyfarfod llawen. *Eich brawd anwiw, William Morris.* W. to R. contd.

P.S.—I fancy you've heard that Mr. Meyrick joins Mr. Owen, of Presaddfed, which they both have signify'd by their letters to their friends, this was done upon casting up their respective numbers when it appeared that Mr. Owen had the majority of Mr. Meyrick, when the latter gave the other his interest per agreement. Lord Bulkeley and Mr. Bayley are busy a-canvassing, but in all probability to no manner of purpose, only for sake of opposition.

Saturday, the 14th.—Dim llythyr oddiwrthych heddyw na newydd o un lle. Ni feddaf ddim chwaneg o franks, felly bydd raid imi yrru fy nesaf drwy law Mr. Vaughan. Byddwch wych.

Eich brawd penbrydd, Gwilym Tew.

HOLYHEAD, 6th April, 1741. W. to R. XXXIII.

Dear Brother—I received yours of the 31st ult., and I see this fatal truth confirm'd by all hands. I have inclos'd a letter I had the other day from brother Lewis, with a further account of that affair, with some reflections, etc. Duw a'n llawenycho' oll. I went to my father's on Good Friday and tarried till Monday. Our poor mother is almost inconsolable. I endeavour'd then to diswade her from her grief by telling her of the likelyhood there was of some other person of the same name dying aboard (for there was one, John Morris, of this country, in the Fleet, but not, I believe, on board the *Torbay*). My father has, I hope, more reason than to grieve intollerably. In short I never saw, and God be prais'd we never had, such reason for gruddiau gwlybion in our family, but if we live we must expect worse, or as bad, o ran chwedl chwithau, nid oes ir hwya' ei oes o honom mor hir aros yma. I send yours this day to brother Lewis, who is still detain'd at yonder cursed place, but Providence, I believe, order'd it, for the bloody flux being very rife there he has been instrumental in saving the lives of many. Our collector's father (who was Patent

W. to R. contd.

Comptroller of Bristol) is dead, intestate, and, it's suppos'd, worth a deal of money. He comes up sometime this week or the next. Roedd ar hwn ddigon oi heisiau. His father allow'd him upwards of £30 per annum whilst he liv'd. Roedd hynny cystal ag un chwechant. He is a good-natur'd man—dim bai mawr ond bod ei dafawd yn ddodrefnyn anwarddus a rhidwll.

I never heard of any will brother had made. I thought that you mention'd something in a letter formerly as if he had left a power of attorney at Portsmouth. Its now quite out of my head. I knew blind Parry, formerly at Cefn Amwlch, before he went to Dublin. He played then a fine harp; I'me glad he does so well. I've had a present of some rare seeds from a friend, a seedsman in Dublin, which includes some of them I nam'd you, viz., nigella, capsicum, basil, mar'l, Peru balsam. If you can pick up a few of the others please to send 'em pretty soon, otherwise 'twill be too late to sow 'em. Rhaid i chwi faddeu imi am sgrifenu cynrhwg for I've been quite mop'd since I receiv'd this newydd brwnt.

Your affectionate brother penbrydd, William Morris.

Da fydde glywed tipyn o hanes y delyn newydd honno.

W. to R. XXXIV.

HOLYHEAD, 23rd April, 1741.

Dear Brother,—I am now to own the receipt of yours of the 11th, 15th, and 18th, with the newspapers, etc., for which I return you thanks. As to poor brother John's affair I suppose it must rest till the ship's return. If it be worth while the old people must administer in order that others may be paid. I am afraid he ow'd a good deal of money, but more of this another time. Our collector is now in London and expects great matters after his father, which, if he gets, I fancy he'll remove hence. Perhaps brother Lewis may succeed him; if he had not an eye upon the thing I would try fair for't. You'll hear of Mr. Griffyth (for that's the collector's name) at the Exchequer Coffee House, Westminster Hall Gate. Brother wrote you last post from Aberffraw, so shall mention nothing of that affair. I sent Coetlogon's proposals to brother Lewis as to the work. The title of it is plausible enough, and the man's character and abilities are all that a body could form a judgment from of such a performance before it appears to the world. I don't like his name; that's a weakness, you'll say, tippyn oi hanes a fydde o'r ffeinia gaffael. Mi welais dri neu bedwar or *motional prints* rheini cyn chwerwed ar bumustl. Digrif yw gweled yr hen Syr yn sefyll er maint sydd yn ceisio ei godymmu, a digrifach fydde ei weled yn gadpen ar y Senedd nesa'. Nage, meddwch 'itheu. Nid oes ymma newydd yn y byd, ond bod y tywydd yn rhwydd sych ag yn oer greulon. Rhyfedd oedd gweled yn eich llythyr ei bod yn glauar ffordd yna. Ni throis i heibio etto mo bwmp o groen arth a wisgais i dros fy 'sgwyddau drwy'r gauaf. Mae gennyf bump neu chwech o ffrancs, pa beth y mae nhw dâ os cyfyd y Senedd cyn ei hiwsio? Dim newydd o Ddulas yn ddiweddar, felly byddwych wych am y tro yma. Deg i un na sgrifennaf attoch etto y Sadwrn. **W. to R. contd.**

Eich brawd anwiw, Gwilym Hiraethog.

[No Address, but endorsed by Richard Morris.]

Whitefield's Journal, p. 46.—Mrs. Edwards is a woman adorned with a meek and quiet spirit, talked feelingly and solidly of the things of God, and seemed to be such a helpmeet for a husband that she caused me to renew those prayers which for some months I have put up to God that he would be pleased to send me a daughter of Abraham to be my wife. I find upon many accounts it is my duty to marry. "Lord, I desire to have no choice of my own. Thou knowest my circumstances, Thou knowest I only desire to marry in, and for, Thee. Thou didst choose a Rebecca for Isaac. Choose one for me to be a helpmeet for me in carrying on that great work committed to my charge. Lord, hear me. Lord, let my cry come unto Thee."*

Query: Who are the executors of Justice Raylton, and where do they live?

* See the Works of Rev. G. Whitfield, 1771, vol. iv., p. 479.

CAERGYBI, 26ain Ebrill, 1741, sef Duw Sul. **W. to R. XXXV.**

Anwyl Frawd,—Derbyniais eich llyth'r ar papurau, a diolch am danynt, etc. Daccw nhw wedi mynd i gyd ir Aberffraw er doe. Gerwin oedd i bod wedi troi yn auaf gida chwi, hi fu ymma yn dywydd gwineu, ond mae hi wedi troi ar *ymendio* rawron, ond eisiau glaw sydd ymma yn fawr. Ni welais i mo'r Sion Pris'

W. to R. contd.

ers ugain mlynedd agos. Ce's lythyr oddiwrth y câr Salbri yn dywedyd ei fyn'd i Fôn. Gerwin oedd iddaw ei yspeilio ei hun yn y modd hwnnw; yn wir, fe heuddai O'Hara gael ei ddarn ladd ag os daw byth ffordd yma, gwae fo ei eni—ceiff hên wrachod Cybi ei labyddio. Ond, yn y diwedd, Duw a faddeuo iddo am y cam a wnaeth an diweddar frawd. Gwych ydyw'r Foundling Hospital yna ar lês y genethod trythyll. Mi a adwaen yr hên Thos. Coram o herwydd bwyta ag yfed yn ei gwmni yn Lerpwl, pan ydoedd yn adeiliadu magazine i gadw powdr gwn yn y fan honno. Clywais ef yn manegi ei hanes o bant i bentan. Ddoe roedd Ffair Fari yn Llanerchmedd, ag un fawr ydoedd meddant imi, ond nis gellais i fynd iddi o ran fy swyddau, sef yw rheini: deputy customer, collector, deputy comptroller, comptroller of the coal duties, deputy searcher, coast waiter and searcher, water bailiff, deputy vice-admiral, collector of the Skerry lights, surgeon, florist and botanist to the Garrison of Holyhead! Par sut yr ydychi yn meddwl yr wyf yn cael amser i huno yn fy ngwely'r nos gan ofalon? Roedd y nhad yn y ffair yn iach, ag hefyd ein chwaer ar brawd Owain, a mam hitheu gartref yn lleccyn. Y newydd brwnt hwnnw wedi rhwystro yr hen wraig tra bo hi byw, rwy'n ofni. Mae nhad, moliant i Dduw, yn well ei amunedd. Rwy'n meddwl oni buasai i fagad o farsiandwyr ŷd awyddus godi'r farchnad o wîr wenwyn, y naill i'r llall, y b'ase rawron fwy o lawnder yn Môn nag yn nemmawr fan, oblegid roeddynt yn rhoddi mwy pris am dano ymma nag yr oedd yn gwerthu yn Lerpwl, a dwad a orug llawer o honynt ar un llafur yn ei ol yw werthu am y mawr bris. Mae'r awron haidd wedi dwad o Lerpwl i Gaergybi (y peth rwy'n tybio na bu erioed or blaen), ag i bob man o gwmpas y wlad yma ag Arfon. Mae'r haidd goreu yw hau yn gwerthu yn Llanerchmedd am 48s. y pêg, ond mae rhyw fath yw gael am 35s. We have at this place plenty of fish and flesh; bread and butter are the dearest articles. Dyna i chwi brisiau amrafael bethau fal y gwerthir yn Nghybi y dyddiau ymma:—

Prynnais ddoe y bedwaredd ran, aelod ôl, o lwdn lloi da yn pwyso 12 lb. am 14*c*. Menyn 4½*c*. a 5*c*. y pwys; prynais tri o forleisiaid (Angl. whiting, Pollock's delicious fish), bob un yn bumtheg modfedd o flaen ei gynffon yw drwyn, am 2*c.*; young blockings neu chwitlengiaid gleision, cymaint a phenwaig, saith neu wyth am geiniog. (N.B.—They take upon this coast this spring abundance of the last, which they call *Cwding Ebrill.* One fisherman has caught with a hook 200 a day of the above size. Ni welwyd ers llawer o flynyddoedd mo'r fath beth. Here are plenty of cod and codlings, whitings, base, and mullet, and other fish). Eggs, four and five a penny; fresh pork, the carkass at 1⅝*d.* and 1¾*d.* per lb.; lamb, very reasonable; mutton, so and so. Prisiau gwychion am fuchod, o achos bod wmbredd o warthegau wedi meirw, yn enwedig hen fuchod; Jack Hughes (Llugwy gynt) has had upwards of forty black cattle died this season. The best wheaten bread from Dublin, oblegid oddiyno yr y'm yn cael ein bara yn y dre ymma, h. y. bwytawyr bara gwyn, the 12*d.* loaf, six lb. averdupois, llefrith gwmpas; ale, pint a penny. Felly dyna i chwi dippyn o hanes belly timber. The Justices of the Peace at the last Assizes settled a House of Correction here, and agreed to put the late Poor Act in force in this country, ond rwy'n meddwl na ddaw dim o ddaioni o'r peth o ran mae ganddom amrafaelion a phleidiau yn ein mysg. The House of Correction was open'd yesterday, tipyn o gwt ail i un mochyn. It's intended chiefly for Irish vagabonds who come in swarms from England, being driven thence by law, etc. **W. to R. contd.**

Monday, 27 April.

I have received your last, a chwedl chwithau trât gwych hwn pei daliai yn hir. Ond ysywaith rwy'n ofni mae dyma'r Pasg diwaetha a gewch drwy'r cyfleu ymma o Lan y Gwyddyl. Ce's lythr oddiwrth Lewelyn ddoe, roedd yn iach, dim son am eich llythr, h. y. ei atteb. By a letter from my brother comptroller of Beaumares of the 25th I don't find there is any order come about the tobacco. Daccw fy eisiau yn greulon, felly byddwch wŷch.

Eich brawd ungalon tra bwyf, William Morris.

P.S.—Rwan hyn yr aeth ein dwy nîth ai modryb adref wedi bod yma dros 24 o orriau: a brace of fine girls. Duw a roddo ynddynt râs. Gwynt Dwyrain coch gethin yn deifio'r blagur.

W. to R. 8th May, 1741.

XXXVI. Dear Brother,—I received yours of the 19th, debygai, a chan diolch am y papurau, etc., ond gresyndod oedd wel'd y newydd o Garthagena; rwyn ofni mae un drwg, drwg yw pan ddelo oll i oleuni. Nid hwyrach na base waeth in brawd Ioan farw a'i ben ar y gobennydd na syrthio i ddwylo'yr Yspaengwn cigyddaidd fal y gwnaeth cantoedd os collasom y fatal. Daccw mrawd Llewelyn yn dechreu sgrifennu attoch ag yn tyngu i facheglîs fawr y lleinw sit o bappur ei hunan felly pawb drosto ei hun, etc. As to newspapers we have the *Gazzeteer* and *London Evening Post* regularly in this place, likewise y^e^ *Com. Senate.* We have also by each pacquet boat from Dublin the Irish newspapers, which take in all the English news, both from the printed and written letters, with ye abstracts of the votes of the British House of Commons when sitting, etc. But as brother and self don't take any of these papers in we are allways glad of those you send us. Gresyn oedd farw Robinson Crusoe, dyn diddan iawn ydoedd tra bu. There is a new weekly paper which Dick Evans takes in, called the *Weekly Oracle.* How much would it cost a week, suppose you were to send it in a frank? Rwyn meddwl mae *2c.* mae'r Dr. yn ei roi, nid rhaid i chwi yrru run o'r London Evening, oni chewch un newydd tanlli ond hynny. Diolch am a gaed, too much for nonsense. Gwybyddwch ddarfod i wenidog ein plwyf a phedwar o wyr bonhegion eraill a minneu gymeryd taith ddechreu'r wythnos ddiwaetha i ben yr Wyddfa, neu'r Eryri, rhai er mwyn cael gweled y byd o'i hamgylch, eraill er mwyn gwarrio eu harian a chael digrifwch; ambell un er mwyn cael edlyw yw cymydogion y buasent yn nes ir nef na hwynt (Pythagoriaid oedd rheini), a minneu (chwedl y mochyn) er mwyn dyfod i hyd i lysiau a deiliach y rhai a dŷf yno yn anad unlle arall o dir Brydain Fawr. We had very bad weather, so that the prosperous men were quite disapointed. I picked up about a score curious Alpine plants, most of 'em on the very top of Snowdon, ond roedd hi'n gwlychu a chin oered nad oedd dim byw yn hir yn y fan. I call'd in my way home at Pentrerhianell, roedd yr hen bobl at yr un gyflwr ag y byddent arfer a bod, ynhad yn fynych yn salaidd gan gnofa yn ei frest: inward impostume, yr hwn mae arnaf ofn ai disodla o'r diwedd.

Nid wyf i yn deall mor Lexicons ymma oll, mi fyddaf yn meddwl yn fynych that there is not a member chose in England, Wales, or Scotland heb ddigon o gastiau o bob tu, os bydd ymryson, a phan fo Dôxi yn edliw bribery a chorypsion i chwi y byddaf bob amser yn meddwl am yr hên ddiareb, "Tîn ddu medd y fran wrth yr wylan." Mae ganddom ymma glwyf sydd waeth na pholiticks pe bae bosibl hwnnw yw, prinder bwyd cristnogion, oni chawn lawer o ŷd o wledydd eraill sicr y bydd newyn yn ein plith cyn y cynhauaf. Mae llongau, i Dduw bo'r diolch, yn dyfod yn fynych ir Beaumaris, Carnarvon, Traeth Côch, Dulas, Pwllheli, etc., ag ydau or cwr yna or deyrnas. Oni bae hynny nis gwn i pa beth a ddaetha o gantoedd o bobloedd dlodion. Roedd Ynghaernarfon ddwy long yn carrio o ddeutu 170 o dynellau yn llwythog; ni bu'r wlad hauach yn ei brynnu oll. Roedd yn Nulas long o Woodbridge (debygai) ag nid oedd ir llwyth mor hanner digon ir cwr hwnnw or wlad, roedd gwas i nhad yn dyfod yn ei ôl oddiwrthi ddydd Sadwrn wedi ffaelio cael dim am arian, y cwbl wedi ei werthu. Ni fedd yr hên bobl ddyrnaid ond a brynant am bris anfeidrol, 40*s*. y pegaid haidd, a llawer o dylwyth yw porthi, hi amdwya bobl y wlad hon. Mae yma sychdwr mawr, yr ŷd a'r borfa wedi eu anafu, dim gwair i sôn am dano, a pheth sydd ryfedd maent yn Sir Gaernarfon yn cael glaw eu gwala, ag mae'r ŷd ar borfa yn edrych yn hyfryd. It would shock you to see the face of this country, especially about Dulas and those parts, a melancholly scene. Duw ai newidio; mae lle i ofni nad yw ein caledi Ymrydain Fawr ond dechreu, ag yn wir mae eisiau rhywbeth i ddyfod ar bobl attynt eu hunain, oblegid mae'r rhan fwyaf o honynt wedi mynd allan oi cof a thros y gwaharddol. Fe addawodd y Cynghorwr Lewis y cwbl i Dwmi ond ni ddarfu iddo seinio mor llythr cymmun, felly mae'r tir ymynd i Drysglwyn, a queer conduct, when he had so many necessitous relations, lodesi tlysion ag eisiau gwyr arnynt, etc., ac yn disgwyl ir hên Forus ei cynhysgaeddu. Rwyn ofni nad oes dim sicrwydd o farwolaeth yr Aeres, am a fedraf i glywed. Da clywed fod Sion Prŷs ai gâr wedi priodi cystal, yn rhodd dywedwch ir cyntaf fy mod yn dymuno llwyddiant iddo. Dim chwaneg am y trô, ond can ffarwel. **W. to R. contd.**

Eich Brawd Caredigawl ddigon, Wm. Morris.

W. to R. XXXVII.

HOLYHEAD, Sunday Evening, 31st May, 1741.

Dear Brother,—I am now to own the receipt of yours of the 21st, and before I undertake to answer it, must give you a short account of our bywoliaeth in these parts. Dymma fi newydd ddyfod adref o Lanerchmedd, wedi bod yn ymweled ar Brawd Llewelyn, yr hwn sydd dan ddwylo y Doctor er's gwell nag wythnos, wedi bod yn hir o amser yn glâf yn yr Aberffraw. Rhyw anwyd gerwin a gadd yr hwn a drôdd yn asthma, ag aflwydd, has been purged, vomited, bled, blister'd, etc., and I don't find he is much better, though I hope he's past all danger, his cough to-day being come to something of expectoration. I met father there, and says all the family at home are well. The old man is much troubled with (I'me afraid) an inward impostume; gripes him violently at times, otherwise he is very hearty. Mother is in tolerable good health. Rwyf wedi blino yn greulon. Ni bum ond naw awr oddi cartref. Ni lyfaswn aros yn hwy, obleit roeddwn yn disgwyl llong bôst i mewn, heb neb gartref i warchad! Dyma'r Collector wedi dwad adref om blaen; ni che's i ond ysgwyd llaw ag ef etto. Rwy'n deall wrtho na chadd ddim gan y fam-ynghyfraith; desir'd me to send his service to you, etc. He must wait a twelve month. Fei anafwyd. Mae arna'i ofn golli'r tadws.

Monday Morning.—A Thursday last came on the Election for this county, which held till yesterday in the forenoon, when Mr. Bayly, finding Mr. Owen about 40 ahead of him, gave up the poll. The other had above forty more unpoll'd, among whom were Fyrth Morrus Pritchard ag Owain Parri ei gefnder. So Mr. Owen was duly return'd. Notwithstanding, they were pretty much afraid of the acting Sherriff (Counsellor Williams, son of Rice Williams, Quirt, High Sherriff). You see as above brother could not go there. This town, which produces a good many electors, were with Mr. Owen to a man (we had two or three in the parish of Bayly's side), and upon the arrival of the news which a Saturday night we had, no less than five bonefires, most of windows in town illuminated, abundance of ale given the populace, the night concluded in drinking loyal health and success to our worthy member, etc., etc. Nid oedd dim rhyfedd ir gŵr ennill, roedd holl wyr mawr y wlad oi du. Ni feddai'r llall ond yr Arglwydd Bwlclai, whose interest is quite ruin'd in this county.

Gwelwch y rhagoriaeth :—

For JOHN OWEN, Prysaddfed, Esq.
Owen Meyrick, Esq.
Owen Meyrick, Junr., Esq.
Edmund Meyrick, Esq.
William Lewis, Llysdulas, Esq.
William Lewis, Trysglwyn, Esq.
William Bulkeley, Brynddu, Esq.
William Jones, Pentraeth, Esq.
Hugh Owen, Penrhose, Esq.
William Roberts, Bodiar, Esq.
Thomas Rowlands, Caera, Esq.
John Griffiths, Llanddyfnan, Esq.
Richard Hughes, Castellor, Esq.
Henry Williams, Tros y Marian, Esq.
Hugh Williams, Chester, Esq.
Kyffin Williams, Chester, Esq.
Morris Lewis, Esq.
Sir Arthur Owen's interest.
Miss Lloyd, Llwydiarth's do.
William Thomas, Coed Alyn, Esq.

For MR. BAYLY.
William Bodvell, Esq.
Henry Morgan, Esq.
Lord Bulkeley.
John Williams, Tyfry, Esq.
John Griffiths, Careglwyd, Esq.
John Hughes, Plascoch, Esq.
Llanidan Interest promis'd 'em but most voted for Mr. Owen.
Herbert, of Oakley Park, stirr'd prodigiously but had neither vote nor interest.
Chancellor Wynne, Bodewryd.

Fe gadd yr hen Dad warning i ymadel a Phentreyrianell am na b'ase yn votio gida Bayly, ond rydis yn meddwl nad oes gan neb bower yw troi allan nes y gwerthir y tir ; fe geir gweled ar fyrder. Daccw'r post yn mynd heibio : fe geir newydd yn y man. Fe ddwad Griffiths glywed o honaw Ynghaer gymeryd o Vernon Carthagena by storm. Your last but one cost dau swllt yn arian sychion. Digrif oedd newydd Carthagena yn eich llythyr diweddaf, a gresyn fod y byrsun wedi ei lygadtynnu. Merch i Mr. Hughes or Plâs-yn-rhoscolyn yw'r eneth honno, un pur dlos y'w, ond nid un o'r rhai cyffredin. Dynion drwg yw eich mobs chwi, ewyllyswyr da ir gwydrwyr. Ni chadd mrawd Lewis ddim chwaneg o hanes'r Admiralty. Pan wel Mr. Meyrick nid hwyrach y ceiff. Ned Edwards gave but a lame account of brother's death, dont mention the time or place. He says he was taken ill and recover'd a little ; then taken ill a second time and died of convulsions ; says his things will be sold before the mast ; had made no will ; had about 40s. in his chest which he ow'd aboard. Had received but 3d. pound of his wages (I don't understand what he means), and out of that the 40s. was part. I suppose he means one pound £ out of three, or each three pound. Drwg bod Mr. Vychan yn gorfod aros ymlith plant Alis. Brother, I believe, wrote to Nanney (but I forgot to ask him) and has sent a cowydd Haint y Marchogion.

W. to R, contd.

The catalogue of seeds came here amongst the newspapers. Dim colled. Mae hi yn rhy hwyr yw hau leni. Rwyf ar anfeidrawl frys ymynd i dynnu allan fy nghyfrif misawl, a dyna ddiben ar fod yn Gollector. *Eich caredigawl frawd, William Morris.*

Dim sôn am Garthagena. I suppose tis only an Irish intelligence.

[No address, but endorsed as follows by Richard Morris].

W. W. W., 1352; J. M., 933; 419 majority. Price turned out Llwyd; Vychan re-chose; Owen *versus* Bailey; Conspiracy Gibralter; 4th Bridge Lottery.

W. to R. XXXVIII.

15th July, 1741.

Dear Brother,—I wrote you a long letter or two without an answer. Pa beth yw'r achos? Mae'n debyg y dywedwch mai trafferth. Wala gore oll, ni fydde golled yn y byd pei medrwn inneu ddywedyd yr un peth heb fod yn gelwyddog. Ond ysywaeth ry'm ni yma yn cael gormod o segwryd o lawer. I wrote a line some time agoe and have since received an answer from Owen Jones, son of John Prichard Prŷs y prydydd, who is a gardiner at the Earl of Tilney's at Wanstead House. He has promised me some curious flowers in case I can get 'em convey'd here, desires to know where he shall meet you in London, for I wrote him that you might likely find some opportunity of forwarding some things down. This young fellow was a gardiner in this county ere he went to England, where he has been now for some years. My brother Lewis is well acquainted with him. He is a sober, carefull, ingenious fellow, and in good way of business. A brother of his, who died lately at sea, was an apprentice att Mr. Prichard's when I was there, a lad of surprizing genius, and had he lived would have been soon master of a ship. Had learned arithmetick by an English book ere he could speak hardly one word of English. Was a good artist when he died. Mae Owain yn blant y cyfyrdyr a ni. Gadewch imi wybod ymhle y caiff afael arnoch, oblegid da iawn fyddai cael rhywfaint o wreiddiach a hadau o'r cwr ynna i'r byd. Mi fum i efo Charn yn Wanstead ryw Sulgwaith yn gweled y gerddi gwychion, pan oeddych yn Stratford. I am to send Owain a catalogue of my annuals and roots in order he may know what to send me. Four kinds of the seeds you sent came up, viz., laburnum (thriving), bladder sena (ditto), lobell's catchfly (in blow), red candy tufft or mithridate mustard (in blow). Mae hi'n rhy gynnar i son am hadau etto. I have a fine catalogue of flower seeds, roots, etc., sold by one Fuller, in London. So much for gardening. Daccw i chwi fotani o'r tu draw. Father and mother was here last Saturday and Sunday night. Mae'r hen bobl druain wedi mynd yn fusgrellaidd. Bum i'w danfon hyd at Garna, i ymweled a Mr. Robert a Mrs. Anne Lewis (qu. your godmother) y rhai sydd dri musgrellach na nhwytha. Un yn fyddar ag yn dra egwan, a'r llall yn gruples wrth ei maglau. Dim chwaneg yr awron. W. to R. contd.

Eich brawd, Gwilym Morris.

[Here follows a catalogue of Alpine plants found by W. M. in and about Snowdon,] Then follows:

Da ydyw gweled eich bod ar ffordd i wneuthur cymwynas i'r brawdLlewelyn. Mae'r hâf ymma agos a mynd heibio. Mae'n debyg na cheir fawr ddaioni o honaw bellach. Pa beth yw opiniwn y Caerluddiaid yna ynghylch Sir John Morris? I ble maent yn dywedyd ei fynd? Mae'n debyg fod Ned Edwards wedi mynd i bant: nid oes dim o'i hanes ymma. Chwi glywsoch farw'r Cadpen Bodvel (mae'n debyg) a'r Cadpen Morris, mab Deon Bangor, y rhai aethant i ymladd a'r Carthaginians. Daccw ystâd Mr. Bodvel ar ffordd i fynd i gadffwll, sef yw hwnnw un Peter Hughes, un o'n coast waiters ni, ag yn awr dan awdurdod eich brawd Gwilym. Cefnder yw i'r Fawdfel,a chyfiawn aur treftadaeth y gwr hwnnw, sef Bodfaen; ond gan nad oes ganddynt ddim nes, na chyn nesed carrenydd o arall, mae'n debyg y caiff stâd Fadryn, y cwbl yn agos i 2,000 o bynnau, oblegyd deg ar hugain i un yprioda'r seneddwr byth, ai chwaer hithau yn rhy hen i blanta. Once the greatest toast in North Wales, yrwan yn hên forwyn. Daccw ddwy chwaer i'r hen Feyrig wedi marw yn ddiweddar, sef gwraig Lewis Nanney, siopwr o Gaernarfon, a gwraig W. Hughes, y Person o Dre'r Ddôl. Y ddiwaethaf a gladdwyd echdoe.

CAERGYBI, Dydd Sul y 27ain o Fedi, 1741. W. to R. XXXIX.

Anwyl Frawd,—Derbyniais eich llythyr or 11eg, a da ydoedd clywed eich bod yn iach, oblegid roeddym yn dechreu ofni eich myn'd i bant. Ond eres na chawsid peth 'chwaneg o hanes y More hwnnw, ni welais i na fyddai ir merched fys ymhob drygioni

W. to R. contd. felly am rwystro ir Gorbed ar Stainby siarad ar Arglwydd Vere. Gwych or cyfrif yr ych yn ei roddi o Delyn Williams, a gw'chach fyddai ei wêled yn canu arni. Gobeitho eich bod cyn hyn wedi cael rhyw hanes or *Navy Offis* a *Phortsmwth* ynghylch helyntion mrawd Sion ag Edward Edwards. Da fyddai gael rhyw faint i dalu d'led y cyntaf. Drwg y clywed fod y priodasau Cymreig yna yn digwydd mor anhapus, gobeitho na chyll Sion mor clôs, onte Duw ai helpio. Rwyf y dyddiau hyn yn dra thrafferthus yn llunio ag yn darparu *a new pleasure garden;* roedd y llall rhyngwy ar offeiriad yn rhy fechan. Ond ple mae'r gwraidd ar hadau a addawyd immi o Wanstead a Llundain? Rwy'n ofni fod y llys yn eich llygru oll ffordd yna; mae hynny yn beth rhyfeddawl iawn! Dyma'r adeg i blannu gwraidd blodau yn myn'd heibiaw, a phwy a wyr pa rai o honom a fydd byw yr adeg nesaf? Ond am yr hadau mae digon o amser o hyn i fis Mawrth, I wish you would send Owen Jones a line where to wait of you in town, and if he could get me a few roots I would not begrudge to pay carriage for them by a wagon. Na siomwch monof, da mrawd. His Grace the Duke Devonshire, Vice-roy of Ireland, embark'd here for Dublin ye 22d. N. B, That person is always a yellow boy to each of your brodyr. Bu yma yn ddiweddar briodas fawr rhwng Hugh Owen, of Penrhose, Esq.. barrister at law, â Margaret Bold, or Duwmares, a most celebrated beauty, with about £2,000. Chwe mîs ir amser yr ympiriodd o ai wraig yn ein heglwys (sef oedd hynny wythnos i heddyw) y claddwyd ei haeddedigawl frawd am hanwyl gymydog Mr. Edward Owen. Felly mae'r byd yn myned heibiaw.

Bu fy chwaer ai mab Sion ymma ddechreu'r wythnos ddiwaethaf, roedd pawb yn rhesymol iach Ymhentre'-rhianell. B'ase mam yn bûr sâl yn ddiweddar, ond rwan wedi mendio yn dda iawn. Mae nhw a rhan fwya' or wlad o'r Beaumaris i Gaergybi gida glan y môr wedi myn'd i gost fawr yn darparu am benwaig ag nid oes ymma fawr iw cael etto. Gwelodd y *Commissioners of the Salts* yn addas yrry immi gomhisiwn im gwneuthur yn Swyddog Hallt, ag felly gorfydd arnaf fod Dduw-Sul nesaf yn y Duwmares in order to be qualified at the Quarter Sessions; felly collaf Wyl mabsant Penrhose, ond mi gâf odfa i ymweled ar rhieni cyn dychwel. Ni chwanegaf yr awron namyn fy mod fal arferawl.

Eich caredigawl frawd, Gwilym Morris.

P.S. October 1st. Your letter to my brother Llewelyn, begun the 29th, came in the nick of time to convince me of an error I had like to run into, viz., that ye citizens regard your promises as little as gwyr y Llys, er y gwyddwn or goreu na waeth ganthoch gael eich cyffelybu i haid o williaid or Nawgyll. So much for an apology but the case is this. If Owen brings you any quantity of roots, etc., and you think it worth while, I should be glad you would make 'em in papers and pack 'em in a box with some things brother Llewelyn may write you about, and send by the Chester waggon directed as per margin, and any charges you are at shall be repaid. Our members will be going up about the end of the month; I can send by some of their retinue the cash. I have had a present made me of late by a gentleman coming from London of a set of songs done on copperplate in red and blue, cost 4d. a piece; they are call'd the Ladies' Amusement or Vocal Harmony: most of 'em with tunes for the flute. Mine is from plate I. to VI; if they are continued I should be glad to have 'em hyd y diwedd yn y box, and any other nick nacks which you may judge acceptable here. **W. to R. contd.**

Box to be addressed for Richard Evans, Surgeon at Llanerchmedd, to the care of Mr. William Goodwin, Grocer, in Chester.

CAERGYBI, Nos Fercher, 28th October, 1741. **W. to R. XL.**

Mrawd Rhisiart,—Mi sgrifenais attoch lostryddyn o lythyr ryw ddiwrnod ers dyddiau byd ynghylch gwraidd, etc.; ond gan ddarfod i mrawd Lewys settlio'r matterion rheini, nid rhaid imi'n awr ond ei crybwyll. Dyma fi wedi derbyn eich llythr heddyw ar pedwar pacced. Daccw mrawd Llewelyn wedi mynd er doe i edrych am y Meistir Bawdfel o Fadryn, i anfon rhyw fapp iddaw ag i dderbyn tâl am danaw; nid hwyrach y bydd yn ôl y foru cyn ir bost fynd allan: os felly cewch glywed. Digon tebyg mae cnâ yw'r Marshal yna, for he acts like a miner; mae rheini i gyd yn ddau wynebawg. Rwy'n meddwl mae llyfr odiaeth yw hwn er na che's mor amser prin i ddarllain tu dalen o honaw ond y peth a brofais ydoedd bur flasus. I could wish now that you had not sent the box this week, for this day I had a letter from y câr Owain ab Sion Brydydd, wherein he writes thus: "The reason

W. to R. contd.

of my not writing to you sooner was because I waited for an opportunity to get some of our own flowers and now I got twenty roots of tulips, of which I believe you have not many such in Anglesey, and about four dozens ranunculas, and some anemonies and jonguils and tulips mixed." He tells me the catchfly is a perennial, so not the same as I have. Gwaed crŵst, pa beth a wneir os cychwynodd y Boccys? Yn y Bala y bwyf os gwn i. I wrote to Owain this night and told him how matters were order'd, and that you would reimburse him if he was any thing out of pocket. If this opportunity is lost we must think of some other.

Dyma lythr gida'r post heddyw oddiwrth yr Evan Delynior yna at y brawd i erchi ei gymorth; mae ef a Mr. John Parry ar fedr gwneuthur gwrthiau. The letter is an elaborate piece; all Welch; bad orthography, ag englyn i'r gelfyddyd. Drwg yw clywed fod eich dinas mor afiachus. We had not long agoe the same kind of fever here which ran through whole families, but few died, God be prais'd; its now in a manner quite over. Mae gennyf ddigon o gwyn i chwi os yw'r gwayw bonsia yn eich nychu; mae i minneu ysgwydd yn ddrwg ei hwyl yn fynych iawn gan y clwyf hwnnw. Fe fyddai mrawd yn achwyn mwy na mi o'r hanner, ond er pan ddarfu i Ddoctor y Bendro flistro ei wàr ni chlywodd e byth na siw na miw oddiwrthaw. Mi adawaf i i'r brawd hynaf yrry gynghorion rhag y clwyfau yna. Nid oes ammau na fynnir cael llymeirch (*oysters*) i'r gwr yna; mae'n rhaid eu dal ai trin yn y Duwmares mae hi'n adeg ar fyrder bellach. Rwy'n meddwl fod y Tylwyth Teg wedi newid y cefnder Salbri ers dalm byd, oblegid roedd y cyntaf yn llencyn llawen, diniwed, cymdeithgar, yn sgrifennu at bobl ag yn dyfod yw hymweled rwan ag yn y man. Ond am hwn sy'r awron mae o'n debycca dyn a welsoch i erioed i'r hen Selatar a welsoch gynt (yn perchen dwy o ferched) yn Modafon, ond ei fod yn llawer culach. Mae iddo ddwy goes pei gwelech nhw heb ddim chwaneg o honaw, chwi dyngach y mawrllw mae perthyn grintachaidd gybydd y maent; ni welsoch i fawr erioed ei meinach. Ei weinidogion yw hen ddyn o ddeutu deg a thrigain oed neu fwy, a hen ddynes o gwmpas pedwar ugain, a hogyn o lanc gwmpas pedair ar ddeg oed, a hogan weithiau. Ni chred meddanhw gysgu yn ei welu'r nos; a rhai a deura nad yw'n credu bwyta llonaid ei fol main o fwyd ba'se unwaith yn yr wythnos, oddigerth efo Meirian. Mae honno hitheu o'r un rywogaeth ag yntau; gresyn na baent wedi ei cwplysu. Dyna i chwi ddarluniad or Salbri, ag yn wir nid oes ynddo fawr air ond y gwir. Mae'r hurthgen yn gaddaw dwad ffordd yma ar fyrder. W. to R. contd.

Mab yw'r Will Williams hwnnw i William Williams y gôf, o Glawdd y Park yn Llaneugrad; a'i fam oedd gyfnither i mam, sef oedd honno merch i William ab William Gruffudd, o'r Figin. Rwy'n meddwl yr adwaenochi ei frawd Owain anraslawn. Dyn a haeddodd y cryg ganwaith. Ond am y Will ymma, y nhad a mam a roddasant y rhan fwyaf o'i fagwraeth iddaw er yn llencyn bychan wedi marw ei dad a'i fam: a chyd ami y bu y siwrnai gynta yn morio; ag mae'r cyfaill rwan yn glŷd arnaw wedi bod ers talm yn feistyr ar y mân lestri ymma. Dyn gonest, cwrtais, yw'r Blerwm, ond bod arno fai anesgusodawl, sef yw hwnnw yfed gormodd o gwrw, a bod yn rhy ddiniwed ped fae bosibl. Mae iddaw unig chwaer wedi priodi yn bur ddedwydd yn ymyl Treffynnon, yn byw yn odiaethol; bum yn llettyfa yn ei thŷ ar fy siwrnai, ag anaml y gwelir tenantiaid yn byw yn daclusach: bendithion yr hen bobl ai para. Hanes y ddwy herlodesi, h.y. Marged ag Elin*, y gyntaf yn ddeg er gwyl Fair, ar llall yn naw flwyddyn ir un dydd; yr hynaf yn balffas o lodes frongoch yr un agwedd ai thâd, ar ifa' yn eneth lwydwen ei gwynebpryd yr unlliw ar papur ymma. Yr hynaf yn dysgu'n odiaeth, ar ifa' nis gâd iddi; yr hynaf yn ddistaw ac yn feddylgar, ar ifa' yn llawn yspryd ag yn gymenddoeth (i.e. witty). Ar air maent yn debyg i fod yn ddeunydd gwragedd da, for they are fine children. They are now boarded at cosin Lewis ab William Morris, and are at school in town. Mae'r Lewis hwnw yn byw yn bur daclus—is one of our extra tidesmen and a coalmeter which brings him about £12 or £14 a year, besides his trade as a joyner. You must excuse this prolixity, for I'me tonight in a scribling cue, being alone, and being tired with playing at cards for some nights past with the ladies with bad success; felly, nos dawch heno.

Eich caredigawl frawd, Gwilym Gontrowliwr.

P. S. 29th.—Nid oes hanes am y brawd Llewelyn yn dyfod adref, felly gyrraf hwn ymlaen rhag i chwi fod heb ddim, a byddwch wych,

* The children of Lewis Morris by his first wife.

W. to R. contd. Os cewch amser ryw brydnhawn Dduw Sul bydda da gennyf gael llinell heb ddim tôn fwngloddiau yr Amralti, a phethau dyfnion o'r fath. Ni chlywais i un gair oddicartref, h.y. o Ddulas, er pan gadd ynhad eich llythr ynghylch pethau mrawd Sion,—W. M.

W. to R. XLI.

CAERGYBI, 25th November, 1741. Ympryd.

Dear Brother,—I received yours of the 21st with an account of the box, which I was impatient for, and I heartily wish it may receive no damage this terrible wet weather; sure 'twill be at Llanerchmedd soon. I had wrote a few days agoe to the Doctor to give directions about it to the carriers. Where is the invoice of the goods? I suppose you've heard from brother concerning some accounts I sent him, ei fod ar y ffordd i gael anffortyn o achos y daith front yna; oblegid hyd rwyf yn deall ir Commissiwners (y rhai mae'n debyg oedd yn meddwl ei fod yn myned ar ei survey) yrru at y *Patent Seals* i achwyn ar ei *Ddeputy* ag ynteu. Sgrifennodd yma lythyr o warning y gyrrai fo yn sydyn gomhisiwn i arall to supersede my brother, am iddo fod mor fynych a chyhyd oddicartref. Nid oes dim cyflog yn perthyn ir deputy searcher yn y borth yma, eithr y ffîs y mae yn ei gael am ei boen am weini. Gresyn oedd colli ychydig yn y gongl lom ymma. Dyma'r Collector mae arnaf ofn wedi ei andwyo; mae twysgen o arian Brenin Lloegr yn ei law ag ynteu yn bur dlawd; fe yrrodd Collector y Duwmares ymma dydd arall yw holi, ond nid oedd dim yw gael, o'r achos hwnnw 'r aeth achwyn arno at y Commissiwners, y rhai mae'n debyg a'i diswydda. Mae'n ddrwg gennyf drosto a'i dylwyth; pump o blantos na fedr yr un o naddynt prin wisgo am dano. Rwy'n disgwyl y caf inneu yn nwrdiaw yn dda am na baswn yn achwyn arno; ond gwaeth gennyf drosdo fo na throstai fy hun: felly chwi welwch ein bod ni ymma mewn drysni bod y gynffon. Gobeithio nad oes dim anfoddlondeb or fath yn eich cynllyn chwi rawron, pan f'och yn dywedyd eich bod mewn llwyn mieri. Ni chlywais ddim o Ddulas ers dyddiau. Er mwyn dyn a aeth y *More* yna i lawr etto ai peidio? Os nid aeth, ymlidiwch ef i i ffordd iw grogi. Fe fase gwell gennifi na llawer pe base erioed heb glywed son am Lywelyn. Dyma fi yn dibennu'r bregowthen ymma. Am heno, felly, Duw'n 'ch plaid.

Eich brawd anwiw, William Morris.

HOLYHEAD, 18th February, 1741. W. to R. XLII.

Dear Brother,—I had a line from brother Lewis by which I find that he left you the 14th, felly ni wybod tua pha le y mae bellach. I had a letter last post which mentions fod meichiau y Colector yma wedi erchi i Golhector y Duwmares yrru am extent yn erbyn hwn, felly nid oes bosibl iddo sefyll ond ychydig ddyddiau or achos hwnnw. Rydis yn fy nghyngori fi i ymwthio yn ei le os bydd modd, felly dymma fi yn sgrifennu at bawb mae fi yw'r gwr ffittia o lawer. I've sent you my letter to Mr. Meyrick, open which if you can possibly spare time, I beg you'd deliver and discourse ye good old man and I desire you'll let me know his oppinion of the matter. I've also wrote this post to Mr. Brereton (my former patron), who though a friend of Mr. John Manley's, may now perhaps be out of play. Sgrifennais hefyd linell at Mr. Vaughan am ei fod yn wr mwyn, (pwy a wyr par sut yr ydis yn trin y drêth yna rwan). Perhaps the promise Mr. Bodvel had through Lord Cholm'ley's interest may be laid aside, and perhaps you may have an opportunity of waiting on Mr. Vaughan, who, I find by brother Lewis's letter, is now in the majority—whatever charge or loss you are at in this affair you may depend of being satisfied. I wrote a line to Mr. Pritchard of Leverpoole sometime agoe to your care, and have not heard since whether he is with you or gone, or not come; he promised, or rather offered, his good offices in this same affair, and when last in London applyd for me (the collectors then ashaking), and says he in his letter, "I believe if the person had been removed you would have a fair chance"; felly os yw yn Llundain, either wait of him or write a line on the subject of this letter. I had a letter this morning from Dulas. Darfu ir chwaer ddychrynnu Dduw Sul diwaetha a ganwyd iddi, y plygain Mawrth, ferch fechan fis cyn ei hamser. Fei bedyddied hi yn Sian, ag ni wyddis ai byw ai marw wna etto; mae'r chwaer gobeithio ar y ffordd o ddyfod trwyddi hi, er cael o honi amser tost,—pawb eraill (ond un o ferched y brawd sydd sâl) yn rhwydd iach. Abundance of poor people dying here. Dim amser i roddi newydd yn y byd. I beg a line as soon as possible, for no time must be lost in the above affair.

I am, your affectionate brother, William Morris.

W. to R. contd.

We never had so much business upon our hands in this place before—occasioned by ships being cast away, others stranded, others drove in by stress of weather. We are now adischarging a cargoe of tobacco and going about another of rum and sugar, shipping off teas, indigo, etc.

W. to R. XLIII.

HOLYHEAD, March 8th, 1741.

Dear Brother,—I received yours of the 27th ult. Am very much obliged to you for delivering my letters to Messrs. Meyrick and Prichard, and am impatient to hear your negociations with Mr. Vaughan and Mr. Owen : rhyfedd na f'ase lythyr ymma heddyw. I wrote another letter since to Mr. Meyrick to acquaint him that the customer was under suspension, etc., and never like to be restored here. Daccw fo yn Nulun yn ffaelio cael daioni yn y byd, ai dylwyth ymma yn dra thlodion. I wish Mr. Meyrick had stirr'd in this affair, and push'd on Mr. Brereton who is a particular friend of Mr. Manley, the Patent Customer. Mr. Vaughan could do more service than any of 'em at this time, ond nid yw'r gwr ond estron imi. I'me sorry for the hint ynghylch fy hen feistr. Brother is come and confirms what you say of your being much hurried : nid oes mor help, rhaid bod yn fodlon i'r dynged. Ces inneu lythr oddiwrth y câr Salbri ; rwy'n ofni nad oes iddo siawns yn y byd gan na b'ase Bodsgallen o'i du ; mae pobl Watkin agos wedi ei nychu, yn benllefain yn ei glustiau ag yn llosci coelcerthi oi amgylch, ag yn gwneuthur pob camwri ag ef, druan gwr. Ni waeth er bod ffrancod o amgylch eich llythyrau, a chan ein bod wedi colli ein Gazetteers, digrif fyddai gael pappur newydd 'rwan ag yn y man. Mae'r rhieni a'r tylwyth yn iach : ni che's amser i biccio hyd yno ers gwyl Fihangel *diwaetha*. Nid af i ymhel i sgrifennu mwyach y tro ymma, but refer you to brother Lewis's.

I am, your affectionate brother, William Morris.

Mae'r brawd yn naccau rhoi pin ar bappir, felly byddwch wych.

W. to R. XLIV.

CAERGYBI, 11eg Ebrill, 1742, sef dydd Sul.

Dear Brother,—Ai gollwng dros gof eich brawd Gwilym a wnaethoch ? Ni che's i linell oddiwrthych er's cryn hanner blwyddyn. Mi welais eich llythyrau at y brawd Llew a da ydoedd clywed eich bod ynhir y rhai byw. Mi faswn i wedi gyrru i chwi ryw nonsens cyn hyn oni bae drafferth y byd enwir a phechadurus hwn ; for I have in a manner been oblig'd to do all the business ot this port for five months past, having had but little assistance from either collector or surveyor ever since brother went first to Shropshire. Ni welais mor hen bobl o Bentre'rianell ers gwell na chwe' mis. But now I hope the tables are turn'd a little, for here is a new collector whom I expect will ease me of a great part of the burden. I was lately appointed a Salt Officer here in room of brother, with a small salary, which I expect to be advanced if a fishery comes. W. to R. contd.

Ωαλα, ωαλα, Δυω αχ λλωυδο, παρ δηλω συδδ αρ υ ωραιγ αρ πλαντος ροεδδων υν μεδδωλ αρ ὑδ υρ αμσερ ειχ βοδ υν βριοδ. Ρωυβι υν φαελιο καελ γαν ρυν ωρ μερχεδαυ υμα βυ νγ'υμρυδ ι ερ α δδωετωυβ ωρθυντ, α δεγ ι υν ναδ ῥαιδ ιμι γαριο βυ μορωυνδοδ εβο μυβι ιρ βεδδ! *

I had a letter yesterday from brother at Carnarvon; 'roedd yn dywedyd sgrifennu o honaw attoch yn ddiweddar, felly ni soniaf ddim chwaneg am dano. I think you seem'd desirous in one of your letters to brother to have something of an account of the roots sent down in the box. Mi fynegaf i chwi, 'roedd y tulips agos i gid wedi llygru, mal na ddaeth o'r ddaear o honynt namyn pedwar allan o hanner cant o'r lleia'! Ni wn etto a geir chwaneg. The ranunculas and anemonies, I believe, are all coming up. The narcisus's, some in blow, proves to be of the ordinary kind. One hepatica, one campanula, alive. The rest all dead and gone. In short we made a broken voyage as to the roots. The seeds are most of 'em sown. Fe geir gweled eu prydferthwch ar fyrder gobeithio. I had the best collection of flower seeds this year (I daresay) of any one in Welch Wales, dyna air mawr! onte? I am much oblig'd to cousin Owen Jones. Can you put me in the way how to make him amends for the favours granted me in roots and seeds?

Here endeth this day's work.

P.S.—28th April, 1742.—Dyma fi newydd ddychwelyd yn ol wedi bod yn ymweled a'r hen bobl ein rhieni, ag amrafael ffrindiau eraill o'r gymydogaeth honno. Bum hefyd yn y Beaumaris yn y Sessiwn Mawr, heb achos yn y byd ond i rodiaw. Roedd yr hen bobl yn rhesymol; yr ifainc, sef fy mrawd Owain, yn mynd y

* Wala, wala, Duw a'ch llwyddo. Par ddelw sydd ar y wraig ar plantos? Roeddwn yn meddwl ar hyd yr amser eich bod yn briod. Rwyfi yn ffaelio cael gan 'run o'r merchedau yma fy nghymryd i er a ddywedwyf wrthunt, deg i un nad rhaid imi gario fy morwyndod efo myfi ir bedd.

W. to R. contd. symydo (h.y.) i fudo i'r Duwmares rwan, Galanmai; ag yna e fydd y rhieni heb neb i edrych ar ei hol, pe bae achos; ond rwy'n meddwl y blina'r chwaer ar y dref yn o fuan. Er mwyn rhoddi'r plant yn yr ysgol ynghyd a dwy herlodes ymrawd y maent yn mynd yno. Gwelais lythyr Parry a Will efo'r Doctor a darn oddiwrthych chwitheu. Gwelais hefyd eich llythyr at y nhad. Gresyn na chae yr hen wr yr arian, oblegid mae hi yn gaeth arno am beth i dalu; yr oedd dau yn dwrdio ei siwio yn y Sessiwn yr wythnos ymma.

Daccw elynion Llewelyn wedi dechreu o newydd, ag wedi gwneuthur cyngrair a Satan yw friwo os bydd modd; ond gobeithio nad allant. Daeth mrawd Owain oddiwrth y Fox Dduw Sadwrn o Bwllheli, lle y mae rwan yn *soundio* Sarn Badrig. Pob peth yn mynd ymlaen ar y goreu. Nid wyf yn cofiaw dim yrwan a dâl ei fanegu; felly byddwch wych, a brysiwch sgrifennu at

Eich caredigawl frawd, William Morris.

P.S. 2.—Mr. Lewis Lloyd, a subscriber to the *British Musick**, being now collector of this place, desires his name may be inserted in the list as follows :—Mr. Lewis Lloyd, Collector of Holyhead. William Roberts, of Bodjar, Esq., spoke to me some time agoe to have his name sent up, which I did to brother Lewis when with you. Quere if he has not forgot? The money will be paid here. Dyma frawd ynghyfraith Dick Morys, Caer Reinallt, newydd farw.

P. S.—Messrs. Parry & Williams may please to call of Mr. Richard Jones (of the Kentish Hoy, gynt) for 4s. subscription money for Mr. Henry Roberts, officer of the Excise at Holyhead, who desires his name may be in the list of subscribers. Mr. Lloyd and the Messrs. Roberts's books must be sent here. Dymma Mr. Owen, Penrhose, yn mynd i farw.

HOLYHEAD, 8th May, 1742.

W. to R. XLV. Dear Brother,—The Bishop of Bangor, at the representation of the Rev. Mr. Ellis, of this place, having undertaken to get the Society for the Propagation of Christian Knowledge to print two or three Welch pamphlets annually for the benefit of Wales in general, and as his Lordship has wrote last post to Mr. Ellis to desire he would recommend some accurate person to correct said pamphlets

* "Ancient British Music," a collection of Welsh airs, was published in 1742, by John Parry, the Harper, commonly called "Blind Parry." There are several references to Parry in these letters.

(which I suppose will be only a sheet each), i gael ohonynt fod yn beth gwell na'r rhai a *brintir* yn y Mhwythig; roeddwn inneu yn meddwl y gallach gael awr neu ddwy i'w sparrio o hyn i ben y mis i'r cyfryw orchwyl, ag i ynill ceiniog a chlôd ag er mwyn llwyddiant y grefydd yn'ch gwlad, ag er disodli y Methodistiaid, etc. So Mr. Ellis this post has named you to the Bishop as a proper person, and assured his Lordship (who is very sanguine for ye thing) that you would either wait of him or give him a line, when you could do it. N.B.—Rhaid bod on the reverse of the title page ye Welch alphabet with ab, eb, etc. This he likewise mention'd to his Lordship. I hope you'll be able to do this small jobb. It may be an annual perquisite to you, ag yn llês i'r cyffredin. Mr. Ellis mention'd you to his Lordship as an acquaintance of Mr. Meyrick. Pray write or wait of the Bishop so soon as you can whether you can do it or no. You need only direct to his Lordship at the Lobby of the House of Lords maen debyg. I wrote you two lines some time agoe and should be glad of your answer to that and this. I have heard nothing of the Hydrographer* since. Pawb yn iach yn Nulas ddoe. Ein chwaer wedi mynd ir Duwmares. Duw fo ich plaid. *Eich brawd anwiw, William Morris.* W. to R. contd.

Oes dim gobaith am gyflog y brawd?

HOLYHEAD, 3rd June, 1742. W. to R. XLVI.

Dear Brother,—Ce's 'ch llythyr or 25 ultimo, ag fal hyn yr attebir ef: Gwr ieuanc o sir Feirion, yn cyfagos i Abermawddach, yw'r Golhector ymma. Bu'se yn glark i Mr. Nicolson, Surveyor General dros gwmpas saith mlynedd o'i ysgol. Mae'n debyg y dylai yr holl lyfrau canu a siaradawdd y Dr. Evans ar brawd Llewelyn ddyfod efo ei gilydd, ond i grogi iddo a ŵyr par sut. Mae'n rhywyr cael ei gweled i dorri blys. Mae Mr. Owen o Benrhose yn lled fyw byth; mae'n beth gwell nag y bu. Mae'n sôn am gychwyn yr wythnos yma tua Bristol i yfed y dŵr, ond ni fedrai mor credu y dychwel byth yn ol; mae'r wraig yn bur feichiog. Gwych a fa'se fod gyda chwi yn Wanstead i rythu llygaid ar rai o'r pethau rhyfeddol hynny. Rwyf yn dra rhwymedig i'r câr Owain; yn rhodd fy ngwasanaeth atto pan weloch. Mae fy ngardd

* Mr. Lewis Morris, who was at this time employed on his survey of the Coast of Wales, afterwards published in 1748.

W. to R. contd.

inneu yn dechreu sirioli; ni choeliai fod moi bath yn y parthau, (h.y.) am amrafael flodau a llysiau dieithr. Mawr na phicciach i hyd ymma yw gweled. Yn wir fe fyddai or ffeinia i Owain gael mynd yn arddwr ir hên Feiryg, ond does he not stand a better chance for preferment where he is? I presume you've heard from brother Lewis ere now. He's still upon the coast of Sarn Badrig. I had a line from him about a week agon, he was well; mention'd to have had a letter from you, but not a word of More. I fancy he is gone to meet him bellach. Y cyngrair a soniais am dano a wnaeth . . . . . bagad o feibion Belial, y rhai maen debyg a glywsoch i ef yn sôn am danynt pan ydoedd yn Llyndain dan enw Tomos Jones, o Aberffraw. Dyma ddau o honynt wedi tynnu ymaith yr hugan oddiam danynt, ag wedi achwyn arno yn ei enwau ei hunain. Bu yma examinasiwn o'r achos y dydd arall, ag nid yw'r cwbl ond gwenwyn glas. The person he recommended to the Commissioners to act for him here is run mad, ag felly nis gwn i par beth y wneir wrth hynny: there must be another appointed. Fe fydd hynny yn fwy o gost ar Lewelyn. I heard from father not long ago; they were well. I suppose he has received your letter ere now. Duw a wnel i chwi gaffael yr arian ir hên ŵr. Mae yn fy mryd fyned y ffordd honno wiliau'r Sulgwyn yw hymweled. I thank you for the news papers; nid rhaid i chwi ymhel i yrru 'run ond hynny, oblegid rwyf wedi myn'd yn gydiwr efo bagad o boblach ymma mewn pappur newydd, sef *St. James's Evening Post.* Mae Mr. Ellis yn gorchymyn attoch yn fawr, ag nis gwn i pei'm crogid pwy un ohonoch sydd fwya rhwymedig i'r llall. Mae'r Grono * wedi mynd i Rydychen. Nis gwn i etto par sutt a fydd iddo drin y dreth: mae arnafi beth ofn am danaw. Oes, mae yma ddigon o bysgod rhywiog, sef whiting, codlings, whiting pollocks, blockings, also crabs and lobsters. Fe gafad tua Dulas rai pilchards yn ddiweddar. No penwag or mecryll to talk of. I can't send you the Noble Race this time, but my next will certainly cover it. We have had delightful weather of late: ni welwyd er's blynyddoedd mor fath olwg ar ydau a phorfeydd! Mae hi'n dal yn afiachus ymhlith y gwerinos. Fy ngharedigol orchymyn at'ch teulu, bod ag un, a Duw fo gida chwi oll. *Eich brawd anwiw, William Morris.*

* This is the first reference to Goronwy Owen in the letters. He was born in January, 1722, and was therefore about twenty years old at this time.

HOLYHEAD, 10th July, 1742. W. to R. XLVII.

Dear Brother,—I have been a long time in expectation of an answer to two letters wrote you some time agoe. In one of 'em I desired you to get the books of the Navy Office examin'd to know how much money there was due to Mr. Henry Welch of this, who died in the hospital from on board of a man-of-war; but as the said Mr. Welch's sister (Doctor Wheldon's widdow) is now in London about her late husband's effects and her pension, so you may manage y[e] above affair under one. I therefore beg you'll give her a line of what you have done, whether anything or nothing, that she may know how to proceed. Direct for Mrs. Ellin Wheldon, at Mr. Daniel Baily, in Flagon Row, Deptford.

Several of the Anglesey subscribers for the *Brittish Musick* have spoke to me to have 'em sent down in a small box by the waggon. I wish it could be contrived some how. I would take care to pay for a box, etc., and collect y[e] money of the several persons. If you or the publishers could send 'em directed for Dr. Evans to the care of Mr. William Goodwin, Grocer, in Chester, the carriage would come easier. Where's the Welsh pamphlet you promised to send me? Duw a wnel eich bod yn iach. Dyma fi newydd dderbyn llythyr oddiwrth y Dr. Evans; he is ill of a fever. I'm just a setting thither, in order to settle some [of] his affairs rhag ofn y gwaetha. Duw ai cadwo yw deulu. Brother was well about ten days agon. I hope all is well at Dulas. I beg you'll let me hear from you and give Mrs. Wheldon a line.

I am, your affectionate brother, William Morris.

HOLYHEAD, 10th August, 1742. W. to R. XLVIII.

Dear Brother Richard,—Mi ge's o'r diwedd afael ar eich llythyr or 31 ultimo, ag yn wir roeddwn agos wedi rhoddi'r swydd i fynu o'i ddisgwyl, ond gwell yw a ddêl ymhen y flwyddyn, na'r hwn ni ddêl byth. Mr. Meyrick is arrived at Bodorgan and his family, together with y[e] *Musick Books* I presume, ond ni che's i mor amser i fynd i ymweled ar hen ŵr etto, ag nis gwybod pa bryd y caf. Yr achos am llesteiriodd oedd marwolaeth ein ffyddlon gyfaill y Doctor Evans, yr hyn a glywsoch, deg i un, cyn yr awron. Gweddw pwy un sydd ymhlith brodyr a ffrins cyfoethogion, heb un a wna iddi ond ychydig iawn o lês ai chwe' phlentyn, ag un ond odid dan ei gwregys

W. to R. contd. (oddigerth Owain ei brawd ifa'): ag rwy'n meddwl mae'ch brawd Gwilym a fu'r ffrind oreu a feddai hyd yn hyn, or amser y clafychodd y Doctor. Bum yno dridie neu bedwar gidag ef pan oedd yn ei glefyd, ag yr oeddwn yno pan welodd Duw yn addas alw am dano. Neithiwr y daethym adre, wedi bod yn nghylch wythnos yn cymryd inventory, etc., etc. Un Alderman Ellams, o Gaer, wedi dyfod yn ungwaith. The doctor's apprentice died a few days after him, so that the poor woman, who is obliged to follow midwifery, has no body to keep the shop open. I wrote to Mr. Willoughby Clay the day he was buried, as there was upwards £45 due him, and shall this post write him again, that as Mr. Ellams and others takes what goods of theirs that are untouched or in good order, the widdow hopes he will do the same. He had a vast stock of drugs by him. How stand you with Clay now? I had a kind letter from him in behalf of Mrs. Evans. Jones's madness is owing to drinking. I don't mean that he is like Davidd Wynne neu'r cyffelyb. His madness consists of a mixture of drinking, swearing, cursing, lying, thieving, and committing ye vilest actions possible. He continues still to be under suspension, and I fancy will never be restor'd. We have got a coxon of one of our Customhouse cruizers now to cut for my brother, who, if we can fix him, will do extraordinary well. I wish I had been with you at Wanstead Gardens. Mine is in a most flourishing condition, and exceeds most in this country (though but of about nine months' standing). I wish I had some good roots from Owain. I am sorry you can't compass brother John's money. Captain Parker, Master of the *Torbay*, who was here the other day, said if he had known of the affair when at London, he would have got it you in a day's time, having received some for others of the said ship's crew. I came from father's yesterday morning; the old man said he never had more occasion for't, having, on account of brother Owen's throwing up his part of the tenement, being obliged to stock it and buy corn for seed and bread all the year. I hope you've heard of Mr. Welch's money and acquainted Mrs. Wheldon. I wish George Williams was in the country now to fill up the poor Doctor's place—no man could do it better. I am sorry for Sion Prŷs. Do you know of e're a young fellow that is a surgeon and apothecary that wants a good shop and drugs? Rwy'n gobeitho na bydd ini fawr golled ar secretary Manley, oblegid nid oedd ond gwr rhwng gwr ar gordd. I b'le yr aeth budd yr holl fŵn? Daccw Lywelyn wedi eich gwneuthur chwi am finneu yn fwynwyr, heb na chenad na chyfarch, ymhle y ceir cydeidiau o arian yw sinkio yn y ddaear? Roedd Owen Williams yma nos arall, wedi gwerthu ei hettiau, yn ffaelio dyfod i hyd i ddim priddach wrth ei fodd. Yn wir, mi roddais eich gwasanaeth ąt Mr. Ellis, archodd ynteu yrru ei un ynteu i chwithau. Mae'r Esgob yn Mangor, mi gwelais ef yn Llanerch-medd dydd arall, yn rhoddi bedydd Esgob i gynifer a ymgynnullasai ynghyd. Pan welwy Fodiar mi ofynaf iddo ynghylch y llyfr muwsig. Mae Griffydd yn Nulun gin dlotted a Jôb pan ydoedd waetha arno, ag yn drâ aniolchgar, fal mae gwaetha ei fod. Ni fedraf feddwl pwy oedd y ddynes oedd wedi troi yn Babist yn y Madeira, ag ni chofiais ofyn ir rhieni, nid hwyrach y basent hwy'n medru dyfalu. Bum nos Sadwrn ddiwaetha' yn y Duwmares; 'roedd y chwaer ar plantos, i Dduw bo'r diolch, yn iachus ddigon. Diolch i chwi am y llyfr Cymreig a benthyg y bregeth. Mae nhw yma yn meddwl mae un o rywogaeth y tylwyth têg yw'r hogyn pan fo mor ffraeth. Gorchmynnwch fi at eich teulu, a byddwch wych am y tro. Dyna i chwi noble race of Shenkyn. *In haste, William Morris.* W. to R. contd.

P.S.—Nis gwn a ddywedais i chwi or blaen fy mod newydd gael llythyrau oddiwrth y brawd Llewelyn; mae wedi cymryd *lease* i fwyngloddio a chwedi eich rhoddi chwi a minneu yn rhannog, etc. Pa beth a wneir a'r holl gyfoeth a ddaw am ein pennau? Should be glad of your opinion of that affair. You must have heard of it.

HOLYHEAD, October 21st, 1742. W. to R. XLIX.

Dear Brother,—It is a long while since I had a line from you. Ai gollwng dros gôf eich brawd Gwilym a wnaethoch? I have this day a line from Mr. Meyrick, of Bodorgan, who desired me to write for Dick Morris (whom he once hired) to come down to be his buttler, if he can quit his present post. The good old gentleman order'd me to tell him that they shan't differ about wages, and says that if I did not know how to direct to him, you

W. to R. contd. did; desires his service to you, so have sent ye enclosed to be directed by you. I think I heard his sister say that he was at Bath with his master some time agoe; but I fancy you know best or can enquire. The old gent. is in great want, and would be glad of this man on account of brother Lewis and your recomendation. Father and mother and the family at Beaumares were all well a few days agone. Brother Lewis a-recovering off a late terrible fit of the rheumatism at Aberystwyth. Owen Jones has been wrote to by me lately to come to Bodorgan. I expect his answer soon. I am sincerely glad it lyes in my power now and then to oblige Mr. Meyrick on account of his kindness to brother Lewis, you, and brother John. What's become of the *Torbay* affair? We have had the best fishery in Holyhead this year that has been this fifteen or eighteen years; not so good at Moelfra. Your brother Gwilym refused lately the place of a collector's chief clerk at Chester, worth about eighty pounds per annum, having been courted to accept it. I daresay there will be great interest made for't. I expect to hear from you soon, and am, with love to yourself and family.

Your affectionate brother, William Morris.

W. to R. L.

HOLYHEAD, January 2nd, 1742.

Dear Brother,—I received yours of the 30th November, which I would have answered sooner but that bydol drafferthion prevented me. I am glad Dick Morris comes to Bodorgan, though I know him not pei t'rawn i fy nhalcen wrthaw. His sister, poor woman, is mighty glad. Owen Jones paid me a visit sometime ago; liked his place much. Ni che's i byth mor amser i fyn'd i edrych am yr hen ŵr gonest, sef yw hwnnw, Mr. Meyrick, ag fe ffaeliodd gennyf fynd hyd yn Nulas y gwiliau ymma, er bod y nhad wedi gyrru march i'm cludo yno—yr achos ai para ydoedd fod llong fawr wedi torri yn gyfagos ir fan ymma ar holl wyr wedi boddi, a minneu yn fawr fy ffwdan yn ceisio cadw ag ymgeleddu'r pethau ir amral o achos mae mrawd yw'r deputy. Mi ges anwyd ag oerfel i'm hesgyrn or achos. Ni safiwyd fawr or petheua, pob peth trwm yn y gwaelod, a phob peth ysgafn yn dippiau rhyd y creigiau, mi a fum ddiwrnod neu ddau yn auctioneer of hên goediach na thalant mo'i cadw. I am in hopes of coming at the anchors and guns when

the wind and weather comes fair. She was call'd *The Farrant* W. to R.
Joseph Young, master, in the cheese trade, would carry near 200 contd.
tons—she was in ballast. Gwych a fydde i chwi ddibennu materion Londonderry* with applause. A mendiodd y bachgen ynteu marw ar ol ei chwaer a wnaeth? Pa sawl plentyn sydd i chwi? Ni chlywa inneu ddim hanes o gaffael mŵn. Mae arnaf [ofn] mae adventurers trwstan ym ni oll. Ces lythyr oddiwrth y brawd, o fewn ychydig yma—roedd yn llabi. Celwydd bod y gair a glywsoch ynghylch yr Arglwydd a Jones Trefoll. It was occasioned by a drunken whim which made some noise—but all diniweidrwydd. Mae gwr Beggi Morgans honno yn un or progiwrs o gwmpas y llong ymma a dorrodd—bywiolaeth wych! Ni wnaed dim diben ar faterion y Doctor, nid oes neb wedi prynnu mor siop etto, na dim journeyman nid oes ynddi, disgwyl beunydd am rywun. Mae'r plant i gyd wedi rywun neu gilydd ei cymryd, dros drô, beth bynnag, ar wraig yn cael purion gwaith, sef dwyn plant i'r byd. Gresyn hefyd na base Sior yn y wlad, nis gwn i par sut fydd trin Mr. Ellams, the chief creditor. He is to be in the country this month, and I am desired to meet him. Mi glywais mrawd ynghyfraith (yr hwn a fu i'm hymweled y dydd arall) yn dywedyd fod y marsiant Owain ab Catrin Arthur yn caru rhyw wraig weddw yn y Traeth bychan, mae rwan yn Leverpool merchant. Aie rydych *χωιθευ υν δυσγυ Γροεγ, ρωυβ ιννευ ωεδι γολλωνγ υ γυβαν υν ανγοβ.*† Let us have a specimen of yours yn eich llythyr nesaf, da chwithau. Roedd ein rhieni yn iachus dydd arall. Dim newydd ffordd ymma. Bu farw yr dydd arall Mr. Coytmore, o Goetmore, y diweddaf or hennw. Gadewch glywed oddiwrthych gynta galloch, a gorchymynwch fi at eich teulu, a Duw a fyddo gida chwi oll. Hang politicks!

Your affectionate brother, *William Morris.*

N.B.—Fe fu agos i mi a gollwng dros gof ddymuno i chwi a'r eiddoch Flwyddyn Newydd wrth eich bodd, a llawer o naddynt. Ni welais i byth mo Mr. Bodiar i gael y pedwar swllt ganddaw. Pethau bryntion yw'r boneddigion yma.

*Richard Morris was employed for a time upon the accounts of Lord Londonderry's estate.

Aie rydych chwitheu yn dysgu Groeg, rwyf inneu wedi gollwng y cyfan yn angof.

W. to R. HOLYHEAD, 4th February, 1742.*

LI. Dear Brother,—I have for a long time past resolved to write you a letter in form, but one nonsensical thing or other has put me out of my byas. I've inclos'd a line for Mr. Pritchard, who told me he would be in your city very soon. I am a little ruffled at my not hearing from brother Lewis this fortnight past. Pray what is become of him? Our parents were well the other day, so are the family here. We had yesterday an account that a ship loaden with 200 hogsheads of tobacco and odd is stranded near Bodeon, bound to Whitehaven. Nid af monwyf ar ei chyfyl om bodd. If brother Lewis ben't set out, please to tell him we buried the other day Gaynor Brimridge, of Newry, his children's old landlady. The poor people die very fast in these parts. We have had nothing but hurricanes of wind, etc., for this month past.

Duw a ddel a thawelwch. Ni chai mo'r amser i wneuthur y brauch arall, ac ond yn unig i'ch dwyn ar gôf mae fi ydyw

Eich caredigawl frawd, Wm. Morris.

The ship stranded near Aberffraw, is called the *Providence*, of Whitehaven, Jno. Williamson, Master, bound from America to Whitehaven.

W. to R. HOLYHEAD, 7th February, 1742.

LII. Dear Brother.—You are in my debt of a long letter, which I would advise you to discharge as soon as conveniently you can. The inclos'd I've sent you presuming that brother Lewis will be with you ere it comes to hand, ag onite nid oes mor llawer o fatter. I received a letter this day from Edward Edwards, directed for brother Lewis. He is at London, and say'd he would enquire you out a Sunday last. He has a ring of brother John and promises an account of his things. If he has not met you, you may send him a penny post letter directed for him at the Newcastle-upon-Tine, near Gun Dock, a dyna'r holl hanes. Is there such a place as Gun Dock? Tell him his sister was well this day. I called at her house: she has buried a girl lately of the small-pox. She lives at Rhydbont—keeps a publick house. Dick Morris I'm told is at Bodorgan. Father and mother and brother's girls and the family at Beaumaris, I thank God, are all well. I'm in great hast.

P.S.—My love to sister. *W. Morris.*

*This letter is probably misplaced. It was probably written in February, 1741, but the year is indistinct.

LLANERCHMEDD, 30th October, 1743. W. to R. LIII.

Dear Brother,—I am now in my way home, having been to see father and mother and our nieces, viz., brother Lewis's daughters, at Beaumaris. Found 'em all in tollerable good health ond bod yr hen bobl yn fusgrellaidd. I received yours of the 29th ult. and 15th and 22nd inst. Hir y buoch yn ei orphen. Fe weddai nad oedd dim brys mawr ar y meddyg am atteb ynghylch siop, etc., Mrs. Evans. I wish the poor woman could meet a person that would buy it. The furniture of the shop and still house, including the drugs, etc., were valued at about 120 pounds, but there has been a good deal of drugs returned and made use of since that time, so that if any person comes to treat about 'em there must be another inventory made. She would let the whole house, or part of it. The conveniencies are very good. Anyone that is qualified may make a handsome livelyhood and may be assured of a great bargain. Your old friend, Mr. William Roberts, the Hamburgher, called of me a few days agoe in his way from Ireland. I wrote by him in a hurry two or three lines with what I knew of Lord Londonderry's affairs, all the sum and substance of which is this: that his Lordship came as far as Holyhead in company with the Earl of Anglesey (senior); that he missed his passage by Monday's Pacquet and had, therefore, a day or two to spare; that I knew his sister* and the rest of the family at Bodorgan would be glad to see him; that I made myself known to him as a friend of Mr. Meyrick, his sister, etc.; that with much adoe I prevailed upon his Lordship to take a ride thither; that he came in a hired chair and pair to Holyhead, attended by two livery men, only one of which came along with us to Bodorgan; that we there found only the old man and Lady Lucy at home; that what passed between the old Don and the penbwl about your affair was in my absence, but the old gent. mentioned you often at our cups and told his Lordship that you had parted with Stainsby and was then with Smyth, etc. Mr. Meyrick told me that he press'd your affair very home to him, that he could not do without such an one, etc. Ond nid oedd y llall yn gaddo dim daioni. He

*Lucy, sister of Lord Londonderry, was married to Pierce, second son of Owen Meyrick, of Bodorgan.

W. to R. contd.

was capable of managing his own affairs and did not want such a person at present, and some such stuff. Gwr gwêllt. Gwych y darfu i ni dermio am un noson. His Lordship carried one saddle horse with him over. Mi glowais ei fod yn traenio yn dêg yn Nuflun, yn hoffi genethod prydferth etc.

Boreu 31st.—I'me confined here by a most violent storm so shall miss this day's post on account of not being at home betimes. Dim franks yma. I'll send you the method of cyweirio crŵth at foot. As to one of our best Welch enterludes, I think it may justly be said of 'em, what is generally own'd in regard to puns, that they may superficially divert, but there never was a good one. I'll endeavour to procure one; old Owain Parry y Crypul I think is the likelyest to apply to with hopes of success. Pa beth ydych nês er bod ymhlith dysgleidiau o fwyd heb gaffael amser i'w fwyta? That I take it to be your case in Smyth's library. Drwg yw clywed eich bod yn afiachus a bod yr eppil yn naccau ffynnu. Gwell i chwi medd yr hen wragedd enwi'r nesa yn Wilym. Mr. Owain Pritchard called at the Head and shewed me your letter which he had in South Wales, llawn ffwdan. Thomas à Kempis was translated by one Huw Owen o Wenynog yn Môn, Esq., and *not Gwenydog*. He was known in this country by the name of H. O. Gwenynog. Has been dead about a hundred years agone as I take it. Brother Owen and sister and your brother Gwilym have lived together at Holyhead since the middle of September. We have taken a good snug cabbin. I left them and children well. Plant yn dysgu yn rhyfeddol, ail i blant Pentrerianell ers talwm. Direct for the Surveyor of Customs at Holyhead if you have a frank, if not, to the company. Brother Lewis's daughters are two fine girls. Duw ro'r gras iddynt. Yn wir mae'n rhieni yn bur fusgrellaidd a than bwys mawr; bydd raid benthycca galan gauaf i gau safn Dorset. Dim gofyn am ŷd nag anifail. Mae'n rhyfedd na byddai rywbeth iw gael oddiwrth gyflogau Brenhin Sior. Ce's lythyrau yn ddiweddar oddiwrth Lewelyn o Dre Benfro. Had the perusal of one from him to the Company of Beaumaris the other day—was brave and hearty. My garden is not to be sufficiently commended for the exquisite beauty of its flowers, etc. Chwi fyddech yn gyrru cardod o hadau immi rwan ag yn y man. Mae gennyf goed o'ch rhywogaeth cyhyd a chwithau from Richmond Gardens. A few choice flower seeds against the Spring would be of infinite service to my paradise. My love to you all, a Duw fo'n gwarchad trosoch yw dymuniad eich caredigawl frawd, *Gwilym Morys.* W. to R. contd.

Holyhead, Dydd Calan Gauaf.—I read this day in the Dublin News Letter the following paragraph: "October 29th. We hear that the Right Honourable the Earl of Londonderry is to be introduced to the House of Peers this day." Mr. Meyrick gave me some time agoe a guinea to remitt to you, being a token of his friendship. I desired brother Lewis to remit it to you and that I would give him credit for it. I suppose he has acquainted you of it; if so, no doubt but you have own'd the favour to Mr. Meyrick. I've accounted with brother Lewis for it.

HOLYHEAD, 17th February, 1743. W. to R. LIV.

Dear Brother,—Dymma fi newydd ddyfod adref wedi bod yn hebrwng Arglwydd London Derry i Fodorgan, lle tarriodd ef a minnau deirnos. This day about noon his Lordship set forward on his journey, accompanied by Counsellor Meyrick and Mr. P. Meyrick, who proposed to go with him as far as Chester. The old gent. was pleased to consult with me what part of your letter to him was proper to be read to his Lordship. Accordingly he imparted to his Lordship what related to Stainsby (i.e.) of your waiting of him for Custom Papers and of his positive denial, etc., at which treatment his Lordship's wrath was much kindled. Mr. Meyrick took several opportunities of speaking of you to his Lordship, and how his Lordship stood in need of such a one, and what an unfit person Capt. Stringer was to manage his Lordship's affairs in Teagueland. It seems he's fallen out with said Stringer, says he has suffered by his indolence, etc., and is to go to law with him, a chant o bethau. All the answer Mr. M. could get out of his Lordship was that as to your part, if he should want such a person, he would think of you. Mr. M. told him what great service you would do his Lordship in settling his affairs, etc. Nid oes dim ond ynfydrwydd yn ei ben, nid aetha' mo hono i ymweled ai chwaer y trô ymma er ei fod yn mynd o fewn 6 milldir at y ty oni bae myfi, mae honno yn dywedyd wrth bawb mae fi yw'r goreu o feibion dynion. Gresyn na sobreiddia'r hurthgan dippyn. Nid ffŵl a

W. to R. contd. fyddai pei gwnâi. I presume it won't be proper that you should mention to his Lordship that you had received any account from me of his Bodorgan, etc. Aiê son am fynd ir West India, rheitiach ymgroesi ag aros o gwmpas y cartref tra gellir cael tamaid a llymaid.

For God's sake what is become of brother John's affair? Oes dim gobaith ir hen bobl fusgrell ymma gael dim byth or peth adawodd ar ei ol? Roedd hi gin gaethed arnynt y leni oni buase iddynt gaffael benthyg £9 neu £10 buase Dorset yn sesio ar ei dâ am yr ardreth ag yno, rhaid a fase mynd i dy a gardd. Mae mrawd Llywelyn a minneu yn gwneuthur goreu ag allom yw cynorthwyo, ond, nid eill neb namyn ei allu. It seems brother John had borrowed £4 or 4 guineas of Wm. Hughes, the silk throwster. This fellow plagues my father with letters by post continually, wrote in a scandalous manner, charging him with keeping him out of his money, etc. I undertook to answer one of them some time agoe, which produced the inclosd and which I presume ends the correspondence between me and that gentleman, though I dont know how to blame him. Duw a wnel i chwi fedri gwneuthur rhiwbeth yn y matter yn fuan er llês ir ddau hen bobl onest. Dyma fy chwaer wedi geni iddi fab, yr hwn a fedyddiwyd o fewn y pythefnos yma, ei enw yw Llywelyn; maent yn rhesymol. Daccw yr hen Dwmoris wedi marw yn gelain gegoer; dim newydd arall yr awron. Fy ngharedigawl wasanaeth attoch oll.

Wyf eich brawd anwiw, William Morris.

Rhaid esgusodi beiau yn y llythyr hwn oblegid fod y pen ar llaw allan o drefn, chwi ellwch ddyfalu'r achos.

W. to R. CAERGYBI, 9th April, 1744.

LV. Anwyl Frawd,—I have yours of the 24th ulto. in answer to about a dozen of mine, *ονδ γωελλ νω'ρ γωρ α δδελ υμ'εν υ βλωυδδυν να'ρ 'ων να δδελ βυθ** was a saying of a famous Graecian. Mr. Robert's ring will be delivered any one that pays me half a guinea for him, its worth little more. Roeddwn inneu yn meddwl fod lleccyn meddal ar ei siol pan ydoedd ymma. Ynghrôg y bwy os medraf gael un enterlude a dâl yw gyrru; mi fynna' edrych etto ar fyrder. I seldom go into the country and then make but short stays. I received the 4s. from Mr. Bodiar, and paid 'em brother Lewis, i.e.

*"Ond gwell yw'r gwr a ddel ymhen y flwyddyn, na'r hwn na ddel byth."

settled for 'em in account. Aie mae'r tir wedi blino ffordd yna, ai nid oes dim modd iw wrteithio? Lewis yw enw'r etifedd yma. I am glad you're resolved to pay that scoundrel Hughes off, it will be doing your aged parents an infinite service; my father was never so ill-used by any man—for God's sake dont neglect it. I should be glad to hear your hanes with my Lord London Derry. Pray dont be so backward in writing. It is something odious to tell a brother that one is glad of his success, etc., oni wyr pawb hynny, felly nid rhaid immi ddim ddywedyd i chwi fod yn dda genyf glywed fod y byd yn gwenu tippin arnoch. I was a night at Dulas about ten days agone, and had the perusal of yours to father; the old people were pretty well. There is no such person in being as a daughter of Uncle W. Morris; he had but one, and she died at his house about a month before him. I am witness to her being interred, oni chododd hi o farw yn fyw. 'Tis pity she was not brought before De Veil and sent to Bridewell. He had no illegitimate children but Sion Gloff, who died in Greece. We are much exposed here to the Privateers. We are in hopes of having a fort, etc., to keep 'em off; we have petition'd. Dyna i chwi hanes hadau sy'n eisiau yma. My love to you all. Brother and sister joins me. W. to R. contd.

William Morris.

P.S.—I had a letter from brother Lewis of the 28th ulto.; his affairs were quite disconcerted on account of the French war. Gwae fi na feddwn lwyth llong o flodau gwychion oddiyna i roddi yn fy ngardd. N.B.—It exceeds any in North Wales for varieties! Dyna air mawr, onte? Hast, hast, post hast!

[This is a Memorandum written by Richard Morris on the back of the previous letter of April 9th, 1744, and it may represent the contents of a letter sent by him to his brother William. As so few of Richard's letters have been preserved, it is inserted here to show the diversity of the subjects he was interested in.]

MEMORANDUM.

Pope Dead — Welsh Bibles — Epitaphs for . . . . . . —French Prizes — Insurance — Privateering — Dutch Wrangling — Prussia dubious p. East Friezland—Sardinians—Lobkowitz in Naples—Queen Hungary, declaration war against—Matthews—Lostock—Kouli Kan's Religion—Foundling Hospital—New Bridge—Mansion House—Weather, Hay and Corn—French Ambassador—Russia—

W. to R. contd. Prince Charles, passing Rhine with 80,000 Men. will Conquer all Lorraine and Alsace—Anson—Treasure come to Town, about One Million — Privateer's Great Succees — The French prodigious losses at Sea — Genoeze bul[d], by Mathews — Several Fortified Towns lost in Flanders—Prussians coming to assist Queen Hungary—O. Prichard—Brother Lewis—Brother William - Father —Corbett — More — Donally — W. Vaughan — Dover 15 Ships, Chester, etc., 8, in all about 30—2 Millions Sterling demanded since commencement of War—Levant Ships taken by Mathews—Ranelagh, Vauxhall, Ruchett, Liquors, etc. — Marybone, 3 Wells, Musick, Alehouses, etc., Playhouses, Extravagance to Excess—297 Chests Silver, 16 Gold, and 21 Bags Gold Dust ; in all 48 Tons in 32 Waggons—Guthrie, 2 Hists.—Rassin, Chambers, Harris, Voyages, 4to. and . . . Salmon, Geography, Journeymen Taylors and Barbers—Wages—Parry and Sir Watkin—Interview with Guthrie — Chamberlain to subscribe £50 for seven years to defray Carte's charges in writing History of England—Vulture privateer (Bristol) lost with prize £30,000.

W. to R. LVI.

HOLYHEAD, 4th JANUARY, 1744.

Dear Brother,—I wrote you a few lines by Jones, the sailmaker, lately, to which I refer you (as the tradesmen say). I'me resolved now to make an attempt of answering your letter of the 10th November. Mr. Ellis tells me that he has wrote to you, so saved me the trouble of saying much. Dr. Davies, of the Temple, did not use me well. I sent an order by him for some things in his way for the winter, and I have not had 'em yet, though parcels has come from him several months agoe. Gadewch iddo, dyna'r tro cynta'. I am glad to hear that you are so much involv'd in business, but if your health and eyes ben't impaired by it, all's well. Gwell bod felly na pheidio oni bae i ddyn gael pwn ceffyl neu ddau o drysor yn rhywle i fyw arnynt, er hynny bydd rhywbeth 'n ôl.

Da syrthio o'r Beibl i'ch dwylo. Gobeithio y cewch glod a budd oddiwrtho, hynny yw, yr haeddwch hwynt. The opportunities you have are extraordinary, and without 'em I fancy you'd have been greatly at a loss. Nid gwr onest oedd Moesen, ag felly nid gwiw disgwyl daioni o'i waith, and his altering Dr. Davies's orthography was an instance of it, ffei hono. Ni wybum i erioed fod gan Mr. P. Lewis,* Llanfihangel, law mewn argraphiad Beibl? Was not he register at Bangor fawr yn Gwynedd? **W. to R. contd.**

Cell wych yw honno o eiddo ein cydwladwr Mr. Jones.† Ni feddyliais i erioed fod y fath un yn Llundain. O ble y ca'dd o yr holl lyfrau Cymraeg? Ai sgytor Moses Williams‡ ydoedd? Odiaeth fyddai gael trin peth ar yr hên weilch rheini, sef y MSS:—*Χωι ωυδοχ υρ αχος ιρ βραωδ σορρι* (you'll excuse the pun). I am sorry for it. *Μαε ο'ν κυμρυδ λλαωερ ο δραφερθ αρνο ι γεισιο βυωολιαεθ ιδο εβ αι βλαντ μωυ νογ α ωναων ι. Δυω α ροδο ιδο ιεχυδ ι βυνδ υμλαεν, ος ωες υν ειχ γαλλυ, κυμοδωχ αγ εβ, ονιδε νιδ ωες μορ ἐλῶ, κεβαις λυθυρ οδιωρθο ο βεων υρ ωυθνος υμα, ῥωεδ υν ιαχ.*§ Rogers is a madman. He'll be with you soon. Dyn celwyddog, caredig, enbydus, digrif, an odd composition! Drwg oedd torri o'r masnachwr hwnnw, ond da cael ûs gan ddrwg dalwr. Da fydd y goron oni cheir y bunt. I can't tell you anything about the Welch Almanack. I know there are three publishers, if not more. All sorry stuff; na thalan yw codi ar y maes, ond ar y goreu i'r bobl gyffredin. Ni phryn neb arall monynt. N.B.—Only two publishers this year, both printed by Durston at Salop.

7th.—Dyma Rogers wyllt newydd ddwad drosodd, yn gorchymun attoch yn fawr. Don't reproach him for the idle story he told me some time agoe. I believe he would not mention it to anyone else; the fellow has a regard for you, and has been very civil to brother's

* Piers Lewis is said by Richard Morris to have edited the 1690 folio edition of the Welsh Bible. Greal 1806, p. 282.

† William Jones, F.R.S., father of the celebrated Oriental scholar Sir William Jones. On the death of Moses Williams, his library of Welsh books and MSS. was purchased by William Jones, who bequeathed it to the second Earl of Macclesfield. The library has recently been bought by Sir John Williams, Bart. Many of the MSS. contain Notes and Indexes by Richard Morris. Historical MSS. Commission, Llanstephan MSS. Catalogue, by Dr. Gwenogvryn Evans.

‡ Rev. Moses Williams, Editor of the 1717 and 1727 Editions of the Welsh Bible.

§ "Chwi wyddoch yr achos i'r brawd sorri. Mae o'n cymryd llawer o drafferth arno i geisio bywoliaeth iddo ef ai blant, mwy nog a wnawn i. Duw a roddo iddo iechyd i fynd ymlaen, os oes yn eich gallu, cymodwch ag ef, onide nid oes mor elw, cefais lythyr oddiwrtho o fewn yr wythnos yma, 'roedd yn iach."

W. to R. contd. family. Car yw i Wion Gwagfost o Bentre Berw. You may depend upon it that I will send you an almanack or two shortly. I'me promis'd some of the last year's. Ond mawr na fedrwch berswadio rhai o'r bobl yna to print a new edition of the Welsh Common Prayer. We never had but one good one, which was done in London—I mean for the pocket. Those done at Salop are intolerable—bad paper, bad print, bad orthography, bad everything except the subject matter, ag mae rhai'n dywedyd y gellid tacclu hwnnw. I wish you would send me a number of two of the songs mentioned in the enclos'd advertisement. If I like, would take 'em all along. I suppose a frank would bring me one at a time. Our parents were well not long agoe, as we are all here. God be praised. I am, with love to you and yours, dear brother,

Your affectionate brother, *William Morris.*

'Fydd dim hadau iw cael y leni. You are at the fountain head.

CUSTOM HOUSE, HOLYHEAD, 19th July, 1745.

W. to R. LVII. Dear Brother,

Wedi bod yn disgwyl nis gwn i pa hyd am attebion i ddau neu dri o lythyrau, I've at last received one from you of the 17th ult° about two days agoe, by the canal of Pentrerhianell (where, by the way, God be prais'd all are well). Rwy'n cyfaddef fod arnaf beth bai am na buaswn yn rhoddi i chwi hanes fy nhgyfnewidiad, yr hyn yn sicr a wnaethum, oni bae feddwl eich bod wedi marw neu or hyn lleiaf yn ddibris am wybod fy nghyflwr, oblegid fe a ŵyr pawb y gallech pe bai ewyllys anfon i'ch brawd lythyr dairgwaith neu bedair yn y flwyddyn, ond bynag par fôdd i wirio yr hen ddihareb, *Γωιριον παωβ αρ ει αιρ ει 'υν.** I presume the Counsellor forgot the guinea. You may, if you please, make use of my name upon that score; you'll ten to one meet him at George's Coffee House in Chancery Lane, where his letters are directed. I dare say he has nothing to say to Dick Morris. How should that fellow know anything of the matter? The lawyer to whom I've wrote last post about some other affair is for leaving the City soon, felly gwell i chwi ymorol cyn bo rhy hwyr. I don't rightly understand what you mean by saying that I stopt the other guinea for brother Lewis. I received a guinea from the old gentleman, which I desired

*"Gwirion pawb ar ei air ei hun."

Brother Lewis to forward to you, and gave him credit in an account settled with him 11 May, 1744, for the same. I presume I advis'd you of it; what could I do more? I'me sorry for Dick Morris, for he is partly past his labour, and nobody would bear with his infirmity except such a good-natur'd man as his present master, which is scarce to be met with. Duw a δελο α χωι ι αλλυ ταλυ ιδδο βοβ κεινιαωγ.* He never mention'd a sillable of the debt to me. I design to go to Bodorgan next week. I'll talk over this affair with him. I have not heard anything of Roberts since he went over. What made the fellow marry a mad woman? Drwg oedd bod Wil Gwredog wedi cael fath golled, etc. No, we have no fort. We have petition'd the great ones for one, but no redress. Our poverty is our safeguard from French and Spaniards. I can't guess who that Price you mention can be. No clergyman of this country to be sure. I fancy it must be a Methodist—religiously mad. This country, which some few years ago might be said not to have six persons within it of any other persuasion than that of the Church of England, is now full of Methodists or Independents or Presbiterians, or some other sect, the Lord knows what. I believe they don't themselves. The Welch name for 'em is pennau crynnion; they've licenced preachers and chapels.

Your apprehensions about the Leeward Isles I hope are dispell'd. You've met with a rare knott of customers! Par sut dâl ydych yn ei gael gan yr Esgobion am drin y llyfr? I'me obliged to you for sending me the Universal Harmony; they would have been much more acceptable sometime agoe, for I made a musical screen all cover'd with such. I wish I had a few numbers more, and the money with you for them. I fancy Counsellor Meyrick's man might pack 'em up safe. If you can contrive to make these up half a score perhaps I may send for the rest some time. The lawyer would pay for 'em if you would but speak to him. Purion esgus i chwi gael eich guinea. I did your compliments to Mr. Ellis, and communicated to him some part of your letter. We are glad to hear that we are to have a perfect Common Prayer Book, and so many improvements in the Bible. Ond gresyndod mawr yw fod y gwaith yn mynd ymlaen mor ddiog. Drwg fod eich golwg

*"Duw a ddelo a chwi i allu talu iddo bob ceiniawg."

W. to R. contd.

cynddrwg. Ni welais i erioed mo Berson Llanbrynmair* er y gwn mae dynan digrif ydyw. Gan bwy y mae stori Dyssilio ar femrwn? Diolch i chwi am hanes ein cydwladwyr, clywsom son am Evans a Gr. Jones. I fancy the first wants a good living. Digrif oedd y dyn a daera that our British Bible had been translated out of the English. Oedd arno ddim cywilydd pan brofasochi ir gwrthwyneb? How goes Carte's History on? When will it be finish'd? I'm glad to hear he gives the Britains fair play for their characters, etc. I have a letter of the 6th inst. from brother Lewis, wrote at Cwmsymlog and Llanymddyfri. He was agoing on some business of the Crown's to Presteign in Radnorshire! dim newydd ond ei fod yn llawn ffwdan fal arferol. Father and mother were both here this month, though at different times; mae eill deuwedd yn bur fusgrellaidd yn enwedig y mam. Deg i un y gwelwn moni hi yma ond hynny. They buried lately their next-door neighbour and the best, viz., Edward ab Owain William (or Nant Bychan) yr hwn Edward oedd yn byw ymodafon Griffith Prisiart gynt, math ar gybydd ydoedd. Bu farw ag ar ei helw 1500 o bunnau, ond rhyfedd na base Mr. Angeu yn cymryd ffi. I've a letter this day from Cousin Jack Salisbury; 'roedd y wraig ar bachgen yn glaf yn ddiweddar. Bu farw iddo dri o feirch ag ynteu ei hun 'rawron yn lleccyn iawn. Pob peth yn ammorth i wann.

Mae' nghylch chwe mis er pan ge's Gywely, er hyny hyd yr awron rwy' fwya dyn ei ffwdan dan haul—repairing, furnishing, projecting, gardening, improving, etc. Rwyn gobeitho bod yn hapus, os gwel Duw'n dda, ag onide rhaid bodloni. My wife joins me in love to you and yours. I'me in great hast.

Your affectionate brother, William Morris.

The Surveyor here, I hope, does very well; has a housefull of fine children. Sister and him desires their love to you. What say you to our foreign warr nowadays? I sent you two Welch almanacks by Rogers five or six months agon. I can get no enterlude as yet worth a rush. I owe Mr. Davies, cordwainer, about 50s.

* William Wynne, the Welsh poet (1704—1760).

for a parcel of shoes and boots I had of him last spring. Please to tell him that I shall answer his draft if he'll give anyone a bill upon me. Brŷs, Brŷs, anferth frŷs. **W. to R. contd.**

CAER GYBI, 17 o Awst, 1745. **W. to R. LVIII.**

Δεαρ Βροθερ,—I received yours of the 1st August, and one of the same date from Counsellor Meyrick. His I answer'd by the return of the post, and sent him the certificates he wanted. All I could tell him of the guinea affair was, that I had been at Bodorgan soon after he sett out for London, and that his father told me that he either had or would (I don't remember which) give him orders to give you a guinea. I wrote since to the old gentleman and conveyed him your thanks, and mention'd the same story, a dyna i chwi ben a thewi am hynny. I'me glad you got me some more numbers of the Universal Harmony. It's suppos'd here that the Counselor will betake himself to a wife upon his arrival in Mona. Miss Rowlands, of Caera, is to be the happy bride. By this match it's to be hop'd the country will be united, and that cursed party quarrels will subside! What the Cardinal told you of Pentraeth and Llanddyfnan I believe will turn out to be fact. Rowlands, the Methodist,* it seems, makes a rare hand of his Gospel harvest— offeiriad to the truth. Price you mention is one Jones' curate, of Llanvair and Llanbedr, an empty fellow. Mi ddyweda i chwi chwedl digrif yn ei gylch ef a'r hen ewyrth Owain Parri'r saer. Mae Owain yn byw mewn tŷ i Mr. Meyrick a elwir Glyn Llanbedr, a chidag ê y lletteua Jones yr offeiriad, a rhyw noswaith fe glywai Owain ryw dwrwf ag ameu wnaeth fod y forwyn yn mynd at yr offeiriad, a chodi a orug Owain yn ddistaw deg a myned a sefyll mewn congl yn gyfagos i stafell y gwr, ag yn y man Owain a welai y forwyn yn dyfod allan yn lladradaidd oddiyno ag yn myned i'w gwely ei hun, ag Owain ynteu aeth at ei wraig. A'r boreu pan gododd, ebr ef wrthi, Sian, ni cheiff y llances yma aros ddim hwy yn fy nhy i, obleit mae hi'n godinebu efo'r offeiriad, o ran mi ai

*Daniel Rowland of Llangeitho.

W. to R. contd. gwelais neithiwr gefnant nôs yn dyvod yn ei uncrys oi stafell. Yna Sian a alwodd ar y wasnaethferch, a'r offeiriad ynteu a ddeua i'r fan. Yno tyngu a rhegi a orug y fenyw a'r offeiriad mae breuddwyd a welsai Owain, ag nid oedd dim coel ar ei lygaid, felly rhwng y wraig a nhwytheu, bu raid i'r truan ddal ei dafod. Ond ymhen byr amser cafodd y pleser o weled geni iddi bwmp o gyw offeiriad, er mawr orfoledd i bob plaid. Dyna ddiben ar chwedl Owain. Digrif hefyd fyddai gweled hanes ein hynafiaid wedi ei loywi o newydd gan Carte. Roedd wedi rhydu yn echryslon, o achos y budreddi a daflodd Cambden, etc., am ei ben, a Mr. Amser ynteu wedi ei dywyllu'n greulon!

Direct for me for the future: Collector of His Majesty's Duties on Salt at Holyhead, er mwyn ei cael yn rhad, etc. Rym yn disgwyl Iarll Chesterfield yma o hyn i ddiwedd y mis ag wmbwrdd o boblach gidag ê. Mae'r wraig a mineu yn gorchymun attoch chwi a'r eiddoch. A byddwch wŷch,

Eich caredigawl frawd, William Morris.

Terfyn, 22nd Aug., 1745.

Capt. Davies (as you call him) appear'd in this town for a few days, and then disappear'd all of a sudden, being, it seems, convey'd *nolens volens* to the County Gaol at Beaumaris, where he remains in *salva custodia* for debt. John Evans waited here a few days for a fair wind for Dublin, where he has great recomendations. He met here a gentleman passenger, who took him into private service, and would employ him some weeks in Dublin whilst he might be looking out for a better place. I told him of what you wrote. Twrstan fu yr Rhobin Parry hwnnw ymadel ar *Falkland.* Daccw hi wedi cymryd Spanish South Seaman a dâl 300,000 neu lai, and carried her into Kinsale. I shall pay Mr. Davies's money to Mr. Edmunds's man if he comes this way with an order, who, I'me told, has purchas'd some lands in this parish. Mab a merch ieuaf i'r hen Ned Owain a ga'dd y rhan fwyaf o'i fwnws. Bum ym Mhentre Rhianell dydd arall yn ymweled a'r hen bobl. Maent, Duw yn ei plaid, yn gymaint ei trafferth a phan oeddynt yn meithrin plantos, yn ymdrechu a dyled a thrafferthion er gwaetha henaint a heintiau. What say you to our success at sea? Have we not play'd the vengeance with the French and

Spaniard in the East India and at home? As to our national debt, civil list, etc., etc., I never trouble my head about it, as being affairs out of my sphere, and I don't think I shall ever be employ'd as a Minister. Codan' hwythau drethi mi ai talaf inneu tra gallwyf yn ddirwgnach. Ni waeth imi hynny na gwingo yn erbyn symbylau. W. to R. contd.

Gwych hefyd pe cymerai rhyw Fryttwn cywraint yn ei ben fynd ynghyd a geirlyfr Dr. Davies. Mae Samuel* yn hên, ag nid oes un yng Nghymru ffitiach i'r gorchwyl hwnnw rwyn credu na'r brawd Llywelyn. He has an excellent collection that I believe he would not take 100 guineas for. Ond beth ydis nes, mae *mwyn wall-gofiaid* ar hwnnw, ag ni cheir daioni o honaw. I never heard of any folio dictionary, Welsh-English and English-Welsh, being publish'd. There was a rascally 2nd. eddition of Rhydderch's printed at Shrewsbury, worse, if possible, than the first, done, I think, by one Williams, a clergyman, *βαω πυρ*.† Mae genyf bot i'r hen Wil Jones, Pabo, am ei bicture i'r Beibl Cysegr lân. Mae arnaf flys gweled y gwaith ar ben. I've been at Bodorgan since I wrote to you last. Mi siaredais a Dick Morus, roedd yn dywedyd yrru o hono'r fond efo'r cynghorwr, ag i chwi adael ei thalu yn ddiffael pan allech. Roedd yn dywedyd iddo yrru i chwi lawer o lythyrau, ond ni bu wiw ganddoch atteb yr un, a'ch bod wedi ei berswadio fo i beidio rhoddi ei fond i mewn pan ich cliriwyd, and I don't know what myself. I'me sorry for the poor fellow. Fe eiff yn hen ag yn fusgrell ar fyrder. Gwnewch oreu a galloch iddo. Rwyn disgwyl llythyr bob post oddiwrth y brawd Llewelyn a hanes da o'r mwyn. Chwi glywsoch, mae'n debyg, son am y swydd newydd a ga'dd, sef bod yn deputy steward of all the King's courts in those parts, with an extensive power and tolerable good profit.

I have seen a book advertis'd this week, I think, in the *General Evening Post* or *Old England*, relating to the Laws of the Admiralty—I mean the Maritime Laws. I wish you would let me know whether it relates to the Vice-Admiralty of the Coast, and what you think of it. Oni fyddai wŷch pei medrai ddyn gael

*The Rev. Edward Samuel, of Llangar, translator of several devotional books into Welsh. He died in April, 1748, aged 75.

†The English and Welch Dictionary, etc., originally begun by John Roderick, and now finished and compleated by the Rev. Mr. John Williams, Rector of Willey, in Shropshire, Shrewsbury, 1737.

W. to R. contd.

cymaint o honno yn sgrifen ag a berthyn i'n achosion ni ffordd yma, sef wrecks, anchorage, harbours, etc. Ni welais i lyfr erioed a roddai gyfrif iawn o honynt. All depends on antient customs, and few here know anything of those.

W. to R. LIX.

HOLYHEAD, 26th February, 1745.

Dear Brother,—Gan nad wyf addas i wneuthur gorchwyl yn y byd y dydd heddyw namyn diwynno papir, a rhyw wegni o'r fâth, dymma fi yn taro atti hi i atteb eich llythyr or 8fed cyn pen yr hanner blwyddyn yn llawn (a course compliment, you'll say), nid oes wybod na ddeuwch chwitheu o dipyn i dipyn yn fanylach sgrifennydd nag a fuoch ers talm o flynyddoedd. Lle da disgwyl daioni gan Garte os felly mae o'n prifio. O eppil gwiberod! I think Evans is in some bread in Dublin. Davies was put in here a few days agon in a Conway sloop, bound home from the Isle of Man. I have not seen him, nor do I know how he got out of prison. Wala, wala, rhaid yw manegi i chwi y peth ucha ar y meddwl. Sef yw hynny a ganlyn: ben boreu heddyw y ganed i chwi nai, fab brawd Gwilym, yr hwn yr ym ni ar fedr i wneuthur yn Gristion bedyddiol y foru. He was introduced upon the stage of this worldly theatre by Cosin Evans (the Doctor's widow), who is the most famous midwife in North Wales, hi wnaeth ei gwaith mewn gwmpas teirawr. Dedwydd a fase eich gwraig chwitheu pei cawsai gystal rhyddhâd ag ond odid gystal cywreinrwydd. Mawl ir Goruchaf am bob peth. Brother Davies was the beginning of this month terribly burnt by gunpowder, was blind for some time, but is now able to go about,—lwcc fawr am ei hoedl fo aeth 10 pwys o bowdwr ar dân dan ei ddwylo, neu rhyngddynt yn hytrach. Da bod rhai o eppil yr hen feddyges o'i gwmpas. Sister was brought to bed of a girl latter end of November, and was nam'd Jane; that family are now pretty well recoverd of their fright and are brave, hearty; yn gorchymyn attoch chwi ar eiddoch. Aie gwr mwyn yw Watkin? Gwrda Wynn y Bardd nid oes ammeu na fyddai yn ŵr digon addas i drin y geirlyfr, ond pa beth ydis nes, mae pawb or gwŷr a soniasoch am danynt, neu yr rhan fwyaf o honynt, mor anwyl ganddynt ei gwaith ei hunain, na ymadawant ai casgliad am ddim pris gweddol chwaethach er lles cyffredin. I despair of ever seeing anything done, aie rych chwi gwyr Llundain yn odiaeth ryfelwyr, etc? Bu agos fod yn dda eich bôd felly, pe daetha chwe' mil neu saith o Highlanders tin noethion ar eich cefnau, fe fu'se yn rhywyr i chwi chwareu yn eich bandiau.* A gadd rhyw ddyn ddrŵg am agor llythyr i chwi at Mr. Smith ynghylch rhyw arfau, etc.? Let me hear how that affair was. I saw a letter from that Jones, the saddler, you mention, to a friend of his in this parish, which mentiond something of it, but in misterious manner. Jones is, I believe, an idle fellow, which made me take no great notice on't. Gerwin oedd scheme y Mercers, a destructive one indeed! A gerwinach yw hanes y clwyf ar y gwartheg, Duw a'n cadwo rhagddo! Da fydde cael y llyfr hwnnw a erchais i chwi ymholi am dano. I really can't tell what Rhydderch's Dictionary, 2nd edition, cost. I never saw but one of 'em; it didn't seem much larger than the 1st. The old folks at Dulas were indifferent well a few days agon. Father had received your letter. Mother had the misfortune lately of being run over by some cattle, whereby she was much bruised; otherwise she would have been here upon these occasions. Rym ni i gyd ymma yn gorchymyn attochi a'r eiddoch, felly nôs da'wch heno. Peidiwch a bod yn rhy ddiog. W. to R. contd.

Eich brawd anwiw, William Morris.

Dr. Herbert Jones a glywais fod dydd arall yn Llanerchmedd wedi ymdrobaeddu mewn aur hyd nad oedd (na bo yma ond ei grybwyll) wedi glynu rhyd ei ddillad, fal prin y gwyddechi o ba beth y gwnaed hwynt! He, it seems, is surgeon of the *Swan*, a man-of-war, built at Chester.

HOLYHEAD, 10th May, 1746. W. to R. LX.

Dear Brother,—Derbyniais eich llythyr o'r 26th ulto. am ba'r un (er hwyred y daeth) yr wyf dra diolchgar, yn gystal ag am y ddwy gân a'r cyfieithiadau godidog i'r *Bysg curious*, etc., Gwrda'r hosenydd am ddwyn y glôch. Digrif fydde weled *specimen* o waith y Garte. Enw fy mab yw Rhobert ar ol ei daid, vide Reasons of State, Lib. I. Nid hwyrach mae Cymro fydd y nesa'. I never

* A reference to the invasion by the Pretender, Prince Charles. It would appear that the brothers Morris were stout Hanoverians; but see "Dewisol Ganiadau" (1759), p. 8.

W. to R. contd.

heard anything of Keynton, and, as he is a rogue, I don't care to own him as a câr. Poor mother had had the misfortune of a ladder falling upon her, before the unhappy accident of being trod upon by the cattle. But the first *anlwc* was not nigh as bad as the last. Mae'r hen bobl yn awr yn fwy eu trafferth a'i gofalon nag oeddynt pan oeddym oll bychain a chostus iddynt. My mother will never have the right use of her arm, which was owing to our not having a surgeon in the whole island. Ni waeth ych brawd Gwilym na'r goreu o honynt. I had seen the Order of Council relating to the infected cattle. We were all of opinion in these parts that it was your cyfieithiad, and am glad to find it was really so. Wfft i'r llall o waith y Deheuwr! Nis gwn i etto pa beth a wneir i'r canau ymma, par sut a fydd ei troi ai trosi. Nid oes ymma agos i ddim difyrwch. Neb yn y wlad i gyd ganu mewn deulais yn ol rheol. Capt. Owen, late of Marian (which place he sold), is a good natured young fellow ruin'd wrth gael meddiannau cyn gwybod pa beth i wneuthur a hwynt. He is now, I am told, abandon'd to everything that's poghy. Brother Lewis's affairs were of late pretty much embarass'd, o achos bod ei holl ffrindiau yn Nghaerludd yn sefyll ar ei huntroed, ag ni wyddid pwy fydde iâr na phwy fydde geiliog, ag rwyn tybio fod yn digwydd iddo ryw faint o gantoedd o'r drysorfa, a dêg i un y cawsai hatling byth pei digwyddasai newid dwylo. Gobeithio fod pob peth wedi ei sefydlu rwan. Ces lythyr oddiwrthaw heddyw o'r 28th ulto. Chwi welwch cyhyd y maent ar y ffordd o'r Deheudir yma! Few comes sooner. It seems he has purchased part of an estate situated in such a place that I would not have accepted of it gratis to live upon't. No doubt he has some inducement,—mwyn neu riwbeth. Duw a'i diofalo ag a ddel ag ef yn ol i blith Cristioniaid. Mae ganddo ymma o gwbl oddeutu £22 per annum mewn amrafael dyddynod, enw'r mansion house yw Ty Wridyn, ymhlwy Rhoscolyn, gwmpas £10 per annum.

Roedd y nghywely i *υν αερες ω γωμπας* 25, *αλλαν ο ὕννυ μαε* 5 *υν μυνδ ιρ ωεδω ελυ ἥν στεντ υω Αλλανβιγελ.* £10 *φ αν. αγ μαε ἅννερ Εγλωυς υ Πλωυβ υν περθυν ι νι! Μαε γενομ γωμπας* £10 *υμμα, α φαν γαφομ διγον ο αριαν ι αδαελιαδυ μι αλλων ει ωνευθυρ υν δαυ κυμαιντ, Ονδ Δυω α ωυρ παρ βρυδ α βυδ ὕννυ, βυθ ονδ οδιδ. Μα'ρ βυδ υν αβλ καλεδ αρ ειχ βραωδ Γωιλυμ ρωαν, αεθ ι γοστ βαωρ ι φιτιω αλλαν, αγ ι*

φωρνεισιω τυ ἐβ γαελ ονδ υχυδιγ ιαων ο ελῶ νεβ, υ βοβλ υν γυβραιθ W. to R.
*ωεδι σορρι αμ δωυν ει μερχ.** Y Pretender ynteu, melldith ei fam contd.
iddo (llwyr y cafodd hi), wedi mynd a hynny o *fusnes* oedd yma yw ganlyn i Scotland neu riwle, ag nid oes ond ychydig gida'r *κυβλογ ωαελ*. Wala, wala, fe ddaw Duw a gwell amseroedd pan wel y byddent oreu ar ein lles, a dyna i chwi. Rych yn dra anffortunus o daro wrth ddrwg dalwyr. Ai nid oes gan Smyth ddigon i dalu i bawb? Mae'r lleill yn abl pe bae 'wllys.

Lord and Lady Castledurrow, who are my very good friends, told me not long ago that Lord Londonderry would be in Dublin this summer; if so, I fancy he'll call at Bodorgan. The abovementioned lady (whose name the other day was Flower) is a great florist and a very ingenious woman. Pei gwelechi'r blodau gwychion sy genyf! Mi fum dra thrafferthus y Gwanwyn yma yn gwneuthur gardd newydd, ag etto heb ei gorphen. A ngwaith i beunydd yw canu.

Gwell imi na chastell gorchestol i run
Dy bâch ar ben erw ar fy helw fy hun.

Drwg iawn y'w bod y Beibl yn mynd ymlaen mor ddiog, ni wybod pwy a fydd byw ymhen yr wythnos chwaethech ymhen y deunaw mis. Oedd yr hen Wil Sion† yn cofio mae yn Llanfihangel tre'r bardd y ganed ef, o fewn llai na chwarter milldir i'r fferem. Do, mi welais Repertt. Poett. y Foesen.‡ Mae'n debyg mae ar ei

* Roedd y nghywely i yn aeres o gwmpas £25, allan o hwnnw mae £5 yn mynd i'r weddw, elw hen stent yw Llanfigel, £10 per ann, ag mae hanner Eglwus y plwyf yn perthyn i ni! Mae genom gwmpas £10 ymma a phan gaffom ddigon o arian i adeiladu mi allwn ei wneuthur yn ddau cymaint. Ond Duw a wyr par bryd a fydd hynny, byth ond odid. Ma'r byd yn abl caled ar eich brawd Gwilym rwan, aeth i gost fawr i ffitio allan ag i ffwrneisio ty heb gael ond ychydig iawn o elw neb, y bobl yn gyfraith wedi sorri am ddwyn ei merch.

†William Jones, F.R.S., father of Sir William Jones.

‡The reference is to the Repertorium Poeticum, etc. (London, 1726), an index to Welsh Poetry compiled by the Rev. Moses Williams. The Collection of Welsh Manuscripts brought together by Moses Williams and his father (Samuel Williams) were purchased by William Jones, F.R.S., from the former's widow. Jones bequeathed them to his pupil, the second Earl of Macclesfield, and they were sold in 1899 to Sir John Williams, Bart. Richard Morris made indexes to a large number of the manuscripts, but when they became the property of Lord Macclesfield he was refused permission to consult the collection. The Manuscript referred to in the letter as S.W. is a very large volume, mostly in the writing of the Rev. Samuel Williams. It now forms MS. 133 in the Llanstephan Collection. Hist. MSS. Commission. Reports on MSS. in the Welsh Language, Vol. II., p. 664.

W. to R. contd.

ol ef y cadd yr hen wr y llyfrau hynny. I always thought that the S.W. was a collection of Moses's father's, Samuel Williams. I think somebody told me so. Aie mae gwendid ar bawb, nid oes mo'r help, felly yr oedd ein tadau a'n teidiau ni erioed hyd yn heddyw. Ni bydd un amser ddim cyfeillach rhyngwyfi a Dafis. Mae gormod o rawn gwynion yn ei gynffon. He's gone either to the island or to the Deel's Arse-a-peak. He got his late wife, who was heiress of a pretty little place, about £14 or £16 per annum, in this parish, to join with him to take up 200 and odd pounds upon a mortgage, and he has left the interest to run on ever since, and continues to receive the rents, so that in a short time the mortgage will be foreclosed, and the poor young fellow, his son-in-law, trick'd out of his inheritance for ever. The mortgagee is the late Captain John Prichard's widow, whose son, if he lives, will be heir of Llanfawr. In short, Davies is a sad dog; have now't to do with him.

Dyn drwyddo yw Ifan Delynior. I should be glad to see a Psalm tune or two which he designs to put in the new Bible, if they are not of Playford's. Perhaps you only mean that he'll alter the shape of the notes and not the tunes. What have we to do with cathedral music? You must know that I've been a meer dab at Psalmody, though that trade is almost quite over with us at the Head. We had about 40 good singers, viz., first and second treble and bass; of the last there's only myself left, chwedl yr hen Elias, etc. Mae yma bawb yn rhwydd iâch, yn gorchymun attoch chwi a'r eiddoch, a Duw a roddo i chwi iechyd a bodlondeb.

Your most affectionate brother, *William Morris.*

P.S. — Do you remember one Dick Owen, formerly an old servant of father's, who has been these good many years in the Navy? He was a brother of Morris Owen. Some say he is dead, intestate, whereby a poor young fellow, who served his time to father, is to have his effects. Peidiwch a bod mor ddiog am 'sgrifennu, da chwitheu.

12th June.—I've this day a letter from Ned Edwards, dated at Bordeaux, the 9th December, where he was prisoner. He beg'd interest to have his liberty by exchange, etc. Says he has wrote to you, and desired you to acquaint us of his misfortune. Sure he must be releas'd before this time. However, I send his letter this day to brother Lewis. Oes ganddoch ardd a blodau gwychion ynddi, cymaint a honno oedd gennych yn Stratford? I've some hundreds of fine tulips now in blow, besides varieties of anemonies, ranunculas's, auriculas's, etc., but they don't bring in any money; that's the worse. Chwi fyddech yn gyrru immi dippyn o hadau, etc., ddydd a fu. Oes dim cydnabyddiaeth ganddoch efo blodeuwr yn y byd ffordd yna? Pray can you enquire what kind of a man is one Alex. Wilson, Esq., that lives within a door or two of old Lady Bulkeley at Westminster; married lately the widow of General Tatton, whose son is now here, recovering of the small-pox, and the daughter is the present Lady Castledurrow. Wilson has sent me an offer of service, etc. I should be glad to know, yn ddistaw, pa beth yw ei allu, etc. Brys anferthol o faint! The d——l's in the Dutch if they've signed a neutrality with France. **W. to R. contd.**

CAERGYBI, Gorffenaf 1af, 1746. **W. to R. LXI.**

Δεαρ Βροθερ, — Bum dra thrafferthus er pan dderbyniais yr eiddoch or 7th ulto., oni bae hynny attebaswn yn gynt. Can diolch yr had Gwylaeth, maen't yn dyfod i fynu yn doreithiawg, a diolch am y mesur Salm. I like Mr. Williams's plan greatly. I find it's the old tunes you design to make use of. I was in hopes that he would have composd new ones, or pick up some choice ones, mae hon wedi taclu peth arni. Dyna i chwithe un fal yr 'ym yn ei chanu yma. As the tunes in your Bible, I presume, are intended for the benefit of those who sing in country churches or private families, and not for cathedrals, etc., where there are organs, I should imagine the long tunes, such as the 1st Psalm, etc., would best be left out and a select parcel of plain short tunes, such as the Windsor, Cambridge, etc., be inserted, together with a few proper tunes, such as the Psalms 148, 113, etc. I would by all means recomend that in all the tunes the three parts begin unisons or octaves, for it's a very great inconveniency for the singers of Psalmody in the country (where great part of the performers are ignorant and sometimes illiterate) to begin a tune with different notes or sounds; it too often occasions confusion. If you are at liberty to remedy these things, Ifan Delynior a wna'r gwaith. Dymuno arnochi ag ynte gyd ddwyn am gwendid yn yr hyn a ddywedais, for I pretend to very little knowledge in musick. Na

W. to R. contd.

dderbyniais i ddim arian gan H. Roberts, exciseman. Mae'n debyg mae ir brawd Llewelyn y talodd, for he received from the subscribers in these parts, and I thought had accounted for it. My old friend, Mr. Davies, disobliged me so far as to discourage me from troubling him any more with my custom, but still I shall always bear a very great regard for the man, though I don't care for the cordwainer; tell him I am not ungrateful. The person whom, I presume, he means is one Ronald Campbell, formerly coxon of a cruiser in these parts, and since a tidewaiter or boatman in the Port of London. What's become of him? I heard he went abroad, mate of a ship. Aie 'rydych yn ffrind fawr a Syr Wat, ni bu gynnes gennyf mono erioed. Gwr a allasai wneuthur wmbwrdd o lês iw wlad, yn lle hynny, drwg. Ond etto er hyn pei gwnae gymwynas im brawd, mi faddeuwn iddo lawer o bethau, gan fod y bŷd fal y mae, ar rhôd wedi troi. Neithiwr y daethym adre' wedi bod efo' mhriod rhyd y wlad a'r dre'r Duwmares yn ymweled a'n ffrindiau; buom ddwynos yn yr hen gartref. Gô fusgrellaidd yw'r hen bobl, mae mam yn llawer gwell nag y bu gan ei braich, mawl i Dduw, hi gadd godwm oddiar ei thraed yn ddiweddar ag a frywodd beth ar ei haelodau, ond fe ddihangodd y llaw yn dda iawn. Ni chlywais ungair oddiwrth y brawd Llewelyn er pan fu Ynghaerfrangon. Mi glywaf o Lerpwl ei fod wedi cael gwythïen wych o blwm, i.e., solid ore, 11 inches broad, ond mi glywais gymaint o newyddion da oddiyno ag o Russia, fal mae anodd gennyf goelio dim a glywyf or ffyrdd hynny. A welsochi'r Corbedyn? Par newydd a gawsoch gannddo o Sir Abernoeth? Ie gwr or mwyna yw, fo gadd imi bum punt yn y flwyddyn gan Gomhisioners yr Halen, bendith Dduw iddo. Mae arnaf eisiau codi'r cyflog hwnnw etto, yr wyf yn gwneuthur cymaint am £10 per annum a nemawr un am £40. If the Fishery continues I design to apply to my friends.

Rwy'n deall mae gwr mawr yw Alexander! Nid wyf mor hŷf arno as to intercede in favour of any one, ond mae iddo fab ynghyfraith (yr hwn a fu'n glaf yma yn ddiweddar) yn awr gida ei chwaer Arglwyddes Castledurrow yn yr Iwerddon. Rym yn ei ddisgwyl ffordd yma beunydd, ag mae'n fy mryd eich crybwyll wrtho, ag nid hwyrach y geill hynny lês. Da iawn fyddai gennyf pe ba'e yn fy mhower wneuthur i chwi gymwynas; ond ail yw'r matter hwnnw i'r dall geisio tywyso'r dall. You complain'd of bad weather: so may we now, dryghin er's pythewnos. Ned Edwards was releasd in May last; is now at Bristol. Yr hen Anne Lewis (eich mam fedydd onte?) o Lanfihangel gynt, a gladded yn forwyn wythnos i foru, about as old as my mother. I hope the Bible will go pursuant to the Vice-Chancellor's order. Gwŷch a fyddai ei weled! Gobeithio fod y Scotiaid wedi casau digon ar ryfela yn erbyn ei brenin, ag mae dyma'r tro diweddaf y daw terfysg or cwr hwnnw o'r deyrnas. O garn lladron! Mae'r wlad yma yn sicr ddigon wedi llygru yn aruthr er's ychydig o amser. Lladron a Methodistiaid yn heidio, wfft, ie, dwbl wfft, iddyn nhw! Rym ni yma oll yn iach, mawl ir Goruchaf Dduw, ag yn gorchymun attoch'i ar eiddoch. **W. to R. contd.**

Eich caredigawl frawd, William Morris.

Pray let me hear from you soon.

CAER GYBI, 27th October, 1746, Dydd Mawrth. **W. to R. LXII.**

Dear Brother,—Eich llythyr diweddaf oedd o'r 7fed o Fehefin yr hwn a attebais mewn pryd, roeddwn yn meddwl cael clywed oddiwrthych cyn hyn, ond fe'm siommwyd. Yr achos a bair imi sgrifennu attoch yr awron yw glywed o honwyf heddyw gan un o ymyl Bodorgan fod Iarll Llundain Derry wedi cychwyn oddiyno tua Llundain ddydd Gwener diweddaf. I went to Bodorgan last month with Lord Castledurrow, who, in his way, went to visit Lord Londonderry, y pryd y dywedais ir hen Feiryg, fal yr oedd yr Arglwydd yn eich cadw heb eich arian am fil Smyth. Mr. Meiryck told me that Smyth was dead at Bath, and at the same time promis'd me that he would take an opportunity of speaking to his Lordship in your favour, though I could not positively tell whether you were still unpaid or no. As you knew he was in the country you should have wrote about it. My father, who is now here, tells me that he has been since at Bodorgan, and that Mr. Meyrick told him that Lord Londonderry had promisd him to do something for you, ond nid oes wybod beth. His Lordship was here about a fortnight agoe; did me the honour to breakfast at my house with Mr. P. Meyrick, ag nid oes pennach ffrindiau na nyni. He attempted to make my father drunk at Bodorgan, but fell in the field of battle. Pwy a wyr na wna i chwi gymwynas er ei fod yn

W. to R. contd.

bend—au. Captain Tatton (Mr. Wilson's son-in-law), who had been ill here, and his sister Lady Castledurrow returned by Chester water, or I would have endeavourd to get him to speak a word to his father-in-law in your behalf. Cadd y nhad, medd ef, lythyr oddiwrthych yn ddiweddar, ond fei gadawodd yn angof gartref. Mi glywais ddywedyd fod llythyr imi oddiwrthych efo gun William Roberts, ond ni welais i monynt. I should be always glad to have mine by post, diddig ydyw hwnnw, a Sior a dâl oni bydd ffrank. Rwyfi yr awron yn gwneuthur y peth a ddylaswn wneuthur 15 neu 18 mlynedd i rwan; sef yw hynny, dechreu trin y byd a magu plant a chann mil o bethau a thrafferthion ag anghenion. A phe' sydd waeth na'r cwbl, dyma henaint a haid o gymdeithion aflafar, sef anwydau yr corph yn chwareu mig ymguddio a dyn. O genhawon hyllion! Gwir a ddywedodd rhyw hen Gymro yn amser ein teidiau.

Pan bassio wr ei ddeugain oed,
Er bod y coed yn deilio,
Fe fydd swn goriadau'r bedd
Yn peri ei wedd newidio.

Wala, wala, nid oes ond gwneuthur y gore o'r amser, a draen am henaint. Aie ni chawn i ddim Beiblau dan fis Mai, rydych yn hir iawn yn ei gorphen. Par sut y mae Syr W. Irby? Mi glywa eich bod yn wr mawr gidag ef. Y fo yw ein meistir tir ni am y Costwmhows; ni byddai waeth genyf pe bawn inneu mewn ffafor efo i fâth. Mae'r chwaer ai gwr ai pum plentyn yn iâch, ach brawd Gwylim ar eiddo yn rhesymol; da fyddai gennym glywed eich hanes chwitheu gynta galloch. Gorchymynwch fi at y chwaer a byddwch ŵych.

Eich caredigawl frawd, William Morris.

Mae'r brawd Llewelyn yn bwgwth dyfod ir wlad yr haf nesaf. A ddeuwch chwithau i roddi tro' i gymryd eich cennad efo'r hen bobl os byddir byw?

W. to R. LXIII.

CAER GYBI, 2nd January, 1746.

Anwyl Frawd,—Wele'ch llythyr o'r 11 ult° om blaen, gresyn na fase'r Iarll cystal ai air. I imagin'd Mr. Meyrick had more influence over his Lordship. Am glad you have hopes of being paid; er mae gwell un hwde na dau ti gai. Aie mae Smyth yn fyw etto? Your blessed sett of Masters puts me in mind of the old saying, "Arglwydd gwan, gwae ei wâs." I remember that formerly you were a famous adventurer at lotteries, and always came by the lee. Pray, how do you order it now? No prize fallen to your share, ynteu, rydych yn ei adnabod yn well? Pa beth y'ch yn ei gael am fod yn clarkio iddynt, hyn a hyn yr awr, mae'n debyg. Ag felly, ni wiw cwyno wrthych chwi ar gledi'r byd. Na welais i mo Roberts na'r llythyr, he must be a worthless fellow that would keep a thing of that nature that could be of no manner of service to him. Ond mae iddaw ddigon o gymariaid ar hyd y byd, ond ni thal y fâth i son am danynt. Am y ddwy gainc salm, nis gwn i pa beth iw ddywedyd wrthynt. Mi ddywedais wrthych or blaen nad oeddwn ond dwl ag anghelfydd mewn peroriaeth, yn gystal ag mewn pethau eraill, the adding a note or adapting the music to the Welch Version was, in my opinion, a happy thought. St. Cybi is a good tune enough, but then the parts—I mean the first treble and the bass—are of too large compass for our voices in this country, and must occasion the treble to squeak or the bass to growl, mae'r llall hitheu'n geincan or ffeinia i bobl Clynnog. Ond bynnag, par fodd, mae'r Telynior yn well barnwr yn y pethau hyn na myfi, a dyna i chwi ben a thewi. What! not a sillable of the Bible? How go you on? Mr. Ellis has been wrote to by the Society that it would be ready by Lady Day, and that the 3,000*l* was compleated, but that the binding was still behind. A glywsochi son am y 10 gini a roddes y Siawnsler Wynne, of Fodewryd, tuag attynt? It went up by Owen, Prysaddfed. I think the Society proposed selling 'em at the value of the binding. Ond gwell a fydde iddynt werthu cymaint am bris gweddaidd o honynt ir Cymry rhwydd gywaethogion (oblegid mae ar lawer eu heisiau), ag a dalai am gauadu'r cwbl? Gwych a fydde gael copiau o lythyrau Sion Morgan,* ni wiw immi ddisgwyl monynt drwy law Llywelyn. Er carriad ar ddyn gyrrwch imi eu benthyg, a chwi a'u cewch yn ôl gin siccred ach bod chwi yna, mae gennyf opiniwn da odiaethol of his prose and poetry. Gresyn marw dyn or fath. Ond ydyw gywilydd na roddai ryw Gymro cywrain allan ail argraphiad o eirlyfr y Doctor Dafis? Rwyn tybio mae gan y brawd Llewelyn y W. to R. contd.

*Rev. John Morgan, M.A., of Matchin, Essex. He was a correspondent of Moses Williams, and one of his letters was published in the "Cambrian Register," Vol. ii., 536. He also translated some devotional works into Welsh.

W. to R. contd. mae'r casgliad goreu o eiriau ag sydd. Dymma fineu (chwedl Tomos Dions, y Sywedydd chwyslyd)* *drwy fawr boen a diwydrwydd* wedi casglu, neu yn hytrach wneuthur Botanologium† (dyna air caled brwnt) o Gymraeg, Lladin, a Saesoneg yn gystal a Gwyddelaeg, fal y byddai hardd ei weled a llesol ei ddeall. Ni thalai hwnnw sydd yn Dictionary Dr. Davies f——w nid er amharch arnoch. Cywilyddus y taflodd Tomos Jones enwau llysiau ar draws eu gilydd heb na synwyr na chynghanedd, a Sion Rhydderch‡ ni adawai iddo, but I must ask your pardon. If I mistake not, Dr. Evans and you had a hand in the latter. Par fodd bynnag, hyn a wnn i yn dda, na waeth i ddyn geisio mynd yn Ustus heb erioed ddarllain *Coke upon Littleton*, neu fynd yn Esgob heb erioed ddarllain y Bibl, na cheisio gosod i fynu i fod yn llysieuwr heb gymorth ag addysg yr awdwr tra godidog hwnnw Mr. Ray. But what is all this to a citisen that sees not a green plant once a year except in the markets? But you can indulge in a weak brother, can't you? Captain Fortunatus§ had been but one voyage at Mahone before he went out on this Privateering expedition to the Levant. I've had account of his proceedings all along from Leverpool. I'me afraid the estimate at 400,000 is rather too much. He is now at Leghorn, where he stays to get his prizes condemned and to settle his affairs with his factors, and has sent his first lieutenant out in the *Fame* on a cruize of three months.

I've not the happiness of being acquainted with Mr. Vaughan, of Gors,‖ though I am one of his well-wishers. O na bae ei fâth o fewn Ynys Fôn! Gorchmynwch fi at y Câr Huw Dafydd, ni adwaen

* Thomas Jones (1648-1712?). He published his first Welsh Almanack in 1680, and continued to bring it out annually until 1711. In his almanack for 1699 he devotes eleven pages to a lengthy account of his illnesses, from which it appears that he suffered from thirty different disorders, one of which he calls "y chwys anferthol," or "sweats immoderate." He also published a Welsh-English Dictionary, printed in 1688.

† The Rev. Hugh Davies was much indebted to this work. Welsh Botanology, 1813, p. vii.

‡ The references are to the Vocabularies of Plant Names published in the Dictionaries issued by Thomas Jones in 1688, and by John Rhydderch in 1725. Second Edition, 1737.

§ Captain Fortunatus Wright, of Liverpool.

‖ William Vaughan, of Corsygedol and Nannau. M.P. for Merioneth, 1734 to 1768.

mo'i wraig. Bum Ymhentre'rianell o fewn y tridie yma yn ymweled ar hen boblach, mae mam yn glâf er's saith wythnos heb allu symmud or gwely at y tan. She was taken ill of a pleuretick fever, which settled in her foot and thigh and broke several times. I am affraid will do so again; she begins to pick up her crums, but is extream weak. Sister has been there continually this six weeks. Father is pretty hearty; would write to you this week by a son of Rowland Owen, of Gadlys, a trooper. Gwelais eich llythyr yno ag arall oddiwrth Lywelyn, ond ni che's i'r un oddiwrth hwnnw ers talm byd. Rym ni yma oll yn rhwydd iach ag yn dymuno i chwi a'ch teulu flwyddyn newydd happus. Can ffarwel. W. to R. contd.

Eich brawd ungalon, Gwilym Fynglwyd.

P.S.—Should be glad to hear from you as soon as convenient.

CAER GYBI, 3rd February, 1746. W. to R. LXIV.

Anwyl Frawd,—I wrote you some time agoe in answer to your last, and should have waited a little longer for a reply had it not been for the following accident—or incident, call it what you will. Am fi neithiwr yn eistedd wrth fy nhân efo'm cywely o ddeutu 10 o'r gloch, mi glyw'n dwrwf meirch yn dyfod tua'r annedd, ag ni chae'm ni gydtrym, nad dyma *gnockio* yn drws, mi a dybiais fod rhai or hên gyrph diddan gynt, megys Tomos Owen Lewis neu Risiart William Gloff wedi codi o feirw ag yn dyfod a gwirod ini or byd arall. Ond yn lle hynny wele balf o wr 'nheddig yn piccio i mewn, ag yn cyfarch gwell imi. Nawdd Duw rhagot ebe finneu, o ble yr wyt yn dyfod ag i ble yr ai, yr amser yma or nôs? Cyfaill wyf, ebyr ynteu, i'ch brawd Risiart yn Llundain, ag mi addewais alw efo chwi yn fy ffordd ir Iwerddon. Yno rhoddi iddo wa'dd i eistedd ai groesawu a bwyd a llyn. Yn y man fe ddywedodd mae ŵyr ydoedd i ryw wraig a fuase fyw yn Sarn Fraint, ag mae ei enw ef ydoedd Williams, ai fod yn byw yn Llundain ers 10 mlynedd, ag nad ydoedd briodol. Rydoedd o Lundain ers mis, ag wedi bod ennyd mewn tai gwyr boneddigion yn Nimbych ag Arfon, efo pha rai yr ydoedd yn cymryd arno fod yn dra chydnabyddus. He was well dressed, had a good cutteau at his side, his fingers ringed, and acted the gentleman very prettily. He went off that night in the pacquet, and promisd to make a longer stay on his return. I supplyd him with some sea store. Ffarwel gidage.

W. to R. contd. After he was gone I recollected that you had wrote me some time agoe about a grandson of Sarn Fraint, whose name you said was Keynton, and who had opened a letter of yours, for which he had been two months in Bridewell, and since married and turnd pedlar, etc. Mi ro'f genad im crogi ond hwn ydoedd, ac mîl i ûn nad *imposter* ydyw, for I find his behaviour to the boatmen that waited of him here and carried him aboard was not of a piece with the fine gentleman. Pray let me know by the return of the post whether he was the Keynton you mentiond, and whether he's a bite or how, that I may behave accordingly (if he returns). He told me sister-in-law was miscarried, drŵg o hynny. Tippyn o hanes y Beibl da chwitheu. Oes dim hadau gwychion yw cael o hyn i ganol y Mawrth? Attebwch ychydigyn or llythyr arall. My wife joins with me in love to you both.

I am, dear brother, yours affectionately, William Morris.

Pray, how came our hero to meet brother Lewis at Sir A. Owen's in Pembrokeshire? What was he doing at Newcastle-upon-Tine, from whence he came, he says, by sea to London? I should have begrudged my throwing away my time in so useless a manner as this, if I had not been confind to my cabbin by a sore shank, which I have unmercifully mangled above a month ago. I heard lately from the Seneschal; he and his family were well. They are somewhat better at Pentre Eirianell. Mother begins to walk about the house with a stick, ond yn bûr fethiant, Duw ai helpo. Mae'r teulu'r chwaer a'r eiddof finneu yn rhwydd iachus. Gerwin y darfu'r newyddwyr gamgymeryd ynghylch pris y llongau a ddaliawdd y Cadpen Wreit yn y Canolfor, os gwnant 10 or pedwar canmil da fydd y gwaith; dyma lythyr a sgrifennodd o Leghorn ddiwedd Rhagfyr ai hanes o bant i bentan. Gwaed gwreinyn glas! Dyma Mr. Ellis wedi rhoddi allan bwmp o Lyfr Cymraeg yn erbyn y Methodistiaid, y rhai a elwir yn y wlad yma pennau crynnion. Argraphwyd yn Nulun.* Dyna lle mae pabwyr yn yr iaith Gymroaeg! Mi yrraf i chwi un o honynt os tarawaf wrth gyfleu. Pray let me hear from you by the return of the post without fail.

*The reference is to the following book: Byrr Grynhoad eglur o'r Grefydd Gristianogol ynghyd a gair o Gyngor ag addysg mewn perthynas i'r Schismaticiaid sy'n ymneillduo oddiwrth Eglwys Loegr. Argraphwyd yn Nulun, MDCCXLVII. [20pp.] A second edition, enlarged to 32 pages, was printed in the same year.

CAER GYBI, 8 o Fawrth, 1746-7, D. Sul. **W. to R.**

LXV.

Anwyl Frawd,—Wele om blaen yr eiddoch or 14 ult°. yr hwn a ddaeth i ben i siwrnai wedi hir o hwyl. Am yr amseroedd euraidd yr y'ch yn crybwyll, sef gwirotta, etc., gallaf ddywedyd gida'r hên Brydydd Gwylld o Fon, "Megys gweled breuddwyd gynt, yw gennu'r helynt honno." Aie'r Geynton oedd y gwr—pei b'aswn ŷn gwybod, llai a fa'se ei groesaw. O Garn Lleidr! Had you forgiven him the breach of trust? Afrwydd-deb cathod Bangor iddaw, ag i bob gwr oi fath. Gresyn fod y Beiblau mor ddiog am ddyfod allan; mae'n Gweinidog ni ymron mynd yn ofer, am iddo ddywedyd cymaint o anwir o'u plegyd. Cywilydd a gwradwydd erchyll! Mae'n debyg fod eisiau rhywun a byw ynddo ymhlith y Society, oblegid gwir yr hen ddywedyd Seisnig, "What's every one's business is nobody's business." Aie naccau argraphu gwaith yr Offeiriad Deheuig a wnaethant, mae'n tebyg na thala'r swydd yw gwasnaethu. Drŵg yw bod y weilgi i'ch herbyn hyd yr amser, pwy a ŵyr pa gin gynted y daw troiad. 'Rwyf inneu yn ymrwyfo yn erbyn y ffrŵd, ag yn caffael gormodd o waith i dorri ymlaen, ond etto yn byw mewn gobaith. Am Owain, o Brysaddfed, ni waeth gennyf i mor llawer ymhle y bo, gwr diddrwg didda, gwaeth yw hwnnw nar c——l, meddant hwy. Ond cywilydd i Seneddwr yrry gorchymun iw weision gartref i gau i fynu y naill hanner oi ffenestri, rhag rhoddi ychydig o drêth ir Brenin tuagat dalu y peth sydd anghenrheidiol, nid felly y gwneuthid ped fase yr peth nad yw yn bod. Ni fu ddim boddfa yn Aberystwyth; yr oedd y brawd Llewelyn yn iach o fewn yr wyth-niwrnod yma. I have Johnson upon Gerard of my own, with Davies of Gwasaney's British Catalogue. I've also all the names of plants from Meddn. Myddfai; dim cywirdeb yn un o honynt. Gŵych a fyddai gael ambell henw Cymreig or hen lyfrau yna, mae llawer yn eisiau, ond ni wiw disgwyl fawr ddaioni, ni adwaenai'r hen Gymru mo'r llawer o honynt, na'r Saeson mwy no nhwytheu, hyd yn ddiweddar. Na fedraf i siarad dim i son am dano or Gwyddeleg. Nage sisemon oedd tad Keynton, ei eni a wnaed rwy'n tybio yn Sir Fynwy, a dyfod yma at ei nain, yr hon a dygodd i fynu er yn grynddyn.

Cefais eich llythyr oddiwrth Roberts, ond ni welais mo'r gwr, mae'n debyg fod cywilydd arno. Mae'n debygol na bydd llythyr

W. to R. contd. Morgan ond double letter, os felly, fe dal y gwr o Saint Iago am danynt. As for John Prichard's note, if he sends it me I'll endeavour to get the money from his brother and send him a London bill for't, but you must not expect that I shall make a purpose journey as soon as the note perhaps may come to hand. I will call of his brother the first time I go into that part of the Island, which will be 'twixt and May; and as to a London bill, one must sometime wait a good while before one can get a good draught. If he approves of this slow but sure way of proceedings, I will, for the sake of himself and friends, negotiate his affair; otherwise, pawb yn iâch, cenwch. I returnd but last night from a Pentre-'rianell journey. I found our parents in tollerable good health, barring mother's foot; she's extream lame, y gwrnau wedi cwttio medd hi. It's, I presume, owing to a bad cure, i.e., too sudden healing up a tumour which had been laid open, and which was arrisen on the crisis of a pleuretick fever, mae arnaf ofn na bydd byth diasgloff na thebyg ir peth. Dywedais ir hen bobl eich hanes yr hwn oedd dda ei gael, maent yn achwyn yn drwm ar y byd brwnt yma sydd yn ei mastroli heb yn waetha iddynt. Gwrolwych yw'r hen Wil Sion Siors, fod iddo grynddyn gin iauaid yn yr oedran yna.* Cyfoedion a'n tâd, waeth pwy un oedd y cynta a gâdd. Pa beth a wna'r henddyn ar llyfrau gwychion yna eu gyd? Nid oes bosibl nad oes ganddo ddigon o arian ag ynteu yn cael y fath gyflogau! Ag felly gwr brwnt yw'r Iarll byth, mi glywais ei gychwyn o Lundain i ddyfod i Gymru ar Iwerddon. Digon da yw bod gobaith i gael peth oddiwrth y Smyth hwnnw. Pwy ond yr hen Gadpen Edward Butler (a fu gynt yn cludo ceirch oddiyma i chwi) a sgrifennodd attaf lythyr y dydd arall o Fanaw i ddeisyf gwybod pris ydau. Ni chlywswn ddim oi hanes ers blynyddoedd lawer. He's lately commenced malster at that place, os attebai'r farchnad 'roedd yn dywedyd y deuai ffordd yma ei hun. Dyna i chwi'r "Noble Race" yn ei hôl. The alterations, I should imagine, are not material, o'r ffeinia fydde ei gwel'd yn argraphedig mewn pedeir iaith. As to seeds, a few curious ones pe bae gyfleu yw hanfon, a fa'e da iw cael, nid oes gennyf fawr o fath yn y byd y leni, fe allai ffranc gludo rhai. I don't mean that you should lay out

*A reference to the birth of Sir William Jones in the previous September.

any money, but if you can pick up a few among your curious friends, either for the parterre or kitchen. Rym ni (yma) ei gyd yn gorchymun attoch ar eiddoch, mae fy etifedd yn crynnu or lusus bob dydd er's mis. Nid yw ei fam bur iâch ar chwaer Ellin yn o laccaidd, yr reliw yn rhesymol. Duw a fo ich plaid a byddwch wych. W. to R. contd.

Eich caredigawl frawd, William Morris.

Our Parson says that you owe him a letter, yr hyn medd ef sydd bechod mawr amhosibl!

HOLYHEAD, 4th April, 1747. W. to R. LXVI.

(O'm Hannedd, sef yw honno, Summer Hill, neu'r Bryn Hafog).

Anwyl Frawd,—I write this upon a suppossition that you have not ta'en up my last letter; and good reason why, for some unlucky goblin (I suppose a Methodistical elf) put it into my head that a frank with two ounces in't would pass free, upon which I packd up Mr. Ellis's pamphlet, the "Noble Race," etc., etc., dispatch'd 'em away, but soon after a kind, good-natured sylph buzz'd me in the ear that I had been impos'd upon, ni cheisiai ond barn person y plwyf eb ef, upon which I waited of the Doctor, though too late, who, to my comfort, told me that whatever weight there was above an ounce would be charged, a dyna ben a thewi. Os y chwi ni chymerasoch y llythyr anfonwch am danno, a minneu fal yr haeddwn, a dalaf drosto pan welwyf gyfleu, oblegyd ni fynnwn iddo fynd yn siêd am bris yn bŷd, o ran pwy a wyr i ba law y digwydd? 'Rym ni yma at yr un gyflwr ag y d'wedais or blaen, byddai wych gennyf glywed oddiwrthych gynnta galloch i ddifyrru tippyn ar yr amser, ni welwyd Ynghybi erioed mo'i fâth. Ein caredigawl orchymyn attoch oll, a Duw a fo ich plaid.

I am, your affectionate brother, William Morris.

HOLYHEAD, 9th May, 1747. W. to R. LXVII.

Dear Brother,—Llyma eich llythyr or 11 ulto om blaen, da iawn oedd clywed ddianc o'r Bystol heb ei drethu. I expected to meet John Prichard's brother at St. Mark's fair at Llanerchmedd, but did not. I spoke to his cousin, William Lewis, who promisd me his answer in a short time, a dyna fo i chwi fal y cefais inneu y Mercher diweddaf. What must be done with the note? Roedd y nhad a mam yn rhesymol iachus o fewn y tridie ymma, ond bod yr hen wreigen yn dal yn fusgrell. Aie nid oes daioni i gael gan yr Arglwydd Pwtt? I beth y mae dyn or fath honno da? I have not

W. to R. contd. heard from Cardiganshire of a long while. Mae'r byd yn mynd yn ŵysg ei din yn y fangre yma, ni welwyd mor fath farweidd-dra yn oes neb sy'n fyw heddyw. It was at first occasioned by some mismanagement in the pacquet boats; the owner first and then his widow dying, left things at sixes and sevens, ag nid oes wybod par bryd y cawn ddaioni o honynt. Notwithstanding, envy and malice with all their concomitants, are as busy as ever. A bold stroke was made at the Surveyor and myself the other day. A busy fellow of this place, a taylor by trade, was made a boatman about some three years agoe, who, presuming upon his interest with Sir Nicholas Baily, whose voter he is, and eggd on by a discarded officer, one Hugh Lloyd,* complained first to the Salt Board and lately to the Surveyor General of certain pretended crimes we were guilty of. We had, last week and this, an examination, when all appeared to

* Lewis Morris wrote a mock awdl to this man, which runs as follows:

OWDL GADARN I HUW LLWYD Y SWYDDOG.

Owdl a ganaf ni wadodd—un erioed
Yn ei raid a ganodd
Cerdd clod i Fab a gododd
Yn wr mawr, mi enwa'r modd.

Crupliaid a deilliaid a dwyllodd—yr hyll-fab
A'r holl-fyd a speiliodd
D'iaren faith, dwr un fodd,
A'i ddrewllyd law a ddrylliodd.

Canhwyllau a gwer cynhullodd—yn dwyllfawr
I'r Dollfa fe'i cludodd,
Ni chae druan mewn anfodd
Gan y Llwyd moi fwyd o'i fodd.

Am Goffi a Thea fe'mgwffiodd—i'r Gwrych
Nid oes gwrach nas curodd,
Cyfeiti a Brandi heb rodd
Yn ollawl a enillodd.

Duwiau arian a dyrrodd—mewn trafferth
Tir uffern a brynnodd,
Rhoddes i ddiawl fawl o'i fodd
A'i ddelw a addolodd.

Llawer gwrach afiach a anafodd,
Llawer lleban ag egwan a gogiodd,
Llawer llythyr cymmun a luniodd,
Llawer o'r eiddo'n llwyr a roddodd;
Ei deulu ei hun fab diawl a henwodd,
Yn aur, yn arian cyfan fe'i cafodd,
Hyd yn oed y cerrig fe'i carriodd i'w ffau
A'r gwiail clwydau i'w gofl a'i cludodd.

ac felly ymlaen.

the Surveyor General, to be but a malicious scheme. What makes me be somewhat particular in this affair is, that I understand you are acquainted with Sir W. Irby. The first of these chaps, viz., Robert Griffith, holds a lease under Sir William, and the latter (H. Lloyd) is a tennant of his in this place. He is a fellow that made himself infamous by his tricks; was formerly collector of this place, but turned for defrauding the King, as he was out of the Salts and out of being Coastwaiter of the Customs a second time. This was the chief person concerned in the scheme of Thomas Jones against brother Lewis, where a sett of villains joind to ruin him, but were repulsed with shame and infamy. He has the best bargain in the county under Sir William. A large inn, with abundance of out-houses, barn, stable, a fine field well waterd, garden, etc., and all for £10 per annum! Gresyn na byddai fodd i wneuthur ir hen leidr gymwynas, am ei ddrwg weithredodd. The other fellow (rhyngwy i a chwitheu) I believe will be out. If Sir Nicholas won't intermeddle (I wish Sir William mayn't), for he is not capable of the duty, and is disobedient and insolent. None but a villain of the blackest dye would have offered to hurt such a person as the Surveyor, who has a housefull of small children and nothing but his business to maintain 'em. He is a sober, diligent, careful man, and perhaps discharges his duty as well as any officer in the Revenue. As matters are circumstanced the two barronetts cannot suspect any partiality; it is what this fellow allways buzzes Sir Nicholas in the ear with, that he is oppressed upon account of being his friend, though without the least shadow of truth. I never concern myself with party affairs, and my voice in this country, as well as at Liverpool, is at the disposal of my patron, Mr. Brereton, who, I dare say, will be for Sir Nicholas; and as to my father, I presume his will be at Sir William's service. I could name some others if I had been biazd the other way, would not have been now for Sir Nicholas. All this stuff is only to shew that Sir Nicholas is imposd upon, and I fancy Sir William too. Perhaps you may one time or other have an opportunity to put in a word. However you must excuse your brother's prolixity! Rym ni oll yn rhwydd iachus, ag yn gorchymyn attoch, a Duw a fo yn amddiffynwr i chwi beunydd. *Eich brawd ffwdanllyd, William Morris.*

W. to R.
LXVIII.

CAER GYBI, 5d o Fehefin, 1747.

Anwyl frawd,—Ce's eich llythyr or 21 ulto. mewn pryd, a da ydoedd cael eich hanes. Yn wyf yn ofni wrth yr hanes yr y'ch yn ei roddi yn llythyrau nhad, mae un or rhai anwadal yw Syr Wiliam, ail yw Gâr o Plâs Newydd; they seem to answer the character of the modern W—gs ni rown i rwynen am garriad or fath. Hawdd ammor i'r hên rai. Mae'n debyg na fedrwch wneuthur fawr gymwynas ir Lwyd, oddigerth i chwi ddigwydd ymgomio efo Syr ynghylch Sir Fôn a chael cyfleu i roddi iddo ei hanes. Wythnos i heddyw y dychwelais i am gwraig adref o Bentre'rianell, Boderwyd a Brynddu. Gan fy mod yn myn'd heibio i Wrêdog (tŷ brawd Sion Prisiart) mi elwais yno i gael clywed o'i enau ei hun pa beth oedd yn ei frŷd; nid oedd ganddo i roddi ond yr un atteb, sef y talai yn ddiffael o gwmpas Gwyl Fihangel. Bid rhyngddo ai frawd am y llôg. Aie ni chaiff Davies moi wraig ei hun? Caled iawn yn wir, mae'n debyg nad oes i'r un or ddau fawr golled,—mi a wn nad oes iddi hi. Vickers has the Pacquet untill new ones are provided by the new contractor, he seems to do well, but query no one here interferes in his business. He has bought the small estate that belongd to Davies' wife out and out, so now Davies is not worth a penny, gwiliwch ei goelio. Can diolch i chwi am lythyrau Sionyn Morgan, chwi gewch ryw drô fy meddwl i ynghylch y pethau 'rwyf fi yn ei amgyffred ynddynt. Dynan cywraint digrif ydoedd, nid tŷb wael yn y byd oedd ganddo o honaw ei hun. Mi a'u gyrraf i Lewelyn or Deheu. Rwyn cofio weled yn llyfrgell fy hen gyfaill David Foulkes, o Wern y Gron (yn ymyl Llanelwy), Esq., yn y flwyddyn 1734, gymmar ir llyfr hwnw or eiddo W. Jones, Esq. * The Note by the Transcriber was the same except "a Harri 6" after H. 5, ag ar ol y gair Dolgellau, "Sgrifenyddiaeth y llyfr hwnw oedd fal hyn y llaw hynaf" and at the bottom of the same page, thus: Totum scripsi, ego John Davies, finis 16, April, 1617; ag mewn lle arall "Totum transcripsi, etc., ego Guil Mauricius, Llansilinensis, Anno, 1662, Nov. 24, Laus Deo,—Magna nec, etc," and then "Ex. p. Llyfr Coch, Llyfr Du."

In the margin all along were certain words inserted out of the Poems by Dr. Davies, who (as Mr. Foulkes was told) borrowd the

* Probably Llanstephan, MS 31.

said book when he was collecting materials for his Dictionary. Chwi welwch mae'r un gwaith yw—Oian a Pharchellan, Arwyrau, etc., on'te? Nid hwyrach y medraf ei gael gan yr Ysgwier Foulkes ryw dro. Ni welais i ond rhyw ychydig o ymrysonion Edmund Prys a William Cynwal, a rheini ydoedd rwy'n meddwl gan y brawd Llewelyn. Ië yn wir ddiau, newydd gwych yw fod Anson wedi dal y Ffrancod! Fe haeddai ei wneuthur yn Arglwydd am ei boen. I deliver'd your compliments to Mr. Ellis, ond y mae e' druan gwr fal chwitheu yn llawn ffwdan, *ynghylch dim yn y byd.* Dyma ryw walch gwamal* (fe dybir mae un o Ustusiaid Heddwch ein gwlad) wedi sgrifennu atteb i'w lyfr ag wedi ei dynnu'n dippiau oddiwrth ei gilydd, ag hefyd wedi talu'r pwyth yn ol o amarch, etc., gida llog! It is a manuscript and dispers'd among the Methodists, who look upon the author to be their deliverer. The parson will appear in print a second time. Cewch weled ar fyrder. The author of the remarks is an Arian and defends that doctrine, dyna dorri gwaith allan ir Bersonyn ffremwyllt! onte? Am yr arian bryntion y soniasoch am danynt, nhw aethont i gyd oddiyma, ffarwel gida nhw. Duw a wellhao'r amseroedd. Aie ni fedrwch ddim cwbl faddeu i fab dihenyddwr y Bardd; mae'n galed ir plant ddioddef dros ei rhieni. Yn wir, diog iawn mae'r Bibl yn mynd ymlaen. Ped fuase ryw wagedd na thalasai i son am dano, fe wneuthid mwy brys. Cebyster ir fath Arglwyddi, chwyn ydynt. Ni ddywedais i yr awn allan i ryfel yn erbyn y Bodorganiaid; ond os fy nghadpen a orchymyn i hynny fod, rhaid yw gwneuthur. So it stands upon the Counsellor to look out, perhaps he may have a good understanding with the Commissioner. Mae'n rhy anwyl gan yr hên gorph ai blentyn

W. to R. contd.

*"Un Mr. Ellis, Ciwrad Caergybi, a ddyfal bregethodd, ac a ysgrifenodd yn eu herbyn. William Bwckle (Bulkeley), Yswain, o'r Bryn Du, a ysgrifenodd ateb iddo." Trysorfa (T. Charles), Medi 1812, tud. 435. Methodistiaeth Môn. Parch J. Pritchard, tud 31. A second edition of the book by Rev. Thomas Ellis was published in the same year, with some additional remarks, in answer to Mr. Bulkeley's written pamphlet. It does not appear that Mr. Bulkeley's pamphlet was ever printed, for Mr. Ellis in his answer refers to a written copy, and says that many of these copies were circulated. The printed pamphlet is written in terse, idiomatic Welsh, and is in itself eloquent testimony of the hold Nonconformity had gained in Anglesey at this early date.

W. to R. contd.

fwnws arian bydol, felly yn bur anghyfaddas i osod i fynu am uchel leoedd. Fe ddywedir ir cyfreithiwr aros yna o bwrpas i ochel gwario. Ni wna nhad ei gwyrthwynebu oi fodd, ond os bydd rhaid iddo ufuddhau iw feister tir, neu droi allan o'i annedd, lle bu ers deugain mlynedd; chwi ellwch feddwl pa'r un a wnâ. This was the meaning of what I mentioned in my last, sure ye took it in that sense? Though as to my own part I've my liberty as to that family, dim rhwymedigaeth iddynt, ond cymydogaeth dda. Father and mother was as usual as to their healths. My mother still decrepid and like to continue so. All here in tollerable good health. Had a letter this week by Alderman Prichard of Leverpoole, from Llewelyn who is like to fall out with his great masters, waits the turn of the scale. Here's a fine Cywydd ir cŵd, chwi ai cewch ryw dro, rwyf rwan mewn brys anfeidrol, felly Duw a fo gida chwi oll.

Eich brawd anwiw William Morris.

Gadewch glywed oddwrthych fynycha galloch da chwitheu.

L. to R.

LXIX.

GALLTVADOG, 21 June, 1747.

Dear Brother,—I received yours of ye 16 June but last night, and the tables of ye Bible, etc., and that no time may be lost, here you have them again. There is very little to be said to them, and as I have neither books nor leisure to compare them, when there is so much uncertainty, even in our common measures, weights, etc., I had best let them as they are, for they are but tolerable guesses at best. When our *Foot* was different from what it is now, such an author might be in the right when he compared the Hebrew measures, etc., with ours, but in another age, since there is no universal standard of magnitude known in ye world, the proportion must fail. That of ye royal pendulum was a noble standard for a yard, if pendulums had not been found to alter in different parts of ye world. I have read somewhere that a certain King of England ordered a yard (standard) to be made according to ye length of his arm; and it is well known that the standard foot we have now was settled by ye instrument makers of London not a great while ago. Where then is ye certainty of ye proportions? Quite dark to be sure. Perhaps the Roman foot on ye monument of Cestucius and

Statilius may be ye only certainty we have, and even there the stone might wear.—Now to words. Tabl (pl. Tablau) is a good word enough to answer the English *Tables*, and though it is not in our dictionaries, it is natural to suppose the Roman *Tabula* might be borrowed from it according to Pezron's rules. I have lost that valuable book, I wish you could get me another. **L. to R. contd.**

"Enw Iesu fu ag a fydd yn dafl o henw Dafydd."

L. G. Cothi.

Instead of *Tablau Seisnig* I think you ought to call them *Brutanaidd*, for they also belong to ye Welsh and Scotch. Write *Testun*, *Testyn*; or write thus, Tablau Arian, Pwysau, a Mesurau Crybwylledig yn yr Ysgrythyr Lân, gwedi eu troi yn rhai Brutanaidd drwy awdurdod y gwyr mwyaf a 'sgrifenasant ar y Testyn hwnnw, a gyfansoddwyd gan R. M., golygwr yr argraphiad hwn o'r Beibl. Then the Table. Nodwch, E gyfrifir yr Arian yn y Tabl hwn yn ol Ystandart y Mint, etc. Tabl Pwysau Iuddewig yn Bwysau Troye Brutanaidd, and so *Troye* everywhere, etc. Tabl Gwlyb fesurau Iuddewig yn Win fesurau Brutanaidd. Nodwch 76 pwys Troye o ddwfr croyw cyffredin a leinw lestr o droedfedd *Bedronglog* 28¾ modfedd *Bedronglog* yn y Pint, etc. Tabl sych fesurau Iuddewig yn Fesurau Yd Brutanaidd. Nodwch 33 3-5 modfedd bedronglog yn y pint, etc., ag 8 galwyn yn y Bwsielaid neu fesur Caerwynt, etc., yn ol yr Ystatut. Hestoraid is a word peculiar to Anglesey, *Bwsiel* may be an antient Gaulish word. Tabl Hyd-fesurau Iuddewig. I think *cam-lath* is better than cam. Nodwch, 5 troedfedd yn y Gam-lath, ag 1056 cam-lath yn y Filldir. Tabl Arwyneb Fesurau Iuddewig, gwedi eu cymharu a mesurau Brutanaidd. Rheol, Amlblygwch [multiply] yr hyd wrth y lled a bydd y cynhwysiad yn Gyfyddau Ysgwar. Amlblygwch y rheini wrth 3 32-100 (y troedfeddau ysgwar mewn cyfydd) a bydd y cynhwysiad yn Droedfeddau Ysgwar, etc. Yr hyn yw 16·634 88-100 troedfedd, neu 1 chwarter acr ystatut, 21 perc., 27½ troedfedd. Tir y Lefiaid, etc. a wna 78 acr, 1 chwr., 20 perc., 80·97 troed.

Rhwd and *pawl* are very bad words and nowhere used. *Rhwd* is a running measure in Anglesey, but no square measure. *Pawl* is no measure. But perc or perk is a common name in South Wales for a rod or perch which is here 13½ foot. The word *acr* we may

L. to R. contd. venture upon (upon Pezron's rule) from which came the Latin Iuger and the bastard Latin *acra*, but *rood* is an English square measure, which chwarter acr will very well explain or *chwart* or *cwart*, as they call the quarter of any thing in this country, as llathen a chwart—a yard-and-a-quarter, etc. But as to ye word cyfair, cyfer and cyfar, Dr. Davies and everybody have been mistaken in it. The word ought to be wrote cyfâr from aredig dydd cyfa, being a certain quantity of land in this part of the world, i.e. as much as a yoke of oxen ought to plow in a day; for what they plow is more or less. A cyfâr and a half makes another square measure called *ystang*, which is a kind of an acre and contains 160 of their square perches of 13½ foot each, which is 107 square statute perches=oa. 2r. 27p., so that a cyfar here is but 71·32 statute perch=oa. 1r. 31p. 4″. And this cyfar in translating can fit no other measure known amongst mankind. It is of no determind quantity in Anglesey, Carnarvonshire and Merionethshire, and I believe not in Denbigh and Flintshire, for there they run to the English measures. It is very wrong then to call any measures by ye name of cyfar, but what is actually a cyfar, the Iugerum of the Romans. The ignorance in these things and following dictionaries hath spoilt many a translation. I dont like the word *noda*, it is a bastard of the Latin word *nota*. Nodwch, is *note you* or take you notice. So much for that half sheet. Now to ye other, the quarter sheet. Tabl arian Rhufain a grybwyllir am rai o honynt yn y Testament Newydd. *Ysten*, any vessel of an undeterminate measure, is a foolish translation of Sextarius a determined known measure. No doubt Solidus is *swllt*. The fractions of a hundred is enough to express thus 30-100, and then they are easily reduced to decimals upon occasion. I think they will do well enough: who can mend them? Compare what I have said above with your own papers, which come to you by post, each singly directed to Mr. Richards as this is; and if I am right make use of my observations, but I think you ought to take Mr. W. Jones's opinion, to whom I desire my humblest service, when I have my senses about me, clear from the noise and nonsense of this world which hath almost distracted* . . . . me. . . . . . .

*Word cut off by binder.

Three years in the prime of my days is now at stake, and like to be lost by the craft and art of worldly men. . . . . ny curious things to impart to Mr. Jones if I was intimate with him, for if I dont live to publish my Natural History of Anglesey, it will be pity my materials should be lost. I have examind into all the British fish, and have given them as many of ye Welsh names as we have from the real knowledge of ye fish, not from ignorant dictionaries. Have rectified several mistakes in Ray and Willoughby. My collection of plants, birds and fossils are better and correcter than anything I have met with. I never [me]t a man yet that understood fossils, and but few that knew anything of birds. I have been digging among fossils for many years and have made them my study, and if I had leisure, I could give better quaeries and answers about mines than any in the Phil. Transactions. The art of Mining is but in its infancy. God be with you, I have no time to spare to write further, but that I understand Mr. Corbett will be here next month, and then I shall be off or on. L. to R. contd.

I am your affectionate brother, *L. M.*

The charge to ye court Leet is but a trifle to what I do here. I dont doubt but I understand those things better than Mr. Guidot, I have puzled the King's Sollicitor and Council about them. They are but men. I wish you could get Mr. Middleton's business, and I wish I was his agent.

From my hermitage at GALLTVADOG, 31 July, 1747. L. to R. LXX.

Dear Brother,—I have yours of ye 18 and 25th July about ye Bible weights, measures and prayers. I have laid aside some very urgent business I had to answer this; for I suppose it will be ye last upon this head. First to ye prayers. The title of ye large prayer seems to me quite idle. A godly prayer to be said at all times. I never heard of ungodly prayers, and all prayers for our good ought to be said at all times. Pray without ceasing. It would have been better, a prayer to be said daily. And I am sure gweddi feunyddiol is the best title in Welsh, let the English be what it will. Beunydd is every day or daily, beunos is every night or nightly (by ye Poets beunoeth). Now to ye prayer. I think Dâd *o'r nefoedd* ought to be *Dad nefol*, yn rhad ag oth ewyllys, etc., divines may make a distinction between electing and choosing, but I know none, but I

L. to R. contd. wont quarrel with the maker of ye prayer since you are only to translate it as it is. Ethol and dewis is ye same and will stand well enough for elect and choose, achub is better than cadw. *Na ad* for *na ddiodde*, pleser is a provincial Latin word, but may do here as we have none so good, but is generally taken for pleasure in y[e] loosest sense. *Plessio* indeed is to *please*, but *Boddio* there is y[e] best verb, but it hath no good substantive. However *Pleser da* mends y[e] matter. Instead of *i'n camweddau*, I would write *wrth ein camweddau*. *Mai mawr* is better than *gymmaint*. Holy name is *enw sanctaidd*, iechydwriaeth and athrawiaeth must be aspirated, as well as ymddiffyn. So much for y[e] long prayer. In y[e] title *cyflwr* is better than *stad*. *Cyffesu* and *cyfaddef* is ye same thing, and is tautology in y[e] English, which to cover, you must write for *cyfaddef*, *addef*. *Cenhedlu* better than *cael*. Here are two *oestads* together, that sound ill. Say for ye first *bob amser*. For *addysg* I would write *athrawiaeth*, ag felly yn enill ini ein hunain drwy dy gyfion farn di angau a cholledigaeth. *Barnedigaeth* makes too many *aeths* i.e. [*caniad y gog*, a good word for tautology]. Anfoddhaus wrthym ein hunain, *o wraidd ein calonnau*. *Tueddiadau* for *Tueddau*, yr ym yn *siccr* gredu, for *symmudo* say *droi ymaith* dy râs a'th ffafor. So much for the short prayer. Now to ye letter. The plural of testyn is testynau. D. G. and all ye poets take many liberties, as *doeth* pro *daeth*, etc., which was a weakness in following the vulgar stream. Troi is a good word enough for to *translate* or to reduce, you may use *trosi* if you will, which comes from the same original, to turn round, about, upside down, backwards, forwards, to bring to some order, etc. The Latin word is bad enough. Custom makes words. As for *Troy* Weight which I write Troye, our moderns say the name was borrowd from Troyes, a city in Champagne in France. I had an eye upon Caerdroia when I wrote it, but I did not know how to write it with proper letters for y[e] Welsh. Pwys Troia I thought did not look so well as Troye, which is so near y[e] English, they would hardly find y[e] difference. The critics will fall foul of poor *Caerdroia* and *Brutus* if they smell the least tracks of them. However, if you will venture it, with all my heart, as for my part I think it very probable the English might have their Pwysau Caerdroia from us, and I have made a note of it in my History of Anglesey. Wythonglog or chweochrog will not do for a cube no more than pedronglog. Chweonglog is rather a hexagon, wythonglog an octagon, we have no words for their ideas, they are lost, and language is arbitrary. We have no word for solid, and the Latin word sounds odd with us as yet, but must be made use of and wrote solid and not *solud* nor *soled* nor *solyd*. Dr. Davies knew nothing of arts and sciences. Corph pedronglog is ye way to convey ye idea, though I would not have it a standard. The word I would use, whatever the original was, is Bwysel or Bwysiel rather, because easier understood, and Mwysel might be made from Bwysiel as modfedd from Bawd. You may use amblygu for amlblygu and is proper enough, it is a better compound for that idea than any in use. *Amblygwch a Thri* may be better than *wrth*. Pawl is not used anywhere for a measure, but perc is all over South Wales, and some parts of North Wales.

L. to R. contd.

The measures and weights in Scripture ought to have been exactly done, to take away all occasion of contempt to that book, because it ought to be truth and to agree with itself, and all translations, but it is the work of an Hercules or rather a hundred Hercules's; we laugh at all other books if they are guilty of these mistakes, and no doubt but other religions laugh at our Bible. Read Mr. Folke's account of Cossutius's foot in No. 442 of ye Phil. Transactions and you'll find the reasons of my objections, and you'll find in Mr. Hookes' Posthumous works, published by Richard Waller, p. 457, that the English foot is quite uncertain, and nothing certain under the sun, and there let them lie. Y sicl yw'r darn arian a *grybwyllir am dano*, etc. Saesonaeg and not Saisonaeg. The inches column in ye Tables of Capacity are I think not necessary, neither of them will be understood but by curious men. Arian is ye word used now for money, but very improperly. Mwnai is ye good old Welsh word for coin used by ye poets, and derived from *Mwn or Mwyn*, from hence money is derived, but the word is now dark: advise with Mr. Jones whether it is proper to use it. Tablau Mwnai would look odd at first, and would be carpd at, but time would make it agreeable. Erwydden may be a good old word for a Rod, but it will not do now; for *erw* was a determinated measure or quantity of ground, though it is now any quillet,

W. to R. contd.

and if erw now signified an acre, I cannot see how this *Gwydden* can take its name properly from an acre no more than from a rood. Then let us stick to our provincial word perc from ye Latin Pertica or the French *Perche*. So much for your querries.

The Duke of Somerset's Rectories are about a day and half's journey from hence. I know some of ye Parishes, but I know very little of the men you mention. What salary had Howel Williams? Could I be of any service to His Grace in those parts? I suppose I may have so much time to spare if there is anything tolerable to be got by it. I hope Gambold will not publish that dictionary, I dare say (by ye Grammar he hath published) it is a foolish one. I never saw a man nor 2 or 3 heads together fit for it. Even Mr. Ed. Llwyd was not. If we send shoemakers to propagate ye Gospel in Germany, the Germans send us chymists or pretended ones, to teach us mining. There is one at Holywell, Diederich Wessel Linden, who hath wrote something lately on mines, on which I have wrote notes. He is as great a mountebank in philosophy, as the shoemaker can be in religion. As for the dinboeth or piles, my father was afflicted with it for 30 years and we tryed all medicines that are in use. Dr. Evans cooked him up for several years, but at last we found a country specific which cured him, so that they never returned again.

The Hebrew and Greek names in their proper characters would be proper enough, for so the learned may better compare ye weights and measures. Ysgwar is a word used of old, and it may as well stand as any other, and it is accepted of by custom as a good word. It is not long since the English knew the right use of it. Three square was a common word among writers till of late, for three cornerd. I was at my father's lately, the 5th year since I saw Anglesey. My mother is very decrepid. She drives on still, doing all the good she can, but stirs too much. My father is turn'd a great farmer, they have a vast plenty of corn and cattle. I saw Evan Bedlar's wife. I fancy the son broke and run for debt as well as on account of ye ship. You dont mention a syllable of Roderick Richards who is lately promoted to be pay clerk at Plymouth. How will you get letters hereafter? I have not yet been with Mr. Vaughan. Have just seen him upon the road, in my way to ye Anglesey elections, when Mr. Meyrick was fairly bit by ye Tories, who ran over from their engagements to Sir Nicholas Bayly, in hopes he would stick to them; but he'll certainly be a courtier. Mae ef yn bur dlawd. I was one night at Bodorgan with the good old man. Pirs is there as usual, and all upon ye old man's back. Dick Morris is superannuated, and he is to be allowed three pound a year and a tenement. Owen Jones is married well, and hath quite left Mr. Meyrick. I had not time to go to Holyhead, to see our sisters, etc. I expect Mr. Corbett and some great men here daily, and am very busy in drawing maps, accounts, etc. So farewell at present. I have a great swimming in my head this great while. It is a weakness in ye nerves which I am afraid will not end well. Service to sister and Meirian. L. to R. contd.

Your loving brother, *L. Morris.*

Let me know if you have contracted any friendship or acquaintance with anybody in ye Navy office during your acquaintance with Rod. Richards. I had desired him to do me a few jobbs there which I suppose are now all over, and I must employ a fresh hand. I have heard from Tom Evans. I believe he will be here soon about business.

CAER GYBI, 20 Awst, 1747. W. to R. LXXI.

Dyma fi'n cael tippyn o amser i gymeryd fy anadl attaf; ag i atteb eich dau lythyr sef o'r 30 Fehefin ar 8d or mis hwn, a sicr yw fod arnaf gywylydd am na wnaethwn yn gynt, now for the first Mi welaf eich bod yn anferth ffrind efo'r cynghorwr Meyrig. Dyma Ddick Morus wedi cael i droi allan. Os gwir a glywaf ni chadd na thyddyn nag ychwaith mor cyflog a gytunasai am dano, a dyna'r modd y gwasanaethwyd ag Owain ap Sion Prisiart Prys. Da oedd cael 7 yn lle 10 punt per annum. Nid oes dim ymddiried i blant dynion ysywaeth. Nid oeddwn yn meddwl y gwnae'r henddyn y fath hagrwrthiau. Gwrthyn y gwaith yr Arglwydd Pwtt yn eich siommi yn y modd yna, what can't we expect from such senators. Na welais i erioed mor abridgement hwnnw o eiddo Sion Morgan, his Thoughts on the 4 last things with englynion Marwnad Ed. Lloyd I have. Mae'n edifar gan y person Ellis sgrifennu mor ddigllon at Frougton, ag mae'n deusyf arnaf ddywedyd wrthych mae gwr rhwydd wyllt, ffrom ydyw, ond yn dychwel atto ei hun yn

W. to R. contd. union deg, ag yn ddrwg ganddo mewn munud y peth y wnelo ondodid! His defence against the Justice is no more than some few additions in a second edition of his former tract, which I will send you by the first opportunity. Fe dybir mae y Mr. Brynddu* is the author of the remarks, ag nid yw yn gwadu, ond mwy allan o ddireidi na dim arall. I believe the Methodists in general are trinitarians. John Westley embarked here for Dublin, did not preach but dispersed his sermons.† Mr. Ellis was from home else there would have been a scuffle perhaps. Mr. Brereton met no opposition at Leverpoole, he did send to desire my vote in favour of Mr. Meyrick, ag felly fase, oni bae aflwydd, cewch yr hanes yn y man. Aie mae'r Gownsler yn o law helaeth pan fo yna? Gwell a fase iddo warrio ei arrian yn ei wlad ag ynteu yn disgwyl iddi ei ddewis yn ben arni. Mae gobaith medd Fortunatis‡ wrthafi (yn ei lythyr or 19 ultimo, N. S.) na bydd raid iddo dalu mor arian ir Twrciaid, obleit his captures were made long before the instructions were sent from the Admiralty to the Commanders of men of warr, privateers, etc., concerning the effects of Turks in French bottoms. Par sut roeddych yn gyrru ei lythyr ymlaen? I mean brother Lewis's letter to him. You must have heard that Mr. Bodvell came off with flying colours at his election—90 odd majority! Er dolwyn rhowch fy nghorchymyn inneu at Sior Feddyg, aie gwr nheddig yw'r gwr bod y fodfedd? Huw ai catto fo. Conolly is gone to Dublin by way of Parkgate, he comes this way often, I know his gentleman.

Aie fe gadd gordderchwraig y Geynton y cryg, nid oedd fatter yn y byd. Na welais i erioed mor William Roberts hwnnw, I fancy he must be an idle chap to tarry in the country a starving. Gwych hefyd fyddai weled gwaith y *Garte*, ond beth ydis nes? Echryslon

* Mr. Bulkeley of Brynddu.

† A Welsh tract entitled "Gair i'r Methodist: o waith Mr. J. Wesley, was printed at Dublin in 1748, and probably circulated by Wesley on his travels through Wales.

‡ It will be proper at this stage to give some particulars of the career of Fortunatus Wright, to whom there are many references in the Letters. He was the son of Captain John Wright of Liverpool, who died in April, 1717, after gallantly defending his ship for several hours against two vessels of superior force. This is recorded on his tombstone in St. Peter's Churchyard,

ydyw'r hanes rych yn ei roddi o'r Iarll Cholmondley, wfft iddo ! a dwbl wfft ir Dug Siando. Chwi glywsoch mi a wranta son am fwgan or henw hwnnw. Ni enillodd y Ffrancod fawr wrth y gwaith yn Flanders, ond yn unig gadw'r ymladd faes. Every dog hath his day. Gwilanhw attynt os eiff hi'n heddwch rhyngom a Spain. Mi faswn yn sgrifenu attoch hanes y lecsiwn oni bae fy mod heb gymaint ag un ffrank ar fy helw, ag nid oes ar y ddaiar a wyr a wna'r cast yma ddyfod a hwn i chwi yn rhad ai peidio. I told you I had had orders to join the Counsellor's Corps and had prepared to set out for the metropolis. The day before the election came on, there came an order that all Mr. Meyrick's friends should tarry at home, that Mr. Owen had gone over to Lord Bulkeley*. The case was thus:—Mr. Lewis Llysdulas, who was Mr. Meyrick's chief manager, having on Sunday the 12th made a calculation of the votes on both sides, and finding Mr. Meyrick had but a small majority of perhaps 6 or 8, 16 says others, and finding that Sir Nicholas had partly despaired of gaining his end, so in order to play a safe card, took it in his head without the previous knowledge of the Councillor or his father (as they say 'emselves), to write to Sir Nicholas to desire a meeting at Llangefni the next day, of the principal gentry of both sides, which was gladly accepted of, and Mr. Owen invited to the Congress, but he would not appear. When it was propos'd by Mr. Meyrick and his friends that Sir Nicholas

W. to R. contd.

Liverpool, where it is stated also that "Fortunatus Wright, his son, was always victorious, and humane to the vanquished. He was a constant terror to the enemies of his king and country." Soon after the outbreak of war with France in 1744, Wright, conjointly with others it is thought, fitted out the brigantine "Fame" "to cruize against the enemies of Great Britain." One of his chief exploits was to capture sixteen French ships in the Levant, worth £400,000 sterling (see ante p. 98). On another occasion in 1756, he successfully drove away a French privateer of 16 guns, which had been sent to capture him, although his own ship and armament was much inferior to that of his rival. So much was he feared by the French that it is said the French king promised the honour of knighthood, a pension of 3000 livres per annum for life, and the command of a ship of war, to whosoever should bring him into France alive or dead. For a long account of this extraordinary man see "The Liverpool Privateers" by Gower Williams, 1897, pp. 32-78.

*Lord Bulkeley was M.P. for Beaumaris. Owen Meyrick of Bodorgan was defeated by Sir N. Bayley, of Plas Newydd at the 1747 election.

W. to R. contd. should yield the election this time to the Counsellor and go up next time, he (Sir Nicholas) readily agreed to it and all concluded except signing, which was to be done next day at Beaumaris when all Sir Nicholas's friends were to join, but when Mr. Owen understood that the parties had agreed and that he was excluded from . . . to Parliament, this or next sessions, he went immediately to Baron-hill and made a tender to Lord Bulkeley of his interest which was about 30 voices, so upon Mr. Meyrick's arrival at Beaumaris a Tuesday he was acquainted of it by a letter from Mr. Owen himself, Sir Nicholas immediately was invited to accept of this unexpected supply, and so the poor Counsellor was jockied. There is abundance of reason to suspect that Mr. Owen from the beginning intended to desert the Councillor; however, if Mr. Dulas had not been over-busy, deg i un na chawsai'r gwr gwirion siawns, and it is suppos'd that notwithstanding Mr. Owen going over to the other side, if Mr. Meyrick had poll'd his men, he would have had a fair chance for a majority. Several of Mr. Owen's friends would have given him their voices, most of 'em condemning his perfidy. Nid oes dim hyderu ar blant dynion, Duw a gadwo pawb! ag felly chwi welwch mor anwadal yw'r byd. Bu orfod ar fy nhad sefyll o blaid ei feister tir Sir W. Irby, ag felly roedd dau fab yn erbyn eu tad. I met brother at Dulas and went with him to Bodorgan, mae o'n anferth lwdn! Rhaid cael ceffyl cryf yw gludo or fan bwygilydd. I am greatly troubled to find your piles are turned to a fistula. God Almighty grant you may get rid of 'em, a gwyn ei fyd a allai eich cynorthwyo mewn modd yn y byd, ond nid yw yn fy ngallu ysywaeth. I shall be very glad to hear that you have got well. Duw a wnel fod eich meddygon yn prophwydo'r gwir pan oeddynt yn dywedyd y byddech yn gawr mewn pythefnos. You prophesied right as to mab Ifan bedlar, a Mari'ch Risiart Prys a Mhorgan o Ben y coed gynt. Diog iawn mae'r Bibl yn myned mlaen. Ai ni fydd hi'n wyl Fair cyn y bo i ben? Nid yw hynny fawr ar ôl y Nadolig. Ni chawn yn fy myw amser i ddywedyd amgen yr awron na'n bod i gyd yn rhwydd iachus, ag yn gorchymun attochi ar eiddo, roedd nhad a mam yn rhesymol o fewn y tridie aeth heibio.

Eich brawd anwiw, William Morris.

P.S. Ni wn i fwy oddiwrth yr argraphwyr, awdwyr ar sywedyddion no chwitheu, o ran anaml iawn y byddaf yn symyd or gongl dywyll yma. Here's a couple of officers (viz. Boatmen) that has been endeavouring to hurt the Surveyor in his reputation as an Officer, newydd ei troi allan oi swyddau, i wirio yr hen ddihareb, "a ddymuno ddrwg iw gymydog," etc. They had been the means of getting £5 per annum in the Salts lately. Duw fo gida chwi, let me hear from you as soon as you can. W. to R. contd.

CAER GYBI, 4dd dydd o Fedi, 1747. W. to R. LXXII.

Anwyl Frawd,—Mi yrrais i chwi'r 2od or mis diweddaf bapuraid o ryw brygowthen, nis gwn i amcan a gawsoch ef yn rhad ai peidio. Neithiwr y deuais adref wedi bod yn marchowca ar hyd y wlad dros yspaid saith niwrnod. I went this day se'night towards Beaumaris where I was summoned to appear upon the Grand Jury, na bo yma ond ei grybwyll! Called at father's in going and returning. The old people are indifferent well, had had their harvest in, in rare order, so has all the country, the finest season ever seen in the memory of man. I came last from Bodorgan, lle y cyfarfum ar Arglwydd London Derry. Ni che's prin eistedd i lawr cyn ir hen wr alw arnaf or neill du, i ddywedyd imi ei fod wedi siared ar Arglwydd ynghylch y ddlêd sydd arno i chwi. "Gwir yw" ebr ef, "mae arnaf i Richard Morris £32 ac mi ai talaf iddo ar fyrder"; ond ebr ei chwaer, "mae ar hwnnw arrian i Ddick Moris dlawd ymma sydd yn awr allan o lê ag fe ddylae eu talu i hwnnw bod a ffyrling"; "o' wllys y nghalon i," ebr ynteu, "os caf i ryddhad am danynt." Ond darfu ir hên wr eu bodloni fod arnoch ddyledion eraill oedd mor gyfreithlon eu talu a hitheu, ag ei fod yn yspys y cae Ddick Morys ran, ond ebe fe "nis gwn i par ran a fydd Mr. Morris fodlon iw roddi." Fe fynnai'r Arglwyddes 'r hanner o leiaf, felly fe addawodd yr hen wr fynny gwybod. Chwi welwch y drafferth sydd ar boblach yn ceisio rhanu yr eiddoch. The old gentleman desired that I would write to you to know what you could allow the poor fellow. His Lordship insinuated that he might choose whether ever he paid you or no, but query Mr. Meyrick told his Lordship what a vast deal of service you had done his Lordship in the settling of his accounts, and that he was sure his Lordship must have occasion for such as you to assist him to settle his affairs. His Lordship promised he would certainly employ you. A fynnwchi waith ganddo? Mae'n rhy'wyr ganddom glywed oddiwrthych i gael

W. to R. contd. gwybod a ddaethoch drwy'r afael ai peidio. Duw a wnel mae do. Yn rhodd pa beth yw'r dwndr yma sydd gan y Cymru yn eich cym'dogaeth: sef yw hynny, eich bod yn mynd yn offeiriad, oes dim lliw na llun ir chwedlau hynny? Digrif fyddai'ch gweled mewn llostryddyn o wn purddu yn pregethu'r Efengyl, gadewch glywed 'r hanes da chwitheu. Alderman Prichard, whom I saw yesterday in his way from South Wales told me, that he left brother about a week agoe and with him Mr. W. Corbett and Mr. Chambers, Deputy Surveyor General of His Majesty's Honours, Lordships, etc., who had come down on purpose to see into brother's affairs which gave satisfaction, and the Alderman said that brother was in a fair way of getting something extraordinary under said Chambers. I fancy he has parted with Corbett and has sold him his part of the lead mine. I long to hear from thence. Brother was gone with Chambers further south. Nid oes genyf ddim chwaneg i ddywedyd yr awron gan fod cant o fudr drafferthion sydd im rhwystro. Rym ni ymma oll yn iach (mawl ir Goruchaf) ag yn gorchymun attoch chwi ar eiddoch.

Wyf eich caredigawl frawd, *William Morris.*

Yr oeddych yn dymuno hanes yr Argraphweisg a gwaith y dysgedigion yn y parthau hyn, indeed you have a specimen of what is done at Carmarthen, and that will shew you what monstrous pitch of handiwork mankind are about to arrive at!!!! Mi glywaf eich bod yn mynd i symud eich cartref, gadewch wybod i ble i yrru attoch rhagllaw os hynny sydd wir. Remember me to my London friends. How does Squire Jones and his library do? Is there any prospect of having a new edition of the Folio Welsh Bible, I think I told you that a second edition of Mr. Ellis's tract is out with answer to the remarks of a certain gentleman, I fancy the anotator will appear in print soon, gwaith ir argraphwyr.

5d.—Dyma fi newydd gael llythyr oddiwrth y brawd Lewis or 26 ulto. a sgrifenasai Ynghaerfyrddin, lle rydoedd gida Mr. Chambers, Deputy Surveyor General of His Majesty's Land Revenues, under whom he expects some pretty pickings. Ymadawse ar Gorbedyn (who had us'd him like a scoundrel) yn ffrindiau mawr or danedd allan. Pwy fase'n meddwl fod yr hen Gorph mor rhonwyr? Nid oes dim ymddiried ir ganfed ran o ddynolryw, ysywaeth.

Anwyl Frawd,—I have your letter dated 10ed o Fedi but the post mark 10 October, a da gweled o dan eich llaw eich bod yn fyw ag ar y ffordd i fod yn iach ddianaf, i'r Goruchaf bo'r diolch am ei holl drugareddau ini. Aie geiriau peraidd a gawsoch gan Mr. Wynn or Glyn? Mae ef wedi gollwng dros gof mae'n debyg fal y bum i un tro yn dysgu iddo ganu penhillion Cymroaeg Ymodorgan. I suspect that he has appeared at the Board of Customs or wrote letters in favour of these vilains at the request of Sir N. Bailey. Nay, I've been told that Sir N. has wrote to him to get them restored. If Mr. Wynne interested himself in this affair, I presume he did not know that was either supporting of delinquents or hurting the innocent, os ydoedd, drwg yr ydoedd yn talu am ei addysg—more of this affair by and by. I've not acquainted Mr. Meyrick with your resolution about Dick Morris, but shall do it in a day or two in the best manner I can (i.e.) the mildest. Nid fal chwi yn ffrochwyllt, Duw fo'n geidwad! yn ddigon er dychrynu pobyl. You certes is the best judge of your own affairs, women will be medling, but ladies must (to be sure) be excus'd, mae gwendid ar bawb, ag ond odid fwy ar y mawrion na'r gwerinos, ni welais i fawr un erioed am boddia i yn enwedig o uchel radd. 'Tis a great gift of Providence that the more we see of the world, the worst every honest considerate man must like it, felly mae'n rhybudd da i ni ymorol am well trigianle, the bulk of mankind is compos'd of knaves, fools, and now and then by meer chance an honest fellow, but they are cursed scarce in these parts ysywaeth. I'll send you 2d edit. of Mr. Ellis's works by the first opportunity, mae'r gwr yn achwyn yn erchyll arnoch am naccau ei atteb, da iwch ei fod ymhell oddiwrthych obleit pry ffyrnig yw! Aie Saint yw Sion Westley? Mi glywais ei frawd yn pregethu yma dydd arall yn nrŵs ty tafarn, naill yr oedd o wedi ynfydu neu yn tybio fod eraill felly, tebyg i un yn pregethu'r Efengil i fagad o baganiaid digred, diwybodaeth. Fortunatus is a letter in my debt, felly ni cheiff linell gennyf i nes cael o honnwyf atteb, tho' if I had leisure I would perhaps scribble him one sheet of paper. Dynan mwyn gonest rwy'n llwyr gredu, oni newidiwyd ef. Mi glywais yr hen wragedd yn dywedyd y newidir pob llwdn dyn unwaith yn y saith mlynedd. Beth meddwch chwi? Roeddwn yn

W. to R. contd. meddwl yr ai wyliai'r Nadolig i wyl Fair, ond ni thybiais i y cyrhaeddant i haner y Gwanwyn! Ail yw'r beiblau Cymraeg i ryfelwyr ym'rhodreth Russia, nid hwyrach mae at yr un amser y cychwynant. Aie ni fynnwchi mor wenwisg? Byddwch chwitheu yn wr llwyd ynteu, na choeliai mo'ch Cymry Seisnigaidd, ond esmwyth gwaith gwrando. Aie mae Zachariah yn gaddaw i chwi waith, goreu oll, gwell ymhel ai fath nag Arglwyddi gwylltion, diolch am ei hanes. Ar fendi mae'n ddrwg gennyf glywed fod y Sgwier Jones yn sal, gresyn ei golli ag mor gymwynasgar ydyw. Ow ai nid oes yna neb yn physygwr a feidr iachau'r Bfb, ah? Nid hwyrach pei bu'se yn Llanbabo y rhoese ryw hen wrechyn doppyn ynthaw, os marw y tro yma a wna hawddamor iddaw, mi awn i gyd ar fyrder ar ei ol (os ar ei ol y byddwn, chwedl y dyn wrth ganu gwirod *mi ganaf ar dy ol, os ar dy ol y byddaf*), nid oedd y cantor ddim yn sicr na ddigwyddai iddo fynd nôt oi flaen wrth diwnio. Rwyn deall wrth y brawd Llewelyn ddarfod ir Gorbedyn wneuthur cast cna ag ef, fe fydd yna o hyn ir Nadolig, yno cewch glywed yr hanes o bant i bentan. Mae'r ddau wr yn ffrindiau mawr or dannedd allan, ag felly nid oes ond ymddwyn felly os trewch wrtho ar dro. O. P. is still a partner with Corbett, ag rwyn deall yn rhy feddal i drin y fath but this inter nos, na soniwch un gair wrtho na drwg na da bid rhwng y din ar wialen. I have a letter from the Alderman the last post and I think to write to him by this, but query whether I can compass it. As for the expenses of this or that year, I never trouble my head about it. I know nothing of the Machine of State, let the managers take care how they act, they are to answer to God and their country, what signifies my being anxious about affairs I can't alter in the least (without my prayers may effect them). I always thought Walpole a frail mortal, felly y bydd y rhai a ddel ar ei ol. Seldom comes a better, medd yr hen ddihareb, and very lively it holds true at this time o' day. I hear nothing as yet from Sion Prisiart's brother, when I do, will let you know. Dyma'r brawd Owain newydd ddyfod adref or Deheu wedi bod yn anfon ei fab at y brawd Llewelyn, pawb yno yn iach, ynhad a mam yn abl afiachus, Duw ai helpio, pwys henaint a dled, ag afiechyd, pob un or tri yn rhy drwm ei oddef. Daccw'r cefnder Ioan Salbri newydd gladdu merch dan ddwy flwydd oed, a dyma ei dad ynghyfraith wedi bod yn yr Iwerddon yn derbyn i Sion scutoriaeth oddiwrth ewythr y wraig, £50 digon o le yw roddi, dlêd fawr! Mae'n rhaid imi roddi ngherdd yn fy nghôd heno, felly nos dawch a Duw a fo yn noddwr i chwi ar eiddoch, felly y gweddia. W. to R. contd.

Eich caredigawl frawd, William Morris.

Two boatmen are appointed to succeed the two turn'd out, one of the new ones is Lewis ap William Morris, ein cefnder, who had given Sir Nicholas his vote last election, and they've had their commissions, etc. I mean the new boatmen. Digrif fydde i chwi deimlo pulse Mr. Wynne, os digwydd i chwi ei weled ag ymddiddan ag ef. I have writ by this post to Mr. Prichard with one inclos'd for Mr. Brereton to be delivered him if there be occasion. I have desired Mr. Prichard to wait on Mr. James Clark in the Secretary's office, who, perhaps will let him into the secret, i.e. whether these fellows can do us any harm, for they will swear anything right or wrong. Mr. Woods if he was acquainted with their character might do wonders. Nawdd bomond i grybwyll! The whole sum and substance of the affair is this that the collector, surveyor and myself (nid er dywedyd o honwyf i) are a set of careful, diligent, sober officers, and the persons who accused us of conniving and everything that's bad are a set of malicious, wicked, troublesome (drunken one of 'em even to stupidity) sad dogs as ever was p—d upon, and we apprehend they are backed by the great, abetted by the most abandoned vilain that perhaps crawls upon the face of the earth, but he fights in close quarters. Hu Lloyd, alias Thomas Jones, alias William Roberts, alias Hu Roberts, alias Charles Macartney, alias John Gledstan, alias Walter Symond, etc., this fellow was discharged years agoe for the blackest of crimes, from being collector here, and since turned out of the customs, being unknown to the Board, a coast-waiter, ordered also out of the Salt whom I succeed, a hyny sy'n llosci ar ei galon.

CAER GYBI, 5ed Rhagfyr, 1747. W. to R. LXXIV.

Anwyl frawd,—Gan na welaf ddim atteb yn dyfod oddiwrthych im llythyr diweddaf, a chan im fod eusioes yn sgrifennu at yr Aldermon Prisiart, ni fedrwn lai na'ch cyfarch. Dyma lythyr oddiwrth y gwr hwnnw yn dywedyd eich bod yn iach ddianaf, mawl i Dduw am

W. to R. contd. bob newydd da. 'Rym ni yma oll yn rhesymol yr awron, ond nid oes neb ond yr Hollwybodawl a wyr pa hyd y byddwn felly. Mae'r wraig eiddwyf fi ar chwaer Ellin yn disgwyl beunydd fyned ir gwellt, roedd pob un o naddynt yn tybied y b'ase bob peth drosawdd cyn hyn, ond nid felly y digwyddodd.

Mae y nhad yn abl salaidd er's dyddiau gan ryw ddolur yn ei frest, digon tebyg mae rhyw 'nafad sydd oddimewn iddo, mae mam yn fynych yn llaccaidd, Duw a helpo yr hen bobl, yr amseroedd yn galed a phob peth yn ei crugo. Ni chlywais ddim or Deheudir er's agos i fis, nis gwn i a gychwynnodd y gwr ai ferched, etc., tua'ch dinas chwi bellach. I find by Mr. Prichard's letter that the Commissioners have not perused the Holyhead Examinations, etc., surely they must have read the Surveyor General's report. If so, I imagine, as all are silent, we shall hear no more on't, be it as it will we have nothing to fear unless our accusers are strongly back'd, if so, adieu justice. I was loath to rob you of so much time (and you not being well), by desiring you to wait of Mr. James at the Secretary's office, I thought Mr. Prichard had more time upon his hands. Mae'n wych gennyf glywed drwy lythyr yr Aldromon eich bod ar y ffordd i fod yn gefn dyn, Duw a wnêl hynny, nid oes ammeu na bo llawer blwyddyn ddedwydd yn ol i chwi etto, diboen i ddyn, dybiaw 'n dda. Ai nid oedd eich gwraig chwitheu yn son am ddyfod ar ei gwely? Pwy a welais i yn y fangre yma heddy ond W. Roberts or Ddrydwy, ni wyddwn i pryd hynny mae efe ydoedd, fo weddai ei fod ymma er's deuddydd neu dri yn termio efo Hughes or Neuaidd, one of the idlest fellows in the country. Roberts came hither to procure a licence to marry his or his mama's maid, and this morn word was brought him that she is brought to bed, mae'n debyg mae gwr yw wedi prisio ei râs. Mae'r Arglwydd Pwtt yna er's dyddiau, ai tybed y cewch ddim daioni ganddo y trô yma. Ce's lythyr oddiwrtho o gwmpas wythnos cyn ei gychwyn, yn dymuno arnaf gasglu iddo fwsoglydd a gwmonydd, mi attebais iddo nad oeddwn yn cael mor amser, ag felly nid oeddwn. Mae lle i ofni y try'r gŵr allan yn Virtuoso mawr; realy his sister is an ingenious curious lady. I ba beth yr af ir drafferth i ddywedyd chwaneg o wansens felly nos da fo i chwi ar eiddych, a Duw a fo yn gynhaliwr i chwi oll

Wyf eich caredigawl frawd William Morris.

Dear Brother,—I have yours of the 27th-28th ultimo, a chan diolch am dano. Ond cyn im daro atti yw atteb mae'n rhaid imi ddywedyd i chwi ein hanes. Ddydd Calan y ganwyd i mi fab, yr hwn a fedyddied y dydd arall a'i enw yw William. Mae ei fam ag ynteu (i'r Goruchaf y byddo'r diolch) ar y ffordd i ddyfod drwy'r afael yn dda iawn. A'r ail nos sef y 3dd y ganed i'r chwaer Ellin fab, a doe y bedyddiasom ef a rhoddasom Forus arno. Mae nhwytha, mawl i Dduw, yn ddigon da yn ol yr achos, a chwedl chwitheu am y *lotteri*, these affairs are finished or I should have had time to answer you. Now for't. Oni wyddoch i y bydd raid i'r gwragedd gael eu ffyrdd eu hunain y rhan fynychaf? Ag yr oedd rhaid cael William pa beth bynnag a fae. Yr enw ffeindia yn y byd meddan 'hw! Ewyllys y mam ydoedd cael Morris, ag yr oedd raid i'r hen wreigan gael ei bodloni, ag felly lle da oedd i chwi ddisgwyl na Llewelyn na Brychwel. Aie ni fydd yna yr un ond hynny? Pa beth a wyddoch i nad eill rhywbeth ddigwydd.

Ces lythyr oddiwrth yr Alderman ar ei ddyfodiad adre, ie, gogr rhŵyll yw'r gwr. Buan y daethoch iw adnabod. I'me sorry that poor Mr. Wright's affair is in such bad plight. Rhaid iddo ymroi i aros yn *Italy* rhagllaw, mae'n debygol. Gwr go anwybodawl yw'r Baynter. Bu ymma yn hir yn gla' a minnau yn ei *dendio* gin fynyched ag a allwn, ag yr oedd yn cymeryd arno fod yn dra diolchgar, ag yr 'sgrifenai attaf, etc. Ond i dd—l damaid ni chlywais gymaint a son am dano er hynny hyd yr awron, ond prin iawn, ffei o'r fath. Rwyn ofni fod Edward Edwards wedi mynd ynteu yn walch di ddaioni. He uses his poor sister ill in not writing to her, and she is so foolish as to be doating fond of him and fretts herself to pieces. Ni thal o i son am dano.

You were mistaken as to the papers which I mentioned. They were the Surveyor General's charges and our answers thereto. Likewise the examinations upon 'em, and the Surveyor General's Report of the whole. A few days ago we had the Commissioners' directions upon the said Report, for their Honours or their Secretary never did nor ever will peruse the charges, answers or examinations (which lasted about 11 days), so they lumped the whole, and all ended in this, that the Surveyor and boatmen were to

W. to R. contd. pay duty for 20 gallons of French wine, which the two informers said had been left on board at 4 different times: some of it in 1744. The Surveyor to pay a moiety which comes to about 48s., too great a sum for him to pay in the circumstances he is in, and this perhaps for an article that never was in being ; but this is owing to Nicholson's misrepresentations. The Surveyor and myself were blamed for suffering a gentleman's baggage to be examined at a public house. I presume they meant the collector and my self, who had suffered the Marquis of Rockingham's agent to bring his luggage to an inn and there examined by the Collector and Surveyor. We were ordered to be good boys for the future ag onite. But what signifies all this, as long as these villains are unhanged, we expect no quietness provided they are heard by the Surveyor General and the Board. The former is still plaguing us upon pretended informations from said . . . . seals. Mêl ar ei fysedd ef yw'r fath beth. If we find any fresh disturbance breaking out that has a bad aspect with it, we must trouble you. The Surveyor thinks of petitioning the Board to have the duty of the wine returned him. When brother Lewis comes to town, I mean your city, we'll bestirr in't for he knows the nature of the Surveyor's Office and the grievance. I'll send you the 2nd edition of Dr. Ellis on Methodism by the first opportunity. He is glad to hear that you intend him a letter. Mae'n debyg mae gwell i chwi beidio a mynd yn gyfoethawg, oni bae hynny buase Rhagluniaeth yn eich gwneuthur felly, ag felly ni welai i y gwiw gwingaw yn erbyn symbylau. Hope is an excellent antidote against despair. Deliwch afael ynddi yn ddiffael.

How came you to declare war in France against the Dutch, that *innocent Republic* chwedl nhw hunain? Ni welai i ddim o'r fath beth yn y papurau. Da bod eich hen gyfaill Pabo wedi mendiaw. Aie mewn yspytty mae Dafis. Par syt y cadd o yno? Mae Salbri yn ymwino a'r byd ag yn grwgnach arno'n greulon. Roedd iach dydd arall. I've seen Jones the architect here, and his works. Na, welai i ddim o frawd Sion Prissiart. A fynnwch i imi yrru'r nôt yn ôl? Mi fynaf ymofyn ynghylch y Geynton ryw dro. Digrif fydde gweled llyfr Garta, you promised me a specimen some time agone. Aie celwydd i gyd a ddywaid Sieffrai o Fynwy? Ow, ai nid oes dim gwir a berthyn iddo? A dark affair, Llywelyn Ddu is a great advocate for Geff. Bid rhyngochi a'ch gilydd. Rhyfedd na tase'r Derwyddon yn medru darllain, etc., pa beth a ddywaid Cesar yn ei *Gomentaries?* Carte's refusing to let you correct his British is an instance of his being a conceited fellow, ag o'r achos hwnnw yn ŵr anweddus iawn, debygwn i, i rodio yn y tywyll ymhlith boncyffion, lle byddai sicr bob yn awr o dorri ei grimogau oni bae gael gan eraill ei hyfforddio. Ffei hono. Aie mae clod fawr i Lewelyn. Ni fase waeth ganddo hebddi na'i chael debygwn i. You'll forgive Dick Morris's indiscreet behaviour, *ignorance* ai parai. He's a poor helpless mortal. Ni bu monwyf tua Bodorgan er's talm mawr o amser, nag yn wir yn un lle arall o'r fan yma. Mae ganddoch i ormod o drafferth ar eich dwylo y rhan fynychaf, a minnau rhy fychan. Mae'r fangre yma wedi mynd i'w chrogi: dim ond tlodi ymhob congl. Duw a wellhao'r amserau ag a'n gwnelo oll yn hapus pan elom oddiyma tua draw i'r dyffryn. We all join in love to you and yours. W. to R. contd.

I am your affectionate brother, William Morris.

CAER GYBI, 24 Chwefror, 1747. W. to R. LXXVI.

Anwyl Frawd,—Mae ennyd fawr o amser wedi mynd heibio er pan attebais i'ch llythyr diwedda', deg i un y ba'swn yn eich cyfarch yr awron oni bae fy mod yn sgrifennu eusioes at yr Aldramon. My last gave you an account of our increase, the young ones were for some time out of order, but are now in a fair way of keeping up the number. Bum ddechreu'r mis hwn yn edrych am ein mam yr hon ydoedd agos ar drancedigaeth. She was ta'en ill with the ague, and drove it off, then had a fever, but God be prais'd she is pretty well recover'd. My father has been much indisposd for these 3 weeks past with the reigning cold (which carries off a great many in this island), but Thomas ap William Owen Pyrs, Glochydd, was here yesterday, says that he now begins to recover a little. Yesterday was buried at Amlwch gweddw Ifan Bedlar, the son is with you. Ni chlywais ddim or Deheudir er's talm o amser, 'roeddwn yn meddwl y base'r brawd yma cyn hyn, ni wyr dyn i ba lê i sgrifenu atto yn iawn. Ffei, ffei, na bae fodd i weled llyfr y Garte yna, mi wela'r papurau yn ei rostio am ei goel grefydd ag nid heb achos rwy'n tybied. Gyrrais i chwi yr ail argraphiad o lyfr y Berson efo gwas Counsellor Meyrick. Dyna'r Counsellor Bwclai ynteu yn

W. to R. contd.

eich plith, dynan mwyn. Gorchmynwch fi atto, bu agos yw fab a marw yn gelain. Dywedwch wrtho am fod yn siwr o ddyfod a rhai hadau gerddi gwychion oddiyna, chwi fyddech chwitheu arfer er's talm o yrry i ddyn gardawd ambell dro. I wish the Alderman and Counsellors may be able to do poor Captain Wright any service. I understand that he is in bad bread, though his ships are successful. Roedd teulu Bodorgan yn iach ddoe, gwelais un oddiyno. Gadewch glywed oddiwrthych gynta galloch, mae yma bawb yn gorchymun attoch chwi ar eiddych wyf.

Eich caredigawl frawd, William Morris.

P.S.—I met John Prichard's brother the other day when I was at Dulas, he told me plain down right that he could not then pay his brother's bill, nor could he tell when he would be able, as there was no prices for cattle. We have no further account of our late informers, perhaps they are silenced. Goreu oll meddwch chwitheu.

W. to R. LXXVII.

HOLYHEAD, 31st March, 1847.

Dear Brother,—I received your letters of the 19th and 26th inst, ag i ddywedyd y gwir, gwnaeth y diweddaf imi wylo y dagrau halltaf yn fy nghalon, o wir lawenydd weled eich bod o'r diwedd wedi cael gafael ar rywbeth conffyrddus. Duw a'n gwnelo oll yn ddiolchgar. Roedd gennyf burion gobaith pan ganfyddais yn eich llythyr cyntaf, fod y Bedyn yn gaddaw o hono ei hun wneuthur erddoch. Rhaid i Lywelyn bellach faddeu iddaw. Bellach am atteb i'r llythyr cynta'. Of the two lads you wished us joy of, one is dead, viz. Morris Owen, gorwyr hwnnw o Fodafon gynt. My boy had been a long time a lingering, but begins to come on apace. I much pity poor 'Natus. Dyn gonest ydoedd gynt. I long to hear how his affair is determined. Gresyn fydde ei libindio i fwrdd Man of Warr a'i gludo a'i helcid adre heb yn ddiolch iddaw. Mae arnaf ofn mae gŵr go annaturiol yw'r Ned Edwards, ag ni waeth i'w chwaer ymhle y byddo. Mae'n debyg ei briodi yn Boston efo rhyw hogan. He was a good natured boy, and very dutiful to his parent, ond fe aeth llygoden gôch drostaw. Rwy'n meddwl fod yn gystal gan ei chwaer ef ai gwr ei hun! Gobeithio na bydd arnoch bellach mor caledwaith. Mae'n debyg mae rhyw oriau penodol sydd yn eich *offis* chwi fal yn y dollfa, o 9 i 12 ag o un i bedwar y byddwn i yn trin y dreth; mae'r relyw o'r amser inni to manage the other affairs of life. Bydd tra da gennyf gael gennych gyflawn hanes o natur eich swydd o ben bwygilydd. Mi roddaf hwn mewn ffrencyn o achos nis gwn ai gweddus imi ddwedyd *clerk* ar ei gefn, ag nid hwyrach heb hynny mae'n gost yr â. The clerks in the Customs House, London, send their letters free of charge to the persons sent (i.e. post paid and allow'd 'em). Mae'n debyg fod hynny gida chwithau. Aie fe aeth y Beibl i ben? Mawl i Dduw a roddes hoedl ag iechyd i chwi fynd drwy'r gwaith, gan ei fod mor bwysfawr. Gresyn fase ei adael yn anorphen, ag iddo syrthio i ddwylo anghelfydd. Mae arnaf flys ei weled. Aeth llawer pen dan bridd a fase hoff ganddynt hynny. Ni wela ddim hanes o frawd John Prichard yn dyfod i hebrwng yr arian. Pan ddel cewch glywed. Ai £11 9s. 6c. ydynt? Rhyfedd na bu'sent yn gweled y Gownsler Meyrig ar hyd yr amser. Gwr o'r mwyna, ond ei fod fal dadi yn wr mwyn galed. Ni bydd neb llyfn heb ei anaf. Nis gwn i par un ai coelio ai anghoelio Carte a wneir ynghylch y Derwyddon, matter tywyll anial. Rhyfedd na base fwy o sgrifenadau ar gerrig ym Môn, os oeddynt wyr lytherennawg. But Carte's explaining away Caesar's meaning is ridiculous I think. He must advance something new, otherwise his history would not go down with many. It would take too much time to write out sufficient direction to learn Auley Mc Auley's characters as I imagine. I make use of Weston's most days of my life, setting down daily occurrences and trifles not worth any other person's perusal but myself. **W. to R. contd.**

Aie mae Mr. William Wynne yn Berson? Ydi vickeriaith Llanbrynmair yn ei law hefyd? Ni ches i erioed mor anrhydedd o adwaen y mwynwr o'r Gors. Gresyn yw. Gorchymynwch fi at y Cardinal. Na, phriodws Roberts ddim. He leads, as I'me told, the most dissolute life of any man in the county. Has ruined his poor mother, who was a charitable good woman, ffei leidr. Aie mae'n eich bryd efo'r hen ustus Pabo daro F.R.S. wrth enw Llewelyn? Mi glywais ryw son am hynny. Ces lythyr oddiwrthaw dydd arall. Gwmpas canol y mis nesaf roedd yn tybio y bydda yn cychwyn tua'ch dinas. I am glad Wheldon Jones does well. Pray return my compliments to him. His mother, etc., are well. Fe ddylae sgrifennu yn fynychach at ei fammi. Hi fu dda wrtho yn ol ei gallu. Nis gwn i par sut sydd ar y byd ffordd yna.

W. to R. contd.

Yn ddiamai mae'n myned yn waeth waeth beunydd yn y cyrrau ymma. The late conflagration with you was shocking. Mawl i Dduw eich bod chwi yn digwydd bod ar eiddoch yn gadwedig rhagddo. Duw a'n cadwo i gyd rhag y fath artaith os gwel yn dda. Father and mother were pretty well in health the other day. Haint y marchogion sy'n blino nhad yn fynych. Rwyn ei ddisgwyl ffordd yma beunydd i'n hymweled. Pan fo'r hên ŵr yn ei lawn iechyd, fe a gerdd ag a ferchyg yn well na chwi na minneu, ond er hynny mae henaint ai gymdeithion yn fynych iawn yn groesion ag yn fryntion. Fe wna'r newydd eich bod wedi newid eich cyflwr at y goreu adnewyddu ieuengctyd yr hen bobl. Gorchmynwch fi at yr Aldremon a'r cyfreithiwr Bwlclai. Duw Goruchaf a roddo i chwi râs ag iechyd i fwynhau eich lle newydd, ag a'ch cadwo chwi a'r eiddoch rhag pob drwg. Felly y gweddia

Eich caredigawl frawd, William Morris.

P.S. Mae yma bawb a'ch câr yn gorchymun attoch ag yn erchi ar Dduw eich llwyddo. Amen. Dyma ddrull o bapur a yrrodd Mr. Ellis. Ni chaf mo'r amser yw sgrifennu gan fy mod ar frys mawr anferth.

W. to R.
LXXVIII.

CAER GYBI, 15 Mai, 1748.

Anwyl Frawd Rhisiart,—Dyma fi yn amcanu atteb eich llythyr or 30 ultimo. Ni fydda'i yn gadael iddynt fynd yn fis oed cyn ei cyweiro ai nodi rhag iddynt fynd ar gyfrgoll, etc. Gerwin yw'r orriau a'r dyddiau sydd yn digwydd ich rhan. Fe feddyliai bobl Môn mae gwŷr o gred y Presbiteriaid yw'ch pennaethiaid. Gweithio ȧr yr ŵyl, na bo mo'nd i grybwyll! Nhw fyddant ei hunain yn cael chwareu yr amser hwnnw mae'n debyg. Da yw eich bod yn gallu cwmpasu peth or hên orchwylion heblaw'r swydd newydd, Duw a ddel ar pelydr rheini nes nes ag i ddisgleirio yn amlygcach arnoch i yrru ymaith niwl a tharth pob tramgwyddiadau, pethau echrys mewn teulu yn enwedig un lle. Diolch yn fawr am y newydd da ynghylch fy hen gydymaith Captain Fortunatus Wright; fortunate indeed! Dyna ddyn wedi eu eni dan *flaened ddedwydd*, chwedl yr hen wrachods. Fe fu yn hir yn anffortunus o achos ei wiriondeb ei hun gan mwyaf. Aie rhyw waith anorffen a rodded ich rhan chwi? Ni chlywsom ni erioed son am Gomissioner Russel; yn y ne' mae enaid, chwedl yr hen Râs Williams, or

Mynydd gynt. Gwiliwch i foddio'r Duc Bedford yn rhy-fawr rhag iddo eich gwneuthur yn arglwydd. Yn wir ddiau mae cerdded gormodd yn ddigon er crugo y neb a fynnoch a fae'n dwyn blonhegen rhwydd dew, —— ach cadwo efo'ch *seat*, nid oes ammeu nad ych yn ŵr mawr anfeidrawl! Gwych yw clywed fod y Biblau wedi eu gorphen o'r diwedd. Mae ar Mr. Ellis a minneu flŷs mawr am gael eu gweled, it seems he is entitled to some of 'em. I should be glad of one with paying for't, but the case is this: if there was a possibility of having three or four of 'em down in sheets we might have 'em bound by a friend in a better manner than the common run, *i.e.*, than what the rest are done at London, and sooner. I presume the whole must be bound before any are deliverd. Gadewch wybod pa beth a wneir yn y matter yma. Brother Lewis by ymrwbiaw yn y gwyr mawrion yna wedi mynd i sgrifenu llythyrau byrrion anial, heb ddim o hanes y byd a'r amseroedd ynddynt, a chwitheu or llaw arall yn rhy drafferthus, felly yn iach ymenyn glan. Rwyn deall fod y Bedyn yn gawr ai frawd Tomos nis gad iddaw. Hoedl hir iddynt, os hynny sydd oreu, ond nis gwn i. Chwi ellwch feddwl y bydd hoff iawn gennyf glywed oddiwrthych fynycha'r y galloch, pe bae ond dwy lein neu dair i ddangos bod einioes. Mae pawb yma yn rhwydd iachus, y plantos yn gridwst mwya. W. to R. contd.

I am, your affectionate loving brother, William Morris.

If there were four bibles sent down in sheets for Mr. Ellis I might have one of 'em; he begs it as a favour of Mr. Broughton, he received the books, though rather too late, desires his compliments; anfeidrol frys.

HOLYHEAD, 2 June, 1748. W. to R. LXXIX.

Dear Brother,—Sgrifenais attoch er's dyddiau bwmp o lythyr ag yr wyf yn disgwyl atteb iddo beunydd, yr achos a bair imi yn awr eich cyfarch yw e'ch yspysu, ddarfod i frawd Sion Prisiart ab William Sion dalu i'm llaw echdoe ddeg punt. Rhoddes imi lythyr a gawsai oddiwrth Sion, dat. 18 ult., yn erchi iddo ddyfod ar deg punt yma ag i mineu roddi'r *Note* i fynu. Mae i hwn dalu hanner gini yw chwaer a 29s. 6c. iddo ynteu pan allo. Bid rhynddynt ai gilydd, brodyr ynt. Mi fynaf edrych allan am *London Bill* cyn gynted ag y medrwyf. I chwi ynteu iddo ef y gyrraf? Rhoddwch

W. to R. contd. linell gida dychweliad y post; os atto ef, a fydd yn ddigon ei lwybreiddio ich tŷ chwi for John Prichard. I writ lately to brother Lewis; ni che's yr un llythyr oddiwrtho er's deubost neu dri. Rhowch dipyn o'i hanes, mae ei lythyrau fo wedi mynd yn dra fyrrion. Pa beth sydd yn dyfod or 3 llythyr F.R.S.? Pa fodd yr ych yn leicio y teulu ieuainc yna, onid yw Sion yn herlod rhyfedd? 'Ry'ch i yn arwain pin sgrifennu buan, ni fyddech i dro yn rhoddi i ddynan foliaid o newyddion. Mae ngwraig a minneu yn eich annerch bod ag un, yr ym ni yma oll yn rhwydd iach. Byddwch wych, a Duw a fo'n gwarchad drosoch.

Eich caredigawl frawd, Wm. Morris.

P.S. Mae'r tywydd ffordd yna fal y byddai yn y dyddiau gynt yn mis Mawrth neu ddechreu Gwanwyn, gwynt a glaw a niwl oerllyd, dim tês! Mae gennyf yr ardd w'cha yn y Fro. Mae yn awr yn tyfu ynddi agos i bob llysieuyn syn hadu hâd (i.e.) pob un dieithrawl a godidawg, o'r *Rhodia Radix*, yr hwn a dyf ar ben y Wyddfa yn Arfon, hyd yn oed y *Pinguicula*, yr hwn a dyf ar Dywyn Tre Owein yn Mon! Ag hefyd goedydd a manwydd beth difesur! Och na bae ambell un cywraint gwybodawl yn dyfod yma ei gweled, ail yw i ganwyll dan lestr. Daccw'r brawd Owain ynteu yn s'fennu. W.M.

W. to R. LXXX.

HOLYHEAD, 7 July, 1748.

Dear Brother,—I have yours of the 11 ult. before me, a da gennym glywed eich bod oll yn rhwydd iachus. Ow, ai nid dim rhwydd-deb ir Beiblau, ynteu llygaid tynnu'r bobl a wnaethpwyd? Rwy'n ffaelio'n glir lan daro wrth fil dan law saff am arian Sion Prisiart ab William Sion; roeddwn yn disgwyl un gan Vickers yma, ond fe gadd arian am fil oedd fwy felly yn well at ei bwrpas. Mae'n debyg ddywedyd or brawd Llewelyn wrthych fy mod wedi petisiwno fy meistryd heilltion am fy nghyflog am harian a roddais allan drostynt y flwyddyn a aeth heibio. I expect an order to draw (upon their Honours) daily and then I can give you a bill on the Salt Board—mae'n debyg mae dyna'r ffordd mwya diogel ar gynta am a welafi. I agree with you that a certain father is rather too rigorous, pe ba'ent ddiriaidus peth arall fyddai, but they were otherwise, ie, bachgenyn rhyfedd yw Sionach. Ni welais i erioed mo ei ail am ddysgu; gwaed Pentre'rianell sydd yn rhedeg yn ei withi mae'n debyg. Nid yw'r brawd Llewelyn yn son dim am yr R.S. yn ddiweddar yma. Pa beth a ddaw or tair llythyren debygwch chwi? Rwy'n deall fod y gwr yn mynd i argraphu ei hen orchwyl, felly fe fydd eu heisiau'n erwin dost. Nis gwn i par sut y dygymydd Meirian a Môn wedi bod holl ddyddiau ei bywyd yn ninas Lundain, rhagor mawr rhwng bywoliaeth y naill fan a'r llall. Fe ffaeliodd genyf gael maint yn y byd o hanes y Robert Roberts hwn, nid o'r pentre yma nag or gymdogaeth yr oedd rwy'n mawr gredu, gofynnwch i Ddafis. Roedd y Gobed Lewis (at yr hwn y sgrifenasai'r brawd Llewelyn ynghylch Will Parry) yma'r dydd arall, roedd yn dywedyd iddo ymofyn ynghylch y matter. Roedd brodyr a chwiorydd Parry wedi rhoddi power ir Huws hwnnw yw derbyn, ag mae ynteu wedi eu rhannu rhyngddynt, digrif fydde wneuthur ir gwalch hwnw ei talu yn ol am fod mor rodresgar, chwi adwaenoch y cono mae'n debyg. Gresyn chwedl chwitheu, ydoedd claddu'r dynan cyn ei farw. Bu Ddic Morus yma'r dydd arall, mae'n dlawd anial; roedd yn crio dagrau heilltion wrth son am ei gyflwr. Rwyf mewn rhyw ffwdan yr awron fal na allaf s'fennu mwyach, felly Duw a fo'n gwarchad drosoch ar eiddych, 'rym oll yn eich hanerch. W. to R. contd.

Eich brawd anwiw, *Wm. Morris*.

LONDON, Sept. 20, 1748. (Charming weather). L. to W. LXXXI.

Dear Brother,—I have a long letter from you 'n achwyn, etc. Mr. Nichylson called here last night and staid with me till 10. He is doing as much as can be done with a Member of Parliament about your affair of ye Salt. You need not fear ye old man—you must write a letter to me to this effect to shew him. That B—o is a sad man for abusing his benefactor, and that M—n is a fool for being brought into his measures, that he is very sorry for what he hath done, and that he owns himself to blame for intermeddling with their disputes, etc. That Mr. N. hath been good to them all, and it is a shame they should endeavour to hurt him, with abundance of religious stuff, etc., and that you are afraid they'll hurt you too. Chwi enillwch galon yr hen wr, mae arno eich ofn chwi a phawb ond y fi. Enquire whether there be any kelp in your parts or Anglesey, and at what rate it can be sold. I can fix a trade here for ever, if it can be had in plenty. Let me know as soon as possible. Let me [know] also if Dick Siencyn fawr is alive, and it

L. to W. contd.

you can send me his dimensions I shall be glad. A man wants him here for a show. Nid oes possibl imi gael amser i ddwedyd i chwi hanes yn y byd am Lord Anson na neb. I have new acquaintances here daily, and am a great virtuoso among the greatest—15 of my plates are finished and more. Diolch am Arglwydd Castell Durrow, I'll go and see him. Stori yw'r cwbl am roi dan law am arian Sion Prisiart. Gwiliwch eich brawd Risiart. I cannot get my money out of his hands, though he hath now I dare say £150 a year. It all goes foolishly, y dyn meddala ar a welsoch i erioed! Gwirion, gwan, credulous and wants common cunning. Duw a helpo pob gwan, tebyg iawn i fy merched i ag i Sion Salbri ydyw—anifeiliaid rhywiog! Mae'n debyg mae gorau i chwi dynnu *power* imi yn hytrach ynghylch yr arian a soniasoch am danynt, canys nid eill ef wneuthur dim ond a wnelo drwy fy ffrinsip i gida'r Commissioner C— H—, ag ni feiddia'r clercod ymddangos yn y cyfryw beth eu hunain. Mi wnaf fy ngorau i Sion Huws . . . .

W. to R.
LXXXII.

CAER GYBI, 3d October, 1748.

Nos D. Llun o ddyddiau'r byd.

Anwyl Frawd,—Mewn difrif mae arnaf gywilydd anfeidrawl am imi esceuluso atteb 'ch llythyr diwaetha cyhyd. Mi fum allan o hyd yn y byd yn disgwyl taro wrth rywun a roddai i'm fil am arian Ioan ap Rhisiart, a ffaeliais yn y diwedd. Roeddwn yn hyderu y medrai'r brawd Llewelyn gael gan Gomisioners Halen £14 10s. oedd yn digwydd imi oddiwrthynt er y 25 o Fawrth, ond y mae'n debyg fod gormod o drafferthion gartref. Ddydd Sadwrn diweddaf y gwelsant yn dda rhoddi cennad imi dynny arnynt fil (30 days after date) gwyr mwynion iawn yn wir! I sent brother Lewis the bill to negociate and to pay Sion as soon as he can get the cash. A dyna i chwi'r hanes o bant i bentan. Bellach am y llythyr. Gwaed swllt! Dyma'r Berson Ellis wedi cael llonaid cist o'ch Beiblau. Mawl i Dduw am gael golwg maes arnynt! A dymma finneu wedi prynnu un o honynt tra bwy'n aros cael un heb ei gauadu. Cadd y Berson un heb ei wisco; drwy ffafr fawr mae wedi gyrru am 3 cistiaid etto, about 25 or 26 each, but query where he will have 'em. Yn wir ddyn, gwaith godidawg ydyw, chwi a ellwch chwi orwedd yn eich gwely bellach, gwyn eich byd! Ni bu erioed y fath daro yn Mon ar lyfrau, fo fu agos i boblach dynny llygaid Mr. Ellis am y rhain, nis gwn i par fyd a ddaw o honaw oni cheiff chwaneg. Gresyn na ba'sent yn rhôdd ac yn rhâd (chwedl Llewelyn) ir tlodion, ni bu'se'r cyfoethogion byth yn grwgnach talu am danynt. Yna ni a gawsem fappia'r brawd yw canlyn. Os y chwi neu fo a fedr gael un imi heb ei gauadu byddai ddigon hawdd ei yrru yma efo rhai'r Bersonyn os daw rhai iddo. Gan fy mod yn myned echdoe i ymweled a'r rhieni i gynal Gwylmabsant gida hwynt (y peth ni wnaethwn er's llawer blwyddyn hir), dygais y Beibl yn fy nghoden yw ddangos iddynt, ag nid difalch oedd ganddynt ei weled er bod y golygon yn rhy henaidd yw ddarllain yn iawn, rhaid a fu imi ei adael yno ar f'ol, i gael or hen wr ei ddangos yw ffrindiau ai gymdogion. Daeth y nhad a mam ar eu meirch efo mi ir Llan. Da iawn oedd eu gweled yn gallu gwneuthur hynny, pur fusgrell yw mam gan ryw ddolur a adawodd y *Ffever* yn ei haelodau yn enwedig un oi thraed. Nid oedd yno fawr or hen boblach gynt yn fywion, cenedl arall sydd yno yn awr ; the few remaining were Twm Rolant, Sion Bifan, Twm ab William Dafydd (dall fal ei dad), Hwmffri o Ddulas ai feib Rhobert a Harri, William Owen Pyrs, byth yn glochydd a chin sythed ar gorsen ag ymhell wedi 80, yn briod a Sian Sion Oylfer, Lewis Sion Oylfir—dyn croes cyfreithgar, Mrs. Williams o Fodafon, ag wyr gida hi agos cymaint a minneu, Twm Wiliam glochydd o Fryn Eithinog, Wiliam ap Huw Williams y seinar, Owain Wmffras, Sion Lewis or Gadlys a'i wraig Alis, ni welais i fawr neb arall or hen stondards, ŵyr i hwn a hwn fydde pawb agos, nid oedd rhyfedd i chwi a minneu frig lwydo. Ni chlywaf ddim son am yr F.R.S. y dyddiau yma. Pa beth yw'r matter? Wala, wala, dyma ryw rai yn dyfod am fy mhen, rhaid cadw noswyl am heno. W. to R. contd.

D. Iau y 6ed.—Mi welais eich llythyr Ymhentre'riannell a hanes e'ch bod yn fyw iach ar euddoch ; sgrifenwch fynycha a galloch at yr hen bobl, mae'n gymffwrdd iddynt glywed hanes pawb o honom. Hi wnaeth flwyddyn iawn dda oi tu y leni, prisiau digon da ar wartheg. I am glad you have an order from Arglwydd Pwtt for your money, better late than never. Nid hwyrach y medrwch roddi codwm ir gymdeithwraig yna sef Ffortun, ag wrth hynny gael ganddi fod yn dippyn mwynach wrthych o hyn allan. Mi fyddaf finneu yn lled ddig wrthi weithiau, pe bae fatter yn y peth. Daccw rai o deulu Bodorgan yn dyfod yna i fyw, nis gwyddis etto

W. to R. contd. a â'r hen wr ae peidiaw, mae ei frawd Iemwnt yn sal iawn. Mae'r brawd yna yn symud yn fynych iawn, ni wyr dyn i ble i gael monaw ond ambell dro, rwyn deall ei fod mewn ffafor fawr efo'r Arglwyddi ar bonheddigion yna,——'n geidwad! Sgrifenaf atto'r post nesa' a henwau subscribers. Par sutt y cadd Sion Fach afael ar eich llaw chwi? Rym ni yma oll (mawl ir Arglwydd) yn rhwydd iachus ag yn gorchymun attoch chwi ar eiddoch, er nad wyf yn haeddu llinell oddiwrthych yrhawg byd, etto er hyn i gyd rwy'n gobeitho'r sgrifennwch attaf o hyn i ben yr wythnos a hanes y byd ar amseroedd, ag yr wyf yn addaw ar fy ngair gwir y bydd fy nesaf yn fwy ystig na hwn. *Eich brawd caredigawl, Wm. Morris.*

P.S.—Cewch griticisms ar 'ch Bibl yn y nesaf os oes bai yw gael mewn ffordd yn y byd, mi fynnwn ddyfod i hyd iddo os yw bosibl. Mae'r Berson i'ch annerch.

W. to R. LXXXIII.

GARTREF, Gwyl Andreas, '49.

Anwyl Frawd,—Gan fod Llewelyn ein brawd yn bwgwth beunydd ymadaw a'ch dinas, mi yrrais hwn dan orchgudd atto chwi. Erdolwyn gyrrwch iddaw, os yw yna. Rwy' bob post yn disgwyl am globyn mawr o lythyr oddiwrthych, ond mae'n debyg nad ych yn cael mor amser gan enill arian. Gwyn eich byd. Cewch ein hanes gan y brawd, felly mi a derfynaf am y tro, oblegid bod yr amser yn fyr. Ein gorchymyn attoch a'r eiddoch.

Eich caredigawl frawd, Wm. Morris.

W. to R. LXXXIV.

CAER GYBI SAINT, Nos Calan, Rhagfyr, 1748.

Anwyl Frawd,—Dyma'ch llythyr or 25 yn gorwedd ger fy mron wedi hir ddisgwyl am tanaw. Nid oes yma fawr *Gritics* a dâl i son am danynt, mae'r Esgob Ellis yn ei dybied ei hun yn un o rhai penna o naddynt, ar pethau mwyaf sydd yn rhoddi llosc calon iddo fo, yw'r gair Salmau yn lle Psalmau, Beibl yn lle Bibl ambell dro, a dilyn gormod ar ol Moesen or Deheu, a rhyw fan droseddiadau, ag aml ffrigwd a fu rhyngom or achos, ond am y relyw or Gwyr Duon, ni chlywais i un o honynt yn rhyfygu beio. Ond er hynny i gyd mae'r Berson Ellis yn canmol y llyfr allan o bob rheswm, ag nid oes bregeth yw chael y dyddiau hyn heb son am danynt, a'u canmol a chanmol y gwyr mwynion ai bwriadodd iddynt hwy y tlodion, a'u cynhyrfu hwythau i weddio yn ddygn trostynt.

I am heartily glad that the Society has resolved to give 'em to the poor, according to the intention of the contributors to the charity. Cywilydd erchyll oedd eu gwerthu i'r tlodion. I am much obliged to you for your intended present, and as the Society pays for the binding, should be glad to have them in 2 volumes, viz., the Old Testament in one and the rest together, and numbered upon the back 1 and 2. I presume it would be too chargeable to letter 'em and gild the backs? Mr. Ellis has sent the one he had in sheets over to Dublin to be bound sumptuously, and to have some writing paper added at the beginning of each book of the Old and New Testaments: he has ordered 6 or 8 shillings to be bestow'd upon 'em. I was obliged to fold 'em lest Teague should blunder. I did design to go on much the same way had I got one in sheets, but since the Society will coat 'em, goreu fyth; os bydd modd i roddi dalen wen neu ddwy yn rhywle, fal y gallwyf gadw cyfrif or plant (oblegid y mae gobaith wmbwrdd o naddynt) da fydde. Rwy'n disgwyl y caf un yw roi lawr o gwmpas y Nadolig, Duw a fo i'n plith. Sister would have hers in one volume. You would win old Bodorgan's heart if you would send him one, he has one of Moses' handsomely gilt, etc. Chwi gewch sport yn cofftio *Rum-punch* pan ddel eich *venture* adref, gwiliwch frwysgaw. Duw a gadwo i chwi eich iechyd, ag ach gwnel yn ddiolchgar am y ffynniant a roddes ich matterion. Mi glywswn eich hanes gan y brawd Llewelyn. Nis gwn i par un or ddau ddwrn i ddewis, if the D— is a generous man, he bids fairest, otherwise gwell y sicrwydd yn yr offis. Duw hefyd ach cyfarwyddo chwi ir hyn a fo goreu ar eich lles. Amen. Aie mae 3 llythyren i fod ar ol yr henw, fe werth y llyfr yn well o lawer a chywreiniach fydd y gwaith yn marn y rhan fwya' or byd. Gresyn bod ein trysorwyr ni mor ddiog am dalu yr hyn sy' gyfion,—lle da disgwyl arian anghyfiawn gan y rheini. Bribery aud corruption must be banished in course, ni wiw i chwi son bellach am y fath beth. Matter tost a fase ir hen Frenhin golli ei fywyd ag Anson ynteu wedi amgylchu'r holl fyd, ni choeliai ei fod mewn cymaint perigl ag y buasai yn y *Centurion*, nid hwyrach mae anwir a ddywed ei siaplan. I find by the papers that the engagement in the West Indies was something of a piece

W. to R. contd.

W. to R. contd. with the rest of our modern proceedings. My wife joins with me in love to you and sister, wishing you health and happiness.

I am, your affectionate brother, Wm. Morris.

P.S.—If your daughter is wild, I have a son that will match her,—y llanc dirieitta or faint Ynghymru.

W. to R. LXXXV.

HOLYHEAD, 20 February, 1748.

Dear Brother,—Mae llawer o amser wedi myned heibio er pan sgrifenais llythyr attoch, dan obaith cael atteb oddiwrthych ag ychydigin o hanes par helynt sydd arnoch, ond ni welai fawr obaith, felly dyma attoch unwaith etto. Byddaf yn cael llythyr ambell dro oddiwrth y brawd Llewelyn ond y mae'r gwr hwnnw, ynteu naill ai cymaint ei drafferth neu ddiogi, na sgrifena'r unwaith oddiar ddwy linell neu dair, a phrin y cair ganddaw dippyn oi hanes ei hun, chwaethach crybwyll am neb arall. Gwyr mawrion sydd yn eich llygru! Nid hwyrach na bydd waeth gennych er clywed par fyd sydd arnom yn hen Ynys Fon. Nid oes i chwi le i ddisgwyl newyddion mawr yn y byd or fath le anghysbell, oddigerth marw o un a geni un arall ar cyffelyb. Dyna'r 'smonaeth sydd yma gan eich brawd Gwilym, claddu'r dydd arall globyn o fachgenyn, sef oedd hwnnw fy ieuaf, ag wythnos i heddyw geni pwmpog o herlodes yn ei le. Ni cheir yma roddi 'run henwau Cymroaeg ar blantos, felly Sian y galwyd hi. Claddu echdoe ei hen nain, sef oedd hono hitheu Sian, wedi iddi fendithio ei gorwyras, a hi yn 85 o oedran ai holl synhwyrau ganddi hyd y dydd diweddaf. Bu 'r gyfnither Margaret, merch Elsbeth, merch Risiart Morus, yma o Bentre'rianell; roedd ein rhieni yn rhwydd iachus ganol yr wythnos ddiweddaf. Ymhle mae'r Biblau ar oeddych yn ei addaw i boblach? Mae yma yr hen ddisgwyl am danynt. Mae'r Bersonyn yma yn ffaelio cael gwybod par bryd y daw chwaneg o honynt ir wlad. Ai cysgu mae'r rheolwyr yna? Pa fodd yr ychi y dinasyddion yn archwaethu'r heddwch a gyhoedded yn eich plith chwi yn ddiweddar? A beru o yn hir meddwch chwi, ynteu un byr oesawg yw? T'rewch ddiogi yn ei dalcen a diwynnwch un llen o bappir ar hanesion, etc., sydd yn eich plith, ni thal y newyddion argraphedig yw darllain. A fu ddim chwaneg o ymgomio rhyngoch ar D— o Fedfordd? Ai gwell gennych aros yna mewn difrif? Wrth son am leoedd daccw'r hen William Lhwyd, o Dre'sgawen, wedi cael ei droi allan oi le neu ei swydd o fod yn *Foatman* Ynghaernarvon, a dyma fo wedi gyrru brief attaf am gymorth swyddogion. *His case is a very cruel one*, mae'r byd fal cynt, nid oes ond *y trecha treisied ar gwannaf gwaedded*, nawdd Duw rhag meibion dynion. Ni weled yn yr oes hon mor fath ddryghin a gwlybaniaeth ag a gawsom er calan gauaf hyd o fewn ychydig ddyddiau yma,—wmbwrdd o golledion ar for a thir. Mae gwyr y glennydd wedi ymgyfoethogi yn odiaethol, a minneu'r eulyn amral agos wedi torri ar fy nhraws yn ymwino a nhw am ran, ond ni ches i ond megys *rhan y gwas o gig yr iar* er maint fy nhrafferth. Dedwydd yw'r sawl sydd ganddaw fodd i gael tamaid a llymaid a thipyn am ei gefn heb orfod arno ymhel a lladron a gwilliaid moroedd a thiroedd. Son a wna'n nhw am Iddewon a Thyrciaid, mae ffordd yma genedl (ai geilw eu hunain yn Gristionogion), sydd gan gwaeth na nhw. Par ddelw sydd ar boblach ffordd yna, ydynhw ddim gwell na rhain debygachi? Mi wranta eich bod wedi blinaw wrth ddarllen gwansens, felly o wir resyndod drosoch, mi a roddaf fy ngherdd yn fy nghod, ond nid cyn imi draethu i chwi fod y wraig yma a mineu yn gorchymun attoch chwi ar chwaer a Meirian ag yn erchi ar y Goruchaf Dduw warchad drosoch bod ag un. Byddwch wych. *Eich caredigawl frawd, Wm. Morris.* W. to R. contd.

P.S.—Pray let me have a line from you as soon as you can, I hope I shall have a letter to-morrow from brother Llewelyn with an account of his daughter Margett's recovery.

CAER GYBI, 12d Ebrill, 1749. W. to R. LXXXVI.

Anwyl Frawd,—Derbyniais eich llythyr or 7d o Fawrth advising you had sent the box with Bibles, etc., last Saturday. Father brought the Bible (and tea) here last Saturday, ag yn wir ddiau tlysau gwerthfawr y'nt, mawl i'r Goruchaf Dduw am danynt a chan diolch ir rhoddwr. I've seen the Society's printed resolution, dynion trwyddyn' y'nt bod y pen. Gwych y llaw oedd eich pen clark yn ei wneuthur o honi yn amser rhyfel, rwy'n deall na waeth gennych am yr heddwch brwnt yma. Dyna fal y mae, pawb drosto ei hun, etc. Mi wela fod y brawd Llewelyn yn ddrwg ei ystum yn ddiweddar, da oedd iddo gael ei einioes er mwyn llawer heblaw'r brawdgarwch, mae o'n ddiog erchyll am yrru ei lyfrau allan, mae llawer o waeddi am danynt. Father and mother are, God be prais'd, in pretty good

W. to R. contd.

health. You would be surprizd to see the old man, sioncach ar gefn march nai fab Gwilym, ag ond odid na 'run oi feib fal y mae mwya'r gwarth, y mam hitheu yn rhwydd iachus ond ei bod yn gloff anial, ni welais mor hen wreigan er Gwyl Penrhos. Father designs to be at Bodorgan with the Bible on Saturday next, when I propose to meet him, i gael tippyn o ymgom efo'r hen Fodorgan ynghylch y byd ar amseroedd. Rwy'n drafferthus iawn finneu y dyddiau hyn rhwng gwasanaethu ei Fawrhydi a gosod fy ngardd mewn trefn, hau, plannu, impio, etc. Leiciwn i ddiniweidrwydd or fath hynny pe bae ond digon o fwnws yn dyfod i mewn. Rhywogaeth Morus Owen o Fodafon ar llafurwyr rheini sydd drecha mae'n debyg. Y ty hwnnw a gedwir gan fy mam ynghyfraith hyd na chaffo denant wrth ei bodd ai cymero; ie'r goreu yn y dre ydyw yn sicr hyd yn hyn. Mae fy nheulu i ar euddo fy chwaer, mawl i Dduw, yn rhwydd iachus, ag yr ym oll yn gorchymun attoch chwi a phawb o'ch tylwyth. Duw a fyddo yn noddwr i chwi, byddwch wych. *Eich brawd caredigawl, Wm. Morris.*

P.S.—Mae yma englynion a wnaed ir Bibl ond ni cheir mor amser y tro yma i yrru monynt. Er bod y car Sion Salbri ai wraig ai dad ynghyfraith yn gleifion drwy'r cynhauaf ar gauaf diweddaf, etto mi glywaf fod un o honynt yn feichiog, dyfalwch par un. Moeswch dippyn o hanes y brawd ai deulu, ni cheir ganddo ond rhyw lythyrau byrrion anial, a thippyn och helynt 'ch hun, a natur 'ch swydd. Adieu.

W. to R. LXXXVII.

CAERGYBI, 27th July, 1749.

Anwyl Frawd,—Wala hai, dyma fi wedi bod yn chwilio i fynu ag i wared, ag yn y diwedd yn ffaelio taro wrth eich llythyr diweddaf yn un lle, a phar sut yr atebaf iddo yn y llun ymma? Ymhle mae'r brawd Llewelyn? Ni che's ddim oi hanes er ysdyddiau; ddoe y daeth ei lyfrau ir wlad wedi hir o hwyl. Roedd Sir Thomas Prendergast, or Marl, yma'r dydd arall; he had found out a most unpardonable error in my brother Lewis' books (one of which he had with him), in the description of Skerry Lighthouse: page 5 of the letterpress he says the lighthouse lies NNW. from Holyhead harbour whereas it lies NNE., a monstrous mistake which may occasion the Lord knows what losses, for a stranger steering his course by that direction must inevitably knock his ship in the head. Er mwyn Duw os yw'r brawd yn dre' sgrifennwch linell atto oni welwch ef, that he may take care to correct as many books as he has by him and advertise as to the rest. The Surveyor here says that the letters SE. by S. in page 18 should have been SW. by S. So much for books, now for men. Rym ni yma at yr un gyflwr ag y byddwn arferol a bod pawb yn rhwydd iachus, mawl ir Goruchaf Dduw. Roedd ein rhieni yn rhesymol iachus 'r dydd arall, gobeithio eich bod chwitheu yn ymendiaw o'r peswch fal y galloch fwynhau tippyn o ddedwyddwch ar ol hir ingder a chyni. Mae'r arian wedi dyfod attochi *Gwyr Llundain* bod y beil nid oes yma ond lle buont: gwae ni oi myned ymaith. Byddai da iawn cael llinell oddiwrthych ambell dro a rhyw faint o'ch helynt, ni chaf mom cof na'm synwyr i ddywedyd yn rhagor, na Duw a fo'n gwarchad drosoch. W. to R. contd.

Eich brawd caredigawl, William Morris.

P.S.—I intend you a long letter ryw ddiwrnod ag englynion, etc., ynddaw, but let me have a line from you in the meantime da chwitheu. Gresyn oedd farw'r hen Wil Sion Pabo, colled i chwi onte?

CAER GYBI, 2d dydd o Fedi, 1749. W. to R. LXXXVIII.

Anwyl Frawd,—Eich llythyr o'r 17 ulto. a ddaeth i'm llaw mewn pryd. Daccw'r brawd Llewelyn gartref, ond ni welais i etto mo'r Wm. Jones, o'r Bagnio. Mae'n debyg ei fynd i Ddulun ryw ffordd arall. Cordwainer Davies called of me the other day,—refused absolutely to tarry a night, too much ta'en up with the great, na bo'nd ei grybwyll! Aie mae Llewelyn ar y ffordd o fod yn anfeidrawl fab, bydd pawb yn ymfalchio wrth ymrwbio yn yr rheini, sef yr *Iarglwyddi* mawrion! Felly ni wiw disgwyl fawr hawddgarwch. Digrif fod y Gorbedyn, Davy ag ynteu yn unfryd ai gilydd, digrifach os byddant eill trioedd yn werth 10,000 bob un cyn ei marw. Your remarks of two of 'em are just I do believe. Mae'n debyg fod y llall felly. Mae'n dra drwg gennyf glywed fod pawb yn beio ar Lewelyn am fod yn rhy greulon galed wrth y ddwy lodes. Mi a wranta y bydd edifar iddo os bydd ef byw. Ill usage will never do; da iawn fyddai clywed. Tesni llyfrau Cymreig Pabo Post Prydein ai gwerthu a wna'r weddw ai peidiaw; erdolwyn ychydig o'i hanes a'i deulu, pa sawl plentyn, a pha gyfoeth, etc., oedd iddo. Mae'n odiaethol genym glywed eich bod yn

W. to R. contd. rhwydd iachus unwaith etto, Duw a'ch cynhalio felly. Mae arnaf gymaint o ofn y gauaf a chwithau, have had lately a violent cough, ag ni waeth tewi na siarad, mae o'n rhedeg yn ein gwaed. Ydychi yn cofio fal y bydde'r hen Elin Owen, o Waun y Grinach, yn adnabod pesychiad Forys Prisiart y boreuau wrth fynd i'r gwaithdy? Pesychu yn ddidrugaredd y byddai (ag y bydd etto) 'r hen wr, ag felly y bydd ei dri meib. Nid oes yn Eglwys Gybi un uwch ei beswch na'ch brawd Gwil,—nobody catches cold sooner. Beth pe buasid yn hwsmyn-tir neu'r cyffelyb? Rhagluniaeth a wyr oreu pa fodd i'n trin a'n gosod allan. Duw a'n gwnelo'n ddiolchgar.

Coelwch fi, mi chwiliais hyd nad wyf wedi blinaw am yr englynion rheini, ag yn ffaelio eu cael yn y diwedd. Gwaith y Bardd Coch, etc., oeddynt. Nid hwyrach imi daro wrthynt ryw dro. Ai tybied y medrwch gael amser i drin yr argraphiad nesa or Beibl? Mi ddywedais wrth fab Ellis, yr offeiriad, ynghylch beiau, dywedyd y mae ynteu mae'r ffordd oreu yw dilyn edition Dr. Davies, oblegid fod hwnnw yn ddifeius oddigerth beiau'r argraph-wasc. Digrif fyddai meddwch, weled y Bedyn a'r Llewelyn yn croesawu eu gilydd, ie'n wir i'r sawl na welodd mor *seremoni* honno o'r blaen, ond myfi a ga'dd yr hapusrwydd hwnnw pan ddaeth Llewelyn i'r Benrhynmawr i gyfarfod y Bedyn *about five years ago*. Fo fu yno'r hen gusanu; nid oeddid yn cymeryd mwy o *notice* o Wilym y brawd nag o Gostog Tom (er na welsid mono er's blynyddoedd) nes darfod gwneuthur diben ar 'sanu, ysgwyd dwylo, a mynd o'r neilldu i ymgomiaw, etc., dros awr neu fwy. Wala, wala, pwy na bai gywaethog i gael ei fawrygu cymaint hyd yn oed gan y rhai na waeth ganddynt pe bae wedi ei grogi. O ynfydion!

Sunday 3rd.—Edward Edwards' sister was here to-day. I read her the paragraph in your letter concerning him. Da ydoedd ganddi glywed ei hanes, ond er hynny yn abl anfoddlonus am na basai yn sgrifennu atti hi ei hunan. Mae'n falch fod gobaith o'i weled ym Mhrydain Fawr; yn deusyf ei charedigawl orchymun atto, os y chwi a sgrifennwch. Mi welaf yma gynhwysiad eich llythyr at y nhad (yr hwn oedd dydd arall yn bur sal), ynghylch ei hen brentis Wm. Jones. That chap whom you mention (Owein Roberts) writ to me of the 11th July from Spithead, acquainting me of Jones's death on the 17th May "that he had made no will and that it would be worth my while to come to the ship because he was worth some money, and if I did not come the money would go to the chest at Chatham," and some such stuff which cost me sevenpence. When I received this billet, I could not guess who it was from, nor who that Jones should be; but upon enquiry found that this O. R. is a son of one Robert George of this place, a fellow I've no society with, the family bearing but an indifferent character and therefore no doubt on't, this O. R. hath made a good hand of the other's effects which in all reason and justice should go to the deceased's sister, and I don't doubt but she has a will and power by her. I am sorry for Jones's death, for he was a promising young fellow, mab Sion ab Wm. Morris o Ligwy gynt, bengwas. My father had brought the young fellow up from his infancy and took him apprentice (arian y plwyf). He must be worth more money than you mention, perhaps he hath some effects in Liverpoole. Its much that there was no better care taken of his effects on board when he died. It's a pity the officers were not called to an account for it. Gwaeth na lladron, first to deprive a man of his liberty and then suffer his effects to be run away with by a parcel of their own thieves. Wala, wala, fe ddaw dial. What Roberts told you of the deceased leaving his effects to you must be meer stuff, for he had allways a regard for his own sister. I presume father will stir in this affair for her. Duw a'm ceidw i rhag eiddo anghyfiawn. So much for this affair. W. to R. contd.

Fe addawodd y Cardinal ddyfod ffordd yma cyn dychwelyd adref, yno cawswn gyfle i yrru i chwi un o lyfrau newydd a gant Mr. Ellis i'r ysgolion Cymroaeg. Roedd carn yn achwyn yn dost ar ei 'Anglesey customs.' Nis gwn i par sut y darfu iddo eu trin. Rym ni yma oll yn rhwydd iachus, mawl i Dduw, ag yn rhoddi ein caredigawl orchymyn attoch chwi ar eiddoch.

Wyf eich brawd anwiw, Wm. Morris.

P.S.—Dyma f'Arglwydd Castledurrow wedi rhoddi imi gorn Ffreinig i.e., a *French Horn*, a chan fy mod yn cyfaneddu ar lethr gallt goruwch y Gaer, fy ngorchwyl ambell noswaith dawel yw chwthu yn fy nghorn er difyrwch i'm fy hun, ag er mawr ddiddanwch i'r Caeryddion a'r relyw o'r Cybeaid. Ond etto er hyn, nid yw

W. to R. contd.

mo'm creglais mor seingar a soniarus ag y dymunwn, achos da paham, na che's i erioed ond ychydig iawn o addysg, a minneu o ansawdd swrn fwngleraidd, na fedraf o honwyf fy hun prin leisiaw corn cystal a Sieffrai Fongan porthwr Tal y Foel, neu Ronwy ap Simon 'r Ast, dispaddwr hychod a moch, o herwydd paham oes yna ddim cymorth i gael tuag at wneuthur fy llais yn rhwydd beraidd. I've no new tunes adapted for this instrument, lessons are wanted, etc., etc. Mae'n rhaid myfyrio am ryw beth i lenwi hyn o ddalen . . . at y gwaelod fal y gallo fod yn llythyr o'r hen ffasiwn. Felly am yr Ardymmyr. Mae hi ymma yn ddryghin echryslon ys deuddydd, taflu a lluchio ydau poblach rhyd y meusydd dinben, drosben! Ysgyttiaw a sgerbydiaw pob peth yn fy nghardd hyd nad yw resyndod eu gweled! I have the Granadilla or Passion Tree now in flower, a strange appearance at Cybi.

Os oedd yn chwythu ddoe ag echdoe gida chwi mal yma, mi a wna'n dda y cawn glywed digon o son am gychod a llongau wedi eu hanafu a da os diangodd y bobl. Dyma fi yn darparu llythyr i Lewelyn efo'r post yma, a hanes y byd ar amseroedd ynddo. Ai yna mae Pegi Morys etto? Pa beth y mae'r Aldremon yn ei wneud yna rhyd yr amser, ond ffitiach fyddai bod gartref yn trin y dreth gyda'r hen wreigan, ah? Felly yr oedd erioed. Roedd carn yn canmawl llawer ar ryw glark sydd yn eich offis chwi, sef mab David Owen a adwaenwn gynt, ag i nith i Risiart William Dailiwr o'r Efail Fawr. Gadewch glywed mewn difrif par sut ddyn ydyw. I have had the loan of the MSS. which I told you Mr. D. Foulks had in his library, the same with that you saw at Jones Pabo's, gwaith prydyddion yr 12d a'r 13 ganrhi. Llyfr gwych yw, the first page is lost. Oes modd yw gael oddiyna? Wala oni wnaethym i sgil go ryfeddawl i roddi llanw yn hyn o bapurun? Byddwch wych, ag na byddwch yn rhy ddiawg i sgrifennu at W. M.

W. to R.
LXXXIX

CUSTOM HOUSE, HOLYHEAD, 14 September, 1749.

Dear Brother,—Mi sgrifenais lostryddyn o lythyr cyhyd am braich attoch dydd arall, to which I refer you, yr achos a bair im eich cyfarch yr awron yw hyn: nid amgen the widow of the late Dr. Wheldon shewed me the other day a letter she had received from Mrs. Bayley, of Deptford, who transacts business for her, receiving her pension, etc., wherein she says that she had done what she could in order to come at the money for the doctor's cloaths' bill which it seems are in the hands of the executors of the late purser of the *Experiment*, man of war. The case was this: Dr. Wheldon, whom I fancy you remember and who was married i fodryb yngwraig i, chwaer ei mam, ag oddiwrth bwy un ond odid y ceir ryw dro dipyn o ryw dda byd, I say the Dr. being surgeon of the *Experiment* man of war died in the Cuba expedition; his wife, or rather widow, came up to London and obtained a pension, and received through the hands of one Barlow, who was his chief creditor, his wages, etc., but the purser being abroad the cloaths' bill which amounts to £10 odd money could not be had. Barlow had it made out but dying soon after, his son who left off business delivered the bill to Mrs. Wheldon's order, viz., to Mrs. Bayley above-mentioned who writes that she apply'd several times to Mr. Ashley (I think she calls him) the present purser, who says he can't find the executors of the late purser, etc. Now, dyma fal y mae, ydych chwi yn meddwl y medrwch wneuthur dim yn y matter yma? Mrs. Wheldon is willing to allow very handsomely if you can procure the money. A power will be given you and the bill deliver'd you if you'll take the affair in hand. Pray favour me with a line as soon as you can with your sentiments. Nid oes gennyf ddim chwaneg yw ddywedyd yr awron ond ein bod ni yma i gyd yn rhwydd iachus, mawl ir Goruchaf. W. to R. contd.

Wyf eich caredigawl frawd, William Morris.

C. GYBI, D. Calan Gauaf, 1749. W. to R. XC.

Dear Brother,—Wawch! wfft i hyn! Na bo mo'nd i grybwyll! Daccw'r brawd Llew wedi ymbriodi ag un ieuanc o lwyth Ceredigion! Gŵr o haner canmlwydd oed yn ymglymmu a benyw oddeutu 25! "Glew fydd y Llew hyd yn Llwyd,"* ebr rhyw hen brydydd gynt; mae'n debyg glywed o honoch y newydd cyn hyn. Duw a roddo ir cwpwl lwyddiant. Ces eich llythyr o'r 17 ult., a hanes materion Dr. Wheldon, yr hyn a ddarllenais i'r weddw. Mae honno yn gweddio gida phob migwrn ag asgwrn o honoch heblaw talu, os ceir y mwnws arian bydol. I ba beth y gadawodd Mrs. Bayly ei phower yna? Ai gwedi hurtio yr oedd y wraig? Gwrda'r

* Lewis Morris married Anne Lloyd of Penbryn, as his second wife on 20 October, 1749. He married his first wife, Elizabeth Griffiths, on March 29th, 1729. His second wife Anne Lloyd died in 1786.

W. to R. contd.

Cardinal am fod ysbryd calonog! Pwy a leteua yng nghabandy gwr gwreng a gai dŷ Arglwydd yn agored? Drwg iawn cynrhwg tesni llyfrau Pabo, yn iach ddisgwyl daioni o honynt. Llyfrau Cymraeg yn nwylo plant Alis sydd ail i fodrwy aur yn rhwyn hwch. Ffarwel gyda nhw. No I have no instructions, the Broad Sheet you mentioned would be most acceptable. I'll assure you I am no dull performer. Nid Siarles Watkin mo'r mab, ond Watkin downright medd ei ffrins. Iĕ, gwr mawr a fydd os byw a wna. Gerwin oedd marw y Dick Ionsiaid yna. Daccw un o'r henw yngharchar Ynghaernarvon am ladd ei chwaer, sef yw hwn Dick Jones bach, alias Dick Sion Greulon, alias y waiter bach, alias Quiken, etc., some time ago one of our coast waiters; ond moliant i Dduw we had got rid of him.

Dyma'r nith Ellin Morris yn ein plith, herlodes benffol rwy'n ofni, achwyn yn erwin ar ei thad, ag ynteu o'r tu arall yn gridwst yn dost. Gresyn na roddasai nhw mewn rhyw wasanaeth, neu mewn rhyw ffordd i enill eu bara, nid oes wybod par sut a fydd bellach. Mae'n debyg y bydd llin arall. Nis gwn i a ddywedais i chwi or blaen farw o'r gyfnither Margaret Salisbury a gadael ar ei hol 5 neu 6 o blantos, yr isa oddeutu haner blwydd oed ar hyna ond 13 neu 14. Colled anferth! Mae wedi mynd yn hwyr, felly mae'n rhaid cadw noswyl am heno. Duw a fyddo gida chwi ar eiddoch hyd y diwedd. Pawb yn iach, cenwch.

Eich caredicaf frawd, William Morris.

. . . Daccw fi drwy fawr gost a thrafferth wedi ffittio allan globyn o dy i'r brawd ar chwaer Dafis i fynd iddo y foru. Och fi ha wr fab, nid ewch byth i adeiladu heb bwn ceffyl o arian, wfft, a chan wfft!

W. to R. XCI.

CAER GYBI, Nos Calan, 1749.

Dear Brother,—I received yours of the 2nd inst., a diolch yn fawr am dano, ag am y Tantan tavern; ni che's ddim amser etto i'w studiaw, pan welwyf gyfleu mi fynnaf yrru i chwi ryw doccyn. Mi ach gwelaf chwi yn achwyn, a daccw'r brawd Llew ynteu yn dywedyd yr un peth, fod y beswch yn eich anafu. Duw a ddel a chwi'n iach yn eich ôl. A fu i chwi erioed yfed colt's foot tea? Fe ddywedir i rai gael y mawrlles oddiwrtho. Tussilago y geilw'r Lladiniaid 'e a'r besychlys, neu ddail carn'r ebol y galwn ninneu fo;

ond i ba beth yr âf i gyngori pan ych ymhlith blaenion y physygwyr? Gwaeth agos nag afiechyd yw aflonyddwch ag aniddigrwydd, wala, wala, Duw a roddo ini râs i'n parodtoi ein hunain am le lle mae gwir happusrwydd iw gaffael, nid oes mo honaw tu yma ir bedd. Mrs. Wheldon hath writ to Mrs. Bayley to the intent you mentioned. I wish you may be able to do something in the affair. Aie gwasnaethgar ir Cybeiaid a fase Killingbeck, nid hwyrach hynny, mi a fyddwn ddydd a fu yn arfer a chael newspapers o Ddulun, y rhai a adewid ynhy ei fam ynghyfraith Benbow ambell dro. Mae'n debyg mae dyna'r rhwymedigaeth, ni thybiais i fod yr un. The pacquet boat people now uses another house. Na welais i erioed mo'r Gatecism hono, a phar sut a fydd imi ei gael? Mae arnaf eisiau gyrru i chwi lyfr newydd y Bersonyn Ellis, fal y galloch weled madruddyn yr iaith Gymraeg! Bu'r car Salbi ai wraig, gwr ei chwaer Margaret ai ferch, a Peggy Morys yma yn bwrw'r Gwiliau. Dyma nhw newydd gychwyn tua Dulas. Penrhyddion iawn yw'r ddwy gares yma. Duw a roddo iddynt râs, mae'n ddigon enbyd, mae'n siêd yr ant heb yn ddiolch i bawb. W. to R. contd.

Dydd Calan.—Ni welai ddim o hanes Trentham a Vandpn. heddyw, pa beth y maent yn ei wneuthur? Gadewch glywed par sut yr ych yn trîn y peswch, sef pwy sy'n mynd ar goreu, etc. Mae 'ngwraig i (yr hon sydd abl afiach) a minneu yn dymuno i chwi flwyddyn newydd happus. Duw a fo'n gwarchad drosoch chwi ar eiddoch. *Eich brawd anwiw*, *William Morris*.

CAER GYBI, 15 Ionawr, 1749. L. to R. XCII.

Anwyl Frawd,—Gan eich bod mor ddiog neu drafferthus na fedrwch atteb mo'm llythyrau, dyma i chwi un chwaneg at y lleill aeth o'r blaen. Dyma nhad wedi dyfod i'n hymwelyd. Mae mam, mawl i'r Goruchaf, yn dyfod i fyny yn dda iawn. Fe gadd y nhad lythyr oddiwrthych lately ag ai attebawdd. Dyna i chwi gyfiawnhad Joan Wesley* wedi i Mr. Ellis ei ddwrdio am droi pobl yr Eglwys yn Bresbiteriaid, etc. A dyna i chwi ddarn o lyfr arall, sef "Anrheg i'r Cymro,"† a roddes y Mr. Ellis allan dydd arall. Cewch y relyw ryw dro. Pan na yrrwch chwitheu eich Catecism

*The reference is to a small pamphlet entitled, "Gair i'r Methodist, o waith Mr. J. Wesley. Argraphwyd yn Nulun yn y Flwyddyn 1748." 8 pp.

†Printed at Dublin, 1749.

W. to R. contd. yma i gael ei weled? Gwaeth na dim, a'r peth sydd ucha gyda mi yw bod yngwraig allan o bod trefn yn afiachus er's talm o amser. Da fyddai clywed oddiwrthych par fodd y mae'r peswch. Ni ches i gymaint a llinell oddiwrth y brawd Llewelyn er pan ddychwelodd i'w allt ei hun. Peth rhyfedd yw hynny! Pa beth a ddaeth o'r commissiwn? Chwi glywsoch oddiwrth yr Aldramon yn ddiweddar, on' to? Duw a fo'n gwarchad drosoch a'ch teulu. Rym oll yn gorchymun attoch a nhad yn eich bendithiaw.

Y fi ydyw eich caredigawl frawd, Gwilym.

Oes dim gobaith i Mrs. Wheldon? A fyddwch i yn cael Almanacau yn rhad yn yr offis yna? We had no fishery this year, so I crav'd no stores from the Salt Board.

L. to W.

XCIII.

GALLT VADOG, February 16, 1749.

Dear Brother,—You may think it strange that I cant spare an hour now and then to write to a brother. But so it is. I pulld my house down in order to make it comfortable to breath a few years, months or days; I find the workmen here the same as everywhere, a parcel of idle good-for-nothings, I am obliged to do half ye work myself, and if I am absent from them a minute there is something done wrong and this is ye reason that I have not a minute to spare till, like another bird I make my nest. I have made my little study up with a fireplace in it; I have floor'd and ceil'd my parlour, I have done abundance of work but not a great deal to be seen. You may imagine it is invisible work. It is so to vulgar eyes. Well, but what is all this . . . letter for? Why, nothing but to let you know I [am] alive, and to tell you this is ye first letter I have wrote in my *myfyr* (library or study) and that you are to expect letters oft'ner hereafter. Today also is the first change for good weather we have had this month—continual wind, and rain and blustering weather; but my mercurial thermometer hath been all the while above temperate, though Mr. F. Wright writes me word that his thermometer at Leghorn, 28 January, N.S. was 12 degrees below temperate at mid-day. Gallt Vadog climate is far preferable to Italy. The steams of the mine perhaps makes us warmer. My service to all yours and mine, and expect to hear from you for I wrote last.

Your [affec]tionate Brother, L. M.

Anwyl Frawd,—Nid oedd yn fy mryd atteb mo'ch llythyr tan yr wythnos nesa oni bae ddigwydd iddi fod yn foreugwaith glawog heddyw fal na allwn fynd i . . . . unlle allan . . . . Diolch yn fawr am y Catecism. I think it's an exceeding good thing, is there not a good deal of Southwalianism in't? The parson had sent to the Society for some of them; seems to like the work much. Dyna i chwi yr relyw o lyfr yr enwog ddifynydd hwnw! Mi ddywedais wrth y Mrs. Wheldon yr hanes ag mae'n llawen iawn glywed fod gobaith ryw dro. Gwych yw'r Phenix snuff hwnw sy'n dwyn pobl o farw i fyw, ag yn gyrru ymaith y tylwyth teg. Gobaith Duw fod y rhod yn troi efo chwi, ag y cewch gysur a diddanwch o hyn allan, ond ni wiw disgwyl mor llawer yn y byd brwnt yma, rhaid ymorol am well. Da gwnaethoch yrru'r lodes oddiyna i gael addysg, rhag ei chyfargolli. Duw a roddo iddi râs, ag a'ch cadwo i'w dwyn i fynu yn ei ofn. Gerwin fod y gorchwyl mor galed na cheir mynd i'r deml —nid felly yma, dim gwaith i wneuthur er enill ceiniog, ond ychydig yn y dollfa, llai na digon yno, mân gymwynase ddigon a digon, trwsio briwiau, etc., fal Boba o Bentrerianell a hen wrageddos da eraill a chant o wâg swyddau. Nid euthim i gam ymlaen ar y Tantan Tavern, fe anafwyd fy nghorn i a rhaid ei yrru i Ddulun yw daclu. Mae'r nosweithiau yr amser yma ar y flwyddyn yn oerion i ddynan sefyll allan, nid ellir udo yn ty rhag ofn gwlldio'r bobyl i gyd i ffordd. Mae'r ddwy herlodesi yma yn ei hunfan etto—Margaret ynhy nhad, ag Ellin efo fy chwaer, ni thrig moni efo ngwraig dros ei berwi, gormod o gynghori ag addysg yn ei dychrynu. Gwirion anial ynt eill dwywedd, bu Farged yma'r wythnos ddiwaetha yn ceisio rhyw ddillad, mae eu tad wedi rhoddi imi gennad i dianghenu am ddilladau. Digon tebyg mae treio triciau y buwyd ar llythyr hwnw, o ran nid dim o'm gwaith i oedd yr ôl tan hwnw, gwych a fase i chwi yru'r ddarn losgedig yn ôl; perhaps it would have been a means of bringing to view a scene of villany. Ale mae'r Gownsler yn gawr efo ei wraig ieuanc? Cerbyd euraid hefyd! wala, wala, mae'r hên dadi druan gŵr ynteu yn cynhilo'r geiniog gôch! Dyna fal y mae, ag felly yr ydoedd o'r dechreuad, ag felly, mae'n debyg, y bydd rhagllaw. Gresyn na basech yn cael amser i fynd i lwyddo'r gŵr, 'rwy finneu o achos afiechyd fy ngwraig yn ffaelio mynd er's 4 mis neu 5 i

W. to R. contd.

ymweled a'r hen gorphyn o Fodorgan i ddwndrio dros ddeuddydd neu dri. Mae'n dda iawn genyf fod y Berocheon yn fyw iach, nid adwaen i mor rheolwyr yna, ag nis gwn i par sur y mae'nt yn trin y drêth, gobeithio'r goreu. Yr oeddych i ag arall yn ddigon dig wrth Walpwl, mi feddyliais lawer gwaith na ddeuai moi fath ar ei ôl, ag ni ddaeth etto moi well, ni waeth tewi na siarad, dynion y'nt i gyd, yn llawn o wendid fal pobl eraill; dedwydd yw'r sawl sydd ganddo leia o honynt, i.e., gwendidau. Anaml y trewir yn y wlad yma wrth neb a ddywaid air da am weision y Brenin, a da os dianc ei Fawrhydi heb gael anair. Wfft i'r hen Golhector Griffith; dim ofn Duw ysywaeth yno. Collais i rywfaint o arian wrthaw: ffitiach fase talu dled na chadw puteiniaid. His sureties lost considerably by him, it was entirely his and her fault—pobl falch, wirion, ffôl. Dychrynadwy o'r ddaear-gryn, Duw a'n gwaredo rhag cael ein llyncu yn fywion fal pobl yr Idal ambell dro, nid oes ammeu nad oes cymaint o ddrygioni Ymrydain ag yn unlle arall, ond gobeithio fod rhai da o honom, er mwyn pa rai y cedwir y lleill. Na wn i ddim oddiwrth y ddynes ordderch hono or eiddo'r Methodist, yr wyf yn credu eu bod yn dywedyd llawer o chwedlau celwyddog ar felldith eu mamau. I heard those stories you mention and many more, but I choose not to give credit to them though I have a very poor oppinion of 'em in general. Os bydd yn unlle undyn yn rhagori ar ei gymydogion mewn castiau drwg a chnafeidd-dra, bydd sicr i hwnw droi'n bengrwn (mal y gelwir nhw yma), ag o hynny allan fei tybia ei hun yn angel y goleuni a phawb oi ddisgyblion hwytheu o'r seintiau, ag a ddiystyra bawb arall o ba radd bynnag y bônt. Griff. Jones had the direction of the Welsh Schools. The clergy here, most of them, hath insisted upon naming their masters. Jones has an agent who comes quarterly to pay and inspect into the management. Mr. Ellis had a school on that footing for a half year and about 60 or 70 children taught to read, etc. Mr. Ellis is tired in battling the Methodists, he now takes 'em by fair means, dyna y ffordd oreu i drin ynfydion a fai direol. Aie mae Dafis yn fyw fyth, pe bae fatter yn y peth, nid oes ffordd yma fawr fywioliaeth iddo i gael. Mae Sion yma etto, yn son am fynd at ei ewythr ar fyr. Dyma fi wedi cael i waelod eich llythyr, nis gwn i pa beth i ddweyd ymhellach. A welsoch i Ganiad y Gôg o waith Llew o Allt Vadog iw wraig pan ydoedd yn caru? Pa sut y digwyddodd cymaint o ragoriaeth between your tables of Jewish and Roman coins, weights and measures, in the Bible and those of Dr. Arbuthnot's inserted in the preface of the Universal History, dywedwch? W. to R. contd.

Ce's lythyr dydd arall oddiwrth Natws Wright, o Leghorn; roedd wedi bod yn Rhufain, etc., etc., mae'n gadael rhoddi hanes o'r wlad hono, yr Idal; yr oedd yn disgwyl i'r wraig esgor ar fab oddeutu canol y Mawrth. Mae arnaf gywilydd na b'aswn yn gyrru i chw cyn hyn ryw anhreg am y rhai a dderbyniais gennych, nid oes yma ddim a dâl i'w anfon. Would a few pickled sampier and some other pickles be acceptable? Er mwyn dyn os meddwch feddwl am ryw beth a fai gymeradwy gadewch i mi wybod fal y gallom ddangos yr ewyllys. Perhaps one may meet a ship by chance bound your way. Father and mother were pretty hearty 'tother day, 'rym ni yma oll felly ond fy ngwraig i am merch sydd yn o salaidd. Duw a fo yn eich cylch. Sgrifenwch gynta galloch.

I am your affectionate brother hyd angeu, Wm. Morris.

GALLTVADOG, April 9, 1750. L. to R. XCV.

Dear Brother,—I received yours of ye 17th and 24th March, and am obliged to you. Digon a digon ynghylch predestination, etc. I do not wonder at anything the wrech can say or do. I had the kindest letter from her you ever saw by last post—a mere rascal, the spawn of Lucifer and the Queen of Hell. Gwrda Amral Griffin; gwnewch gymwynas i chwi eich hunen, na rupiwch, na brenin, na brenines, dyna fal y mae pawb o'r rhai synwyrol yn gwneuthur; a da fuasai i minneu pei gwneuthwn felly, mi gollaf o achos bod yn lled onest. Gwych yw'r Phœnix snuff, a iacha wragedd gwallgofus. Gyrrwch lwyth o hono i Aberystwyth, da bod Meirian mewn order. I am sorry for poor Ben Jones. Never trouble your head about Mr. Paynter, of Dale, nor about the other Paynters. I shall order ye money for Blankley's book soon. Well done Whiston and his millenium! He knows as much of the matter as Dafydd y Bugail defaid. Thank you for Jones's catalogue. Och y fyrred yw gwychder dyn. I have not time to send memoirs of old Jones. I know nothing of the girl and the Methodists, nor of their tricks, for there are none of them here. [I have my]self heard Howel Harris tell a congregation at [Llanfairmuallt], in

L. to R. contd. Brecknockshire, that God was come among them that night. "Take hold of His skirts," says he, "for He never hath been among you before"; with a great deal of the like fulsome stuff that made most of his audience weep.

Well done, Lord Vere gynt, and Lloyd Peterwell. Dyna siccrau Sir Aberteifi yn y teulu hwnnw. Dick Davies is here yn gwneuthur wyneb, yn cau cloddiau, yn edrych ar ol yr adar, etc. Go and see Meyrick by all means. Mae edlin yn cynhyrfu yn . . . . y wraig, trafferthion ddigon. Cyfreithiau yn un tew oi hachos hi. Duw a ddelo a ni drwyddynt. I have not had a letter from Commissioner Vaughan, since I left London, and I dare not presume to give Ben a letter till I renew my acquaintance with ye Commissioner, which I intend soon. You cannot imagine how busy I am sowing, gardening, and cutting down a coppice of wood I bought towards ye mines. Darren doth not yet go on with vigor. God be with you. You shall hear from me again soon.

Your affectionate brother, L.M.

W. to R. XCVI.

HOLYHEAD, 21st May, 1750.

Dear Brother,—Rwy'n deall fod John Owen wedi sgrifennu attoch hanes marwolaeth fy anwyl wraig, yr hon a welodd yr Arglwydd yn dda gymeryd atto y dydd cyntaf or mis hwn, er mawr dristwch a cholled i mi am plant gweiniad; ni fedraf ddwedyd dim chwaneg ar y testyn galarus yma, mae fy nghalon yn rhy lawn yn berwi drosodd. Duw am diddano i ag ach cadwo chwitheu rhag tristwch. Mrs. Wheldon, who had sent an affidavit to Mrs. Bayley, of Deptford, in order to receive her pension, received a letter from her this day mentioning that she had left her Power of Attorney with you and desiring that she might write to you to deliver her said power (all needless work). However, please to deliver it to her when she calls for it. I hope the cloaths bill will be decided soon Pray give Mrs. Wheldon's compliments to Mrs. Bayley, and tell her that she hath sent her by one Richard Hughes in the *Providence*, Captain, Henry Stewart :—one flitch and one ham of bacon as a present. I hope you will excuse this freedom. I long to hear from you. Peggy Morris is with me and is a good girl; have writ to her father for leave that she may continue here for some time. Father and mother were in tollerable good health a Friday last. *I am, your afflicted brother, William Morris.*

CUSTOMHOUSE, HOLYHEAD, 18 June, 1750. W. to R. XCVII.

Anwyl Frawd,—Nid oes gennyf esgus yn y byd i sgrifennu attoch yr awron ond yn unig i ddangos mor rhyfedd gennyf na chefais gymaint ag un llinell oddiwrthych er's cymaint a chymaint o amser yn atteb i'r rhai a sgrifennais attoch er's cyhyd o amser Yn wir, mae'r prawf diweddar a gefais o freuolder hoedl dyn wedi fy ngwneuthur yn fwy ofnus ac amheuus ynghylch bywyd fy ffrins nag a fyddwn arfer a bod. Mae'r amser yn neshau y pryd y bydd raid i'r hwya ei einioes o honom ymadaw a myned i gartref y bedd, felly gadewch i ni tra bo'm yma efo'n gilydd ddiddanu tippyn y naill ar y llall, oblegid mae digon o drwblaethau yn rhan y lwccusa o honom. Canol yr wythnos diwedda y daeth y nhad ar chwaer adref o Allt Fadog, lle buont yn anfon Sion Owen ac yn ymweled ar tylwyth. Roeddynt yn rhwydd iachus, disgwyl y wraig ar ei gwely ar fyrder. Duw a roddo iddi amser da ag etifedd i'r gwr ag onide gwae Lewelyn. Mae ei gyfreithiau a phob aflwydd yn ei flino yn erchyll. Daccw'r car Salbri yn dechreu codi allan o'i glaf wely lle bu dra hir a thra gwan ddiobaith. Mae yma sychder mawr, dim gwlaw a tharanau mal yna. A fu Mrs. Bailey gida chwi am y Power? Mi welais lythyr Esgob Bangor at y person yn dywedyd fod y Society yn mynd i argraphu Bibl Cymraeg allan o law, a'i chwi yw'r golygwr? Pray let me have a line from you if you are in the land of the living, who am, dear brother, with love to you and yours, a Duw a fo'n gwarchad drosoch oll.

Eich caredigawl frawd, William Morris.

P.S.—Mae hynny sydd o honom yma, mawl i Dduw, yn iach. Mae Peggy Morris yn gorchymyn attoch. Bum yn ymweled a mam dydd arall. Roedd hi'n resymol iachus.—W.M.

CAERGYBI, 30 Mehefin, 1750. W. to R. XCVIII.

Anwyl Frawd,—Wrth hir ddisgwyl derbyniais lythyr oddiwrthych dated 16th inst., ac yn wir ddiau da iawn oedd i gael, a chan diolch am tanaw. The case is thus. In one of my letters I desired, or should have desired, you to send me in a frank 6 papers of the Phoenix Snuff for Mr. Ellis, etc., but you did not take any notice on't, or perhaps could not, if I forgot. I am plagued out of my life about it by the Doctor and a sister-in-law of mine both valetudin-

W. to R. contd.

arians, and to mend the matter, here's brother Davies wants a couple more, and if you don't make hast to forward these 8 papers, a thousand to one but in a few posts the order will be increased to a dozen or two. If you could somehow contrive to receive the 4s. for 'em from Mrs. Bailey of Deptford it would do, and I would pay Mrs. Wheldon here. Mewn difrif, nid oes dim byw yma hebddynt. Y nhad a ganmolawdd gymaint a'i para. Mi eisteddaf i lawr ryw ddiwrnod ben boreu i atteb eich llythyr, da iawn bod y byd mor hafog efo chwi, ni bu erioed anifyrrach gyda myfi. Ond odid ceir gweled gwell dyddiau. Duw a eill ein bodloni oll. Mae'r Bersonyn yma yn abl afiachus—corphilyn salw ydyw. Balch yw gennym glywed eich bod yn cymeryd yr argraphiad arall o'r Bibl yn llaw. Duw a roddo i chwi hoedl ac iechyd i fynd trwy'r gwaith ag a gadwo'r golwg i graffu yn ddiwyd. I read the Doctor your remarks upon his letter, etc., ag mi debygwn ei fod crio crecc. Fe fydd yma'r hen chwilio am feiau, etc. Rhaid tewi heno. Cewch lythyr digon ei hyd ar fyrder. I am, with my kind love to you and yours, dear brother,

Yours affectionately, *Wm. Morris.*

P.S.—Since I writ the above I've spoke to Mrs. Wheldon. She returns you many thanks for your care of her affairs, says that Mrs. Bailey will not receive her pension till next month. In the interim she'll send you an order for the snuff money. Dyma fi'n cychwyn tua Bodorgan i ymweled a'r Gownsler a'i wraig, etc.

W. to R.
XCIX.

GAERGYBI, 23rd July, 1750.

Anwyl Frawd,—Wrth hir ddisgwyl ce's eich llythyr or 16 ulto. a chan diolch am dano. Yn atteb iddo, mae imi fachgen a lodes, y cyntaf yn agos yw bedair blwydd a hanner oed, yn mynd i'r ysgol beunydd, ac yn siarad Cymraeg dda a Saesonaeg resymol. Herlod llawn o ddireidi tebyg iw ewythr pan oedd yn ei oed. Pob castiau gwaharddedig, etc. Yr ail o gwmpas blwydd a hanner yn dechreu cerdded. Yr acsus wedi ei dal yn ol yn erchyll. Y mab, sef yw ei enw Robert, gartref yn gywely yw dad, a'r eneth, sef Jane, gyda mamaeth yn y gymydogaeth, lle bydd raid ei chadw dros ennyd. They are, God be praised, fine children. Gwyn y gwel y fran ei chyw, meddwch chwitheu. I delivered the account of Edward Edwards. His sister lives tollerably well. Her husband is a millwright of good business pe bae ddim yn ei phen hi. Wfft i'r Arcana Celestia yna! Mae'r gwr, pwy bynnag yw, wedi colli ei bwyll yswaeth. I told you that I had read to Dr Ellis that part of your letter which relates to the Welch Bible. He owns his mistake in brenin, etc., and is not a little pleased at your resolution of not changing the initials of proper names. Your remarks upon Moses Williams's improvements are just. Few of our clergy knew anything of them except the Mynegai. What you mention of the Act of Uniformity, Canons, etc., to be left out of the Common Prayer, I think, is quite right. I wish the Apocrypha was left out also. Rym ni yma o'r un feddwl a chwi ynghylch y Salmau. Broughton's additional references must be of great use. Aie ni waeth gennych par un am ddyfod a dynion cyndyn i mewn, a gadael y rhai diniwed allan, boddlon wyfi, er fy mod yn llwyr gredu fod bai'n rhywle. Bid rhyngochi a'ch gilydd ynghylch eich Catechism a'ch Schism. Ynteu is surely better than yntef. Mae'r bersonyn yn abl piniongar weithiau. He condemns a thing violently one day and is sorry for't the next. W. to R. contd.

Ie digrif fyddai cael hanes cyfraith y Baltimore pan gaffoch gyfleu, fel y gellir gweled par law a wnaeth y gwyr o'r Duwmares o'r peth. As to my Herbal I have not half a quarter finished it, nor perhaps ever will, though the materials are collected, sef y coed ar cerrig, y clai a'r calch, ond nid oes neb a wyr par bryd yr a'r adeilad i ben. Nid hwyrach os caf hoedyl ac iechyd y gwnaf rywbeth y gauaf nesa. Duw yn unig a wyr. Dedwydd ydych (er lleied o amser sydd gennych i'w *spario*) gael bod yn gydnabyddus a'r Warburton yna a'r cyffelyb. Nid oes yn awr o fewn Ynys Fôn—er pan fu feirw rhai ac yr ymadawodd eraill—ddyn a dim diddanwch ynddo. Wala, wala, rhaid myned ar eu hol ar fyrder, felly ni waeth mo'r llawer pa beth a ddigwydd yma, etto er hyn mae arnaf hiraeth am glywed pa beth a ddaeth o'r addewid a gawsoch i'r brawd Llewelyn or degymau, a gwych fyddai gael y newydd fod etifedd yng Ngallt Fadawg. Gordderchwraig ddigrif oedd hono o'r eiddo'r gwr o'r Gors, anaml iawn y bydd y creaduriaid rheini yn cyfoethogi eu gordderchwyr, aie am aur melyn, etc., yr haeddai nef yw henaid? Do, do, fo ddarfu am bicklio ar cyffelyb hyswiaeth yn y ty yma, ond etto er hyn mae yn fy mryd

W. to R. contd. osod fy nith Marged ar waith i biclio rhai sampier neu gorn carw môr. The best of pickles for strengthening the stomach, procuring "appetite and removing all obstructions" medd y doethion. Gresyn fod cywely bynwes wedi hurtio! Oes dim gobaith gwellhâd? Da yw clywed fod yr herlodes ar y ffordd i fod yn *gonffwrdd* i chwi ryw dro. Duw o'i fawr drugaredd a roddo iddi ei ras, heb hynny ni thal yr holl fyd ddim. Nid yw Esgob Bangor mwy na gwr arall yn boddio mo'r llawer o bobl. Fe wnaeth lawer o ddrwg i'n Caer ni, drwy rwystro ir bersonyn a'r holl esgobaeth briodi Gwyddhelod, in Ireland called clandestine marriages, but in Great Britain deserved a genteeler name. Peth brwnt yw gormod o grefydd, neu o rith crefydd. I daresay that man has an eye upon York or Canterbury fal Herring a Hutton, ni waeth o'r cynted.

Aie apostol Cymry oll? Pa radd ydyw Prys ynteu, archapostol mae'n debyg. Fe gair clywed ar fyrder hanes yr High Bailiff, ond mewn difrif, nid oes dim dyfod at y gwir where party matters are concerned: every man thinks himself in the right if he but sticks close to his text. Gormod o ddrigioni sy yna ag yma ysywaeth! Aie gormod o ddrwg or achos? Nid rhaid mor llawer o ofn os y Senedd sydd i roddi barn. Ai tybiad na fedr y Rupeliaid drin y dreth yno or ffeindia? Beth meddwch? Siawns go wael i Vandeputain. Dirty work of both sides by all account. Ffei honyn' bethau hyllion! Ni fase mor llawer o fatter be busai y naill hanner o gyfreithwyr y deyrnas yn mynd yr un ffordd a'ch arglwydd Maer chwi. Ni chadd cyfreithiwr erioed swllt o'm harian oddigerth wrth *gwaliffeio* am fy swydd. Gresyn na chaent eu trin yma fal ym Mhrussia er lles ir deyrnas yn gyffredinol. O chwiw garn lladron! I have seen a brother of Lord Egremont here agoing and coming from Ireland, viz., Wyndham O'Bryan, a plain countryfied chap, have had of his franks, and am known by him, though not familiarly. Ie, ie, meddyginiaeth dda iawn yw *codaid* o arian rhag anesmwythder meddwl, ond etto maent ymhell oddiwrth roddi boddlondeb mewn myrddiwn o bethau er dywedyd o'r hen brydydd hergloff gynt mae:—

Arian a drwsia bob dryswch, o'r byd
Er na bâr na thristwch
Er digwydd affwydd tramgwydd trwch
Y Nhwy'n hawdd a wnan' heddwch.

Wele yma eich ail ebystol o'r 14 July yn canlyn 8 bapuraid o ysnising i'r bersonyn, a'r brawd Owain, a'm chwaer ynghyfraith. Daccw'r cynta wedi cymeryd dau eisioes, ag yn llwyr gredu ei fod yn llawer gwell. Ie, ie, tlodion yw pawb ffordd yma felly mae 6d. yn ddigon ar yr rheini. Fo fydd y bersonyn yn llawer gwell i chwilio am anafau, etc. Mae yn gorchymyn attoch yn fawr. Mi fum dydd arall yn ymweled ar teulu ym Modorgan, lle teriais dridie a theirnos yn ol yr hen ddefod, ond ar fy ngonestrwydd i fe fu agos iddynt am llwyr ddifa. Wfft i'r bobl fawrion am yfed. Roeddwn wedi bod er's gwell na chwarter blwyddyn yn byw yn dra rheolus, hyd nad euthym yno. Mi debygwn (yn ddistaw bâch) nad pur fodlongar yw'r hen gorph wrth yr etifedd am na buse yn priodi aeres ag un o'r wlad. Gwreigan o'r ffeinia debygwn i, ond ni welaf fi ddim hudoliaeth mawr yn perthyn iddi, ag ni chlywai fawr son am y gynhysgaeth. Beth a ddywedir ffordd yna? Mae rhyw anfoddlondeb ymhlith y rhai cyfoethogion yn gystal a rhai o isel radd, ond pwy a feddyliai hynny? W. to R. contd.

26th day.—Doe yr aeth Ellin Morris oddiyma, wedi bod i'n hymweled y Sul y creiriau. Mae arnaf ofn na wna'r eneth hono (beth bynnag a wnâ hon) fawr ddaioni. Mae hi byth yn llamhurtio ar ol y llanc brwnt hwnnw, ac ynteu ar ei hol hitheu. Roedd y nhad heb fod yn bur iachus, yr wythnos ddiweddaf. Y mam yn rhesymol. Rym ni yma, mawl i'r Goruchaf yn rhwydd iachus, eich brawd Gwilym fal llwdn dafad a fai a'r bendro arno, neu un a fai wedi ymddyrysu mewn drain a mieri yn ffaelio cael yn rhydd oddiyno. Somewhat between hope and despair. Ni waeth tewi na siarad, rhaid ymwroli a rhoddi hyder ar y Goruchaf yr hwn sydd Hollalluog. Nid adwaenwn i mo'r Harri Bemwnd na'r Will Parry chwaith. Newydd drwg i'r Boba Wheldon fod yr elusen yn mynd lai, lai. Ni chlywais i erioed sôn am Ddick Huws y sclatar. Pwy ydyw fo? Na, ddygodd y môr mo'r tir i gyd a ynyllasid oddi arno yn afon Gael, ond bu yno anfeidrawl golled y gauaf diweddaf. Ond mae'n debyg y byddis yn ei gymryd i mewn etto. A mi'r dydd arall yn ymweled a hen ffrind, yr hwn a gâdd golled am ei wraig yn ddiweddar, fal finneu, sef y Dr. Lloyd o'r Monachdy, pwy oedd yno wedi cymeryd ei letty dros dro ond y Doctor de

W. to R. contd. Linden.* Mae'n debyg glywed o honoch sôn am dano. He was in the King's Bench or some of your prisons not a long ago. Fe'ch hadwaenai chwi a'r brawd Lewys yn well na mi o'r ddau, er na welsai yr un o honoch erioed. A most impudent fellow. Mae wedi bod yn Sir Fflint er's llawer o flynyddoedd, wedi dianc o'i wlad ei hun, sef Prussia, rhag cael ei grogi maen debyg. He hath a mind to bring in some of our gentry to his schemes, says Sir Nicholas is his particular friend. O chwiw leidr! Wala, wala, rhaid imi roddi mhin i lawr, a mynd i fwyta gymhychiaid a chath môr, felly ni ddywedaf chwaneg, ond fy mod yn gorchymyn attoch a'r eiddoch. A Duw yn eich cylch. *Eich caredigawl frawd, Wm. Morris.*

Dyna i chwi fil am bedwar swllt. Rwyf finneu yn cynhill beiau yn y Bibl. Chwi a'i cewch ryw dro cyn Gwyl Fihangel. Rhowch lythyr gynta galloch i ddifyrru tippyn ar eich brawd trwmbluog.

HOLYHEAD, 4th August, 1750.

Dear Brother,—I am now to acquaint you that I have this week put on board the *Racehorse* of Carmarthen, Thomas Rees, Master

W. to R. C. from Beaumaris, for London, two pots of pickled sampier which the said master promised to deliver safe and sound; perhaps it will be proper to put a little vinegar to 'em when they reach you as I presume there are more than you will use in your own family for some years. A pott will be a handsome present to some of the great, for they are of the right sort and well done; however, please to accept of them, a rhwyddeb iddynt i ben i siwrnai. Wawch! na bo mond i grybwyll, dyma'r newydd fod mab ag aer Yngalld Vadawg, er y 25 ult—bellach am dani hi! Mawl i'r goruchaf Dduw am ei haelionus ddaioni ini oll, yn wir yr oeddwn yn dra anesmwyth eisiau clywed yr hanes. Fe fydd y gŵr gefndyn bellach, gwae'r Ceredigioniaid! Och fi ha wr fab, pa beth a wnair? Dyma eisiau dwsing a hanner o bapurau snising, ag nid oes i'ch brawd Gwilym na hun na heddwch nes y ceffir hwynt. If you have any bowels of compassion for a brother pray send the said number (for the poor) in a frank as soon as possible; ag onite fe fydd 'nghroen i ar y pared, the money shall be returned you. It's the parson that wants

* Probably Diederick Wessel Linden who published a work on the Medicinal Waters of Llandrindod (first edition, 1756; second edition, 1761), and another on the Waters of Llangybi, Carnarvonshire in 1767. See also ante page 114.

'em for his parishioners, and some friends, mae ô a minneu yn dyludo beiau yn goreu glâs. I have gone through Matthew, Marc and Luke, mae ynteu yn yr Hen Destament. Roedd y nhad a mam yn rhesymol iachus 'n ddiweddar, 'rym ni yma hefyd felly, mawl i Dduw, bydded iddo eich cadw chwitheu a'r eiddoch rhag pob drwg yr hwn yw taer weddi, dear brother, W. to R. contd.

Yours most affectionately, Wm. Morris.

P.S.—Captain Rees will be heard at the sign of the City of Bristol, Irongate, London, you may expect him in about ten days or a fortnight. Daccw'r chwaer yn dywedyd y gyr hi gosynun i chwi efo'r llong uchod. Byddwch wych, ag sgrifenwch efo'r powdwr, pen gynta galloch.—W.M.

W. to R. CI.

HOLYHEAD, 29th August, 1750.

Anwyl Frawd,—Wele yma eich llythyr o'r 25, a'r hanes galarus o farwolaeth y chwaer ynghyfraith. Duw a'ch diddano ac a ddelo ar byd wrth eich bodd, 'rym ni i gyd yn weiniad mewn wmbwrdd o bethau, er hynny, mae ini le i obeitho y cawn drugaredd a maddeuant drwy haeddedigaethau ein Iachawdwr, ag nid oes ammeu nad yw hitheu mewn anorphen esmwythdra a dedwyddwch. Duw a'n gwnelo'n barod oll yw chanlyn. Yn wir, nid yw cadw tŷ heb wraig ond gorchwyl tra gwag; rwyfi yn gwybod hynny yn rhy dda yn barod. Er hyny, mae'n fawr gwerthu dodre'n a gostiodd lawer, am hanner a dalont, a bod heb letty i ffrind pan ddeuai im hymweled a lle i rhoddi pen i lawr, etc. Ond nid yr un fath mor byd ffordd yna, 'rych chwi ar yr union, mi wnawn inneu yr un peth pei yn Llundain y bawn. Ond dyma'r lle'r wyf, a rhaid ymguro oreu gellir i fynd i ben y tir, fal yr arddwr. Dyma Mr. Ellis yn rhoddi ei wasanaeth attoch, ac yn gridwst yn dost na baech yn ceisio gan y *Societi* yna brintio rhai Gweddi Gyffredin ar eu pennau eu hunain er lles ir gwerinos, mae o agos yn yspys y medrach i gael ganddynt yr erchiad. Ie'n wir peth rhyfeddol iawn yw bod eich cyfocthogion yn troi yn garn lladron, digrif oedd eu gweled yn mynd i Newgate yn eu cerbydau. Ai tybied na wnant ffrindiau a'r mammon anghyfreithlon, beth meddwch? Heddyw yr aeth merch hyna Captain Fortunatus Wright oddiyma, wedi bod efo Mr. Mosson or Duwmares, ai fab in hymweled dros wythnos. 'Rwyf wedi cael fy 'sgegio yn dost drwy eistedd i fynu yn

W. to R. contd.

hwyr, a bolera, ni ddaw mo'm corphilyn yw hwyl un wythnos mi wranta. Y diwrnod y daethant yma yr aeth fy nhad adref wedi bod i'n hymweled dros ddwynos neu dair ; mae'r hen bobl yn rhesymol ar eu iechyd, mawl ir Goruchaf, oedran mawr! Ni chlywch i ddim sôn mi wranta amgylch y Powdwr Snising, mae Mrs. Wheldon . . . . lecyn oni bae cawsech fil, yn y nesa y daw. Ces lythyr or deheu dydd arall, roedd y ddau Lewelyn ar chwaer yn rhwydd iachus ; achwyn ar gyfreithiau sydd yno o hyd a chant o drafferthion. Duw a'n diofalo ni oll. Nos dawch!

Eich caredigawl frawd, William Morris.

P.S.—Esgusodwch *flynders* obleit mae'r mennydd wedi mynd yn *succan*. Er mwyn dyn anfonwch yma dippyn o lythyr fynycha' galloch, i ddiddymu y meddyliau duon yma, sydd chwanog o ddrysu dyn. Ymhle mae Ned Edwards bellach? Mae'r brenhin ynteu? A phar fyd sydd ar yr holl hen ffrindiau yna, Cardinal Davies, etc? Mae'r chwaer yma ai gwr ai phlant ar eiddof inneu yn iachus yn gorchymun attoch oll.

W. to R. CII.

C. Gybi, 13 Medi, 1750.

Anwyl Frawd,—Ce's eich llythyr or 8d. Mae'n dda cael clywed eich bod yn iachus, diolch am dipyn o hanes y Bibl, etc. Wfft i'r arian a dalasoch am helcyd y corn carw môr yna! A villainous place indeed! I thought the Captain would have been more reasonable in his freight. Gadewch iddo, cynt y cyferfydd dau ddyn na dau fynydd. If the liquor about the sampier turns moldy, you must boil strong pickle, viz., salt and water, and add when it's a little cold the same quantity of white wine vinegar, so cover the plant with the liquor ; we eat 'em sometimes chopt small and mixt with melted butter with mutton, which is seldom eaten here without 'em. Sometimes brought to the table upon a saucer and chopt by the eater as you do capers or other pickles ; if you design to keep 'em long you should pour some melted suet upon 'em to keep off the air. Dyna i chwi'r tu arall fil am naw swllt ar y Failies. Ai tybied na dderbyniodd hi arian y weddw yma cyn hyn? Aie comhisiwner yw'r cardinal, iechyd i'r galon, oes llawer o wyr mor ddoeth a dysgedig ag y fo yn ei plith? Mi welais lawer o sôn am y Cwrt Consiens yna, nid oedd ryfedd. Ni chlywai ddim sôn am wrthiau'r snising, mae'r Bersonyn yn achwyn nad yw fawr well erddo, ar lleill at yr un fath. Aie yna mae'r marsiant Fychan o'r Bala, gorchymynwch finneu atto ynteu os gwelwch yn addas. Ie, ie, bywoliaeth front yw bod yn adyn diymgeledd! Rwy finneu yn cadw tŷ a thendans, ond er hyny yn ddigon drwg fy nhrefn lawer trô. Nid yw fy housekeeper ond ieuanc, ag heb erioed gael fawr hyfforddiant, rhaid yw 'morol am ryw fath arall os hoedl ag iechyd a gair. Duw a'n cyfarwyddo at y goreu. Aie'r cenhedloedd gan y Spaeniaid ar Ffreinsh ydych yn ei feddwl a'n cospa am ein drigioni? Pe cae'm ein heiddiant ni byddem chwaith hir ar wyneb y ddaearen hon, ond y mae trugareddau'r Arglwydd yn dra helaethion. Ai tybied na chafodd y Ffrancod lonaid eu boliau ar ymladd er's dyddiau? A thybied na bo'r cenhedloedd rheini cynrhwng a ninneu a pheth gwaeth? Os felly, p'am na chawn inneu ei paffio nhwythau weithiau? Rwyn llwyr gredu ei bod yn haeddu golchfa rwan ag yn y man yn enwedig y Ffrancod. Is it not evident that they don't mind treatises nor have any regard to faith; witness Nova Scotia and the Caribee Isles. O chwiw ladron ffeilsion, yr wir nid oes le i weled mor llawer o fai ar y Spaeniaid. Gibraltar is an eye sore, and their logwood is their own, ond er hynny, nhw ddylent dalu eu dledion. Gadewch ich brawd Gwilym unigol glywed oddiwrthych fynycha galloch a byddwch wŷch. Roedd y nhâd a mam yn rhesymol dydd arall ag yr y'm ni yma oll yn rhwydd iachus. Mawl i'r Goruchaf am ei drugareddau. W. to R. contd.

Eich brawd anwiw, Wm. Morris.

Ai tybied y gwnâr tipyn bil yma hwn yn llythyr dwbl? Nid oes yma ddim ffrancodiau i'w cael. Mae'n harglwydd ni wedi ei briodi (ag yn gwneuthur gŵr gerwin). Mae Mr. Vychan ynteu yn ddigon pell o ffordd oddiyma. A welsoch i gowydd y gariadwraig Haras am adael cyfoeth i'w marchog? Mae'r brawd Llewelyn yn gadael ei yrru yma, rwy'n credu ei fod yn un digrif oblegid y mae'r testyn yn un llawen. Mae Mr. Ellis yn gweddio am weddi gyffredin ar ei phen ei hun. Pa'r ddelw sydd ar Feirian? Duw yn eich cylch. Yours as before, W. M.

C. Gybi, Hydref 23ain, 1750, Nos Fawrth. W. to R.

Anwyl Frawd,—Dymma fi newydd ddyfod adref o daith, o ba un y bydd da gennych gael tippyn o'i hanes, oblegid fy mod yn ymweled a'r hen gartref gynt. Boreu dydd Sadwrn cychwynais i CIII.

W. to R. contd. a fy mab tua'r dwyrain, ag wrth drafaelio yn ffest yn galed, ni a gawsom i Bentre'rianell cyn y nos. Roedd yno hen wr a hen wraig i'n croesawu yn rhwydd iach ac yn llawen, dyna lle bu dd'ri'r badell fawr am ben y badell fechan, etc. Tranoeth mynd a wnaethom ir Llan, lle trewais wrth ambell un or hen drigolion i ysgwyd llaw a hwynt, nid amgen, na Mrs. Williams o Fodafon, Wmffra o Ddulas, Twm Rolant y go', Sion ab Ifan, Owen Wmffra, Lew. Sion Oylfer, William Sion Oylfer a Sian eu chwaer (yr hon sydd wraig William Owen Pyrs glochydd yn agos i 90), Rhobert Wmffra, Rhobert a Harri ap Richard William, dailiwr or Efel fawr gynt, Twm William Glochydd. Digwyddodd fod priodas i fab iddo fo, a merch i Elsbeth 'ch Rhisiart William ag i Huw Probert, fab y Melinydd. Dydd arall roedd eu rhieni yn hogiau, onte? Bu agos imi anghofiaw Gruffydd Dafydd, mab yr hen William Dafydd Lewis gynt, a Thomas ab William Dafydd, yn awr yn ddall, felly yr oedd . . . . flaen. A dyna i chwi hanes yr hen "Stondards," ond nid y . . . . ynt yn awr ag oeddynt 27 mlynedd i rwan, pawb yn hen ag . . . . llwyd. Yn wir ddiau b'ai ryfedd gennych weled yr hen rieni, mae mam er ei bod yn cerdded ar ei 80 yn dra sionc oni bae fod un troed yn pallu. Roedd hi ddoe yn canu penhillion i fy mab a minnau. Mae nhad ynte yn dda iawn ar ei iechyd, yr anwyd ar peswch sydd yw drwblio yn o ddrwg, mae'n gwaeddi am Imperial Phoenix Snuff yn erwin dost, mae'n dywedyd yw fab Rhisiart adael gyrru iddo beth ryw dro. Taro yn Llanerchmedd wrth Tom Bryan, Dic Morys dlawd ddrwg ei ystym, Will Bedo, ffidler, pur dlawd ynteu, Mredydd yr hen was gynt, yn awr yn sadler, a dyna i chwi gyfrif o honynt bod y pen. Mawl i Dduw dyma ni wedi cael y cartref arnom yn llwyddianus a phawb yn iach ynddaw, felly nos dawch heno. Duw a fo'n gwarchad drosoch chwi a ninneu.

Eich caredigawl frawd, William Morris.

P.S.—Dyma fi wedi taro wrth lyfr ysgrifen ag ynddaw well na phedwar ugain o gowyddau yr ardderchog fardd, D. ap Gwilym, roedd gennyf lonaid llyfr o honynt or blaen, sef oddeutu 90; mae yma o 30 i 40 nad oeddynt gennyf na chyn neb arall yn y brofydd yma. Let me have a line from you as soon as you can, da chwitheu. W.M.

HOLYHEAD, 3rd December, 1750. W. to R. CIV.

Dear Brother,—I have yours of the 22nd ult. a chan diolch am tanaw. Gwych or bwriad oedd yn eich pen ymgyfarfod ar brawd Llew a minneu ym Mhenrhos, peth a eill ddigwydd ydyw, a phwy a wyr nad eill yr hen bobl gael y dedwyddwch hwnw before they make their exit? Brother Lewis and yourself, when you get over some difficulties that you have both to encounter with, a fyddwch yn gefn dynion os Duw a rydd yr hoedlau ar iechyd. Dyma finneu yn ymrwyfo ngoreu (wedi cael fy rhan o drwblaethau'r byd brwnt yma) i ddyfod i hyd i chwi, nid hwyrach y byddaf cyn darfod y Bibl ar gefn fy march; nid hwyrach, ynte, mae gwr traed fyddaf. Duw yn unig ai gwyr, rwy'n meddwl fod yn dyfod i mewn yma o gwmpas deg a thriugain yn y flwyddyn ond och or rhif sydd yn mynd allan, ni choeliach i byth! Mae'n dra drwg geny glywed eich bod yn cael eich nychu gan y peswch, Duw ai lleddfa. Ow na fase snising yn eich mendiaw; ie, ie, peth mawr yw ymgeledd. Nid oes dim llonychrwydd hebddi; rwyfi, mawl i Dduw, yn cael fy iechyd yn rhagorawl, drwy fyw yn dymherus, etc., er bod y meddwl yn afiach. Oes y mae genyf dwysgen o gywyddau D'ap Gwilym na fedd y brawd Llewelyn monynt; mae imi o ddeutu saith ugain, ond daccw Ynghallt Vadawg well nag un ugain ar ddeg o naddynt! Ie, digon digrif fyddeu ei hargraphu, gresyn bod cymaint o honynt mor fasweiddgar. The horse distemper has reachd this place, but I hear of none dying, ag yn ddistaw fe ddywedir fod y clwyf ar y gwartheg yn agos, but this under the rose, dan obeithio'r goreu. Yr anrhas ir printiwr efo i *dypes*, pan nad eiff o mlaen? I have time enough on my hands to write a line to a brother, though I can employ it pretty well, ond nid er cael chwaneg ir bocced, dyna'r gofid. Ymhle'r watch paper. I am glad you writ to Aldroman Pritchard. I have had a letter from him lately chiefly about Hughes's affairs. Mae ar yr Aldroman ddiwredd eisiau cymodi a Llewelyn, mae yn achwyn arno yn greulon am ddigio wrtho; rwyn sgrifenu at Lewelyn heddyw ag yn dywedyd iddo fal y mae'n bod. Father and mother were in a tollerable state of health the other day, felly mae pawb yma. Write as often as you can these dull times. Duw oi fawr drugaredd a fo'n gwarchad drosoch ar eiddoch ag a roddo i chwi iechyd. *Eich brawd caredigawl, Wm. Morris.*

W. to R. C. GYBI, 1st January, 1750.

CV. Anwyl Frawd,—Mae arnoch imi lythyr neu ddau er's dyddiau, ond er hynny i gyd ni fedraf lai na rhoddi i chwi hanes fal y mae'r byd yn bod ffordd ymma. Dyma'r chwaer yn dechreu ymendiaw (o glefyd mawr a gadd er's tair wythnos) er mawr gysur iw thylwyth mân ddigon; mae darpar chwaneg yno. Daccw ein mam wedi bod yn llesc iawn er nos Nadolig y pryd y torrodd y postwm arni, roedd hi heddyw yn beth gwell, a gobaith da rwan yr erys yn ein plith rai blynyddoedd etto er maint ei hoedran; mae nhad ynteu yn cael ei scerbydio yn erchyll gan yr anwyd, fal y bydd o agos i bob gauaf. Mae'r relyw o honom yn rhwydd iachus, mawl ir Goruchaf Dduw am ei drugaredd. Gwych y dywedodd un o'n diweddar brydyddion:

Dyma gyflwr dynol ryw
Yn iach, yn gla', yn farw, yn fyw.

Par sut y mae'r peswch gyd a chwi? Gadewch wybod, da chwithe. Ni welai ddim o hanes y papur waitsh. Nid yw Mrs. Wheldon yn clywed dim oddiwrth Mrs. Bailey o Ddeptford. Ai ni dderbyniwyd mor Wido' Pensions, etto? Pa beth ydyw'r matter? Ce's lythyr ddoe ne echdoe o Allt Fadawg, y gwr hwnw yn achwyn yn dost ar y byd; felly y gwnawn inneu pe byddai gwiw imi. Mae fy hen ffrind, sef Gobaith, yn ceisio sio yn fy nghlustia mae diboen i ddyn dybio yn dda, ag y daw pob peth well, well. Ond y peth goreu wedi'r cwbl yw disgwyl yn ddyfal wrth yr Arglwydd, a rhoddi ein hyder a'n goglyd arnaw. Dyna'r feddyginiaeth oreu allan; oni bae honno, nis gwn beth a ddeuai o honom. Duw a roddo i chwi flwyddyn newydd hapusawl a llawer un o naddynt yw taer erfyniad anwyl frawd.

Yr eiddoch yn garedigawl, Wm. Morris.

Pa wedd y mae'r Bibl newydd yn mynd ymlaen? Par drefn sydd arno?

W. to R. CAERGYBI, 30th Ionawr, 1750.

CVI. Anwyl Frawd,—I received yours of the 5th with the watch paper and seeds, a diolch yn fawr am danynt; ond etto erbyn yr y'ch llythyr yn fy n'led i cofiwch. Ni choeliach i byth falched ym ni yn y cwr yma or byd o gaffael tipyn o hadau oddiyna, ag och na bae'ch yn arddwr, telwn y pwyth ar y ganfed. Mae yma rai o bob cwr ar y byd, but they soon degenerate in this climate, rhaid a'u newyd bob yn awr. Ie yn wir gwaith odiaeth sydd ar y pappir waits. Par sut y daethoch i wybod mae hwn a hwn yw'r pechadur mwyaf? Nid yn ol y cystydd a dderbyn dyn y mae ei farnu. Ond dedwydd i ni gael tipyn o gosp yma, rhag ofn drwg draw, peth ffeind ydyw gobaith, coeliwch fi nid oes dim byw hebddaw. Gwilwyr meddwch ar byrth Mon rhag y clwyf, y mae ein ustusiaid wedi gorchymyn na ddel neb rhyw anifail corniog carnol o Arfon, ond beth ydis nes? Ofer yw ymwared dyn. Gwell yw Duw yn gar na llu daear. Nid oes ini siawns yn y byd oni wel yr Arglwydd yn dda attal y clwyf o gwbl, yr hyn y mae ein gobaith a wna ef yn ei amser da. Aie yr ydych i (ag eraill) yn pesychu am yr hoedl glas? Gresyn na chai ddyn eich cwmni dros awr neu ddwy i gyd besychu, oblegid nid oes yma nemawr un yn dyfod i fynu i'ch brawd Gwilym yn y grefft honno, ag etto rwyf inneu, mawl i Dduw, yn llawer gwell nag y bum. Da ydyw'ch bod yn gallu bwytta digon, felly finneu, a draen hefyd i bob peswch tra bo dyn yn cymeryd ei luniaeth yn rhywiog. Da yw bod y nith Meirian yn gawres neu'n gorres; mae yma un gyfnither iddi yn ei hannerch sef Marged, yr hon yw fy housekeeper i! Am y chwaer arall mae hi mewn gwasanaeth er's talm byd (heb ddim cyflogiad etto) efo Morgan, or Henblas. Mae hon yn lodes rhwydd dda, ond nis gwn i par sut a fydd ir llall drin y dreth, un bengaled ydyw. Rwyf hyd yn hyn yn cadw ty oreu gallwy sef yw fy nheulu, fy hun, am mab, ar nith, a morwyn, a chi a chath a dim arall. Mae fy herlodes etto gyda'i mamaeth; nis gwn i par sut a fydd trin y dreth pan ddel hi adref, ond ni waeth tewi na son am gartref, gwell a fai i minneu werthu'r creglach yma a mynd i letyfa fal chwitheu, nid wy'n enill fawr ar y gwaith yma. W. to R. contd.

Salaidd iawn oedd ein rhieni'r dydd arall. Y mam yn mendiaw yn bur araf deg, a nhad ynteu yn allan oi iechyd ymhell gan ryw anwyd a chnofydd yn ei frest; mae o yn ddewr iawn pan fo iach ond anwadal iawn yw henaint. Dyna i chwi ryw faint chwaneg or beiau ar anafau. Gresyn bod yr argraphwyr yn mynd 'mlaen mor ddiawg, ffei ladron, what do they blunder more than the Cantabs? What's the meaning on't? Daccw'r Mr. Meyrig o Fodorgan wedi talu i law Mr. Ellis bum gini aur tuag at argraphu'r Bibl, mae'n ffaelio

W. to R. contd. ettwa gael cyfleu iw gyrru i fynnu o achos eu bod yn ysgafn o bwysau, ag nid oedd dim edrych dannedd march rhodd. How do they manage the light gold with you? Mae yma'r rhwystr gerwina fu erioed or achos, most of the gold that's stirring are too light, English and foreign. Will nothing be done this sessions of Parliament for the relief of the subjects? If light guineas will be permitted to pass at 21s., no rogue that can afford to buy a file will ever pass a heavy one. We are worse off in this corner than anywhere, all our silver is carried to Ireland for I know not what, and light gold is all the species we have. Mae hi yma yn rhew ac eira echryslon, ag mae'n rhywyr imi ddarfod hwn fal y gallwyf fynd i dynny allan ryw accounts ag yno mynd i saethu adar gwylltion. Duw oi fawr drugaredd a fo'n gwarchad drosoch chwi a ninneu in cadw rhag pob drwg. *Eich caredigawl frawd, William Morris.*

P.S.—Dim newydd o Allt Fadawg er's dyddiau byd. Mae Margaret Morris ieuainc a minneu yn rhoddi ein gorchymyn at Feirian. Mae yma globyn o gefnder iddi yn dysgu mynd yn Esgob, un o'r llanciau digrifa a ganfu hi erioed; nid yw mor llawn bump oed, etto er hyn mae ganddo burion Cymraeg a Saesonaeg ag yn ysgolhaig rhagorawl! Ag am ei gampau eraill, nid oes rifedi arnynt. Mae fy herlodes yn dechreu dwndrio a cherdded ei goreu hitheu, tebyg yw nain o Bentre'riannell yw. Sgrifenwch gynta galloch da chwitheu.

W. to R. CVII.

CAER GYBI, 2d o Fawrth, 1750.

Anwyl Frawd,—Cefais eich llythyr or 23 a diolch am dano, a thrannoeth ar ol ei dderbyn daeth y nhad yma a chanddo'r eiddych yn ei bocced a phapir Irwin, etc. Ydynt, mawl i'r Goruchaf Dduw, wedi ymendiaw'n rhagorawl. Ni bu bo nhad er's llawer o flynydd-oedd cystal ar ei iechyd ag yw yn awr, a mam yn dechreu ymdreiglaw o gwmpas y ty, ag yn gallu bwytta tamaid yn dda iawn. Ddoe yr aeth y nhad adref gyd a'i gymydog Ffoulk Jones, officer Dulas, yr hwn oedd gynt Fowkyn y trwmpeter, brawd i Sion yna a fu'n drwmpeter ir Gards. Dynan cwrtais diniwaid yw hwn yn byw yn Rhos Fadog (Hu Bwiliam Tomos gynt). Gwych a fyddai ir Parlment yna fedru wneuthur argau i lestair ir *gin* brwnt ymledu dros yr holl deyrnas a boddi o'r holl wragedd sychedig. Temperance is a most amiable thing! Lle da i'r un o honom ddisgwil mynd cyn hyned an rhieni tra b'om yn bolera ag yn gloddesta beunydd mor ddigydwybod. Ond ni choeliach i byth gased gan eich brawd Gwilym ddiotta yr dyddiau hyn; mae'n debyg mae'r achos yw am nad ydyw yn cytuno ai dymer wneuthur felly, ag nid i unrhyw rinwedd. Inclosd you have a ffrank to send Mrs. Wheldon's printed paper. She is very uneasy to know if she has any chance for the remainder of last year's pension, Mrs. Bailey having given no reason for the deduction. Gwych yw bod y Bibl yn mynd yn mlaen mor hoyw. W. to R. contd.

Dyna i chwi lythyr ag erratas Mr. Richard Bulkley, Person Mechell, hen wr mwyn diniwaid, cywraint, llariaidd, cwrtais, Cymroaegydd goreu mae'n debyg ym Mon. Mi ai symbylaf i fynd ymlaen. Mae Mr. Ellis yn gorchymun attoch, mae o'n awr fal y byddai arferol, ond yn taeru na lefys gymeryd dim cywreinwaith yn llaw gan ei ben ai frest; mae pryf yn y pen, hynny sydd sicr, ni wn i pa beth yn y ddwyfron. You'd think your self happy if you could exercise your self as much as he may, having a good horse and master of his own time, Sundays and holydays excepted, a theiau gwyr mwynion o'i amgylch ar hyd y wlad. Na atto Duw chwedl amgen na'ch bod wedi meistroli'r peswch am y tymor yma. Mi ge's inneu fy sguttiaw gantho yn o dost, ag yr wyf fyth ag ettaw yn cael ambell loes. I will enquire about the ticket affair, though am affraid the fellow is the Lord knows where. Dyma fy nau grwtyn i wedi bod yn glaf or frech goch,—yr archlod ir haint, fe ai trinodd yn abl anfoesawl. Daccw blant y Syrveyor tan yr un clwyf; fe ddywedir fod y *Wen* yn y plwyf. Duw a gadwo bawb o honynt yn ddianaf os daw in plith. Mi af yn y cyd ar Weddi Gyffredin, par bryd y bydd arnoch ei eisiau debygwch? Wala, wala, rhaid tori'r eda' i gael mynd ir farchnadfa i brynnu lluniaeth erbyn yr wythnos nesaf. Duw a fo'n gwarchad drosoch chwi a'ch herlodes. Mae Marget Morris yn gorchymun attoch.

Eich caredigawl frawd, William Morris.

P.S.—Roedd yma ddoe un Mr. Ab. Morris, brawd i'r Captain Will Morris, who signd Irwin's Certificate. I presume this gentleman was a merchant in Cork, a phur falch ydoedd daro wrth namesake. Dyn mwyn digon. Par ddelw sydd ar Irwin? Mi ach gwela yn y pen ucha o'i Receivers, tipyn oi hanes da chwitheu—

W. to R. contd.

a good undertaking. Mae ar y Bersonyn Ellis flys garw am gael gweled un sheet or Bibl yna. Stwffio ddigon o ryw bethau yn y ffrencyn yna, na yrrwch monaw yn weili da chwitheu. Have you no acquaintance with ere a florist that a body may have a few curious seeds. I've now a hot bed with frames and glasses that I could raise anything almost. Dyma genym dair o longau pyst newydd brafia a welwyd yma erioed. Hyspyswch i bawb o bell ag agos y newydd pwysfawr hwn! Dydd Mawrth diweddaf y boreu y bu yma'r gwynt echryslona ar a welwyd, glywyd neu a glybuwyd yn oes neb yn fyw; gerwin y torrwyd ein teiau ar tô gwellt arnynt. Dim drygau ar y mor ffordd am a glywn ettwa. "Piliwr adail pa le'r ydwyd, planed wyllt pa le nid wyd," ebr rhywun.

W. to R.

CVIII.

GARTREF, 12d Ebrill, 1751, N.S.

Anwyl Frawd,—Dyma fi newydd ddyfod adref o Bentre Eirianallt. Mae'n yspys gennyf mae da gennych glywed fod ein rhieni yn dda iawn ar eu hiechyd, yn ol yr achos, sef eu hoedran. Mae mam wedi bod ddwywaith yn yr eglwys ar ol y clefyd diweddaf, ag y mae hi'n gweled ag yn clywed cystal cynt ond ei bod yn ô fusgrell. Mae nhad yn achwyn bod y golwg yn pallu peth, ond y mae yn clywed yn well nag y bu—mawl ir Goruchaf Dduw am ei drugaredd. Byddai ryfedd gennych eu gweled gin sionced ag ydynt; mae'nt yn gobeitho cael golwg maes arnoch cyn eu marw. Digrif fyddai cael un ymgyfarfod yma, ond nid hwyrach mae draw y bydd, Duw a ddel ag un llawen bydded lle y mynno. Do, mi gefais eich llythyr a phapur i Mrs. Wheldon, chwedl abl tlawd ir druanes honno, ond mae llawer un yn waeth eu cyflwr. Nid têg oedd gwaith y dynion yna, addaw 20 a thalu dim ond 6. Yr oeddwn inneu yn meddwl mae gwell ieithydd Bwclai nag Ellis, mi sgrifenais atto i erchi iddo fynd ymlaen, ag a elwais ddoe yn ei dy, ond nid oedd mo hono gartref. Buan y daeth Iorwerth ap Iorwerth yn ei ol o Foston. Ni chlywais i gael oi chwaer yr un llythyr oddiwrthaw. Rym ninneu yn gorchymun atto yntau, pe bai fatter yn y peth. Ie yn wir gwych iawn fyddai gael rhai o'r hickry nutts o'r Shagbags, fal y gallwn wneuthur coed o honynt. Won't the cranberries grow here? Roberts, the sailor, is daily expected at Liverpoole; his parents have promisd to let me know when he arrives. Ie, yn wir, da chwitheu ymorolwch am dipyn o ryw hadau dieithr. I have all the common annual flowers and common perennial plants, ond er hynny, nid digon i foddio'r golwg. Os Gwyddel cynhwynol yw Irwin, lle da disgwyl daioni o honaw; nid oes mewn mil un o honynt a dâl ei godi oddiar y maes; er y gwelais yrwan ag yn y man ambell un or gweddeiddia, rare birds! Ond felly mae pob cenedl, meddwch chwitheu, ie, yn wir, felly maent yn sicr ysywaeth ir cywiriaid. Och y finneu'r golled ir deyrnas am y tywysog, ond Dûw yn unig a wyddai oreu pa beth i wneuthur ag ef a ninneu. Perhaps things may turn out well; if they do, its more than we deserve—a wicked and perverse generation. Do you know whether a certificate of the minister, churchwardens, and principal officers of the Customs here might not do to obtain Mrs. Wheldon's pension, instead of going to a Justice of the Peace; the pension is but small and the justice far off; os gwna, gadewch glywed mewn amser, obleit rhaid iddi yrru un yna'r mis nesaf. Daccw Huw Huws, Lligwy, hwn a welsoch gynt yn Llundain yn saerniaeth, wedi marw a chwedi gadael yr hen Lowri Huws, ein modryb ynghyfraith, yn wraig weddw. Nid hwyrach y myn hi ŵr arall; he died of a dropsy and was become a drunken old fellow! Dymma Farged Morys ieuanc, yn gorchymun yn fawr at ei chyfnither, felly mae pawb o honom attoch eich deuwedd 'Rym yn awr yn rhwydd iachus bod ag un. Mi af ynghyd ar Weddi Gyffredin pan ddarfyddo imi roddi fy hadau, etc., yn y ddaear; rwy wedi bod yn segur drwy'r wythnos yma felly rhaid gweithio a mwstrio yn ffyrnig y nesaf. Ni chlywais ddim o Allt Fadog yn ddiweddar, digon da os ceir llythyr oddi yno rwan unwaith y pedwar amser; mae'r cyfreithiau ar planta ar hwsmonaetha wedi spwylio'r dynan hwnnw. Wrth gofiaw. Nis gwn i pa beth a wnaf am dipyn o sgrifen or Customhouse, yna, sef: "A certificate to discharge a coast bond given here for a parcel of tobacco shipt on board the *Francis and Mary*, Thomas Archer, ... from hence for London in the name of Peter Fearon." The Cocket was dated the 6 or 7 April, 1749. Perhaps there is no charge attending it, for we here take the fees of the certificate at the entry of the goods; it may be so there, but if you are obliged to pay 2s. or 2s. 2d. nid oes mor help, mi ai talaf inneu nhw i chwitheu y cyfleu cynta a gaffwyf. Da chwitheu

W. to R. contd.

W. to R. contd.

picciwch hyd at y dollfa ryw dro a mynnwch gael certificate ag onite fe a fydd digon o ddrwg yn y dref. Duw a fo'n gwarchad drosoch.

Eich caredigawl frawd, William Morris.

W. to R. CIX.

HOLYHEAD, 6 May, 1751.

Dear Brother,—I received your two pacquets containing Evans contra Whitfield, and Richards' proposal, likewise the seeds, which were more acceptable than either of them, a chan diolch am danynt. Rhyfeddol iawn fydd gweled Cedrwydd Libanus yn gorchguddio naill hanner o Ynys Fôn, yno hi a â yn ynys dowell yn ei hôl, a chenid cywyddau iddi mal cynt. Gerwin yw bwriad Richards* yna! Par sutt gymorth ydych yn ei feddwl—cymorth *subscribers* ynte geiriau? The book would certainly be very useful if well conducted, and 'tis pity that it had not been ta'en in hand by some Northwalian such as Samuel, Wynne or Morris; mae pawb yma yn ofni na wna'r dyn Deheuig yna law yn y byd or peth. He sets out pretty well, his specimen should have been quite inexceptionable. Pam y dywaid o mae Syr A. Owen yw *proprietor* Aber-ffraw? Mae yno *broprietors* heblaw fo, Mr. Meyrick, etc., though Sir Arthur has the greatest estate in the village. If the thing had been well recommended I doubt not but a great many subscribers would be had here. His inserting the name of bishops, clergymen, and esquires as patrons is all stuff. Beth a ŵyr y rheini oddi wrth y mater? Is there to be a botanic part to it? Who manages that? Gresyn na bae'r brawd Lewis yn cymeryd y Doctor Davies yn llaw, rhoddwn inneu iddo y botanologium goreu (o un Gymreig) ar a fu erioed ar wyneb y ddaear! But that man, the Lord help him, hath brought upon himself troubles and vexations in abundance, base well bod yn weddw ganwaith na'r gwaith accw. Ce's lythyr trist oddiwrthaw yr wythnos ddiweddaf. Duw ai dycco allan oi dramgwyddiadau, a phawb o honom gydag ef, os gwel o'n dda. Rwyf inneu wedi digio yn erchyll wrth y byd brwnt yma, nid oes dim daioni i gael ynddo ar a welai i, ond i ambell rôg a chnâ; oes mae ffyliaid yn ffyny'n rhyfeddol, ond i paradwys nhw ydyw fo. Ie, yn wir, gresyn na bae'r mes a'r cnau yna yma, fal y gellid eu hymgeleddu.

*The Rev. Thomas Richards, of Coychurch, Glamorganshire, published his Welsh-English Dictionary, in 1753. It is a translation of Dr. Davies's Welsh-Latin Dictionary with some additions from Lhuyd's vocabularies.

Rwyfi yn cyweirio ar y Weddi Cyffredin ngoreu glâs, chwi gewch fy ngorchwyl ryw dro, pawb eraill yma yn ddiog anial. Diolch yn fawr am y certificate (heblaw talu). You were sadly imposd upon by the clerks, the original certificate should have been but 2s. 2d., and this about 14d. O chwiw ladron! Ymhob crefft y mae coggiaw, felly yna mae'n debyg. Dyma Ddic Morris bwt wedi bod yn cymeryd ei gennad, mae o am gychwyn tua Llundain rai or dyddiau yma medd o; roedd yn dymunaw arnoch ymorol ymhlith eich ffrindiau am wasanaeth iddo, fe fedr wneuthur peth o bob peth a llawer o bob un. Nid oes yma ddim lle iw fath; fe wnae'n burion i dendio ar rhyw hen ddynan neu hen forwynig, os medrwch helpu tippyn arno, gweithred enaid a fydd, nid taclus y trinwyd mono Ymodorgan. W. to R. contd.

Pwy yw'ch cyfaill Evans, awdwr y pamphlet yma?* Mae o gida'r chwerwa yn ei ymadrodd, gweddusach bod yn hynaws. Diammeu fod yr hen Ruffudd Sion, Llanddowror, yn gwneuthur llawer o ddaioni, o achos paham yr haeddai barch a thrugaredd gan ddynion gweiniad fal ef ei hun, o ran pwy sydd heb wendidau ag wmbwrdd o honynt hefyd? Er hynny i gyd, gadewch gael y darn arall or llyfran. Par ddelw sydd ar Feirian? Ni soniasoch am dani yn eich llythyr. Par sut y mae hi yn dyscu yn y Boarding School? Dyma fy merch inneu yn dyfod adref yr wythnos nesaf oddiwrth y famaeth yn 2¼ mlwydd oed, ag yna ni fyddwn bum nyn o dylwyth. Mae Pegi Morris yn tario yma dros un hanner blwydd etto, ag yno i fynd i wasanaeth a fo gwell, naill ai Lundain, ai Lerpwl, ai Dulun. Mae Ellin yn glynu yn yr Henblas ag yn leicio ei lle o'r goreu. Beth a dâl cadw ty heb wraig ynddo? Ni thâl o ddim yn y byd, ag ni waeth roddi'r swydd i fynu na pheidiaw. Beth meddwch chwi sydd wedi treio'r ddwy ffordd? Rhowch gyngor, da chwitheu, i ddynan ymddifaid. Roedd y nhad a mam yn rhwydd iachus oddeutu canol yr wythnos ddiwaethaf. Bu Ruffydd Dafydd yma ar ryw neges iddynt. Ag yr ym ni yma oll yn iachus, i Dduw y byddo'r diolch. Mae fal yr ysgrifenwch gynta galloch, a Duw a fo'n gwarchad drosoch bob amser.

Wyf eich caredigawl frawd, William Morris.

* This refers to the scurrilous pamphlet issued by John Evans, Vicar of Eglwys Cymmun, Carmarthenshire, in 1752. See Llyfryddiaeth y Cymry, p. 432.

XC Dear Brother,—I received yours of the 3rd on my return from Shropshire, and am glad to hear you are so well in health and so well situated. God be thanked for all happiness and peace. Nag ydwyf ar fedr bedyddio 'run dri mis etto. What put it in your head that Tywysog Cymru was a good man? Dyn gwirion dros ben oedd ef. What goodness was there in that? Woe be to ye country that hath a fool for its Governor! Beth a wn i pa Gymraeg sydd am dowager? Gwaddoledig mae'n debyg. Y dywysoges waddoledig sydd air newydd iawn, dyna'r gwaethaf. Pa fodd y gelwir hi ynghyfraith Howell Dda? It is impossible for me, and I am sorry for it, that I cannot send you remarks on your proverbs. I am so confounded with lawsuits and troubles that I have not a minute's cool time to spare, and a few days ago I was within an ace of *mynd i garchar*.* That trial at Chester being unknown to me it was a great chance they did not get an execution against me before I knew anything of ye matter and before the writ of injunction could be serv'd upon them. Duw a ddiofalo pob dyn gonest oddiwrth gyfreithwyr. Nid oedd Corbed o'r Amralty ddim ffrind imi ers talm, mwy nai frawd, ped faent ar gefnau eu gilydd ni waeth gennyfi. Chwi oedd y cynta a ddywaid imi pa le oedd gan Lord Lincoln, a phawb eraill yn gwybod o'r papirau newydd, a minneu fal llo yn gwrando arnyn. Fe fydd ar y gwr lai o eisiau arian bellach, ag nid hwyrach y cofia fo ryw ddynan truan ryw dro. I have discovered some frauds of ye late steward lately, ni wn i gaf i glod am hynny ai peidio. The Welsh Dictionary may be a tolerable thing, but far from being perfect for want of a general correspondence. I beth y dwedai'r fulen mae Syr Arthur oedd y piau'r Aberffro? Mae yno dir i Mr. Meyrig a phobl eraill. Pa fodd y gellwch i gael amser i roi coppi och casgliad o eirieu Cymraeg iddo fo? Ni chawn i yn fy myw amser i sgrifenu iddo un *sheet*, chwaethach deugain. I gave you my reasons for writing (g) in ye word *ieuangc*, and why I write *ieuengctyd* and not *ieuengctid*. It is for the same reason that I write bywyd, iechyd

* For a full account of Lewis Morris's connection with the Cardiganshire lead mines, and the legal proceedings he was engaged in, see the excellent monograph written by Mr. D. Lleufer Thomas in the Cymmrodor, vol. 15.

clefyd, etc., and not bywid, iechid, clefid, from byw, iach, claf. Anghenogtyd ought also to be wrote so. Mi glowais yn Sir Amhwythig ddwedyd briodi o Arglwydd Powys. Diolch i chwi am ddywedyd pwy, fe allai mae hynny oedd yn rhwystro iddo atteb fy llythyr i; gwae fi na attebai fo, mae'n fy mryd i sgrifennu at y Mr. Bodvel ar fyrder i siarad ag efe. No, I had no letter from Ned Edwards, I suppose he blunderd in his direction. I hear Roderick Richardes* is come home. Goreu pei pella yr elo eich controwler chwi mae'n debyg. Mi wranta yma werth mil o bunnau o fwyn i'r penwyn, ond ni wn i pa hyd y pery. Da iawn, Murdoc Macensi, ag och o druan Pickering, ni waeth dyn mud nag ynte. Gyrrwch yr hiccory nuts ar New England acorns, yn llong Catterel neu rywun sydd yn dyfod i Gaerfyrddin, a'r almanac hefyd, to be left for me at John Griffith's, the attorney there, and I can have them. Er mwyn Duw oes dim gobaith cael mynd yn ddegymwr? Fe wnae hynny help fawr mewn adwy wan—chwi wyddoch amcan wrth wyneb Guidott, a ydyw ef mewn difrif? Duw fo gida chwi. *Eich brawd digon mawr ei drafferth, L.M.* L. to R. contd.

Ynghylch pa amser y bydd y Parliament i fynu! Ni wn i na bydd raid imi ddyfod yna cyn hynny.

CAER GYBI, Mehefin 6, 1751. W. to R.

CXI.

Mon Cher Frere,—Yr achos a bair im sgrifennu attoch yn awr ydyw hyn: Neithiwr y dychwelais adref wedi bod bedair nos ym Mhentre Eirianallt yn ymweled a'r hen rieni, sef fy hun am mab Rhobert. Yr wir, musgrell ag afiachus iawn yw yr hen bobl. Mae nhad yn lleccyn er's dyddiau byd, rhyw gnofydd yn ei frest, y piles, etc. Mae o yn gorwedd yn fynych ai sprydoedd yn bur isel, which is generally the case in that distemper. Are you quite clear of it? Mae mam hitheu yn bur gloff; prin y medr hi ymlwybran rhyd y ty. Duw a helpio y ddau; mae'n dosturus ei gweled weithiau, ag yn hyfryd ei gweled dro arall. Bum efo offeiriad y plwy a nhad yn gwneuthur llythyr cymun yr hen William Owen Pyrs, glochydd, yr hwn sydd 87 oedran agos, yn ddall ag yn orweiddiog. Sian 'ch Sion Oylfer ei wraig yn scutores ar y cwbl am ymgeledd. Rym ni yma oll yn rhwydd iachus, wythnos i forri y bedyddiwyd mab ir

* Roderick Richardes, of Penglais, Aberystwyth. He was a friend of the Morrises, and is constantly referred to in the letters.

W. to R. contd. chwaer ar brawd Dafies, yr hwn a enwyd Rhisiart, nage, nage, Richard. Mae'r fam yn dda iawn yn ol yr achos, dim newydd arall. Duw a fo gyda chwi. *Eich caredigawl frawd, Wm. Morris.*

P.S.—Pam na ddywedwch ai Biblau William Jones, Pabo, oedd ar werth dydd arall ymhob ieithoedd. Er mwyn dyn sgrifenwch at y nhad fynycha galloch. Mae rhyw chwaer i'r Wil Jones hwnw agos a thynu ei lygaid am arian; mae hi'n clywed fod eraill wedi cael rhai, scutorion Lieutenant Edmonds, etc.—W.M.

W. to R. CXII.

CAER GYBI, 12d Fehefin, 1751.

F'anwyl Frawd,—Mi sgrifennais attoch dydd arall a hanes yr hen rieni, etc., ag yno cefais eich llythyr or 4dd a chwaneg o waith Evans contra Whitfield, etc. Diolch yn fawr am danynt, a chan bod y tywydd yn rhy wresog (poeth allaswn i ddywedyd) i weithio mewn gardd neu rhyw orchwyl arall allan, dyma i chwitheu linell neu ddwy yn atteb. Aie mae hi yna yn rhwydd wresogaidd? Digrif fod y fath hin yn eich bywhau chwi ag yn fy lleddfu inneu. Ni welai mo'r cedrwydd yn eginaw mor pethau, er bod ffawydd a hauwyd yr un amser allan o'r ddaear er's dyddiau. Have you such a thing as a whole cone which contains the seed? I'me afraid the seed you sent were crushed in the carriage. Er dim ar y fo cedwch imi chwaneg o'r had fal y gallwyf ei hau y Mawrth nesaf—roedd hi gyda'r diweddaraf pan gafed y rhain. Mae gwyddau breision yn anhawdd eu llochi, ag ni thal rhai culion i gymeryd y drafferth efo nhw, felly heb ŵydd y byddis ni wybod par hyd. Par fodd yr y'ch chwi yn amcanu treulio y rhan arall och bywyd, ai'n ddwbl ynteu'n siengl? Om rhan i, ni waeth cyfaddef y gwir na pheidiaw, pe cawn fy ewyllys ni byddwn chwaith hir heb newid fy nghyflwr, er ond odid mai gwell fyddai peidiwch. Duw yn unig a wyr pa beth sydd oreu ar ein lles, nid y'm ond megys dynion ag *amhugwd* neu ymhugwd, myhugwd, mwhwgwd, neu rywbeth dros eu llygaid. Na chlywais i erioed son am Sion Evans y Darllenwr. Ai ni fydd o yn pregethu dim yddynt? I am sorry that I must answer in the negative to your question concerning the herbal, which I'me obliged to do upon many accounts. My catalogue (for so it's called) is drawn, the Latin first, then Welsh, and then the English names, and last of all the Irish, Cornish, Armorican, etc., with the virtues and receipes annext, so that it is a pretty large book; it would be a monstrous piece of work to model it anew by setting the Welch first alphabetically, though I have begun it, i.e., the Welsh first, a long time ago; yet it will require a long while to perfect it, perhaps more than I shall ever bestow upon't but query. If Mr. Richards publishes a botanic part I would willingly revise it, were it possible to have it sent here, all that have been done in the Welch hitherto are intollerable. He'd better not meddle with it without he can exhibit a better herbal than Dr. Davies and his followers Jones and Rhydderch, confounding one plant for another and playing the vengeance. I have shewn the proposal to many of our clergy and gentry, most of whom were willing to subscribe towards carrying on so useful a work, provided Mr. Richards would appoint some responsible person to receive, etc., in this country. I have been consulting with some friends who might be a proper person, for booksellers we have none, nor shopkeepers that will do any good. We have fixd upon the Rev. Mr. John Evans of Treban (a brother of Mr. Thomas Evans, the lawyer of your city). Mr. Evans is a person that lives in the middle of the island, and as he is a considerable farmer and an agent for some gent, frequents most fairs and publick meetings, and is acquainted with all the gentry and clergy in the county. I daresay if Mr. Richards would apply to him by letter directed for him as above, near Llanerchmed d, he would take upon him that trouble, though I have not spoke to him yet. I have desired Mr. Thomas Owen, Rector of Aberffraw, to do it. Mr. Owen liked the work greatly and will recomend it, he is the oracle for dysceidiaeth ffordd ymma. What says Llewelyn to do this work, doth he countenance it? Perhaps it may prejudice his scheme of publishing Davies's lexicon. Ie, yn wir, rwyn ofni mae chwithig ydoedd y naid a gymerwyd er maint y synwyr, a digon o siampl i boblach gymeryd y mawr ofal wrth neidiaw rhag ofn y gwaethaf. Roedd yn disgwyl i'r Arglwydd Powys wneuthur erddo yn y Drysorfa, nis gwn i a wnaed dim ai peidiaw. Mae subscribers Dulun yn prifio'n bur fawaidd (nid er amharch arnoch) wedi cael eu llyfrau plans, ni welai fawr arian yn dyfod oddiwrthynt. Gwyddhelod ydynt. Pray my compliments to Alderman Prichard. Roberts, his rider, was here two days ago and had left all well at home. I presume Huw Roberts, his factor here, will write him next

W. to R. contd.

W. to R. contd. post; he hath bought for him, I believe, upwards of 50 tons of kelp. Gobeitho hefyd y prifia Meirian yn lodes dda. Gweddiwch drosti tra bo heb allu hynny drosti eu hun, a Duw a rydd ei ras iddi, os y chwi a hitheu a'i cais yn ffyddlon. Yn wir ddiau aneirif yw'r temptasiwnau sydd beunydd yn amgylchu ieuenctyd; chwi wyddoch fod gormod o lawer yn gosod arnom pan fo'm mewn gwth o oedran, chwaethach hwynt sydd yn feddalion. Aie mae'r wasc yn peri codi'n foreu, ni waeth fyth, gwyn ei fyd a fedra gan ddiogi wneuthur yr un peth, ag mi fyddaf yn fynych pe ba'i fatter yn y peth, ond yn lle chwynnu beiau llyfrau, chwynnu gardd lysiau y byddaf innau, oblegit dyna'r amser goreu i weini allan o dy, ag o mor hyfryd y boreuau yn y wlad. Ie, yn wir, peth digon erchyll yw 'spectol ar draws trwyn gwr tan 50 oed. Hyfryd fase ganddoch weled ein tad a'n mam yn darllain dydd arall pam fum Ymhentre Eirianallt heb spectol na dim arall. Mae mam yn gweled ac yn clywed cystal ag yr oedd pan oedd 40 oed, ond y mae'r ddau yn pallu gan fy nhad er y medr ddarllain print eglur heb ddrych. Duw ai cadwo nhw i'w gilydd. Mae fan yma ryw wâg drafferthion yn llestair i ddyn wneuthur dim daioni. Wawch, dyma Gadpen Weller (Commander of the *Dublin Yatch*) newydd yrru imi hanner dwsing o ryw win braf, braf. Rhaid a mynd i gerdded ag i rodienna efog y fo ai wraig ieuanc a briodws e'r dydd arall ffordd yna. Mab hynaf yw hwn ir hen Gadpen yr hwn a roddes y swydd i fynnu er mwyn y mab. Ffrind mawr imi ydoedd yr hen. Dyma Arglwyddesau, ni wn prin moi rhifedi, yn dyfod i lygadrythu ar fy ngardd i ag i fwytta fy holl fefus i; rhaid rhoddi pob peth heibiaw a mynd i wneuthur sîr iddynt. Duw a fyddo'n gwarchad drosoch ar eiddoch yw dymuniad *Eich anwylaf frawd, Wm. Morris.*

P.S.—Nid oes yma a roechi yn eich llygad o newydd yn y byd, oes yna ddim gydag a welwn yn y papurau argraphedig yma? Ba beth y mae'r Counsellor Meyrick yn ei wneuthur yna ar hyd yr amser? Mi glywa fod ei hen was Robin wedi chwareu castiau cadi ag wedi cymryd y goes. Wfft ir fath ddyn ag efo. A fyddwchi yn gweled y Bwrsun ddiniwed weithiau ai Arglwyddes? Par sut y daeth oddiwrth yr Arglwydd Pwt? A gesochi'r mwnws ganddo? Oes digon o rheini ffordd yna? Nhw aethont oddiyma bod y beil, ffarwel gyda nhw. Byddwch wych, yr eiddoch fal or blaen.—W.M

HOLYHEAD, 17th July, 1751.

Dear Brother,—I have before me yours of the 29th July (June oeddid yn ei feddwl), gresyn fod y piles ar peswch yn ymgydiaw a chwi, cymdeithion o'r dihira', fo'i gwyr Duw a dynion. Aie roeddych yn gweled llawer o ryfeddodau yn eich pererindawd o 15 milldir? Yn wir nid wyf inneu ond ymdeithydd diog iawn, ni bu monwy' bellach Pentre Eirianallt ers dwy flynedd, nag or Ynys yma er's pedair mlynedd neu bump. Mae gwahawdd mawr i'm i deiau'r bonedd o'r cwmpas yma, er hynny nid wyf yn clywed arnaf symud oddi yma, o achos ei bod yn gostus mynd i blith y mawrion ag yn enbyd hefyd o achos y tra yfed sydd yn eu mysc! Mae gormod gartre ysywaeth. 'Roedd yma ddoe hen ffrind ir brawd Llewelyn a chwitheu, sef Mr. Thomas, pen gwas Syr Thomas Wynne gynt. Dyma fi'n llesc ar ol pottiaw efo hwnnw ag arall, pottiaw heddyw efo Chaptain Weller ynteu, a chroesawu'r wraig yn fy ngardd a mafon a chan mil o bethau eraill. Pwy oedd yr Arglwyddesau oedd yn bwytta fy mefus i, ond Countess of Meath, Lady St. Leger, Lady Prendergast, etc., gwragedd cymhedrol ddigon. I am glad you stopt that impertinent silkman's foul mouth, ffarwel gydage, chwedl Huw Parri'r hen was pan framiai. Aie *a sour morose man*, meddwch am y cadpen, mi ai hadwaenwn er yn las lanc, a mwyn ddigon y gwelais i o erioed hyd yn heddyw, nid yw'n cofiaw monoch chwi yn yr offis. Mr. Evans seems to decline the office of receiving subscribers for the Welsh Dictionary; however, Richards may try him. Gerwin or hyd sydd yn llythyr Evans at Whitfield! Fo debygai ddyn ei fod yn mynnu cael y gair yn drecha ar naddynt; ond nid wyfi farnwr ar fatterion mor bwysfawr. Aie mae'r benywiaid (na b'ond i grybwyll!) yn barod i dynnu eich llygaid och pen? Wfft ir rhywogaeth arglwyddi yna! Mae'r cnawd yn sisial yn eich clust, mi a wranta, fod y Bibl yn beth o'r ffeinia, ond llawer ffeiniach yw gwraig rinweddol. Mae'r yspryd yn dywedyd yn y gwrthwyneb mae gwell priodi'r Bibl nag ymherodres, rhaid im wiliaw meddwch, ni wiliwn yn fy myw. Daccw lydnes o ddynes wedi fy nal mewn rhwyd ag etto yn naccau ymborthi arnaf, a phe ymgrogwn nis cawn yn rhydd oi hafflau. Yr anrhas ir golud bydol yma, ni bu erioed ddaioni o ormod o honaw. Gwir yw'r penill:—Ymhob man mae cryf a gwan
Am arian yn ymorol.

Deg i un nad ydwyf yn ddedwyddach efo'r ddau giwtyn yma W. to R. CXIII.

W. to R. contd.

nag a fyddwn pei cawn ryw wilog benffol, ond pwy a wyr os ieuanc a fydd rhaid gwneuthur plant, a dyma fineu mewn gwth o oedran i drin y rheini. Os hen a fydd y feinir, ni waeth mor llawer hebddi na'i chael. Un ganolig sydd raid gael yn rhywle, nag oes yma ddim dewis na thebyg ir peth. Lle brwnt anghysbell, ffei hono! Da clywed eich bod wedi cael bara i Owain y Garddwr. Ni chlywais byth inclin gair oddiwrtho. Aie nid oes dim buwiol'aeth i Ddic Morys bwtt, pa beth a ddaeth or hadlaeth? Rwy'n gobeitho fod y nhad yn dippyn gwell, bu yma lanc dydd arall oddiyno yn nôl Pegy Morris a fy herlodes inneu i ymweled ar hen rieni, nis gwn i etto par sut a fu iddynt drafaeliaw. Ni chefais i un llythyr oddiwrth y brawd Llewelyn er's agos i chwarter blwyddyn. Mae'r dyn hwnnw wedi ei lygad tynu yn ddiamau. 'Roeddwn yn meddwl gwneuthur llythyr hir o hwn, ond dyma ryw wag drafferthion ym rhwystraw. Nis gwn i pa beth i ddywedyd ynghylch y *dowager*, nid wyfi yn leicco mor gair gwaddolig oll. Mae *twysoges weddw Cymru* yn chwithig iawn, mi a debygwn mae'r *dywysoges weddw* fyddai, neu dyna'r enw ym yn ei arfer yma wedi hir synied y matter. Rwy'n cofiaw weled mewn rhyw lyfr a argraphwyd yn amser Siamas II. (rwy'n meddwl) y gweddiau dros Catherin y Frenhines weddw. Y fam Frenhines, a arferid yn amser Charles II. Ni thal dim rhoddi i lawr mewn gweddi air ni ddeallir gan y bobl. Pwy sydd yn cymeryd arno gyfiaethu y *Proclamation* sydd yn dyfod allan ynghylch gweddio am y teulu, etc. Yr archlod iddo, mae'n gwneuthur trefn ddrwg ar iaith. Duw fo'n gwarchad drosoch a'r eiddoch.

Eich caredigawl frawd, William Morris.

CAER GYBI, 16 o Awst, 1751.

W. to R. CXIV.

Anwyl Frawd,—Mae ennyd fawr o amser er pan gefais lythyr oddiwrthych yn rhoddi hanes eich bod yn sâl ar eich iechyd, ag roeddwn yn gobeithio cael cyn hyn y newydd o'ch bod wedi mendiaw; os y'ch felly, pam na roesech i ni y melus cystal ar chwerw? Mae imi frawd (rwy'n gobeitho) yn Nehaubarth Cymru na rydd imi na'r naill na'r llall, mae hi'n well na chwarter blwyddyn er pan ge's lythyr oddiwrthaw, ag ni chlywai fod neb arall yn cael yr un mwy na minneu ffordd yma. Nid hwyrach fod yr hen elyniaeth gynt rhwng Gwynedd a Deheubarth yn tarddu allan o newydd ag y bydd brawd yn erbyn brawd. Par sut yr ydych chwi ag ynteu yn sefyll, oes llythyr yn dyfod yna weithiau? Wala, rhaid ceisiaw ymfodloni pe bai'r holl fyd yn anghofiaw dynan unig. Pawb drosto ei hun, a Duw dros y cwbl, yw'r hen ddywediad sydd yn cael ei le yn fynych. Roedd y nhad a mam yn rhesymol iachus echdoe, ag yr y'm ni yma oll yn dda iawn ar ein hiechyd, mawl ir Goruchaf am ei drugaredd ai fendithion. Nid wyf yn gwneuthur llaw yn y byd or Weddi Gyffredin yma, rhwng gan anhawsed yw, o eisiau na fase yn adnodau neu wersi, etc., a minneu yn cael fy nyrysu gan ryw wag drafferthion y rhai sydd im blino neu yn fy hudo beunydd, nad wyf yn cael mo'm cof na'm synwyr mal y dylawn. Gobaith sydd yn fy nghynnal rhag mynd gyda'r weilgi. Dyma ddiwrnod wedi mynd yn ofer heddy wrth rythu fy llygaid ar Esgob Bangor yn rhoddi bedydd i fagad o bobloedd *hen* ag ieuanc; ni welswn mor seremoni er pan fu'r Esgob Evans yn rhoddi ei fedydd i chwi ar brawd Llewelyn yn Llanerchmedd er's yn agos i 40 mlynedd, mi a wranta. Nid wyf yn leicio mor peth hanner da, fal y maent yn eu drin, rhy debyg i rodres a rhiolti Eglwys Rufain. Nos dawch heno, Duw a fo'n gwarchad drosoch a'r eiddoch. **W. to R. contd.**

Eich caredigawl frawd, William Morris.

CAER GYBI, Awst 28, 1751.

Anwyl Frawd,—I ddangos i chwi mor ddiolchgar ydwyf am eich llythyr llawn o ddiddanwch, dyma fi yn eistedd i lawr iw atteb agos cyn gynted ag y daeth i'm llaw, ond nid wyf yn disgwyl i chwi wneuthur felly, gan gymaint yw eich trafferth ach anhunedd yn pentyrru dâ byd. Gwych a fyddai gennyf inneu gael digon o waith a thâl am ei wneuthur; mi a ymegniwn yn hoyw, ond nid dyma'r fan i enill mwnws bydol—lle odiaethol yw gwasgaru. We Officers of the Customs' hands are tied, that we can't do anything but our own business, no dealing, no farming, nid oes yma un ffordd arall. Aie diddaioni o'r Wiltwrn accw? Wala bydded ynte' felly, ni wnaf i ddim ond hynny o groesaw iddo. Par sut y cair gweled pregeth Befan i'r Cymru Wyl Ddewi? Ie yn wir eisiau gwaith i wneuthur sydd ar bawb a ymhelio ar benywiaid, nid hwyrach na bydd i mi a wnelwyf ag yr un o honynt tra bwyf byw. Os hynny a ddigwydd, nid arnaf i y bydd y bai, mi a wnaf yng ngoreu ar ymgadw rhag y Penrhyddion, ond nid oes ameu nad allaf gael fy siomi wrth borthmonna. Hen ddyn digrif yw'r Esgob yna, rhai a ddywaid nad **W. to R. CXV.**

W. to R. contd.

yw mor sanctaidd ag y mae yn ymddangos; roedd iddo frawd yn ei ganlyn o ddarllowydd i'r Brenin meddant, o ŵr sych foneddigaidd. Mae'r Esgob yn cael y gair o fod yn dra chynil. Aie yr ych yn cael yr anrhydedd o dderbyn ambell lythyr yn fynych o Sir Abernoeth? Ni che's i yr un byth oddiyno. I remember formerly Llewelyn took it in his head to be affronted about some management of his daughters at Carnarvon, who had taken up more goods, etc., than he thought they had need of, so blamed me for not being a check upon 'em, a minneu'r pryd hwnw newydd briodi yn cael mo'm cof na'm synwyr gan gant o drafferthion. I suspect there is some foul play now somewhere pe bae fatter yn y peth. Aie ni chafed mo arian y drysorfa etto? Drwg iawn yw hynny, yn boeth y bo'r holl arian sydd yn y deyrnas, y nhw ydyw mam pob drwg anian, etc. Pa beth a ddaeth o Ywain (ŵyr Gornelius) y Garddwr, ni chlywais i byth na siw na miw oddiwrthaw, er dolwg rhoddwch dippyn oi hanes. Och o fi, ce's globyn o lythyr oddiwrth y car Huw Davies dydd arall yn llawn o ddifyrrwch, ag yn dadcan cystal oedd ganddo Mr. R. M. Mi debygwn wrth ymadroddion y gwalch ei fod yn o gynnes arnaw. Aie Rhys Ifan sydd yn anafu'r iaith bob yn awr? Ffei hono, wlan groen brwnt! Gwyn eich byd am daraw wrth Ddoctor Dafis Sion Morgan.* I dare say his additions are curious, a benthyg un arall or fath meddwch! Wala, wala, i chwi mae'r lwc, neu fal y dywaid yr hen ddihareb, "chwi biau'r byd c——ch ynddaw." Ni fedda inneu ond benthyg hen eir-lyfr D.D. a fu gynt yn eiddo yr Dr. Evans, druan gwr, ag yr wyf yn ofni beunydd ir gwr arall ddyfod yw gyrchu adref yno; ffarwel gyd ag ê, pa beth a ddaw o honwyf gwedi? Gresyn na chymerai Lewelyn y gwaith yn llaw i gyhoeddi un iawn, fe gai ddigon o gymorth o bob parth, hyssiwch o 'mlaen. Nag oes yma neb yn derbyn mwnws ir Domas Risiart yna am a glywaf i pam na ymeryl o am rywun? I have been wrote to from Beaumaris to know if any one was appointed. Mr. Evans, mentiond in a former letter, seemed to decline the office, but recomended one Richard Owen, a shopkeeper and bookseller, at Llanerchmedd, who if writ to, probably would take the task upon him. I will chearfully revise the botanical part if sent here. I can't

*This probably means John Morgan's copy of Dr. Davies's Dictionary. John Morgan was a Welsh scholar of some repute.

guess how Osbourne should send his catalogue for me, for I needn't have heard anything of it, doth it cost anything? If not, pray send it with the above by some opportunity or other. The story of L. Lucy is merry enough; I thought her ladyship had more prudence than to go to brag of favours done by her family to ours. I know of one of your family that is not much obligated to her if the truth was known, ag os adwain i yr tylwyth maent yn abl digolled ar bawb o honom. Par fodd bynnag fe fydda da yn fy nghalon i pe bae'ch wedi cau safn y cadffwl yna gin Ddic Morys. Necessity hath no law, and he really is necessitous, a dwndrio a dadwrdd a wna tra bo chwyth yn ei ffroenau, hyd na ddigonir, nid oes iddo base hanner pwyll dyn cyffredin. Yr archlod i'r dyn, na bu'sai yn hebrwng y Gatechism i chwi mal y cawswn ei weled—da fydd ei gael y tro nesaf. Pwy oedd yma'r dydd arall ond yr Aldromon Prisiart o Gael Nerpwl, ni welswn monaw erys llawer blwyddyn, ag yn wir ddiau roedd y gwr wedi cynhyddu llawer iawn mewn cnawdoliaeth a boneddigeiddrwydd, ond etto er hyn yr un dyn yw ef o hyd y bwa hen, ond bod y tu allan wedi newid twysgen. Darfu ini ddwndrio llawer o bant i bentan dros gryn bedair awr ar hugain. Nag oes yma rhof a dyn fawr ffrancodau odid dyna i chwi rai or ychydig sydd; mae'n debyg fod digon yng Ngallt Vadawg o'r eiddo Mr. Vaughan or Gors. Och y fi, hâ ŵr fab, daccw fy anwyl ffrind Natws wedi gyrru imi o Leghorn gryn longaid o *rarities*, sef, turtle doves, terrapins, various creatures and insects preserved in spirits, garden seeds, etc. But as the d——l would have it the s——n of a captain who carried them jockyd me fairly. Instead of five had but three turtle doves, instead of four had two terrapins or land turtles or tortoises; two potts of choice flowers all gone, barbary partriges none, insects, etc. a few, ni waeth tewi na siared, rhaid bodloni heb yn ddiolch. Er mwyn dyn byddwch siwr o gadw hâd y cedrwydd a'r hickry erbyn y Gwanwyn. Gwyn ei fyd a gai ychydig o hâd *the white cucumber*. Oes gennech ddim cydnabyddiaeth efo'r gentlemen gardiners yna? We have had hitherto a glorious harvest: may God continue it. Rwyf inneu yn llafurio 'ngoreu; mae gennyf im llaw o gompas 25s. o ardreth, sef tir ŷd. Dyma fi wedi bod yn ystyccio fy ngoreu glas, tippyn o haidd i wneuthur brâg, a hwnnw yw ddarllaw'n gwrw rhwydd fain gô

W. to R. contd.

W. to R. contd.

fŷglyd i ymbesgi arnaw. The people in these parts are very fond of your porter, and I cant say but I like it well enough, far fetched, etc. Mae pawb o honnom yma, mawl ir Goruchaf, yn rhwydd iachus, ag yn gorchymun attoch chwi a Meirian. Dim newydd o Ddulas yn ddiweddar. Duw oi fawr drugaredd a fo'n gwarchad drosoch. Byddwch wŷch. *Eich caredigawl frawd, Wm. Morris.*

The termination of your letter put me in mind of the following pennill:

> Nid wy'n deusyf gan Dduw cyfion
> Ond tri pheth (mae hynny'n ddigon):
> Byw'n ddigonol, marw'n ddidd'led,
> A thrugaredd Nef im henaid.

Let me have a long letter from you as soon as you can; nid y'ch yn sôn am Feirian, par ddelw sydd arni hi?

CAER GYBI, 3 Hydref, 1751.

W. to R. CXVI.

Anwyl Frawd,—Doe y daeth i'm llaw yr eiddoch o'r 28 ult., a chyd ag ef *gwitansa* Mr. Richards, heb iddo roddi mo'i law wrthynt, felly gyrrais hwynt yn ol ir perwyl hwnnw, a phan ddelont yn ol (os hynny sydd raid) mi a wnaf fy ngoreu er ei wasanaethu; ond fal y dywedais gynt, ni fu erioed ddyn mwy anghyfaddas ir gorchwyl hwnnw, oblegid ni byddaf yn ymlwybren or gongl anghysbell yma oddiar ddwy waith neu dair yn y flwyddyn, dim myned i ffair na marchnad, felly nid wyf yn gweled namyn y Cybiaid ag ambell Wyddel ar dro unwaith yn y 4 amser. Why don't the author bestir himself and write himself to folks and let the world know how he goes on? People are cautious how they trust strangers with their cash, many have been bit by such proposers: maent heb anghofiaw hagr weithiau Moesen yng Ngwynedd etto. Ydyw'r gwaith yn y wasc mewn difrif? Fe ddywaid hynny fis Mawrth. Dyma Lewelyn ab Gwilym y cefnderw wedi dyfod ddoe o Bentre'riannallt o'r Gwylmabsant, yn dywedyd fod y nhad a mam yn rhesymol iachus. Ces gydag ef Gatecism yr Eglwys wedi ei ddryllio yn ddarna mân, i.e., wedi ei dorri, ond ni chefais i mor amser i ddarllain dim o honaw. I see the word goat in your scheme as in the former; pam fa'sai waeth i chwi roddi gardd na gafr. Fe daerai'r Saeson na fedrwn fyw na siared heb eifr ar bob testyn. Os medra i nar berson weled dim bai yn unlle cewch ei glywed. Gwaith pwy yw hwn? Och fi, ha wr fab, roeddwn yn gobeitho y cawswn y *cedar cone* ar cnau, etc., efo hwn, ond ni chlywa i ysywaeth ddim son am danynt. Os gwraig H.O. clorach ydoedd, yn iach ymenyn glân. Dynes yn cael gair rhesymol drwg o ollwng pobl rhyd ddi, etc. Mi glywswn son gan ryw drafaeliwrs am yr Harris* yna mae dyn cywrain iawn ydoedd, ai fod wedi dyfeisio rhyw fath newydd o gloriannau i bwyso aur, etc. Duw ro'r gras iddo fod yn well nai frawd Hwlyn, os gwir a ddywedir am dano. Gwych bod yn gydnabyddus ar gwyr cywrain yna; un o'r Deheu yw Wmffreys mae'n debyg. Aie mynd i letya i'r Tŵr Gwyn, na bo'nd ei grybwyll? Mae yma offeiriedyn yn dwyn llawer o anhunedd o eisiau gwybod pa gan belled yr ych wedi mynd efo'r Bibl, a wnewch chwi dorri'r gofid arno? Dyma fo wedi cael gan Froughton sheet o honaw, sef o lyfr Genesis. Mi ach gwela wedi ail drin eich chronology, etc. Mi debygwn fod y llythyren o'r ddwy yn fanach na'r argraph ddiweddaf. Gwae finneu, mae'n ddrwg iawn fod y piles yn ymgydcan a chwi. Duw Goruchaf ach cadw rhag y fistula. Bleeding cured me and thousands more, and certainly would relieve you; nid oes ond gobeitho'r goreu. Gresyn oedd golli o Gatteral ei long, ie, digon gwir fod Douglas wedi mynd i Ddouglas yn n'led pawb ar adwaenai. Wfft ir fath ddyn ag ef, yn medru rhoi llŷg dros olwg poblach yn y modd hwnnw. Cefais lythyr oddiwrth Gornelius Agrippa yn llawn o fendithion a chanmoliadau i Mr. Morys or Nafi Offis. Chwi orphenasoch ei wneuthur yn gefn dyn, mi yrais iddo'r dydd arall lonaid sach o gynghorion, addysc, etc. Llencyn glew lwccys. Ces arall oddiwrth Allt Fadawg, y wraig wedi dwad drwy'r afael, ar gwr yn mynd i ymweled ai stiwardiaeth, nis gwn i ble, yn gwaeddi am lês ar wythen o fwyn o ddwy droedfedd diameter. Deliwch sylw mai bai ceryddus yw dywedyd ym Mathew 21, verse 1st, olewwydd yn lle olewydd, oblegyd mae olwydd neu olewydd yw enw'r ffrwyth neu rawn yr olew-wydden. O'r olwydd mae dwy genedl, meddai M. Myddfai, Mount of Olives, mynydd yr olewydd, not mount of olive trees. Mi ymegniaf yrru yn fy nesaf some remarks on the Common Prayer. Rhaid rwan gadw noswyl. Duw yn eich cylch chwi ar eiddoch, a byddwch wych. *Eich caredigawl frawd, William Morris.*

W. to R. contd.

* Joseph Harris of the Mint, a brother of Howel Harris, Trevecca.

W. to R. contd. P.S.—Par sut y mae Ywain y garddwr yn boddiaw ei feistr? A fyddwch i yn myned yno weithiau? Os byddwch, cynghorwch yr Hu'lrhod i fod yn sobr ag yn grefyddol, a Duw a dâl i chwi drosto. Peggy desires to be remember'd to her cosin.

CAER GYBI, 9d Dachwedd, 1751.

W. to R. CXVII. Anwyl Frawd,—Mae llawer iawn o amser wedi myned heibiaw er pan glywais oddiwrthych. 'Roedd eich llythyr diwaethaf yn achwyn ar y Lledewigwst; gobeitho na ddarfu i'r haint echryslon hwnnw mo'ch dihenhyddu. Dyna i chwi ryw faint o ymgraffiadau ar y Weddi Gyffredin; ni thalent ei codi oddiar y maes. I think Moses Williams to blame to deviate from the folio edition of Ellis Wynne's, which is now read by the ministers in most of the churches throughout all Wales, and as that edition is almost unexceptionable, 'tis pity to run away from it, and have such confusion. I dont know whether it is owing to one's hearing that read continually or one's byas to the Northwalian dialect, but this I protest, that I think Bardd Cwsg much the best, though neither his labours nor that of any mortal can be compleat. In my last I returned you Richards' receipts to be signd by himself, ond rhyfedd na ddaethant yn ol, *os yn eu hol y deuant?* I have been writ to by many about the dictionary. Where is the herbal? Dyma fi'n barod iddo er's dyddiau. Mr. Mosson, of Beaumaris, writ to the author to know who he should pay his subscription to. He answer'd him that he knew no one in Anglesey, so desired him to get him what subscribers he could and send him their names; he writes me he hath got a few for him in and about Beaumaris,—one Richard Parry of Llanerchmedd hath promised me a good many. I received the other day from Pentre Eirianallt Osburne's catalogue, about three dozen hickery nuts and some small pieces of the cedar cone (dim pregeth Evans). My father, it seems, had a mind to see whether the cone produced the nutts so broke it to pieces, but as no nutts were hatch'd within it, he threw it away to be hang'd—a few of the pieces were pickd up which I had. Felly nid oes dim lwc ini gael cedrwydd Libanus ym Môn, bynnag par fodd 'rwyf yn dra rhwymedig i chwi am danynt, pan ddeloch yma, cewch rodio ymhlith y coed hickry, or the Virginian walnut. Ces lythyr y dydd arall o Allt Fadawg ag un yr un post oddiwrth yr Aldramon Prichard.

Mae'r ddeuwr rheini wedi mynd yn benna ffrindia, er bod o honynt y dydd arall yn elynion brychion; na bo mond ei grybwyll! Mae'r brawd 'rwan mewn gwell calon nag y bu er's talm. Gwych o'r mwyn a ddadcuddiodd i Fawrhydi'r Brenhin, a gwych yn sicr os ceiff o fynd yn rhannog. Na atto Duw chwedl amgen,—mae'n rhywyr clywed yr hanes. Roedd y nhad a mam yn rhyfeddol o iachus y dydd arall, bu ef yn y Creuddyn yr wythnos ddiweddaf ag yn ol, a gwraig y car Sion Salbri yn ei sgil. A wnewch chwi 'r fath beth pan f'och yn tynnu at eich pedwar ugain? Na wnewch mi wranta, nag yr un o'u plant, os byddant byw cyhyd. Daccw'r gwr a fu yn briod a'r gyfnither Margaret Salbri wedi ffaelio; gorfod troi ei gefn a gadael y cwbl ir meistir tir,—llonaid y ty o blant iddo yntau. He was once a topping farmer. Yr ym ni ymma oll yn iach, mawl ir Goruchaf am ei drugareddau ini. Da fyddai clywed eich bod chwithau felly. Mae'r brawd Llewelyn yn gadael, os ceiff hoedl, etc., y rhydd ef allan, *an edition of Davies's Dictionary.* Duw a wnel iddo gowiro. Dyna lle cewch weled Botanologium! Y fath ni bu erioed er dechreuad y byd. Dyweded Solomon a fynno ynghylch y pethau a fu, nagê, nagê, gwawdio yr oeddwn, gwir a ddywaid Selyf ddoeth. Mae hi'n amser cadw noswyl am heno; Duw a fyddo'n gwarchad drosoch. Byddwch wych! W. to R. contd.

Eich tra charedigawl frawd, William Morris.

P.S.—Fe fu agos i mi a gollwng yn angof achwyn wrthych ar yr anwyd a'r peswch sydd yn fy llibindio i yn greulon! A ydych chwi yn medru dianc rhag y clwyf anwaharddol hwnnw? Da chwithau, sgrifenwch yma gynta galloch.—W.M.

HOLYHEAD, 16 November, 1751.

Dear Brother,—Last night your letter came to hand after having lain in the post office here dridie. This comes to tell you that I am extream glad of your recovery,—mawr ddiolch ir Goruchaf am roddi i chwi allu i ddioddef yr mawr boen, ag am eich dwyn allan o'r mawr berygl y buoch ynddaw. I was much afraid all the while that you were ailing; wala, wala, rhaid ymegnio i fod yn foddlawn; gobeitho na bydd ir Arglwydd geryddu monoch mor dôst ond hynny, a bod Hywel wedi crafu yr holl wraidd ymaith ai dwcca. I observe what you say about the diet, I wish you had mention'd formerly that the money to be received was only a deposite. I would have W. to R. CXVIII.

W. to R. contd.

fall'n to in good earnest, but I took it for granted that the cash was to be remitted to Richards, ag na byddai gan y Monwysiaid ddim i ddangos am eu harian, in case of misfortunes (which all undertakings are liable to) but my receipts, gyrrwch, gyrrwch, nhw gynta galloch chwitheu, gewch chwitheu bwmp o list cyn pen hir ddyddiau. I writ you a long letter last post but one, and sent you some vague observations on the Common Prayer, cewch chwaneg ryw ddiwrnod. Dedwydd y chwi am fod yn gallu rhoi yr mawr arian am lyfrau, ni roddes Gwilym bunt am lyfrau er's pump neu chwech o flynyddoedd. Gerwin o'r taro ar Gorn. Agrippa! Ydynt mi a wranta yn prynnu'r meddyg-lyfr hwnnw. Os caf hoedl a phob peth yn atteb, nhw g'ant well hyfforddiadau yn fy llysieulyfr. "Arglwydd eb y Gronw ddu,"* etc.; ni chaf mor amser [yn awr] i osod ar lawr ddim chwaneg o wansens. Pawb yn [iach] cenwch, Duw a fo'n gwarchad, ag a roddo iechyd i chwi. *Eich brawd rhwydd besychlyd, Gwilym Ddu o Fôn.*

CAER GYBI, November 29th, 1751.

W. to R. CXIX.

Anwyl Frawd,—Mae gennych ddau neu dri o'm epystolau i heb eu hatteb, felly nid oes gennyf nemawr iw ddywedyd yr awron namyn rhoddi o'ch blaen gofrestr o'r sawl sydd yn ewyllysio gyrru ymlaen y gorchwyl tra godidawg hwnnw sef geirlyfr y Meistr Richards. Nis gwn i par un ai drwg ai da wyf yn ei wneuthur oblegid rwy'n rhoddi clod anferth iddaw, oni ddywedasoch'i mae gwaith *glew* iawn ydoedd? Dyma i chwi enwau'r subscribwyr mal y daethent i'm llaw hyd yn hyn, disgwyl bagad etto:—

The Rev. Thomas Ellis, B.D., Minister of Holyhead ...	1
Lewis Lloyd, Collector of the Customs of Holyhead ...	1
William Morris, Comptroller of the Customs of Holyhead	1
Hugh Roberts, Grocer of Holyhead	1
William Roberts, Esq., of Bodjôr	1
Hugh Owen, Esq., of Cae'rberllan	1
Robert Carreg, Esq., Collector Customs, Caernarvon ...	1
John Roberts, Apothecary of Caernarvon	1
Rev. Wm. Wynne of Lasynys, A.M., Rector of Llanaber	2
Rev. John Evans, A.B. Curate of Llanbeulan	1

* A reference to "Breuddwyd Gronw Ddu o Fôn" (Greal 1807, p. 370). The full quotation should be "Arglwydd, heb y Gronw, pa bryd y bydd hynny?" a phrase which is constantly re-iterated in the "Breuddwyd."

CAER GYBI, 18d o Ragfyr, 1751.

Anwyl Frawd,—Mi sgrifenais ryw dro ddechreu'r mis ag yno gyrrais i chwi enwau subscribers to Richards's Lexicon, a llawer o ryw ddwndwr gwâg mi wranta. Ni chawn i gytrym nad dyma yr eiddoch chwitheu or 3dd yn ymddangos a receipts and proposals, ai atteb a wnaf fal hyn. Gwych yr ydych yn mynd ymlaen efo'r argraffwaith yna, yn Luc yr amser hwnw! Rhwydd-deb iw'ch. Wawch! daccw ryw garn lladron wedi yspeilio'r post, a ddylasai ddyfod i mewn heddyw, ar y Mynydd Plwm (i.e., Halkin Mountain) yn Nhegeingl, ag wedi mynd a holl lythyr-gydau y cwr yma o Wynedd ymaith, but left the Irish Mail (i.e. for Ireland) untouched. Beth os oedd llysieu-lyfr Richards ynddaw? Dyna i chwi enwau rhyw ychydig o wyrda Môn. Mae hi'n amser trwm ar y flwyddyn anaml y byddaf yn ymdreiglaw oddiyma i unlle, ni bu monwyf y tu draw i bont Rhydbont er's misoedd, oni bae mwy fase rhif y subscribers:—Walter Williams, Officer of Excise at Holyhead, (had you him before?); Hugh Jones, Esq., of Cymunod; The Rev. Mr. Thomas Owen, A.M., Rector of Aberffraw; John Owen, Esq., of Presaddfed; The Rev. Mr. Henry Morris, clarke, Rector of Llan Fachreth. Pray what does Mr. Richards mean by saying he will deliver the book in sheets? Sure they will be stitched in blue paper or something! I am often asked the above question. Resolve it, da chwithau; rwyf heb gael henw Bodorgan a llawer o rai eraill oedd yn sôn am subscribio,—nid hwyrach y deuant ar fyrder. I hope he will take care to insert the names very correct, oblegid digio a wna poblach pan lysenwir hwynt a'u tai ai swyddau a'u graddau. Rwyf wedi meistroli'r anwyd yn dda iawn, ond etto er hyn pesychu byddis yma o hyn dan wyneb blwyddyn, os byw cyhyd a wneir. Digrif oedd i'ch peswch chwi fynd allan drwy holltas Hywel, gwell gennyf i besychu tra bwyf byw yn y byd na'i ollwng allan ffordd honno. Bydd y llysieulyfr gyda'r mwya i eirlyfr Davies, ond nid oes wybod par sut a fydd etto. Pei bai'r gallu mal yr ewyllys, rhoddwn allan lysieulyfr iawn, nid enwau llysiau yn unig, ond hefyd eu rhinwedd, a'u hamser, a'u cartref, etc., etc.,—bynnag par fodd, nid mynych mae wythnos yn mynd dros fy mhen na bwyf yn casglu at eu gilydd ryw faterion, a hynny er's 10 neu 12 o flynyddoedd tuag at y perwyl hwnw. Nid hwyrach mai gadael heb

W. to R.
CXX.

W. to R. contd. eu gorphen y byddis i ryw genedl goeg sychu eu —— a hwynt. Mi glywaf fod y Duwc yn ymendiaw er mawr orfoledd i rai, a thristwch i eraill. Chwedl penrhydd oedd hwnw a ddywaid y Cardinal wrthych ynghylch y Fwlcleias hono; ni amcenais ag nid wyf yn amcanu fyth gydio a hi, er bod poblach yn dwndrio tan eu dwylo heb achos nag ystyr; nid llawer ffordd yma er cyhyd y bum yn eu plith a adnebydd eich brawd Gwilym, er nad yw mor anhawdd ei adnabod gan bobl onest ddiniwaid. I pursue other . . . game, but this under the rose. Mi welais un a fu Ymhentre Eirianallt ddydd Sadwrn; roedd y mam yn rhesymol iachus, y nhad yn cael ei libindio gan y gnofa, etc. Rym ni yma oll, mawl i'r Goruchaf, yn iachus ag yn gorchymun attoch ag at Feirian. Rhowch dipyn o'i hanes. 'Roeddynt yn iachus Yngallt Vadawg o fewn y pythefnos yma, roedd gan y brawd ryw *scheme* newydd ar droed.

Eich caredigol frawd, Gwilym Tew.

CAERGYBI, Dydd Calan, 1752.

W. to R. CXXI. Anwyl Frawd,—I writ you a letter of the 18th ult., to which I refer you. Neithiwr y dychwelais adref o gynhebrwng y Cownslor Bulkeley, yr hwn oedd ddydd Gwener diweddaf: aros efo'r hen wr noswaith a diwrnod i gwyno iddo etc. Tranoeth mi aethym i Bentre Eirianallt, lle y cwrddais wrth yr hen rieni yn rhesymol iachus, mawl ir Goruchaf; byddai ryfedd gennych weled mor sionc a llawen y bydd yr hen bobl ar droau er hyned yn't. Aethym ddydd Sul efo nhad ar ein meirch i Eglwys Benrhos, yr hon oedd lawn o wynebau dieithr oddigerth ambell un o'r hen 'stondarts —megys Wmffra Roberts o Ddulas, Sion ab Ifan, Owen a Rhisiart Wmffra, Twm Rolant y gof, hen ddyn cûl cwla, ail ir hen Rolant y gof ei dad gynt, Gruffudd Dafydd, Rolant Huws o Ligwy, hen ddyn cul cibddall; y rhan fwya o'r llaill oeddynt blant ag wyrion eich cyfoedion chwi a minneu, sef rhai Harri Prisiart William, Twm William Glochydd, Sion Bifan, etc., wedi hen briodi! Wedi aros ddwynos efo'r hen bobl cychwyn tua'g adref, drwy lôn y Bwlch Côch, ag heibio'r Efail Fawr. Gadael ty Sion Oylfer, a Bryndulas, ar y llaw ddeheu, a myned drwy'r lôn Aethnen, a rhwng Bodafon Ruffudd Prisiart, a'r Gegin Ddu, a hŵi a mi i Fryn yr Orsedd; gadael ty William Owen Pwlkyn ar y llaw dde'au, a mynd heibio'r Tŷ Hyfryd, ag ir ffordd deg, heibio'r Erw Hir, oddiyno ir mynydd, wedi gadael afon Geiri, a thŷ Risiart Niclas, a'r Fedw a Maes y Llan, etc., ar y llaw chwith, i ffwrdd a mi heibio Waun y Gimach a'r Ty Pink, y ffordd y byddwn i yn mynd i dy fy nain ddydd a fu, heibio'r Arwydd Eithin, a thŷ fy'rth Gruffydd Sion Owen, a gadael Ffynhonnau'r helwyr ar y llaw chwith, ar Brynnau Hirion a Cherrig y Llithr, ag at Gors y Mynydd, a thrwy'r llynn heibio dŷ Gras Wiliams, yr hen forwyn, a thŷ Sian Owen or Mynydd, ag i lawr at dŷ Huw Tomos wedi gadael y Glyn, a Bodafon y Glyn, ar Carneddi ar fy neheu, a thŷ Iemwnt Bengam, ar Fferam a thŷ mamaeth, or tu chwith, ag ymlaen a mi at y Maenaddfwyn (wedi passio ffôs Golmon) heibio' dŷ Harri 'r gof, a thŷ Domos Pyrs, etc., ag i dŷ fy nain, galw yno a howd'ye ir cefnder Rhisiart (?) Jones ai wraig, rheini au plant au hwyrion yn gwledda, oddiyno heibio i'r Eglwys (sef Llanfihangl Tre'r Bardd, lle cawsoch chwi a minneu grêd a bedydd) at Glorach, a rhwng Ffynhonnau Seiriol a Chybi, a thrwy Ryd y Badell ag heibio i Foel Lwydiarth i Llanerchymedd, ag odd'yno linkyn lonkyn i Gaergybi, drwy eira ag oerfel ddigon. Thus you have an exact journal of my return, and I daresay, though its a kind of survey of the places as they were called thirty years ago, it will rouse some ideas that have been lurking, the Lord knows how long, and bring to your mind many a circumstance that happen'd in those innocent days of ours before cares and troubles had got any footing in our heads. I have heard nothing from Gallt Vadawg since my last. I have writ post to Fortunate Fortunatus, who was well 3rd December, to hurry him home to take care of the main chance. Is it true that Mr. Hugh Davies, the cordwainer, hath bought an estate in Anglesey? God grant you a happy new year. Adieu. *Your most affectionate brother,*

William Morris.

W. to R. contd.

P.S.—Gwiliwch ollwng yn angof hâd y cucumbers gwnnion, ag o gynull gymaint ag a alloch o bob hadau dieithr gan eich ffrindiau. Oes modd i gael peth o hâd y Phytolacca o'r Virgianian poke, a plant famous for curing of cancers; it must be in the seed shops. Corph crwst, dyma lythyr oddiwrth Owain y Garddwr o Ddatchet, a hanes gerddi a llysiau a hadau, etc., mae ei weddi o'n ddwys gida.

CAER GYBI SAINT, Ionawr 20d, 1752.

W. to R. CXXII. Anwyl Frawd,—Ce's eich llythyr or 7d yn atteb 3 o'r eiddo fi; chwi welwch fy mod yn *leicio'r* fargen cystal a fy mod yn myned ymlaen eilwaith. Ie, ie, gwell o lawer oedd cael peidiaw coleddu'r llysieu lyfr, ni bu ond y dyd rhyngwy a naccau gaddaw, cadd rai subscribers ar hyder cael fy ngorchwyl ffordd honno. Aie drud dwyn i fynu fenyw ieuainc yn y parthau yna? Rhaid i mi ynteu addyscu fy merch gartref. Gwych a fydd gan Farged gaffael llythyr oddiwrth ei chyfnither. Diameu mae gwell ydyw gyrfed. Melldith eu neiniau i'r hen wrachiod gwrthunion rheini r'ych yn son am danynt, ni fynnwn am bris yn y byd fod gennyf i wneuthur ar hafiig bechadurus. Aie 'rych yn clywed yn fynych o Geredigion? Rwyf inneu yn disgwyl, disgwyl, er's mis heb fod ddim gwell. Dyma fi wedi prynnu ir Tew, well na thunnell o gaws i borthi'r mwynwyr gwancus, ag yn ffaelio taro wrth gyfleu yw gyrru iddynt. Gresyn oedd i chwi anghofiaw yr hen Stents. I am sorry that my old friend Mr. Davies can't purchase in Anglesey; mae gennyf bot iddo am gynnig. As you say 'Natus may do this country some service, ond ni wiw disgwyl fawr ddaioni, oni bae fod y boneddigion beilchion yma yn dangos siamplau da—a most worthless set of mortals! Drwg bod y chwiw dwll heb gau, gobeitho'r goreu. Dyma Ruffudd Dafydd (chief mate William Dafydd Lewis pan ddaeth y brawd Llew., y chwi, a minneu, yn bassengers o Gonwy ers talm), wedi dyfod ddoe o Bentre Erianallt i'n ymweled, oblegid fod rhai o honom yn anafus, sef bachgen ir chwaer, 8 neu 9 oed wedi torri ei forddwyd, ond ar y ffordd o ymendiaw; herlodes i minneu yn sal er's dyddiau, gobeitho ei bod hitheu'n well nag y bu, y rhelyw o honom yn rhwydd iachus. Roedd yr hen bobl yn dal yr un fath, weithia'n llaccaidd, ag weithiau'n rhesymol. Gwaed gwreinyn glas! Dyma hi'n amser hau cucumbers, ymhle mae hâd rhai gwynion? Nid hwyrach y medrai Owain gael rhai tua Windsor; mi sgrifena atto heddyw ag a archaf arno yrru i chwi rai os medr, nid rhaid i chwi ond taro dwsing neu 2 mewn ffrank, oni byddant yma erbyn ddechreu'r mis nesaf bydd yn rhy hwyr. How goes on the Bibles? Dr. Ellis is very impatient for them. Yn wir, nid wyf yn clywed ar fy nghalon lygadrythu mor llawer ar y Weddi Gyffredin, gan eich bod chwi ar dyn arall yn cymryd cymaint o boen yn ei geryddu, ag mae'n debyg na wnai fy holl allu i fawr ddaioni i chwi. Duw a fyddo'n gwarchad drosoch a'r eiddoch. W. to R. contd.

Eich caredigawl frawd, William Morris.

CAER GYBI, Chwefror 12, 1752.

Anwyl Frawd,—Bydded yspys iwch gael o honwyf y dydd heddy eich llythyr o'r 8d, ag ynddo dau fath o hâd chwerwddwr, am ba rai yr wyf yn dra diolchgar i chwi, ac i'r marsiant Vaughan am eu pwrcasu. Daccw fi wedi eu claddu dan obaith adgyfodiad. My hot beds were ready to receive them, nid hwyrach y bydd i'r Cibeaid, neu'r Cybiaid, gael ymborthi arnaddynt cyn Mai. Pam na fu'sech yn dywedyd y pris fal y gallwn feddwl am dalu ryw dro? Na soniasoch i wrthyf fi eich bod wedi anfon Meirian draw i Gent. Duw a roddo iddi râs ac a'ch cadwo yw dwyn i fynu i allu byw yn onest ac yn rhinweddol yn y byd twyllodrus yma. Mae'r plantos yma, mawl i'r Goruchaf am ei drugaredd i ni oll, wedi dyfod i fynu yn dda iawn,—bachgen y chwaer yn ymlwybren wrth ei faglau, a'm herlodes inneu cystal cynt, a'r relyw o honom yn iachus, roeddynt yn rhwydd iachus ym Mhentre Eirianallt dydd arall. Ce's lythyr o Allt Fadawg 27 ult., pawb yn iach cenwch. Nid wyfi yn cofiaw mo'r storekeeper hwnw,—gwell a f'ai gan Wilym eu weled ef neu arall yn nhŷ y Mrs. Welsh nag yn nhŷ y Llwyds rheini, rhywogaeth Tomos Jones hwnw a fu yn ceisio amdwyo Llewelyn. Gwaed crŵst nid oes yma ond y prinder bwygilydd am ffrancod; fe gyst imi ddau i yrru i chwi un, onid yw'r aelodau cyn amled ffordd yna a bytatws Ynghaer Gybi! Par fodd bynnag, os medraf daro wrth fagad o naddynt cewch chwitheu rai. Gresyn na buasai'r brawd Llwyd o'r Gors yn dyfod yna, cawsach eich digoni. Aie mae'r chwiwdwll yn egored fyth, os yw'n gwneuthur daioni, mawr les iddaw. Par ddelw sydd ar Hywel y Meddyg? Yn rhodd gorchymynwch fi attaw, ai cô ganthaw'r amser y buom yn consuriaw yn siop y diweddar Ddoctor Evans wirion! Och na buasech yn rhoddi tipyn o hanes y Bibl; mae'r bersonyn yma agos wedi torri ei galon am ychydigyn. What! not a word of Richards with his geirlyfr? Ni ches i ddim chwaneg o subscribers. Aie mae Osburne wedi rhoi imi gatalogue arall, roedd yna'r dydd arall (rwy'n ofni ei gychwyn adref). Ddynan o'r gymydogaeth yma a ddaeth i hebrwng rhyw offeiriad oedd allan o'i hwyl, a fasai yn ei W. to R. CXXIII.

W. to R. contd. garrio yn ewyllysgar, ond ni chaf mo'r amser i ymofyn am ei letty yr awron. Ce's lythyr oddiwrth Gornelius Agripa yngwrthgefn fy un i, ag ynddo y rhan arall o lun gardd ei feistr, a llawer o bethau hynodawl eraill. Canmol ei le yn ddiareb. Pa swydd sydd gan y Fason hwnw? It seems he hath an elegant villa at Datchet, his gardener is no mean man. Mae'ch brawd Gwil byth yn unigol, *un* tŷ, *un* ardd, *un* bachgen, *un* lodes, *un* nith, *un* forwyn, *un* ci, *un* gath, *un* fuwch, *un* —— ar air,—unig yw pob peth a berthyn iddaw, a thebyg i fod felly am a glywafi. Rhaid cadw noswyl bellach i gael myned i gymeryd *un* cyntun, ond nid cyn im ddywedyd i chwi ein bod ni oll yn *un* a chy'*tun* yn gorchymun attoch. A'r unig Dduw a fyddo'n gwarchod drosoch. *Eich brawd ungalon,*

William Morris.

CAER GYBI Saint, 9d o Fawrth, 1752, D. Llun.

W. to R. CXXIV. Anwyl Frawd,—Dyma ddau lythyr o'r eiddoch heb eu hatteb, yr hyn sydd ryfeddod fawr! A pheth sydd fwy, yr oeddynt eill dau yn feichiog o'r hadau gw'cha (ond odid) a fu eriod yn Ynys Fôn! Best in the world! Nefoedd i enaid yr hen Dduc am eu cynnyrchu au gadael ar ei ol. A diolch yn fawr i chwithau am eu hanfon. Daccw rai o honynt yn ymwthio allan o'r gwely; mae arnaf ofn na chant gystal ymgeledd ag a fyddai eu hynafiaid yn ei gael ffordd yna. Daccw'r chwerwddwr gwynion cynta yn eu dail geirwon yn gystal a rhai Datchett. Lle mae Cornelius Agrippa a'i erddi yn mynd ymlaen yn Hafog? Ond och yfi, ai dyna'r modd y ca'dd y Faswn ei gywaith! Drwy dderbyn lledrad na bo'nd i grybwyll! Mae lle i ofni yn ddirfawr na thyf na chwerwddwr na dim arall oddigerth mieri a drain yn y tiroedd taerion hynny. Mae 'Safaids ag yntau yn bennau ffrindiau mi a wrantau, rhag ofn i'r naill achwyn chwedlau ar y llall a chodi clownsia'. Gwant yn llawen ar ei cyfoeth tra bont yn eu perchenogi, ni bydd hynny chwaith hir, a phwy a wyr par sutt a fydd wneuthur y cyfrif i fynu, a phwy a feddiana'r dâ byd yr oes nesaf? Aie tri llythyr Cymreig yn cyd ymgyfarfod yn llaw? Digrif oedd ei gweled gan eu bod oll yn dwyn newyddion da sef o iechyd yr sgrifenyddion, etc., mae'n debyg mae yn y byd arall y bydd yr ymgyfarfod cynta. Ond pwy a wyr pa beth eill ddigwydd? Duw yn unig. Gwych yr ydych yn myned ymlaen efo'r Biblau, a gwych y gwaith meddwch chwi, ond pa beth y dywaid y *critics* ar *snarlers* ar holl genedl goeg am dano? Mae doethion y wlad yma wedi perswaidio eu gilydd na thâl geirlyfr Richards yw godi oddiar y maes, felly ni wiw ceisiaw llaw neb ond hynny. Pethau digrif yw plant dynion, tebyg i hydnod eraill mwy diniwed, os â un i'r dwfr, hwi ar lleill yn llu ar ei ol. Mae'r Gardinal yn haeddu clod am lenwi ei phwrs cystal drwy onestrwydd, gobeithio ei fod wedi cloi'r fargen efo'r marchog ariangar hwnw yr hwn sy'n gwerthu etifeddiaeth ei hynafiaid er mwyn budr elw. O ffei hono 'run rhywogaeth a Safaids! Da iawn yw clywed eich bod yn prifio well, well, yn eich iechyd, bydded i'r Goruchaf ei gynal i chwi rhagllaw. Rym ni yma oll yn rhwydd iachus; roeddynt felly Ymhentre Eirianell yr wythnos ddiwaethaf. Erchyll meddwch o'r drafferth sydd arnoch yn trin dyled y Navi; gwaith brwnt computing interest etc., ffeindiach gorchwyl o lawer trin gardd ai pherthynasau, er hynny, y bydd a ludd y lludded,—nid felly yma. Byddwch wych, a Duw a fyddo'n gwarchad drosoch a'r eiddoch. W. to R. contd.

Eich caredigawl frawd, Y Twrch Trwyth.

HOLYHEAD, 2nd April, 1752.

Dear Brother,—I was the other day at Brynddu upon some business of Mr. Wright, of Leghorne, when Mr. Bulkeley desired that I would write to you in behalf of a neighbour of his, viz., Mr. Edward Warmingham, of Carrog, whose brother, George Warmingham, went to India an armourer in the Company's service and there is a report that he is dead abroad. One Owen Jones hath writ to the country that he will receive his wages if the brother will send him a proper power; it seems he lodged in that man's house at the sign of the Barley Mow before he went to sea, and he knows what ship he belong'd to, but his friends dont. Now what is desired is, that you would enquire of this Owen Jones what ship he belong'd to, then you may know at the India House what is due and let me know by a line as soon as you can, and if it be anything worth while his brother will administer and send you (if you will take upon you the trouble) proper power to receive it. Treiwch, da chwitheu. Ai rhy fychan o drafferth sydd arnaf eisioes, meddwch chwitheu? Ni waeth i chwi par un; ffwdan fawr yn sicr a fyddai ar ddyn nad allai wrth fynd heibiaw, roi help llaw i dynnu ei gymydog or domen. Ni waeth tewi na siarad ni W. to R. CXXV.

W. to R. contd.

wyddom ni yma pa beth yw gormod o fusnes. Mi welais eich enw dydd arall yn y rhestr argraphedig or Clarkod [yn] y Nafi a £90 ich rhan, heblaw mae'n debyg gymain' arall o ryw friwsion; ni welir wrth fy enw inneu druan gwr ond y drydedd ran a llonaid y ty o bobl yw cadw ai meithrin, etc Wala, wala, rhaid ceisiaw ymfodloni (h.y.) rhaid gweddiaw yn daer am y dawn hwnnw, sef yw un or rhai goreu allan. Daccw'r Golhector Dyfi wedi gyrru yma ddyn ifanc attaf i ddyscu bod yn glark iddaw, fal y gallo ynteu aros gartref, etc., i drin ei drethi. Nid oes bosibl na wnai'r mawrion yna ryw beth drostaw o'r diwedd, mae lle i ofni y bydd y gwr yn ustus heddwch cyn y bo hir, na bo'nd i grybwyll! Duw a roddo iddaw hoedl ag iechyd i fwynhau ei freintiau. Daccw fo wedi gyrru imi ddau gywydd o waith Gronwy ap Owen (ap Gronw Owen yr Eurych) offeiriad, un o honynt sydd i Ddydd y Farn Fawr, gwaith godidog iawn; ni feddyliais i fod y fath ddyn ar wyneb y ddaear, ni wiw i Mr. William Wynne na cholhector Dyfi son mwyach am y gadair, os Gronwy Ddu a â ymlaen fal hyn, nhw allant ganu'n iach iddi, ond gwreigdda Sian Parri am ymddwyn y fath fardd? Gwreigdda. Ni ches i mor amser i edrych om hamgylch er's gwell nag wythnos gan drafferth yn trin cyfrifon chwarterawl a blynyddawl. Ond dyma fi wedi ei cefnu nhw wrth siawns. Bellach am awr neu ddwy yn yr ardd, rwan ag yn y man. Hi wnaeth dywydd cas yn ddiweddar ar les y cucumbers a'r melons. Roedd y nhad a mam yn rhwydd iachus dydd arall, 'rym ni felly yma i gyd, mawl ir Goruchaf! Da iawn a f'ai gael llinell neu ddwy oddiwrthych gynta galloch. Duw yn eich cylch.

Eich caredigawl frawd, William Morris.

P.S.—Nid wyf yn cofiaw a ddarfu i mi ddiolch i chwi am yr had sibol o Spaen, ag am y pine plants a amcanasoch imi, by the way of Egypt. Mae arnaf ofn y bydd gan anhawsed ganddynt ymadael a hwynt oddiyno, ag oedd gan Pharoh hen ollwng ymaith Foesen ai lu o Israeliaid gynt, par fodd bynnag can diolwch am danynt. The hickery nutts dont shew their seed leaves as yet. A ddarfu i chwi ddibennu talu'r *Nafi Bils* rheini bellach, fal y galler cael clywed oddiwrthych weithiau par ddelw sydd ar Feirian? Ai mate yw Iedw Edwards o hyd? Par sut ddyn sydd arno, a ydyw ef yn ymwrthod ar diotta, dyna'r aflwydd gwaetha. Ai byw

Cornelius Agrippa? Ai cwbl iach y chwiw dwll? Aeth y Brenin oddicartref? Oes dim o hanes y Geirlyfr? Pa le yr ydych yn eich Bibl? Par bryd yr ewch drosto? Oni feddyliai ddyn a welai'r cwestiwnau gweigion yma, fod ar y sgrifenydd eisiau gwaith iw wneuthur. Wala, wala, byddwch wych. W.M. W. to R. contd.

CAER GYBI, 20d o Ebrill, 1752.

Anwyl Frawd,—Eich llythyr or 14eg a ddaeth ym llaw y Sadwrn diwaetha ynghyd ag un arall oddiwrth Golhector Dyfi, a ysgrifenodd oi Dollfa. Da iawn yw cael clywed eich bod yn iach o gwr bwygilydd; 'rym ninneu ffordd yma oll yn rhwydd iachus, ag yr oeddynt felly ym Mhentre Eirianallt dydd arall. Mawl ir Goruchaf Dduw am ei drugareddau i ni bod ag un. Aie Gwyl Fihangel a Gwyl Ifan y mae i ni ddisgwyl gorchwylion y Mr. Richards a chwitheu? Iechyd a rhwydd-deb i chwi i fynd ymlaen, felly ni waeth pa beth a ddywaid y gweilch rheini sydd au holl doethineb ymhethau bydol, ag a ddibrisiant bob peth na ddêl ag elw amserol yw ganlyn. Ond y chwi a alwodd Safaids yn for leidr gynta? Diolch i chwi am yr hanes or Marchog, y modd y darfu ir hen dad roddi baich anoddef ar ei dreftadaeth, etc., ag rwy'n gofyn nawdd am feiaw ar y gwr yn ddiarwybod dan addaw na wnaf mo hynny ond hynny. Mae'n debyg mae yn ei gastell y trenga'r Cardinal, rhaid ceisiaw sgrifennu atto a letter of congratulation a chanmoliad. Pa beth fyddai gael gan Oronwy wnio cywydd iddaw a barhau hyd ddiwedd byd? Digrif fa'i ych gweled ach boly ymron llusco'r llawr fal y brawd Llew! Nid oes mo'ch brawd Gwilym yn tewychu mo'r pethau er pan gollawdd ei ymgeledd, mynd yn hytrach yn deneuach drwy farweiddiaw'r cnawd ai ddireidus wyniau, hynny a wnaf, Duw'n y blaen. Rwyf agos a llwyr droi heibiaw y tra yfed, oddigerth pan elir i ymweled a ffrind, yno y bydd raid ambell dro bottiaw tipyn heb yn ddiolch i bod adduned. Gwych clywed fod y chwiw-dwll hwnw ar fyned yn holliach, ar peswch wedi myned allan drwyddo iw grogi, byth na ddelont i'ch crugo mwyach, Amen. Aie trwstan yw Dick Morys Bwt o hyd? Ow! ow! Ai nid oes ar neb ffordd yna eisiau hen ddynan gonest yw dendio, mae ei chwaer yn erchi arnaf ddywedyd ei bod hi ar gŵr yn yr un gyflwr a phan i gadawodd hwynt, oddigerth eu bod yn dipyn hŷn nag oeddynt y pryd hwnnw. Roeddynt wedi rhoddi benthyg gini i Ddicws i W. to R. CXXVI.

W. to R. contd.

ddyfod yna, mi debygwn fod ei eisiau to buy . . . . for the kiln erbyn y gauaf, nis gwn i par sut a fydd. I sent Mr. Bulkeley an account of what you said of George Warmingham. I wish I had Langham's Crouch. Pa beth a gostiawdd? Gronw hath overtopt all the bards of this age, and brother says of all others! I am glad Iedw Iedwards is a sober fellow, I forwarded his letter. Dacw wrechyn O.P. wedi marw'n gelain; mi ge's lythyr galarus oddiwrthaw na bo'nd ei grybwyll! He always was tra anfeddylgar. I am afraid he does not think as he ought to do of the affairs of this world or the next, which God grant we may all do, yno, er ein bod wedi ein gwascaru un yma ar llall accw, bydd in obaith cael ymgyfarfod ryw dro mewn hapusrwydd lle ni'n gwahenir mwyach, a phar bryd y bydd hynny nid oes na Whiston na neb arall a ŵyr, pa'r fan na'r lle. Duw a fo'n gwarchad drosoch, moeswch lythyr cynta galloch. Cymwys bod ffrank i lythyr dwbl, onide nid rhaid wrthaw.

Eich brawd anwiw William Morris.

P.S.—Daccw Llew yn gaddaw dyfod yma efo'r wraig tua diwedd Mai!

HOLYHEAD, 27 April, 1752.

W. to R. CXXVII.

Dear Brother,—I writ you two lines the other day to which refer (chwedl y marsiandwyr). By the last post came to my hands the inclos'd odidawg awdl, sef Gofuned Goronwy, and I fell to it to copy it for you whilst it was piping hot (as Llewelyn required) but I was too late for the post, and now you have it, gwnewch yn llawen arnaw. Wfft, a dwbl wfft, ir awdwr. I shall write to him this post a letter of canmoliaeth, and to ask Mr. Ellis leave to print Cywydd y Farn i ddangos ir holl Gymry benbaladr fod bardd wedi cyfodi i goleddu eu hiaith, etc. Roedd y nhad a mam yn bur sionc echdoe, 'rym ninnau oll yn iach, mawl ir Arglwydd am ei drugareddau i ni bod ag un. Nid oes yma ddim hickery yn dyfod allan or cnau. Oes dim o hanes Cornelius Agrippa? Mi sgrifenais bwmp o lythyr dydd arall at Mr. Dafis o Dre Castell i ddymuno llwyddiant iddo ar ei stad, ag iw ganmol am bentyrru, etc. Nid oes yma rithyn o newydd a dâl i son am dano, a minnau ar anfad ffwdan. Duw yn eich cylch. *Eich caredigawl frawd,*

Gwilym Ddu o Gybi.

P.S.—Os dwbl fydd eich llythyr da fydd ei ddidolli ag onide na ymboenwch.

CAER GYBI, 7d o Fai, 1752.

Anwyl Frawd,—Gan eich bod chwi beunydd yn llawn ffwdan a lludded a minnau yn fynych yn rhwydd segur, cymwys i chwi gael gennyf ddau lythyr am un. Y diweddaf o'r eiddwyf a yrrais i chwi o ddeutu'r 27 ult., a llawer mae'n debyg o ryw ddwndwr gwâg ynddaw. Nid hwyrach mai felly y bydd hwn hefyd. Nis gwn i yn iawn etto par oreu ganddoch pan f'och wedi cadw noswyl a rhoddi eich cerdd yn eich côd, gael rhyw rigwm fal hyn i'ch difyrri, yntau cael llonydd i'ch ymenydd i loywi ag i'ch golygon methiedig ddyfod attynt eu hunain. O'm rhan fy hun, rwyn addef mae un o'r pleserau mwyaf gennyf yw darllain yn eu llythyrau, hanesion fy anwyliaid a megys ymgyfrinachu â hwynt o hirbell, gan ddigwydd imi gael fy nidoli fal hyn oddiwrthynt. Wawch! pa beth ydyw yr twrwf erchyll sydd o gwmpas y Neuadd Wen!* Pa beth sydd yn darfod ir siaplan yna pan fo yn y modd echryslon yma yn ceisio taflu i lawr a llarpio mal llew rhuadwy ein hysgolion Cymreig ni. Y rhain ynhŷb pob Crist'nogaidd Gymro diduedd 'ynt dra mawr fendith i'n gwlad. Ai allan oi bwyll y mae'r dyn? Pam waeth pwy a yrro ymlaen y daionus orchwyl, bydded o Dwrc, Iddew brŷch, Pagan neu Fethodyst? Oni fyddai hyfryd gennych a chan bob Cymro diledryw weled yn yr ysgol yma, sef ymhlwy Cybi ond odid 40 neu 50 o blantos tlodion yn cael eu haddyscu yn *rhodd* ag yn *rhad* i ddarllain yr hen Frutanaeg druan ag i ddeall egwyddorion eu crefydd. Y rhai (pe nis cawsid drwy draul a diwidrwydd Mr. Griff. Jones yr eluseni yma) a fasent mae'n ddigon tebyg bod ag un yn anllythyrennog ag ond odid yn anghrefyddol, h.y., heb na dysc na dawn. A chan fod yr ysgolion hyn o leia yn y wlad yma dan lywodraeth offeiriadau'r plwyfydd, y rhai sydd yn dewis meistryd o'u cymodogion eu hunain o ddynion crefyddol, sobr, etc., par fodd y mae lle i neb rhyw elyn in hiaith feio ar y peth? Os oes rhyw *falciau* yngwaith y Mr. Griff Jones, ynfyd a fai'r dyn a dybia'r plantos gwirion hyn yn abl i amgyffred neu ddirnad y cyfryw bynciau neu bonciau dyrys, y rhai'n y bai

W. to R.
CXXVIII.

* William Morris is here referring to John Evans's book "Some Account of the Welch Charity Schools, etc., 1752." Evans resided in London and held a Chaplaincy at Whitehall. It is clear from internal evidence in the book that he was on terms of intimacy with the promoters of the 1746 Welsh Bible. It may be stated, after a perusal of the book, that William Morris's strictures are well merited.

W. to R. contd. harddach i'r gwŷr Eglwysig eu celu naill ar y llall, yn lle bod yn dannod mor chwerwedd iw gilydd, ag yn eglur ddangos ir byd eu gwendidau a'u angharedigrwydd. Drwg erchyll y maent yn copio ar ol eu Meistr. Pa beth a roddasai ein teidiau ni er gweled y fath ddedwyddwch (ag ynt yr ysgolion hyn) yn eu plith, ai gael hefyd yn rhodd, ie, ei gymell iddynt? Lle y clywais fy nhad yn dywedyd nad ydoedd Ymhlwy Llanfihangel tre'r Bardd a fedrai ddarllain yr hen iaith gyffredin onid un gwr gwreng y sef Sion Edwart y Cowper, at yr hwn y byddai'n myned lanciau'r plwyf i ddyscu darllain gwaith Domos Jones y sywedydd, argraphydd, etc. Hen ddynan oedd Tomas yntau a wnaeth lawer o lês er cymaint ei anwybodaeth. "Rhodd filoedd o bobloedd iw beiblau," ebr Huw Morys. Pwy a wyr na bu'sech chwi a minneu yn anllythrennog oni buasai ir hen gorphyn o Glorach (oblegid 'roedd Rhisiart Morys ein taid yn farwol) addyscu i nhad, ag felly rhoddi cychwyn i'r dawn bendigaid hwnnw. Nid wyf yn tybied fod nemawr o blentyn mewn oed yn y plwyf hwnw yn awr heb fedru darllain, os oes, bai eu rhieni ydyw oblegyd bu yno yscol yn gynnar. Aent wedyn i'r wlad a fynnont, deg i un y gollyngent byth yn angof iaith eu bro, fal y mae mwya'r cywilydd gweled y Cymro coegfalch a'i dibrisia, o achos na cha'dd erioed moi sylfaeni ynddo. Diamau fod Rhagluniaeth yn gweithredu mewn amryw foddion nas gwyddom ni bethau cibddeillion par sut iw deall. Digon tebyg mai heblaw tywallt gras i galonau'r gwirioniaid yma, fod i'r odidawg hen iaith hefyd drwy'r modd yma gael, fal pettai, ei hail fwrw ai gloywi. Nid oes ameu na chyfyd digonedd o feirddion o nifer y rhai hyn. Sicr fod hâd rhinweddau a doniau'r Derwyddon ar cynfeirdd yn parhau byth yn ein plith. Siampl hynod a welwn yn awr yng Ngoronwy Fardd, sydd yn mwynhau awenydd Taliesin, Myrddin, neu rywrai o honynt. Wawch etto, dyma'r berson Bellis yn dywedyd glywed o honaw fod yr Evans hwnnw yn beio arno am fod yn canmol yr ysgolion, etc. Ai tybied fod y Siaplan yna mewn difrif yn meddwl y gwyr o oddi yna yn well nac offeiriadau Cymru par sut yr ydis yn trin yr yscolion yma, a phar faint y budd ar lles y maent yn ei wneuthur, ag a wnant, ir gwerinos? Os yw, disgwyliad gan bob dyn synhwyrol gonest o Gristion a fai Gymro, chwerthin am ei ben ai ddiystyru. So much for yr hen iaith. Rhwydd-deb iddi a'r sawl a'i caro.

Hold! Hold! meddwch chwithau, why all this ranting? Why, it would make a saint rant. Oni ddywedasoch i mae ffrind i chwi oedd mab Ifan, os felly onid cymwys oedd dangos i chwi ei fod wedi myned allan o bob cynghanedd? Yn rhodd ymgeged, os hynny sydd raid iddo, a Chwitfield a Jones, ond er corn ei wddwg na soniad am yr ysgolion Cymraeg, rhag ofn i Gymru osod Goronw iw ddryllio yn 4 aelod a phen a chowydd blaen llym miniawg. Byddwch wych? Pawb yn iach, cenwch. W. to R. contd.

Eich caredigawl frawd, Gwilym Ddu.

CAER GYBI SAINT, Mai 11, 1752.

Dear Brother,—Echdoe daeth im llaw yr eiddoch o'r 5d yng nghwmni un arall oddiwrth y brawd Llewelyn a scrifenasai yn ei offis. Mawl i Dduw eich bod chwi oll a ninneu yn rhwydd iachus. Dymma heddyw ynteu lefnyn o lythyr penigamp oddiwrth Oronwy Ddu y Bardd,* mae'n taring mewn man a elwir Donnington yn agos i'r Ymhwythig, lle mae yn giwredyn tlawd mae'n debygol. He calls Collector Dyfi his tutor; nid oes dim oi waith i ymddangos i'r byd heb i'r gwr cywrain hwnw eu golygu. Pam na bai Gornelius Agrip yn sgrifenu yma ambell dro? Yn wir, chwi wnaethoch iddo'r mawr lles; gobeitho y bydd iddo fod yn ddiolchgar i Dduw a dyn. Da clywed fod y Pwt wedi cael tamaid o fara yn rhyw ffordd weddus. Mae Llewelyn yn barod yn dechreu cilio yn ol, ni wn i etto a ddaw'r wraig yma ar fyrder ai peidiaw; mae ar honno ffŷs mawr am weled y wlad y ganed ei gwr prâff! Ie'n wir, digrif ddigon fyddai i ni gael unwaith ymgyfarfod o'r tu yma i'r bedd. Aie mae dau o honoch yn bennau gwŷr efo'r Comisiwner Fychan yna, gresyn na bai William y trydydd hefyd, nid hwyrach y ceid rhyw gymwynas tuag .... chwaneg o enllyn gyda bara. Nid oes yma ond cynnildeb. Na, chafodd Mrs. Wheldon ddim chwaneg o hanes y bill. Hi a fyddai dra rhwymedig i chwi if you would petition for her. Oni bae fod ganddi ffordd arall i gael tamaid o fara nid ellai mor byw ar y pension tlawd hwnnw. Oes dim gobaith y ca'nt y gwragedd gweddwon ddim chwaneg o arian rhagllaw? I thought they had petitioned the Parliament; if so, W. to R. CXXIX.

*This letter is printed in "Llythyrau Goronwy Owen," Liverpool, 1895, page 3. It also appeared in "Tracts of Powys," 1795, and "The Cambro-Briton," iii., 409.

W. to R. contd. what became of that affair? Os medrwch helpu tipyn ar y weddw cewch dâl yn y Drugaredd ag yma hefyd. You say Meirian sends her compliments; is she in town? If so, ours to you and her. 'Roedd y nhad a mam yn rhesymol iachus dydd arall. Bu Ruffydd Dafydd, a Robert Wmffra, a Sion Drinioel grŷdd, yma ddydd Gwener. Gwyr y buoch gynt yn chwareu pel droed efo hwynt yn fynych ag ar y Sul hefyd. Duw f'on maddeu i ni oll, ag ach cadwo chwi ar eiddych. *Eich caredigawl frawd,*

William Morris.

P.S.—Ai ni sgrifenais attoch labi o lythyr yr wythnos ddiwaetha, i ddwrdiaw rhyw Gymro Seisnig sydd yna yn amherchi ein 'sgolion Cymreig; mae fal y rhowch i senn iddo a llythyr i minneu gynta galloch, da chwitheu. W. M.

GALLTVADOG, May 11th, 1752.

L. to R. CXXX. Dear Brother,—Dyma fi newydd ddyfod adref o Ddyfi, a chwedi cael yr anwyd, sef y pâs yno, a chwedi gwaedu drosto, a ffaelio cysgu, ffaelio bwytta nag yfed na dim; ond etto rhaid y ceisio byw tra gellir. My protection from ye Treasury is not yet come down but expect it daily, Mr. Pelham having given his word it shall be sent without loss of time. The money is safe enough, no doubt, in your hands, but if you should die it would not be safe, but would be supposed to be your own, or perhaps pocketed by a servant, etc., so that it is best to lay it out in my name in India bonds, and I believe I shall have a great deal more soon to be laid out in the same manner. Nis gwn i mwy beth yw India bonds mwy nag y gwyr Alsi bach—pray let me into ye nature of that affair and its management, how and where you put money in, to whom, what security, and profit from it, how to take it out, etc.? I am glad Mr. Reade behaved so well: he is a cleaver man. I shall send a box of ye books of plans and some charts by land carriage to you soon. I shall send for ye books to Salop, etc. Give my service to honest Mathews, I have seen his sister lately and dined at her house. Well done, Duke of Lancaster, Linden will make a goose of him. Jack Owen hath not a minute's time to write anything now but mining accounts,—no cywydd half so profitable. Who told you about Lady Lincoln's dreaming? It is as like as can be. I am in ye same condition with her, but she, I suppose, hath more reason.

Pais heb ddim aur ynddi oeddwn i yn ei feddwl, nid pais euraidd; nid yr un peth yw pais dlawd a phais goethawg, eithr arall yw gogoniant y goethawg, etc. Goronwy's address is "To the Rev. Mr. Gronow Owen at Donnington, near Salop." Send it frankd, he is but poor, and let him know how to write free letters to you. Gofuned Goronwy hath more of nature in it than all the rest; he is a most surprising fellow. We must have him into Anglesey, if possible, or at least some part of Wales. There are a hundred schemes by Powell, Jones, and Lisburn about getting into this mine, but I hope I shall overset them all. If they mine, I undermine. I wish Roderick may not prove one of them at bottom. I have some doubts. What think you? He had promised me a lease, but I don't think I shall have it. No letter from you last post. *Your affectionate brother, L. M.* **W. to R. contd.**

HOLYHEAD, 28th May, 1752.

W. to R. CXXXI.

Anwyl Frawd,—Rwyn tybio i mi yrru i chwi ddau neu dri o lythyrau er pan glywais oddi wrthych, a deg i un y cawsech ddim chwaneg o'm prygowthen y dyddiau yma, oni bae fod yn yspys gennyf y bydd da iawn gennych glywed fod y nhad a mam cystal mewn iechyd, a gallu o honynt yr wythnos diwaethaf ddyfod yma in hymweled, a doe y dychwelasant adref,—mawl i'r Goruchaf Dduw,—yn dra sionc yn ol ei hoedran. Nid oedd ar yr hen bobl ond eisiau eich gweled chwi, ar brawd Llewelyn, a ninnau efo'n gilydd i'w gwneuthur gan ddedwydded ag allai fod. Ni feddyliais i y daethai y mam yma byth, mae hi, Duw au helpio, yn bur gloff, ond yn clywed ag yn gweled cystal cynt. Mae pob un or ddau yn o ddrwg gan fy nhad. Dyma fi wedi hanner fy nihenyddu fy hun, drwy fod yn sefyll ar ben y ffordd fawr dros bedwar diwrnod or untu; nid yn di-berchenogi pobl, eithr yn rheoli y rhan oreu o saith ugeinyn o bobl i daclu y ffordd fawr bob dydd, ai gwneuthur fal ffyrdd y Werddon gin wastatted ar geiniog mal y gallai'r Brenin, Duw safo gydai ras, ddyfod yn ei gerbyd rhyd-ddi yn ddi-dramgwydd. Dywedwch wrth y mawr wyr yna nad rhaid iddynt risio dyfod ffordd yma bellach, bawb yn ei gerbyd. Ond wrth sôn am danynt, daccw'r gwr mwya yn ein gwlad ni wedi marw, y sef yr Arglwydd Bwclai, ag iddo ferch gwmpas dwy flwydd oed, ar wraig yn feichiog, ag oni ymddwg hi fab, ffarwel ir Arglwyddiaeth, yr

CXXXI

W. to R. contd. hon a ddescyn i ryw Gyrnol Bwclai yn Ffrainc, neu'n rhywle . . . . Wala, wala, rhaid a mynd i orphwyso, Duw a roddo i chwi nos da, ag a'ch cadw rhag pob dihirwch. *Eich caredicaf frawd, Wm. Morris.*

P.S.—Sgrifenwch fynycha galloch, da chwitheu, yma ag i Bentre Eirianallt. Gyrrwch dippyn o ryw newyddion i ddifyrru tippyn ar boblach sydd fal pettai wedi eu claddu yn fyw yn y gongl fynyddig yma. Ai gartref y mae Meirian ganddoch? Os e, mae Pegy Morris yw hannerch.

GALLTVADOG, June 13, 1752.

L. to R. CXXXII. Dear Brother,—I have read Dr. Free's essay on history, it is a pity he had not some of our British materials, he guesses surprisingly. (He) is wrong in ye etymon. of Caledonia and Strat, and Gambold hath informed him about the word *pen vahel* or *vahal*, or *pen* . . . . . *Gwal* and *gwawl* is an antient British word, perhaps more . . . . than the Latin vallum. We have no other word so common . . . . all over Wales. See Davies's dictionary in *gwal* and *gwawl*. . . . . say pared for a wall. *Pared* is the surface of a wall, 'sgrifennu ar y pared, gorwedd yn nesa i'r pared. We never say adeiladu pared, so gwal seems to be ye right Celtic word, and mur the provincial British, borrowd (from) ye Romans. It is idle to say that the Britains had no [word for] a wall but what they borrowd from the Romans. I agree with him about ye etymology of ye word *Cymro*, (the) Britons were so called from Bryth. . . . . in page 16 is y^e^ *Saracen's stop* and not their works. . . . . allow the Gauls to be called a barbarous nation, p. 16, but on . . . . very, very polite; read Pliny's Nat. Hist. . . . . our language is not *painted*. . . . made some attempt towards distinguishing the antient (the most British) words from ye Provincial words of ye Romans, and it is a most pleasant undertaking, but I have no time for it. Free's opinion of ancient colonies and intermixture of languages in . . . . of times. I have no time to write any more about this at present, ... a will and power of one John Lloyd, an old servant of mine . . . . months ago. He now writes me word the money is to be paid . . . summer. Do you remember anything of it? (I)'ll endeavour to send Mr. Pritchard a bill on another person . . . . have laid out ye money as you have. But if necessity . . . . me I must draw on you. I shall see soon.

I am, your affectionate brother, Lewis Morris.

CAER GYBI, 27 o Fehefin, 1752.

Anwyl Frawd,—Wele yma yr eiddoch o'r 2d a phregeth y Dr. Evans. Ai allan o'ch pwyll yr oeddych chwitheu pan ro'ech fy llythyr yn llaw gwr ffromwyllt or fath yna? Gresyn na base debyg i hwnnw o Lanerchmedd gynt. Wfft i'r rhimynau yma a ddodws yn ei araith. Nid gwell ei orchwyl er canmawl rhai pobl ef, ond ny lyfasai dreuthu fy meddwl wrthych mwyach rhag ofn i mi dynnu gormodd drwg yn fy mhen. However, you may please to give my respects to the Doctor, a phan gaffwyf odfa, ond odid, imi sgrifennu atto yn atteb iw lythyr, ond nid i ofyn nawdd ganddo, oblegid ni wnaethym achos etto, mae rhywun yn euawg ag fe ddylai ddwyn penyd o'r achos mewn cynfas glaerwen i edrych a ymadawai yr yspryd afrywiog ymlidiawg allan o honaw, nid hwyrach y deuai un addfwyn, tyner, llaryaidd, hynaws yn ei le. Rwy'n tebyg fod y Doctor yn meddwl mai darn o Fethodist yw eich brawd Gwilym Ddu, oni bae hynny ni ddodasai ar lawr eu campiau yn ei lythyr attaf. Och yfi ha wr fab, fe gamgymerth yn erchyll! Nid wyf wedi ymhyllu felly chwaith, o ran rwy'n tybied fod pryf naill ar gŷsp ai rhywbeth ymhen pob rhai o honynt, a bod anferth gynrhonyn aflonyddgar ynghoppa pob dyn lled synhwyrol gynt sydd yn ymgynnhennu a nhw. Dyna lythyr oddiwrth y nhad, chwi welwch fod yr hen bobl yn anesmwyth o eisiau clywed oddiwrthych. I writ father this morn by Peggy Morris, who went to visit there, and told him that you were well the 2nd. I hope Jones of Marrian (who is agent for the eldest of the three Lady Dowagers Bulkeley) was mistaken. Ni chlywai ddim sôn am Cardinal Castleton; pa beth a ddaeth o honaw? Nid hwyrach mae aros y mae 'rhyd yr amser i ymryson doethineb efo Goronwy yn Swydd Amhwythig, fal y dywedai Oronwy eurych fod y paun bâch o Wicwair yn Rhos, a Gwgawn wawd newydd o Gaereinion, Ymhowys, y pryd y bu ddoethach Gwgawn o hanner gair.* Dyma un o'ch

W. to R. CXXXIII.

* This refers to the folk tale "Araith Gwgan," copies of which are common in Welsh MSS. of the 16th and 17th centuries. It was printed for the first time in Cydymaith Diddan [1766], p. 42. Y Paun bach and Gwgan gwawd newydd were the two wisest men in North Wales, and the story goes that they once met to decide which of the two was the wiser. They talked through the night, each one exerting himself to the utmost. "Ac ymresymu doethineb onid oedd ddydd dranoeth, ac yna doethaf oedd Gwgan ar y tir gwyllt, a doethaf oedd y Paun bach ar y tir dôf." Gwgan appears to have won the day, or rather the night, for he was "doethach o hanner gair."

W. to R. contd. pobl, y sef Sir Peter Warren, Knight of the Bath. Dynan mwyn cymwys, medd pawb. Fe roddes 36s. i ni tuag at daclu'r ffordd fawr, a digonedd i'r tlodion yma. We have made a coach road from hence to Rhydbont of nine or ten feet wide, after the Irish manner. It's own'd to be the compleatest thing of the kind in Wales, if not in England—a pattern for the rest or the county. Dyna iddyn' nhw! ontê rwan? Nag oes, nag oes, golled yn y byd ar ol Arglwyddi gwirionllyd, nid hwyrach y daw un o'i rywogaeth etto, teulu oeddynt abl di ddaioni. Da clywed fod yr ystât yn mynd yw blant neu blentyn, os dwy ferch rhennir rhyngddynt, os mab, ca'r cwbl. Fe ddywedir fod y Dwm Bifan, dwrnai, yn gwneuthur llaw wych o'u materion. Ydych i yn gydnabyddus a Thomos? Par ddelw sydd arno fo? I had a line the other day from my old friend Fortunatus Wright. I find his Italian children are come to London. I fancy he and his wife will soon follow. Ni chefais ddim llythyr o Allt Fadawg er's pymthegnos, mae yno ddigon o fwstwr gan fod y 1af o Orphena ar eu gwarthaf, wfft i'r gwythenni sydd ganddynt, pwy fydd yn cael y rhan oreu bellach? Ni chefais i byth linell oddiwrth Gornelius Agrippa, ai byw ydyw ai peidiaw? Mae fal y dwrdiwch i fo am beidiaw ag ysgrifennu at ei hen athraw cyhyd a chyhyd o amser. Peidiwch a gillwng dros gof yr haf yma eich gaddawiad o dyrru ynghyd ymhob gardd yr eloch iddi oreu galloch o hadau dieithr, etc., ir brawd o Gybi, da chwithau. Let me hear from you as soon as you can. Mi fum dra trafferthus yn ddiweddar ar y ffordd fawr, gorfu arnaf ginhiewa 13 o ddyddiau ar y dywarchen las,—dyna fyd blin onte? Oni bae hynny 'sgrifenaswn attoch ryw rigwm yn gynt. Duw a fo'n gwarçhad drosoch, a byddwch wych.

Eich caredigawl frawd, William Morris.

Bu'r hen Fawdfil yma dydd arall, roedd yn son am danoch. Dyna i chwi gwpl o'i ffrancodau.

GARTREF, Nos Awst, 1752.

W. to R. CXXXIV. Anwyl Frawd—Mi sgrifennais attoch linell neu ddwy ar ffrwst o Allt Fadawg. Yno y cefais yr eiddoch or 4dd yn atteb i ni-wybod-pa-sawl llythyr oddiyma. Maen debyg glywed o honoch oddi wrth Lewelyn yr hanes fal y darfu i'r wraig o'r Allt a minneu gychwyn oddi yno tua Mon Ynys wythnos i ddoe. Ni gawsom rwydd-deb odiaeth ar ein taith, ag yr oeddym y drydedd nos Ymhentre Eirianell wedi ymdreiglio dros freichiau moroedd a mynyddoedd echryslon. Daethom i hyd ir hen rieni yn iachus dda iawn, terriais yno ddwynos, yno adre yn nerth y carna' i fwrw golwg ar fy neu giw, wedi bod oddiwrthynt dair wythnos gyfan! Cefais bawb yn iach, mawl ir Goruchaf am ei holl fendithion. Rwy'n disgwyl y chwaer ynghyfraith y foru (under the convoy of my father) i darrio yma un wythnos i weled rhyfeddodau Cybi. The morn we set out brother had received ye letter mentioning that his new Commission would be sent the post following, yno edifaru na ba'sem yn aros un deuddydd yn rhagor, ond erbyn i ni fyned i Aberdovey wele bwmp o lythyr oddiwrth y Com. Fychan ag ynddo, na bo 'nd i grybwyll, gommission nawdd D— rhagddaw! a chyngorion oddi wrth yr hen wr ynghylch cwrs y byd, with some dark, very dark, hints of some under-hand dealings, etc. Perhaps you'll be desired to get an explanation; if so, should be glad to know what he meant, otherwise tewi a sôn. Mae'r Tew yn ymdrobaeddu mewn cyfoeth dros ei ben ai glustiau. Duw a roddo iddo iechyd, llwyddiant a hir hoedl i fagu ag i feithrin y plantos bychain accw a rheini sydd i ddyfod (mae un cyw yn y cawell eisioes), nid oes ammeu na bydd digon o honynt. Mae'r tir mewn purion cyffaith. Roedd y nhad yn dywedyd gael o honaw eich llythyr efo'r Cardynal, ond mae o yn disgwyl un arall ynghylch rhyw arian chwaer Will Jones sydd yn ei grugo fo yn erchyll. Mi glywais fod meistr Trecastell yn y wlad dydd arall tua'r Caerau, lle mae'r Arglwyddes, etc. Par sut y mae'r boblach yna yn trin y cyfreithiau hebddo? Ydyw'r Lord Chancellor weithiau yn cadw ei le fo? Mi glywais Mr. Bodvel yn dywedyd ei fod o yn tirrio am lô yn agos ir fan lle mae'r Gardynal, ai fod wedi methu, er gwarrio llawer o fwnws. Nid hwyrach mai gwell lwc y Cardynal. Ni a wnawn ein goreu ar berswaedio'r boblach i dacclu eu ffyrdd o hyd oddiyma i Gaerllion Gawr. Here are mile stones come over from Dublin, a present from the owner of the pacquet, to be set from hence to Porthaethwy, and it's said large subscriptions are raisd in sundry places to carry on the work, felly profeidiwch gerbyd gynta galloch, but if you dont care to be at the expence of keeping a coach-and-six, fel y Fason honno, nid raid i chwi ond llogi post chaise. Rydis yn son am gael rhai yn berthynol ir dref neu'n hytrach y Gaer yma.

W. to R. contd.

W. to R. contd. Nid oeddych ddim ymhell or ffordd, pan na feddyliasoch mai gwr D—w ydoedd y Fwclai hono, tebyccach ei fuchedd ai ymarweddiad i wr i'r F—ll, nolff o ddyn meddwa a gwagca a roes erioed wenwisc am dano, ffei hono frebwl brwnt. Fe yrrws yr hadau imi, ond ni wyddwn amcan gan bwy y cawsai hwynt, roeddynt wedi gwlychu peth, ar enwau wedi colli agos i gyd, felly mi fum yn hir cyn dyfod i wybod pa beth oeddynt wrth y gelfyddyd lysieuawg. Diolch yn fawr am danynt. My service to Mr. Parry the importer, though unknown. Mi glywaf fod Herbert Feddyg yn y gymdogaeth yma ynhy ei frawd arall, Person Maethlu. Da clywed mai celwydd a ddywaid Sions y Marrian. Gwych clywed eich bod yn pesci, nid hwyrach mae chwi fydd y brasa or tri brawd, rhaid i chwi gynyddu llawer cyn mynd o honoch gin braffed ar Llewelyn, nid wyfi ond burgyn wrtho. Aie mae'r Corddyn ganddoch byth yn ffawtys, well, well, y b'o rhagllaw. Syr Peder Warren is mightily carressd by his country men, the Teaguelanders, braidd na rho nhw·aur ar ei glôg o! Aie chwi gawsoch yr anrhydedd o dderbyn llythyr oddi wrth Oronwy or diwedd? Dyn rhyfeddol ydyw. Mae Ngallt Vadawg, mi a wranta, ddau ddwsing oi lythyrau a chywydd ymhob un o naddynt, ag yn wir rhai gwychion ynt. Dyma un odiaethol ir Awen, cystal a'r goreu a wnaed. Ni argraphwyd mo un Y Farn, ag ni choeliai yr argrephir ar frys, oblegid mae Madog yn dywedyd y bydd rhaid ir Berson a minnau (gwyr cymwys iawn i'r gorchwyl) sgrifennu learned notes upon't, those to be sent Goronwy, thence to Madogallt, thence back to him, and thence hither, so the work stands and will stand. Digrif stori Dwm Bifan a Miss Owain, fe gadd ei haeddiant yn llwyr gwbl. Pam na chais yr anifail gymhares gyfreithlon yn lle dilyn drwg fuchedd? Nid oes mor llawer er pan ge's lythyr oddiwrth Nat, nid oes dim gobaith y daw o adref ni wybod par bryd; the Turkey Company are a plaguing of him still, but I hope he will be able to baffle 'em with all their power. O chwiw ladron! Yr anrhas ir Aldromon ap Rhisiart; e'm siommodd yn aruthur drwy beidio dyfod im cyfarfod yn Arfon i gael ei gwmni ir Deau dir, nid oes dim coel arno. Aie mae Agrippa'n gawr! Ni a wn i ydyw fo yn cynnull dim hadau i mi erbyn y flwyddyn nesaf o erddi'r Dugiaid ar Arglwyddi sydd gan dewed oi amgylch a bytatws Ynghaer Gybi.

Dydd Awst.—Dim newydd o unlle. Disgwyl y nhad ar chwaer Madog, a'r mwynwr a ddatcuddiodd y mwyn yn yr Escair, ar gwas, yn un gyr, felly rhaid rhoddi'r pin heibiaw a mynd i ddarparu iw herbyn. Duw a fo'n gwarchad drosoch. **W. to R. contd.**

Eich caredíccaf frawd, Gwilym Ddu.

P.S.—Mi glywaf fod chwigs Lerpwl agos wedi lladd Mr. Vychan o'r Gors am ei fod yn Dori ; bu fwstr gerwin or achos, gorfu gofyn nawdd iddo a chan mil o bethau, dyna lle mae efo i long er's talm byd. Digrif traeth awdlau a wnaeth Llewelyn iddo fo a hithau.* Gwaed hwch! Ymhle mae llyfr Richards? Mae'r bobl ymron tynnu fy llygaid am naill ai arian ai llyfrau. Er mwyn dyn gadewch glywed yr hanes. Byddwch wych. W.M.

August 9th, 1752.

L. to R. CXXXV

Dear Brother,—I have yours . . . I ask pardon, I did not understand ye nature of ye pow(er) . . . Bank ann. Must there be such another power in ye India Bond affair? This is not so convenient for me, when I have occasion to draw upon you now and then for certain sums. I should like the situation of ye money as it is, in ye Bank ann. in your name, better than any way, if it was not subject to an accident of being lost if you should happen to die. For you have no body but strangers about you. Explain this.

Mae golwg braf yn Esgair y mwyn (new discoveries !), ond rwyt etto heb *settlio* gida Lord Lincoln a Mr. P—m, etc., pwy sydd i gael gweithio'r gwaith (as a miner), whether they or I. If I am accountable only for the duty, fe fydd gennyf filoedd o bunnau yma tocc. But if I must work for them I must get pickings in another shape. I can get old silver here in tolerable quantities, but what I wanted was two or three hundred pound in new silver, if it could have been easily got. If I was to make a noise, fe fuase'r mwynwyr yn tyngu mae'r brenhin oedd yn ei danfon imi yn ungwaith. If I had five hundred weight of new half-pence it would make some noise, but how are they to be packd? and is not there a risque in ye carriage? Er gwaetha'r wrach benwen mae Collector Dyfi yn wêll na chanpunt yn y flwyddyn *clear profit.* My fees and salary last quarter came to near £40, but it was an extraordinary quarter,

*Lewis Morris wrote a Traethodl on William Vaughan's ship, "Harlech Castle," in the form of a dialogue between the ship and the poet."

L. to R. contd.

on account of y[e] great quantity of Esgair y mwyn ore we shipd off and enterd there. The best motto I can think of for the British Society is *Yr Hen Drigolion.* That can give no offence to other people. I shall be glad to hear from the Jew. Upon second thoughts, *Yr Hen Drigolion* may admit of some bad turns, as if they grumbled because there are trigolion newydd. But I think *Y Cymrodorion* (i.e., Y Cynfrodorion) throws a sort of disguise over it. Now I must have your opinion by return of post, what motto I shall have for my seal of office of superintendent of y[e] mines. If the following will do in your opinion, get an engraver immediately to cut a seal on brass the size of figure *A*, with a tail to fasten it in wood as in figure *B*, or a socket as usual.* I will have one cut in chrystal or cornelian if this pleases our friends. If the seal could be made smaller than figure *A*, it would be better, because of sealing on wax; or if cutting on steel be not too dear, I would have a steel one. As the first painters in y[e] world were obliged to write under their pictures: "This is a horse," "this is a man," etc., so I must tell you this is a hand holding a pick or pickax striking a rock. I fancy those must be my arms when I have occasion for arms, and the motto '*O for ag o fynydd, da i ddedwydd.*' Upon third consideration, might not the words *The seal of* be left out, everybody that sees the impression will know that it is done by a *seal.* This third consideration is best, y trydydd tro mae'r goel. My wife is still in Anglesey, mae ei heisiau yma yn fawr iawn—y plant yn gweiddi ar morwynion yn diogi. Dyma Ifan brydydd hir Yngallt Fadog, yn darllain (chwedl Gronwy) "cain acceniad beirddion, hil Derwyddon olau adroddiad." He grows drunk and a mere poet in all respects. Gronwy (though I am told he loves liquor too) is ten degrees above Ieuan. Gronwy is a prodigy. Bonedd a Chynneddfau'r awen is an admirable inimitable piece! But what do I talk of poetry? Esgair y mwyn calls. Farewell for this time. *Your affectionate brother, Lewis Morris.*

HOLYHEAD, July 30th, 1752.

W. to R. CXXXVI.

Dear Brother,—Ces lythyr o Bentre'rianell dydd arall; roedd y nhad yn abl afiachus. Dyma un o Allt Fadawg heddyw (y 30),

*Lewis Morris draws a sketch of the seal in his letter. The seal was to be a circular one, with the words "The Seal of the Superintendent of the King's Mines" around the edge, and a hand holding a pick-axe in the centre.

pawb yn iach ag yn llawn trafferthion bydol ffordd hono, ni chaf mor amser i ddywedyd dim chwaneg na'n bod ni i gyd yma yn rhwydd iachus. Mawl i'r Goruchaf Dduw am ei holl drugareddau i ni oll. Bydded iddo warchad drosoch a'r eiddoch. Sgrifennwch yma gynta galloch. Byddwch wych. *Eich caredicca f frawd, W. Morris.* W. to R. contd.

P.S.—Peggy Morris desires her compliments to her cousin Meirian and would be glad of the favour of a letter from her.

HOLYHEAD, 13th August, 1752.

W. to R. CXXXVII.

Dear Brother,—I writ you two or three lines the 1st inst. That same day our mother was taken ill, and she hath continued ever since extream sick; hath been speechless for some days, and God only knows the event. Disgwyl clywed naill ai newydd da neu ddrwg bob munud. Duw a ŵyr oreu pa beth i wneuthur. Ei ewyllys bendigaid ef a wneler. My sister-in-law set out homewards the 10th, and I hope she reached Gallt Vadawg last night. Hi gadd dywydd go afreolus a hitheu debygwn i yn magu mân esgyrn; mae'n rhywyr clywed ei myned yn ddidrwc i ben ei siwrnai. Dyma Nelly Morris wedi ymadael or Henblas, lle bu hi ddwy flynedd; mae'n rhaid ei swccrio hi hyd na chaffo ryw le etto. Mi debygwn fod blŷs am fynd i wasanaeth i Lundain neu ryw ddinas fawr. Lle anghymwys ddigon i herlodes rhwydd ynfyd. Ni chefais er pan ddaethym adref or Deau prin amser i edrych o'm hamgylch gan ryw wâg drafferthion, felly esgusodwch y llythyr cwtta yma. Dwg y nesaf, mae'n debyg, ryw newydd oddiwrth y mam. Duw a fyddo gyda ni oll. *Eich caredigawl frawd, William Morris.*

HOLYHEAD, 16th August, 1752.

W. to R. CXXXVIII.

Dear Brother,—This day I returned home from my father's and am extream sorry to acquaint you that this morning about three o'clock the Almighty was pleased to take to Himself the soul of our dear mother after a fortnight's illness. I need not tell you what grief it must occasion to us all, especially to our poor father, whose loss is inexpressible, for few people loved one another so well, and lived so long without any broiles and contentions. Mae'r hen ŵr wedi mynd yn fusgrell ag yn ddwl. Y clywed a'r gweled yn ffaelio, ag y rwan Duw ai helpio yn dra ymddifad. Trennydd y bydd y cynhebrwng. Duw a'n diddano ni oll, ac a roddo ini, ei phlant hi, râs i ddilyn ei llwybrau hi. *Eich brawd galarus, Wm. Morris.*

W. to R. contd. P.S.—17th August. Roeddwn yn disgwyl llythyr oddiwrthych cyn hyn, ond ni ddaeth yr un. Dyma ni yn cychwyn tua Phentre rianell bod ag un. Duw a fo'n gwarchad drosoch chwi a minneu.

HOLYHEAD, 20th August, 1752.

W. to R. CXXXIX. Anwyl Frawd Richard,—Gynneu y dychwelais adref o fod ynghladdedigaeth ein mam, ag yn wir roedd yno gynhebrwng mawr iawn, yr holl geraint o'r ddwy sîr ar gydnabod o bob cwr i'r wlad. Ni ai claddasom yn Eglwys Benrhos or tu deau iddi, roedd rhy fychan o le i'r bobl i fynd ir eglwys, felly bu raid dyfod ar allor ir fynwent a darllain ag offrymmu yno. Nid eill neb amgyffred y golled a gadd yr hen wr musgrell; mae o'n dra hiraethus a thrist; Duw or nef ai diddano. Nis gwn i par sut a fydd ir hen wr drin y tyddyn bellach—weithiau mae o'n meddwl cymeryd rhywun i mewn i fod yn gydwr iddo. Mae fy chwaer ai merch a Neli Morys wedi aros yno i ddiddanu tipyn arno, gobeitho y bydd well i hamdden ar fyrder. I received your letter this day but have not time to answer, nor is my head fit for anything. Brother Davies and self came through Llanerchmedd this morn. I went streight through; he stopt, and overtook me after, and told me that there was some English boy at Mredith Parry or Richard Parry that wanted to see me, but it was too far for me to turn back. Who is that boy? My father spoke something of him, but I did not then mind it. Cousin Jack Salisbury tarried three nights with us at Pentrerianell—yr un dyn yn union deg. What are these red drops? Ni waeth tewi na siared, I am not fit to write or anything else. Duw a fyddo gyd a chwi ag ach cadwo rhag pob drwg.

Eich caredigawl frawd, William Morris.

P.S.—Daccw'r post wedi mynd i ffordd, felly rhaid gadael hwn tan ddydd Sadwrn heb ei yrru ymaith. Rwy'n lled ddîg wrth Huw Dafis, eich cymydog, fe yrrodd efo dau o bobl attaf i'r cynhebrwng iw escusodi ei hun am beidiaw a dyfod yno, er ei fod yn y gymdogaeth, dan daeru na wyddai mo'r diwrnod (though both the people could tell him), and mountebank-like sent me word that he would be such and such nights at Presaddved and Caera', and that he wanted much to see me. Unparaleld impudence! What! did the b—k he--d think I would wait of him, or did he give himself airs to make those folks think him a man of consequence? Ffei honno, wag bren. Gerwin or daith a gymerasoch i ymweled a Meirian yn eich cerbyd, ar dail ar llysia a welsoch; roedd Parry ynteu wedi colli ei adnabod ar ddail ei wlad mi wranta. Da iawn oedd cael yr hadau rheini ganddaw, a phe bai gyfleu, or ffeinia fydde gael rhyw faint chwaneg o naddynt. Aie ymadaw ar Faswn a orug Owain, pam na yrr yr hulrhod ei hanes i mi, fal y gallwyf atteb ei bobl, etc.? Fe ffaeliodd gennyf fi fyned ir Deheudir pan oedd y Commissioner Vychan yno, oni bae hynny cawswn fod yn gydnabyddus ag ef, ag ond odid cawsid ryw dro gymwynas ganthaw, yn wir digon rhaid wrthi, anawdd iawn trin y byd yma. Cewch yn fy nesaf hanes y mwyn a Mr. Vychan or Gors, a chant o bethau; mae'r galon yn drom yr awron, felly ni cheir ganddi mor ystwytho at ddim diddanwch. Mae'n bur anhawdd atteb Bifan rhag mor chwerw ydoedd. Ffei o hono'r Richards yna yn hudaw poblach i ddywedyd gau chwedlau ar ei ol. Maent yn anesmwyth o achos ei fod yn ddyn dieithr iddynt.—W. Morris. W. to R. contd.

HOLYHEAD, 29th August, 1752.

Dear Brother,—Mi sgrifenais attochi'r dydd arall, a chan fod gennyf awr segur rwy'n cyfarch yr awron. Dyma ferch fy chwaer wedi dyfod adref ddoe o dy nhad. Mae'r hen wr yn bur drist, mae o'r dydd yn difyrru tippyn arno ei hun ymhlith eu weinidogion, ond y nos nid yw'n medru cysgu ond ychydig, felly mae hi'n galed ag yn hiraethus iawn arno. Duw ai diddano! Roedd yn rhyfedd gennyf glywed y lodes yn dywedyd na ddaethai ddim llythyr oddi wrthych atto. Er dim ar y fo 'sgrifennwch fynycha fyth ag alloch yno. Gadewch ini bawb wneuthur goreu gallom tuag at ddifyrru tippyn arno tra byddo yn y byd trallodus yma,—nid llawer o gymffwrd sydd wiw i'r un o honom ddisgwyl yma. Ychydig yn sicr a ddigwydd yw ran ef, yr hwn sydd yn ymdrechu beunydd a heintiau a henaint. I should be glad of a line from you if you have not writ already. Y Duw goruchaf a fyddo yn gwarchad drosoch chwi a ninneu. *Eich caredigawl frawd, William Morris.* W. to R. CXL.

HOLYHEAD, Yr Hen Wyl Fathew, 1752.

Dear Brother,—Mae llawer er pan dderbyniais eich llythyr or 29 Awst hyd yr awron, yn enwedig os oes coel ar y rhif newydd, mae'n debyg fy mod wedi ei atteb but query. Echdoe y daethym adre o Bentre Eirian Allt wedi bod yno yn setlio amryw fatterion W. to R. CLXI.

W. to R. contd. a berthynynt ir hen wr. Mae e' mawl i Dduw yn rhwydd dda ar ei iechyd yn ol ei oedran, y nos y mae'n achwyn ei fod yn dra anesmwyth mewn corph a meddwl, nid oes disgwyl chwedl amgen. Wala! wfft i chwi am ddodi i lawr y brygowthen honno, ni chymeraswn yr holl fyd (agos) er gwneuthur hynny, mae'r bonedd yma yn barnu ag yn goganu llawer o'r achos.

Mi glywaf gan 'Ronwy yrru o honno i chwi Gowydd y Farn Fawr. Par sut yr ydych yn ei leicio fo? Onid yw e' yn waith godidawg iawn? Daccw fo yn mynd iw argraphu. Dyma arall oddiwrtho, y sef yw C. Gemm, ac yn wir ddiau un campus ydyw, ni ddeuir i ben i sgrifennu moi holl waith. Mae arnai ddiwredd gwlad am ei gael i Fon, mae yma le neu ddau ar ddyfod yn weigion, gobeitho y ceiff y bardd ei ofuned ryw drò. Mynych mae Rhagluniaeth yn ein canfod ymhell bell allan o ffordd yn ein gofunedau, ag och mor ddeillion ydym tra bo'm yn gwisco cnawd am danom. Nid oes ir bardd ond disgwyl wrth Lywelyn, fe eill hwnnw fod yn wasanaethgar iddo a Duw yn y blaen. An excellent motto that! Daccw nhad wedi ymroi i gadw pob peth yn yr un modd dros un flwyddyn parfodd bynnag. Anhawdd iawn yw caffael cydwr a foddiai ddyn, ie, amhosibl ydyw, a digon anhawdd taraw wrth hafodwr gonest diwyd, felly wedi amrafael ymgyfarfodydd, ni a droesom bob peth ir hen ffrwd. Mae merch fy chwaer, yr hon sydd ddynes lysti, mae'n debyg o ddeunaw i ugain oed, i fod yno yn wastad, and 20 other regulations made. Your ward at Llanerchmedd is a good looking boy, but a very wicked one. I am affraid his master is too easy with him, bachgen ag araith fudraidd ganthaw ag heb arno fwy o ddawn nag ar anifail gwyllt. He wont eat this and that, he must have white bread, ale, etc. Pan wnelir uwd ir plant eraill i swpper, sef mab fy chwaer a mab y gares Marged Salbri gynt, ni fedr o prin edrych arno, a throi ei ben ol at ei landlady pan fydd hi newydd roddi brechtan o fara gwyn iddo. Sgrifenwch atto a dwrdiwch o yn ffest ag yn galed, rwyn meddwl na chadd ei feistr ddim llythyr oddiwrthych; give him likewise a charge for to keep him under. Mae yno achwyn tost ar yr hogyn. Rwyn disgwyl ceffyl yma beunydd i gyrchu Nelly adref i Allt Fadawg. Yr ym oll yn iach ag yn gorchymun attoch. Duw a fo'n gwarchad drosoch.

Eich caredigawl frawd, Gwilym Ddu o Fon.

CAERGYBI SAINT, Medi 20d, 1752.

Anwyl Frawd,—Y gwr ieuanc a ddyd hwn yn eich llaw sydd fab i wr bonheddig or wlad yma, yr hwn ydoedd yn byw yn Nulun ag yn mwynhau yno swydd ardderchog, ond gan fod iddo ddisgwiliad mawr ar wr cyfoethog arall, byw a orug i fynu i'r dyfodiad i mewn oedd iddaw; yno marw or cyfoethawg heb adael iddo beil, ac ymhen ennyd bu farw ynteu hefyd. Felly gorfu arnaddynt ei blant fynd i ennill eu bywoliaeth. Gwasnaethodd hwn ei amser i wneuthurwr tlysau, ag mae'n awr yn dyfod yna i enill tippyn chwaneg o athrawiaeth yn ei gelfyddyd. Mae ganddo ychydig o dir yn y wlad yma a adawodd ei daid (sef oedd hwnnw Morris Parry, o Asgellog, yn Amlwch), heb ei werthu. Anferth ffrind oedd tad hwn i'r brawd Llewelyn. Dynan cwrtais iw hwn o Wyddyl, gwaed y Cymro sydd ynddo, a Will Parry y gelwir. Os bydd arno eisiau cymwynas, a chwitheu yn gallu ei gwneuthur, gwnewch ran cydwladwr obleit Cymro y myn y gwr ei fod, ond y tafawd sydd yn gwneuthur ei frâd. Ni wiw imi ddodi ar lawr ddim chwaneg yr awron, oblegid geill y pererin fod yn hir ar ei siwrnai. Duw yn eich cylch. *Eich caredigawl frawd, William Morris.* W. to R. CXLII.

GARTREF, 22d September, 1752.

Dear Brother,—Llymma'r eiddoch o'r 29 ulto yn addef 3 or eiddwyfi ar yr achos galarus o farwolaeth y fam oreu, ond odid aeth ir pridd yn yr oes yma na nemawr un arall. Duw a alwodd am dani i dderbyn ei gwobr, felly rhaid ymfodloni iw ewyllys bendigedig Ef. Fe ymgysura pawb o dippyn i dippyn ond yr hen wr hiraethus. Rwy'n meddwl mynd ffordd hono y foru os medraf. Gobeitho os cewch hoedl ag iechyd na bydd hynny ich llestair rhag dyfod i Fon yr haf nesa', gan fod yn fwy elusen ymweled ar hen wr ymddifaid nag a fuase pe byw eill deuwedd yn ddiddanwch y naill i'r llall. Mae ini gefnderw o fab i'n modryb Elsbeth 'ch Richard Morris o ddynan, sobr, gonest, gofalus, yn byw gyda mam fynghyfraith iddo erioed hyd yn heddyw (a deu frawd eraill gyda e')—y dyn yma mae nhad yn amcanu gymeryd i mewn yn gydwr gyda ei chwaer Marged, yr hon sydd lances ofalus, ag Ymhentrerianallt y mae er pan fu farw ei mam (h.y.) er pan oedd blentyn. Ond mi debygwn (gan fod yr hen wr yn awr yn o dacclus ar tir mewn cyffaith da, a newid arno wrth fal y mae'r byd yn bod yr awron), fod gan y chwaer W. to R. CXLIII.

W. to R. contd. ryw dueddiad i gadw eraill allan er mwyn ei hun neu i phlant. Da fyddai pei gellid lles iddynt, mae nifer mawr o naddynt ar ieuaf ar ei bronnau'r dydd arall, ag yn ddistaw 'r gwr yn beth pottiwr.

Mae'r tywydd yma yn dal yn llaith erchyll—gwynt a glaw agos bob dydd. Dryghinoedd mawrion a mawr ddrwg ar fôr a thir ysywaeth. Duw a helpo'r sawl sydd yn dioddef o'r achos. Dyma fi, mawl ir Goruchaf, wedi cael fy nghynhauaf i mewn im scubor — "Mention" (says you) "what seeds, etc., and Parry will order 'em to be sent hither by first opportunity." What! From Jamaica? Or how do you mean? Ni waeth gan Wilym par hadau a gaffo am y bont rai dieithr a rhyfeddol. Bu feistr y bachgen Parry hwnnw yma'r dydd arall yn ciniewa efo mi, mi debygwn mai da fyddai ganddo gael orders gennwch i reoli'r llanc bob modd, oblegid un gwyllt ydyw. Ces lythyr Owain Arddwr ag ai hattebais hefyd. Wala! A gawsochi'r dirgeloedd allan or gwyn bychan? Ymadawodd Nelly er's dyddiau, mae ei thad drwy ddeusyfiad y fam ynghyfraith debygwn i, yn lled ildio yw chymryd adref. Herlodes ynfyd ddifeddwl! Duw a roddo i ras i ymgroesi rhag drwg ddynion; rhaid yw thad ei phriodi yn y man i rywun neu gilydd, a rhoi pwrs o arian am ei chymryd. Mae'n debygol y bydd Marged hitheu yn mynd ir Deau ar fyrder, mae tueddiad ffordd honno. Aie y mae'r Great Seal of Wales dan law'r ymgrafwr? Nid oes bellach ond eisiau mynd yn heddychwr! I am glad that Ned Edwards is well, pray my compliments a buan y bo fo gadpen. Ai nid oedd (yn ol yr hen ddefod) ddim hadau coedydd y fordaith yma? I brought the pine cones with me from Madogallt, wedi rhoddi addysc i Lewelyn par sut i drin ei rai ynteu; ni wyr hwnnw i wrth ardd mwy nag y gwn innau oddiwrth bwll mwyn. Gresyn na bai ddigon o gyfoeth i gael wrth arddio. Wala! wala! Ni wybod pwy sydd yn *profeidio* i ddynan. Dyma lythyr o Allt Fadawg, wfft o'r mwyn sydd yno! Mae'r brawd yn meddwl roddi o hono godwm i Groxton. Da iawn y newydd. You desired some little account of the discovery of the mwyn ar yr Escair. My brother had been trying at the place five or six years ago but could not light of a vein. Digwyddodd i ddau frawd o weithwyr, h.y. weinidogion a fase yn gweithio mewn llefydd eraill a chanddynt dippyn o arian, gymeryd lease dros flwyddyn ar y mynydd a elwid

Esgair y Mwyn gan y mrawd (and though it bore that name yet they have no traces of any tradition that ever any one workd there since the antient Britons or Romans had). These men, or rather the eldest brother David Morgan (of whom perhaps you may hear more anon), discoverd immediately a body of ore yn agored ir haul heb ddim agos yn ei guddio o olwg pobl, naill fe ddarfuasai lladd neu newynu'r hen bobl gynt, oni bae ni adawsid mono felly,—yno gweithio a orug y ddau frawd am yr hoedl glas, ond gan na allant o eisiau digon o arian a dysc, a phower, yrru'r gwaith ymlaen yn hollol, cymeryd a wnaethant ddau eraill i mewn yn gydwyr, sef yr oedd y rheini debygwn i Llew *als* Sion Owain, medd rhai yn ddistaw hwn a hwn, ar llall ar llall, ag enill ynghorph y flwyddyn fil o bunoedd bob chwarter heblaw talu i wydd ag i bannwr. Dyna i chwi ar frys yr hanes dyrys. Duw a fo'n gwarchad drosoch. W. to R. contd.

Eich caredigawl frawd, William Morris.

CAER GYBI SAINT, 29th November, 1752.

Anwyl Frawd,—Dyma'r eiddoch or 21, 23, ar 25 inst. Da oedd ei ddyfod rhag yr ofn oedd arnaf eich myned i ffordd pob cnawd. Yr oeddwn yn bygwth gyrru llythyr arall i ymofyn fy un diwaetha. Diolch yn fawr am hanes y Gymdeithas odidawg yna. Rhwydd-deb i chwi fyned yn mlaen yn eich caredigawl amcanion. Gwyn eich byd chwi gael bod ymhlith Christnogion; nid oes yma ond rhyw baganiaid. Mae yn y pentref yma (Caer oedd hi gynt) er ys dwy flynedd neu well fath ar *Glub*, ond nid yw eich brawd Gwilym yn perthyn iddaw na'r Bellis chwaith, o achos bod ei aelodau yn yn ymgyfarfod i dra yfed, etc., a llawer o naddynt y cyfryw rai ag yr ych chwi yn eu gau allan och Cymdeithas. Father some time ago desired that I would write him a draught upon you for £10, which he was a long while endeavouring to get cash for, and the other day he sent me word that he had received from Mr. Jones, of Marian, money for't. Perhaps he has acquainted you of it ere now. He enjoys his health better of late than he used to do, fo fydd y peswch yn chwannog oi helcyd rwan y gauaf. Gerwin or newydd yna ynghylch Powel o'r Nant. Ai tybied y bydd y Person ei frawd ddim gweddeiddiach gwr; par fodd bynnag na atto Duw i neb lawenychu o'r achos. Mi ddywedaf i chwi pa beth a wnewch i Feirian. Tyrrwch iddi lonaid sach cras geirch o gymysc aur ac W. to R. CXLIV.

W. to R. contd. arian, a cheisiwch iddi wr, o ddyn iachus, synhwyrol, gonest, lled ddyscedig gynta galloch; gadewch iddynt hwytheu enill Llywelynau a Meiriannau, etc., hyd ddiwedd y bennod, ag felly eu plant hwythau ond odid hyd ddiwedd byd. Yn y Bala bo'r Richards yna efo ei eirlyfr, bu edifar gennyf erioed gymeryd arian dynionach i'm llaw. Mae rhai mor ddrwg dybus a meddwl, mi wranta, fod i'm enill mawr or achos; those are your mean, pitiful fellows that imagines that no one doth any thing for his neighbour without what they wisely call a view! A pox o' their views. I wish all such vermin were at Grand Cairo. No, I dont want any Bibles for myself, for thanks to my good brother Mynglwyd, I have got a neat sett, but some friends may be obliged. Ni gawn weled par brisiau a roddir arnynt meddwch. Ydyw'r Gardinal yn un o'ch Cymdeithas chwi? Oes yno lawer oi fath o? Os yw'r pendefig yn cyfaddef ei fod yn euog, and upon making proper submission, he may perhaps be receiv'd into favour again, but let him beware of relapses.

Nid ydych yn son un gair am yr hen Gommissioner Fychan. Roedd Arglwydd Madawc yn y llythyr diweddaf a ge's oddiyno, yn achwyn fod yr hen wr yn ddrwg o fath arnaw, ag yn ofni ei golli'n erwin dost. Digrif fyddai i Filtwn gael Nanneu. Pwy ydyw Miss Bladen honno? Ai nid oedd ar hen ddyn yn y byd ffordd yna eisiau etifedd? Base hen gywelu Powel yn gwneuthur yn burion. Cawsai ond odid fab yn ddidrafferth. Roedd y fenyw bert honno mewn anrhydedd mawr iawn yr ha' leni pan fum yn y Deaudir. O ddilin hir ddrwg y daw mawr ddrwg, ebe'r neidr wrth y swynwr ers dalm. Roedd iddaw'r Bowel fab ordderch yn byw gyd ag ef, 28 neu 30 o oed,—a captain of his mob. A drow'd hwnnw allan hefyd? 'Rym ni yma oll yn rhwydd iachus, mawl i'r Goruchaf Dduw. Mae'r frech wen wrth ein drysau, disgwyl iddi alw wrth fynd heibiaw; it is of a very favourable kind, nid oes ond gadael pob peth o'r fath i ewyllys Rheolwr nef a daear. Bydded iddo warchad drosoch chwi ar enethig yna a'ch cadw rhag pob peth a'ch dryga. Peggy desires her love to her cousin Mariana.

I am, your most affectionate brother, William Morris.

P.S.—Inclos'd you'll receive a bit of paper which I dare say will divert you, and bring to your mind 'r hen gofion gynt, a ddigrifed oeddym pan oedd pyttiau o esgyll gennym fal cywion hwyaid yn ceisiaw dyscu ehedeg—an unlucky comparison, for those are but poor flyers at best. Llawer troad ar fyd a ddigwyddawdd mewn naw mlynedd ar hugain, onte? Oes yna ddim son fod y Llew yn cael rhyw beth gwell na Dyfi, mae ffordd ymma rhyw ddwndwr ei fod, beth meddwch? Ni ches i ddim llythyr oddiwrthaw er's dyddiau. A welsoch i byth ddim oddiwrth Parry'r jeweller hwnnw? Os do, moeswch dippyn o'i hanes, da chwitheu. Daccw'r frech wen yn nhy'r chwaer. Gadewch i mi gael llythyr gynta byth ag a alloch, a byddwch wych. Pam na ddywedwch i pa lun oedd ar y seal fawr honno a wnaed i'r Llew? W. to R. contd.

GARTREF, Rhagfyr 29th, 1752.

W. to R. CXLV.

Anwyl Frawd,—Mi glywais ryw dro son am wr, yr hwn wedi mendio o sias o glefyd, a ollyngasai yn ango ei enw ei hun. Nid llawer gwell mo'ch brawd Gwilym ynteu, wedi rhyw drallod a fu arno yn ddiweddar, prin y gwyr o ragor rhwng ci a buwch gan nolffder a hurtrwydd. Gwybyddwch mae'r 9fed y clafychodd fy machgennyn, a'r 13 yr herlodes o'r frech wen, a chan drymmed yr haint, a daed oedd gennyf fy nghywion, ni ches na'm cof na'm synwyr i feddwl am ddim ond y nhw er hynny hyd yr awron. Ond bendigaid a fyddo enw'r Arglwydd maent eill deuoedd yn dechreu ymendiaw ag yn ddianaf. Mae'r bachgennyn yn cerdded 'rhyd y ty, ar lodes hithe yn ddigon ei hamdden ond heb ddechreu codi etto. Hi ai cadd yn dra erchyll ag yr oeddwn yn ofni am dani yn dost. Bu'r llanc ynte yn llesc iawn. Ni bu monwyf ddeu can llath o'r ty yma er's tair wythnos i foru. Mae'r frech yn lladd yn abl aml ffordd yma. Rwy'n meddwl fy mod i yn ddoctor brêchwen go gywraint, wedi bod yn myfyrio arni ddydd a nos cyhyd o amser. Gynneu yr aeth Gruff. Dafydd adref wedi dyfod ar gefn ceffyl i nhad with an annual present of red herrings. Roedd y nhad yn rhesymol iachus. Dyma hefyd Dda 'p Morgant a ddaeth o Allt Fadawg wythnos i ddoe, y pryd yr oedd pawb yno iach, y chwaer ymron cwmpo i'r gwellt dros y pen a'r clustiau. Fe ddywaid Dafydd mae i ymofyn menyn a chaws Mon y daeth, tebygach mae i ymofyn merch Madawg, peth enbyd iawn yw mil o bunnau D—w 'n geidwad! Bid rhwng y din a'r wialen. Mae'r Fadws yn rhwydd fodlon debygwn, ond na soniwch un gair och pen. I had some time ago a letter from Goronwy with a Cowydd

W. to R. contd. Coffadwriaeth am yr hen wreigan o Bentre Eirianallt, ni fyn alw mono yn Farwnad am bris yn y byd. I'm tyb wael i un cywraint ydyw. Gresyndod gerwin na fedrid caffael rhyw fywioliaeth i'r truan yn rhyw gwr o Fon yn ol ei ddymuned. Mi sgrifennaf atto'r post nesaf os medraf a hanes rhyw fan betheuach na thalant prin i son am danynt. Oes dim o hanes Cornelius Agrippa? Mae ei bobl yn ymofyn yn ei gylch yn fynych. Ymhle mae'r geirlyfr bellach? Beth am yr Arglwydd Bwlclai ieuanc yma? Er carriad ar eich brawd Gwilym, gadewch gael llinell oddiwrthych gynta galloch i helpu cyfodi tippyn ar fy ysprydoedd trwmbluog sydd wedi mynd na thalent iw codi oddiar y maes. Daccw bedwar o blantos y chwaer wedi'r frech wen eu coethi yn abl tost, yn enwedig y ddau ieuaf. Gobeithio eu bod oll wedi passio'r gwaethaf. 'Rym oll yn gorchymun attoch. Duw a fyddo yn gwarchad drosoch.

Eich caredigawl frawd, Gwilym Cybi.

P.S.—Ond ydych chwi yn o gydnabyddus ag Esgob Bangor? Mawr na roddech i air i mewn dros Oronwy, er mwyn ei wneuthur yn wybodawl fod y cyfryw ddynan cywrain agos a llewygu o eisiau cael rhent neu giwradiaeth go dda ym Mon Ynys.

CAER GYBI SAINT, 9d o Ionawr, 1753

W. to R. CXLVI. Anwyl Frawd,—Gan fyned o'm llythyr diwaetha i yngwrthwyneb yr eiddoch o ddydd Nadolig, rhaid imi ei rhoddi ar do nesaf, yn ol cwrs natur. Chwi gawsoch yn y llall hanes brêch wen o bawb i bentan, prin y medraf etto son am ddim arall ond y hi, yr anrhas iddi. Mae hi rwan o wir ddig na chawsai ddihenyddu fy nau gywtyn i, yn lladd ac yn anafu plantos yn erchyll ffordd yma. Wfft, a dwbl wfft iddi hi genhawes! Da gweled eich bod ar wyneb y ddaear, rych ar yr union am beidio chwenychu byw ymhlith y Monwysiaid yma, nid oes ysywaeth fawr o honynt a dâl i son am danynt, ag nid oes yma gan mwyaf ond tlodi; ag os digwydd i ddyn gaffael bywioliaeth rhwydd dacclus, ni wybod par un ai'r bonheddig ai'r gwreng fydd yn ymwenwyno fwya wrthaw—y cyntaf am na thelid iddynt y deyrngad honno y maent yn tybied fod yn ddyledus iddynt, sef mawr barch ag urddas a dilyn eu siamplau da hwynt, etc., ar ail am i neb un oi cydwladwyr ryfygu ymgodi yn uwch na hwynt a chymeryd arno wybod gwell pethau na phenbyliaid eraill. Ond felly mae'r byd, er yn amser Cain eiddigus. Aie yn Nover y mae Meirian yn bwrw'r gwiliau? Par ddelw sydd ar Sior Feddyg? Aie anhawdd yw llenwi codau yna, er agosed ych i'r Twr gwyn? Nid rhyfedd fod gyn anhawsed llenwi gobwrs cyn belled a hyn oddiwrth y crewyn. Digon o waith a geir yn ceisiaw tamaid a llymaid ar greigiau Cybi, chwaethach hel ynghyd. Dyma Wilym er's gwell na mis yn llenwi bolia wyth neu naw o boblach bob dydd, heblaw cost arall, y cyflog yn gwtta, y *fees* yn gwtteuach! Nid ellir byw'n hir fal hyn. Gerwin or amser, ond mawl i Dduw am Ei drugaredd, nid oes lle i achwyn mor llawer. Aie fo mendiawdd yr hen Gommisioner? Da iawn y newydd er mwyn Madogyn, ond nis gwn i a fydd neb arall honom well er hynny. I had a hint from Liverpool, where Llew himself must have dropt it, concerning old Nick—y byddai ef debyg o fyned yn ei le yn o sydyn. I mentiond it to him in a letter and that a report prevaild here which had its rise in South Wales. But he seem'd to be greatly surprized at such a rumor, ag na byddai fo Nicol trai bai'r llall byw, gwell ganddo fo yr Escair, etc. Reconcile these oddities if you can, and what means these inconsistences? Ymhentre Eirian Allt mae'n debyg y trewais wrth hanes yr awdwr hwnnw, ond oedd o yn ddigrif? Do, mi welais sêl y mwyn; gresyn na base'r dyn yn torri'r llythyrenna cystal ag a gwnaeth lun y llaw. Gan fod arfau ar sêl yn sicrhau llythyrau poblach ag yn gwneuthur y papur megys yn gysegredig, (I mean a coat-of-arms nid llun pigau a dwylo pobl), ond gweddus ddigon fyddai cymeryd i fynu gan fod gennym hawl i hynny rai o arfau ein hynafiaid, oblegid chwi wyddoch mae'n debyg fod gan bawb a fai'n deilliaw allan o unrhyw lwyth ymhlith y Cymry gystal hawl au gilydd i ddwyn yr un arfau, without the modern differences or distinguishing brethren and houses; consequently we see the Arms of Hwfa ap Cynddelw wore by most of our Anglesey gentlemen and others without any difference. Gwerydd ap Rhys Gôch, Lord of Talebolion, in Môn, was one of the 15 tribes of North Wales, lived about the year 1170. He bore argent on a bend sable three leopards faces of the field. (By some MSS. three lions heads couped regardant which is the same in effect) and his descendants were the Humphreys of Bodlewiddan extinct, Lloyd's Gwaredog or Lligwy extinct, and the Wynne's of Bodewryd, only one of which

W. to R. contd.

W. to R. contd. now living, viz., Dr. Wynne. NOW KNOW YE that we are descended by the father's side from Bodewryd and by the mother side from Lligwy, consequently have a title to Arfau Gwerydd ap Rhys yn ddiddadl. I writ to Madog about this affair. Ebr ynteu, "Bydd arfau Gwerydd ap Rhys Goch or goreu, pe bai ddigon o diroedd a meddiannau, and my motto when I have regular Arms shall be 'O For ac o Fynydd.'" A'm un innau a gaiff fod "Duw yn y blaen."* Gadewch glywed pa beth yr ydych chwithau yn ei dybied ynghylch y matter yma. Mi a welais arfau ambell dro ar eich llythyr a berthynai ond odid i ryw garn Sais coesgam, ond pa wedd bynnag nid oedd a wnelom ni a hwynt. Byddaf finnau ambell dro yn taro ar gwyr ryw seli a berthynynt i bobl fy ngwraig, nid o ran gorchest yn y byd ond o ran gwneuthur y seliad yn siccrach. This letter will be seald with the Arms of Gwerydd which I have had by me some time, but the shield is properly a clergyman's. The crest of Madog, I suppose, will be the "hand and pickaxe"; the "hand and pen" fydd ganddoch chwitheu, mae'n debyg. Ond i grogi iddo a wyr pa beth fydd gan Wilym, perhaps a hand holding a flower, beth meddwch? So much for pais arfau. Roedd y nhad yn iach dydd arall, rym ni yma, mawl ir Goruchaf Dduw, yn dda iawn mewn iechyd, y bychain yn dechreu ymlwybren ar hyd y ty yn ddianaf. Mae'n rhy'wyr cael typpyn o lythyr oddiwrthych, nid y'nt ond byrrion y leni; nhw ddylynt ddyfod yn amlach. Duw or nef a fyddo yn gwarchad drosoch ich cadw rhag pob peth a'ch dryga. Amen. *Eich caredigawl frawd, Gwilym Amhorys.*

O'M HOFFIS INNAU, 12 Chwefror, '53,
Diwarnod yr Eiry mawr!

W. to R.
CXLVII.

Rwy'n tybiaw fod arnoch i lythyr i mi er's dyddiau, ac nid hwyrach na baswn ddim yn eich gyrru mewn chwaneg o ddyled yrwan, oni bai'r matter a ganlyn, ond arhowch dipyn bach. Yn gôch y bo mhais onid wyf yn meddwl mai yngwrthwyneb eu gilydd y trafaelws y ddau lythyr diweddaf einom, os felly nid oes lle i achwyn arnoch y tro yma. Y matter sydd fal hyn: marw'r dydd arall a orug Person Aber Gwyn Gregin yn Arfon, a living in the gift of the Baron Hill family, ag mae'n debyg y bydd cynnwrf

* Richard Morris has added in the margin here "a'm un innau 'A Gair Duw yn uchaf.'"

a symudiadau ymhlith yr offeiriadau cywradiad (i.e. cywion y rhad, etc.), ac fe allai y ca Oronwy siawns o daro i bawl yn y llawr yn eu plith. Llyma fi yn sgrifennu atto heddyw ar y perwyl hwnnw, nid hwyrach i chwithau gael odfa i roddi gair i mewn gyda'r Escob o'i blaid. Fe dybir mai naill ai vicar Llanidan ai viccar Eglwys Vach a ga'r rhent accw. 'Rych yn dywedyd fod Goronwy wedi gyrru i chwi gowydd marwnad y mam, mae ynteu yn dywedyd ei fod wedi tacclu llawer arno er pan gawswn i yr ûn ûn, o herwydd pa ham yr wy' yn adolwyn arnoch roddi benthyg hwn yna fal y gallwyf fi altrio hwn, mae ganddoch ddigon o' francs y dwthwn yma. I will send it you back without fail in a post or two. Bu nhad yma bumnos ddiwedd y mis diwaetha, yn rhwydd dda ar ei iechyd. Gwych o'r cywydd a wnaeth Goronwy ir calan, onte? Ni che's ddim newydd o Allt Fadawg er's dyddiau, disgwyl beunydd fod y chwaer honno wedi cwympo ir gwellt. Aie chwi gawsoch lythyr oddiwrth Felics Farley? Maen debyg fod y geirlyfr yna bellach. Aie gwaeth yr ysprydol na'r tymhorol Bowel, oes yno gyfraith ar droed yntau pa'r aflonyddwch sydd ar y Ceredigions? Gwrda Osburne am beidiaw a gollwng yn angof ei hen ffrindia. Aeth y Forgant hwnnw i bant heb ei neges, ond mae'n debyg y bydd raid iddo ei gael ryw dro. Rydwyf agos a llewygu gan anwyd er bod eirias o dân brenin wrth fy nghlin. Duw gyd a chwi. W. to R. contd.

Eich caredigawl frawd rhynllyd, William Morris.

P.S.—Yn y Duwmares y mae'r Aldromon yn taring, wedi gwerthu ei holl fatterion yn Lerpwl ond ei stât; mae o yn marsiandiaeth yd, etc., fal cynt, ag yn cadw gwin a chwrw i werth (wrth gofio) yn Nerpwl.

HOLYHEAD, 15th February, 1753.

Dear Brother,—Mae'n debyg dderbyn o honoch linell neu ddwy oddiwrthyf y post diwaethaf; mae'r llythyrau wedi cael blâs ar fyned yngwrthwyneb eu gilydd, rhaid ei gwarchad yn well rhaglaw. Well, in answer to yours of the 10th the Dictionaries would best be sent down in a bundle, 15 for my list and 5 for father, directed to the care of Mr. Thomas Bryan, merchant, in Llanerchmedd. But who is to pay the carriage? Mr. Richards should. Brother Lewis was at the charge of carriage of his books sent down to the subscribers. I know some of them will grumble W. to R. CXLVIII.

W. to R. contd.

to pay perhaps 1½d. or 2d. extra. However, we must have 'em down. A box will be too chargeable; if they are well packd in good thick brown paper will do as well, but they must be directed to the care likewise of Mr. Goodwin, grocer, at Chester, who will take care to forward 'em per carrier to Llanerchmedd. The names of the Beaumaris subscribers were sent the author by Mr. Thos. Mosson, comptroller of that place, to whom I've writ this post, and told him to give you directions which I presume you'll receive next post. They might have been sent much cheaper by sea to Carnarvon where vessels often come from Bristol, or at least to Chester. I can get mine bound in Dublin, it would make some difference in the carriage. You see how very exact we are about trifles! How is the money to be remitted when it comes to hand? Dick Morris's sister [is in] the same house. She and her husband lives in the same mann[er as] when he left them: she desires her love to him as doth his bro[ther Will] who was in town yesterday. She mumbles something about a g . . . . and would be glad of it if possible, heb yn wybod ir gwr anniddig. Can` diolwch am yr almanac hwnnw, ceiff ei barch ai groesaw ai ddodi yn y cwr goreu o'm hoffis. I writ my father to-day about it, etc. Gerwin gwaith Ceredigion! Ni chlywais ddim oddiyno ettwa. Dihareb y mae'r *motto* "A Gair Duw yn ucha'" yn dygymydd ar Beibl yn y *crest*. Pan wneloch eich seal gadewch weled ei llun a pha'r faint a gyst torri un daclus. Pan ydoedd y nhad yma fe ddigwyddodd fod yma *hard wareman* a chanddo wmbwrdd o spectolau, ond nid oedd yr un a helpa ddim ar ei olwg. Perhaps they can't be much assisted as he is so antient, Duw a'ch cadwo rhag dallineb o bob rhyw. Mae fy ngoleuadau i, mawl i Dduw, yn dda iawn. Ow, ai nid oes un gair yngylch y Beiblau? Well, I must leave off, having arrived at my *ne plus ultra*, felly, byddwch wych. *Eich caredigawl frawd,*

William Morris.

W. to R. CXLIX.

HOLYHEAD, 10th March, '53.

Dear Brother,—Wele yma yr eiddoch or 6ed a hanes bocys a llyfrau, etc., a gair neu ddau ynghylch y brawd Llewelyn. Na chefais i lythyren oddiwrthaw er's tair wythnos neu fis. Echdoe daeth yr Aldromon Prichard yma ar ryw neges, ag a ddywedodd iddo glywed gan ryw ddyn or Deheu yr stori echryslon a ddywedsoch chwitheu, sef bod llu o wyr wedi cymryd yr Esgair a mynd ar Llew i garchar, ond ni wyddai am ba beth.* Cyn y nos wele ddyn o longwr o'r Abermaw yn dywedyd yr un peth dros yr holl bentref yma. Yn wir ddiau ni fedraf ddywedyd i chwi faint oedd fy sannedigaeth or achos, na pha beth wdwyf arnaf er hynnu hyd yr awron, rhwng gobaith ac annobaith, rwyf wedi lled hurtio. Fy ofnaid mwya ydoedd iddo (mewn ond odid wylltineb) daraw neu ladd rhywun, ag felly iddynt ei ddihenyddu o'r achos. Duw a'n cadwo oll rhag ein caseion. Rwy'n cael gormod o waith i ddangos wyneb rhwydd lawen ar meddwl ynteu cyn drymed ar plwm. Mae yma bobl a lawenycha am ei gwympiad, ond 'rwyf yn hyderu ar Dduw na chant moi gwynfyd. Duw a ddelo ag ef yn ddiangol allan oi dwylo. Yn wir nis gwn i pa beth i sgrifennu, er mwyn Duw oni byddwch wedi sgrifennu cyn y del hwn ich llaw, moeswch linell neu a thippyn o hanes y gwaith melldigedig accw. Rym ni yma oll yn iach, mawl i'r Goruchaf Dduw; roedd y nhad yn iachus ddechreu'r wythnos, Duw a'n diddano. W. to R. contd.

Eich caredigawl frawd, William Morris.

CAER GYBI, 24th March, 1753.

Anwyl Frawd,—Chwi welsoch yn llythyr Mr. Mosson fy mod wedi derbyn eich epystol chwi ar tra chysurus newydd fod y Llew W. to R. CL.

* Lewis Morris got into this trouble on account of his action with regard to the lead mines on Crown land in Cardiganshire. It appears that on the 23rd of Feb., 1753, two of the county magistrates, with the sheriff or his deputy, and a "mob of several hundred armed and tumultuous people," came to the banks of the mine and threatened not only the life of Lewis Morris, whom they regarded as the author of all the mischief, but also "the lives of his agents and miners on refusal to deliver up the possession of the mine," and further to enforce their threats, "one of the ringleaders, a Justice of the Peace, presented a cock'd pistol at Morris's head, and threatened to shoot him, while the rest surrounded him with firearms," and seizing him carried him a prisoner to Cardigan Gaol. (Cymmrodor, Vol. xv. p. 15). From the deposition made by George Evan, keeper of the Common Gaol at Cardigan, it is shewn that on the 24th of February, "Lewis Morris, gentleman, was committed into the deponent's custody and was put in the Common Gaol, where he continued for the space of fifteen minutes or thereabouts." He was then bailed out and was permitted to go at large within the precincts of the borough. He stayed at the house of William Gambold and was detained at Cardigan until March 9th of the same year. He left Cardigan in the company of his gaoler on March 13th, and went home to Gallt Vadog and from thence, the gaoler still accompanying him, went to London. In due course Lewis Morris appeared before Sir William Lee, Lord Chief Justice of the King's Bench, and was discharged on April 4th.

W. to R. contd. ar y ffordd i gael ei ryddid, ai wynfyd ar ei gaseion, mawl ir Gorucha' Dduw am Ei drugareddau. Mi yrrais Peggy Morris a'r hanes i nhad; 'roedd yr hen wr gwirion wedi clywed y rhan waetha or stori, ag yn dra anesmwyth o'r achos; yn ffaelio cysgu yn ei wely'r nos gan drymder, a phar sut y peidiau a chlywed gan fod y peth yn safn pob dyn yn y wlad, er mawr orfoledd i laweroedd. Ag etto ni dderbyniodd neb o honom un llinell o'r wlad felldigedig honno er pan ddigwyddodd y drîn, hyd y dydd heddyw, which by the bye is both unkind and unnatural. 'Roeddwn i mor anesmwyth o'r achos, pan glywais ei garcharu, fy mod weithiau yn amcanu llogi ceffyl a mynd yno drwy'r tew ar tenau. Ond yr oeddwn yn ofni na fedrwn wneuthur iddo fawr ddaioni, ag y tybiai pawb fod ei gyflwr ond odid yn waeth nag ydoedd, ag mai gwell oedd aros gartre' i ladd dieithr. Roedd y gwr a ddŷg y newydd gynta yma, yn fy nhy i neithiwr dan wadd, sef one Parry, a South Wales clergyman, goes about for subscriptions towards publishing some sermons preach'd by him at St. Albans, Wood Street, in London. He is vicar of North Shobury (or some such name) in Essex. He is a monstrous, lusty man and walks it afoot, but certainly he must be under a cloud or some trouble. He is an acquaintance of the Anti-Methodist of White Hall*; er mwyn dyn tippyn o hanes hwn. Mae o'n son am fynd heddyw i Ddulun ag oddiyno i Frysto, Llundain neu rywle, ni waeth ganddo ple, mi debygwn wrtho. Dyma Peggy wedi dyfod adref neithiwr, hi adawodd y nhad yn iach lawen, fe roes newydd da ail einioes iddo. Fe ddarfu ir Ceredigioniaid (chwedl Cibber) outdo their usual outdoings. 'Roedd rhai yn dywedyd fod y Bowel† yno ei hun, eraill nad oedd. Gwych ystori Roderick Richards. Dim hanes o'r box, mae lle i ofni y llygra'r orains. Mi ge's inneu bwmp o lythyr i wrth y Gownsler ynghylch y fôt honno, oni egyr o ei bwrs yn llettach nag y byddai ei dad ag yntau arferol, rwy'n ofni mai colli fal cynt a wna. Aie pethau tost yw'r biliau rheini sydd raid i chwi ei drin, dyna fal y mae. Dyma finnau agos am lladd fy hun yn impio coed, a hau a phlannu, swrn debyg i chwareu plant yn y pistyll yw'r pethau hyn. Fe fydd Mr. Mosson yna mae'n debygol o hyn i ben yr wythnos Cewch ganddo ef, uwch ben potel, hanes y byd ar amseroedd

* Rev. John Evans.

† William Powel, of Nanteos.

Deg i un na bo'r brawd Llew yna bellach, gorchmynnwch ni oll atto, nid hwyrach y ceir llinell oddiwrtho. Rym ni, mawl i Dduw, oll yn iach. Byddwch wych. *Eich caredigawl frawd, Gwilym o Gybi.* W. to R. contd.

P.S.—Roeddid wedi dywedyd wrth y nhad fod y brawd yng ngharchar am bedeir mil o bunnau, a chan na roddasai feichiau ar y cyntaf, 'roedd rhaid iddo aros yno tra bai byw, a chant o chwedlau eraill; ond oedd hynny ddigon er torri calon yr hen wr ag yntau'n ffaelio cael clywed dim ir gwrthwyneb? Och·o fi, pa beth sydd yn dyfod o Oronwy; roedd yn dywedyd ei fod yn ymadael a Donnington o gwmpas hanner gwanwyn oni throdd arno, mae dialedd o eisiau cael clywed hanes Cywydd y Tywysawg; a ddarfu ei argraphu? Mi sgrifenais at y bardd dydd arall a gair fod y Mr. Ellis wedi rhoddi iddo Ramadeg Sion Dafydd Rhys heb fod fymryn gwaeth na newydd, yr oedd arno eisiau canllaw yn anguriol. Gresyn, ie, can resyn, na bai iddo fywioliaeth drefnus yn rhywle, yn lle bod yn llewygu o eisiau bara, nid yw fawr gwell debygwn. Peggy Morris sends her compliments to Meirian if in town. Gwych a fyddai llinell oddiwrthych. Yr eiddoch, *W.M.*

HOLYHEAD, 15th April, 1753. W. to R. CLI.

Dear Brother,—Mae ennyd fawr o amser wedi llithraw heibio er pan 'sgrifenais attoch, ac er hynny hyd yrwan mi ge's, na bo'nd ei grybwyll, ddau o lythyrau oddiwrth y brawd Llew. 'Rwyn deall ei fod yn llawn trafferthion fal y mae yna. Fe ddaw Duw ac e yn y man i'w iawn hwyl, ni cheir dim tycciant arno dan hynny. Gerwin o'r aros sydd raid iddo yn y ddinas yna ag ynteu gyn belled oddi wrth ei deulu, etc., wala, wala, rhaid bodloni. Nid oes arnafi ofn dim ond ir Ceredigioniaid ei dyngu o allan o'i feddiant, os tyngu a wna'r gwaith, yn iach ymenyn glan. Yr archlod ir cludwyr ni ddaeth mor boccys ar geirlyfrau yma ettwa. Mi glywa Oronwy yn son gael o honaw ganddoch un o honynt. Mi a wneuthym fy ngoreu ar geisio tippyn mwy o fara a chaws i'r bardd, nis gwn i etto a lwyddodd fy nghorchwyl ai peidiaw. Gwyn ei fyd a fedra ei wneuthur yn esgob. Dyma lythyr o'r diwedd oddiwrth Gornelius Agrippa a rhyw faint o hadau a pheth oi hanes, mae yntau wedi mynd yn ddiog. Daeth yma heddyw lythyr oddiwrth y nith Margaret Owen yn dywedyd fod y nhad yn iach. Roedd hi

W. to R. contd.

newydd ddyfod adre o Lerpwl, etc., wedi bod yn prynu marsiandi. Dyma finnau yn gyrru foru wr ar farch i gyrchu Pegi Morys adref wedi bod yno yn ei lle hi. Rwyn deall gael o Mr. Mosson siwrnai seuthug; roeddwn wedi prophwydo mai felly fyddai, felly dyna gost heb fod raid wrthi. Ni rydd y brawd Llewelyn ddim o'i hanes ei hun, er carriad ar eich brawd unfam undad (chwedyl Sion Sittrach) dodwch chwi ar ddu a gwyn dippyn o'i helynt, a gyrrwch o yma da chwithau. Fy ngharedigawl annerch atto fo a chwithau, a Duw a fo'n eich rhagflaenu chwi ag yntau yn eich holl amcanion. Y fi ydyw, *Eich brawd trwmbluog ddigon,*

William Morris.

P.S.—Fe allai Mr. Lew. yrru imi haner dwsing o ffrancods, nid oes yma un bach. Mi 'sgrifennaf atto'r tro nesaf os medraf gael un i werth neu yn echwyn.

W. to R. CLII.

GARTREF, Nos Basc, 21 Ebrill, 1753.

Anwyl Frawd Rhisiart,—Llyma'r eiddoch a llythyr Goronwy a'r farwnad. Mi ai gyrraf yn ol pan gaffwyf ffrencyn ar led ymyl, prinnion iawn ydynt ffordd ymma. The alterations, as indeed all that extraordinary man's productions, are excellent. He had sent me the Prince's Cywydd, I fancy he was too much tied down, gwell a fase adael i'r bardd ei ffordd ei hun. I had also a letter from the bard, 5th instant, with an excellent poem which is not yet to be expos'd to the view of the world; mal hyn y dywaid wrth son am y

"Treiswyr blin trais arw blaid,
"Pobl anwir Pabiloniaid,
"Ou gwledydd tra dyglydynt,
"Gwyr Sion yn gaethion gynt."

ymhen ennyd y dywaid:

"Daear Mon, dir i minnau,
"Yw, o chaf ffun, ei choffau,
"Mawr fy nghwynfan am dani,
"Mal Sion yw Mon i mi!"*

Ond ydyw resyn na chai'r dynan gwirion fywioliaeth rhwydd dda ym Mon? I imagine he is now at Walton, gerllaw Liverpool. Mi glywais ddywedyd mai chwareuwr oedd y Barri hwnnw a fu'n cymmortha ffordd yma. Dyma llythyr heddyw oddiwrth y brawd Llewelyn; drwg iawn bod ei dylwyth yn afiachus gartref, Duw a fo'n gwarchad drostynt ac ai dycco yntau yn ddiangol adref attynt.

* Barddoniaeth Goronwy Owen (Liverpool, 1896), tud. 60-1.

Aie difalch oedd y Gownsler am alw i'ch ymweled—ffafor fawr yn ddiammeu. Disgwylied cymorth gan rai o'ch ffrindiau mae'n debyg a barodd yr ymweliad. Par sut y mae Llewelyn ag ynteu yn dilio! Oes caredigrwydd mawr rhyngddynt mal y bai arferol? Chwi ddywedsoch fod rhai ffrindiau yn syrthio ymaith. Pam na sgrifena Meirian at ei chyfnither? Mae hon yn gorchymun atti hithau yn fawr iawn. Ni ddaeth mor boccys ar llyfrau yma etto, nid hwyrach fod pob peth wedi mynd yn efrydd; mi a yrraf gyfrif i chwi pan dderbyniwyf yr arian ac a'u talaf i nhad. Wrth gofio, daccw ffrind imi yn dymuno cael un or geirlyfrau wedi ei gauadu and letter'd; if you have one to spare, pray send by the penny post one directed thus, "For Mr. Williams, apothecary, at Carnarvon, to be forwarded by Mr. Palmer, druggist, in Barbican," and set down the price opposite the title page, and the money will be paid me here or Mr. Palmer perhaps will lay it down, yr un a fynnoch. Mae'r arian yn bur anhawdd eu cael ffordd yma, oni bai hynny, wedi ei argraphu bu'sai Gowydd y Farn, etc., *cum not. varior.*; it would cost about a couple of guineas to print a parcel of 'em. 'Roedd Mr. Ellis a minneu yn barod i helpu tippyn, ond nid allai Oronwy spario 'run or ceiniogcach. Gwych fyddai gweled peth o waith y bardd yn argraphedig. Wala, wfft ir 'scobion yna! Ai'r c——l a gadd wall ar yr haflug? Paham y cadwant drysor mor werthfawr oddiwrth y tlodion druain? Nid oes dim daioni yn perthyn ir gwyr goludog. Eu trysor sy'n eu gyrru yn ynfyd. Ni choeliachi byth mor drafferthus wyf i beunydd yn fy ngardd, am galwedigaethau eraill, na bo'nd i grybwyll! Fe eill dyn fod cymaint ei ludded yn chwareu ag un arall a fai yn gweithio. Gorchmynnwch fi at y brawd yna; mi attebaf ei lythyr drennydd. Duw yn ei blaid ef a chwithau, byddwch wych. *Eich caredigawl frawd. Wm. Morris.* **W. to R. contd.**

P.S.—Nos Fercher y daeth Peggi Morris adref o Bentrerianell; hi adawodd fy nhad yn iachus, mae o'n dra sionc, ni wna fo ddim o fyned ar eu ddeudroed i Landyfrydog, etc., mwy ystig na'u dri meib fal y mai mwya'r cywilydd. Mae nhw yn taeru ei fod yn son byth am wreicca, y Mrs. Williams o Fodafon, y mae yn ei hoffi: hen wreigen dew sychedig, agos gin hyned ac yntau, ymgro dda i bawb! Oni fyddai gweddusach i chwi a minnau geisio rhyw huttog bob un? Ymhell y bwyf os medraf fi gael hanes yr un yn

W. to R. contd. unlle am bodlonai, felly rhaid bod yn unig, but query. Dymma lythyr tosturus ddigon heddyw oddiwrth y gefnder Sal; mae o ar wraig yn bur afiachus ac yn llawn trafferth bod y fodfedd. He is afflicted with a pleuretic disorder, yr hwn mae'n debygol ai gerphyn ryw ddiwrnod cyn pen hir. Duw yn eich cylch. Yr eiddoch, mal or blaen, *W.M.*

CAER GYBI, Hen Wyl Farc, 1753.

W. to R. CLIII. Anwyl Frawd,—Mi sgrifenais at Lewelyn y post diweddaf a'r hanes, nid oes gennyf fawr yn rhagor iw ddywedyd, ond hynny sydd dyma i chwi. Llymma Farwnad y mam yn ol, a diolch am y benthyg. Yr wythnos ddiwaetha y daeth y boccys ar geirlyfrau ynddaw i ben ei siwrnai, ag yn wir y mae yn waith glew iawn,—ond wfft, a dwbl wfft, ir Botanology! Yr wyf newydd yrru'r pump i nhad, a phan gaffwyf yr arian am y lleill gan y bonddics yma, mi au gyrryf iddo. Diolwch yn fawr am y pethau eraill, 'roedd yr orains ar lemons wedi llygru oddigerth 3 neu 4, a chwedi arteithiaw tippyn ar y llyfrau. Bland's version of Gen. is a curious thing, ond och or dynged mai 3 pennod neu 4 yn ol. A fyddai modd iw cael am aur, nog am arian, nag am eiriau teg? Dyma fi wedi gyrru' ngeirlyfr ag eraill gyd ag ef ir Iwerddon, i geisiaw sippog newydd interleaved, etc. I sent Mr. William Jones's by Mr. Mosson, who came here to relate his adventures. Beth am Oronwy sydd mewn meddiant o'i gawradiaeth yn swydd Hirgaer, £35 per annum salary, gobaith am £13 yn chwaneg? Mae o'n ymyl Lerpwl, the mother church of that flourishing sea-port—bydd hawdd cael angenrheidiau o Fon. Rym ni yma yn ddiweddar yn cael y tywydd gw'cha a welwyd er's talm; mae hi heddyw yn des 'splennydd. Mae eisiau tippyn o lythyr oddiwrthych a hanes y byd ar amseroedd. O pei gwelech i fy ngardd i mor hyfryd a blodeuawg ydyw! Och y fi ha wr fab, ni anaich yn eich croen o lawenydd, par bryd y deuwch i'w hymweled? Wala, wala, rhaid i mi fynd i gadsio penwaig, ond arhowch, dyma glamp o lythyr oddiwrth y brawd Llew. Moliant ir Goruchaf Dduw am Ei drugaredd iddo fo ag i bawb o honom. Gorchymynwch fi atto, a Duw gyda chwi bod ag un. *Eich caredigawl frawd, W.M.*

Y post nesa a ddwg lythyr iddo ynteu.

GARTREF, yr Hen Nos Galan Mai [1753].

Dear Brother,—Wele yman yr eiddoch or 5d., a diolch yn fawr am danaw. Ni choeliach i byth y daioni mae'ch ebystyl yn ei wneuthur drwy fywhau ysprydoedd trwmbluog eich brawd Gwilym. Oni ddywedais i chwi'r dydd arall ddyfod or bocys i ben i siwrnai. Yn rhodd i ba beth y mae'r cregyn llymeirch yma da wedi eu gwneuthur yn dippynnau crynion? A ddeuwyd i hyd i ryw rinwedd newydd arnaddynt, heblaw'r hon sydd ar bob cregynlwch? Na wnaeth yr orains druan fawr niwaid heblaw pydru a drewi, oddigerth llygru'r hadau, a niweidiaw tippyn ar y pamphledau, etc. Can diolch am bob peth. Na ddaeth un or pine i fynu nag or hickory nuts chwaith, rhy hên mae'n debyg, ag ni ddangosawdd un o'r hadau Jamaica mo'i drwyn or ddaear, er fy mod wedi eu coleddu a'i helcyd mewn gwelyau brŵd. The seeds from abroad seldom answers. I have had some often from Mr. Wright, at Leghorn, but they generally are either of a wrong kind or don't come up at all. Nid oes neb debyg i'r Saeson neu'r Cymru am onestrwydd. They stand upon their character, I mean the seedsmen. Am y peth a ddywaid y Brysaddfed nid oes mo'r goel arnaw. Llandrygan, etc., oedd yn ei feddwl, a thing not fixed, and perhaps never will, gwael yw ei *interest* ô gyd ag Escob Bangor, mae o'n rhy hen i ddechreu gwneuthur daioni i ddynolryw. Gronow might have had 30*l.* per annum a twelve month ago in Môn, but he refused accepting of it. If he has the school at Walton it will be worth him upwards of 43*l.*, paying another 5*l.* for teaching, the whole being 48*l.* Mi fanegaf Iedw Edwards iw chwaer; aie nid yw yn tyrru fawr arian ym Mostyn? I suppose that is the meaning of trade being dull. Aie 'roedd y gelyn-ddynion yn medru hau celwydd yn y drysorfa ag ymhob man? Par sut y mae'r penwyn talog yn ymddwyn ar yr achos yma? Ai tybied na bo yn rhoddi benthyg llaw i'w gydwladwyr gonest, dan din? Mae gennyf bot ir Bèlam ar Bèlammes* ar bychan mawr hwnnw, taled yr Arglwydd iddyn' nhwytheu am eu caredigrwydd. Digrif o'r L.C.J.'s warrant; mi glywaf fod rhai or Gwilliaid wedi cael ei gwasanaethu. Dô, os chwareuwr ydoedd, fo dyrrodd lawer o arian yn y wlad yma ar gymdogaeth, ond i

W. to R.
CLIV.

* Henry Pelham was First Lord of the Treasury. He befriended Morris at this time. "Cymmrodor," xv, 16.

W. to R. contd. wenwyn beil a gadd o gan Wilym; rhoddais iddo lonaid ei groen o fwyd a llŷn un noson o ran ffasiwn. Pam na roddwch ei hanes? Mi 'sgrifennaf at Oronwy ynghylch Cowydd y Farn, but while your hands were in you might as well print a whole sheet, then that would contain Cowydd yr Awen beside; ond beth a fyddai'r dynan truan gwell er hynny? oni bai roddi o honoch hyn a hyn o gantoedd iddo i wneuthur ceiniawg o naddant. Aie'r gŵr o'r Gors yw'r cadpen arnoch? Gwych a fai gael gweled eich rheolau, etc., wedi eu hargraphu.* Rhwydd-deb i chwi yn eich holl amcanion tra b'ont ganmoladwy. Aie Calan Gauaf y daw'r 'Sgrythyr oddiwrthych? Diog iawn yn wir, da fydd caffael tippyn chwaneg o'i hanes. Aie shuttlecock yw'r main, felly mae'r rhan fwya o'r bonedd; balchder Nic† sydd anoddefadwy, mae'r llall yn dippyn llarieiddach, un yn gwarrio gormodd, ar llall yn rhy gynnil, nis gwn i par sut y maent yna. Goreu ar lês yr hen ŵr gwirion fyddai aros yn y cyflwr y mae ynddaw, mae henaint wedi cael y llaw ucha arno, ar synwyr wedi pallu, oni ba'i hynny ni sonniai am y fath beth a gwreicca yn awr o fewn blwydd neu 2 i bedwar ugain; mae ô yn cael ei iechyd yn dra dâ, ag y mae ô'n sionc ryfeddol; roedd ddydd Llun diweddaf yn ffair Llanerchmedd ar ei ddeudroed er bod iddo 8 neu 10 o geffylau; ni chymerasai yr un o'r tri meib lawer er gwneuthur hynny, mi attebaf i am un, na cherddasai saith milldir neu 8 o'i fodd.

Chwi glywsoch son am gynghor tad iw fab, digon rhaid yma roi cynghor ir gwrthwyneb; os byddwch yn sgrifennu atto touch gently upon that topic. Felly mae arnaf inneu ofn y benywiaid rhein, ag etto er hyn mae o'n ffolineb mawr geisiaw trin ty a thylwyth heb ryw fath ar gymhares; nid wy'n ammeu na b'ont yn beth gwell yma nag yna, ond etto er hyn, mae yna godau llawnion y rhai a wna iawn am bob gwendidau agos. Pur anhawdd yw taro wrth nemawr un ffordd yma a thwysgen ar ei helw, heb ormodd falchder, a rhodres, a gorwagedd y byd enwir a phechadurus hwn. Mae Marged yn atsias yn ol orchmynion ei chyfnither. Aie cadw ty, par sut dy ydyw? Och fi ha wr fab, mi wela yma

*This refers to the Cymmrodorion Society, originally founded in Sept., 1751. The rules referred to were approved by the Society on April 4, 1753. William Vaughan, M.P., Corsygedol, was the first President.

†Sir Nicholas Bayley, Bart., of Plasnewydd, who was M.P. for the County of Anglesey at this time.

eich enw ymhlith y cynfeirdd Cymreig, a dyma aml R.M. ynghorph y llyfrau, sef yw'r geiriau hynny Morrisisms—ewch ymlaen i ennill clod ac anrhydedd, tra bo Gwilym wirion yn ymdroi mewn priddach ag yn dom hyd at ei benelinoedd. Chwi chwerthasech pei'm gwelsech heddy' yn chwnny, ag om hamgylch 4 neu 5 o hen wrageddos yn cymeryd dybacco ag yn dywedyd hen chwedleu, ag yn diwreiddio ambell chwynnoglyn wrth eu pwys. Ond deg i un na basech yn medru tynnu mo'ch llygaid oddiar yr aneirif rywogaetha o dulips, ranunculas's, anemonies, jonquils, iris's, narcissus's, crown imperials, hyacinths, auriculas's, hepatica's, polyanthus's, saxifrage's, martagons, a mil myrddiwn onid dwy (chwedl Sion Olifer am ei geinciau) o bethau gwchion eraill. Wala, wala, mae'n rhywyr cadw noswyl fal y gallwyf godi'r boreu foru bump o'r gloch iw trin. Mae'n debyg y clywsoch son am hŷd y llythyr a sgrifennais at y brawd Llewelyn ddoe; nid yw hwn ond erthyl wrtho. Ceisio yr oeddwn yn hwnnw ddeg punt yn y flwyddyn i esm'ythau arnaf. Sure the people will not be so uncivil as to refuse so small a request. If I had ask'd a hundred a year fo f'ase lle iddyn' nhw nacca; be it as it will. I am, dear brother, **W. to R. contd.**

Yours most affectionately tra bwyf yn y cnawd, Wm. Morris.

P.S.—Dyma fi newydd gael llythyr oddiwrth glark y Captain Weller, o'r Dublin yatch, now abuilding at Deptford, yn dywedyd i bydd hi parod o hyn i ben chwech wythnos, ag ymhen y ddeufis yn Nulun os cânt rwydd-deb, ag yno mae bachgen y chwaer Davies i entrio yn brentis ir Cadpen, who is my particular friend (as his father was before him). Os gwelwch y Cadpen, o'r ffeinia fyddai i chwi roi gair i mewn o dŷ'r hogyn, ond odid y ca'i fwy o barch. He is a lusty, ingenious lad, writes a good hand, casts accounts well. The birth is a good one, for the Captain's apprentices attend the cabin, and as they carry so many of the nobility to and fro Dublin, they get a good deal of money. I hope the boy will be sober; he's a stouter, stronger-made lad than his brother John. Perhaps, after he has been awhile aboard, some of you may do something for him. Dyma fi wedi rhoddi hi ar dô. Chwarewch chwitha'. What came of that affair which you said was of a similar nature with that of Mrs. Wheldon's cloaths bill? Hyssiwch Lewelyn ymlaen i goethi'r Rheolwyr yna, am y neges a

W. to R. contd. sgrifenais atto oi blegid. Onid oedd y swyddog Hallt diweddaf yn cael yr hyn yr wyfi yn ei erchi, er ei fod yn ddyn yn cael gair rhwydd wrthyn; cadd ei droi allan or Dollfa ddwywaith, or Post Office unwaith, ag or Halen yn ddiweddaf oll, nid am ei daioni, nid oedd ganddo ddim vote i roddi i'r gwyr mawr, ag ni wnaethai erioed ddaioni yddynt. Whereas dyma Wilym a chanthaw ddwy fôt (na bond i grybwyll) iw gwasnaethu, ag wedi gwasnaethu'r Brenin, Duw safo gyda Ei Ras, er's gwell nag unmlynedd ar bymtheg yn gywir ac yn onest, ag yn ffyddlon ddeiliad iddo erioed hyd yn heddyw a phaham na cheiff o ei neges, ag ynteu yn ei ofyn? Dymma'r bîb (nid er amharch arnoch) agos a dwyn hoedl y bersonyn yma. Ni thal y fan ymma ddim hebddaw. Nid oes yma ddyn a fedr ddarllain chwaethach deall llythyrennau, namyn y Dr. Bellis. Dynan onest yn gymysg o rinweddau da a gwendidau. Colled ir tlodion ar ei ol. Er mwyn dyn bwriwch lythyr gynta galloch, a byddwch wych. Yr eiddoch mal cynt, *W. M.*

GARTREF, Mehefin 4d, 1753.

W. to R. CLV. Anwyl Frawd,—Mae hi'n fy ngolwg i yn gryn chwarter blwyddyn er pan ges lythyr oddiwrth yr un o honoch; yn enw Duw pa beth ai para? Gobeitho nad oes yna ddim rhwystr ar fatterion Llewelyn, etc., nid oes yma ddim o'i hanes o'r deheu nag o'r dwyrain. 'Roedd y llythyr diwedda a gefais oddiwrthaw yn achwyn fod y beswch ymron eich nychu chwi ag yntau; gobeitho fod y tywydd mwll yma wedi eich gwneuthur eich deuoedd yn holliach a bod y meginau cystal cynt: peth hyfryd yw cael ganddynt chwythu yn rhywiogaidd. Gwae ninnau, mae'r boblach ar hyd y wlad yma yn beiaw yn echryslon ar y mawrion yna am droi yn Iddewon brychions. Ni wiw imi geisiaw dywedyd yn ei herbyn, mae'nt yn taeru yn fy nannedd fod y B——, a phawb wedi mynd drosodd at hâd Abram. Er carriad ar ddyn rhoddwch dippyn o hanes nattur yr act honno fal y gallwyf wybod pa beth i ddywedyd. Ces lythyr oddiwrth y nhad echdoe, y pryd yr ydoedd yn iachus dda iawn; 'rwyf yn ei ddisgwyl ffordd yma rai or dyddiau yma. Och y fi, hâ wr fab, dyma'r Doctor Bellis wirion yn mynd heddy i'r Iwerddon i chwilio am iechyd. Duw ai dycco iddo, ag a ddel ag ef yn hawntus adref, ag onide bydd anfeidrawl golled i werin Cybi, yn enwedig ir tlawd ar anghenus. Ni edy nemawr oi fath ar ei ol yn y parthau yma, nis gwn i pa rywogaeth bobl sydd ffordd yna. Dyma ddogn o ddybacco Siamaica yn tyfu iwrth had Wilym Parri; fo naccaodd yr hadau eraill a dangos eu trwyna allan or ddaiaren. Mae'r hwsmyn ffordd yma yn gwaeddi yn erchyll am law, a'm gardd innau nis gad iddynt. Dihareb, mor brydferth yw honno, mi wranta i pe bai Miller o Chelsea yn dyfod yma y blysia lawer peth sydd ynddi. 'Rym oll yn gorchymun attoch ar brawd arall a Meirian, a Duw yn eich cylch. W. to R. contd.

Eich caredigawl frawd, *William Morris.*

P.S.—Ymhle mae rheolau eich Cymdeithas Gymreig? Ymhle mae arfau Gwerydd ap Rhys Goch? Ymhle mae can mil o bethau eraill sydd eisiau eu gweled au clywed? Ni ymadewais i ar holl eirlyfrau etto, mae'r bobl yn ddigon diofal wedi clywed eu bod yn y wlad. A roesoch i un i Mr. Owen? Dyma fi wedi bod yn anfon Mr. Ellis ddarn o ffordd i Ddulun rhyd y môr, gwynt croes iawn ysywaeth, ag heb fawr o hono, tywydd drwg o hwn ar les pobyl dewion. Da chwithau, 'sgrifenwch lein neu ddwy allan o law. Adieu.

HOLYHEAD, July 2nd, 1753.

Dear Brother Richard,—Dyma fi wedi sgrifennu llythyr digon ei hyd at y brawd Llewelyn ag ynddo gymaint o newyddion ag a fedrwn eu casglu at eu gilydd,—gwnewch yn llawen arnynt. Mi delais i nhad am yr holl lyfrau er bod rhai ar fy llaw etto. Fal hyn 'roedd y matter yn sefyll: W. to R. CLVI.

15 llyfr yn ol 6s. bob un sydd yn dwad i... ...	£4	10	0
1 llyfr i Williams y Pottiau	0	7	3
Telais	4	17	3
Am gludo'r Box	0	7	0
Nett Produce ...	£4	10	3

Roedd y nhad yn achwyn am lythyr oddiwrthych ag felly finnau. Ymhle mae hanes y Beiblau a'r Gymdeithas a chant o bethau sydd yn eisiau yma? Pawb yn achwyn fod y geirlyfr yn ddrud anial. Da chwithau, sgrifennwch bwmp o lythyr gynta galloch, fal y gallwyf inneu ei atteb. Nid wyfi yn cael maint yn y

W. to R. contd. byd o newydd gan y brawd arall. Daccw'r 5 July wrth ein drysau, felly rhaid torri cynffon hwn ai adael yma. Duw a fyddo gyd a chwi. Remember me to Meirian. *Your affectionate brother,*

William Morris.

Gwerydd ap Rhys Goch, Lord of Talybolion, in Môn, bore Argent on a Bend Sable, Three Leopards Heads regardant Or. Davies in his Display of Heraldry* has it thus: Argent on a Bend Sable Three Leopards' Faces *of the Field.* But all other books says they are Or, ag Or y ca'nt fod.

HOLYHEAD, 16th July, 1753.

W. to R. CLVII. Dear Brother,—Yn enw'r Arglwydd pa beth sydd ich rhwystro na sgrifennach linell yma weithiau? Nis gwn i a ddeil y llythyr yna Lewelyn cyn iddo droi ei wyneb tua'r Deheubarth. Mi glywaf ei bod hi'r gymdeith'rag gan y frech wen wedi ymaflyd yn ei deulu ieuanc. Cenawes ffyrnig ddigon cynrhwg a Gwilliaid Teifi, neu waeth pe bai bosibl. Duw a ddycco'r gwirioniaid yn ddianaf drwy'r afael. Ag felly ni chafad dim diben ar gyfraith yr Esgair, wfft ir cyfreithwyr am nyddu. Par ddelw sydd ar Feirian? Oni adawodd hi sgrifennu at ei chyfnither Marged ond do? Adwaenoch Ddai Morgant? Mi glywais ei fod yna yn byw er's talm byd. Chwi fyddech'i arfer a rhoddi tippyn o hanes y byd ar amserodd i Wilym wirion sydd mewn congl greigiog, lle na wêl ag na chlyw ddim ond mulfranod, gwylyn a ffwffingod yn crôch waeddi. Pa beth sydd yn peri fod llais drwg gan bob aderyn y dwr? A mwyned lleisiau adar y tir, yn enwedig y rhan fwya o naddynt. Ni wn i a ddywedais i chwi fod yr Aldroman Prichard yn settlio ei holl fatterion yn y Duwmares ag yn mynd efo ei wraig farfog i fyw i Gaer Nerpwl, 'roeddwn yn meddwl y blinai'r gwr ar ei esmwythder. Mae yma olwg gwych a hyfryd ar ydau'r maes a phob creadur yn iachus iawn, mawl i'r Goruchaf am Ei drugareddau i ni. Ychydig a haeddem oddiar ei law. Gerwin o'r glawiau a gawsom yma yn ddiweddar rwan. We all join in love and service to you and Mariana, dear brother.

Yours most affectionately, William Morris.

P.S.—Och fi, ha wr fab, na bae'ch yma i fwyta rhai gooseberries, strawberries, rasberries, currans, o amrywiau rywogaetha a

* "Display of Herauldry" by John Davies of Llansilin, Salop, 1716, p. 47.

digonedd o honynt. Pa beth, meddwch chwithau, dâl frwythau coed heb arian? Nid oes dim byw heb y rheini, yr archlod iddynt. Gwell yw digon o arian heb ŵsberries, na digon o ŵsberries heb arian. W. to R. contd.

CAER GYBI SAINT, 22nd July, 1753.

W. to R. CLVIII.

Anwyl Frawd Rhisiart,—I have at last had the pleasure of a letter from you, wedi bod yn disgwil nis gwn i pa hyd am dano, a da iawn yw gweled eich bod yn symmud, yn byw, ac yn bod. It is a weakness I can't get the better of, to be too anxious about my friends when I don't hear from 'em as often as I could wish. Chwi adwaenach Rhisiart William, y tailiwr o'r Efail Fawr; fo fyddai ar yr hen wr ofn ei gysgod lawer tro pan ddigwyddai iddo ei weled a chîl ei lygad wrth loergan lleuad. Unwaith y dychrynodd gwydd aradr fo yn erchyll, ag ni ddaeth atto ei hun dan dranoeth a chael gweled wrth liw dydd o ba ddefnydd y gwnaed y bwgan lol. Ni waeth tewi na siared nid o'r un math ar bridd y crewyd ni oll. Wrth son am bridd mae'n ddrwg yn fy nghalon gennyf fod y geirlyfr wedi dihenyddu Ffelics yr argraphwr,* wala nefoedd iddaw. Mi dalaf y tri swllt i nhad. Pam na attebasech ynghylch Geirlyfr Siaplen Madfryn? Aie mae'n rhaid cymryd llawer o drafferth i ennill llawer o arian, codi 4 neu 5 or gloch, etc? Wala! Ond ydis yn gwneuthur hynny yma yn ddigon mynych heb fawr fudd yn dyfod i mewn. Och fi am lonaid bol o fusnes i edrych a gwynwn i nemmawr. A fyddan nhw yn beiaw, meddwch? Byddan, byddan, Gwnewch a fynoch, ai da ai drwg, fe fydd rhywun yn anfoddloni—gwell siawns i'r drwg weithredwr nag ir llall. Gwnewch chwi'r sêl, ac na chymeroch arnoch glywed na gweled y coeg-ddyn cenfigennus a wel fai heb achos yn y byd. Pam waith pa beth a ddywedynt os bydd Gair Duw yn uchaf. A Duw yn y Blaen fy motto innau. Rwy'n cofio eich bod o'r blaen yn dywedyd mai dyn balch, morose, etc., o'r Gadpen Weller. Ymhell y bwyf rwy'n meddwl ei fod yn cael cam. I have known him these 15 or 16 years, and of late years have bin intimately acquainted with him, but could never discover in him those bad qualities attributed to him. Dynan mwyn ddigon y gwelais i ef, a phawb o'i swyddogion a'i bobl yn rhoddi gair da iddaw; nid oes ammeu nad oes tippyn o

* Felix Farley, of Bristol, printer of the Welsh Dictionary, edited by Thomas Richards, so frequently referred to above.

W. to R. contd. falchder, a phwy or cadpeniaid sydd hebddo, yn enwedig y rhai ieuanc? Ond oes nifer o bobl y fann hon yn perthyn ir yatch a llawer o lanciau ieuanc odd'yma yn brentisiaid ynddi, a phawb yn rhoddi geirda ir cadpen. This affair I thought incumbent upon me to clear up, otherwise I might be thought to have given too little attention to my nephew's welfare. Profeidiwch chwithau le iddo fynd yn gadpen llong o ryfel erbyn y delo allan o'i amser. Aie ar eich ysgwyddau chwi mae pwys yr holl Gymrodorion yna,—gresyn na bai gennych fwy o amser i'w hepcor fal y gallech fod yn gyfrinachwr iddynt. Mae arnaf ofn nad oes yna neb arall a wna'r gwaith. Nid oes yn y cyrrau yma fawr o bobl sydd gymmwys i wneuthur aelodau or Gymdeithas. Mr. Ellis is an invalide, Mr. Owen, o'r Aberffraw, upon his last legs, ni thal Huw Huws iw godi oddiar y maes, fo fu yn rhesymol, ond mae'n llawer gwaeth er ei wisco. Na wnaeth y Llew gymwynas yn y byd i mi yn yr Halen, nac allan or Halen, er darfod i mi grugo llawer arno er pan mae yna. Dywedyd y mae, nad yw hi ddim yn adeg i drin y matterion hynny, a minneu'n ofni mae gormod o drafferth sydd arno yn ceisio ei gynhauaf ei hun i mewn yw scubor. Par fodd bynnag rwy'n ofni mae ar yr ol y bydd fy llafur i. Rwyf yn ceisio dyscu'r wers galed honno i rhoddi fy holl ymddiried yn Nuw yn hytrach nag ar ddyn yn y byd. Fe wnaeth yr Arglwydd bethau rhyfeddol erof hyd yn hyn, a pham i mi wanobeitho na wna o hyn allan? Oes yna ddim gobaith cyfodiad i chwi ar ol marw yr hen Bedyn? Oni fyddan nhw yn mynd i fynu o ris i ris yn yr offis yna? Dyma'r brawd Llew wedi rhoddi hanes da iawn or Cymrodorion a pha wrthiau ydych ar fedr eu gwneuthur. Gwych a fyddai eich gweled yn mynd ymlaen yn hoyw. Rwyf heddyw yn anfon Cowydd y Farn at Oronwy fal y gallo ei gymwyso i ymddangos ir byd. Mae Wil Owen yn mynd i gopiaw Cowydd yr Awen; mi a yrraf hwnnw ynta cyn pen yr wythnos. Oni bydd Llewelyn yna, mae arnaf ofn na thal y gwaith mor llawer, I mean Gronw's performances, for they deserve to be well lookd into. Daccw un gwr a wna aelod odiaeth i chwi, sef yw hwnnw Owen Holland, of Plas Isa', in Conway, Esq.,—dyn cywraint a gar ei wlad ai hiaith, meddyg, llysieuwr da, a knack in Natural Philosophy, etc. Fe ddaeth yma'r dydd arall im hymweled ag i lysieua, ac mi ddywedais wrtho y byddai raid iddo fod yn aelod. Fe fydd yn dyfod i Lundain ambell dro; fe eistedd yn eich cadair mae'n debyg. Fe ddywaid i mi hanes Mr. William Wynne efo'g Esgob Elwy. Yr Esgob ar ei giniaw efo'g offeiriada' a goreuwyr y wlad, oi fawr ddoethineb a ddywedodd ei fod yn tybiaw mai gwell a fyddai ped fai'r iaith Gymraeg wedi ei thynnu o'r gwraidd, etc., a speech worthy of a Welch bishop! O na ba'sai Risiart Davies neu ryw rai eraill or Hen Esgobion Cymreig yn medru cyfodi o farw'n fyw i grafu llygaid yr Alban allan o'r tyllau,—ond beth bynnag, fe ddechreuodd y bardd gynhyrfu, ac a roes i'r Scottyn wers y persli. Ni sonnia fo mwyach am ddifa yr hen iaith o flaen y cadarn fardd. Ie, drud ddigon iw ymdeithiaw i'r Wyddfa, chwaethach i Rismunt a Siattam, a daccw Hwlant yn tyngu i'r cyrs ag ir coed y bydd raid i mi fynd etto y leni rhyd fryniau Arfon i ymofyn dail, etc. My father was tollerable hearty about four days ago, when my sister came from thence. Mae'r caru drosodd am a glywa i. Nis gwn i par sutt yr wyf fy hun yn sefyll, pe i'm crogid. Something must be done, but whom, or where, or why, or wherefore, or when, or what will be done, nid oes dan haul a ŵyr. Nid oes bosibl mae'r hen Felial a biau'r merched yna bod ag un, os ê, deg i un na bo iddo gyfran o'r rhain, ac os felly gwell ymgroesi o bob cwr. Duw a wnel i'r Secundus hwnnw a soniasoch am dano wneuthur daioni. Wala, wala, rhaid i minnau bellach roddi fy ngherdd yn fy nghôd a thewi a sôn. Duw a fo'n gwarchad drosoch bod ag un. Mi ysgrifenaf at y Llew y post nesa. *Eich caredigawl frawd,* W. to R. contd.

Gwilym Ddu o Fon.

P.S.—Os daw gofyn ymhle y ganed Gwilym Ddu, attebwch mai yn yr un plwyf ag y ganwyd William ap Sion Siors, Pyrs Lewis, Morris Prisiart Morus, Marged Morys, Lewis Morys, a Rhisiart Morys y beirdd, sef yw'r plwyf hwnnw Llan Fihangel tre'r Bardd neu'r Beirdd. O fynydd Bodafon y cawsoch oll y rhinweddau a berthyn i chwi. Rhos Fawr a roddes gerdd i Oronwy. Ni thal pobyl nag anifeiliaid y tir rhywiog ddim yn y byd mewn cyffelybiaeth i'r rhai a gair or tir garw mynyddig, etc. Mi wela fod y Llew wedi rhoi codwm ir Bowel, byth na chotto. I have desired Gronw to send you the Cowydd in a frank I inclosd to him. Dyma'r Aldremon Prisiart yn un cawr; mae o'n mynd yn union

W. to R. contd. deg i Lerpwl efo i gywely, nid oes yn fyw a wyr par sut y mae'r matter yn sefyll rhyngddo ai fab ynghyfraith. I've seen both their letters on that subject, ag nis gwn i beth i feddwl. Llythyr etto gynta galloch, da chwithau. Adieu.—*W.M.*

LONDON, August 4th, 1753.

L. to W. CLIX. Dear Brother,—Pa sawl cynnyg a rois ar fyned tuag adref? Dyma un cynnyg etto ymhen'r wythnos; a dyma fi, mawl i Dduw, gwedi cael diben ar lawer o'r materion caledion yma, a chwedi gorthrechu llawer o'r gelynion, fe fedr Duw eu gorthrechu i gyd, ag efe ai law ei hun a wnaeth hyn i gyd. I have seen lately some very curious collections of fossils, and among the rest I believe I have seen your *llun pen dyn Sion Owen.* I am afraid strength of fancy hath assisted you in making it a man. Ai nid llun pen rhyw chrysalis gloywyn Duw ydyw, fal plentyn yn ei amdo? Neu'n hytrach rhyw bryf mawr or rhywogaeth honno? I have seen three or four of them, the face was about an inch wide or more, with two lumps like eyes, and a raising like a nose, and the place of ye chin turning under like the tail of a chrysalis, a rhicciau hyd ddo, dyna fo mi wranta osowaeth. They are extreme curious here, and they think me so, though I am not. Mae yma ymryson mawr am danaf i fynd i weled casgliad pob un. I took in hand to explain the ores of one of them, which I did better than he could himself, though his ores and other figured fossils were foreign chiefly and there were several fossilists present that were much pleased. The generality of learned people is not so knowing as you imagine,—a little happy nature, assisted with a very little diligence and application will outdo ye forced study of common unanimated clay such as ye mass of mankind are made of. But there are some of these that are very uncommon spirits and of ye superior kind, though they have not the right opportunity of enquiring into ye nature of things. I have bought a stout mare yesterday which I hope will do for me in the room of my favourite mare that died lately; I shall try her to-morrow. *I am your affectionate brother, L. M.*

My service to good Mr. Ellis.

LONDON, August 14th, 1753.

L. to W. CLX. Dear Brother,—I have yours of ye 8th and though it required no answer it is a sort of sin against a brother not to answer him, besides giving a bad example. Ni waeth i chwi dewi nid pen anifail o'r byd yw'r cerrig yna, na phen dyn *yckwàith* (na chwaith Cardiganshire). It is some worm they call *anthropomorphites* or some such name in the winter state, a gwyneb pur debyg i ddyn, ond mai ei gynffon yn troi yn rhicciau ar ei gefn megis gwedi cammu yn ol. Whether there was ever such a worm or chrysalis, I know not, but the fossilists imagine there was. I am not yet learned enough to discuss ye point, having neither books nor opportunity at present, but I told them ours was a child's face, which made them all stare! 'Rwyf finau yn ffwdanus iawn. Commissioner Vaughan just come from Wales. Mr. Pellham and him at Greenwich—minnau'n disgwyl cael mynd adref, a thousand interuptions and ten thousand enemies. Had I been a master of all these difficulties I could have got something for Gronow. I am afraid this London affair will not do, though it is a good thing too. The greatest philosopher in England waited of me at my lodging last night to invite me to dine with him—mwy'r twrw na'r taro. He is now publishing the *Host of Heaven* and a glorious thing it will be. If it had not been an election year Gronow might have had a chance for Aberffro, but none at present. All well at Galltvadog, I hope to be with them soon. I have a lawsuit going on there also in the beginning of September, but am afraid I cannot attend it; for I was not certain of it till to-day L. to W. contd.

I am, in great hast,

*your affectionate brother, L. M.**

LONDON, August 14th, 1753, Tuesday.

L. to Mrs. Morris. CLXI.

My dear,—I received yours of ye 6th and am glad to hear you are well and the rest of ye family. I am glad the harvest is so forward, as you are so scarce of corn. Dont be under any uneasiness, my dear, about Cwmbwa, we must do as well as we can, I have wrote this post as full instructions as I can to Mr. Stephen Edwards to carry [on that] trial. I endeavourd to put it off till the Spring Sessions, but upon the Council on the other side promising to produce all deeds and papers relating to ye estate on the trial, I was obligd to yield to come to trial next Cardigan Sessions. The greatest thing against us is the Deputy Sheriff. Mr. Stephen Edwards will consult with you about witnesses to prove that all the

* Copied by Mr. G. J. Williams, H.M. Inspector of Mines, from the original.

L. to Mrs. Morris contd.

tenements are called Cwmbwa Estate, you know them better than I can recollect in the middle of all my hurry. Let Mr. Edwards have what money he wants to carry on the cause. I am afraid it is impossible for me to be at Cardigan by September 1st, when the Sessions begins; because I have a great many things to prepare here which will take up several days, and it was not determind till to-day whether we should have a trial or no till they would answer the bill I had filed against them. I must send a Proctor with the original will to Cardigan Sessions from Doctors Commons here. I must send subpoenas to serve Dr. Hayes and Mr. Taylor to go to Cardigan to prove the will. I must stay here to take out those subpoenas, and to get some instructions next post for Mr. Edwards, if I can, so upon the whole the weight of the matter must lie upon Mr. Edwards and you. And if I don't come home in time, you must go, my dear, with Mr. Edwards if you can, to Cardigan Sessions, or meet him there; and take some money with you as he may think will be wanted to remove the cause into Chancery, if we lose it by common law, and to pay all charges. Take courage, and don't be in the least cast down, for God will help us, as He hath done hitherto. And if there is law or equity to be had for money, they shall have their belly-full of it. If it is possible for me to come to Cardigan Sessions I shall come by Gloster and Hereford to meet you there, but it is very uncertain as yet. I shall know better by next post. I have no more to say at present, but that I beg of you, my dear, to keep up your courage, for I am strongly of opinion we shall conquer all our difficulties in time.

*I am, my dear, your affectionate husband, L. Morris.**

LONDON, August 18th, 1753, Saturday.

L. to W. CLXII.

Dear Brother,—Is it not enough to drive a man of little sense stark mad to be kept in this place so long, and no certainty yet of the time of setting out? But we must have patience perforce and I don't know of any other cure for our distempers in Cardiganshire. Mr. Pelham is just come to town from Scarborough, and is now at Greenwich, considering upon this affair how to do for the best, *iddo ei hun ai deulu, ag nid i neb arall.* I wrote to you that

* A few letters written by Lewis Morris to his wife will be inserted in their chronological order.

the Esgair y Mwyn Justices were struck out of their commissions, but have not yet had an account how they behaved under their excommunication. I think I wrote to you also that Ned Edwards, had got to be master of a ship of 150 tun, to trade from Boston to Jamaica, thence to London, thence to Portugal, thence to Boston, I think that is the rout. Mae gwedi mynd yn rhyw hwndriwr o ddyn rhyfedd, and may possibly do tolerably, for he doth not want spirit, though he wants learning. My lawsuit in Cardigan this Sessions about Cwmbwa goes on in spight of me, and cannot possibly attend, but have given directions for it to go on as well as we can. Old Dr. Hampe, a German physician to y[e] *Princess of Wales*, was at my lodgings this morning. He is a mineralist, and he and Dr. Shaw are about publishing a book of mining and smelting, and neither of them know anything of the first. Dyna lyfr gwych! Mae Duc Cumberland yn erbyn Pelam gymaint ag allo, mewn lecsiwn a phob peth, ag yn pallu gyrru milwyr i gadw mwyn Sir Aberteifi, felly mae'n debyg y bydd raid mynd at yr hen frenin yr hwn yw'r mwrthwl mawr a eill yrru'r hoel, ond na ddwedwch mo hyn i'r bobl a fydd yn carrio chwedlau; canys mae'r Duc yn dwedyd fod yn ffittiach i fab y brenin gael lease o'r Esgair Mwyn na mab Pelam, etc. Mae'r hen Dr. Hampe yn fy nghyngori i yrru peth mwyn i'r brenin, y bydd wych gantho ei gael allan o'i Welsh mines; ond mae'n debyg mae gwell yw peidio rhag digio Harri.* I have bought here a charming MS. on vellum, finely wrote in Latin, containing among other things the History of y[e] Britons, translated by Galfrid (sef Stori Tyssilio), Giraldus Cambrensis's Itinerary of Ireland, and Conquest of Ireland with verses of y[e] Sybils, articles of Munster, etc. This MS. is well bound, and formerly belonged to y[e] Monastery of the Blessed Virgin Mary, near Dublin. Pray enquire where that monastery was, and when it was dissolved. The book is so fair and whole that it may last again a thousand years or more. It contains also Dares Phrygius's Siege of Troy, Explication of Merlin's Prophecies, verses on Ireland and Scotland, the Nature and Properties of Animals from Aristotle. It is remarkable that the writer took particular care in mentioning that the History of y[e]

* Henry Pelham.

L. to W. contd. Britons was translated from ye British, both in the beginning and end of ye book. Would not you think that I had no cares upon me when I can write about such light things? But it is far otherwise, I do assure you; and it is this way of thinking that keeps me on my legs among my great troubles, I consider myself as an animal of one day's duration, and must fight it out while that day lasts, and then give room for another. All our affairs, great as they are, are quite trifles compared with something that is to come, *that* I am sensible of, though I dont know what it is, nor how it can be. But God that governs these things knows everything, and in His hands we and our enemies are, let Him do with us as He pleases. My best respects to Mr. Ellis, and if you know any other honest friend. Remember me to my sister and brother in law, and God bless you all. Roedd *Iarll* yn fy 'stafell yn ddistaw y boreu ddoe, a Duw wnel i'r peth ddyfod fal ag y mae ef a minneu yn bwriadu; then we can help our friends. I was obligd to sell off a hundred pounds stock yesterday i gael arian i'w gwarrio; nawdd Duw rhag y difethiant. Dyma rywbeth arall wedi dyfod yn fy mhen, nid oes modd i sgrifennu dim chwaneg. *Eich brawd ffyddlon, L. M.*

Ni choeliach i fyth gystal peth yw *ysbectol*, beth yw ei henw yn Gymraeg? If Wheldon Jones's mother is alive you may let her know that her son is like to be a very great man. His honesty and good work has got him the favour of the Navy Board so far that their chief contractors are discharged and all the work ordered for him, which will cause him to employ over 200 men, and bring him in perhaps a thousand a year. My brother hath been of some assistance to him to fight against the stream of ye Navy Office, who were all against him, and he has fought a great battle. He has the crasder and plainness of his mother and is well liked by the principal officers, i.e., commissioners. A few days ago the Comptroller of ye Navy called him to the board and spoke to him thus, "Mr. Chwel-don Jones, I am told there is a *little* [fault in] your work." "I am very glad of that" says Wheldon. "Glad of it" said the Comptroller, "what do you mean by that?" "Glad that it is but a *little* fault" says Wheldon, "for other people commit *great* faults." "Well," said the Comptroller to the other commissioners "I have done with him, and I turn him [over] to you," and Wheldon was so *dewr* and so *cras*, that he out talked them. His needles had been too large in some sail and ripd the cloth, and . . . . . . they perhaps deducted a few shillings from his bill, when pounds are deducted on [those] of others, and he really produces better work than any other contractor. L. to W. contd.

CAER GYBI, 26 Awst, 1753, wedi nos.

W. to R. CLXIII.

Anwyl Frawd Rhisiart,—Wele yman eich llythyr o'r 18d ag och o ddaed oedd ei gael. Your last conjecture about the sea-birds I think is the best. Birds of prey are generally poor singers, oddi gerth i ddynion eu drwg ddyscu. Ar ddryghin y bydd hi'r gaseg yn gweryru fwya, for its the bad weather that drives them from the mountains, ag ni welwn ni un amser monynt, ond ar rew ag eira. Ie, yn Nerpwl y mae yr Aldremon ai wraig; mae wedi cymryd rhan o dy, debygwn, i dreio par sut y digymydd hi ar fan. Gerwin o'r glaw ar gwynt a wnaeth yma heddyw; fe ddarfu am long gynna' o flaen ein llygaid ni, ond fo ddiangodd y bobl. O Gaernarfon roeddyn', ceisio mynd ag yslatis i Ddulun,—mae'r ddryghin drosodd am y tro. Digrif fyddai eich gweled ym Mon (yn enwedig yn y rhan sancteiddiaf o honi) yr hâf nesaf, ni fyddach i dro yn dyfod mewn post-chaise; fo fydd y rheini yn dyfod yma bob yn awr. We had about a month or six weeks ago 8 coaches, chariots, and post-chaises in the compass of 48 hours from Chester, dyna hogan o ryfeddod yn y fangre yma! Ni fyddynt ers talm yn ymdeithio drwy Gymru yn y fath gerbydau; gofynnwch i mrawd Llewelyn. Ie, ie, mrawd Rhisiart, peth digon anghysurus yw dwyn ar got yr anhwsmonaeth a wnaethom o ddyddiau ein hieuenctyd; pa beth na roddem er cael ei rhoi hi ar dô unwaith etto? ond och druain gwyr, nid ellir galw doe yn ol. Gwnawn ynta'r goreu o'r ychydig ddyddiau sydd i'n rhan ag edifarhawn am y cam dreuliad a *Duw yn y blaen*, ni a wnawn o'r goreu. Amser mawr iw 31 o flynyddoedd pan ystyriwn fyrred einioes; ai tybied yr adwaenem ein gilydd pei tarawem y naill wrth y llall ar fynydd? Nid oes imi le i achwyn, fe roddes Duw imi, moliannus a fyddo Ei enw, iechyd a hawddfyd gan mwyaf, ond etto er hyn rwyf wedi mynd yn rhemwth o ddyn anystwyth, diowc, swrth, llawn o anwydau ystyfnig, a digonedd o le i bob hadau heintiau a llygredigaetha' gynnyddu eu gwaetha glas.

W. to R. contd. Rydych yn cofiaw mae'n debyg, mal y byddech i yn fy ngalw er's talm y *llanc main*, ag yn ddiau mi fyddwn y dyddiau hynny yn llwyr ddymuno bod yn dewach rhag cywilydd. [Mae] i mi fachgen o'r un lun a minna' pan oeddwn ieuanc, pin o wr main tal hir (chwedl y dyn) yn crymmu tippyn yn ei ysgwyddau fal Morys Owen o Fodafon. "Gwyn y gwel y fran ei chyw" medd yr hen ddywedyd, nid hwyrach mae dyna finnau. Meddwl yr wyf fod Duw wedi fy mendithio a dau o blant braf os caf hoedl iw dwyn i fynu yn ei ofn Ef. Ond digon o hynny Gwilym, soniwch am ryw beth arall heblaw eich hunan ach plant, wala, wala, mi adawaf: Turn over, ie, parottowch eirlyfr ir Berson Williams; mi fynnaf dal am y ddau. Ag felly, mewn arian yr y'ch ar fedr cael yr arfau. Would not steel be better, as it takes a better polish? Ond bod yn ddrud ei dorri; pa beth a fynnent am ei dorri mewn dûr? I like your scheme of the old women on Tower Hill well enough; os dengys siampl dda ir herlodes wirion. Pur anhawdd meddwch iw taro wrth yr un or gwrageddos yn y fangre yna heb fod a rhiw gastiau gwaharddedig arnynt. God direct you for the best. Nid ydis ymma chwaith bur fodlon i'r cyflwr, pe gellid ei newid am un a fai gwell. Ond Duw a wyr pa beth sydd oreu, fe fydd rhyw rwystr deued y byd fal y mynno, a dymma fal yr ym yn ymdeithiaw drwy ddyffryn y trueni, a sicr yw na chawn orphwysfa wrth ein bodd nes mynd i ben ein siwrnai. Gwych a fyddai weled eich gosodedigaethau (dyna air hir erchyll, oes yr un sydd fyrrach a geidw ei le?). Chwi welsoch fy meddwl ynghylch Grono yn llythyr Llew. Dyma'r Aberffraw a Rhoscolyn yn ddiberson,—one in the Crown's gift, the other in the Bishop's. Oh na chair truan un o'r ddau. Fal hyn y digwyddodd i blant yr Efail Fawr: Rhobin (ag iddo lawer o wyrion, chwaethach plant) a ddrwg ladded y dydd arall gan bowdr gwn, wrth chwthu cerrig oedd ar ffordd llongau yn y Glaslyn, ag a fu farw dan law meddyg, eisiau na basai ei dad ynghyfraith yn y byd mae'n debyg. Harri yn dailiwr meddw, ag iddo blant, etc. Elsbeth a Marged ag iddynt blant ac wyrion eill dwywedd yn byw Ymhen y Coed; ag yno mae Gryffudd Dafydd, yr hwn sydd ganddo blant ac wyrion, a Siwduth Edward, a gwraig Huw Owen yna oedd yno hefyd dydd arall, a rhain yn byw gan mwya ar Bentre'riannell. Sian 'ch Sion Oylfer yn yr hen dy, lle busai ei thad; erchyll or celwydd a ddyweddodd rhywun yn y *London Evening Post* ynghylch ei gwr hi, William Owen Pyrs, a fusai farw er's cryn flwyddyn. Mae Wil Peters hên (oblegid fod iddo fab yn briod er's talm a elwid Wil Peters ieuanc, a chan hwnnw fab mae'n debyg a elwir Will Peters ieuaf) mae ô meddaf gyn ynfytted a chyn feddwed ag ungwr, er ei fod wedi mynd heb ewin i ymgrafu, wedi gwarrio'r cwbl mewn oferedd a bryntni. Gorchmynwch fi at y Cadpen Iorwerth ap Rhisiart Iorwerth. I wish him success in his new ship. What, no seeds nor plants from abroad? gadewch iddo. 'Rwyf ar y ffordd i gael y peth a fynnwyf o Siamaica a Barbadws os deil y trât yma yn hir, sef dilwytho siwgr. His sister has a good pretty lad if she would let him come up; let him write to her if he cares to do for his relations. Rhaid a rhoddi'r pin heibio er difyrred iw dwndrio fal hyn. Duw Goruchaf a roddo i chwi ras ac iechyd, ac a fendithio Feirian. Let me hear from you as soon as you have a spare hour. W. to R. contd.

I am, dear brother, yours most affectionately, Wm. Morris.

P.S.—Nid oes yma ddim lle i roddi drecsiwn, felly rhaid chwilio am ffrencyn Captain Barry. Yr iot yn Nulun, a llong a siwgr arall i fod yma foru.

HOLYHEAD, [29th August, 1753].

Dear Brother Richard,—Mae fal y ceisiwch argraphu'r paragraph a ganlyn yn y *London Evening Post*, da chwitha', fal y gallo'r byd weled ein bod wedi cael morwyndod yr yatch newydd. Dyma Begi Morris wedi dyfod adref neithiwr o Ddulun yn iach lawen, ag yma pawb yn iach, cenwch. Aeth y brawd Llewelyn adref? Os naddo gorchymynwch fi atto, a Duw a fyddo gyd a chwi. Dyma'r nai William Owen yn mynd i gymeryd meddiant yn ei le yng nghaban yr yot. I hope he'll do well, he's a sober, stout, strong, genteel lad. Lle buddiol y mae yn ei gael, ag os efe a ymddug yn dda, nid wyf yn ammeu nad allaf wneuthur cymwynas iddo dro arall. W. to R. CLXIV.

29th.—His Majesty's new Dublin yatch, *The Dorset*, Captain Weller, commander, is arrived at Holyhead, and is to carry over the Right Honourable the Lady Ann Connoly, who was expected there the 30th inst. Get this inserted as an article of news. I am in a great hurry, dear brother, *Yours most affectionately*,

William Morris.

CASTLE BROMWICH, August 29, 1753.

L. to W. CLXV.

Dear Brother,—So far I am come in my way homewards, pretty much tired, and my horses (i.e., mares) too, and it being rainy, I have stopd at ye end of 26 mile for this day, the mare I ride being but 4 year old, if so much. It is most charming weather for the harvest, for ye little rain does more good than harm to ye corn. In these counties the corn is more backward than we are in Wales. Here is some barley and oats that wont be fit for reaping this three weeks. But fine grass and hay, and the face of plenty all over ye country. Och i blant Alis am ddwyn y fath wlad oddiar yr hen Frutaniaid, sef y Cymrodorion. It is really my opinion that the bulk of ye people are still the old Britains. They have the same dress, the same customs and manners, and all except the language, and I dare say the words which we suppose were mostly borrowd by us from ye English are words the English found in ye country among ye natives. Where could the Loegrian natives go to on ye Saxon [conquest]? There was not room for them in Wales. I was [highly diverted] on the road till last night by a mongrell Welshman, a brother of Jarvis of Dinerth, such another hairbraind mortal as O. P., a tide surveyor in London. But last night he dropd me, because I told him his horse was able to travel sixty mile a day, and to shew the goodness of his horse that cost 50s. he left me with my fine horses, and I shall see him no more. Such another whiff as Dick Jones bach, but . . . . .

[The rest is gone.]

GARTREF, 3dd o Fedi, 1753.

W. to L. and R. CLXVI.

Anwyl Frodyr,—Dyma linell neu ddwy i'ch mysg i ddangos ein bod ni ymma oll yn iach, mawl i'r Hwn sydd yn rhoddi iechyd a phob bendith arall. Daccw Ddeon Bangor wedi marw, a chwedi gadael ei renti, etc., ar ei ôl; Llanbeulan, etc., ym Môn, Llanfair gerllaw'r Penmaenmawr. Ag mae'r gair farw or Siawnsler, ond nid oes dim siccrwydd o hynny. Mae'r bobl ym Môn yn taeru fod rhai o honoch yn mynny cael rhai o'r rhenti yma i Gronwy, yr Aberffraw maent yn ei roddi iddo, na atto Duw chwedl amgen, meddaf innau. Dyna'n porth ni yn llawn o longau. Mae'r Dorset yatch yma etto, ac yn ddiau llestr gwych ydyw, mi fum ynddi ddwywaith. Rym wedi setlio Will Owen. Un bachgen arall ac yntau sydd i fod yn y caban pan bydd gwyr mawr i mewn, a lle buddiol iawn ydyw, ag yr wyf innau nid er brol nag er gwawd yn anferth ffrind ar holl officers sydd ynddi na bo'nd i grybwyll! Nid oes ameu na bydd William Owen yn gefn dyn ar fyrder. Da iawn yw ysgafnhau tippyn ar faich y chwaer ar brawd. Mae yma Arglwyddi ag Arglwyddesau fwy nag a aing yr inns yma, felly mae'n gorfod arnynt orwedd mewn teiau a thô gwellt arnynt! Daccw Huw, mab Syr Bodeon, ym Mhresaddfed, pawb yn erbyn Bodorgan ond haid o offeiriaid sydd yn ymbleidio o'i du, ag ambell wr 'nhêddig. Mae'n rhywyr cael tippyn o newydd oddiyna bellach; ai ydych chwi ym mrawd Lewis yna, ai nid ydych? Dyma'r cefnder Gobed ab William Morris yn dywedyd fod yr holl *personal estate* ym Modowen wedi eu prisio, ag mae'n debyg y gwerthir y cwbl yn y ty ag allan (oblegid i'r ddau gyrnol y perthynant). Cywilydd anial. Duw a fyddo yn nodded i chwi. W. to L. and R. contd.

Eich caredigawl frawd, William Morris.

Peggy desires a blessing.

GALLTVADOG, September 11, 1753.

Dear Brother.—I met three letters of yours here, the last of 25th ult. Bydd y Mynglwyd* yn brwysgo yn ddi-drefn weithiau, ond yn o anaml. Parry, I believe, will go again to Jamaica. I am glad you have sugar enough. Ie, ie, ynghroen dyn fal y chwilcath roedd y sarph a dwyllodd Efa. Ffarwel i awen yr Aberffraw, gresyn oedd iddo ei boddi mewn cwrw: L. to W. CLXVII.

Boddodd awen lawen loyw
A gwawr hoywlith y gwr hyloyw,
Porthed ar eurgred ir-gwrw
Mae'n gorwedd mewn hên hên gwrw. Etc.

I have no time to add, being extream busy in setting things in order. All well. *I am, your affectionate brother, Lewis Morris.*

[The following notes in the handwriting of W.M. are on the back of the previous letter dated Sept. 11th, 1753.]

I often endeavor to draw a comparison between my correspondence and my garden affairs, and that to little purpose. The intermediate state of the two are somewhat similar; at proper seasons I commit my garden seed to the ground, and then I wait perhaps a fortnight, three weeks or a month, and sometimes another

* Richard Morris, who often called himself Rhisiart Fynglwyd.

L. to W. contd. year ere I can judge whether I shall have any return, so by my letters there are certain seasons when a body is disposed to scribble to all his friends: this is sowing. Then I wait and wait again till I am tired and out of all patience at last. Some friend that's better natured (or perhaps to give it a softer turn), one that has more leisure than others will oblige me with a line, and some of the others may by and bye favour me with one line for . . . Nature I know is regular in her returns, making some little allowances for the weather, but I find often to my great mortification that the humane productions are quite irregular and that the comparison will not hold good. Be sure of good seed and deposit it in proper soil, you may be certain that it will come up, but on the other hand those you mostly depend upon will often deceive you,—perhaps a brother will be the last that will reply.

CAER GYBI SANT, 15d o Fedi, 1753.

W. to R. CLXVIII. Anwyl Frawd,—Echdoe'r boreu daeth gwr'nheddig im offis ac a roddes yng nghîl fy nwrn i ebystol oddiwrthych, sef oedd y gwr hwnnw Woodward eich cyfaill, a chydag ef 'roedd cyfathrachwr iddo, un Dr. Smyth, o Rydychen. Dynan diniwaid fal yntau debygwn. Mi ddangosais iddynt fy holl ryfeddodau, ag a wneuthum iddynt gymmaint o sir ag a allwn. They favoured me with their company to drink tea, and then we passed the evening over a little punch and Liverpoole ale. It happend I had both good in their kind, a phwy a ddeuai ar ein cefnau ennyd o nos ond yr Aldroman Prichard, ag felly ni bu diffyg digon o ddwnddwr lle roedd ô ar Berson. Y boreu ddoe darfu'r Berson a minnau fwyta boreu-fwyd efo hwynt hwythau yn ei lletty, ag o ddeutu hanner dydd nhw a hwyliasant am dre Ddulun, mae'n debyg eu bod yno bellach! Roedd Woodwarth yn dywedyd yr ysgrifennai attoch or Iwerddon, but in the mean time desired his compliments. Ce's lythyr oddiwrth y Llew. o Castle Bromwich, dated 29 August, yr hwn lythyr a fase ynghylch pythefnos yn mynd i Lundain ag yn dyfod yn ol, ag oddiyno yma. Ond nid oedd waeth mor llawer i ble yr aethai, nid oedd ynddo un gair oi hanes. I mean as to his affairs, so I must depend upon you for a little inteligence, par sut a fu rhyngtho a'r Belam, etc. Ces lythyr dydd arall oddiwrth Oronwy. Ni cha'd byth ddaioni or dyn hwnnw er pan ddaeth o swydd

Ymhwythig, fe adawodd ei awen ar ei ol, neu ryw andros. The man's head, I'me affraid, is too much bent upon preferments; he was made to believe that Aberffraw was his, though without foundation, and Mr. Vychan o'r Gors, yntau wedi bod yno'r dydd arall, a chwedi tyngu i'r cyrs ac i'r coed na cheiff mo'r aros yno (Walton) flwyddyn, felly lle da disgwyl na chywydd nag awdl. Roeddwn yn disgwyl llythyr oddiwrthych cyn hyn dan sêl Gwerydd ap Rhys, nis gwn i a geir yr un y boreu foru, par fodd bynnag rhaid rhoddi i chwi nos dawch am heno, a Duw a fyddo yn gwarchad drosoch. *Eich caredigawl frawd, W. Morris.* **W. to R. contd.**

P.S.—Dymma Peggy Owen wedi dyfod o dy nhad echdoe; roedd yr hen wr yn rhesymol iachus. Dim llythyr oddiyna heddyw, 17th, gadewch ei gael gynta galloch, da chwithau. We expect the Viceroy of Ireland here in a day or two. Gwych a fyddai ir gwynt ddal yn y Gorllewin dros wythnos er mwyn gwragedd Kybi. Ni feddai i ffranc yn y byd i sgrifennu ir deau dir nag i unlle.—*W.M.*

HOLYHEAD, 23rd September, 1753.

Dear Brother,—I received yours of the 11th and 15th inst, yngwrthgefn un i minnau sydd yna cyn hyn, a hanes Woodward, etc. Gerwin y nifer o lythyrau oeddych wedi eu gyrru ar ol Llewelyn ir wlad. Digrif a fai eich gweled ym Mon eich deuoedd a ninnau i gyd yn fyw ac yn iach i'ch derbyn, yn ddiau bydda yma lawenydd mawr. Dyn a feddwl, Duw a ran. Fe eill hynny ddigwydd, ag os ni wna, rhaid i ni ymfodloni ag ymgysuro dan obaith y cawn gyd gyfarfod mewn man a fo gwell pan elom ir nefol wlad. Roeddwn yn dywedyd wrth y nhad, yr hwn a ddoeth ymma echdoe i'n hymweled, fod yn eich bryd ddyfod eich deuoedd, roedd yr hen wr yn ymlonni yn fawr glywed fod y fath amcan ar droed. Pwy a ddigwyddawdd ymma yr un amser a nhad, ond y cefnder Morris ap Sion Prisiart, ai wraig ai fab, ag yr oedd gyda nhad gymydog iddo, sef Foulk Jones, y swyddog, an excellent hand on the violin, felly rhyngddynt ar berthynas yma roedd gennyf echnos lawenydd mawr—cerddoriaeth ar dafod a thant, etc. yr un fath ag y byddid yn y dyddiau gynt. Heddyw yr aethynt adref, chwaneg o hanes y car Morys yn y man. Mi glywais y Tew yn son am Bowys, mai ffryndiau mawrion oeddynt, etc., a bod **W. to R. CLXIX.**

W. to R. contd. rhyw anferth *scheme* ganddynt ar droed, pawb drosto ei hun a wela'i ymhob man. Ce's lythyr oddiwrth y Llew. ddoe yn cynnwys naill ai dwy lein neu 3, heb gymmaint ag un gair o newydd. Dyn diflas ar droau, onte? 'Roedd arnai ddialedd eisiau clywed par sut y base rhyngddo a'r rhai mawrion yna cyn cychwyn, a pha'r sut a fu yn y gyfraith yn Aberteifi ynghylch Cwmbwa. He has got a way of acquainting one with most of his schemes, but then he always or generally leaves me in the dark as to the success of 'em; gwell a fai beidio clywed son am danynt, na gadael dyn mewn disgwyliad diddiwedd. Fe ddywedir ymma mai un Vincent a gâdd yr Aberffraw, roedd yr Esgob wedi rhoddi un o renti'r Deon or blaen. Ond nid oes dim cyfiawnder iw gael, ag nid ydyw'r mawrion yn prisio mo'u addewid ddraen crin? Gresyn na base Bowys a'r Tew yn dre pan ddaeth y newydd yna o farw'r câr Tomos Owain. Gwych y gymdeithas yna a rhwydd-deb i chwi i fynd ymlaen. Pan elir yn aelod o honoch rhaid sgrifennu rhyw ryfeddodau attoch, gobeitho na byddwch yn dangos yr un o'm 'pystolau i iddynt, oblegid diofal y byddaf yn dodi fy ngeiriau ynghyd wrth sgrifennu attoch chwi, ni wêl brawd feiau. Bu yma *riolti* mawr yr wythnos ddiwaetha pan oedd Brenin y Gwyddelod yn ein plith, llonaid y dref o boblach. Gorfu ar y Cadpen Weller ddiniwaid adael i Lord George Sackville gael ei wely lle y gorweddai ar y lan, a minneu a gymerth drugaredd arno ag ai dygais im cabandy. Wrth son am y Navy Offis, digwyddodd iddo ddywedyd fal y basai raid ddwrdio a tharo ei d—n wrth y nen bren o achos rhyw gyfrifon, which he had left in the Comptroller's Office when he returned from Smyrna, etc. He complained of the head clerk. A dyna fe weddai yr achos oedd i chwi feddwl fod y dyn yn falch, yn gostog, etc. Camgymeriad mawr, oni yrrodd i mi'r dydd arall, cyn i mi roddi gwely iddo, fascedaid o win Ffreinig yn rhodd ac yn rhad; ai costog a fai'r dyn a wna hynny? Nag oes un ;defnyn o waed Gwyddyl yngwithi'r gwr. Yng Nghent y ganed ag y maged ef ag yno mae ganddo enedigaeth fraint, sef tir a daear lawer ydoedd gan ei deidiau oi flaen, ag mae iddo lawer o stât yn Nghilgwri a brynodd yr hen Weller, tai a gerddi gwchion, a minnau iw ffwrneisiaw a blodau, etc. Nage Cockney iw'r D. Doughty yntau, apothecary o'ch dinas gynt; torri mae'n debyg a orrug—dynan gwag digrif ddigon. Camgymerodd Ierwerth, fe eill yr yatch wneuthur cystal llongwr o'r nai Gwilym ar llong oreu allan. Gwych or hanes 'rych yn ei roddi o'r Florentius hwnnw, wfft iddo fo. Do, mi welais hanes y Veronica (i.e., Llys Llewelyn) yn y papurau; roedd gennyf dŷb odiaeth o honynt o'r blaen, a chan gynted ag y gwelais pa beth a ddywaid yr Abbe Perneti am danynt mi aethym ag a heliais wrâdd or dail, a dyma fi heddyw yn mynd i yfed yr ail boreu-bryd o naddynt, bellach ni wiw ir physygwyr ddangos mo'u trwyna. I know several sorts of the Veronica growing in this country and the next, but the *Veronicamas Supina* and *Vulgatissima* is the officinal one; few knows it here beside my self. Our countrymen, the Cambro-Britons, had always a great opinion of the Veronica and attributed many virtues to it; incredible stories are told by 'em of cures performd by the help of llys Llewelyn. Cymaint ag a fedraf i ddywedyd ynghylch pais arfau Llewelyn ap Gruffydd yw hyn: that the Arms of the Sovereign Princes of Wales before the English took upon them that title were thus, they bore quarterly Gules and Or, Four Lions Passant, Gardant, Counter changed, meddai'r Hen Feirdd. So that Llewelyn Amhadog was mistaken. Aie roedd Dick ap Tomos Lewis yn fyw flwyddyn i heddyw! Wala, da iawn druain, pwy a wyr nad eill ddyfod i brynnu tir yn lle'r llall. Gwyrda'r Saeson am baffio'r Ffrancod a'i cyfeillion melyndduon. Ie, ie, achwyn yn erchyll y bydd y porthmyn bob amser er däed eu budd. Ond dynion digrif o'r John Hughes a'r Will Jones? Nid adwaen mo frawd Benja! Och y fi ddrytted yw'r geirlyfr a rwymwyd. A dalodd y Fawdfel am y llall, ynteu 15 swllt sydd arnaf am y ddau? Gadewch wybod.

W. to R. contd.

Ni welodd y nhad erioed w'chach cynhauaf nag a gafed ym Mon,—tywydd odiaethol heb fod nag yn rhy wresog nag yn rhy oerllyd, ag yn sych 'rhyd yr amser. Llawnder mawr, a dymma ŷd brynnwyr yn dechreu rhoddi prisiau braf yn barod am haidd, 15 neu 16 y pêg. Duw a roddo ei ras i ni bawb i fod yn ddiolchgar am y bendithion hyn a'r holl rai y mai Ef (bendigedig fyddo Ei Enw) yn ymdywallt arnom a ninnau mor anhaeddol. Hanes meibion Plas Ofa gynt: mae'r cefnder Rhisiart yn byw lle bu nhaid, gerllaw Eglwys Llanfihangel-tre'r-Bardd; mae'n dilyn yr

W. to R. contd.

hen grefft, saer melinau, ar goreu ydyw yn y wlad. Mae ganddo wmbwrdd o blant ag wyrion. Mae Morys yn byw ar fin Menai tu draw i Borth-Aethwy, yn dal llawer o dir ac yn wr cefnog; ei fab hyna wedi gwasnaethu ei amser i saer llongau o Whitehaven, a llanc cywrant iawn ydyw, yn awr ar y mor o chwant gweled y byd. Yr ail mab ydoedd gydag ef yma wedi ei ddwyn i fynu mewn ysgolion ir Lladin, sgrifennu a thrin rhifyddiaeth—a smart lad about 16 or 17, wants to get him some clerkship; mae o'n nacca ystwytho i wneuthur dim gan iddo gael bod yn ysgolhaig. Oes yna eisiau dim dyn or fath? His parents would rig him out like a gent and would give him money in his pocket to try his luck. Pray let me hear from you for I promisd I would write to you about him. Mae iddynt lodes gyda hynny, bu farw'r lleill. Daccw'r cefnder William yntau'n ffermwr tua Llangefni, ag yn briod a merch Rhisiart Hughes or Hendre (eich tad bedydd), ag iddynt ferch wedi priodi a chan honno blant neu blentyn. Mae Wiliam yntau yn byw yn gefnog, a dyna i chwi eu hanes bod ag un. Mae'n amser i mi bellach roddi fy ngherdd yn fy nghod, chwedl y crythorion gynt. Duw a fyddo yn gwarchad drosoch a'r eiddoch.

Eich carediccaf frawd, William Morris.

GALLTVADOG, September 28, 1753.

L. to W. CLXX.

Dear Brother,—This will only tell you that I have yours by last post and am glad you are well. I have not leisure as yet to answer one paragraph of it, nor have I it by me. We are all well I thank God, and in a continual state of war, law, squabbles, wrangling, enough to make the dullest fellow in ye world rouse his spirits and to make a man of spirit mad. God bless you all. You shall have a long letter as soon as I can. *I am your affectionate brother, L.M.*

Should be glad to know how Mr. Meyrick goes on, and how the old gentleman is.

CAER GYBI, 17eg o Hydref, 1753.

W. to R. CLXXI.

Anwyl Frawd,—Mi dderbyniais yr eiddoch or 6ed presenol, ag yn ddiau roedd yn llawen ei weled er mwyn clywed eich bod yn fyw iach, etc. Na chawsent gwrageddos Cybi hanner digon o gwmni Brenin y Gwyddelod; ni arhödd yma ond un noswaith i gyd; fe ddywaid yr hen ddihareb: Mae'r lle'r ymgreinio'r march y gedy beth o'i flew, felly yntau. Gwych eich bod yn cynhesu fwy

fwy wrth y daith Gymreig. Os Duw a ganiatta ini hoedl bydd falch eich gweled eich deuwedd. Rwy'n deall mai'r un ffunud y mae'r Llew yn eich trin chwi a minnau. Diflas ddigon o wrantu. I had a letter from him since of 4 or 5 lines. Wala, wfft ir dyn! Mae gennyf bot a chaccen ir Bowys am ei ostyngeiddrwydd ai garriad tuag at Oronwy. Gresyn oedd colli'r Aberffraw, o eisiau ——. Ni waeth tewi na siared. *Δυν βαω ο'ρ Βυρσυν*, a meer *νήγρω, φει ὅναω*.* Digrif or daith honno hyd yn nhrigfan Cornelius Agrippa, digrifach a fuasai fis ynghynt i gaffael haelsiad or amrafael ancwyn oedd yno ar hyd y parwydydd yn tyfu. Oes mi wranta ddigonedd o lysiau Llewelyn yn tyfu'r ffyrdd yna, ar hyd bonciau sychion y ceir hwynt, croppian a wnant fal y brymlys a gwreiddio o bob cymmal. Dyna i chwi rai or dail sychion yn sampl, fal y galloch eu hadnabod, mi fyddaf fi yn yfed tea o honynt bob yn awr, nid drwg iawn mo'i flas. I'me glad you are convinced in regard to Captain Weller ddiniwed, rwy'n ei ddisgwyl yma y foru neu drennydd i ddwyn drosodd yr Arglwyddes Prendergast or Marl, gerllaw Aber Conwy. Gadewch wybod pwy oedd ar union ai Llew ai Gwilym ynghylch arfau Tywysogion Cymru gynt? Yr archlod fyth a fo ir hurthgen yna a gerfiodd eich sêl chwi. Instead of 3 leopards' heads or faces he hath put three heads erasd a gyddfau hirion iddynt. Dyna i chwi ar glwt o bappur lun fy sel i pan i gwneler. Pa beth a gyst ei thorri mewn arian, a pha'r faint mewn dur, a pha'r faint mewn cornelian? Aie pan eloch yn Gomisiwnwr y cynorthwywch eich ffrindiau? Arglwydd eb y Gronw (wrth y maccwy) par bryd y bydd hynny? Bid buan y delo'r amser, chwi a glywsoch ganwaith mai diboen i ddyn dybio'n dda. Mi dalaf i nhad arian geirlyfrau person yr Aberffraw, mae rwan gini yn digwydd ar gownt Richards. Gwelwch y cyfrif yna. Mae'n fy mryd fyned tua thy y nhad rai or dyddiau yma. Tacclu'r ffordd fawr iw ngorchwyl y dyddiau hyn, i.e., giving it a coat of gravel. We can boast of having four miles of as compleat a road as any in His Majesty's Dominions, par sut bynnag y mae yr relyw or ffordd oddiyma ir Borth. Pawb drosto ei hun. Rwy'n deall fod Cadpen Tatton yn y Ddinas, y gwr a addawodd i mi'r crocus duon, felly fe ddarfu i Agrippa golli'r ôl.

W. to R. contd.

* Dyn baw o'r Bursyn, a meer negro, ffei honaw.

W to R. contd. Diolch yn fawr am yr hadau. I had some of the seed of the large water melon by me; the East India pampion or gourd, I dare say, must be very curious, nid am ei ddyfod o cymmhelled o ffordd. Gadewch wybod par fath bethau a yrr Agrippa, a phar faint o hadau a gadd Mr. Parry o Siamaica. Pray my compliments to that gentleman. I should be glad to render him any service in my power in this part of the globe. What is become of Mr. Woodward and his Irish antagonist? Gerwin y twng y tystion Gwyddhelig; os eu llyfon a gant, yn iach droedfedd o dir ir Woodwart. 'Rwyf yn deall darfod i'ch Cymdeithas chwi, sef y Cymmrodorion, urddo yn ddiweddar, Mr. Hwlant o Gonwy, a minnau yn aelodau o'r gyfeillach odidawg honno, er mor anhaedd-awl oeddwn i yn enwedig or cyfryw anrhydedd. Och mor dlawd wyf o eiriau i ddatgan fy niolchgarwch am y parchedigaeth hwn, ar peth sydd waeth 'rwyf dra thlawd o allu i wneuthur unrhyw weithred neu orchest a eill gynnal i fynu'r alwedigaeth neu roddi im hawl o fod yn aelod or fath enwog Gymdeithas. Ond etto er hyn, rwy'n deusyf arnoch yspysu ir brodoriaeth, fy mod yn addaw na chaiff fod yn ol yr hyn a allwyf i wneuthur tuag at gyrru ym'laen arddunniant a bri, yn gystal a daioni'r Cymrodorion yng Nghaer-ludd. Nid ydych yn son dim argraphu goreuon gwaith Prydyddion, etc. Pa beth sydd yn dyfod o gowyddau Goronwy? Gwych a f'ai cael gweled rhai o'ch gwrthiau. Dyma i chwi hanes y Salbriaid. Mae Sion yr etifedd yn byw yn Llanwddan, y wraig ag yntau yn afiachus bob yn awr, ag yn dra bydol, a couple well met. Mab a merch oedd ir gyfnither Elsbeth o Huw Evans ei hail ŵr, y mab Tomos Evans (a wasnaethodd ei brentisiad gyda nhad). The heir apparent is a carpenter, follows his trade, is a batchelor; the girl is married and lives at Bodafon, in Creuddyn, a farmer of the orderly sort. Roedd gan Farged Salbri chwech neu saith o blant pan bu farw. Dyn meddw or tad, y plant un yma ag un acw, rhai ir môr a rhai ir mynydd. Roeddynt yn byw yn bur dacclus tra bu hi, ond wedi hynny fe aeth yr holl eiddo gyd ar lli. Catrin yr ieuaf o blant y Fferi sydd yn byw yng Nghonwy yn briod a dyn meddal meddw. He is an officer (i.e., a boatman and tidesman) of the customs. His brother left him lands and a sloop a few years ago. They have a great many children—one boy follows the sloop which trades in Sion Salbri's name in trust for them, a dyna i chwi eu hanes o bant i bentan, a bellach mae hi'n amser i mi cymeryd trugaredd arnoch, ac ych gollwng yn rhydd oddiwrth y rhigwm gwag ymma. Duw gyda chwi. *Eich caredicgaf frawd,* — **W. to R. contd.**

William Morris.

P.S.—Pa beth sydd yn dyfod or Biblau Cymreig? Father was well lately, pawb yma yr un modd. Mawl ir Goruchaf am ei holl drugareddau. Roeddwn yn meddwl fod gennyf rai o'r llys Llywelyn wedi ei sychu, ond erbyn edrych nid oedd. Dyna i chwi rai allan or *teapot* wedi i ddwr berwedig ddwyn eu cyffaith. I drink the infusion sometimes as tea, at other times fasting. I have great faith in them. Richards' Dictionary:—

		£	s.	d.
15 books received at 6s. per book	...	£4	10	0
First payment for Prysaddfed book	...	0	3	0
2 books bound at 7/3 per book ...	...	0	14	6
1 ditto bound and interleav'd ...	...	0	9	0
		5	16	6
Carriage ...	...	0	7	0
		5	9	6
Paid father at twice	...	4	8	6
Remains ...	...	£1	1	0

Mi fyddwn chwannog yr amser ymma or flwyddyn o gael tippyn o naws haint y marchogion, ond yr wyf hyd yn hyn yn ddiangol, i Dduw bo'r diolch ag ond odid ir Abad Ffreinig am roddi hanes llys Llywelyn. Rwyn yfed y drwyth ar achos arall hefyd, to rid me of an impetigo which has been a little troublesome to me er yn llencyn.

GALLTVADOG, October 23, 1753.

Dear Brother,—I write with a head as muddy as a pool on ye high road, and as fluctuating as the tide in ye race of ye Head—all things in confusion and hurry. Just returned from Dovey, endeavouring to settle things there. Things are there in better order than the rest, only they riot a little now and then, break our windows and threaten our officers, etc. Staid there from Friday to Monday gathering shells for Lady Lincoln and some money for — **L. to W. CLXXII.**

L. to W. contd. self, etc. If you have idle people about you, gather as many shells as you can of all sorts, and sort them in strong paper bags, and fill boxes with them, and I will tell you how to make the shells your friends by recommending you to great folks. They have odd names here for shell fish, pidyn Iago, bwl bwlas, ... arglwyddes (concha veneris), pig y barcyd, esgid y for forwyn, pen y for forwyn, etc., etc. Gather also all the sea spoils, bron alarch, sponges, white honey comb, skate and dog spawn bags, sea mosses, etc., to throw among the shells for variety. You may say that a man who can spare time to think of such light things is either light himself, or hath no troubles, no, no, I have my hands full, my back loaden, my head on ye rack. To help all, my daughter Jane is very ill in a quincy on ye point of death, my daughter Elin on ye point of marrying. I want no more cousins from North Wales. I shall be a nation myself here by and by. Lewis is in school and John begins to speak, and I hope the girl will recover. Tell my father I shall write to him soon. I want time to write a long letter, and to give some comfortable news, which I hope to do by and by. Let them electioneer and be d——d ; beth yw i mi? Ni ddown i led fy nhroed i ymladd ag anifeiliaid gwaeth na Theifisieid. My letters directed to me Collector of Aberdovey, to be left at ye custom house there, will come free, but directed to be left at ye post office in Aberystwyth or Galltvadog, must be paid for, so must send you franks for money is dear. A geir dim oddiyna? A oes yna ddim ymenyn am bris yn y byd? Mae ef yma yn costi 4d. a 4½d. y pwys heb fawr o hono. Och na yrrech beth yma am bris gweddol sef 3½d. Mae Iarll Powys gwedi addo cymeryd Gronow yn ei fynwes (i.e., in his care), h.y., yn ei gare, and I hope to see him a bishop. At the same time that the Earl was my *supplicant*, (h.y., yn crefu gennif *rywbeth*), my brother Dick took it in his head, upon news of Tom Owen's death, to petition him for Gronow, without ye least acquaintance with the Earl, imagining, I suppose, that as I had private visits from his Lordship he would refuse me nothing. The petition was indiscreet, for it was not well timed, and besides I knew he had promisd Mr. Bodvel all in that district that he could come at. However, the Earl was so complaisant as to send a servant with a letter in answer to my brother, that if he and I would desire it, or if it was our pleasure, he would take Gronwy into his hands; and a few days ago I had a letter from y^e *Iarll* about business, where he renews the same offer. He and the Countess had promisd me their interest before, and now he has had ye opportunity of making two handles of his promise against one promise of mine, which was not fair, a dyna hanes yr addewid. There are some things a going on, not to be mentiond to ye brawd Rhisiart na brawd yn y byd, na gwraig na phlant, and *that* hath occasiond the above imprudent petition by ill-judging of things by outsides. Mae'r brawd yn meddwl mai fal pobl fychain yw pobl fawr, nage, nage. They have their times and seasons, and like ye old oracles have their particular priests, who they will answer and none other. God be thankd for all his blessings yn codi'r anghenus o'r dommen, a'i osod *uwch ben* pendefigion ei bobl. Mae'r byd yn galw arnaf oddiwrth y pappir yma, felly nos dawch. *Eich brawd ffwdanus* L. to W. contd.

Lewis Morris.

24 Oct. Since I wrote ye above letter my poor little girl died, and is to be buried a Friday. It was too late before I knew her distemper, and Dr. James's fever powder was administered to no effect, which I believe would have saved her life if timely applyed, for it gave her great relief when it was given. Her mother is very disconsolate, being extream fond of her.

CAER GYBI YM MON, Hydref 30, 1753.

Anwyl Frawd,—Wawch! Dyma ddau lythyr oddiwrth ym mrawd Rhisiart. Mae'n rhywyr mynd yn y cyd a hwynt i'w hatteb, ond cyn gwneuthur hynny gweddus fyddai ddatgan *fy niolchgarwch* am danynt, a hynny wyf yn ei yspysu i chwi o ewyllys gwaed fy nghalon. Ag am yr ebystol cyntaf roeddwn yn dechreu llygadrythu o'm hamgylch am lythyr Agrippa i wybod pa beth oedd ynddo oedd mor werthfawr; ammeu'r post offis yn ddigon diachos, ond y bore ddoe rhyddhaodd *yr ail* fi o'm cythrwfl, a diau y baswn yn atteb ddoe (o ran bod yn rhy'wyr cael y gwraidd iw dodi yn y ddaear) oni bai fy mod yn dra ffwdanus yn tynnu allan ddeputation newydd, etc., iw gyrru i Gaerlleon at fy new patentee, who had writ for me to come and meet him there, ond nid oeddwn yn leicco mor daith oll, gormod blinder a chost. Gwyddel o'r gwr, car o W. to R. CLXXIII.

W. to R. contd.

hirbell i Iarll Powys, yr hwn a gâdd y lle iddo. Wala bellach am y gwraidd ar hadau a'r ffrwytha'. Gan fod yn rhyngu bodd i Gornel Agrippa fod cymhelled allan o'i hwyl a thaflu cymaint oi werthfawr olud am ychydig wreiddiach, ag i Wilym Parri yntau fod gan fwyned a gyrru am ychydig hadau dieithr cymhelled o ffordd a Siamaica, ie, a chnau cashew hefyd: y ffordd ar modd iw caffael ymma sydd beth iw ddwys ystyried. Gresyn na fai yma hanner dwsing o'ch esgobion chwi yna, i ddodi eu penna ynghyd, deg i un na ddeuant i hyd i rywffordd neu gilydd (o hyn ir Nadolig) iw cludo i Wynedd. Ond gan nad oes yma ond un benglog a honno, e ŵyr dynnion, yn wâg erchyll, nid oes ond cymryd a geffir, well then it is resolved *nem. con.* that you'll be so good as to get a little box made that will just contain the sundry articles above, and have them neatly pack'd up in it; the tulips and narcissus may be loose, so may the anemonies for the sake of stowage, ag oni bai eich bod chwi yn drafferthus, byddai da iawn gennyf gael tippyn o hadau o'r sioppau yna, nid amgen: 1 ounce of carrots, ½ ounce of onions, 2d. worth of Oriental mallow, 2d. worth of lavateras, 2d. worth ketmia vessicaria, 2d. worth of carnation seed, 2d. finochia, 2d. carthamus or bastard saffron, 2d. worth fraxinella's, 2d. worth American nightshade or Virginia poke, 2d. worth helianthemums, 2d. worth cassida or skull cap, 2d. worth various sun flowers, 2d. worth various sweet sultans and bottles, 2d. worth beech mast. Pray let them be new seed, they are not all to be had but in some of the best seed shops, ni wiw mynd i fwy nag un lle iw ceisio, tippyn o fox hir gwr (i.e.) long square and shallow, hwnnw a fydd hawsa' ei garrio yma. Please to direct for W. M. at Holyhead to the care of Mr. Charles Goodwin, grocer, in Chester, and send it by some of the Chester waggons, a dyna ben am hynny. Wala, dymma hi'n nos Calan gauaf newydd, ond i wenwyn goelcerth ym Mon, dilyn yr hen ffordd a wnant yma. Ymhell y bwyf os gwn i, pa beth i yrru i chwi a fai deilwng iw argraphu, ni welsoch i erioed benbwl o ddyn dylach na mi, yn enwedig i gychwyn ryw orchwyl. Ni chlywafi ddim son am Oronwy, ni cha'd byth ddaioni o hono er pan aeth i Walton, tlodi a ddigymydd oreu a'r awen. Na soniai am Bowys nag am fawr ddim arall wrth y Llew or deheu, ni feddaf yr un ffrancod, ag ni yrr yntau r'un i mi, felly rhaid cadw'r gerdd yn y gôd. Gobeitho y ceidw Duw ef yn ddiangol rhag cyrch ei elynion; anifir iawn debygwn i, o'r byd y mae yn ei fwynhau ymhlith y fath haflug. No consideration of a temporal nature would ever induce me to intangle my self in such manner; he was cut out for it, though no doubt on't he flatters himself that he will be able one time or other to live in quietness and ease. Ofid och o fyrred, ie, freued iw einioes dyn, and how often we see people in the midst of their career to that phantom called earthly happiness, snatched off! The impetigo is a kind of ringworm, yn fynych o ddeutu bôn y glust ag ar hyd y gwddf a chammedd breichiau poblach. Nis gwn i beth i feddwl or lecsiwn front honno, mae lle i ofni'r mae'r Plas Newydd a fydd drecha. Bu'r gwr hwnnw yma'r dyddiau diwaetha ag yr oedd yn ei ganlyn ddwsing o ysgwieriaid. Oni bai'r Esgob ni fyddai siawns yn y byd i Fodorgan, mae haid o bersoniaid ym Mon; nid yw *un* yn prisio par faint o arian a warria, ar *llall* yntau yn caru'r geiniog fal y cara cardottyn ei gwd. Bernwch erbyn hynny par sut a fydd. Digrif y mae'r Belam yn trin y boblach yna sydd yn crefu am leoedd. Daccw dân wedi torri allan yn Lerpwl, fe roddir cynnig ar droi allan fy hen batron, Mr. Salusbury (Brereton gynt), os felly, rhaid fydd mynd yno i daro yn ei blaid ag i roi carreg ar y ffagl. Os rhwydd-deb a gewch gyd a'r mine adventures yna moeswch dippyn or hanes. W. to R. contd.

Aie'r gysp, na bo'nd ei grybwyll, oedd yn eich pen pan angofiasoch lythyr Corn Agrippa, a minnau'n meddwl mai ymhennau defaid a cheffylau y byddai'r pryf direidus hwnnw yn magu? Ceisiwch ei ymlid oddiyno gyntaf y galloch cyn iddo fanu, ag yno bydd anodd ei yrru ymaith pan warrioch bryf du hir, cymalog, ffyrnigwyllt, chwannog i godi ei gynffon ar ei gefn, chwi ellwch dyngu mai hwnnw ydyw fo, lleddwch o yn union deg rhag iddo ddychwelyd iw hen letty. Mae'n ddrwg erchyll gennyf fod yr hurthgan accw o lanc wedi mynd i gymaint cost i brynnu gwreiddiach oblegid 'rwyn ofni na thalent mor llawer, maent yn rhy rad i fod yn rhai gwychion, but query; ni feddaf ddim francs i sgrifenu at y gwr i ddiolch iddo, mal y gwnewch chwi hynny drostai da chwithau. Roedd y nhad yn iach y dydd arall, daccw fy chwaer Davies wedi mynd yno iw ymweled er doe. 'Rym ni

W. to R. contd.

yma oll yn iach, mawl ir Goruchaf Dduw. Bydded iddo eich diwallu a phob daioni, a byddwch wych. *Eich carediccaf frawd*
William Morris.

P.S.—Ddydd Calan gauaf. Ni chofiais ddywedyd y talwn i yr gost, yr hon a syrthiodd ag a syrth ar y matterion yno gyd a diolchiadau lonaid sach.

HOLYHEAD, 2nd November, 1753.

W. to R. CLXXIV.

Dear Brother,—I wrote to you per last post to which I refer, but I forgot therein to desire of you to wait of *Mr. John Ellis*, merchant, in Lawrence Lane, Cheapside, with my compliments, and to let him know that I have had Mr. Meyrick's commands concerning sea plants, but as I don't pretend to any extra knowledge in that article, it would be ridiculous in me to send him what would be of no account, therefore it would be necessary he should send me some specimens as he proposed to brother Lewis, and a small glass to view them with. I have engaged our oyster drudgers to procure me all the sea plants they can meet with in deep water, but they have brought me nothing hitherto worth notice. I have borrowd Dilenius's History of Mosses to enable me to make some little progress in that study. If Mr. Ellis thinks proper to send me specimens, there will be a good opportunity to have them in the box with the garden roots, etc., and if he has any curious seeds or roots that may be managed without a greenhouse, should be glad of a few. When I can pick up any sea plants, shall observe the directions given in Mr. Meyrick's letter. I hear Mr Putland quits Bodorgan on Saturday or Monday.

Gwaed swllt, os bydd modd yn y byd piciwch hyd at dŷ'r gwr accw a dangoswch iddo y rhan Seisnig or llythyr hwn. Mae'r gwr yn dra chywraint yn mynd i roddi allan lyfr o'r môr blanhigion au lluniau, etc. ; fe addawodd yrru imi hadau gwchion am rai, ond ffitiach iddo fo ddechreu ynghyntaf. Hen ffrind ydyw a'r Llew, ag yr wyf innau yn gydnabyddus ag ef er's llawer blwyddyn, gwr o Ddulun a char i'r wraig o Fodorgan. Fe ddywedodd wrth y Llew y gyrrai ef i'm *ddrych* yn rhodd ; pwy ai gwrthodai ? Mae o wedi dyfeisio un o'i ben ei hun sydd well nag yr un or rhai ydoedd or blaen, ond nid wyfi yn disgwyl ond un cyffredin. Duw a fyddo gyda chwi. *Eich caredigawl frawd,* *William Morris.*

P.S.—Nid y gysp oedd yn y mhen i eithr rhyw gynddaredd neu wallgofiad yn deilliaw oddiwrth—ni wn i pa beth. Wala hai, dyma lythyr hir or diwedd oddiwrth Lewelyn or 23/24th ulto., a hanes bod ei lodes fechan wedi marw—galar mawr! Rhaid mynd i hel cregyn i ryw Arglwyddes. Dim newydd a dal ddraen crin. Adieu. W. to R. contd.

Yr eiddoch mal or blaen, *W. M.*

CAERGYBI, 19th November, 1753.

Anwyl Frawd,—Nid oes achos nac ystyr i mi sgrifennu attoch yr awron, ond yn unig i ddiolch i chwi yn dra mawr am y drafferth a gymerasoch efo'r boccys ai gynhwysiad. Yn ddiau yr oeddwn yn dechreu ymofidiaw am glywed ei hanes, gyrraswn i Gaerlleon iw groesawu. Gwrda Ellis am yrru imi hadau a rhai odiaethol ydynt yn ddiamau, a gwrda yn sicr a fase pei cawsid y drych. Druan gwr o'r Barri yntau am gymeryd trafferth i brynnu hada' ag am roddi cnau, etc., i bobl. Os byddir byw ag iach yr hâf nesa mi ddanghosaf i chwi flodau (os dowch yma) na welsoch mo'u bath Ynghent nag yng Ngwent, etc. Echdoe y cawswn lythyr Llew a hanes fod Nelly wedi priodws eich namesake* ag yn wir da iawn or newydd. Gwyn ei fyd na bai'r llall wedi gwneuthur cystal; mae nhw'n son am yrru iw nhol hi, yno bydd raid i Wilym ymorol am benaethes ar ei dy, nid hwyrach eich bod yn gryn Ddewin. Doe neu echdoe y daeth y nith Marged Owain o Bentre Eirianell, roedd ynhad yn rhwydd iachus. Y boreu heddyw y cychwynnodd adref ag efo hi'r gini—gorphen tal am y geirlyfrau. W. to R. CLXXV.

Ni chaf mor amser i helaethu yr awron, rhaid a mynd efo rhyw ferchettos i weled coed orains yn tyfu mewn llong o Spaen a yrrodd y gwynt ir borth yma. Mi sgrifenaf at Oronwy y post nesaf, i wybod a ydyw wedi ei lygatynu ai peidiaw. Duw yn eich cylch.

Eich caredigawl frawd, *William Morris.*

P.S.—Talaf y 4s. 4d. i nhad yn siwr.

GALLTVADOG, Nov. 26th, 1753.

Dear Brother,—I received yours of ye fifth but have been in such a hurry ever since that I could not answer it, and now am but just out of a fit of the hardest labour I ever had in answering an attack of 18 persons against my character and reputation, who had swore against me. There is no villainy but what they have attempted and will still; but God hath been hitherto my support L. to W. CLXXVI.

* Richard Morris of Mathafarn.

L. to W. contd.

and hath defeated them. I shall not know the event of this affair this week yet, but hope the devil shall not prevail. Saturday night arrived here another detachment of ye Welsh Fusiliers to protect me, which hath much daunted my enemies. You never saw or heard of madder work than there is here. The war formerly in Flanders was but a fool to it. I do assure you a veteran soldier told me to-day that the Highland rebels were honest people in comparison to these, and he had been among them long. But who would not fight for ye finest mine in Europe? That mine is now a surprizing prospect, and is like to improve. My wife went yesterday to bring home my daughter Elin with her husband to Mathafarn, and againt all persuasions the heads of two women joined to take ye most rainy day ever since ye great frost. Lewis is my bedfellow and prattles like a parrott, and John begins to gabble, — the diversion of old age. Gwae finnau, dros hanner can mlwydd, ag un arall yn dyfod mi wrantaf—ag wyrion hefyd, hynach, hynach. Pa bryd y ceir llonydd gan y byd, fal y byddai'r hen bobl gynt yn cael rhoi eu pennau i lawr mewn heddwch i ganu cywydd gan dant? Mi glowaf swn mawr yna rhwng yr electionwyr—ant rhagddynt a gadawant y gweiniaid yn llonydd. Duw wnel fod Gronwy'n fyw, ni chlywais air oddiwrtho ers dau fis. Cefais lythyr oddiwrth fy nhad yn ddiweddar, mi a'i hattebaf. Cefais hen MSS. Cywyddau dieithr a fu yn Mathafarn gynt, ond nid oes amser i'w ddarllen. Sad, stormy weather here, rain and wind, a'r gwair a'r gwellt yn fyr. Dyma hi'n llawer o'r nos ag yn oer. Service to Mr. Ellis and blessing to Peggy. Nelly and her husband talk of coming to Anglesey in ye winter, they love bad weather. Jack Morgan is one of my captains in ye mine, a worthy honest fellow, that was with [me] all the time in London, and his brother David is at Portsmouth along with the ship that he and Jack are partners in with Catterel, and I believe are bound to Dublin. They have had a good fishery at Aberystwyth. Herrings sold at 21s. a barrel there, but few to be had for money. They have 25s. or 26s. in Ireland. I expect ye Captain of ye soldiers to dine here to-morrow. I am lame and cannot wear a boot to go to him—nid y gout (govyt) ddim, nage. God be with you and yours. *I am your affectionate brother*, *L.M.*

CLXXVI

GALLTVADOG, Dec. 1st., 1753.

L. to W. CLXXVII.

Dear Brother,—I have yours of ye 17th ulto. which I begin to answer because it is Saturday night, and all other business over till to-morrow. My wife is returned from Mathafarn, and praises the place much, and the neighbourhood, pobl ddiniweidtiach a mwy cymdogol na Sir Aberteifi. I have applyd for a lease for R.M. for Mathafarn in Syr W. W's family after the most prudent manner I could. If we fail there is no remedy. I have not heard from Gronwy this two months, I am afraid he is dead. Wyth galwyn a brynasoch o ymenyn am 5s. 8d., ceisiwch 8 neu 10 etto os cewch ef; a deugant neu drichant o bwysau o faccwn am 3d. y pwys. Fe ddaw cwch neu long yn rhwym i Ddyfi neu Aberystwyth heibio yna ryw dro cyn y gwanwyn llwm. Dyna i chwi rai ffrancod. I am glad to hear father is well, and hope he'll continue so while nature allows it. My brother Dick tells me he guesses that you are about taking a woman unto you. I dont doubt but you will weigh the thing well, but weigh it as well as you can, you have a thousand to one against you: ten thousand I think Solomon said, and not a woman amongst them all—all foolish or obstinate, or had some imperfection or other. Strange that the finest creature in ye universe should be so imperfect! But we must be dabbling with them, and nature requires it; perhaps nature intended them imperfect. Quaere, ask Mr. Ellis, he knows I suppose. Women have taught me patience and humility, and teach me daily. Those are fools that advise us to beware of them entirely; we may as well beware of our hands and feet which we cannot be without. My son Lewis gives his service to his cousin Robin, mae ef yn ei gôt ai *fridys* ers llawer dydd, and is a very tractable boy, and Jack is as fierce as a tyger —an odd contrast.

Since I wrote the other side, I have letters from London that we have given our enemies another fall this term, and drove them off the walls again till next term, when no doubt they will make another attempt upon us. Some of our greatest managers above are my enemies also, which is a sad situation, but they could not help giving it under their hands by last post, that I had very great things, in drawing myself ye affidavits of 16 men, and so much

L. to W. contd.

to y[e] purpose as to defeat our opponents. This brings into my mind a saying which Mr. Addison puts into y[e] mouth of Cato: "The Gods in bounty work up storms about us that give mankind occasion to exert virtues, which shun the day and lie conceald in y[e] smooth seasons and the calms of life." I have no time to add more in this, my next will be more calm. I am now busy in quartering y[e] soldiers in proper places. *Your brother*, *L.M.*

W. to R. CLXXVIII.

HOLYHEAD, 8th December, 1753.

Dear Brother,—I writ you two lines on the receipt of yours of the 15 ulto., and did then intend answering in full and ample manner the said letter long before this time, but an unseen accident prevented me. A friend of mine had his ship sunk in this harbour in a violent storm on the 27 ult. laden with wine and fruit, etc. Since that very day I haven't had an hour hardly to spare, Sunday not excepted. We have but just finish'd store-housing, etc., of the cargo which is large and valuable, bellach gwiliwch atto. Ond ynghynta man, llyma yr goflwch hirgwr wedi dyfod im gafael ag nid difalch wyf or hyn oedd ynddaw. Nid oes gennyf ond diolch yn fawr i chwi bod ag un am yr amryw bethau ar drafferth a gawsoch. Heddyw y gyrrais y Bibl i Lanerchmedd efo Phegi Morris oedd yn mynd i edrych am ei thaid; mi berais iddi ymofyn am y cones. Mae rhai pines yn tyfu yn fy ngardd i, ni wn i a wnant hwylbrenni ir llongau rhyfel ai peidiaw. Rwyn ofni fod rhywbeth gwedi llygadtynnu Goronwy, mi sgrifenais atto on receipt of yours iw symbylu, ond dim atteb nid oes. Dyma lythyr heddyw oddiwrth y Llew mawr yn achwyn yntau na chawsai linell oddiwrtho ers deufis; ond ydyw resyndod mawr fod dyn a ga'dd y fath dalent gan ei Greawdr yn ei chuddio mewn succan. You'll begin to stare at this, ond ysywaeth mae'r peth rwy'n ofni (yn ddistaw rwy'n dywedyd) yn rhy wir, Duw a edrycho yn drugarog ar ein gwendidau, onid ydyw hefyd yn erchyll na wyr dyn par sut i gymeryd neb yw fynwes gan anhawsed adnabod plant dynion! Fe ddywedir fod heintiau ar ein meddyliau gystal ag ar ein cyrph, os felly nid hwyrach y daw'r bardd etto atto ei hun, na chymerwch arnoch wrth neb glywed o honoch na siw na miw ynghylch diotta'r dyn. Ni wybuum i erioed eich bod yn gregynwr, gallech gael digon o gregyn Mon, ond nid oes yma yr un a dal ei chodi oddiar y maes, ond yn unig i lenwi i fynu'r gwaith mewn grotto,—all common shells every one of them. Ni cheir dim craff o honynt dan y Gwanwyn. Ie, mi wranta cadw Hen Nadolig a wna llawer ym Mon, a phwy a eill weled bai ar y gwerinos tra bo'r rhai ai geilw eu hunain yn foneddigion yn dangos iddynt siamplau drwg? Hiliogaeth Iago. Gresyn na bai'r adventurers yna yn gwerthu eu rhan o Geredigion. Dyma lythyr oddiwrth y Llew or 26 yn dywedyd fod deunaw wedi tyngu iw erbyn, Duw Goruchaf ai hymddiffyno rhagddynt. I shudder at the thoughts of 'em. I find he has got another detachment of soldiers to protect him; but God alone must do it. Ydyw Haman Befast ddim car i Haman, a fynai ddrygu'r Iuddewon yn amser Ester? Wrth gofio mi glywaf fod yr Iuddewon wedi colli maes yna er mawr wradwydd ir B—m. Ymhle maer Biblau bellach? Daccw Mr. Ellis fyth yn y Werddon yn ymofyn iechyd. Duw ai rhoddo iddo. Par ddelw sydd ar Wdwart? a phar sut a fu rhyngddo ar Gwyddhelod cynffonnog? Gorchmynnwch fi atto. Ry'ch yn ymofyn hanes y ddau Owen Parry. Mae'r crupl yn y nef gobeitho ers talm byd, felly ni waeth i chwi faddeu iddo na pheidiaw, ag am yr ewythr mae yn dilyn yr hen drâd cowperiaeth o blas y gwrda bwygilydd, ai was yw ganlyn—gronyn o hen ddyn a cheden o wallt llwyd ganddaw, yn briod a hen grimpan o wrechyn foneddigaidd, yn byw gerllaw'r Traeth Coch yn o daclus arnynt. Dyma'r cefnder Rhobart ab William Morris newydd briodi rhyw wraig weddw rhwydd oludog. Dynan go chwannog ir brecci, yr oedd yn amaeth aradr ym Modeon ers llawer blwyddyn a chwedi tyrru tippyn dan ei ewin. Prin yr ydwyf yn medru dal fy ngafael yn y pin sgrifennu gan oered yr hin. Tippyn o lythyr gynta galloch, da chwithau. Pawb yma'n iach, mawl ir Goruchaf Dduw. Byddwch wych. *Eich carediccaf frawd, William Morris.*

W. to R. contd.

P.S.—Roedd y petheuau yn y box mewn purion trefn. Os digwydd i chwi daro wrth Ellis dywedwch iddo fy mod yn diolch yn fawr iddo. Mae'r Llew yn son am anfon ei ferch Marged adref. Pa beth a wneir am gadw wraig ty? Rhaid ymorol bellach am ymgeledd cymwys. Beth meddwch chwi? Yn wir, nid oes dim trefn ar dy annedd heb wreigan. Ond och fi, ha wr fab, dyma henaint yn dechreu ymrithio ymhob man. Daccw mrawd Rhisiart

W. to R. contd.

wedi ei ddeg a deugain, a minnau yn nesaf atto. Wala hai, rhaid bodloni, nid oes modd i adnewyddu'r ieuenctid. Daccw'r Llew yn ymroi i fanu, mae'r wraig debygwn wedi dechreu chwyddo, 'roedd hi'r dydd arall wedi mynd i anfon Ellin ai gwr i Fathafarn, mae o'n ddedwydd weled y lodes benffol honno wedi priodi. Oni bai fi, nis gwn i pa beth a ddaeth o honi pan ydoedd ym Mon. Par sut y mae Meirian? Ydych chwi wedi settlio yn y ty newydd efo'r hen wrechyn honno; tippyn oi hanes?

GALLTVADOG, December 14th, 1753.

L. to W. CLXXIX.

Dear Brother,—I find it necessary to provide against next term some affidavits from the County of Anglesey, to guard against some malignant and spiteful affidavits that have been filed against me last Term, in order to throw dirt on my character, and to insinuate that I was but of a mean family and very little or no fortune, and not to be trusted with such a great concern as the mine in dispute, with abundance of venomous stuff of that kind; praying that a new Receiver might be appointed, and that I might be called to an account. The chief part of their requests were denied by ye Court, but I suspect they will make a fresh attack the first day of next Term by filing more affidavits to ye same purpose, for they now know what answers I have sent from hence to their last attack, and that those are not from my native country. Therefore I have sent the inclosed draughts of affidavits which I presume as to your parts and brother-in-law you will not scruple to make. And as to that of Richard Owen, Lewis Williams, and Hugh Roberts, you may take some out of that into yours if you have a mind, or alter them and vary them as you please. If Mr. L. Lloyd hath a commission to take affidavits in ye Exchequer it will save you a great deal of trouble. Neither he, nor whoever is commissioner, is to know the contents of the affidavit, and I do not care that any noise is made about ye affair, therefore perhaps it may not be very proper to make use of Richard Owen; you best know his inclinations, whether he is friendly and trusty. If you get two or three, or half a dozen more to speak to the same or any part of these affidavits it would be better still, but they should be persons that can write, for a marked affidavit is of very little weight, and they should be particular friends that will not babble, for they may think in Anglesey there is more in it than there is, and make some broad lye of it. I dare say if you were near my old friend Mr. Lewis Owen, of Gallgo, he would not refuse. Can Robert Jones of Tywridyn write? Two or three clergymen would sound well, and an esquire—Hugh Jones perhaps. Pray don't lose time about this affair, for the affidavits ought to be returned me here about ye middle of next month, and they must be in London with the Solicitor of the Treasury by ye 19th or 20th at furthest to be copied, and briefs drawn to Council against ye first day of Term. If you cannot get more than these two affidavits let me have them without loss of time that I may strengthen my forces here in proportion. This is all I have time to write at present. I need not tell you that they are to be drawn on double sixpenny, and if there is none to be got, treble sixpenny will do, and the heading must be exactly as that of Richard Owen, etc. Let no figures or contractions be made use of in ye body of an affidavit. *I am, your affectionate brother,* *Lewis Morris.*

L. to W. contd.

Mae'n debyg na fyddai wiw gofyn i Mr. Ellis. Query.

If you are likely to get a good many, and some people of consequence, don't spare ye expence of sending a man on foot here if it draws near ye time above mentioned, for the post is a great while a coming, sometimes a fortnight.

GALLTVADOG, December 24, 1753.

L. to W. CLXXX.

Dear Brother,—I received yours of ye 14th yesterday, and am glad you are all well in health, a peculiar happiness, if a man hath sense to thank God for it. Nag oes dim i son am dano o waith Dafydd ap Gwilym yn llyfr Mathafarn. Dyma dywydd blin iawn—glaw a niwl anfeidrol ers pythewnos. Newydd glowed oddiwrth Oronwy; mae'n canu etto, ac yn gwneud dychmygion. Am lai na charrai ysgrifennwn at Mr. Hamage ynghylch y postage, ond prin y tal i son am dano; fe allai mai codi mwy o gythraul a wnae hynny, onide mi a'i gwnawn. Pam nad a'r hen chwilcath i'r byd arall fal y cawn i ddyfod yna yn ei le i ddial fy llid ar chwiwgwn fal Brisco ag eraill? Melus yw dial. Ple mae'r chwilcath? Ni chlywai son am ei drwg na'i da. I hope you have received my letter about ye affidavits; a few will do, but they ought to be here as soon as possible, for they should be in London four days before the Term.

L. to W. contd.

If upon receipt of this you find you cannot get them ready time. enough to be sent here you may direct them to Thomas Francis, Esquire, Assistant Solicitor of y[e] Treasury, at his Chambers in Lincoln's Inn, London, or to John Sharpe, Esq., Solicitor to y[e] Treasury at his Chambers in Lincoln's Inn, and you need not mention anything in the letter inclosing them but that you were desired to send such affidavits. Dim son am frawd, etc., and send me here copies of what you send. Perhaps you may add to or diminish from y[e] draughts sent; the whole thing wanted is to corroborate other affidavits made here about my character and circumstances, for after so many detractions and degradings, the Court requires to be well satisfied that things are not so. Aberdovey cleared me last year above £140, plus Cwmbwa £50, plus mines ditto £10, plus Lord Lincoln's salary £20, plus Anglesey £24, plus Penbryn and Tanycastell and Galltvadog clear £26, which is £270, not to mention Esgair y Mwyn, which must be excluded at present. Now if there could be inserted in one of the Anglesey affidavits a clause to that purpose it would not be amiss in these, or the like words, "and these deponents say, etc., and that the said Lewis Morris as these deponents verily believe, hath an yearly income of some hundred pounds a year, besides a very plentiful fortune in money and other effects." I have certainly very hard labour of it to carry things on as well as I have done, and my hands are still full day and night, so that you would be surprised how I have time to write such a long letter as this, but I must own my head is almost giddy, and I can write no more at present but that *I am your affectionate brother*

*Lewis Morris.**

GARTREF, Nos Calan, 1754, cyn codi haul.

W. to R. CLXXXI.

Anwyl Frawd Rhisiart,—Mae yna mi wranta ddau neu dri o lythyrau o'r eiddof heb eu hatteb eisioes, ond etto er hyn rhaid torri'r cosi yma. Ag yng nghynta man rhaid dywedyd i chwi ein bod ni i gyd yn iach yn y fangre hon. Roedd y nhad ai deulu yn iach o fewn y tridie neu bedwar; bu Ruffydd Davydd yma yn dwyn eu flynyddawl anrheg o benwaig cochion, math ar glera, cael dwynos o hanesion gan Ruffydd o'r hen gartref. Mi gefais y

*This letter was printed by Myrddin Fardd in "Adgof uwch Anghof," 1883, and it is here re-produced with his consent.

dydd arall lythyr oddiwrth Oronwy. Nid cynrhwg ond odid y chwedl a glywswn ynghylch y diotta, ag nid hwyrach cystal ag y dymunai ddyn ei fod, chwedl Simwnt Fychan yn araith Wgawn. Pa wedd bynnag, mae'r brawd hybarch yn dywedyd iddo anfon *Cowydd y Farn* a nodau arno, at y brawd Llew (a chyd ag efo briodasgerdd ir wraig o Fathafarn), a dyna'r fan lle'i *trig* mae'n debyg yn ddigon o hyd gan fod y Llew yn cael digon o waith iw ymddiffyn ei hun, rhag cyrch a brad y Teifisiaid, y rhai 'e weddai sydd mor gythreulig a bod yn gorfod arno yrru i Fon am gynhorthwy, a dymma finnau, yn ddistaw rwy'n dywedyd, yn gwneuthur fy ngorau glas ar siommi'r haflug ddigydwybod! Yn lle gyrru hwn ym'ith dduw Calan, ni che's amser yw orphen tan heno sef y 4dd o Ionawr (sef yr Hen Nos Nadolig). Dymma'r gwerinos sef llawer o honynt yn ymroi i gadw'r hen wiliau, a phwy eill farnu gan fod rhai boneddigion yn dangos y ffordd iddynt; fe ddywedir fod ysgwier or gymdogaeth yma wedi erchi a gwneuthur iw weinidogion aredig, etc., ar ddydd Nadolig diwaetha. A rare chap, onte? Os caf bob peth wrth fy modd rwy'n amcanu myned tua Phentre'r Eirianell y fory i ymweled ar hendad, etc. Pam y dywedach'i wrth y Llew fod Gwilym y'mynd i ymgymharu? Nid oes yma ddim tebyg ir peth. Camgymeriad mawr anferth ysywaeth. Duw oi anfeidrawl drugaredd a warchotto drosoch a'r eiddoch. W. to R. contd.

Eich caredigawl frawd, *William Morris.*

P.S.—Dyma hi dranoeth yn ddryghin fawr ag yn enbyd i ddynan trwm musgrell fynd i farchawcca, felly rhaid gorphwys tan drennydd. Dyma lythyr oddiwrth Lewelyn, pob peth yno yn rhesymol. Wfft ir Teifisiaid am anudonedd. Duw ai cadwo rhagddynt. *W.M.*

GALLTVADOG, Jan. 11th, 1754.

Dear Brother,—I received last post three affidavits, which are very well, and if more go up it is very well—they will be too late to come here, for these are rather of ye latest. We are all well, I thank God, and I hope to conquer all my enemies, (Efnys yn Gymraeg). I am excessive busy this post. So adieu. *L. M.* L. to W. CLXXXII.

GARTREF, 13 Ionawr, 1754.

Dear Brother,—Ar fy nyfodiad adref dydd arall o Bentre Eirianell mi drewais wrth lythyr a sgrifennasechi'r llynedd, yr hwn 'e weddai a ddaetha' gyd a Haman eich anwyl gyfaill, nid W. to R. CLXXXIII.

W. to R. contd.

collector or Belfast, ond customer debygwn ydyw. Mi a fuaswn yn ymweled a nhad ag yn ceisiaw rhyw hen gymdogion i wneuthur affidavits o blaid y Llew mawr o Sir Teifi. Daeth gyd am fi yma berson Gallgo, a Mr. Foulk Jones y trwmpeter gynt, yn awr swyddog yn Nulas, the best violin perhaps in Wales. Cawswn efo rhain noswaith lawen yn yr hen gartref cyn cychwyn. Telyn ein nith Marged Owen, who plays very pretty, and Ffoukyn's violin, the parson, father, myself, etc., yn canu gyda'r tannau. As soon as I had leisure I went to wait of Mr. Haman, and found with him a woman whom he called his wife, but as you had told me that he had parted with her, I began to think the man had borrowed one, but upon further examining into the affair (for I believe he imagined I was suspicious) he and her threw some hints that set my doubts aside. I invited them to a dish of tea and to spend the evening at my house. I asked Parson Ellis, who, with the two gentlemen above mentioned, made a jolly company. But what was most agreeable was the violin, which pleased madam prodigiously, and surprised Mr. Haman very much to meet such musick where he so little expected. He seems to be a good natur'd man and very fond of her. We were all invited by him to his lodgings next day but could not wait of him but a little while. I think they are not gone by to-day's pacquet. So much for gelyn Fordecai wirion. Gresyn eich bod yn ffaelio a chyttuno ar hen wrechyn honno, a bod gorfod ymadaw; Duw a roddo i chwi gartref wrth eich bodd, nid oes dim trefn heb un. Mae'n dda gennyf glywed fod eich bywioliaeth wrth fodd eich calon. Dylwn innau ddywedyd fy mod felly, ond etto er hyn nis gallaf. Odiaethol gennyf hefyd glywed fod yr Wdward ddiniwed wedi medru trin y Gwyddelod wrth ei fodd. I like the man much, and wish him success. Pei digwyddai i ffrind i chwi ddyfod ffordd yma ond hynny, I should be glad ye would recommend them to the best house in town, viz., Welch's house. It's kept by my mother-in-law and her sister, and is the house where all the lord lieutenants of Ireland put up at, and all the best of the gentry and nobility of both kingdoms that comes this way. The other (for there are but two inns in town) is kept by the daughter of the late Hu. Lloyd alias Thomas Jones, etc. I mention this as it would be most agreeable to me in regard of waiting on any person at his lodgings, for since Lloyd endeavoured to ruin brother Lewis, I never had any intimacy with his family, or seldom go to the house. Dont mistake me—its not self interest. Perhaps my children may have some pickings after these women, but my dependence is upon Providence to do for them ; however, they've no other friends but them here that could do for them should I be called hence, a phwy a wyr fesur ei ddyddiau? This tattle was brought on on my calling to mind that both Mr. Woodward and Mr. Haman put up at Lloyd's, therefore could not enjoy as much of their companies as I could have wished. Mentioning the women above put me in mind of asking you whether Mrs. Wheldon, the surgeon's widow, is ever likely to have any thing from the Cloaths Bill: you mentioned a similar affair of another person that was to come on, pray how was it determin'd? Dyma'r Berson Ellis yn un cawr! Er na bydd o byth ddiffawt, ag ni bu o ers ugain mlynedd, a sedentary life at college did not agree with him ; he was made or cut out for a labourer or mechanic. Llimwst o ddyn esgyrniog. I am glad you compassd that affair of Mathafarn. It was Gwilym that advised y Llew to get it done. Gwych or hanes yr y'ch yn ei roddi o'r Cymrodorion, ag pe yr y'ch yn ei rheoli mal y rheola Belham y Senedd. I should have been of your side of the question, maugre all that your opponents could say to the contrary, for a good room in a convenient part of the city in an Englishman's house is certainly better than an ordinary one in an inconvenient part of the city though in a Welshman's house. That national distinction too much cherished by many is totally laid aside by me. I love an honest worthy man, let him be English, Welch, Irish, Scotch, or whatsoever nation he may be of. The *man* should be distinguished and valued for his good qualities, and not for the country or family he was born of; ac, yn ddistaw bach, rwy'n ofni fod ein cydwladwyr ni gan mwyaf yn fwy diddaioni na nemawr rai o'u cymydogion ag yn enwedig ein boneddigion, no public spirit or any benevolent qualities belonging to them, balchder a rhodres a gorwagedd, etc., ymhob cwr. Gobeithio eich bod wedi derbyn cyn hyn waith Gronwy Ddu a'r nodau a berthynynt i'r godidowgwaith hwnw, mae'n addaw trino'r lleill yr un modd. Rwy'n meddwl

W. to R. contd.

imi ddywedyd i chwi gael o honwyf innau labwst o lythyr oddiwrth y Bardd, yn atteb ir swmbwl a yrraswn atto, a fy mod wedi clywed iddo roddi heibiaw ryw gyfeddach, a rhy fynych dramwy i Lerpwl. Yn wir ddiau, da iawn gennyf glywed eich bod wedi trin matterion y Mine Adventure Company cystal. Gobeitho y ca'r Llew weled ei ewyllys ar Waller a Ball, ac y daw'r fargen i ben. Mi yrrais ir Llew y dyddiau diwaetha affidavits deg o wyr cymeradwy—rhai eglwysig, rhai bonedd, etc., a phawb yn tyngu ir cyrs ac ir coed nad oedd gonestach, cywreiniach, diwyttach, cyfoethoccach, synhwyrolach, a gwell ei eirda nag e odd'yma hyd yna. Some of 'em I sent to himself, and others have directed per post to Mr. Francis, Assistant Solicitor of the Treasury. Mae'n debyg na welodd y cyfreithwyr yna erioed rai mor gywraint, oblegid nid llai gwr na Gwilym Tew au tynnasai gan mwyaf oi ben ei hun, heb un o honynt fod yn yr un eiriau au gilydd. Er mwyn dyn sgrifennwch yma gynta galloch a rhoddwch fwya' ag a fedroch o hanes y Llew ai fatterion, ni bydd o'n amser rwan yn son am Gommissioner Vaughan. Pa beth yw'r achos? A pha beth oedd yr achos na soniasoch faint yn y byd ynghylch y Biblau Cymreig yn eich llythyr diweddaf? Fe fyddis yn holi llawer yn eu cylch, a minnau ni fedraf roddi atteb cymwys o eisiau gwybod eu hanes. Roedd Mr. Lew. Owen, Person Llaneugrad, Llanallgo, ag offeiriad Penrhos yn dymuno arnoch, os byddai fodd yn y byd gennych, geisio iddo fagad o honynt iw dri phlwy, ni chadd ond rhy ychydig y tro diwaethaf. Os medrwch wneuthur cymwynas ir plwyfydd hynny lle bu ein hynafiaid gynt yn bwhwman mewn tywyllwch dudew, ar lle mae llawer ou hepil byth mewn anwybodaeth, da fyddai, ie, gweithred enaid yn ddiamau. Gan fod y gwr Eglwysig uchod yn Gymro glân (gwr o Sir Feirion o anedigaeth) yn caru ei wlad ai hiaith, yn brydydd glew iawn, yn awdwr llyfrau da yn erbyn Methodistiaid,* etc., oni fyddai yn weddus ddigon i chwi ei ddewis yn aelod parchus o'n cymdeithas ni y Cymrodorion? A fynnwch i Mr. Ellis yn un arall? Gwr crefyddol deallus, yn caru ei wlad ai iaith, yn gwneuthur cymaint o ddaioni ag a fai bosibl iddo drwy gyhoeddi rhai ag argraphu ar ei gost (draul) ei hun

* Lewis Owen published a book entitled "Yr angenrheidrwydd o ddyfod i'r Eglwys a'r iawn gyflawniad o'r addoliad Sanctaidd yno." Mwythig, 1753.

amrafael fan lyfrau iw rhoddi ymaith yn rhodd ag yn rhad, a hynny bob blwyddyn a elo dros ei ben, ac hefyd, drwy ei fuchedd ai ymarweddiad yn harddu ei ymadroddion ai weinidogaeth. Mae arnaf anferth flys am gael gweled eich rheolau, etc., yn argraphedig. Ymhle mae'r sel fawr? a phwy oedd ar yr union? ai'r Llew ai'r Gwilym? Mae'n debyg y gwyddoch mae gwilym yw enw math ar fôr aderyn, 'rhwn sydd gyffredin amser haf yn y moroedd yma, h.y., o ddechreu Ebrill hyd ddechreu Awst, un ŵy a ddydwa ar graig noeth, ag ar hwnw yr eistedda hyd pan ddeora, yno cymryd ei godwm a wna'r cyw ir dyfnfor a byw yno rhag llaw heb osod ei droed ar dir oddigerth i orphwys ar forgraig; math o'r *pwffingod* ydyw. Mae gennym o'r rheini 3 rhywogaeth, unŵyawg ynt oll, ag yn nhyllau cwning y ddydwa un math. These are what's pickled and collar'd at Beaumaris, and sold to London, etc. It's time for me to leave off, for I dare say you'll be heartily tired by reading thus far, so adieu. A Duw'r heddwch a'r cariad a fyddo gyd a chwi, ac a'ch cadwo yn eich holl ffyrdd. W. to R. contd.

Eich caredigawl frawd, William Morris.

HOLYHEAD, Sunday night, the 20th January, 1754.

Dear Brother,—Mi wranta y byddwch yn rhyfeddu weled dau o lythyrau, na bo'nd i grybwyll, yn dyfod efo eu gilydd oddi yma a chwithau newydd dderbyn llostryddun o bystol y dydd arall. Ond gollwng yn angof a wnaethum beth angenrheidiol iawn, sef dymuno arnoch yrru imi un or Stationers' Almanac for the current year (I mean one with a head piece) computed by you, a dyna i chwi ddau ffrenkyn iw garrio. You need only cut it across in the middle and put a moiety in each ffrank; I wil pay the cost to father. I paid him for the seed, etc., 4s. 6d., ond e wedda nad oedd ond 4s. 4d. yn digwydd. Cês linell neu ddwy ddoe o Alltfadog, dim newydd ond byw mewn gobaith o enill y maes yn y Term yna. Duw a'n cadwo i gyd rhag ein gelynion ysprydol a chorphorol, rhag caffael o honynt y llaw uchaf arnom. Byddwch iach. W. to R. CLXXXIV.

Eich caredigawl frawd, Wm. Morris.

P.S.—Oni welais i yn y newyddion yma fod y Belam fawr yn salaidd iawn? Pa beth os bydd marw ynghanol mwstr yr Esgair? Wawch! Dyma lythyr a dau awdl oddiwrth Oronwy—Priodasgerdd a Marwnad—ond ni chaf mor ennyd iw darllain cyn ir post fynd allan. Duw yn eich cylch.—*W.M.*

[GALLTVADOG], January 31, 1754.

L. to W. CLXXXV.

Dear Brother,—I have yours of the 16th, as also a copy of Captain Hill's affidavit which is very well if it went in time. Twelve pence an oath is what is paid for taking affidavits, and neither more nor less. It is fixd by law for King's Bench, Exchequer, and Common pleas, and it is usual to pay in Chancery 2s. 6d. but they can demand no more than 2s. So pay L. Ll's. 10s. for ye 10 oaths. You want to know about Cwmbwa. The affair depends in Chancery; we had no trial about it, but was advised to suffer judgement at Common Law having no chance to try it in Cardiganshire, and because I had a bill then filed in Chancery, and have filed a cross-bill since—troubles enough of all conscience, and not a friend to help me. O. P. hath been here, a mere boy! Hath a fine wife, etc. Digrif o'r amreliaith. It must be so, as things stand. I foresaw it plain enough and there will hardly be a Commission granted before ye election. Well done Tom Roberts, Hu Roberts, R. Owen, L. Ll., etc. Mr Pelham is recoverd. You see a French war begins in ye East Indies. Ni chlywais i son or blaen am ddwyn Cybi; nag oes yn y llyfr ddim son am dano na *mark* Cymreig yn y byd arno. The Galfrid in it is ye first translation that Galfrid made from ye Welsh, being much shorter than the printed one, but the matter (and sometimes the phrase) much ye same. It is a noble MS. I heard this post from brother R.M., who advises me that the motion did not come on the first day of Term as expected, so it is likely they have dropped it when they saw the strength of our affidavits, which were very bitter and biting, and but what they deserved. I should be extream glad if our affidavits were read in court, for they would expose them with a vengeance. I have not time to tell you of some of my successes here. I [shall] be extream busy, and don't expect a night's easy rest till the month of June, however things will turn out. Dyna fywoliaeth ryfeddol! I have heard nothing from Mathafarn this great while, nor have I my senses about me to think about Peggy—my affairs being at sixes and sevens till I have time to breath.

Your affectionate brother, L.M.

HOLYHEAD, 7th February, 1754, Eira Mawr!

Dear Brother,—Rwy'n awr yn cydnabod eich llythyr or 26 ulto ynghyd a dau hanner almanac prydferth ddigawn. Can diolch am danynt bod ac un, yn enwedig y ddau hanner yn rhodd ac yn rhad. Gerwin o'r *codwm* hwnnw a gawsech ac ir *peswch* yntau syrthio arnoch a chwithau ar lawr eisioes. Its well the imperial sneezing and *oppodeldock* stood your friends, onte ba'sai yn gaeth arnoch; aie mae'n eich bryd fyw yn llawen pan ddel Ierwerth ap Rhisiart Ierwerth yna o Siamaica? Wala, chwi biau'r byd c—ch ynddo chwedl y bobl, rhaid byw yma ar uwd a llaeth. Doe roeddych e wêddai yn cymeryd Sir Rhisiart ich nifer, na bo'nd i grybwyll! Er mwyn dyn, rhoddwch dippyn o'i hanes; mae'n debyg mae rhywogaeth Glyn Llifon ydyw, os e mae'n dwyn arfau Cilmyn Droetu. Mae ym Modorgant ddeiol fawr a wnaethai un Richard Glyn o Lundain (instrument maker, mae'n debyg), rwy'n tybio fod yr hen Feuryg yn dywedyd mai un or bobl uchaf ydoedd. Dyma i chwi lun gwraig Haman. Cloben o ddynes lyfndew, landeg, lawen, lygeitu, ddiddan, rhywbeth tebyg i Wyddeles ynddi, nid yw dàl na bèrr ond rhwydd ddynes, swrn foethus, yn son llawer am ei herlodes o gympas 14 oed, son am Kinsale, ni buasai yno er pan briodws yr Haman. Byw efo'g ewythr y byddai ffordd yna. Hi ddywedodd ei hanes o bant i bentan pei bawn iw gofiaw. What confirm'd me most was that he contradicted her now and then in an ill-natured manner, pe basai fenthyg-wraig, nid felly maen debyg y basai yn ei thrin; cawsai honno ei mawrygu'n fwy. Yn wir mae yn dda gan fy nghalon i glywed fod yr Woodwart ar y ffordd i gael ei dreftadaeth; ni welswn i mo hanes Bouchier yn y papurau. Wawch, dyma lythyr oddiwrth Llewelyn yn dywedyd ei bod hi wedi mynd yn heddwch rhyngddo ar Arglwydd Lisburn, er mawr dristwch i'r Teifisiaid, a pheth oedd mwy fod *Cywydd y Farn* wedi mynd i Lundain a'r nodau (a gatwo pawb!) arno. Ceisiwch ei argraphu gynta galloch, da chwithau. Ce's lythyr mwyn digrif dydd arall oddiwrth ein cydfrawd, Mr. Hwlant, o Gonwy; mae o'n *studiaw* Cymraeg gymmaint ag allo, er mwyn ei wneuthur ei hun yn gyfaddas o fod yn aelod o'r Gymdeithas. Mae'n deusyf ei wasanaeth at y gyfeillach yn fawr iawn, ac yn dra diolchgar am yr anrhydedd a wnaethynt iddaw. Digrif oedd talu'r pwyth i *Ball* ai

W. to R. CLXXXVI.

W. to R. contd.

gydymaith. Rwy'n disgwyl bob dydd lythyr oddiwrth Offeiriad Penrhos, sef Person Gallgo ac Eugrad, a hanes par sawl faint o Fiblau sydd yn eisiau yno fal y gallwyf eich gwneuthur yn gydnabyddus. Dymma rywbeth im galw ymaith, felly byddwch iach, Duw yn eich cylch! *Eich caredigawl frawd, William Morris.*

W. to R. CLXXXVII.

GARTREF, Chwefror 15d, 1754.

Anwyl Frawd,—Mi sgrifennais attoch bwt o lythyr y dydd arall, ni fedrwn ddywedyd i chwi mo neges y Mr. Owen, Person Eugrad, ag Allgo, ac Offeiriad Penrhos Lligwy, cystal ac y dywaid ei lythyr ei hun, a dyna fo i chwi fal y cefais inne, ond ei fod yn dippyn anhymoreiddiach. Roedd y nhad ynteu yn gwaeddi yn groch am rywfaint o Fiblau i ryw rai ydoedd wedi dymuno arno ei ceisiaw. A fydd modd iddo eu caffael? Pam na thâl aelod Anghyttrig am goresbonding member? Par sut y gelwch i lawer o honynt, ai Anghyttrigion yntau Anghyttrigiaid? Gronw a ŵyr. Brysiwch a'r cywydd yna, da chwithe, ie, a'r diplomas, a'r constitutions hefyd, rhag ein caffael yn gelwyddog. Daccw'r Berson Bellis wedi gyrru i Gaerlleon Gawr am Oxford Almanack; a pha beth debygwch chwi a gadd yn ei le ond y Stationers' Almanack, o'r un rhyw am hun i. Gerwinol son y gweithio rwyf y dyddiau yma yn fy ngardd i gael lle i hau'r hadau braf rheini a ge's oddiyno. Mae'r gwraidd yn y llawr er's talm mawr o ddyddiau. Rhowch lythyr gynta galloch. Duw yn eich cylch, pawb yn iach. Cenwch! *Eich caredigawl frawd, William Morris.*

W. to R. CLXXXVIII.

HOLYHEAD, 21st February, 1754.

Dear Brother,—I writ you two letters of late, to which I refer you, chwedl y masnachwyr. Gan ddarfod i Mr. Owen o Brysaddfed y dydd arall ymadaw ar byd hwn, mi dybiais na byddai anghyfaddas imi grybwyll wrth Sir William Owen mae fi ydoedd y water bailiff yma er's cwmpas deuddeng mlynedd, etc. I have therefore writ him the inclos'd letter setting forth a fwyned oedd ei dâd wrthyf yn fy ngwneuthur yn water bailiff a fy mod hyd yn hyn yn cadw'r offis anrhydeddus honno, a fy mod yn gobeithio y byddai wiw ganddo ei rhoddi immi rhagllaw a thrwy hyder ar hynny fy mod wedi gyrru blank deputation, air yn air a hwnnw sydd gennyf o'r eiddo ei dad, os gwela ef yn dda ei seinio, etc. I have likewise mention'd to him that I had been ever since Brother Lewis Morris fixing in Cardigan

Shire (till of late) his father's deputy vice-admiral of the coast, and had done some signal services in securing for him wrecks, and that if he thought proper to grant me a deputation for my late district *or any part of it*, I would do him all the service in my power. Ond nid wyf yn disgwyl dim oddiwrth y matter ymma. Now the case is this: I must beg that you will wait of the baronett and deliver my letter, but first of all to apply to his *gentleman*, and as the fees of my last deputation (to Sir Arthur's gent) was half a guinea, I desire you would pay him the same *provided Sir William doth sign the deputation* herewith inclosed. Os ni wna nid yw ond'ergyd ir gwellt, os gwnâ, minnau a dalaf yr arian i nhâd yn ôl. If you dont care to undertake this affair, perhaps you may think of some friend that's acquainted with the baronett that may do it either in conjunction with you or *per se*. Its odds if our old friend Mr. Hugh Davies of Trecastell be not intimate with him, or at least with his gentleman; put your heads together, perhaps as Prysaddfed is gone that Sir William may not trouble his head about the Anglesey election. Be that as it will, nid oes ond ei dreio fo; os neccy nid oes mor help, ni thal y peth prin i son am dano, I mean the *anchorage*, ond etto er hyn, mae'n fawr gan ddyn weled ryw chwiwgi yn ei gael, a hynny ond odid o eisiau ei ofyn. Whatever expense you may be at on this account, charge it to me, and I will pay it to your order. Na sonniwch wrth y Llew am hyn dros dro, deued a ddelo. Success attend you, a byddwch wŷch. *Eich caredigawl frawd,* W. to R. contd.

William Morris.

CAER GYBI SAINT, 11th of March, 1754.

Dear Brother,—Myfi attebaswn eich dau lythyr or 23 and 28 ulto yn gynt oni bai fy mod yn disgwyl llinell oddiwrthych a hanes Gwyl Ddewi, ond gan na ddaeth dymma attoch'i ryw fath a'r ebystol, ni wn i etto ai hir, yntau byrr, neu gwtta a fydd, wrth fal y ceir defnyddiau ac odfa. Ond gweddus ddigon fyddai yn y fan gynta ddywedyd i chwi pa mor ddiolchgar yw eich brawd Gwil am danynt, y cynta oedd (mi dynga i chwi) yn glamp o lythyr trefnus, yn cynwys llawer o ddiddanwch a newyddion da odiaethol! a'r llall yntau yn cynwys (na bo'nd i grybwyll) bwmp o gomhisiwn i Wilym Tew, a dâl ni wybod pa'r faint hir-oes ir Marchog urddol ai rhoddes, ac ir Hen Frenhin yna, W. to R. CLXXXIX.

W. to R. contd.

ac ir ceryn yna gan Gwilym Parry am fod yn gyfryngwr, ac ir llywydd Mynglwyd am ei osod ar waith. Bellach am attebion. Yn ddiau mae yn dda iawn gennyf weled eich bod wedi gyrru y'mlaen lythyr y Person Owain Gallgo, fal os bydd modd, i roddi tippyn chwaneg o oleuni ir hen gymydogion accw i ganfod y ffordd i'r tragwyddol bebyll. Oes modd i gael yr un o'r Weddi Gyff. a'r Salmau Canu ynghŷd? Bydd cyfleu efo *Biblau* Mr. Ellis, mae iddo fo addewid o laweroedd o honynt. Gresyn eich bod mor drafferthus na cha'ech amser i lywodraethu y Cymrodorion a'u matterion yn iawn. O na bai Oronwy yn agos attoch, neu ryw ddyn arall celfyddgar. Llug-eirian y gelwir y grawn rheini, yn llysieu-lyfr Cybi, oblegid eu bod yn edrych yn brydferth, ond yn dra surion, fal na wyddai'r Hen Frutaniaid i ba beth yr oeddynt yn dda; I think the North Americans calls them hurtle berries or huckle berries, they infuse 'em in rum as we do black cherries; in the North of England they're calld cranberries; in Ireland bogberries. Mae chwaer Dick Morys bwtt ai gwr yn iach yn gorchymun attoch maen debyg. Nid oes bosibl eich bod yn tyngu eich aelodau cartrefol yna bod ac un. Nis gwn i par sut y cadd y Glyn yna yr eryr dû yn unig, arfau Cilmyn Droetu o Lynllifon cyff genedl yr holl Glynniaid yw, 1st argent, an eagle display'd (i.e., spread) with two necks sable; 2d argent, 4 firey ragged stukes (i.e., billets) gules (in some MSS. but 3), the 3rd as the 2d, the 4th as the 1st. Over all upon an escutcheon argent, a man's leg coup'd below the knee sable. Cilmin or Cilmyn lived about the year 843 yn amser Rhodri Mawr ai dad Merfyn Frych. Digrif anial o'r advertisements yna ynghylch y Cymrodorion yn y papurau newydd, a digrifach fyddai gael ambell un o rheini mewn ffranc; mae yna ddigon o fembers. Diolch am gyfieithiad Goronwy. Llawer un ond odid a feia ar y gair grann. Gwŷch y trinasoch y Mine Adventures, er mawr dristwch ir Bowel a Ball. Ce's echdoe lythyr oddiwrth y Llew ar hanesion oddiyno, he's now in tip top spirits. Nid oes modd ir *Brice* hwnw fynd yn fwrdais dros y Duwmares yr awron; he must be one of the 24 and elected into that honour at Michaelmas; its supposd Mr. Rowlands, of Caera, Lord Bulkeley's grandfather, must be chosen. Our candidates seems to be in good earnest. Meyrick has been here last week.

Presaddfed's death was a loss to Sir Nicholas, so was Kyff. Williams's. Nid oes wybod par sut a fydd, digon o lid, cenfigen, a gelyniaeth, par fodd bynnag. Yn atteb i'ch ail ebystol, it was an agreeable surprize to me to find the commission in it, oblegid rhyngwyfi a chwithau nid oedd fawr obaith o honaw a phei byw a fa'sai Brysaddfed, ni welswn byth mono, for he had gone so far as to order another person to act (a voter iddo chwi ellwch dyngu), but I would not let him proceed without a commission, which Owens would have had him, pei cawsai gan yr angau glas ddyfod yna. Chwi welwch mai gwir yr hen ddiareb, "Dyn a feddwl, Duw a ran." Mae'n rhaid sgrifennu diolch iddo ar fyrder sef ir Marchog. Dylem oll ddiolch i Dduw bob awr ac ennyd am ei drugareddau. Nis gwn i pa beth a wnaf ir câr Gwilym Parry, gan rwymedicced wyf iddo. A geiff o stenaid o fêdd? Ceiff yn ddiamau; a pham na cheiff? Ac yntau gan fwyned a chyn rhwydded oi gymwynas. Stenaid a ddywedais i, ceiff gryciaid yn llawn lloned pan ddel i ymweled ac ysgrin Cybi Sant. Mi yrraf y dernyn aur i nhad, onid af yno fy hun yn o fuan. Och y fi, ha wr fab, par sut a fu i Oronwy esceuluso hebrwng y Cywydd i chwi i roi ir Tywysog? Mae arnaf ofn y cyll o'r siawns o fod yn lawrydd-fardd iddo o'r achos. The letter must be miscarried, or some accident befel it, otherwise you would have had it, for he writ me some time last month that he was preparing one for you. Ni wn i a wyddoch i fod Cilmyn Droe'tu yn un o'r 15 llwyth Gwynedd, sef yr ail o honynt (Braint hir oedd y cynta), cil a myn, i.e., mynnu ir gelynion giliaw, yntau cil and min i.e., cilio a wna pawb rhag min cleddyf y troedtu, na bo'nd i grybwyll, rhag mor awchus ydoedd. Dywedwch y Marchog na ddylae am bris yn y byd fod heb droed du yn ei arfau. Hi a wnaeth dymyr odiaeth ar les garddwyr yn ddiweddar. Ond dyma'r rhod wedi troi, ar gwynt or gogledd-ddwyrain yn dwyn rhew a chenllysg yn ddigon er rhynnu poblach a fai'n trin y ddaiaren. Daccw'r Gwyddelod wedi colli eu cô-au, yn gynrhwg eu cwrs ac ydoedd uchelder-wyr Alban ers dyddiau, mae'r ychydig sydd yn eu hiawn bwyll yn ofni dim llai na rhyfel gartrefol, mae pob peth bendramwnwgl yn Nulun, nothing but tumults and confusion. The Government mobbd and insulted! W. to R. contd.

W. to R. contd.

Gorfod ir Duke a Duchess (fe ddywedir) ddianc or theatre am yr hoedl! Then the mobility tore all the play house furniture to pieces and did, as 'tis said, thousands of pounds worth of damage. Dyma Gatteral o Aberystwyth wedi dyfod drosodd efo'r llong bost i ymorawl llwyth o ŷd iw long sy'n gorwedd yn Nulun. Nid oes yno ddim yn mynd ymlaen ond mobbio. Nid hwyrach mai yn ail ir Corsicans yr â'r Gwyddyl. Os felly, gwae Gybi!

Wel, dyma post wedi dyfod i mewn; dim hanes Gwyl Ddewi.

Pa beth a wneir a chwithau mor drafferthus? Wawch! dyma lythyr oddiwrth fy hen gyfaill Captain Tatton, a hadau gwychion ynddo, a gwadd i yrru am fwy, os bydd raid wrthynt, pobl fwynion o rheini. Gresyn bod Wilson yn gna. Roedd y nhad yn iachus dda iawn y dydd arall; 'rym ni yma'n rhesymol, bu'r chwaer dydd arall yn o leccyn, darfu iddi ysgarrio. Mae'n awr yn abl hawntus. Duw gyd a chwi, a byddwch iach. *Eich caredigawl frawd,*

William Morris.

HOLYHEAD, 23rd March, 1754.

W. to R. CXC.

Dear Brother,—Fe ddywaid y Cymru fod newid gwaith neu orchwyl cystal a gorphwyso; os felly, oni fedrwch gan ludded sgrifennu gair neu ddau attom, chwi ellwch ddarllain pwtt o lythyr wrth eich pwys. Llawer o amser aeth heibiaw er pan wyf yn disgwyl am hanes Gwyl Ddewi Sant. Llawer rhingyll a yrrwyd i'r offis accw i ymofyn llythyr ar y testyn dymunol hwnnw heb fod ddim nes. Pa beth, ai colli'r fatal a wnaethoch? Yntau *marwolaeth y Belham* fawr a'ch dychrynnodd? Yn wir, yr oeddwn yn meddwl y byddai hynny'n golled i Lewelyn, ond dymma lythyr oddiwrtho heddyw i'r gwrthwyneb, ar papurau nhwythau yn rhoddi hanes fod y brawd hyna wedi myn'd yn ei leoedd, felly ni bydd, mae'n debyg, fawr dröad ar fyd. Os mawr eich ffwdan a'ch trafferth chwi efo'ch Navy Bills, can mwy fy llafur am lludded i y dyddiau hyn—yn hau, plannu, impio, gwneuthur gwelyau brwd, ysgythru coed, heblaw cyfrifon heilltion a chroywon yw tynnu, teulu iw trin au coleddu, etc. Roedd y nhad yn iach y dydd arall. Poblach yn taeru ei fod yn mynd yn ofer am wraig, peth anhawdd ei goeliaw pei gwelid chwedl rhyw rimmynnwr. Duw a fo'n gwarchad drosom oll.

Eich caredigawl frawd, William Morris.

CAER GYBI, 6-8d o Ebrill, 1754.

Anwyl Frawd,—Am fi 'r dydd arall yn ymofidiaw ynof fy hun am glywed oddiwrthych, ymddanghosawdd im mawr gysur eich llythyr or 26 ult. Can diolch iwch am tanaw, ond aruthr y chwedl nad oedd Mr. Lewis Owen i gael yr un o'r Beiblau, gobeitho'r goreu. Er cariad ar eich geirda chwi a minnau, ag ar yr hen blwyfydd accw, gwnewch ryw ddyfais i gael rhyw-faint ir gwr, ag onide, ni feiddiafi byth ddangos mo 'ngwyneb iddo. Mr. Ellis, I presume, will have his full complement, notwithstanding what the sgrifennydd told you, for he had the other day a letter from Mr. Broughton that the moiety of what he had sent for would be sent him out of hand, and the other in course. Duw yn unig a wyr par bryd y daw argraphiad arall allan, oni ddygaswn i eich bod wedi rhoddi diofryd na chymerach byth fath orchwyl yn llaw ond hynny. The secretary did not mention anything to Mr. Ellis about the account of families. Bum innau ennyd yn ofni am Oronwy, ag fe weddai nid oedd eich ofnad chwi a minnau yn ddiachos, oblegid ce's lythyr heddyw oddiwrtho, yn dywedyd mal y darfuasai ir oerfel ar ddryghin, etc., fagu'r peswch arno, ar peswch yntau a fu fam ir pigyn, a rhwng y ddau bu agos iddo fynd i blith y meirwon, ag yno b'asai oni bai borth Duw a chymorth physygwyr. Dyna'r modd y collawdd y Tywysawg ei awdl. Rhoddes y bardd i mi tri phennill o honaw, ond och o'r gresyndod na allasai ei orphen ; but who can help sickness, chwedl y Sais. Mae marwolaeth fawr ymhlwy'r Bardd y tymmor yma. Gwalch diofal yw Huw Sion Marian—un o blant y byd hwn. Ni sonniodd o, mae'n debyg, am y cog a roddes o imi y llynedd ymhrynniant march ir Llew ; cymerais ei air am y llwdn, a rhoddais iddo fawr bris am un na thalai ond ychydig. Ymhell y bwyf, ond yw'n ddrwg erchyll gennyf glywed fod y Wilym Parri wedi mynd oddiwrthych, poed buan y delo yn ol. Onid yw yn golled i bawb am dano, a rhwydded o'i gymhwynas ydoedd? Gorchymynnwch fi atto, da chwithau. Gwych or riolti oedd yna Wyl Ddewi. Mae hi'r awron yn fwy na dwy flynedd ar hugain er pan fum i yna'n gloddestu gyd a chwi ar gyfenw'r dydd hwnnw. Nid ydych yn son un gair am y gwyr gwellt oeddid yn ei crogi i fynu ich croesawu or Eglwys ir Neuadd. Gwaith cymmwys ddigon oedd dewis Syr Rhisiart yn drysorwr ac yn stiwart. Nid oes

W. to R.
CXCI.

W. to R. contd.

ammau na bydd yna ddigon o fwstr pwy bynnag a fydd byw i'w weled y flwyddyn nesa! Ai nid ydych yn cofiaw mo'r Captain Alexander Wilson a briodws fam y Captain Tatton, ac fal y cogiawdd yr holl fyd? Ni chlywais i ddim newydd a dalai ddraen o Allt Fadawg er's dyddiau, llythyrau byrrion 'rwan ac yn y man. Gerwinol son fod y sawdwyr wedi myned i bant heb yr un yn eu lle. Gadewch glywed par sut a fu rhyngoch a'r Iarll yn yr ail ofwy, a phwy sydd iar a phwy sydd geiliawg ymhlith y mawrion yna. Os y Dûg o'r Castell* a fydd eistedd ar ben bwrdd yn y drysorfa, deg i un y bydd mor troad ar fyd yn yr Esgair. Digrif o'r Iarll yna sydd am chwareu bys yn y bastai. I would give my vote for a lion and a lamb for the supporters, whatever might be used (if any there were) of old, ag i dorri'r ymrafael, os bydd raid, llew for the crest, a chael plu a chenin i mewn. Rhowch chwithau lew naill ai coch ai melyn. Coch fyddai oreu, mae'n debyg, yn ei eistedd yn rhythu eu lygaid arnoch, ac yn dal yn ei bawen ddeau y plu, a'r genhinen laswyrdd yn y llall, undeb a brawdgarwch o gwmpas y sêl. Rhaid rhoddi coron ar ben y llew, mi wranta, but you say that sêl *Cymdeithas y Cymrodorion* is to be about the seal and undeb, etc., for the motto, bydded felly. Ie, yn wir, cymwys ddigon fyddai Cymraeg loyw lan yn lle'r Lladin budr yna. There must be, I presume, a chapeau of dignity upon the helmet for the lion to sit upon, beth meddwch—bydded a fynno, nid yw Gwilym yn rhyfygu tybiaw nad oes yna a wyr amgenach pethau nag efe, therefore the whole is most humbly submitted. Rhwydd-deb ich petisiwn, par un bynnag ai i chwi eich hun, yntau ir gymdeithas yr y'ch yn ceisiaw'r FSS. Bu'r chwaer y dydd arall Ymhentre'rianell, a gwir ddigon yw'r gair fod yr hen gorphyn ymron ynfydu am wraig, a phwy debygach i mae o yn ei hoffi ond merch yr hen Williams dew, o Fodafon gynt. Gobeitho y bydd rhagluniaeth yn well wrtho na gadael iddo ei chaffael. Sgrifennwch dipyn o gynghor mab iw dad. Ond am Wilym, nid rhydew mono i ail *ymaflyd* a gwraig ettwa pe deuai un i'w arfod, ond ni welafi ddim hanes yr un a dâl ei chodi oddiar y maes, mae yna ddogn o ddewis o bob math a phob cynneddf, ond congl yw hon heb ei bath. Ces

* The Duke of Newcastle, who became Prime Minister of England on the death of his brother, Henry Pelham, in March, 1754.

lythyr dydd arall oddiwrth Gornelius Agrippa, a rhai hadau i'm gardd; os daw'r gwr yna'r Gwiliau fal yr oedd yn amcanu, dywedwch iddo fy mod yn dra diolchgar am danynt. Mae ei bobl oll yn fywion ac yn iach am a glywaf i; mi welais ei chwaer Sarah o fewn ychydig yma yn ymofyn ei hanes; diog erchyll yw'r gŵr am sgrifennu. Rhoddes Goronwy imi dri phennill o'r awdl, ag yn wir rhai enwog ydynt. Fal hyn y mae'r cynta ar fesur gwawdodyn hir:—Dwyre, wawr fore, ,erfai arwain, W. to R. contd.

Dymmawr dydd eurwawr, da ei ddwyrain,
Dyddwaith ar euriaith i arwyrain
Dryd fawr briodawr, Eryr Brydain
Dwysawg llym aerawg llu mirain—Dewi·
Dewr Ri Lloegr wedi Llyw goradain. †

Chwi welwch mae bâs gan Oronwy ddynwared beirdd y canrhifoedd diweddaraf ai fod yn myned yn ol, tu ac oesoedd Taliesin, Myrddin, Llywarch hên, ac Aneurin, ac weithiau yn dyfod cyn nesed attom ar 10d, 11eg, ar 12fed ganrhi, ac yn canu ar ddull y Gwynfardd Brycheiniawg, Gwalchmai, Cynddelw Brydydd Mawr, etc. Yn ddiammau mae Duw wedi rhoddi 'roddiad fawr anfeidrol, rhodded iddo hefyd hiroes er mwyn yr hen iaith, etc. Gwyn ei fyd ai gwela mewn personoliaeth rhwydd frâs. Mae'n dywedyd ei fod yn darparu Cywydd yr Awen. Did you ever see a cywydd of his (i'r Awen) in imitation of the 3rd Awdl lib. 4 of Horace? Onid yw e'n un digrif? Mae newydd dderbyn o Allt Fadawg y llyfr Arabaeg, a chwedi dysgu ei ddarllain mewn byr amser, ond bod eisiau lexicon, neu ynta' ddwned o'r iaith. Dyma fi wedi bod yn clandrio par faint a dalodd y flwyddyn ddiweddaf i mi, or 5d Ebrill, '53, ir 5d o hwn, a chwedi gwneuthwr allan fod y cyflogau, tippyn tir, etc., wedi dyfod uwchlaw pedwar ugein punt, heblaw y ty ai berthynasai, lle'r wyf yn byw yr hwn a dâl £6 neu £8. Mawl i'r Goruchaf Dduw am bob llessiant, mae hyn yn fwy nag oeddwn yn ei ddisgwyl, neu yn ei erchi pan ddaethym yma, nid hwyrach y geill blynyddoedd eraill fod cystal. Ond par fodd bynnag, mwy na'r haeddiant. Wala, wala, rhaid i'm derfynu bellach heb yn ddiolch imi. Duw gyda chwi.

Eich caredigawl frawd, William Morris.

† See Goronwy's letter to William Morris, dated April 1, 1754, and Robert Jones's edition of Goronwy's Works, vol. 1, 151.

W. to R. contd.

P.S.—Os un or Siamesiaid ydoedd y gwr a gynhygiodd y dwyfil punnau, nid oes ammeu na byddynt gymeradwy. Ond os un or Sioriaid, pei rhoddai bummil ni bai ddim nes. Ynfydrwydd mawr o hynny, onte? Dyma Syr Nicholas newydd fod yma efo ei lu yn curo i fynu am *volunteers*, ac yn broliaw, meddynt, yn ddigydwybod mai fo a eiff ar maen ir wal, a Bodorgan yntau yn tyngu ir cyrs ac ir coed nas gedy iddaw, a phwy a ellir ei goeliaw nis gwyr Gwilym. Er mwyn Duw cofiwch am Allgo ac Eugred, a phlwy Penrhos Lligwy rhag i'n cael yn gelwyddawg. Daccw wr y gyfnither Catrin Salbri wedi marw. Tidesman yn Aberconwey ydoedd. Yno mae chwech o blantos, a phrin y medr yr hynaf enill tammaid o fara. Duw ai helpio. Mae chwaer Ddick Morys bwtt yn gwaeddi yn groch am ei hanes; mae hi yn disgwyl rhyw beth oddiwrtho. Byddwch wych, a sgrifennwch gynta galloch.—*W.M.*

GARTREF, Dydd Llun y Pasg, 15 April, 1754.

W. to R. CXCII.

Dear Brother,—Wawch! Dyma lythyr oddiwrth y Gownsler Meurig yn adrodd fod y lecsiwn fawr i fod yn y Duwmares (sef am Farchog y Sir) y 25 inst, ac yn dymuno arnaf yrru am Lywelyn i ddyfod yno iw gymorth, a dymma finnau yn sgrifenu dyfyn iddaw, pe baid gwell er hynny. Ond gan fod ei lythyrau ambell dro bythewnos neu un niwrnod ar ddeg yn trafaelio, tybiais mae'r ffordd sicrra f'ai treio'r ddwyffordd; felly dymuno arnoch chwithau sgrifennu yn union deg lein neu ddwy atto'r modd yna, nid hwyrach y bydd yno ddeuddydd neu dri o flaen y llall, felly os oes gan y gwr ewyllys a gallu i wasnaethu ei hen gyfaill, bydded felly. Gyrrwch gymaint a galloch o uchelwyr or iawn blaid tuag yma, ond gwaherddwch ir lleill ysmician o'u hunfan. Oes dim gobaith Biblau i Lewis Owain? Dyma Mr. Ellis yn rhifo'r bobloedd oi blwyf sydd arnynt flys rhai. Ai llygoden gôch aeth dros y *Gymdeithas?* Ai nid oes ir naill blwy cystal ar llall achos i ddisgwyl rhan or elusen? Ai ni chadd pobl Cybi a phlwyfydd eraill lle mae aelodau anghyttrig yn tarriaw lawer mwy na'u rhan y trô o'r blaen? Ac oni fyddai gyfiawn i'r plwyfydd eraill (sydd heb gael ond odid un bâch) gael y'rwan ryw ychydig o nifer? Er carriad ar elusengarwch, dywedwch wrthynt eu bod yn gwneuthur cam erchyll ac eneidiau'r trueiniaid yma ar hyd y wlad, ag nid oes amau nad felly y mae mewn mannau ereill. Pawb yma yn iach, mawl i Dduw am ei dramawr drugaredda'. Byddwch wŷch. *Eich carediccaf frawd,* W. to R. contd.

Gwilym Amhorys.

P.S.—Wawch etto! Dymma lythyr oddiwrth y Llew a hanes ei helyntion, ai fod drwy gennad Duw i gychwyn tuag yna ddechreu Mai ag ynghylch 60 o wyr i dystiolaethu oblaid Coron Loegr goch.* Lle da disgwyl mono yma ir lecsiwn. Gerwin os cyll y Gownsler or achos, beth bynnag rhowch hi ar dô os pymtheg a fydd, nid oes mor help.

CAER GYBI SANT, Ebrill yr 28, 1754.

Anwyl Frawd,—Mae'n debyg gael o honoch lythyr y dydd arall a yrrais ffordd i roddi gwa'dd i Lywelyn ddyfod ir *lecsiwn* eiddom ni. Neithiwr y daethym adref o honi, wedi colli'r maes yn lanwaith, y Plâs Newydd a gadd y llaw uchaf ar Fodorgan, ysywaeth ir bobl.† Daethym echdoe law yn llaw efo nhad i Bentre Eirian-Allt er ein bod (na b'ond i grybwyll) yn elynion brychion in gilydd yn y Duwmares. Mae'n debyg, meddwch chwithau, fod y byd ar ben pan fo'r mab yn erbyn y tad, etc. Mi welais yr Ardderchog Gardinal yno a'r llythyr a ddygasai i nhad. Mae'r Gardinol wedi gaddaw dyfod yma dros noswaith cyn myned or wlad, ond ni wiw rhoddi mo'r llawer o goel arnaw, gan ddaed ganddaw gwmni'r boneddigion. Mae nhad wedi darllaw styntiaid o gwrw odiaethol erbyn y delo y Llew a chwithau ir wlad yr haf draw,—dyna lle bydd ei hyfed hi! Gerwin o'r gwaeddi yr oeddid am Lywelyn i fotio, ac yntau mae'n debyg yn ddigon mawr ei drafferth ffordd arall. Fe ddarfu i nhad a minneu alw wrth ddyfod adref i edrych am yr hen ewythyr Owain Parri ai wraig yn y Glyn yn Llanbedr, lle y dywedir fod yr hen Feiryg yn mynd i fyw. Mae Owain yn hen sparbwch digrifa ar a welsoch, yn llawenychu'n erchyll fod gobaith eich gweled cyn ei farw. Roedd y nhad fal yr W. to R. CXCIII.

* Lewis Morris took no less than seventy witnesses up to London with him on this occasion, to give evidence for the Crown in the suit of Attorney General v. Lord Lisburne and others. Some of the witnesses were very old people, and it is not surprizing that one died in London. After reaching London, however, a peace was patched up, which amounted to a victory for the Crown, and the witnesses returned triumphantly to Cardigan, wearing favours in their hats in token of Morris's success. Cymmrodor xv., 22-27.

† The result was as follows: Sir N. Bayley, Bart., 231; Owen Meyrick of Bodorgan, 126.

W. to R. contd. oedd, mwya'r cywilydd i Wilym, yn llawer sioncach na'i fab ar ei farch a'i draed; roedd hwnw ar bildin a chant o anwyda eraill iw grugo. Dyma Mr. Ellis wedi cael tair cistiaid o Fiblau a darnau o Fiblau, moliant i Dduw am y golwg prydferth! Nid oes ammeu na wna ef gymaint o ddaioni â hwynt, a nemawr ddyn o'r aelodau. Roedd arnaf gwilydd edrych yng ngwyneb Mr. Lew. Owain er na wyddai'r gwr nad ydoedd i gaffael baich ei gefn o honynt. Er cariad ar yr Arglwydd gadewch glywed gynta galloch oes gobaith iddo, fal y caffo ymorawl am rai os bydd bosibl gan rai o'r aelodau, ond mae'n debyg ei bod hi bellach yn rhywyr. I am vastly pleas'd with the Common Prayer, Testament and Singing Psalms bound together. As the Society seem'd to hint that Mr. Ellis might have as many as he would of them (he took only 50), perhaps you might have a parcel of them, I think they'll go off extream well. Ceisiwch o rheini 80 neu 100 i Benrhos, Eugred, a Gallgo, a Duw a dalo i chwi. Ped fa'i ganyf inneu un o honynt wedi ei rwymo mewn garw-groen lloi yn daclus ac yn drefnus, da fyddai, minnau a dalwn i nhad am danaw gyda diolwch. Gweddus a fyddai gael un or fath yn yr eglwys, obleit bydd'ch brawd Gwil bob Sul, brydnhawn a bore yn darllain o uchder ei ben gyda'r offeiriad, bob yn ail bob yn eilwas o Gymraeg loyw lân, tra bo ambell waith oi ddeutu haid o Wyddelod, Ysgwidiaid, Saeson, ag o bob cenedl yn llygad rhythu ac yn rhyfeddu wrth ddyfnder ei ddysgeidiaith! Bum ddoe yn Eglwys Llan Babo yn ymweled a bedd (neu o leiaf carreg fêdd) Pabo Post Prydain, the most curious piece of antiquity (I ever saw,) perhaps to be found this day in Britain. I have seen a draught taken of it formerly by brother Lewis, ond ni thybiais i erioed ei fod mor odiaethol! Ond gresyn bod ei fath mewn hen eglwysig fechan ddrwg ei threfn ar syrthio ai phen ynddi, nid llawer amgenach ei thaclusrwydd na beudy. Mae Pabo yn ei frenhinawl wisg, ai goron ar ei ben, ai deyrn wialen yn ei law, ar ei hyd gy'd, a'r llythyrennau gan amlycced a chan gyfäed agos ac unrhyw o'ch monuments yn Abadty Westminster. Chwi welwch nad yw fy llaw na'm clol wedi dyfod iw eu hiawn hwyl, felly esgusodwch wendidau eich caredigawl frawd, yr hwn sydd ar feunyddiawl weddi ar i Dduw warchad drosoch ar eiddych tra bo'ch yn ymdreiglaw yn nyffryn y trueni.

Byddwch wych, Gwilym o Fôn.

P S.—Mae Mr. Ellis yn erchi arnoch (os medrwch gael 40 neu 50 or Common Prayer, Testament and Singing Psalms i Mr. Lewis Owen), siared a Mr. Broughton neu Watts am iddo yntau gael 50 yn rhagor o honynt allan o law. Ond os ni chewchi rai i Benrhos, etc., mae o yn dywedyd y caf i hanner 40 neu 50 os ca yntau nhw felly. Siaredwch chwi drosto, ag yntau a sgrifena at y Gymdeithas os bydd gwiw. Chwi ellwch ddywedyd wrthynt ei fod wedi derbyn y cwbl yn ddianaf, sef 150 Bibles and 50 New Testaments, Common Prayers and Salms, and that he will send bills for the money immediately. Duw gyda chwi. Sgrifenwch gynta galloch, da mrawd Rhisiart.—*W.M.* W. to R. contd.

CAER CYBI, Mai'r 5d, 1754.

F'anwyl Frodyr,—Dyma'ch llythyr chwi mrawd Rhisiart o'r 27 ulto, wedi dyfod yn ei adeg; diolch yn fawr am danaw. Oni fydda'i yn maddeu i chwi bob yn awr pan fyddoch yn ol llaw am atteb fy llythyrau? Felly rwan. Gwaeth par un o'r ddeuwr a fai aelod o'r Palment? Mae un o naddynt yn Gymro, o waed coch cyfa, yn wr difalch, diniwaid, fal ei dadws, ag yn sefyll bob amser o blaid y Brenin. Hir oes iddo, a llawer o rinweddau eraill arno, a'r llall ——. Ie'n wir cymmwys ddigon a f'ai gwneuthur i Oronwy orphen ei awdl. Fe ga ddigon o amser o hyn i Wyl Ddewi i'w gaboli. Gwych clywed fod Sir R. Glyn yn ymroi i fod yn Gymro o ddifrif. Gwr oi fath o sydd deilwng o fod yn drysorwr. Ni wn a gafodd o ei ddewis gan eich dinasyddion i fod yn seneddwr. Och na chawn weled Anacreon yn saired, neu yn hytrach, yn canu Cymraeg. Os daw Sion Ywain yna, efo'r Llew, mae fal y rhoddwch e ar waith i goplo yr odlau hynny. Efengyl och genau mewn perthynas i'r bersonoliaeth honno a ddaw o'r Castell Côch. Os rhodd yr arglwydd his word and honour, ni phalla wneuthur ei air yn dda. Bid buan y cywira. Gwych o'r rhodienna a gawsoch efo Gwil Parry. Mi fum innau yn ciniewa ynghylch tri saith mlynedd i'r amser hwnnw, efo'r Sion Jones hwnnw yn Woolwich. Cofiwch fi at Wredog pan i gwelwch. Mae 'nhad yn tyngu i'r cyrs ac i'r coed nad oes un sillaf o wir yn y chwedlau rheini ynghylch priodi, er y gallai gael gwraig heddyw heno; ond ni fyn o 'run, ni waeth tewi na siarad. Na atto Duw chwedl amgen, meddwn innau. Rwy'n ei ddisgwyl yma yr wythnos a ganlyn i'n hymweled. Fe fyddai W. to L. and R. CXCIV.

W. to L. and R. contd.

hyfryd gan eich calon weled a sionced ydyw. Mi glywaf gael o honaw ryw *grwyds* anwyd yn y lecsiwn. Mi sgrifenais attoch ryw 'strodwm dydd arall a hanes ein colled ni'r cywiriaid, ac erchiad ddwys ynghylch y Biblau, a'r Gweddi Cyffredin, etc. Gobeithio eich bod wedi llwyddo. Fe ddarfu Mr. Ellis ddoe sgrifennu at Froughton am chwaneg o'r rhai ola. Chwi welwch yn y papurau newyddion hanes fal y mae'r Gwyddelod wedi ymgynddeiriogi o achos i'r Brenin (Duw ai cadwo) droi allan y cyfryw rai o'i weision ac oeddynt wedi myned dros y gwaharddol, a dodi o honaw eraill ydoedd fwy gostyngeiddiach yn eu lle hwynt. Rydys yn disgwyl y bydd yno waith eurych pan el yr hen Dduc i fynd ymaith, a hyn a ddywedir a fydd rai o'r dyddiau hyn. Ni feiddia fo prin ddangos ei drwyn iddynt, gan eu hofn au harswyd rhag mor flyngderddus ydynt! Gwir a ddywaid Mabclaf ap y Llywarch: "nag anifeiliaid ar gefn rhôs, llywodraeth gwyr sydd anos." Och fi, ha wr fab, llyma y Mr. Ellis wedi rhoddi benthyg i mi bregeth yr Sgottyn gwenwynllyd hwnw sydd wedi ei ddodi yn fugail yn Llanelwy,* yr hon a bregethasai yn Eglwys Grist, 26 Ebrill, 1753, o flaen trinwyr yr ysgolion elusenaidd yna. Rhag na welsoch mo'r cywreinwaith hwnnw, dyna fo i chwi air yn air sef a berthyn i'm testyn. "Among many other pious designs pursued by this Society (i.e., that of promoting Christian knowledge), I cannot omit their reprinting and dispersing at a low price 30,000 Bibles in the Welsh tongue for the use of the poor in that country, *which may be necessary* till that people see, *that it is their true interest to enlarge their views and notions and to unite with the rest of their fellow subjects in language as well as Government.*" Wala, beth meddwch? This great reformer of languages as well as morals, had not the effrontery to put this bombast in the body of his sermon, but placed it *yn lladradaidd* as a note upon his enconium upon his Society! Ond gwych y mae'n canu yr un cowydd a'i frawd o Fynyw gynt,† yn ei bregeth ar yr un achos, y 30 Ebrill, 1747. Wala, wfft i'r fath esgobion! O na bai Ddewi yn gwybod par fath gymdeithion sydd yn eistedd yn ei drŵn, ac yntau Elwy, a'i ddylynawr Rhisiart Davies yn gweled par fath goegyn sydd yn llenwi eu cadair!

* The Hon. Robert Hay Drummond, Bishop of St. Asaph, 1748-1761.

† Richard Trevor, Bishop of St. David's, 1743-1752.

Gresyn na bai Ronwy wedi cael ei ddyrchafel ennyd yn uwch, mal y gallai dalu'r echwyn adre i'r 'Sgot. Ond mae'n enbyd iddo rwan, rhag iddo ddigwydd mynd dan faner y gwalch, fal y bu yn swydd Ymhwythig yn cael ei gystwyaw gan y genedl genfigennus honno.* Digon o hynny bellach. Mi glywais yr Aldramon o Lerpwl yn manegi boethed lecsiwn a fasai yno, a bod ym mryd Llwyd betisiwno'r Palment yn erbyn fy hen ffrind Mr. Salisbury, ac y trŷ ef allan etto, ond nid oes mor llawer o goel ar y chwedl, oblegid fod O.P. wedi sorri wrth y gwr ola er däed ffrind a fu iddaw. Diau yr aethwn yno i wasnaethu'r hên wr pei cawsai amser i alw ynghyd ei luoedd, ond ni chadd. Ni wn i pwy yw stiwart yr Archesgob Caergaint; mi adwaen ei feistr. Aie'ni wybod pwy fydd y trô nesaf; wala, ni hwyrach hynny. Mae Duw wedi anfon i ni yn ddiweddar ddigonoldeb o wlaw; moliant iddo am danaw. Roedd yn yr ynys yma ei fawr eisiau. Prinder mawr o borthiant milod o bob math; ni a gawn bellach, Duw yn y blaen, ddigon o borfa, etc. Mae fy ngardd i yn dechreu gwisgo ei gwychder, a phrin y clywaf ar fy nghalon ddyfod allan o honi y nosweithiau chwaethech gefn dydd goleu. Brysiwch gynta galloch i'w hymweled, ag i fwyta o'i ffrwythydd. Ni wn i a fyddwch chwi y mrawd Llywelyn wedi cael gafael ar ben eich siwrnai erbyn y delo hwn yno; par fodd bynnag, dyma fi wedi derbyn eich dau lythyr, un o Leominster, p'le bynnag y mae'r fan honno, a'r llall o Gaer Wrangon a hanes y deng hynafgwr a thrugain oedd gennych yn eich gosgordd. Rhwydd-deb a'ch dilyno chwi a nhwythau, a llwyddiant ar a fanegynt pan ddelont o flaen eu gwell. Digrif oedd fedru cludo'r hynafgwr hwnnw oedd yn ganmlwydd namyn pump. Nid gwyr ieuengaidd iawn mo'r rheini sydd uwchlaw eu pedwar ugain mlwydd. Mae'r berson Bellis yn gaddaw ystwytho gweddiau o'ch tu chwi. Ni soniasoch inclyn gair pwy ydoedd eich cydymdeithion eraill heblaw'r Septuagint. Rhai a dybia fod y gwr o Fathafarn, eraill yn taeru fod Ioan Ywain; os yw'r cynta dâ fydd gennyf gael llinell oddiwrtho par fodd y gellir *fforddio* gwerthu'r coed yma. I received no directions about 'em, and they are such that are not usually brought hither. I shall defer proclaiming a fair of them untill I hear from him. Pan gaffoch

W. to L. and R. contd.

* Goronwy served as curate under the Rev. John Douglas, at Donnington.

W. to L. and R. contd.

amser sgrifennwch linell neu ddwy at y Gownsler i ddywedyd iddo fal yr ydoedd gyda chwi. Fe ddywedir nad oedd Syr Nicholas drech nag e ond o gwmpas 30 neu 35. Pei basai ddim byw yn y teulu, mae pawb oi ffrindiau yn meddwl yr enillasai'r maes, er bod y Siamaisiaid bod ag un pen yw erbyn a llawer a'u galwont eu hunain yn chwigods hefyd. Wala, mae'n rhaid cadw noswyl. Duw a roddo i chwi eich deuoedd nosweithiau a dyddiau dâ. 'Sgrifennwch fynycha ag alloch. *Eich caredigawl frawd, William Morris.*

W. to L. and R. CXCV.

CAER GYBI, Mai y Deunawfed, '54.

Anwyl Frodyr,—Mae hi ynghylch wythnos o amser er pan yrrais i lythyr yna gyda'r post; nid oes gennyf yr awrhon nag achos nag ystyr i sgrifennu ond yn unig i gyfarch gwell i chwi, ag i ddywedyd ein bod i gyd yn rhwydd iachus, mawl i Dduw. Y Syrfaeor sydd ar gwaetha' gallo ar ei droed, sef yw'r haint hwnnw y droedwst, alias y gymalwst, alias cryd y cymalau, alias y gouyt. Llymeitiaw ai dygodd arno, nid oes wybod pa beth ai gyrr ymaith. Daccw'r Arglwydd Deputy wedi cael mynd adref o'r Werddon yn groen gyfa wrth siawns fawr, a daccw Sir T. Prendergast yn dyfod trosodd y foru, ag fe ddywedir mae yna y daw rhag ei flaen i drin y dreth ynghylch yr offis o Bostmaster General yr Iwerddon. Dyna lle bydd mwstrio! Gwae i feistryd y llongau pyst! Gwae i gantoedd o boblach a berthynynt ir post offices! Ni chânt na hun na heddwch bellach, os y fo a fydd feistr. Ni chafed dim llythyr oddiyna er's talm byd, beth bynnag ydyw'r achos, parottoi erbyn y ddadl fawr, mae'n debyg. Ond chwi ellachi, mrawd Rhisiart, ddodi llinell neu ddwy ar lawr wrth eich pwys. Mi welais yr hen Nicol yn y lecsiwn. Roedd y peswch arno, ag edrychiad abl cwla; mae hi'n amser iddo bellach roddi'r cardiau iw cadw. Er mwyn Duw gadewch gael llinell oddiwrthych gyn gynted ag y bo' bosibl a hanes y treiol pan el drosodd. Rwy'n hyderu mai newydd tra da a fydd. Duw gyda chwi, a byddwch wych. *Eich caredigawl frawd, William Morris.*

W. to R. CXCVI.

CAER GYBI, Dydd Llun y Sul Gwyn, 1754.

Fy Anwyl Frawd Mynglwyd,—Daccw ryw hen philosophydd wedi dywedyd y gylch y môr ymaith bob haint oddiar ddynolryw. . . . . O wir grediniaeth ir hên Roegwr ag ich cymydog y Doctor

Richard Russel,* sgrifennydd rhinwedd yr Heli, dyma fi wedi taro atti hi i yfed y mor, na bo 'mond i grybwyll! Ac or achos hwnw gorfod aros gartref yn lle mynd i wrando ar Ioan aur-enau yn pregethu, sef yw hwnw y Mr. Ellis ddiniwed, sy'n gwneuthur ei oreu ar gael gan y gwerinos wrando'r Sgrythyr Lân yn lle'r *anterliwts* bryntion. Dyma'ch llythyr o'r 18 ulto. yn crochwaeddi am atteb. Ac atteb a roddaf iddo fal hyn: nid amgen na'm bod wedi sgrifennu yna ddwywaith neu dair yn olynol o fewn ychydig yma; ond nid oedd dim meddwl am unrhyw beth yr amser hwnnw (ag nid oes fawr ettwa ond am y gyfraith fawr yn Llundain). Mae'n fwy na rhy'wyr clywed par sut y mae rhwng y Llew ar bobyl fawrion yna. Nid oes bosibl na bydd cusanu llaw, a gwneuthur o hono ustus bellach, ar ol y gwroldeb yna—digon bychain a fai ir hen Unben wneuthur marchawg urddol o honaw, pe bai ddogn o stad. Bellach pwy a fydd debyg i enill wrth chwareu'r bastai? Nid hwyrach mai gwell a f'ai gael cnwff o honno na'r holl wag anrhydedd uchod. Gobeithio y bydd ir Bowys gael rhoddi bys yn y bastai, ac yno nhwy allant reoli'r Ceredigioniaid. Pa'r hyd y mae'r brawd yn aros yna? A ddeuwch i efo' ge i lawr y tro yma, ah? Mi ollyngais yn angof mai atteb llythyr yr oeddwn. Gwych clywed fod Llewelyn ap Owain Gallgo i gael llyfrau. Pa'r bryd y deuant i lawr? Chwi gewch (meddwch) Destament, etc., wedi ei rwymo mewn garw groen lloi, os mynnwch. Os mynnaf! Mynaf yn siwr dda ddiamau; a gadewch ei gael wedi ei gauadu yn weddus ac yn drefnus, da chwithau. Gwych y newydd i wrth Ierwerth ap Ierwerth, mi ai gyrrais iw chwaer, a gwych yn sicr y newydd fod yr Wdwart ddiniweid wedi enill ei dir ei hun. If you see him, though perhaps I never shall, pray tell him that I am extream glad to hear of his success, and that I desire my compliments. Ni ddaeth mo Gardinal Castleton im hymweled yn ol ei addawiad. I am afraid his Excellency is affronted. I happen'd to meet him at the election, as I told you, but the same instant met

W. to R. contd.

* Dr. Richard Russell was the author of a treatise "On glandular consumption, and the use of sea-water in diseases of the glands," which was published in Latin in 1750, and translated in 1753. The new remedy acquired an extraordinary favour, and was the means of giving a great impetus to the fashion of sea-bathing, while it also increased the popularity of sea-side resorts. (Lecky, vol. ii., chapter 5).

W. to R. contd.

O. P., my quondam Master, and old Nicholas, our Surveyor General, and Mr Wynne, Bod'sgallen, etc., all my old friends, etc., and it seems I did not pay that deference to him as he perhaps thought due to so eminent a person, for he seemed to complain a little of it then. Mi r'of gennad im crogi ond dyna'r achos, wfft ir bobl fawrion yma! Rych yn dywedyd fod Cymdeithas y Cymrodorion yn fy annerch a llaw ddeheu brawdgarwch. Rhynged bodd i chwi f'annerch inna' attynt hwythau a deheulaw brawdgarwch drwy fawr ostyngeiddrwydd ac ewyllys da. Ni ddaeth mo nhad i'm hymweled etto. Y mae'n gaddaw bod yma y foru efo ei gymydog Mr. Foulke Jones, y swyddog a gwr wrth gerdd. Dyna lle bydd llawenydd, gobeitho! Mae fy chwaer wedi mynd i Bentre Erianell er's cryn wythnos, ai phedwar plentyn gyda hi, i aros yno dros dro, tra bô Peggy Owen ei merch yn mynd i Fathafarn i ymweled ai chyfnither. Daccw ein cyfnither Margaret Williams (sef merch William Prisiart ac Elsbeth'ch Rist. Morys) yr hon oedd Ymhentre'rianell er yn blentyn wedi priodi, hogen o golled ir hen dâd am weinidog gwybodawl. Mae'r bobl wedi blino ar roddi Mrs. Williams Bodafon iddo, mae'nt yn llunio un waelach iddo rwan, ond nid wyf i yn medru mo'r coelio ei fod mor ynfyd. Mi glywais fod hanes y treiol yn rhai o'r papurau newydd, *General Evening Post*, debygai, a bôd sôn am ryw false survey, or some survey, made without the direction of the Court. Was there a survey produced by Powel, or how was it? I could not get sight of the papers. Er dim ar y fo gadewch glywed par sut a fu. I suppose you were at court. Gorchmynnwch fi at Lywelyn a Meirian, a Duw gyda chwi oll. *Eich caredigawl frawd,*

William Morris.

CAER GYBI, Mehefin 6d, 1754.

W. to L. CXCVII.

F'anwyl Dew-Frawd,—Dyma'r eiddoch o'r calan yn cynwys 5 llinell, nid oedd y llall ond 2½, felly os cynnyddant wrth reol bydd y nesaf, cofiwch, yn 12 llinell. So much for a preface. Can diolch am olwg ar y ffafr felen. Gwych oedd gweled yr hynafgwyr yn mynd drwy berfedd Lloegr gôch ar tlws yn eu hettiau. Mi wranta fod digon o rythu llygaid arnaddynt. Ond can gw'chach oedd yr achos a barodd eu gwisgo, sef cyflawniad prophwydoliaeth Sibli ddigri ddoeth. Ond i roddi heibio bob gwawd, Duw a'n gwnelo oll yn ddiolchgar am ei anfeidrawl drugareddau i ni bod ac un, ac yn fwy enwedigol am y drugaredd a ryglyddawdd drwy roddi i chwi'r fuddugoliaeth. Dyma nhad wedi dyfod i'n hymwelyd ac yn son am fyned yn y man tuag adref; mawl i Dduw, y mae yn dra sionc; mae'n hyderu y deuwch chwi ar brawd Rhisiart iw ymweled cyn y bo hîr fal y gallo [eich ben-]dithio cyn ei farw. Par bryd y bydd wiw eich disgwyl? Gwych oedd gennyf weled enw Powys ar gefn eich llythyr, rwyn mawr obeithio (er nas gwn pa'r un ai drwg ai da a fyddai hynny) y bydd ir pendefig hwnnw gael rhoddi bŷs yn y brywes, sef brywais yr Esgair pan elir i rannu'r wlêdd. Mae'n debyg eich bod chwi yn meddwl i'r Mynglwyd roddi imi beth o hanes eich matterion yn y dadleu. Na ddo, na ddo; ni chefais i gymaint o hanes o unlle ag oedd yn eich llythyr at fy nhad a hynny wrth siawns. Wfft, a dwbl wfft, i Lwyd y Pottiau, ni ba'swn byth yn meddwl y profiasau'r lloercan hwnnw yn gymaint cnâ, nid oes dim ymddiried i ffylied o holl bobl y byd, ffei arno *leidir* diffaith, ni byddai fatter pei b'ai arno eisieu llymaid o gwrw, mwy côsp nag eisieu tammaid o fara iddo ê ar wraig. Mae'r newydd da accw wedi gwneuthur 'nhad yn ieuengach o ddengmlwydd o'r lleiaf, mae'n dymuno ar un o honoch gynta byth ac alloch roddi iddo dippyn chwaneg o'ch hanes. Gresyn i'r tŷst farw yna, na chawsent fynd adref yn eu cyfrif, ond ewyllys Duw a wneler, ni wiw gwingo yn erbyn ei symbylau, mae arnaf ddialedd eisieu clywed par hŷd yr y'ch ar fedr aros yna, a chan mil o bethau eraill angenrheidiol i ddyn wybod a'u dysgu. Par sut y mae'r B—n—n? Hiroes iddo a'i fab Wiliam! Mi yrrais hanes y fuddugoliaeth i bawb o'ch hen ffrindiau. Oni haeddai'r Brynddu hynny yn fwy na neb? Fal hyn y dywaid 'r hen ŵr y dydd arall yn y llythyr: "Duw a wnelo i mi glywed newydd da oddiwrth fy hên gyfaill, os y Brenhin a geiff y cwyn, fe fydd y ffonnod yn anferth ar warr Powel, trawsglwyddo 70 o hen bobl cyn belled o ffordd a'u traul yn mynd a dyfod, ac aros llawer o ddyddiau yn Llundain. Nid eill fod lai na llawer o gantoedd o bynnau, ac os y Brenhin a gyll ni bydd dim costau yn ei erbyn ef, ond pa un bynnag Duw a ddycco fy nghyfaill anwyl adref yn ddiogel, sydd ddeusyfiad diragrithiol eich, etc." Ac nid wyfi yn ameu un gair; diragrith oedd yr hen ŵr erioed hyd yn heddyw. Rwyf wedi gadael yn siccr fyned efo mrawd llysieuwr Mr. Hwlant

W. to L. contd.

o Gonwy i olrhain planhigion i'r Wyddfa o ddeutu diwedd y mis yma. A ddowch'i efo nyni frodyr? Wala, wala, rhaid tewi a son bellach. Duw a fyddo'n gwarchad drosoch bod ac un, a byddwch wŷch. *Eich caredigawl frawd, Gwilym Rwydd-dew.*

W. to R. CXCVIII.

CAER GYBI YM MON, 27ain o Fehefin, 1754.

Anwyl Frawd,—Wele yma eich ebystol o'r 15d ac ynddo ychydig o hanes y maes mawr yng Nghaerludd, etc. Can diolwch am dano, tra digrif o'r araith o'r eiddo Hume Campbell, a digrifach oedd y Bowel am fynnu roddi câd ar faes, heb achos nog ystyr yn y byd oddigerth i gyflawni darogan y Bardd Du, allan o brophwydoliaeth y Sybli; na sonniwch bellach am Robin Ddu a'i gyfoedion, ni ba'sai iddynt siawns yn y byd pe'i basai Oronwy yn eu plith. Cyfieithiad Seisnig meddwch o'r Ddarogan, ag eisiau £5! Ffei, ffei! Gresyndawd anfeidrawl na bai'r cyfieithiad yn fy llogell i, ar pum punt yn un y Bardd. Rhoed Duw yng nghalon Powys i roddi rhent gynta gallo. Byddai ddrwg gennyf pei troid Salbri gerfydd ei ysgwydd or Senedd, gobeithio na ddigwydd mo hynny. Echdoe y daeth y chwaer adref o Bentrerianell, roedd yn nhad wedi bod yn o salaidd yr wythnos ddiwaetha gan y tor llengig ar anwyd. Digrif oedd yr Aldremon amachwyn ar y wraig a hithau wedi mendiaw. Pa beth y mae'r hen chwilcath, i.e., Nicholas yna yn ei wneuthur? Aie, mordaith wêch a wnaeth Iorwerth? Ymhle mae'r hadau etc? Mi glywaf iw chwaer gael llythyr oddiwrthaw. Daccw Farged Morys wedi mynd iw atteb, ac i edrych am ei thaid. Ni ffromodd y Gardinal ddim; camgymeriad mawr ydoedd! Fe ryngawdd bodd ir Pendefig hawddgar ddyfod i'm hymweled a tharing a orug efo mi bumnos i fwydta, i yfed, i ymresymmu, ac i ymbynciaw; ac yn y diwedd nid oedd wybod pwy oedd iâr na phwy oedd geiliawg! Mae'r Gardinal cyn fynyched ymhlith y *gwyr 'nheddigions*, ai fod wedi dysgu ei drwg arferion, eistedd i fynnu i bottio yn dra hir, gorfedd drannoeth drwy'r boreu, rheol iw honno ni ddigymmydd a Gwilym; ond rhaid weithiau dioddef. Ymhen y tridiau neu pedwar wedi'r gwr fyned i bant, mi bicciais hyd ym Modorgan, lle 'rydoedd mwy na llonaid y tŷ o'r creaduriaid uchod. Arhosais yno wythnos i ddysgu mynd yn un o honynt, ond nid wyf fymrun gwell, ffaelio'n glir lan ddyscu'r gelfyddyd. Pwy a ddaeth yma echdoe debygach i, a llythyr yn ei law oddiwrth y brawd Hwlant i dorri'r garw, ond eich cyfaill y Mr. Penant, the fossilist, etc., of Downing, in Flintshire, a surprizing man in his way! We've been ransacking the sea and land for curiosities, ac nid pennach dau gyfaill oddiyma hyd yna. Daccw fo wedi cychwyn tua'r Iwerddon iw chwilio hi o ben bwygilydd am bethau ar y ddaear a than y ddaiar. He is to send me the L—d knows what from all parts. Nid brwysgaw y bydd y Surveyor ond llymeittiaw'n lewdost. Gerwin o'r prisiau ar gig ffordd yna; maent yn achwyn yn Nulun yr unmodd ac etto er hyn, nid sôn mawr a fu am farwolaeth milod, mae pob peth mal arferol ffordd yma, ond ei bod hi'n dal yn oerllyd. Yn gôch y bo mhais, ond ydych i ar Llew yn ddeuddyn digrif amhosibl, am ein rhoddi ni i gyd mewn disgwyliad o gael golwg maes arnoch, ac yr'wan ein sommi? Wala, gadewch iddo, ni choelir monoch o gwbl o hyn allan. Ymhle mae'r llyfrau bellach? A rwymwyd un i Wilym mewn garwgroen lloi? Ni che's i ddim llythyr oddiwrth Lewelyn etto. Daccw'r nith Peggy Owen wedi dyfod adref o Allt Fadawg a Mathafarn; pawb yno yn iach, y Ceredigionaid yn groesion erchyll achos bod y Brenin yn drêch na Phowel. Mae pawb o honom ffordd yma yn rhwydd iachus; i Dduw y byddo'r moliant a'r diolch. Bydded iddo warchod drosoch chwithau ar hyn oll a berthyn i chwi. Sgrifenwch gynta galloch at **W. to R. contd.**

Eich caredigawl frawd, Gwilym Lwytu.

P.S.—Pray my compliments to Captain Edwards and to Mr. William Parry, am hannerch at y Gymdeithas, sef y Cymrodorion. Mae'n rhywyr gweled tippyn o'ch gorchwyl yn argraphedig.—W.M.

ESGAIR Y MWYN, July 8, 1754.

Dear Brother,—I received yours of the 29th ulto this morning and am glad you are well and that there are no bonddigigions to be visited in your country. I don't know what colours they are of. Digrif yw Penant fossilist. Gwych fod Cymro oi fath, yn lle rhyw bendewion dogs. I am here now at ye Quarters pay, paying miners, carriers, washers, witnesses, etc., nid llai na mil o bunnau a gludais i o arian oddicartref i dalu iddynt—a prodigious affair, no wonder people should run mad about it! Mae'n debyg mae fi yw'r sobraf o'r holl genedlaeth, ag yn cadw lleiaf o swn yn ei gylch, ac yn cadw fy lle yn lew hyd yn hyn er gwaetha'r gelyn ddyn. I have a fine prospect of lead ore on a tenement that I have a lease of on **L. to W. CXCIX.**

L. to W. contd.

ye forefield of Esgair y Mwyn, the same vein. This will drive them madder than ever. We are raising some ore there, and I believe it will answer. I have given you an account of a girl, and my wife is pretty well. Notwithstanding all the surprizing schemes of my enemies I have defeated them surprizingly, and I trust in God I shall hereafter. Poor Dick Morris of Mathavarn was like to drop of a cholera morbus, but I hope he recovers. Yr ydym ni gwedi gorthrechu'r gelyn am *fobbio* yn glir lân. Ni fu'r fath *lachio* erioed yn Llanerchymedd ag a fu yma yn ffair Ystrad Meurig yr wythnos ddiwaethaf; fe ddarfu ein pobl ni drwy nerth *cocâdes* ar cwrw ei sgwrrio nhwy'n *Deifis* ag yn Wyddelod drwy'r ffair yn ôl ac ymlaen, dros bedair battel a wnaethont. Roedd yno gantoedd o gloliau cochion i bawb a waedda "Bowel for ever." "King George a Mr. Morris for ever" oedd yn ei charrio hi yn dêg. Would any man believe such a thing possible? But so it is. Fair honest dealings and punctual payments, and an open behaviour hath outdone all their schemes and villanies, and hath brought the body of ye country of our side. I have no time to add but that

I am your affectionate brother, Llewelyn.

P.S.—Gronwy hath been helpd for ye present.

CAERGYBI, 13th July, 1754.

W. to R. cc.

Anwyl Frawd,—Mae encyd o amser wedi llithraw hebiaw er pan sgrifennais attoch ac etto heb gaffael dim atteb, fal y mae mwyaf y cywilydd. Chwi ddywedsoch y gyrrai Lewelyn hanes i gâd i mi mynych iawn,—ni che's i byth fymryn. Dyma hanes ei ferch Elsbeth ai mam. Aie treiol arall sydd debyg ei fod? Mae'r gwr yn achwyn ar rai o hen ffrindiau sydd wedi mynd yn elynion brychion. Ai Fychan or Dollfa a droes yn gî glâs, beth meddwch? Gobeitho fod y Bowys yn gywir ac yn onest. Os chwildrôdd Fychan mae'n debyg na cheir daioni mwyach o'r Drysorfa. Rhowch dipyn or hanes, da chwithau. 'Rym ni yma ag Ymhentrerianell yn iachus dda iawn. Mi glywais weled Goronwy dydd arall yng Nghaer Nerpwl yn un cawr (ond yn . . . . y sgrifen o hi). Pwy sydd yn ei le meddwch chwi? Ni bu monwyf ymhen yr Eryri ettwa, ag mae lle i ofni nad âf yno y leni, o eisiau na bawn yn feistir ar fy amser ac ar ddigonedd o ddâ bydol. A fyddwch i yn gweled y Mr. Ellis o Lawrence

Lane weithiau? Gwyn ei fyd ai gwela fo yma i gael dangos iddo'n môr blanhigion yma sydd yn tyfu rhyd greigiau Cybi. I think that I have discoverd lately three or four sorts of the animal flower as Hughes of Barbados calls it. When does Mr Ellis's book come out? Bendith Dduw i chwi am gyd a'ch bys ddwywaith o lythyr, ni choeliach i fyth ddäed fyddai ei gael. Rhaid rhoi'r swydd i fynnu ar sgrifennu i fynd ir farchnad i brynnu bwyd i 5 neu 6 o gegau. Duw a fyddo gyd a chwi. W. to R. contd.

Eich caredigawl frawd, William Morris.

P.S.—A fyddwch i yn gweled Jack Evans, mab yr hen Ddoctor. ambell dro? Dyma frawd iddo yn yr ysgol yn y fangre hon yn dysgu sgrifenu a rhifo, a bachgennyn ffeind ydyw. Ces lythyr ddoe neu echdoe oddiwrth y car Salbri yn achwyn yn greulon fod y golwg yn pallu, a chant o anffortunau er'ill. Yn iâch byth weled na chlywed Anacreon yn canu Cymraeg na'r Sibli ddoeth. Mae mis er pan sgrifenasoch yma or lleia.

HOLYHEAD, 20th July, 1754.

Dear Brother,—I have a long time expected to hear some account of the fifty New Testaments and Common Prayers, but hitherto in vain. W. to R. CCI. Mr. Ellis has received his fifty some time ago, and he expects that his second parcel of Bibles are now at Chester, the secretary having acquainted him that orders were given some fortnight or three weeks ago for sending of them, but not a word of the others. The inclosed I received from Mr. Owen, but do not know what answer to give; your being disapointed of the promised Bibles makes me terribly affraid of the same treatment in regard to the Testaments, which God forbid! Er cariad ar yr Arglwydd ymegniwch ar ddyfod ar matter yma i ben dâ, rhag gormod gwarth a ch'wilydd; os digwydd ir gwrthwyneb, ni choeliach i byth (pei medrwn ddywedyd i chwi) faint yr anhunedd a barodd imi eisioes, gan nad mai peth ysgafn ag ofer iw *iechydwriaeth* dyn, ac nid hwyrach na bo rai llawer yn ymddibynnu wrth y neges yma. I shall continue to be uneasy untill I hear from you; the money shall be paid for them when and where you please to order them. 'Rych i gael 50 chwaneg o Fiblau i'r mwynwyr. Ow cofiwch am yr hen gartref yn anad unlle, ond y cartref newydd. Dyma lythyr oddiwrth y Brâs o'r *Esgair* a hanes fod gobaith dogn o fwyn mewn rhyw dyddyn

W. to R. contd.

gyferbyn ar llall. Beth os ceir yno wythen o deir llath neu bedair o ddiameter? Roedd nobility y Brenin a Mr. Morris yn ffysto *rhai'r Bywel* iw crogi, ni lyfasant ddangos mo'i trwynau mewn ffair na marchnad. Beth ydys nes os câ rhyw goegyn diddaioni arddelw gan Sior ar yr Esgair; yno ni bydd, ond odid, ond sychu trwyn mewn llawes. Mae pawb o honom ffordd yma yn rhwydd iachus, a nhad felly ddoe neu echdoe; rwy'n ei ddisgwyl yma Wyl Iago i'n gwylmabsant ni, yr hwn a drôdd y meistr Ellis oddiar y Suliau. Roedd tri Sul y'mis Gorphena ar ba rai y byddid yn dangos, ac mae'n debyg yn carrio o amgylch greiriau Saint Gybi, etc., ac er hynny hyd yr awron fe'i gelwid Suliau'r Creiriau. Byddai'r holl wlad yn dyfod yma i wylmabsanna arnynt, sef i fwyta, i yfed, i feddwi, i ymbaffio, i dyngu ac i regi, etc. Beth a wnaeth y Preiddiawr yma ond cyhoeddi drwy'r wlad y byddai'r Gwylmabsant ar Wyl Iago ag y byddai gadachau sidan i redeg, i ddawnsiaw, etc., am danynt, hynny a hudodd yr holl *ynfydion* i anghofiaw'r creiriau er mwyn gwychder y sidan sidani; ag ni welsochi nemawr waith yn ffair Llanerchmedd fwy o honynt nag a fydd yma ddydd Iau nesaf. Mi glywaf Lewelyn yn dywedyd iddo ddianghenu Goronwy. Gwyn ei fyd allu gwneuthur y fath gymwynas; rhaid imi dewi am lol heb yn ddiolch imi, neu golli'r bost. Duw a f'o yn gwarchadw drosoch a byddwch wych. *Eich caredigawl frawd, William Morris.*

HOLYHEAD, 29th July, 1754.

W. to R. CCII.

Dear Brother,—Chwi welwch fy mod i yn ymroi i sgrifenu attoch, er eich bod chwi wedi rhoddi'r swydd i fyny er's talm mawr o amser, ni waeth pa peth a fai'r achos, os ydych iach ac wrth eich bodd, mae'ch distawrwydd yn ddigon er peri ofned i'r gwrthwyneb. Ni ddaeth mo'r hen ŵr ein tâd ddim i'n gwylmabsant Sant Jago, ond fe ddaeth ei wyres Margaret Owain; mae hi'n dywedyd ei fod yn llecyn yn ô fynnych gan y Fors sydd yn ei grugo. Os uchel, bloedd Gwilym am glywed oddiwrthych, mae'r tad yn gwaeddi tri mwy, medd Marged. Ni chadd lythyr oddiwrthych er's gwell na chwarter blwyddyn, neu bedwar mis, medd hi, er maint a sgrifenodd. Mae'r ddau hogyn wedi mynd yn noeth lumaniaid nid er am'arch arnoch, ni fedd yr hynaf grŷs am ei gefn, a phobyl yn dyfod a'u biliau am arian drostyn ag yn dechreu siarad yn uchel, na bo'nd ei grybwyll, felly ni wyr yr hen wr pa beth i wneuthur o eiseu clywed oddiwrthych.

"Yn wir Marged," meddwn innau, "nis gwn innau, rhaid i chwi berswadio'r bobyl i fod yn amyneddgar dros dro. Naill (chwedl Elias brophwyd) y mae'r gwr ar ymdaith neu yntau'n cysgu, ag y bydd ei ddeffro. Tra adawodd yrru i ffrind imi yw rhannu ymhlith plwyfolion Penrhos, Gallgo, ac Eugred, hanner cant o ryw lyfrau, ni chlywa i na siw na miw yn eu cylch." "O ho!" eb'r hitheu, "mae nhaid yn breuddwydio bob nos yr elo iw wely ynghylch y Biblau a addawyd iddo yntau. Ag nid yw Mr. Owen ein person ni yn gorphwyso gan sôn am ei Destamentau Newydd, a braidd y gedu o nhw allan o'i bregeth y Suliau, mae o'n dywedyd pei gwyddai fewyrth Rhisiart Morys gymaint sydd o'u heisiau a chynifer o fendithion a ddeuai iw ran fe wnai fwy o frys iw hanfon iw hen gymdogion." "Wala, yn wir nid hwyrach hynny," meddwn innau, "Ond chwi welwch fy nith fal y mae'r byd yn bod, a rhaid gwneuthur y goreu o'r gwaetha" felly dyna i chwi'r ymgomio a fu rhwng yr ewythr ar nith. Dyma ei brawd Will wedi cael cennad i ddyfod adref i ymweled a'i rieni, ag yn glamp o ddyn lysti, gwrawl, cyfoethog ddigon. I must contrive to get him out of the cabin, for he begins to be too much a man and a sailor to bear with the slavery of it, though it is a beneficial post. I must leave off abruptly. I am, dear brother, *Yours most affectionately*, *William Morris*. W. to R. contd.

ESGAIR Y MWYN, July 29, 1754.

Dear Brother,—I have yours of ye 20th this day, and am glad you are all well. I have a very sparing line from Peggy, too much upon the laconic. I intend a letter for her in this. Though she may be ready, I am not yet in ye condition to give her a husband and baich cefn o arian, unless I give other people's money, but hope I shall be able to do handsomely for them all if I live a few years. I consent to pay for ye deal boards if Robert Jones gives the work. There is some boundary to be set to ye first but none to ye last, unless you fix a few days which you may guess it may be done in. Had a letter from father lately. Gorchmynnwch fi at y berson onestaf or rhywogaeth yn y wlad yna, sef Mr. Ellis, ag archwch iddo yfed diod ysprydol os myn fyw, mae natur yn gofyn mwy nag oedd Paul yn ei lwfio, oblegid nid yw ef ddim apostol yn mynd ar led i droi pobl at y ffydd. Rwy'n gobeithio y ceiff Gronwy fara, onid oes rhyw dynged yn dywedyd nad â prydydd byth yn gyfoethawg. L. to W. CCIII.

L. to W. contd.

Daccw fi gwedi sgrifennu rhyw stwff at yr Aldramon Prichard. Nawdd Duw rhag ei ddŷled. Where is ye magnetic sand found that you sand your letters with? Is it not the iron stone powderd? Or what is it? Dyma'r diwrnod teg cynta leni; the wind N.N.W., and wandering clouds, we have had such continual rains that we have neither fireing nor hay in as yet. I intend for home in a few days, but cannot be there long. Upon the hoof again.

I am, your affectionate brother, L.M.

W. to R. CCIV.

CAER GYBI, Awst yr 11eg, 1754.

Anwyl Frawd,—Ar fy nyfodiad adref o Bentre'r Eirianallt mi dderbyniais eich llythyr o'r 3dd; wedi bod mewn hir ddisgwiliad diball am danaw, ac mewn anesmwythder rhag ofn bod rhyw anlwc wedi digwydd iw 'sgrifenydd; ond moliant ir Goruchaf Dduw fod [pob] peth yn ddiogel. Mi eithym wythnos i ddoe i ymweled a nhad ac i fwrw'r Sul yno—mynd i Eglwys Benrhos i glywed y Gair, lle'r adwaenwn oddeutu dwsing o bobl. Ond pe dywedwn i chwi gy'd a chywydd prin y rhoisai'r person ei droed dros agorddrws yr eglwys i ddyfod allan nad ydoedd yn y cy'd a mi am y Testamentau, ni feddwn innau air i ddywedyd yn eu cylch ond gwrido a chywilyddio, a dywedyd y gwir sef fy mod yn gobeithio eu bod ar ddyfod. Mi welaf yn y llythyr yma eich bod yn tybiaw ei fod wedi derbyn y 50 a ddaeth gyda rhai y Mr. Ellis. Naddo, naddo, na chlywed dim son am danynt. I presume the Society never sent them or they would have writ to somebody here about them. However, I writ yesterday to Mr. Bryan to desire that he would order the carrier to call at the warehouses at Chester, but I am affraid to no purpose. Ow pam na fuasech yn 'sgrifennu lein (oni allasech gael amser i ymweled a rhai o ysgrifenyddion y Gymdeithas) i wybod a yrasant hwynt. Nid wyf yn ammeu dim nad oes gennych ddigon o waith ar eich dwylo, os oes gormod eich bai chwi ydyw. Na atto Duw i neb ymhel a mwy nag a eill gwmpasu iw trin heb wneuthur sarhaad neu gamwri ai gorph nai feddwl (h.y., ei ysbryd). Engraved *yn Gymraeg* meddwch y mae'r 52 Scripture prints, nid wyfi yn deall monoch, but the proposals will explain the thing. I had the perusal of yours to my father where you mentioned your being busy about some printing work, which I imagined was the affairs of the Cymrodorion. My father is in tollerable good health. Y fors oedd waethaf wrthaw. Yr Esgob recommends members to the Society in this country ac nid eraill. O ni fedd Pennant ddim Cymraeg, ag ni wiw disgwyl iddo byth ddyfod iw deall, fal y mae mwya'r gresyndod. I have letters frequently from him, for to me he incloses his friends' epistles. Aie epil y wiber honno a elwir yr hydra yw'r Teifisiaid? Nawdd Duw rhagddynt! Ie'n wir, gwych a fai cael gafael ar ddictionary y Dr. Davies a nodau Wotton arnaw. Gwych fyddai gennyfi gael un heb na nodau na dim arall, ond ni welafi ddim gobaith ysywaeth. Pwy a wyr a fyddwn byw ym mis Mai? Am y cones neu genhawon sedar, lle da disgwyl byth ei gweled os aethynt i Allt Fawdawc; ni chawsem byth y lleill oni bae ddigwydd imi fynd yno, ond ni lwyddodd un o honynt, meirw wedi dyfod i fynu. Ffarwel i Hwlyn, os oes daioni a berthyn iddo, nid oes mymryn iw ddeufrawd, pe basai Forys byw, dyn gwych a wnaethai, i ran hwnnw y digwyddodd yr holl synwyr. Am y Ddoctor Bifan siaplan, ni choeliwn yn fy myw nad gwagbren ydyw, pa wedd bynnag, moeswch weled pa beth a ddywaid am bobyl. It is a discredit to anyone to be halld into such *foolish disputes*. As obscure as I am in this nook I would not for a good deal that my name should have been mentioned, diolch i'r offeiriad tanbaid am beidiaw. Mae'r Llew yn 'sgrifenu attaf innau yn abyl mynych rwan. Dim son yn ei lythyr diweddaf am Esgair y Mwyn fach. Os ceir dogn o fwyn ceir yr hanes, os cynnogni tewi a son a wneir. Newydd da a fai clywed fod y pum cant punnau wedi ei sefydlu ar y distain. Ond os y brenhin a rydd yr Esgair o'i law, bid ir Bowys ei chaffael ac nid arall, oddigerth iddo ei rhoddi ir sawl ai haeddai oreu, sef y Llew ei hunan. Roeddwn yn meddwl mae sorri a wnaethai'r Gommissioner Vychan. Gwae'r mân swyddogion. Gadael gair allan a *wneis* wrth sgrifennu ynghylch Goronwy; mae'r gŵr byth yn Walton ac yno bydd hyd na symud y Bowys bawl ei dîd ef. Sgrifenu y mae ef fal hyn "yn Ghaer Gybi neu yn Ghaer Nerpwl" yn lle yng Nghaer, a gofyn yr oeddwn pa un o'r ddwy orthography ydoedd yn ei lle? Ce's lythyr oddiwrtho'r dydd arall; roedd y pum guinea wedi cau bwlch, er na yngenodd un gair wrthyf o ble y daethynt. I have some pwytri lying at Alderman Prichard's in Leverpoole which were too bulky for a frank; perhaps Anacreon may be among them, os nad yw, mi fyddaf yn crefu

W. to R. contd.

W. to R. contd.

benthyg hwn yna. Mae'n dda gennyf glywed fod Jack Evans yn llencyn da, gobeithio fod rhai or bendithion a enillodd ei dâd wedi dyfod iw ran. Gorchmynwch fi attaw, mae ei frawd Gwilym yma'n yr ysgol, bachgennyn cwrtais cywrain ddigon ydyw. P'ar fodd y mae'r câr Gwil. Parry o Woolwich? A wyddoch i ddim o hanes Will Parry y jeweller Gwyddelig?. Mae arnaf eisiau gwybod os aeth yn siêd, par sut y mae'r stât yn cyttuno ar Woodward? Da bod yr iechyd mor helaeth ffordd yna, rhag mor druenus bod hebddo. Rym ni yma, mawl i Dduw, bawb yn iachus. Nid yw nhad etto yn bur fodlon i fod heb wraig, ac nid oes ond Duw ei hun a eill ei gadw rhag gwneuthur rhyw fargen wirion ffol. Mae'n rhaid i mi dorri cynffon y llythyr yma mewn byrbwyll. Byddwch wych, a Duw'n eich cylch. *Eich caredigawl frawd, Gwilym Lwyttu.*

CAERGYBI, 23rd August, 1754, Nos Wener.

W. to R. CCV.

Mrawd Rhisiart Fynglwyd,—I received yours of the 17th and observed that you had not received a letter of mine in *answer* to yours of the 3rd. I ble'r aeth y chwiw leidr? But lest he should be lost for good and all, will give you a second, though perhaps not of the same tenor with the other, obleit nid wy'n cofiaw un gair oedd ynddo. Mi ddywedais mae'n debyg mal y buaswn yn yr hen gartref, lle y tarawswn wrth y nhad a'i deulu yn rhwydd iach, ag ar fy nyfodiad adref wedi cael eich llythyr, a chwedi gyrru i Gaerlleon i ymofyn Testamentau, ond fe weddai fod y matter hwnw wedi ei ddiddyrysu o'r diwedd. Os gwelwch gyfleu i'w gyrru i Gaer, bydd digon o lestri yn mynd oddeutu Gwyl Fihangel i'r ffair, ac yno bydd hawdd eu cael i bob parth o'r Ynys Dowell. Dyglywch ha wr fab, 'rych yn tuchan ac yn achwyn yn echryslon ar y *bydol drafferthion* sydd i'ch crugo beunoeth, codi'n foreu a mynd yn hwyr i gysgu, a phrin gael amser i roi gylfinaid yn eich pen! Ag etto er hyn 'rwyn deall eich bod yn ymddugwd a rhai a ellid adael heibiaw, o bai ormod o ludded. Y pethau rwyf yn ei feddwl yw tynnu llunia seintia, etc., o *Gymraeg*. Nid gwaith llwyr angenrheidiawl hwnnw, a pham i chwi ddwyn anhunedd o'r achos? More of these by and by. Beth ynta, rhaid gadael y llyfr heb ei rwymaw tan na cheffir y darluniadau a'r ymyla prydferth iw rhoddi ynddaw. Mae'r berson hon yn dywedyd mae'r *Esbog* sydd raid enwi'r aelodau i'r Gymdeithas, ac nid un aelod anghytrig geisio i mewn un arall. Nid oes mymryn o ameu nad y'ch yn cael dogn o blâ efo matterion y Deheudiriaid. Gwyn ei fyd a gai glywed ei fod unwaith ar ben. Mae eppil Iago bod y gynffon yn tyngu i'r fach'lis fawr mae tawel fab Hywel a fydd a biau'r Esgair, er na brenhin na neb arall, ei gyfiawnder o ydyw meddynt, a pham na cheiff o hi. Nid oes gan y Bennant mwy na'r rhan fwyaf o wyr Tegeingl fawr o Gymroaeg, ac ni bydd ganddo byth, oni bae daro o honaw wrth hanes fossils yn yr iaith honno. Ie, da chwithau, gadewch gael y mohogany seed i edrych a fedrwn ni goed o honynt. Arwydd ddigon sal yw bod Hwlyn yn mynd i Siamaica. Deg i un nad yno y bydd ei farw dywarchen. Ni thâl Bifan o'r Neuadd Wen i son am dano. Gobeithio nad yw'r dyn hwnnw yn un o'r Cymrodorion, beth meddwch? Rwyn ofni fod ysbryd eiddigedd a'i holl felldigedig berthynasa wedi cael gafael ar galon y Bychan o'r dollfa, ac nid wyf yn ammeu dim nad ymddangosodd y dydd arall mewn rhyw anghymwynas a wnaeth y Bwrdd i'ch brawd Gwilym. Chwanog a fydd pobl y rhai y bo'r yspryd drwg ynddynt, wneuthur niwaid i bawb a fo'n deiryd i'r sawl ai cyffroa. Da iawn clywed fod Sion ab y Doctor Evans (yn nef mae ei enaid) yn prifio yn llanc da. Ydyw fo yn gallu ymwrthod a'r diotta? Mae Wil ei frawd efo mi bob dydd yn burion bachgen, ai dad ynghyfraith yn gwneuthur yn fawr o honaw. Er dim ar y fo, moeswch fenthyg caniad Sibli Seisnig ac Anacreon. Ni yrrodd Goronwy monynt i mi namyn rhyw bethau eraill, nid o'i waith ei hun. Chwi fyddwch sicr o'u cael yn ol yn ddiogel gyda llawer iawn o ddiolchiadau dwysion. Bellach am yr ail ebystol, a hanes conffyrddus fod y llyfrau iw cael unwaith ettwa. Better late than never, ebr y Sais, felly yna. Nid wy'n ammeu na byddai cyn hawsed cael y llyfrau o Gaerlleon i Ddulas, ac o Gaernarfon, for they seldom have any boats coming from the latter, but from Chester frequently. You ask my oppinion concerning the cutts mentioned in the proposals, but as to my part I am at a loss about the nature of the undertaking, fifty-two cutts t e i ht shillings a sett, meddwch. (Query whether the book and cutts are to be at eight shillings). Mae hynny yn agos two pence bob un, a phar sut i ddwyn pobyl ar ddeall y talent hynny, nis gwn i, nor can I believe that you'll ever get off half the number you mention, for nobody but persons of fashion will lay out so much

W. to R. contd.

W. to R. contd. money, and of them we have but very few in these parts that regards the Welsh. These proposals will do the scheme more hurt than good, as they are in my oppinion but inaccurately done, a school boy of twelve year old would write as good a hand or better especially than the receipt. Os dyna'r drefn sydd ar Philips efo ei *Bewter* ni waeth arall nog yntau. Mi ddaliaf storaid o wenith i chwart o faip y tyr Siac Owain well llythyrennau, yn enwedig y rhai Idalaidd. Pam na fusech yn dywedyd yr y cynnygiadau na fynnech mor arian nes caffael y llyfrau? Dyma'r Berson a mau am y cyfan o honynt. Mi wnaf fy ngoreu ar gaffael chwaneg, ond yn wir ddyn, nid wyfi yn tybiaw y ffynna gennyf, cewch glywed. Mi ddygaswn glywed farw Ifan William y Telynior. Ai ceingciau oi waith ei hun ydynt? Ni chlywais ddim blâs ar y mesur hwnnw a yrrodd yma ddydd a fu, ond na ddywedwch mo hynny wrtho. Er mwyn dynion a da oes dim gobaith gael byth weled peth o waith *Goronwy* wedi ei argraphu? If you think you cant compass to do it, I wish you would send me the copy of Cowydd y Farn with notes. We'll have it done in Dublin by contributions. Several friends are desirous to have it published, and I have told too many stories about it though not designedly. Mae rhai o'r Personiaid a'r bobl 'nheddigions yma'n dechreu cyfaddef fod y bardd yn ddyn abl rhyfeddol. Nid ydych yn son un amser am ein brodyr y Cymrodorion; a'i llaccau y mae gwres brawdgarwch yn eich plith? Par fodd bynnag annerchwch fi at y Gymdeithas pan ymgyfarfyddoch. A fydd y brawd Glyn yn dyfod yn eich plith y dyddiau yma ynta blino a wnaeth ar ol y lecsiwn? Fe ffaeliodd gennyf fynd i lysieua i'r Eryri yr haf yma er maint o'r awydd. I have had no letter from y Tewfras this ten days or fortnight past, mae dialedd eisiau clywed hanes Esgair y Mwyn fâch, a pha beth sydd yn dyfod o'r cyflog. Gwych a fai cael y πυμ καν-πυντ yn y flwyddyn. Mi fyddwn i fodlon i gymryd chwarter yr ariant. Dyma ryw hen wrechyn yn grwnan yn fy nghlustia am gyngor, ac mae'n rhywyr mynd i ymorawl porthiant i chwe-nyn. Duw a fo gyda chwi ag a'ch llwyddo yn eich holl amcanion a fo er daioni i chwi. Amen.

Eich caredigawl frawd, William Morris.

P.S.—Ymhle y cawsoch y gair dau synied neu'r gair mwys yma, sef diwaethaf? Argraphiad diwaethaf meddwch yn y cynnygiadau, h.y., mae'n debyg di-waethaf, heb fod yn waethaf, ac yn ddiweddaf hefyd. Mae'r llongau siwgwr yn dechreu dyfod i mewn. Dyma ni wedi pwysaw llwyth un o well na deucan tunell. Mae ambell geiniog i chael oddiwrthynt, pe caid llonyddwch iw chanlyn, ond ni chair ddim. Mae'r un yspryd wedi myned i mewn i dollfa'r *Duwmares* ac aeth y^{n} mewn i un Gaerludd. Yno y byddai longau'r Gwyddyl yn mynd i bwyso ei siwgwr, etc., ond nid oeddynt yn medru cael pob peth wrth eu bodd, felly dyfod yma a orugant. Hynny a barodd i'r swyddogion yno ymddigiaw wrth gowiriaid Cybi, ac y maent yn gwneuthur cymaint o gamwri ac allant. I'r dollfa honno y byddwn ni yn gyrru ein cyfrifon a'n llythyrau, ac nid at the Bwrdd. So they've the opportunity of representing things in what light they think proper. Duw a'n cadwo rhag ein câs. Roedd y gair ffordd yma'r dydd arall fod yr hen Nicholson wedi marw yna a bod y brawd Tew yn ei le—celwydd bod y gair! A fyddwch i yn gweled yr hen gorphyn hwnnw weithiau? Par ddelw sydd arno? Da chwithau, gadewch wybod a gawsoch i fy llythyr diweddaf sef atteb ir eiddoch o'r 3dd, os nid 'o, fe fu rhyw hagr weithred ar led. Byddwch wŷch.—*W.M.* **W. to R. contd.**

GALLTVADOG, September 8, 1754.

Dear Brother,—I have yours of ye 22nd August with *Cwynfanau* about entring wine in bottles. If you had not a copy from Beaumaris or a letter from ye Board of ye 1st March, 1753, or thereabouts, about wine in bottles, I think you may petition ye Board, as you can produce instances of such entries allowd; but if you had that notice I can see no colour for it. Perhaps I may get a Member of Parliament to hand in ye petition when the Parliament meets, but I believe it is impracticable at present, so that you must pay ye mulct. Inclosed you have a copy of a letter we had a few days ago from the Board, which seems to be a general letter on the same head, so that your misfortune very likely was to act so at an unlucky time, when the Treasury had received an information. I cannot think that anybody from your parts had any acquaintance with Mr. Harding, not even Chwilcath, so I suppose the information **L. to W. CCVI.**

L. to W. contd.

is real from the Sussex coast perhaps of French wines intended to be imported. Ni chlywai son am y Chwilcath yn marw, ni wn i a fentriwn i gymeryd ei lle hi rwan ai peidio. Have had no leisure yet to write to father, I am so excessive busy that I have hardly my senses. As for the Common Prayer cuts they are in my opinion beautiful things and we have subscribed here for about twenty. I would not take a guinea for the book if I had it well bound. There is neither credit nor discredit to my brother about it. If any like it, well and good. It is true the thing is more for ostentation than use. But religion requires its fineries and follies as well as other ladies.

This hath no regard to Gronwy's poems. Those must come from ye Cymmrodorion, but this is a private affair of Ryland's. The cuts are intended for ye Common Prayer and Testament bound together, which I think is one of ye prettiest books of ye kind I ever saw. Have you seen none of them? Y Llwyn Llwyd yn addo fyth. Ydyw mi wranta mae'r Esgair yn digio llawer un, gadewch iddynt; dywedwch iddynt hefyd fy mod mewn cymaint ffafor gida'g Iarll Powys, nad yw'n gwneuthur dim gweithred o bwys heb ymgynghori a mi, and that there is often two messengers in ye same week from him to me, and you may tell them that they are not sure there will be ever a trial more about Esgair y Mwyn, and it is *impossible* there can be any at Hereford or Salop. Bod Powel wedi benthygca gwell na £1500 o bunnoedd i garrio'r treial hyd yr aeth, ag nid yw cantoedd mor hawdd i'w cael yn y Sir yma i chware a hwynt. That he calls for his rents before hand, and curses the hour he ever meddled with this lawsuit. Pawb yn ddigon distaw yma, no places of trust to be given without asking my opinion, and certifying for ye persons! Torri ar ei traws a wnelo'r sawl sy'n chwythu gwenwyn o achos fod dynyn truan yn mynd rhagddo. Gadewch i'r Brysgi fynd ymlaen. It is good sometimes to have such a spur—it will happen one time or other that he may fall in his own snare. It is envy more than anything else I suppose that poisons the mind of Collector Smith, for this affair is vastly magnifyd in all countries to be a prodigious thing for my profit. Duw gyda chwi, nid oes yma ddim amser i sgrifennu ychwaneg, pob peth mewn ffrwst ar draws eu gilydd. *Eich brawd ffyddlon,* *L.M.*

CAER GYBI, 21ain o Fedi, 1754.

W. to R.
CCVII.

'Mrawd Mynglwyd,—Dymma eich llythyr o'r 14 gar bron a chan diolch am fenthyg llythyrau Goronwy, ond nid wyf yn diolch mo'r pethau am y rhan gyntaf o'ch ebystol. Pam i chwi ddwrdio a digio mor erwin wrth Wilym wirion? Nid oedd ô yn meddwl chwaethach amcanu sarhaad yn y byd i neb; nid felly y bydd brodyr, sef yn ffromwyllt naill wrth y llall, ac yn cofiaw'r gwaethaf i'w gilydd. Os bu eich brawd yn anrhesymol (ac nid oes dim ameu nad oedd o dippyn allan o ffordd) nid oedd hyny achlysur yn y byd i chwi daro'ch tîn wrth y nenbren, chwedl yr hen Wen droed lewt. Rhaid i chwi ysgwyd llaw a rhoi cusan ffrins a gollwng yn angof wendidau 'ch brawd; mae crefydd, ie, a'ch dyledswydd yn gofyn hynny gennych; mae yntau'n gofyn nawdd ac yn addaw na throsedda ond hynny o'i wirfodd nag o'i anfodd. 'Rydych chwi wedi maddeu, ond ydych?—mi a wn eich bôd; felly digon am hynny. Mi glywais y Bennant yn son am eich ffrind Mendez da Costa; fe yrrodd iddo ryw bethau a gawsai gennyfi oddiyma efo'r post, ai Iuddew o'r Fendez? Na welis i ddim son am dano yn y papurau newydd; anfynych y byddai'n cael golwg ar y rhai Seisnig gan mor ddrudion ydynt. Gwaed hwch! Dyma fi wedi colli'r ink am ben y papur, gresyn oedd, a ffeiniad o'r ysgrifen a gwastadled y rheswm! Ond i fynd ymlaen. Ni bu uwch bawd na sawdl i un o bobl Drysglwyn er pan fu farw'r hen bobl, a Moi yntau yn South Carolina. Mi adwaenwn Hwlyn* yn llencyn diniwaid ddigon. Wawch! dyma fy nheulu i wedi dyfod adref yn iach lawen o Bentre'rianell, lle buont dair wythnos gyfan yn difyrru'r hen wr, nhw ai gadawsant

* A pedigree of this family may be seen in "Powys Fadog" v. 287. One of the sons of William Lewis of Trysglwyn is frequently referred to in the letters (e.g. pp. 185, 187). He was a doctor in London and attended upon Richard Morris. In an old ballad printed about 1754, there appear the following englynion. Tri o Englynion i Mr. Howel Lewis, y meddig o Lundain, ail mab William Lewis, Esqr., Trysglwyn, yn Amlwch ym Mon:—

Howel wr tawel teg—Lewis feddig
Lwys fiddiol dy anrheg,
Yn fwyn y daeth o Fon deg,
I Lundain, iredd landeg.

Mab Gwilim a'i rim o rad—wyr Morys
Ymyrwr da weithred
A gorwyr er llwyr wellhad,
Howel Wredog ni wridad.

W. to R. contd.

y boreu heddyw yn bur heini, ni buont erioed cyhyd oddiwrthyf or blaen; dô, unwaith pan fum yn y Deheudir,—mewn difrif mae nhw' yn gwpl o blant ffeind, i Dduw bo'r diolch am danynt, ac rwy' yn hyderu y rhŷdd ei ras ai fendith iddynt. Beth pei medrai Feirian siared Cymraeg cystal a Siani, a'i darllen cystal a Robin? Beth pei medrynt hwythau siarad a darllen Saesonaeg cystal a hithau? Ond nid felly mae'r byd yn bôd. Oni addawodd Meirian sgrifennu at ei chyfnither Margaret Morris? Gobeithio fod swn priodi drosodd tua'r hen gartref, but query. Digrif a fai clywed y Doctor Bifan yn canu "Dick aeth yn Hittyn" wedi iddo roddi or neilldu'r gŵn du. Mae'n ddâ gan fy nghalon glywed fod y Gymdeithas o'r eiddoch yn cynnyddu bob mis a brawdgarwch yn ymledu fwy fwy. Budd ir awdwr oedd un o'r achosion mwyafa barodd i mi dymuno'r Cowydd; rhaid bodloni hebddo, oni cheir drwy fwynder a hawdd-garwch. Cefais innau lythyr heddyw iwrth y *Llew*, ac rwy'n cael ambell un yn o fynych, diolch iddo, mae o'n awr yn llawn o ysprydoedd, diolch ir Iarll. Os caf fi hanes fod yr un o'r Personiaid yma ar drancedigaeth mi sgrifennafi attoch chwi, cynt y cewch afael arno, na llythyr oddiyma at Oronwy ac oddiyno yna. Och fi na cha'i yr *rhent* oreu ym Môn! Pe bai Mr. Bodvel, i.e., Arglwydd Powis, yn ceisio gwell un iw gâr Huw Williams ac yn rhoi'r Aberffraw i Oronwy, ond gwych a fyddai? Dyma Wil ab y Doctor Evans yn copiaw gwaith Goronwy Fardd, pan ddarffo iddo, mi ai gyrraf yn ôl yn ddîos. Ni wyddai'r Bardd mae'n debyg mae bil ar yr Aldremon a yrrech iddo, mae'n ddigon tebyg fod tippyn o f—w yn y caws, roedd peth dyled er's dyddiau byd arno i O.P., nid hwyrach fod attal or achos hwnnw, nid oes mymryn o amneu nad yw'r Aldremon yn ddigon diflas pan fo'r *geinog fach* yn brin. Mae yn ddigon drwg gennyf dros yr Wdwarth yna, gan fod y benywiaid mor dost wrtho; ofn mepcyrn mae'n debyg sydd arnaw, pan fo'n ymwrthod a rhai ieuanc prydferth, cym'red ofal mae digon o achos iw hofni, nawdd Duw rhagddynt! Mae nhad yn ei lythyr yn dywedyd i chwi yrru am Dwm Parry yr Sais, mi fynnaf ymofyn oes dim llong yn barod i hwyliaw o Ddulun ffordd yna, fal y gallo gael i basaids efo hi. Bachgen cywraint ond bod eisiau ysbryd arno. Mae'r bychan a chanddo ddigon. Yn y modd ymma yr sgrifennodd fy anwyl gyfaill William Bulkeley or Brynddu, Esq., attaf y dydd arall: "I received the proposals for printing by subscription 52 o ddarluniadau newydd Ysgrythyrol, etc. I am determined to be a subscriber for two Common Prayers with those cutts bound up in them as also Mr. Evan Williams 24 Psalm tunes annex'd, of which you may acquaint your brother, Mr. Richard Morris, and shall therefore return you 8s. for that purpose, but in the meantime shall desire you to inform me what those prints are that I may satisfy others that may be inclined to subscribe, for as darluniad is a general word for prints or pictures of all kinds, whether empires, kingdoms, cities, men, beasts and birds, so shall inpatiently wait for a solution of that word, and what those two Common Prayers will cost me with those prints and Salm tunes bound up in them." Mi attebaf yr hen ŵr ynghylch pob peth ond *y Psalmau*. Pa faint a gyst y rheini? Rhaid i minnau ei cael yn fy llyfr mi wranta, mae'n debyg, obleit rwy'n disgwyl o Fodorgan gomhisiwn am ddarluniadau, ond goreu i chwi yrru yma ryw faint chwaneg or cynnygiadau, os troseddodd un nid eill y lleill mor help. Rhaid cadw noswyl, mae hi wedi mynd yn hwyr anial. Duw a warchotto drosoch ar eiddoch a byddwch wych. *Eich brawd pendew ddigon, Gwilym Fyngfrith.* **W. to R. contd.**

P.S.—Nos dranoeth. Wawch etto! Dymma fyng werthfawr gyfaill Surgeon Gen. Nichols newydd ddyfod ir dref. Roeddwn yn meddwl y cawsech olsgrif digon ei hyd y boreu foru, ond ni wiw sôn bellach, rhaid myned efo'r mwynwr accw i ymweled y claf ar anafus, etc., as the pacquet boat doth not sail till about 2 p.m. The day will be his, a da yr haeddai. This gent is deservedly at the head of his profession in Ireland (a Chester man born), a great botanist, a famous florist, gardener, etc. Dont you think it very kind of him a year or two ago, to give me by a letter from under his hand, leave to send hence as many patients (poor people incureable in our way) as I pleasd over to the hospital in Dublin where they will be admitted, attended, dieted and cured without a halfpenny expense? Did the poor Welsh ever receive such civilities from the Irish before? Ond yn ddistaw, mae'r gŵr yn ddarn o Gymro glan! I have sent many, and all have been cured, and sometimes the hospital surgeons have complimented me that I had done the work to their hands. Mae'n rhaid a brolio tippyn weithiau. Hanner dydd Dydd Llun—Dymma fi wedi bod efo'r meddyg mawr drwy'r

W. to R. contd.

boreu yn ymdreiglo, nothing would give you a better notion or rather idea of the old apostles going about, such flocks of poor miserable creatures yn crefu ag yn cael *cynghorion*, eraill yn dyfod i fendithio am rai a wnaethent lês, nid oedd ond un o ddeg a ddaeth i roddi diolch im Iachawdwr, os daw un o'r ugain rwan mae'n beth go ryfedd. Er bod gan yr hen gorphyn yr ardd wcha ond odid yn y deyrnas hono, etto fe gyfaddefodd that I had more curiosities in mine!! Ie, dwbl wfft! Wala, wala, rhaid rhoi'r pin heibiaw a mynd at y ciniaw, and to benefit by the good old man's discourse, oddiyno ei ddanfon i'r llong a ffarwel gyd ag ef dros un flwyddyn. We have come to an agreement to send each other all the varieties wanting by each yn goed, llysiau, blodau, etc. You see how fond I am of writing about these things. Dry meat to you. Hoff gan bob bwch ei ddigrifwch. Byddwch wych, a sgrifenwch gynta galloch da chwitheu. Mi wnaf fy ngoreu am yrru i chwi ddigon o enwau subscribers cyn y bo hir. Adieu.—*W.M.*

W. to R. CCVIII.

HOLYHEAD, October 11th, 1754.

Dear Brother,—Llyma fi yn gyrru yn ol i chwi, gyda chan diolch eich dau lythyr a gweithredoedd Goronw Ddu o Walton. Ni chlywais ddim oddiwrth y ceryn er's llawer dydd. Rwyn maddeu iddo dan obaith ei fod yn gwario ei amser mewn gorchwylion mwy buddiol na 'sgrifennu epistolau i'r Cybiaid, a bod Cywydd y Castell y'mynd ymlaen, etc. Par fodd bynnag, dymma fi heddyw yn llunio llythyr iddo, ac yn anfon gwrâdd o'r hen Brydyddiaeth o'r eiddo Gwalchmai ai gydoesiaid. Wrth gofio, what becomes of Mr. William Jones's MSS.? Did you petition for them as you proposed? If so, pray what was the event? The Rector of Llandegfan and Beaumaris died lately. A living in the gift of Baron Hill family, and given by young Lord Bulkeley to John Hughes, junior, of Glan'rafon. Dim siawns i Oronwy yno. Dyma linell oddiwrth yr hen wr tlawd o Fodorgan yn deysyf cael *set o'r darluniadau*, but as he dont want (i.e., cant afford to purchase) a Common Prayer, etc., desires he may have 'em loose and will have 'em bound in Dublin. Fe fu Risiart Morys o Fathafarn yma ddiwedd y mis diweddaf. Dynan o'r ffeinia rwyn credu, a bod yr herlodes honno yn ddigon dedwydd daraw wrth ei fath. Wfft o'r maint sydd ynddo; saith droedfedd mi wranta o uchder? He took with him Peggy Morris to be assisting at her *sister's* lying in. I long to hear of her being safely delivered. You remember the Priodasgerdd "O bo't llawn, bŷd da a llanc." Felly y bo, ond digrif gweled y wraig a'r ferch yn planta ar unwaith, ah? Hi eill ddigwydd yna felly, ond nid yn debygol yma. Your friend and mine Mr. Pennant is returned from his Irish travels. He left this place the 7th inst, after giving me a full account of his tour through that extensive kingdom. I told him that you had forwarded the Harwich Cliff's rarities, for which he expressed himself under great obligations to you. By inclosing a line I received from him just now you'll see how proud I am of such an ingenious worthy man's friendship. His fossils, etc., are gone in a vessel from Dublin to Flintshire, so I am to have specimens from thence. I had a letter a post or two ago from y Tew mawr o Allt Fadawg, all was well. Some skirmishes with Powel's clan, a llythyr arall o Bentre'rianell, y nhad yn rhwydd iachus, gweiddi am betisiwn iw roddi yn nwrn Syr William Irby. Mi yrrais iddo rywbeth yw seinio gan y plwyfolion. Ni byddynt fawr nes mae'n debyg, beth meddwch? Rhaid mynd tua'r hen gartref rai o'r dyddiau yma, mi addewais fyned i yfed tê at ryw ferchettos, felly rhaid terfynu. Duw gyda chwi, a byddwch wych. W. to R. contd.

Eich caredigawl frawd,

Gwilym Rwydd-dew.

P.S.—Pa beth sydd yn dyfod o fy hen gyfaill o Drecastell? Wawch! Dyma bwmp o lythyr oddiwrth ymrawd Rhisiart. Oni wyddwn i o'r goreu mae pendefig digon ffromwyllt o'r Llywydd, ond y deuai yw le mewn munudyn. Ni chaf prin amser iw ddarllain cyn gyrru hwn ymaith. A gewch chwi'r gofuned? Cewch yn siwr, a'r peth fyd a fynnoch i gan Wilym. Rhaid tewi a son bellach. Adieu. Cewch lythyr yr wythnos nesaf.

GALLTVADOG, October 14th, 1754.

Dear Brother,—Pray let me know the truth of the report that Huw Llwyd* throws sticks at Newhaven. Pray enquire closely into the affair. I dont think it impossible but the aerial part of such a fellow may be condemned to act like a fool, that so long acted the knave. I have heard it affirmed by very sober men in Merionethshire that Mr. Wynne of Ystymllyn can do some surprizing things L. to W. CCIX.

* See "ante" p. 104.

L. to W. contd.

which are called supernatural, by producing the appearances of distant persons; not that they are perhaps really above nature, but that they are done by some means that are not commonly known, or can be accounted for, as electricity and magnetism are secrets of that kind, though really natural. Be so good as to let me know the common opinion of your part about Mr. Wynne; and whether really he performed those things before sober, sensible, sedate men. I am not over credulous about those things, and scepticism is madness, for we really know in general very little or nothing in comparison to what is to be known. The great Lord Bacon owns it, and that temper of mind in him brought him to enquire into the depth of Nature beyond any man that was born before him. People that know very little of arts or sciences or of the powers of Nature (which in other words are the powers of the Author of Nature) being full of conceit of their own abilities and knowledge, will laugh at us Cardiganshire miners that maintain the being of knockers in mines—a kind of good natured impalpable people but to be seen and heard, and who seem to us to work in the mines; that is to say, they are types or forerunners of working in mines, as dreams are of some accidents that happen unto us. The barometer falls before rain and storms; if we did not know the construction of it, we should call it a kind of dream that foretells rain; but we know it is natural and produced by natural means known to us. Now how are we sure or is anybody sure, but that our dreams are produced after the same kind of natural means? There is some faint resemblance of this in the sense of hearing, the bird is killed before we hear the report of the gun. However this is, I must speak well of these knockers, for they have actually stood my very good friends, whether they are aerial beings called spirits, or whether they are people made of matter, not to be felt by our gross bodies, as air and fire the like. Before the discovery of Esgair y Mwyn mine, these little people (as we call them here) worked hard there day and night, and there are abundance of honest sober people that have heard them; (although there are some people amongst us who have no notion of them or of mines either), but after the discovery of the great ore, they were heard no more.

When I began to work at Llwynllwyd they worked so fresh there for a considerable time that they even frightened some young workmen out of the work. This was when we were driving levels and before we had got any ore, but when we came to the ore then they gave over and I heard no more talk of them. Our old miners are no more concerned at hearing them blasting, boring holes, landing leads, than if they were some of their own people, and a single miner will stay in the work in the dead of the night without any man near him and never think of any fear or harm that they will do him, for they have a notion the knockers are of their own tribe and profession and are a harmless people who mean well. Three or four miners together shall hear them sometimes, but if the miners stop to take notice of them the knockers will also stop; but let the miners go on at their own work,—suppose it is boring—the knockers will also go on as brisk as can be in landing, blasting or beating down the loose. And they are always heard at a little distance from them, before they come to ore. These are odd assertions, but they are certainly facts, though we cannot and do not pretend to account for them. We have now very good ore at Llwynllwyd where the knockers were heard to work; but the knockers have yielded up the place and are no more heard. Let who will laugh, we have the greatest reason to laugh and thank the knockers, or thank God who sends us these notices. This topic would take a large volume to handle properly and I wish an able hand would take the task upon him to discuss the point, perhaps some extraordinary light into nature might be struck out of it. The word supernatural used amongst us is nonsense; there is nothing supernatural, for the degrees of all beings from the vegetative life to the archangel are natural, real, absolute creatures made by God's own hands, and all their actions, motions, and qualities are natural. Doth not fire burn a stick into ashes as natural as the air or water dissolves salt? and yet fire when out of action is invisible and impalpable, but where is the home or country of fire? Where also is the home and country of knockers? *Lewis Morris.**

*(This letter has been copied from a transcript made by the Rev. P. Bayley Williams, in the Editor's possession. The original appears to have been lost, and it is probable that the letter is not complete.)

W. to R. CCX.

Mi ddywedais i chwi yn fy llythyr diweddaf imi dderbyn yr eiddoch o'r 8d, a da oedd ei gael, mi dyngaf i chwi hynny. Peth hyfryd iawn yw bod gan ddyn galon faddeugar, digon anhawdd yw ei hystwytho lawer tro er mynyched y dywedir y pader. Chwi ddywedwch am y Llywydd, mai creadur llariaidd ddigon pan foddir yw, ond erchyll pan ddigir. Ond gwych tymer y dyn a fai lariaidd ddigon pan ddigir. Ah! beth meddwch? Yn wir, dyma fi newydd fod yn ffrochwyllt heb yn waetha yn fy ngên, er fy mod wedi cael digon o amser i'm harfogi fy hun. Dim ond ymgegi a rhyw Wyddelod rhwydd feddwon. Maent yn dywedyd mai balchder yw gwreiddyn pob gwlltineb a drygnaws; nid oes dim o'r ammeu, beth meddwch? Dywedwch wrth Feirian y cyd-ddygir a beiau ei ysgrifen pe digwydda rai lyn ei llythyr at rai o honom. Mae yn fy mryd i (os byddaf byw i weled fy nghywion yn gallu sgrifennu) wneuthur iddynt yrru llythyrau at eu ffrindiau fynycha gallont. Mae Rhobert wedi sgrifennu pwmp o lythyr at ei gefnder Llywelyn o'r Deheu er's dyddiau byd, ond heb gael atteb etto. Dyma i chwi Awdl y Gofuned a gopiawdd Will ab y Doctor Evans. Rwyn ei gymeryd i'r Dollfa yn glarc! [Here follows a copy of the Awdl signed Gronwy Ddu o Fon.]

Dyma'r bachgen wedi darfod ei dâsg, sef ydoedd hwn y gorchwyl cyntaf a wnaeth erioed mewn barddoniaeth Gymraeg. Gwell f'asai ganddo gopio Lladin o lawer bŷd. Rhaid dysgu croppian cyn cerdded. Maddeuwch chwithau'r beiau. It was for curiosity sake that I enquired about the Jew's L. Mendez. He may be as honest a man as the most orthodox of us all, and consequently to be valued. Dyn cywraint gonest, pa grefydd bynnag a fo, a haeddai barch a charedigrwydd, ond cynnesach gennyf y Cristion, os bydd yn ddynan llariaidd. Dyma lythyr heddyw (yr 16eg) oddiwrth fy mrawd Pennant ynghylch ryw dlysau, etc., a brawd mae'n fy ngalw! Cymhesur, meddwch chwithau. Daccw yn Nhre Ffynnon lonaid boccys o drysor i ddyfod imi efo'r cyfleu cyntaf. I send no invoice along with them (medd y brawd) for I think you will be better amused with guessing at the particulars. Fossils bod ag un, for the Museum Morrisianum. Mae yma eisioes gasgliad glew iawn o fossils, shells, sea-plants, mines, animals preserv'd, parts of animals, medals, coins, etc. Chwi welsoch lun Sydrophel yn Hudibras. Mae llong yn mynd o'r Iwerddon, sef o Ddulun, y mis nesaf; os na thery nhad wrth gyfleu i yrru Twm Parri yn'ghynt, rwy'n meddwl y medraf gael ei *basaids* gan y meister â'r hwn rwyf gydnabyddus. Aie marw a wnaeth ei chwaer, beth oedd ei hoed hi? Nid oes wybod par sut a fydd cael y llyfrau o *Ddyfi*. Rwyn deall mae yno 'raeth rhai y Mr. Ellis, ac mae'n debyg yr holl rai oedd i ddyfod i Fôn. Mae'n fy mryd i sgrifennu i'r Dollfa yno i erchi arnynt hebrwng rhai nhad a Gallgo efo rhyw gŵch i Fôn. Fe fydd mân lestri yn dyfod a choed oddiyno i'r wlad hon rwan ac yn y man. Do, yn siwr, mi delais i nhad yr hanner gini yn union dêg pan gefais yr hanes gennych. Ie, yn wir, gerwin o'r llygod Ffreinig sydd yn ceisio ysu, nid yn unig ein dybacco ond hefyd ein planfeydd a dihenyddu ein poblach. O chwiw garn lladron! Gormod cywilydd os gedir iddynt. Gwell i'r hen wr yrru ei fab William drosodd i wanstrio tipyn ar y cenawon haerllug. Nis gwn i par sut bethau a fyddai da gennych gael i'w hargraphu. Oddiwrth Lywelyn neu Oronwy y dylai ryw gampau ddyfod, chwi a wyddoch nad yw'ch brawd Gwilym druan ond annysgedig ag anghelfydd ddigon yn y famiaith Gymraeg, ag heblaw hynny, daccw fi wedi rhoddi benthyg y Delyn Ledr i Oronwy, ag yng nghist honno mae'r holl drysor a feddwn i mewn barddoniaeth a hynafiaeth. Pe baech unwaith wedi torri'r garw, mi wnawn fy ngoreu ar anfon i chwi rywbeth neu gilydd i borthi'r bendro, ni choeliach i byth y blys a'r awydd sydd gennyf am gael gweled peth o'ch gorchwyl yn argraphedig. Myned heibiaw yn ddistaw ag megys yn anwybod i ni y mae'r amser, ac o dippyn i dippyn rym bod ac un yn llithraw i'r bedd, lle derfydd am ein holl amcanion. Nid oes yno, chwedl Selyf ddoeth, na gwaith, na dychymyg, na gwybodaeth, na doethineb. Dyma Robin yn dechreu dysgu canu ffidl. He has "Jenny Jennee" at his fingers ends. Rhaid a dysgu i Siani hithau i ganu gyda eu dannau. Cantores fawr ydyw, digon o benhillion Cymreig ganddi. Wale, wale, rhaid a rhoddi main clô ar y gwaith (am heno pa wedd bynnag), felly byddwch wych, a Duw ach noddo. **W. to R. contd.**

Eich brawd anwiw ddigon, Gwilym o'r Dollfa.

P.S.—17th Roeddwn yn disgwyl fy chwaer adref o Bentre'rianell fal cawsech newydd odd'yno, ond ni ddaeth.—W.M.

HOLYHEAD, 21st October, 1754.

W. to R. CCXI.

Dear Brother,—Mi a wn mai dywedyd ei Bader i Berson yw rhoddi hanes i chwi fod y Doctor Hugh Wynne, Archjagon Merionyth, Person Dolgelley, etc., wedi marw (for in the London papers I saw it). Roedd yn briawd a chwaer i'r pendefig or Gors, a brawd ydoedd i Mr. Wynne o Fodysgallen. Ai tybiad fod dim siawns i Oronwy gael 'run o'i lefydd? Gofynwch ir Iarll or Castell Côch. Dyma lythyr o Fathafarn. Dim hanes mab bâch. Dyma'r Aldremon Prisiart wrth fy mhenelin, ac yn canmawl y Llywydd Mynglwyd yn anad un câr a fedd yn y byd! Lle da ceisio sgrifennu chwaneg. I writ this day to Aberdovy about the Bibles. Father was tollerable well last Thursday when sister came from thence. Duw yn eich cylch. *Eich caredigawl frawd,*

William Morris.

P.S.—The Aldramon desires his compliments to you.

GALLTVADOG, October 26th, 1754.

L. to W. CCXII.

Dear Brother,—Just now returned from an attempt of getting through Rheidiol to Esgair y Mwyn. But to speak after the manner of ye ancients, the principal River God stood upon the bank with a stern countenance and told me it would be my destruction, if I moved a step further. His head was in the clouds and the skirts of his gown in the river, he shook his white beard, and I took his advice and went home again, and sat down to write this account of his Godship. You remember the expression of Cato (or of ye poet, however: "the Gods take care of Cato," and why not of me? You see they do, and everybody sees it. Then what signifys the efforts of little mortal animals to hurt me? It was contrived by some little malicious fellow in ye Exchequer the other day to get an Exchequer process directed to ye Sheriff of Cardigan to distrain on me for £100, money remmitted me in ye year 1745 and 46 to be laid out to lawyers, etc., for the King's service, and for which I was accountable. I had accounted for the money and for several hundreds after that, but for all this the Sheriff distrained, and I gave him a note for £100. Doth not this look odd, think you? The very person on whom depends all their affairs here to be distraind upon by a Tory Sheriff. Now a passionate man (as they call me at the

Treasury) would have thrown dirt in their faces and kickd all about him, but another of y[e] Gods of y[e] ancients, called *Patience*, told me that it was impossible this could come from the leading men—my superiors, for it was too ill timed a thing if they had a mind to fall out with me. And it was the direct way to drive me off with what money I could lay my hands on, and to suffer all to go to wreck and ruin. Therefore I immediately wrote to y[e] solicitor of the Treasury to desire him to put a stop to these Exchequer processes, for that I should be never safe to enjoy one penny of y[e] money paid me by y[e] Treasury for my services while this gate was open. How slippery is our situation! A man may be thunderstruck with a writ from y[e] Exchequer for money he hath accounted for ten years ago, and all his effects swept away, and it shall cost him a London journey, and a quarter of a year's application before he can recover his own, and yet not know as long as he lives from whence the bolt comes. Not from Jupiter, but from some of y[e] rascally inferior gods. This is in y[e] language of y[e] heathens which fits those people. The solicitor was never more surprizd at anything than at this proceeding, and doth not know how it came about, wrote to me that he would get an order of y[e] Treasury to the Sheriff to return me my note, etc., and that I was to have all the countenance, assistance, etc., as I could wish to have,—diolch i chwi, ebr finnau. Well, to be sure, I have honour in abundance done me by y[e] great ones, clod a mawredd; ond nid hynny sydd arnafi eisiau. A patent place for life, ac aros gartref er gwaetha pawb,—that is all I want *of them*. And no body but the God of Gods can do it. These inferior ones are not inclined to do any good to me, they are all for their own dear selves. I hear not a syllable of Commissioner Vaughan; Duw wnel ei fod gwedi bwrw ei wenwyn. My wife and daughter Margaret at Mathavarn expecting my grandson, and here is an order in great hurry for me to go to y[e] mines, but Rheidiol wont let me; os tyr hi'n deg heno yn y nos, ag i'r dwfr ostwng, mae'n rhaid mynd. Mae yno le conffyrddus ddigon, a very good warm house, pretty well furnished and fireing enough, a digon o *lineing* mewn bol. Abundance of fish (herrings) in ye bay at Aberystwyth, but ye weather so bad that they cannot go out to take them.—*L.M.*

L. to W. contd.

HOLYHEAD, 11th November, 1754.

W. to R. CCXIII.

Anwyl Frawd,—Echdoe y daethym adref o siwrnai fâch wedi bod ddwynos Ymhentre'rianell, noswaith ym Modewryd ac arall yn y Brynddu. Gerwin o'r llifeiriant sydd rhyd y wlâd, y pontydd tan ddwfr gan mwyaf, ag roedd im cwmni innau yn mynd ag yn dyfod o Fodewryd haid o ferchettos, ni chadd dyn erioed y fath drafferth ag a ges yn llusgo rheini drwy afonydd a ffosydd! Ond i wneuthur iawn (oni cheir ganthun' nhw) am yr holl ludded, pa beth ydoedd gartref im croesawu ond llythyrau oddiwrth fy neufrawd, oddiwrth fy nith Marged Morris o Fathafarn, oddiwrth fy nghyfaill Mr. Pennant o Downing, a chyd ag e flychaid o bethau gwerthfawr anial, viz., fossil shells, plants, animals, mines minerals, etc. Wala, ni bu erioed wr mwynach ar wyneb y ddaearen hon rwyn llwyr gredu. There are twenty-six parcels of these curiosities. He told me in a former letter that he would send me no invoice of them, for I think (says he) that you'll be better amusd with guessing at the particulars, ac felly fu fe weddai. Rwy finneu i gynull iddo yntau loniad y boccys o ryfeddodau Môn ar fyrder. He sent me some fossil shells of chalk which came, I presume, from Harwich. Gresyn na chawsai Gronwy well siawns am Ddolgelley, ni chlywais i byth na siw na miw ynghylch y matter. You'll receive herewith Owdl y Briodasgerdd, pray send it me back again when you get a frank, you shall have an index of all the poems I have of his, then you may have the loan of any of them. Fe eill Twm Parry glafrllyd eu copiaw i chwi. You imagine, like most of the English, that the scrubado hath over spread all Wales as well as Scotland, but you and them are much mistaken. Particular lads may have it in most schools, which is entirely owing to their poor nasty way of living; people of fashion know nought on't, and its but seldom clean children catches it; mine or sister's never did. Dont you think that some of your poor are infected with it? I daresay they are. Diolch am y cynghor. Oni wyddechi that my esteemed friend Surgeon General Nichols hath dubb'd me his deputy the other day, nid ffwl o feddyg mo Wilym. Ond rhyfedd gweled pobl gymeradwy yn dyfod i Fodewryd (wrth glywed fy mod i yno) i ddangos ei harchollion, etc. Gresyn oedd marw chwaer Dwm a hithau gystal geneth. Aie prynnu'r lease a wnaeth y Downsend hwnw? Ai

Chwig ynteu Tori o'r Chauncey? Er mwyn Duw gadewch glywed par sut a fydd yn y term yna da chwithau; its said here that there's nothing in that affair of Captain Price. Pwy gymerai ddyn a fai eiddigus cyn priodi, ah? A gewch i samphire—cewch yn siwr, os medraf innau eu cael am aur nag am arian nag am eiriau têg. Er mwyn dyn rhwymwch ddarluniadau yn y llyfrau fal hyn:—A Common Prayer, Testament and Singing Salms with the Cutts and Williams's Salms bound in rough calf and letter'd, for the Rev. Mr. Richard Bulkeley, Rector, Ll. Fechell; two done in the same manner for William Bulkeley of Brynddu, Esq.; one done in black, Cutts and Salms for Mrs. Catherine Bulkeley of Brynddu; one done for Mr. Ellis like the others; and mine and Mr. Meyrick's loose. My father was tollerable well, no tidings of the Bibles. Duw yn eich cylch. *Yours most affectionately*, *William Morris.* **W. to R. contd.**

ESGAIR Y MWYN, November 24, 1754, Sunday night.

Dear Brother,—Just now received yours of ye 1st by way of Gloucester. Where hath it been twenty-four days? Nid oes help. Digrif llythyr Pennant ar fossils. What you call a tortoise is of ye echinae kind, *Pen y for forwyn.* I have seen very perfect ones with old W. Jones, F.R.S., oddigerth bod traed wrth eich tortoise chwi neu ryw fariau cryfion iawn iw bennodi felly. You should have Dr. Hill's book of fossils before you can make any hand of it, it is a vast spacious field, and almost endless. But he hath ranged them surprizingly,—everything but ores and minerals—in which he and everybody are inperfect, and Mr. Pennant may do wonders that way, as he lives in a mine country. I have a great collection of these things but have not a minute's time to range them into order, gwaith sy reidiach. Garw oedd Alaw a Dulas, a digrif oedd Carrog am . . . . . yn Alaw. Pa bryd y peidiodd y Doctor Wynne a bod yn Siawnsler, a phaham? Aie calyn gwragedd bonddigion y byddwch i? Oes dim mwynder i gael ganthyn? Ai nid oedd gair o sôn am *Ganiad Melinydd Meirion* sydd ym Mhentrerianell? Hên felinydd a gododd felin newydd i falu peccaid. O achos y newydd a ddaeth yma'r dydd arall fod wyr imi ym Mathafarn mi drewais atti (er gwaetha trafferth y byd) i ganu *Caniad Hanes Henaint*, canys fe fydd peth canu yn dyfod arnaf ymbell dro, ac mae'r caniad hwnnw **L. to W. CCXIV.**

L. to W. contd.

yn burion yn ail rhan i Ganiad Melinydd Meirion, ac mi ai gyrraf i nhad pan glywaf pa fodd y mae'n leicio y cyntaf. Fe allai mai digio a wna, ond yn wir nid oes le i ddigio, obleid mae'n ddigon gwir ac a bery byth yn wir, ac yn'r un modd Hanes Henaint. Both new subjects I suppose. Afon Ystwyth, o achos nad yw'n *anystwyth*, medd pawb yma, ond pa reswm sydd am afon *Rheidiol?* The names of rivers are generally inexplicable, and we can make but poor guesses at best. Duw helpio Gronwy a phob dyn sy a gwreigan wleb ddifraw. I dont hear a word about Dolgelle; who has got it? Gwych yw'r berllan ar lan Alaw. Perllan comes from *peren* the word here for *pears*. Pêr o achos ei bod yn *felus*, yn *beraidd*, and should be wrote *perain*, I suppose, for it is ye plural of *perenyn* as maip is of meipen.

Afal pêr ac aderyn
A garai'r gwas a gro gwyn

ebr L. Gl. Cothi, and it is probable *pears* were more in vogue among the Britains than apples, as pêr hath given a name to an orchard, and the old liquor perry which some prefer to cyder took its name from pêr on account of its sweetness, and the English name *cider* or *sider* from *surder*, because the liquor was sharper or sowrer. Can you or any man imagine that the ancient inhabitants of Britain wanted these useful liquors *surder* and *peraidd*, i.e., cider and perry? No, no! and perhaps no Englishman knows the derivations of these words. They are but children in ye knowledge of ye ancient tongues of this island. Wele hai pan gaffwyf innau heddwch mi blannaf berllanoedd, ni wn i pa bryd a fydd hynny. Mae gennif ryw fath ar ddwy berllan pei cawn fwytta oi ffrwyth. Ceisiwch 'i Ganiad Melinydd Meirion gan fy nhad, os palla fo chwi ai cewch oddiyma, a Hanes Henaint hefyd. Mi dybygwn y bydd John Owen yn cychwyn tuag yna yr wythnos sydd yn dyfod.

Your affectionate brother, *L.M.*

Wele hai etto, dyma fi newydd ddarfod swppera ar fwdran llygadog, y bwyd goreu a brofais i erioed. Ni fyddai ddyn farw gan mlynedd, tra gallo fo fwytta llonaid ei fol o fwdran llygadog. Ped fae gennif amser mi wnawn ganiad Bwdran Llygadog. O the high life of feeding on Bwdran Llygadog! Oni wyddoch i beth ydyw, ymofynwch.

ESGAIR Y MWYN, SWYDD ABERTEIFI, Dec. 4th, 1754.

L. to W. CCXV.

Dear Brother,—Your derivation of cod wen from the clergy is probable enough, for they knew what was good, and it is probable cookery as an art first got its beginning among them, for they studied good eating while others studied the art of war to defend the country that their sons the clergy might eat their pudding in peace, alias pease pudding. Your pysgodyn is a surprizing affair. I'll return it you when I get home and can take a copy of it in my commonplace book. The purple snail that I found in the harbour of Holyhead was something like yours, but you dont mention any purple colour issuing out of yours. I have no time to answer your objection against knockers; I have a large treatise collected on that head, and what Mr. Derham says is nothing to the purpose. If sounds of voices, whispers, blasts, workings, pumpings can be carried sixteen miles (or a mile) underground, it should be always heard in the same place and under the same advantages and not once in a month or year or two years, just before the discovery of ore. Last week three men together at our work of Llwynllwyd were ear-witnesses of knockers pumping, driving a wheelbarrow, etc., but there is no pump in the work, nor any within less than a mile of it, in which there are pumps constantly going. If it were those pumps that they heard, why were they never heard but that once in the compass of a year? And why are they not now heard? But the pumps make so little noise, that they cannot be heard in the other end of Esgair y Mwyn work when they are going. We have a dumb and deaf tailor in this neighbourhood, who hath a particular language of his own by motion (signs), and by practice I can understand him and make him understand me pretty well, and I am sure I could make him learn to write, and be understood by letters very soon, for he can distinguish men already by the letters of their names. Now letters are marks to convey ideas, just after the same manner as the motions of fingers, hands, or eyes, etc. If this dumb man had really seen ore in the bottom of a sink of water in a mine, and wanted to tell me how to come at it he would take two sticks like a pump, and would make the motions of a pumper at the very sink where he knew the ore was, and would make the motions

L. to W. contd.

of driving a wheelbarrow, and what I would infer from thence would be, that I should take out the water and sink or drive in the place and wheel the stuff out. By the same parity of reasoning the language of the knockers by imitating the sound of pumping, wheeling, etc. is that we should take out the water of a sink and that we have to fall and drive there. This is the opinion of all our old miners who pretend to understand the language of the knockers. Our agent and manager upon the strength of this notice goes on and expects great things. You and everybody that is not convinced of the being of knockers will laugh at these things, for they sound like dreams; so doth every dark science. Can you make any illiterate man believe that it is possible to know the distance of two places by looking at them? Human knowledge is but of a small extent, its bounds are within view of us, we see nothing beyond that. The great universal creation contains powers, etc. that we cannot so much as guess at. May not there be beings and vast powers infinitely smaller than the particles of air, to whom air is as hard a body as a diamond is to us? Why not? There is neither great nor small, but by comparing things together. Our knockers are some of those powers, the guardians of mines. You remember the story in Selden's Table Talk about Sir Robert Cotton and others disputing about Moses's shoe. Lady Cotton came in and asked them: Gentlemen are you sure it is a shoe? So the first thing is to convince mankind, that there is a set of creatures, a degree or so finer than we are, to whom we have given the name of knockers, from the sounds we hear in our mines. This is to be done by a collection of their actions well attested, and that is what I have begun to do and then let everybody judge for himself.—*Lewis Morris.**

W. to R. CCXVI.

HOLYHEAD, 14th December, 1754.

Dear Brother,—Chwi welwch mor barod wyf i atteb eich llythyrau chwi er mor hwyrfrydig 'ych chwi i dalu'r pwyth yn ol. Diolch yn fawr i chwi, meddwch chwithau, eisiau rhywbeth arall i wneuthur, mae'n debyg? Nage yn wir mrawd, mae gennyf lawer peth digon angenrheidiol i'w drin, ond er hynny i gyd,

* This letter also has been copied from the Rev. P. B. Williams's transcript.

mae'n ddyledus arnaf eich atteb, ni wna orrig na'm dwyn na'm gadael, felly dyma attoch chwi. But hold, I must dress a patient first. Dynan wedi gangrene daro ar ei fŷs, darfu i minneu drwy gymmorth rhagluniaeth ei attal cyn iddo fynd ymhellach. Torri'r bys ymaith a wnaethai'r meddygon, ond rwyfi yn treio a fydd bosibl ei gadw iddo. Ni wn i etto par sut a fydd. I have been a battling with it for three weeks past. Gwŷch bod y Sais gan Dwm y'medru trin yr hen Gymraeg cystal. If he had been put under a course of salivation when he first came to town, sure he would have been well long ago. Aie mewn llêd-ty yr y'ch. Roeddwn yn meddwl eich bod wedi cymeryd ty rhiw hên globen ready furnish'd. Ymhle y mae Em-eirian gennych? Na wnant y merchedos na thynnu na thagu, yr archlod yddynt, mae yma ddogn o'u heisiau. Yn wir ni bu yma erioed fwy o brinder ffrancod; pe bawn wrth elin y Llywydd pan fa'e ai law yn y gwaith i gaffael hanner dwsing ganddaw, gwych a fyddai. Mi welaf gowydd Goronwy atto i geisio rhai, nid tebyg i rai eraill a wnaeth. Wrth son am y bardd, mae'n amlwg i bob dyn nad yw'n Esgob ni ar fedr gwneuthur dim gwasanaeth iddo, for he hath had of late opportunities enow. Dolgellau is offer'd a young clergyman, already a Rector, a tutor to Mr. Wynne of Glynllifon, and if [he] doth not accept of it, Andrew Edwards, a brother-in-law of Chancery Edwards, is to have it. *Llanrhaiadr*, one of the best livings in the diocese has been offer'd Mr. Ellis, a vicar of Bangor, and upon his choosing to have the Archdeaconry with what he had, it was given to Syr Thomas Prendergast for a friend of his, one Roberts, who had Conway and another good living. The Archdeaconry of Merionyth has been given as above. Llangelynin, near Conway, which Roberts resigned, is, they say, given away. Conway and Gyffin is also lost. These two last indeed was not in the Bishop's gift; all the rest were. Ffei gan gywilydd. Nid oes bosibl fod y Castell Coch* o ddifrif am helpu'r truan, beth meddwch?

I had read in the papers that young Lisburn had compromised matters with his uncle at court and did expect the poor d—l was outwitted. Roedd eisiau'r Llew neu ryw un dewr i sefyll wrth ei gefn o, druan gŵr. Duw a'm cadwodd hyd yn hyn ac am ceidw

W. to R. contd.

* Lord Powys.

W. to R. contd.

rwyn gobeithio rhag trais cyfreithwyr. Wfft i'r fath haflug ac ydynt. Gerwin o'r Downshend a'r Bywel am uno ai gilydd yn erbyn y goron, na bond i grybwyll! Gresyn na chrogid hwy yn enwedig y Rhonwyn, am y llall mae o yn ymddangos y peth ydyw. Daccw'r Biblau a'r Testamentau wedi dyfod o'r diwedd i Gaernarfon. Mi yrrais air i nhad i yrru am danynt. Mai rhai y Mr. Ellis yno hefyd. Fe dâl y Gymdeithas y freight mae'n debyg. Roedd 17/6 yn digwydd ar rai Mr. Ellis. Ni fedrai Edward Griffith gofiaw par faint yn syrthio ar rai 'nhad. Beth pei prifia'r Sharpe yna'n gna pîg? F'anwyl gydymaith yw'r Brynddu, ond am Fodewryd, un bydol yw ac ni thâl i sôn am dano. Un yn ymdrobaethu mewn cyfoeth, ac untroed yn y bedd iddaw, ac ni bydd mor llawer o griowtan ar ei ôl gan ei ffrindiau ai garrennydd. Duw a gadwo'r llall. Na welais i mo gân Melinydd Meirion; mi erchais i'r nith Pegi Owain, yr hon a aeth adref heddyw, ei gyrru imi yn ddiffael. Mae'r Llew yn gaddaw imi'r llall. Wrth son am dano dyma lythyr heddy oddiwrthaw, o'r 4dd, o'r Esgair, a chant o hanesion digon difyr. Mae'r gwr debygwn yn abl diofal arnaw, pethau ffeind, ffeind ydyw'r mwnws bydol, dywedad a phregethad yr offeiriadau a fynnont yn eu herbyn. Nid oes dim byw yma hebddynt. Gwael iawn y gwelaf fi. "Ben bonedd heb un beni," ebr rhyw hen brydydd, ac yn wir ddiau gwael yw pawb hebddynt. Rydych chwi ac yntau wedi eich gosod lle mae digon o fwnws i'w cael. Ond fe ddigwyddodd i Wilym druan roddi ei bawl yn llawr mewn congl anghysbell, lle nad oes ond y tlodi bwygilydd. Ymma nid oes nag arian na mwyn arian, na dim ond y creigiau noethion, ac ambell heiddglwt yma ac accw. Ond etto er hyn mae Gwilym yn cael cann mwy nag a haeddai, felly diolched i Dduw am tano. Rwyn llwyr gredu mai camgymeryd yr ydych, ac nad *mai Pabist o'r brawd Pennant.* Ond yw ei dad yn ustus heddwch? Ac oni ddygwyd yntau i fynu yn y colas yn Rhydychen? A phar sutt y gellwch i ddywedyd y fath beth? Os yw Babist, he is so in disguise, ond ni choeliwn i yn fy myw. It was odd enough that he and I the same week, heb wybod y naill i'r llall, should commence being cregynwyr. Prin yr oeddwn wedi dechreu trin rhai tramor a chartrefol, nad dyma lythyr y brawd Pennant yn dymuno arnaf gymeryd y gwaith yn llaw. His letter was of the 29th ulto, dim son yr amser hwnnw am fod yn aelod anghytrig o'n Cymdeithas ni yna. You have a worthy brother of him. I sent him lately a box-full of sea-plants, etc., na welodd o ermoed eu bath, mi dyngaf i chwi hynny. Ie, ie, fossilist o'r tad hwnnw ac nid o ran crefydd y gyrrws atto. Mi welais lythyr atto o'r Idal. Yr anhunedd i'r peswch, fe'm blina innau beunydd, ac nid gwiw i minnau geisiaw llwyr ymado ac e tros drimis o'r lleiaf. Nid oes fatter fod gwyr gleision Rhydychen yn cael codwm. Roeddynt yn rhy hyfion yn eu matter. Diau fod beiau lawer, nid ychydig, o bobtu. *Gwiliwch i'r Esgob Elis** oganu yr hen Frutaniaid au hiaith yn lle eu moli. Gwr digon coeglyd ydoedd ym Mynyw oi flaen. Par sut y disgwyliwch gennyf lythyr hir, a minnau newydd gael gafael ar hen sgrifenlyfr, ac ynddaw yn agos i chweigian o gowyddau D'ap Gwilym, a llawer o naddynt nad oeddynt gennyf o'r blaen, a rhai na feddai'r Llew monynt ychwaith. Alas! I have no amanuensis. Will Evans is too young and ignorant in these things, a gwaeth na dim, dymma'r ganwyll yn darfod o dipyn i dipyn. Mae digon o newid ar sebon a chanhwylla yng Nghaer-Gybi, meddwch chwithau. Nid hynny mo'r llall. Canwyll 'r einioes, mrawd Rhisiart bâch, sydd yn mynd lei-lai beunoeth, ac o bydd eich brawd Gwilym fyw i weled dyddiau c'lanmai, fe fydd yn hynafgwr deng mlwydd a deugain oed! A pheth a dal sôn am wragedd, ffosils, cregynach, a masweidd-waith D'ap Gwilym, a chant o bethau gweigion eraill? Rheitiach rhifo paderau ac ymbarodtoi i'r siwrnai faith honno, i gael ymgyrraedd nefol goron, chwedl Goronwy, na bod yn gwilrhin ac yn bwhwman fal plantos gwirion ffol. Beth meddwch chwi? Yn wir mae'n erchyll edrych yn ol. Mae arnaf ofn y gallwn i gyd ddywedyd, i ni dreulio ein blynyddoedd fal chwedl, ac och par sut a fydd edrych ym mlaen? Nid oes ini ond gwneuthur ein goreu tra bo'm, a Duw a rydd ei râd ar ein gorchwyl. Bydded iddo warchad drosoch ar eiddoch. Sgrifenwch gynta galloch, da chwithau, a thippyn o ryw ddiddanwch i'ch *caredicaf frawd penbrydd ddigon,*

William Morris.

W. to R. contd.

* Anthony Ellis was Bishop of St. Davids from 1752 to 1761. He succeeded Richard Trevor.

L. to W.
CCXVII.

GALLTVADOG, December 19, 1754.

Dear Brother,—I have yours of ye 3rd December. Sôn am gregin y mor, thirty kinds collected. I have collected a good many but never counted them. I have Lister printed 1678. He hath but forty-one kinds reckoning pen y forforwyn (echinus), etc. But I have a book printed at Frankfort, wrote by Dr. Johnston, 1649, dedicated to William, the Landgrave of Hesse, which is far more curious than Lister. I find there several kinds of y^e . . . . fôr, which he ranks among the Zoophytes or animal plants, and says the Greeks called them by a bawdy name *mongi* as we do in Welsh. They are called by him *urtica*, but is not very exact in the description of them, following Aldrovendus, etc. Your snail is pretty like his *Holothurius* being the first of Rondeletius, of which he gives two figures, but he makes the *flower* nigher the end of it, and says it is immoveable on ye rock. I dare say it is ye same, for he hath nothing else like yours. Aldrovendus, l. 4, c. 4, also hath it. Johnston hath also mentula marina (. . . . . . môr) in ye same class, you have seen such things on oyster shells. I have no time to mention gerllygen y mor, afal y mor, cucumer y mor, etc., and I think they are wrong in placing your moving snail among the exanguibus aquaticis, for as it is a moving living animal and changes colour there is no doubt but it hath blood in it—and perhaps the . . . . . . *môr* have blood also. Mae fe'n dwedyd fod y . . . . . . fôr yn llosgi dwylo pobl wrth ei theimlo, as you know the Pulmo marinus *mathioli* do, sef *sêr* y mor a fyddem yn ei daflu at ein gilydd yn noeth lumuniaid gynt. But why called by ye name of sea-lungs? It is more like a star with its rayes and is a living creature and not without feeling, as the vulgar suppose. So much for animal plants, etc. What will you do for Welsh names for your cregin? There are some Welsh names about *Dovey*, but I cannot now come at them, and I have found a fish there that is not in Willoughby, but there is something like it in Johnston, with a German name. The names of his fish are mostly German and Latin. The book is in Latin. Ni feddai mor arian nag amser i *Subscribio* at lyfr yr Iddew, though I suppose it is a curious thing. Drwg mae'n debyg fod Mrs. Mary Hughes yn glaf, os e ymendied. Nid oes yma ddim iw wneuthur i Sion Owen, Dwyran dir etto, ni wn i beth a ellir wneuthur iddo pan wastadheir pob peth. All the world here is in confusion, ni waeth er cynted y delo Sion Owen adref, for I suppose I shall be going towards London pretty soon. L. to W. contd.

Dyna fi gwedi bod yn Mathafarn yn gweled fy ŵyr Lewis Morris, gwych o'r cynnyddu y mae'r enw hwnnw, pwy wyr na fydd gorwyrion etto o'r enw?* I long to hear how Father digested *Caniad Melinydd Meirion*. If he doth not like it, he cannot take ammiss Caniad Henaint. Ni chanaf i ddim ond hynny ennyd fawr,—no leisure hours, other things confounding the brains. Chwiwgwn lladron defaid yn cyfarth arnaf. The change threaten'd in y[e] ministry is more like to hurt me than all the *bygythion* and *peryglon* of this country. Duw fo gyda chwi; os oes ceiniog yna iw sparrio gyrrwch hi gyda Sion Owen, rydis yma gwedi gwario arian heb na rhi na rheswm, ag eisiau peth i wneud y cyfrif i fynu. Pawb yn crafu lle bo cosi, a lle bo'r gelain y casgl y cwn.

Eich brawd ffyddlon, *Lewis Morris.*

HOLYHEAD, 9th January, 1755.

W. to R. CCXVIII.

Dear Brother,—Llyma'r eiddoch o'r 28 ulto o'm blaen yn achwyn ar fydol drafferthion ac yn rhoddi hanes Deputy Comptroller y Mint a chan fod Carn yn llymgi dwl, da oedd gael o'r Barri yna'r peth. Hir oes iddo iw fwynhau. Wala, wfft, a dwbl wfft, ir *Llymgi* yna. Ni bydd Llyw Brydain yn torri ei air un amser mae'n debyg, beth meddwch? Mae yn debygol fod y brawd yna bellach efo ei gyfrifon. Gwae fi na chawn glywed fod yr Esgair accw wedi ei sefydlu wrth ei fodd; er carriad ar eich brawd Gwilym gadewch glywed par sut y mae'r materion yn mynd ymlaen. Rhaid credu bellach fod yr Arglwydd Powis o ddifrif ynghylch Goronwy; nid oes modd iddo wneuthur gweithred mwy elusengar, obleit fod y Bardd gyn dlotted ac oedd Job pan oedd dlotta. Gwreigan feddal ni thal dim yn y byd, yn enwedig i fardd a fai ar awen yn berwi yn ei ben yn oestad teg. Mi a wranta y ba'sai un o hen wrachïod Môn a llonaid cragen o eli yr ymgrafu (nid er ammarch arnoch) wedi mendiaw'r Domas ymhell cyn hyn. Mi welais ei hen feistr yma'r dydd arall, ond ni lyfesais i son wrtho am y scrubado, rhag ofn a fa'sai iddo sorri. Cymhesur oedd i chwi ofyn nawdd gan f'anwyl gyfaillt y Benant, a chwithau wedi ei gam-farnu yn euawg. Mi ge's dydd arall lythyr

* Sir Lewis Morris is a great grandson of Lewis Morris.

W. to R. contd.

tra charedig oddiwrthaw, taeru yn fy nannedd i, byddai raid immi droi yn awdwr a chant o bethau, ond bychan a ŵyr o mae *Penbwl gô ddwl o ddyn* yw'ch brawd Gwilym, ac nad oes fawr ddysg na dawn yn perthyn iddo. Mae'n debyg fod y Mr. Pennant wedi cychwyn yna cyn hyn ac yna'r erys tan Ebrill. Chwi ai cewch yn ddynan mwyn cywraint,—mae'n rhaid sgrifennu atto yn y man ynghylch cregyn, etc. Mae'n bur naturiol i ddŷn cyn mynd i ofyn cymwynas, fyfyriaw ynddo ei hun par sut wr y ba'i iw gofyn iddo, a gawsai gêd ganthaw erioed o'r blaen? Ac os cawsai a ddarfu iddo dalu'r pwyth yn ol? Felly yma, yn boeth y bo'r holl sampier; pe buaswn i wedi cael siwgiaid o honynt i mrawd Rhisiart, mi allaswn o hŷd fy nh—n grefu ganthaw yrru i mi Almanack Ryland drwy dalu. Ond f'aeth yr adeg heibiaw tra bum i yn cosi fy llechweddi, ac nid oes yr un iw cael am aur, nag am arian, nag am einioes teg, ond par un bynnag a wnaf ai cael Almanac ai peidiaw [rwyf yn] llawn fryd ar fynnu cael i chwi grochanaid o honynt. Wala, wfft o ddigrifed y ddwy ganhlan yma i Henaint.* Mae'r bobl agos a thynnu fy llygaid am danynt. Roedd fy nhad yn iach y dydd arall y bu'r chwaer yno yn anfon ei mab Sion oedd yn myned tua'r Deheudir, roedd iddo obaith cael dyfod yna efo ei ewythyr. Rym ymma bawb yn iach, mawl i Dduw; bydded iddo 'ch cadw chwithau felly, a'ch merch gyd a chwi, a rhoddi i chwi flwyddyn newydd happus. *Eich carediccaf frawd, William Morris.*

BISHOPS CASTLE, Wednesday night [Jan. 21, 1755.]

L. to Mrs. M. CCXIX.

My Dear,—We got here safe about the edge of night, and everything right. I believe I shall send my baggage by ye way of Ludlow by ye carriers, and go our selves by the way of Shrewsbury, but am not yet certain. Edward did not come here till last night, and tomorrow morning he sets out for home and is to call at Newtown for two casks of powder and twenty pounds of steel, which powder William Griffith is to put in ye long cask which used to keep oats in ye brewhouse, and you are to give him the double padlock (that is upon ye window in ye closet) to put upon it, and take care that no body goes near it with a candle, and when

*This probably refers to the poem "Caniad Hanes Henaint" by Lewis Morris, see Diddanwch Teuluaidd, 1763, p. 170, and "Caniad Melinydd Meirion," for which see the same book, p. 161.

the Cwmervin miners want any of it let Edward Hughes be there to weigh it out for fear of accidents. Thomas Davies of Llanidloes, also brings five or six dozen of candles which are to be put in ye same chest for ye same use, and also some hoop iron. Let the steel and hoop-iron be also put in ye out loft, that it may not be stolen or put to any other use. I have bought a bag here to carry ye powder, and you are to make use of ye bag, but not to take off ye small bags that are about ye powder. I shall endeavour to persuade Mr. Jones to go with me to Salop, but I dont know whether he'll go, I believe he will. I shall send you some flax from Salop. L. to R. Mrs. M. contd.

I am your affectionate husband, *Lewis Morris.*

I shall pay Edward for his journey and all the carriage.

CAERGYBI SANTAIDD, 24th Ionawr, 1755.

Anwyl frawd Rhisiart,—Mi sgrifennais attoch er's dyddiau byd mawr, ac yr ydwyf er's ennyd yn disgwyl gronyn o lythyr yn atteb, Cês lythyr doe o Bentre'rianell yn dywedyd fod y nhad wedi cael un oddiwrthych wythnos ir dydd foru, ar brawd Llew heb ddyfod yna y pryd ysgrifenasech, yr hyn oedd ryfedd gennyf. Nid oes bosibl na bô wedi dyfod yna cyn hyn i wastradedd y bobl yna. Mae'r tywydd yn oer anguriol ffordd yma, a hynny'n codi'r peswch a rhyndod ar boblach crwyn deneuon. Dyma ar y papir, arwydd hynod fy mod yn ffaelio dal y pin im llaw, ac etto er hyn rhaid gorphen hyn o lythyr rhyngoch. Mi ge's eich llythyr chwi ym mrawd Llewelyn or 6ed, a hanes bod Sion wedi dwad a llythyr yn ei law adref, ai arian yn ei bocced. I have answer'd you about Richard Morris of Mathafarn's boards. I can say no more about 'em than that I have received no more money since, and that I writ a pressing letter to my father to egg him on to sell what he has of them. He hath some chance, there's but a poor one here; I am doing all I can to get rid of them heb fod nês. I proclaimed a fair twice, no chaps came to signify any thing. If I can get any money from father, will send you a small bill, but there's no depending. Gerwin or troad ar fyd a wnaethoch yn yr Esgair. Llwydded Duw eich amcanion a ddywedaf fi. Bydd rhywyr clywed eich bod wedi gorchfygu'r gelynion brychion, a gwych a fydd wedi eistedd i lawr i fanegi'r hanes o bant i bentan—pwy a lâs hwn a hwn, etc. A gewch chwi amser i'm clywed yn dywedyd fod gennif yn awr gregin a physg W. to R. CCXX.

W. M. to R. M. contd.

bywion ynddynt a ydoedd yn byw 6 throedfedd ymherfedd y ddaiar mewn clai glasrudd morfa; mae'n debyg na wybu un cregynwr erioed oddi wrthynt. Mr. Pennant is now in London, rhaid rhoddi iddo'r hanes er mwyn cael pob cregyn a'u henwau ganthaw. Nid hwyrach y ceir anrhydedd am eu datguddiaw, beth meddwch? Da clywed fod y Llwyn Llwyd yn gwenu arnoch a digrif a fai sgrifennu nodau ar ganiad Henaint yr archlod iddo. Rwyfi cyn ddicced wrtho ac ydych chwithau, ac a genwn iddo o'wllys gwaed fy nghalon pei medrwn. Gwyrda'r tylwyth teg am gnociaw ac am blympiaw, ant ymlaen. Duw gyda chwi eich deuwedd, a byddwch wychion.

Eich brawd anwiw ddigon, *William Morris.*

P.S.—Dim hanes am gwch i gyrchu'r enllyn. Dyma lythyr 25ain oddiwrth Oronwy a fu agos iddo a marw; mae'n gwaeddi am offeiriadaeth ym Mon gan nad oes yr un yn Llundain.

W. to R. CCXXI.

CAERGYBI, 3dd o Chwefror, 17[55].

Rhisiart fy Mrawd,—Ni choeliach i byth yr anhunedd sy ynwyf o eisiau clywed hanes y brawd Llewelyn. Fe fyddai arfer a sgrifennu tippyn o lythyr ar ei daith yna, ond ni chlywais na siw na miw oddiwrthaw er pan rybuddiodd ei fod am osod allan ymhen hyn a hyn o ddyddia. Gobeitho ei ddyfod yn llwyddianus ai fod yn iach a chwithau gyd ag ef. Nid hwyrach na feiddiwch ddywedyd wrth eich brawd ungalon eich hun ei bod yn mynd yn rhyfel. Wala, ond gwell a fa'sai cadw mwy o longau a morwyr ar droed na'u gadael i fynd yn rheccod, beth meddwch? Dyna i chwi dippyn o ddifyrrwch, by way of relaxation from business. Canu a orug Elisa ryw englynion go drwsglaidd i Huw'r Bardd Coch, i roddi iddo a beirdd Môn, sialens, fal pettai, yno rhyw ffrind arall ai hattebodd yn enw Huw.* Wrth gofiaw, dyna i chwi daflen o holl ganiadau Goronwy ar y sydd gennyf fi, mae digon Yngallt Vadawg nad y'nt ymma. Mae eisiau gyrru'r englynion yna ir Ymhwythig iw hargraphu ynghyd a rhyw faeled, chwedl 'r hen Risiart William y taeliwr o'r Efel Fawr gynt. Fe wyr y brawd Llew hanes Elisa a'r

* It appears that Goronwy wrote the englynion in the name of Huw Huws. They may be seen in the Liverpool edition of his works, p. 122, and see also his letters of October 16th, 1754, and December 2nd. Huw Huws himself wrote a ballad on the occasion, in which he ridiculed Elis y Cowper and David Jones, Trefriw.

modd y bu'n rhyfela ac Owain Goronwy gynt,† etc. Dymma fi yn gyrru llythyr heddyw at y Brawd Pennant a hanes cregyn; a welsoch i yr mwynwr etto? Mae hi'n ddiwrnod teg, felly rhaid mynd ir ardd i weithio er mwyn cynhyrfu tippyn ar y gwaed a sugn y corphilyn brwnt yma, ac er lles a budd ir ddaearen, fal y gallo ddwyn cnwd toreithiog. Duw o'r nef a fyddo'n gwarchadw drosoch y ddeu frawd, ac a ddel a newydd da oddiwrthych. **W. to R. contd.**

Wyf eich brawd anwiw, *Gwilym Morys.*

LONDON, February 11, 1755.

L. to W. CCXXII.

Dear Brother,—I have to-day fixed in lodgings at Hopkins and Taylor, the corner of St. Martin's Church Yard, near Charing Cross, where I hope to have some letters from you for the future, and if I recover this terrible cough that I have you shall have some from me. As for the cheese, etc., you must correspond with my wife about them, for I know no more of my own affairs at home than you know of them; mae yma ormod o bwys ar ben dyn gwan o lawer, yn enwedig dyn a fo'n pesychu fal fi. I thought I should have expired last night in going from home to Tower Hill in a coach through the fog and smoak just at ye edge of night, it kept me a vomiting and coughing all the way, and yesterday I had eat a bit of beef, the first for a great while before, I suppose that assisted the disease. O gwae fi am Sir Aberteifi neu ryw gornel o Gymru lle mae awyr a a dwr da! Honest Mr. Vaughan of Nannau is here; I saw him yesterday. He hath begun a curious translation into English of Caniad Henaint, rhywir yw'r caniad hwnnw gida'g ef a minneu. Well, you'll expect some account of my success in my own affairs; dim ond bod pob peth o'r gorau hyd yn hyn a gobeithio y dont oll i ben da. I have powerful people against me tooth and nail, ag nid gwan yw mhlaid inneu; mae'r morthwyl mawr, mawr, yn dwedyd na chaf fi ddim cam. Ni wiw cyfri'r cywion cyn eu deor—na wiw'n

†For the englynion written on a similar occasion by Goronwy's father, Owen Gronw, see Robert Jones's Life of Goronwy, vol. II., 87. The original may be seen in Addit. MSS. 15027, p. 65. Robert Jones has omitted the last englyn:— Ar frys dweded pawb o'r fro—yn niwedd nos
Nefoedd i enaid Cludro,
Dafydd Sion ag Owen Grono
Tri bardd i harddu'r byd tra bo.

Robin Cludro was a crack-brained poet, contemporary with Sion Tudur and William Cynwal.

L. to W. contd.

wir; mi welais i lawer troead ar fyd mewn diwrnod. Mae yma fwstwr garw ynghylch rhyfel,—pressio'n danllyd; ond gwedi'r cwbl fe ddwedir fod y *French* yn cnoccio danodd, ag yn ceisio nadel ini baratoi. Fe ddwedir fod ein Fleet a'n pobl ni (2000) yn yr East India gwedi ei dinistrio gan y Ffrangcod. Ond beth yw hyn i gyd i ni sydd lawer grâdd yn is na'r bobl sydd yn llunio rhyfel a heddwch, boed rhwng y din a'r wialen? Talu trethi sydd raid ini tra bôm byw. Duw fo gida chwi. Gyrrwch beth o arian Richard Morris os oes peth i'w cael. *Eich brawd*

mwya ei drafferth o'r cwbl, *L.M.*

L. to W. CCXXIII.

LONDON, February 15, 1755.

Dear Brother,—I have yours of ye 9th and am glad you are clear of y^e^ *asthma* except for a minute or two now and then, nid yw hwnnw ond dechreu dangos eu gamp, mae'n debyg. Mine came upon me last night in bed about midnight, or after, a bu raid codi i fynu i gael gwynt ag oerni, a phesychu, etc. Och am *bair dadeni*! A wyddoch i beth oedd hwnnw? Crochan neu badell fawr oedd gan'r hên Frutaniaid gynt, lle byddant yn berwi dyn a fyddai'n hên ag yn glwyfus, ac fe ail *enid* yn y *pair*, ond nas medrai ddywedyd. Fe fydd fy mab Lewis yn gofyn imi, "nhadi, a wyddoch i hynny?" This is when something extraordinary is to be told me; felly finneu, "mrawd William, a wyddoch i hynny?" Mi a eis a'ch llythyr Cymraeg ynghylch Goronwy at yr Arglwydd Powys neithiwr ynghylch chwech, lle bum heb ond y fi ag ynteu yn *constrio* pob materion dan unarddeg. Duw a dalo iddo, ag chwedl y gwyddau oedd yn pesgi, i'm porthi i, y cododd Duw y gwr hwnnw. Gwedi darllain (nage edrych) dros eich llythyr Cymraeg chwi, a gweled enwau Bangor a Llanrhuddlad ynddo, a rhyfeddu weled y fath sgrifen Gymraeg lân loyw, fe ddymunodd arnaf sgrifennu henwau'r llefydd ar bappir, ag fe sgrifen yn union deg at yr Esgob; os gwel Duw yn dda i Ronwy fynd yn Berson Rhuddlad fe a'i ca, ac onide os byddwn byw fe ga y peth cynta a allo'r Iarll iddo. He is really concernd for him; and we agreed it was proper to rescue such a man, lest he should fall into the hands of Jacobites, ond na ddywedwch mor rheswm hyn i Oronwy. I told the *Iarll* that *those people* wanted him to accept of a rectory, but that I persuaded him against it, as he was a Whig. Twyll yw'r byd i gyd, chwi welwch, hyd yn oed wrth wneuthur personiaid. My affairs have a very good aspect as it pleasd God to raise this good man to defend me from all the efforts of my enemies, which are a vast many here as well as in y[e] country. Drwg bod yr arian oddiwrth y coed mor brinion, nid chware teg oedd i R.M. addo'r fath daliad musgrell imi. A war we think is unavoidable, for the hurry we are in seems to shew we have been too slow in preparing. The West India ships refuse to go out till they are sure of the event of these great preparations, and they expect privateers daily in the Channel. But some wise men, that pretend to see through the designs of Providence, say that when the French see that we are ready to fight them *they* will retire into their dens, fal cath goed a fyddai'n chwythu ag yn 'sgyrnygu dannedd. Others say now is the time for us to follow our stroke while we are strong and they weak, for it is agreed they are very poor. Dyna i chwi *bolitics* yn lle sgrifennu peth sydd reitiach. Clywais y post diwaethaf fod pob peth o'r gorau yn Sir Aberteifi; pawb o'r teulu'n iach. Duw fo gida chwi. *Eich brawd, Llewelyn.* L. to W. contd.

Given at my lodgings at Hopkins and Taylor, the corner house in St. Martin's Churchyard, St. Martin's Lane, Westminster. Dydd Sadwrn ar ol y noswaith y bu'r pesychu mawr.

CAERGYBI, Dydd Gwener, 27 Chwefror, [1755.]

*Κυχωυν αρ λυνιαω Λλυθυρ ερβυν υ βωρυ.**

Mrawd Anwyl,—Llymma'r eiddoch or 9d presenol yn dywedyd fod y Rhisiart Forys wedi ymddangos i chwi. Yn angof y gadewais lyfrau Bo Pîp ddiniwaid heb ei anfon gyda'r tal. Drwg bod bygydfa mor flin wrthych, nid oes yma na chymryd monynt na dim arall ond beichio pesychu ar droau. Peswch gauaf yw hwn, dyfod a myned a wna, fal y geffylog, fof y ddyn llabindiaw rhywun yn y lleuad amser Haf, ac a ddychwel yma yn ol tua'r Hydref. Sigo ffer sydd dda rhagddo, fal y mae'r ymgrafu yn dda rhag y droedwst, rwyfi wedi cadw'r ty arnaf bythewnos yn pesychu llai; succan gwyn a gronyn o fêl a menyn, a bara ynddo, sydd well na physgod chwilod yn gwynos.‡ Ie, Robin a dynodd y pictiwr—seems to take more delight in it than in Latinizing. Gwyn ei fyd a allai wneuthur Urbin neu Angelo o honaw, mae o W. to L. CCXXIV.

* "Cychwyn ar luniaw llythyr erbyn y fory."

‡ Hunlle, neithiwr. Rhaid rhoi llai o fara yn y bruchan heno.—(W.M.)

W. to L. contd.

megys yn rhag fwriadu. Beth a gymerai'r Bowen hwnnw am ei ddysgu? Dyn hynnod o hwnnw meddwch, ond digon anghyfaddas i roddi hanes Swydd Amwythig heb ganddo grap ar yr heniaith. Daccw fy meistr Pennant ynta wedi taro wrth "the greatest genius in England (next to Edwards)§ for birds! who, at my instance," (quoth he) "undertakes the history of those of Great Britain with coloured figures. His name is Haultier, an Irishman (cymysg debygwn), a modest, inoffensive, sober creature, is gone over to Dublin for some time to improve in etching. On his return I shall take him to my own house to overlook him whilst he draws the birds of our woods." Fo eilw yma wrth ddychwelyd ac y mae o i dynny lluniau animal flowers, etc. Cewch ei hanes os daw; ie, ac os bydd Robin gartref, fe ga Haultier ddodi barn a ellir lluniedydd o hono, ai nid ellir. Beth a fydd pobl eraill meddwch nes er i Haultier liwo adar Prydain? Byddant, byddant, daccw'r Bennant yn bwriadu giving the public a translation of Ray's Synopsis Avium, as far as relates to those of Great Britain, and therefore hath called aloud upon me for a catalogue of the Monensian birds with their Welch names.† Cewch o ewyllys gwaed fy nghalon, hebai finneu, hyd lle gallwyf, a thyma restr o naddynt ynghylch chweigain. Da chwitheu, moeswch yr enwau Cymreig chwithig gynta galloch, fal o bai bossibl gwthio'r gwaith ymlaen. Oes yna yr un nondescripts debygech i. Oes, oes, mi a wranta yna ac yma. Pa enw Seisnig sydd ar hebog marthin, yoraox ondê, ai bwyta marthiniad y bydd ac oddiwrthynt yn cael ei enwi, fal sparrow hawk. Par un yw'r gwalch llwydlas byresgyll colerog at faint colomen ddof a welir rhyd fryniau Mon? tlws iawn ydyw, ynghoed Glan Alaw y nytha, meddai Wil ab y Doctor. Dyna i chwi bapur iw ddodi ar yr almari; it will stop the mouths of foolish enquirers about Natural History. [Derbyniais] eich llythyr, ac ynddo un i nhad, arall ir Coch moel, ac iddynt yr aethent, roeddwn i yn clywed fawr flas ar y Cywydd o eisiau cnoi cfl arno, fe wedda. Oni ddywedais

§George Edwards, a naturalist, born at West Ham, April 3, 1693, and died July 23, 1773. He published among other works, a 'A History of Birds" in seven volumes in 1743—1751. He became Librarian to the Royal College of Physicians.

†William has added the following note at the side of the letter:—I ba beth y mae hwn a hwn da, meddynt, a pha beth a dal casglu pethau or fath yma yngbyd? Darllenwcb y pappur meddwch chwitha'.

i wrthych lawer tro mai gwan or Sion Twm Offeiriad, he solidity, but then he moistens it too much. No, he knows nothing of antiquity; llanc pedair ar hugain oed, hanner pan, mae o'n Eglwys fach dros y Grawys a Langffwrdd yma, fo fedr hwnnw ddarllain Cymraeg, ni fedr hwn ddim ond brygaldian. Fo fu o ar ffeiriad Gwyddelig yn ymffisto'r nos arall; dewr pob ffeiriad ar ei dommen ei hun, y Gwyddel a gollodd a thorrwyd y cledda'. Dodwch ronyn chwaneg o hanes y Bowen, da mrawd, a chân i'r ddau ffeiriad meddw. Mae'r ffêr in cryfhau o dipyn i beth bob dydd, mi fum yn y Costwm Hws ddwywaith neu dair, ac yn y dref yn yfed tea unwaith, rhaid cerdded yn bur foneddigaidd, *cerecloth* a brandi a gwinegr a thippyn o Capystrors spirit wine weithiau yw'r feddyginiaeth. Ai ni chawsoch i mo'r London bil hwnnw etto? Nid hwyrach fod rhyw chwiw leidr wedi ei gymeryd o'r godgroen. Dyma ebystol o Lerpwl a gwadd i ddyfod i votiaw. Dymma arall yn dwrdio myn'd a thir sydd ynghanol tyddyn Llanfigel, oni rhoddaf fy llef efo Hu Bwiliam Barthur. Och o druain, rhywbeth tebyg i wybed amser hâf. Os ewchi iw hymlid ac ymddigio wrthynt gwaetha'r cwbl fyddynt, ond e meddwch chwi? Ni chymeraf arnaf ei gweled na'u clywed, mi af rhagof wrth oleuni gwan fy rheswm fy hun, gan na wnewch i nag arall ŵr synhwyrol fy hyfforddiaw. Yr un yw Gwalch gweilgi, a Chas gan longwr, medda Sion Dwyran; par un o'r Lari neu'r Mergi ydyw hwnw? Yr 'ych i yn dywedyd fod dwyfath ar Linos Felin, un a nytha mewn eithin ar llall yn yr yd ar y maes, nid wyfi yn cofio ond un ar dir yr Arianell a hono yn yr eithin, yr wryw yn dra melen (Llinos Felin fair), ar llall sef y fenw yn frychach ac yn ronyn llai. Oes yna lawer math o hebogiaid, ie, a llawer math o ieir. Nid oes yma, ond y cyffredin, a'r dragwm, a'r cwtta, a'r dandi, a'r crib cadenfyrddin, a'r coppog. Mi wn eich bod wedi diflasu'n darllain fy hir llythyrau yn barod i heppian u'ch i ben, felly mi dawaf am heno, ond rhowch gennad ym cyn rhoddi fy 'mhin i lawr i gofio ngorchymmun at fy chwaer a'r llanciau mawr yna fydd gartref cyn y cyrhaedd hwn yna. Duw a fyddo warcheidwad i chwi bod ac un.

Eich brawd herglod, *William Morris.*

L'Oiseau St. Martin y geilw'r Ffreins y Pygargus, medd Linnæus Par 17, Synops. Wawch! oeddwn i yn geisiaw ddywedyd ar ben

W. to L. contd.

W. to L. contd.

boreu Sadwrn y dydd diweddaf o'r mis, cyfrifon y mynd ymith, etc. Dyma'ch dau lythyr, ni chaf atteb monynt heddy; rhaid rhoi pob peth heibio. Dyna hadau cymmysg. Duw gyda chwi oll.—*W. M.*

[At the foot of the letter Lewis Morris has added: Brith y fuches = Brith y gro = Sigl din y gwys; Llinos velen = Melyn yr eithin; Jack Nichols = aderyn pentân; Tom-tit, sywidw, gwrach y cae.]

GARTREF, y 7d o Fawrth, 1755.

W. to R. CCXXV.

Anwyl Frawd,—Daeth i ben ei siwrnai eich llythyr bychan bâch yr atteb i naill ai tri ai bedwar om rhai mawr i, ond er lleiad ydoedd, roedd yn dda iawn ei gael. Mi ddarperais globyn o lythyr i gyd gychwyn efo hwn at y brawd arall a llawer o newyddion ynddo tuag at iachau'r pesychu, neu or hyn lleiaf i esmwythau tipyn arnaw, rwyn deall ei fod e wedi ymsymud ymhell oddiyna, gwell a fasai iddo biccio ir wlad dros wythnos o'r mwg ar dewawyr yna sydd gennych. Gerwin ydoedd fod y Castell Coch yntau ar syrthiaw i lawr gan beswch, etc.; Duw a gatwo'r gwyr iw gilydd. Fe fyddis yn llygadrythu llawer am y post y foru i gael gweled a fydd dim newydd oddiyna, hanes yr Esgair, hanes Gronwy, hanes Gwyl Ddewi, ac un or *tickets* ar arfau, etc. Cefais y dydd arall lythyr mwyn ddigon oddiwrth f'anwyl Bennant; roedd yntau yn achwyn am y siomedigaeth a gawsech chwi ag yntau o achos camgymeryd y ty ac aros yno ddwyawr, and went away undeceived. Gwae fy nghadach, fe ddylae'ch brawd Gwil gael rhai o fosils Mahone er dim ar y fo. Oni wyddochi fy mod yn gynhullwr, *Anglice* collector of fossils, shells, etc., ad infinitum! If you were to see the Museum Morrisianum at Holyhead, you would hardly trouble your head with Sir Hans's.* Mr. Pennant will next summer lay my subteranious shellfish before the Royal Society, medd ef. Yr oedd Grono yn iach dydd arall, meddai Dwm Sion Twm gynnau. I can't guess what should hinder the man to earn the guineas. Y boreu heddyw y daeth fy nith Pegi Owen o Bentrerianell, roedd yr anwyd ar peswch ar fy nhad yn greulon, Duw ai helpio, ac ach cadwo chwithau yma ac accw. *Eich brawd cysgadur,*

P.S.—Dim llythyr. *Gwilym Tew.*

* Probably Sir Hans Sloane.

LONDON, March 15, 1755.

Dear Brother,—I have yours of ye 6th. Do fe fu agos imi a mynd o'r byd yma i dragwyddoldeb y dydd arall, ag rwy'n ddigon agos etto, Duw ai gwyr. Ond wrth gymeryd vomit (Cardiganshire, moment) a blood vessel broke and my blood ran as thick as my finger *agos iawn*; dychrynodd y Doctor a phawb, ond y fi. The operation of ye vomit was just over, so I did not take anything to stop ye blood, for I knew it would do me good, felly fe stopiodd, ag y mendiais o ronyn i ronyn yn lew iawn, ond fy mod yn groen deneu iawn a'r bol gwedi gostwng, felly bydd gwragedd ar eu gwelyau. I believe I shall never venture another vomit. Mae'r *Arglwydd* bach anwyl ynteu yn ymendio. Take notice, there is a *Glywydd* or *Llywydd*, and an *Arglywydd*, ond pwy o'r blaen a ddaliodd sulw ar hyn? Am not I happy in having a friend of one honest man—perhaps there are no two people that know one another's minds and capacity's better. Duw mawr ai catto fo imi megys tâd—ond mae fe'n taeru mae fi ydyw'r hynaf. Mae'r Gowntess yn feichiog etto, ag yr ydym yn gweddio Duw yn deilwng roi mab iddo i etifeddu y Castell. That would finish his happiness, for *to that* he is the happiest man alive now. His lady is like Eve described by Milton, and indeed beyond that description; for I cannot believe that any Eve had so much innocence, sweetness and dignity. Duw gatto ini Oronwy hefyd i wneuthur Caniad y Castell Coch, ag onide gwae ni fyth. I dont hear a syllable whether he is recoverd. When my own hurry is over, I shall apply my self entirely to help Goronwy, if alive; ond yn awr nid oes bosibl, nid yw'r hanner awr yma wy'n ei gael i sgrifenu attochi ond lledrad. Gwych o'ch perllan chwi, gwiliwch i'r bobl anifeilaidd droi anifeiliaid iddi i bori, fel y gwnaethant a mi yn Mhenbryn, a phori'r holl goed ifaingc brâf oedd gennif. Wele, wfft i'r Bardd Coch! Diwedd hên yw cadw defaid a geifr. Pan ddelom i Sir Aberteifi, ni wn i na bydd rhyw swydd i Sion Owain, Duw a wyr hynny. Gwych o'r MS. yna. Gwaith D.G. difyrrwch! Mr. Pennant hath been with me several times, I gave him some great curiosity's of chrystalizd lead ores, etc., that drove him madder than ever. He says he is now richer than any man in England, and so he is in *that*. Lloercan o ddynan digon diniwed. I have not been able to see his curiosities

L. to W. CCXXVI.

L. to W. contd.

yet. Gwae finneu, rhyw offeiriad yw Borlase, that pretends to be a great Celtic antiquarian, he hath wrote ye antiquities of Cornwal, price twenty-one shillings. I have seen quotations out of it, llawn gwendid. One Cooke follows him, that is, hath publishd on ye same head, about Stonehenge and Abury, etc., but is a most miserable writer, person hwnnw hefyd. A Welsh antiquary ought to have wrote those things ; pam i'r Saeson dylion ryfygu son am ein hen weithredoedd ni? Mi ddof i or goreu 'n enw Duw fal y llongau yn y teidiau mawr. Great actions must expect great opposition, and that whets the edge of an adventurous spirit to conquer those difficulties. You would be surprizd to hear of ye difficulties I have surmounted, a minneu ond un gwan lledwirion. Mi sgrifennaf at fy nhad etto, mi sgrifennais yn ddiweddar. Mis enbyd yw'r Mawrth, all the juices in ye body are in a ferment, occasiond by ye approach of the sun. Oer iawn yw'r hin yma etto. Eira'n aml. Digrif oedd Twm Sion Twm a Ned William Sion! Pob creadur yn ei ffordd, mi wranta'r rheini'n meddwl mae ffyliaid yw pobl na fedrant rwyfo a hwylio a charrio tywod. A fidler standing at his door observing some very fine dressd gentlemen passing by, wonderd to see people so vain and proud when they did not know the difference between a crotchet and a quaver. A man measures the excellency of all knowledge by his own standard. Cofiwch fi at Mr. Ellis ddiniwaid, ffarwel i Huws Glanrafon, a phawb o'r hen drigolion ; rwy'n mynd iw canlyn hwy fy hun, o un i un, darfuon. Ni choeliai nad aeth hwn yna'n benill. I am told the Dublin bankrupcy was of no great consequence. Mi sgrifennaf at Risiart Morys ag a yrraf eich llythyr iddo, nag ofnwch ddigio, cenedl wirion. Pawb yn iach yn Ngallt Vadog.

Your caredig frawd, Llewelyn.

LONDON, March 27th, 1755.

L. to W. CCXXVII.

Dear Brawd,—I have answerd yours of ye 15th. Dyma'r Benant wirion yn o sâl, ag yn mynd heddyw i Richmond i gael iechyd ag yn crefu mwyn etto i'w mendio, gwedi dwyn oddiarnaf gymaint o fwyn gwych ag a dalai corn i wddwg. Y munud yma yr aeth Iarll Powys lwyd oddiwrthif, he waits on me instead of my waiting on him. Pwy sy wr mawr! Bid a fynno, Duw ai bendithio, amen, ag ai cadwo yn swccwr i mi. Os daw'r Protections yma heno, fal mae'n debyg y dônt, mi ai gyrraf i'r Duwmares; ond na rowch imi'r fath fân swyddau ond hynny,—i ryfogaeth y cewri Basan or holl bobl yn y byd, y cwsgfilod a fyddai'n ymladd a'r ffyddloniaid erioed o'r dechreuad. I have wrote to Gronow to come here, which is, I think, the best scheme of all, and leave his wife and children in ye country for a while. I'm told one of his boys is in Anglesey, ymhen mynydd Bodafon, mae'n debyg fod Gronow yn meddwl mae hwnnw yw Parnassus, lle i ddysgu ieithoedd, etc. Mi ymofynnaf beth a gyst bod yn Notary Public. Rwy'n gobeitho fy mod gwedi taro rhyngof a mrawd Rhisiart wrth le i Jack—y Dr. Evans a'i gwna fe'n ddyn uwch pawb o'i genedl; ie'n, ddigon uchel uwch eu pennau bod ag un, pwy bynnag y'nt. You shall hear more in my next, and then you may write to his mother; but I'm told she doth not mind him. Natur pobl haiarnaidd Lligwy, yr hên Huw Rolant ap Huw'r Cybydd angor, ond llangc calon agored yw Jack fal ei dâd. It is to no purpose to write to you the disputes of ye Parliament here. I mewn ag allan, fal gwr a gwraig, weithiau'n heddwch weithiau'n rhyfel, ond yr hen darw mawr cailliog or Castell y piau hi etto, ag a fydd hefyd tra bo byw y ddraig goch.—[*L.M.*] L. to W. contd.

LLUNDAIN, Mawrth 28, 1755, Dydd Gwener Croglwyth.

Anwyl Frawd,—By last night's post I sent off (directed to Thomas Jones at y[e] Custom-house, Beaumares) as ordered:— L. to W. CCXXVIII.

Two protections—cost at y[e] office	10	0
To y[e] broker for his attendance one morning and night, entering and taking out ...	4	0
	14	0

It is to-day charming weather, and yet I shall hardly venture out, rwyf yn deneu ag yn gul fal Mr. Ellis agos—y clos yn syrthio bob yn awr, pob anhwylusdra. Y mawrion yn mynd o'r dre' yngwyliau'r Pasg, mi wranta! Daccw'r son of a bitch gan Gottrel gwedi diangc a llong y bobl ag arian i minne hefyd, i Venice, siawns y gwelir byth mono: roedd yn onest iawn mi wranta' Ynghaergybi er mwyn cael gwneud yn fawr o hono; ni welais i mono er ys blwyddyn. Mi ymofynaf yn nghylch Notary Public. Nid oes yma newydd ychwaneg ond disgwyl bob munud am glywed fod y ffleet sydd yn Spithead yn cael orders i fynd i Brest—to blockade y[e]

L. to W. contd.

place, a rhyw newydd mawr o'r West Indies. Duw mawr a gadwo pobl wirion ddiniwaid oddiwrth ddrygioni'r mawrion sydd rhwng gwendid a diffaethwch gwedi mynd yn gythreuliaid.

Eich brawd digon trafferthus, *Llewelyn.*

Here is a full answer to your query about Notary Public. It is to be had out of Doctors Commons, the stamps will cost £6, and the whole instrument about £15, besides coming up to London, for it is thought it cannot be done by a proctor in ye country. Mewn pa sawl blwyddyn y daw'r arian i mewn yn ol ?*

HOLYHEAD, 10th April, 1755.

W. to R. CCXXIX.

Dear Brother,—Dyma dipyn bach o lythyr i ddangos fal y mae'r byd yn bod ffordd yma, ac i rydwst am lythyr oddiwrthych. Fe fyddai'r brawd arall yn sgrifennu attaf yn ddigon mynych hyd yn ddiweddar. Dyma dri phost neu bedwar wedi myned heibiaw er pan glywais oddiwrtho, gobeithio'r goreu ac ofni'r gwaethaf y byddwn'i yma yn wastad teg. Par bryd y ceir diben ar yr anhunedd yma ? Fe ddywaid hwnnw imi o amser i amser lawer o newyddion mawr bod Gronwy i ddyfod yna, etc., ond mae dinc erchyll am chwaneg or hanesion. Dyma fi er's cryn bythewnos yn ffaelio cael llonydd i aros gartref, yr wythnos ddiweddaf tua Bodorgan, etc., cymeryd cennad ac erchi siwrnai dda i'r gownslwr a'i wraig sydd ar y ffordd yna. Neithiwr y daethym adref o Chwarter Sessiwn y Duwmares, lle bum yn cymeryd llyfon, etc., o achos newid meistr er's talm. Bum echnos ym Mhentre 'r Eirianâllt, neu Ymhentre Rhianell. Roedd y nhad yn dra sionc, a phob peth o'r goreu. Fe dybia lawer un fy mod yn bur ystig, ac yn hoff gennyf ymdreiglaw or naill fan i'r llall y tywydd gwlybyrog yma. Ond nhw a gamgymerant, ni bu erioed debycach peth i'ch brawd Gwilym na'r planhigion a esyd yn ei ardd, os cant y rheini lonyddwch i aros yn ei hunfan nhw dyfant o'r ffeinia, ac a ddygant ffrwyth yn lew iawn ; ond os eir i'w symud a'i helcyd i fynu ac i wared, ni cheir daioni yn y byd o honynt, felly finna, nid yw'r peth yn dygymydd a mi oll. 'Rwyn llwyr gredu nad oes yn Lloegr a Chymru waeth ffyrdd nag sydd o'r Du'mares i Ddulas, ag oddiyno yma, nhw ddywedant nad da rhoddi diofryd yn unlle ond bol mam ac uffern ; etto er hyn, mi a

[*This letter was copied from a transcript made by the late Mr. Richard Williams, Newtown, from the original.]

roddais i (agos) ddiofryd nad awn byth rhyd y fath ffyrdd os gallwn beidiaw mewn modd yn y byd. Nid oes yma newydd yn y byd, ni wiw son wrthych chwi am goed, blodau, hadau a chregyn, nis gwn inneu mwy oddiwrth fatterion y Nafi nag a wyddai'r Brenin Pabo pan ydoedd byw, ac am *drysor*, y peth 'e weddai y mae pawb yna yn ymdynnu am danaw, nid oes gennyf fawr i ddywedyd yn ei gylch. Da os ceir yma damaid a llymaid a 'chydig o ddillad o ryw fath, a thewi a son am godau llawnion. Er cariad ar eich brawd eich hun, rhoddi heibiaw un orrig i sgrifennu ym dippyn o lythyr, ac ynddo hanes y byd a'r amseroedd, ac i gael gweled eich bod yn fyw, nid oes dim coel bobl eraill. Duw a warchotto drosoch ac a roddo i chwi bob peth sydd raid i chwi wrtho. W. to R. contd.

Eich caredigawl frawd, William Morris.

LONDON, April 14, 1755.

Dear Brawd,—I have yours of ye 2nd April, which I believe I have not answerd, being always in a hurry. Dyma fi gwedi darn ddigio wrth y Benant, o achos pallu o hono aros tridie neu bedwar yn dref yn lle mynd ar oferedd i rodio, canys fe allasai wneuthur imi lês mawr ped fuasai ewyllys y peth, nad oedd ddim: rhywbeth meddal gwirion diddaioni ydyw. Nag oes arnafi eisiau dim llengcyn gonest cwrtais o hiliogaeth Cwyllog, mae rheini cynrhrwg a'r Teifisiaid. Lle da i chwi ddisgwyl daioni oddiwrth ffyliaid fal tylwyth '*Organ*, nid oes ond cnafiaid a gaiff le yno, a chida Mr. Dulas. Ie, goeliai i, naill ai'ch *patentee* chwi neu ei dad yw'r Herbert yma, mae e'n byw yn dref yma. Mae Gronwy yn dyfod yma goeliai, ai wraig i aros ym Môn gyda'g ewythr iddo hyd nad allo yrru am dani. Mae ei eisiau yma yn dost gyda'r Cymmrodorion, ag fe wna fywoliaeth o'r gorau. Dyma'r peswch (cyfaill henaint) gwedi fy ngadel yn hollawl, ag rwyf yn iachach nag y bum er's llawer dydd, y bol gwedi gostwng, a minneu gan ystwythed a'r neidr. Y tywydd yn deg fal cefn haf weithiau a digon o ddail *salet* i'w bwytta gida *buyff*; dyna fywoliaeth! Heddyw mae motion yn'r House of Lords i gael cadw'r Brenin gartref, ond er hynny fe â'r henwr i edrych am ei *gountry house*. Ebr ef y dydd arall wrth y Lord Chancellor: "Ond oes genych chwithe *gountry house* lle byddwch yn mynd i roi trô?" "Oes," ebr y Cangellwr, "but not in *Term time*." Mi gefais yma ddau neu dri o L. to W. CCXXX.

L. to W. contd.

lyfrau cywrain iawn, sydd hyfryd eu cael. Mae Arglwydd Powys, hil yr Herberdiaid yma gida mi bob dydd agos,—dynan mwyn iawn; nage, nid dynan eithr *dyn* trwyddo, yn llawn o synwyr a gwybodaeth, dysgeidiaeth, etc. It is a great honour to be concernd with such a man even in writing, dictating, contriving, and planning letters, etc. Fi'n gweled bai arno fo, ac ynte'n gweled beiau arnaf inneu dro arall, ag oddiyno gofyn imi: Is not this right? Duw a'i catwo ai wraig fwyna'n y byd. Roeddwn yn dywedyd i chwi fod fy mol gwedi gostwng, ond daccw fol Arglwyddes Powys gwedi codi, a'm gwraig inneu o fewn mis iw hamser, a dyna'r peth mwya sy'n fy nhrwblio i achos fod yn amhosibl i mi fod yno erbyn hynny, a Duw a wyr a wela i hi byth ai peidio—mae yno haid o blant digon bychain, digon diswccr. Rwy etto heb gael gwastadrwydd ar fy materion, ond gobeithio dônt yn y man.

*Eich brawd trafferthus, L. M.**

LONDON, April 19, 1755.

L. to W. CCXXXI.

Dear Brother,—I believe I have answerd all your letters, and it is hardly anything but an itch of scribbling that makes me write now. I am obliged to fight hard here and gain ground but by inch and inch, so strong are the party against me in the Treasury, who have sufferd my greatest opponent to do surprizing illegal things against me; ond etto trwy nerth Duw ni ai gorchfygwn, ie, eu *mygu* nhwy, i e, *smoak them*. I have wrote this post to Richard Morris of Mathafarn to send you an order to pay me what money you can get for ye timber or father either. Never mind answering his letter about ye gravestone. Rhaid yw cymeryd pobl bendeneuon mewn ffordd gymmwys a phendeneuon yw'r bobl fawr yma hefyd; surprizingly so! Moliant i Dduw am ddyn fal Arglwydd Powys ag emmenydd yn ei ben; roedd ef yn fy stafell i y boreu heddyw, fal y mae agos bob dydd, weithiau ddwy waith yn y dydd, gwae fi na buasai'n dwysog. Mi rois iddo heddyw anrheg oedd well gantho ei chael nag aur melyn, ie, nag aur coeth o Ophir, sef, dangosiad o achau ar bappir fal ac y mae ef 'n deilliaw o'r Brenin Harri'r Seithfed,† y peth na wybu e erioed o'r blaen, ac yn ei lyfr ei hun y cefais ef hefyd, a most noble manuscript upon vellum, with

* This letter was printed in the Brython for January, 1860, p. 34.

† A copy in additional MS. 14929 in L. M's. writing.

the pedigree and arms of ye Herberts finely drawn, and proved from ancient records, deeds, manuscripts, histories, etc., from their first coming into Britain with William ye Conqueror. But they dwindled immediately into Welsh, and spread over great part of Wales and England, and made a great and noted family, or rather *Tylwyth*, sef *Tylwyth yr Herberdiaid*. There is one curious record in it of a commission granted by Edward 4th in ye year 1462 to Evan ap Rhydderch ap Ieuan Lloyd of Cardiganshire, Esq., to call together to ye Castle of Pembroke the most knowing *bardhs* and heralds in Wales to examine into ye pedigree of the Herberts, in order to fix the pedigree of William Herbert, newly created Earl of Pembroke; he that fought so brave in Banbury field. And the said Evan called there Howel ap Dd. ap Ieuan ap Rhys, Ieuan Deulwyn, Ieuan Brechfa and Howel Swrdwal, who sent to ye king a certificate in four languages—British, Latin, English and French, etc.‡ This is all the time I have now to write, here is business come. *I am your affectionate brother, L. M.*

L. to W. contd.

CAER GYBI, Nos Sul, 27 o Ebrill, 1755.

W. to R. CCXXXII

Anwyl Frawd,—Dymma eich llythyr ffwdanllyd o'r 19 o'm blaen, a diolch yn fawr am dano. Yn wir ddiau roedd arnaf i gryn hiraeth am gael llinellig oddiwrthych, ac 'roedd brawdoliaeth yn gofyn y peth. Nage, nid gwych gan eich brawd Gwilym farchowca o'r fan bwygilydd ac ef yn hynafgwr diawgswrth; e fu ddydd y basai hoff ganddo ymdreiglaw o'r naill fan ir llall, a byw'n llawen efo'r hen a darawai wrthynt yma ac acw, ond fo aeth y dyddiau hebiaw, gwell yn awr gartref a llonyddwch nag aur coeth Ophir. Yn wir, y gwir sydd dda ei ddywedyd, mae'r brawd Llew yn bur dda am sgrifennu, a hynny'n fynych, taled yr Arglwydd iddo. 'Rwyn ofni fod twrw rhyfel yn llestair ei amcanion fyned ymlaen. Gwae fi na chawn glywed ei fod wedi eu dibennu yn hollol. Cadwed Duw Bowys iddo'n gydymaith cywir. Mi sgrifenais at Ronw'r dydd arall, ni chlywais oddiwrtho er's dyddiau byd, mae Llundain yn rhedeg yn ei ben; mae'n debyg nad yw'n meddwl am ddim arall. Gobeitho y medrwch roddi iddo fodd i fyw yn gonffyrddus

‡For a copy of this Commission see Fenton's Pembrokeshire, Appendix, xiv. It is now regarded as a forgery. (Catalogue MSS. Wales in British Museum by Edward Owen, p. 488.)

W. to R. contd.

ddigon, fal y gallo ymgeleddu'r hen Gymraeg sydd wedi llwydo a mynd allan o bob trefn yn y byd Ynghymru chwaethach yna. Llwyddiant a fyddo i chwi ymhob amcan canmoladwy, ac iechyd ich aelodau. Gwych a fai gael gafael ar rai o ffosilod Mahone, gochelwch anghofiaw cadw rhan imi. Doe'r sgrifenais at Fortunatus Wright i erchi iddo yntau gasglu i mi gregynach a fosilod ei orau glas, roedd hwnnw yn son am ddyfod adref 'rwan ddechreu haf, ond mae'n debyg os rhyfel a ddigwydd mai i ddilyn yr hen drat yr â, sef i herw longwriaeth. Aie mae'r brawd Pennant i yrru i chwi dlysau i roddi yn eich ysgrin wag? Gwyn ei fyd a fedrai ei hudo yma dros dridie neu bedwar, mae'n gadael dyfod Awst, mae'n resyndod mawr adael cymaint o gregyn yn afreolus tan hynny. Byddai dda gan fy nghalon i gael gweled peth o'ch gorchwylion chwi y Cymrodorion wedi dyfod allan o'r wasg. Nid wyf innau yn cofiaw yn iawn par faint or darluniadau a yrrais am danynt—first: one set and Salms, Evan Williams,* for Owen Meyrick, senior, Esq.; secondly: one set and the Salms bound up in a Common Prayer for William Bulkeley, of Brynddu, Esq.; thirdly: one ditto and ditto bound in same manner for Mrs. Catherine Bulkeley, of ditto; fourthly: one ditto and ditto bound in same manner for Rev. Mr. Richard Bulkeley, Rector of Llanfechell; fifthly: one ditto and ditto bound in same manner for Rev. Thomas Ellis, Batchelor of Divinity, Lecturer of Holyhead; sixthly, one ditto and ditto bound *handsomely* with the Common Prayer as above, but not in rough calf, for myself. Ymhell y bwyf os gwn i par sut y cair hwynt i lawr, na phar sut y cewch chwithau'r arian pan eu derbynnir oni wasnaetha eu talu i nhad. Ni wyddwn i mae Cymro glan ydoedd Wmffreys; 'roedd Aldromon Prichard yma'r dydd arall yn roddi mawrglod iddo, mi ai hadwaenwn gynt mae'n debyg.

Rwy'n cofiaw ir Foddar Benbow honno neu 'merch eich trwblio er's talm yn fy enw i, na bu rhwngwyfi a hi ddim cydnabyddiaeth erioed. Hi fyddai yn cael y gair o garu ers talm, a'r ferch nis gadawai iddi. Ond "mae cares i bawb yn caru," medd'r hen ddywediad. Ie, ie, iawn i chwi y Cymrodorion gael y tamaid cyntaf o bob amheuthyn fwyd a ddelo yma, a chwi ai cewch hefyd

* Evan Williams was a musician who composed eight of the Psalm tunes bound with the metrical version of the book of Psalms.

deued a ddel, cymerant y R.S. a'r A.S. eich gweddillion. Ond gwaeth na dim nid wyf etto ddigon dysgedig yn y gelfyddyd odidog hono o gregyniaeth i allu dosbarthu'r cregyn ar cregyn, ac i ddywedyd yn 'yspys i ba lwyth a changen y perthynynt; mae'n rhaid ymroi atti hi, ni cheir anrhydedd heb gymeryd poen. Gerwin'r henwr sydd yn mynd iw Hafoty ach gadael oll yn y glud. Duw hefyd a'i cadwo rhag syrthio i grafangau Sion Ffrainc. Rhyfedd clywed fod yr Arglwydd Lieutenant y Werddon yn son am ddyfod trosodd yr awron, ni welwyd erioed fath beth; mae'r Gwyddel yn o anesmwyth arno, gwilied y bydd edifar. Dyma Iarll Kildare newydd ddyfod i'r dre i fynd y foru efo'r llong bost, un o'r Grumbletonians pennaf o honynt. Rym ni yma bawb yn iach, mawl i Dduw, ac yn eich hannerch o waelod ein calonau. Duw yn eich cylch. *Eich carediccaf frawd, Gwilym Rwydd-dew.* W. to R. contd.

P.S.—Dyma linell heddyw (28th) oddiwrth Siac Owain, a chowydd Dychymyg Oronwy; a champus iawn ydyw. Gobeitho y medrwch yrru'r Hunlle ymaith pan ddel yna. Digrif oedd roddi *ystop* ar y Downsend front honno. Ni buasai anifail yn y byd ond y Llew abl i drin bwystfilod or fath a drawodd wrthynt. Roedd yn dda bod "Gewinedd a dannedd da, arw fil i ryfela."—*W.M.*

LONDON, May 14, 1755.

Dear Brother,—I have yours of y[e] 10th. I am glad the cheese are gone part of y[e] way. Pray send the girls cloaths as soon as possible, ni chyst mo'r llawer eu gyrru yn bwn i Gaernarvon; mi wranta fod digon o'i heisiau, Duw ystyrio, nid oes yno faint yn y byd o synwyr pen. Mi debygwn fod rhyw anfodlondeb eisiau digon o ganu a downsio Yngalltvadog, ac felly da cael esgus i fynd i Fachynllaeth i fod yn ffol. Talk what you will, sense as well as other qualifications must be born with mankind. The world may tame a horse, but will never make a horse of sense of him. Da fydd cael panelau, ni chlywais i son erioed am y Doctor Poix; beth oedd e'n i geisio yn yr Aipht? Mi wrantaf i Fostyn sefyll, a chenfigen oedd yn ei erbyn o'r blaen. Mi dybygwn wrth Sion Owen ei fod yn chwenych syrthio allan a mi, mae ef gwedi mynd yn o *stiff* er pan ddaeth yma, felly mae'n rhaid ymadel ag ef mae'n debyg, ond gwell a fuase iddo beidio, o achos roedd ar ffordd wych, dybygai ddyn, i L. to W. CCXXXIII.

L. to W. contd.

gael dyfod i ryw beth yn fy nghysgod i neu ar fy ol i a llawer peth, ond os na bydd peth yn y pen, ni wiw i chwi geisio ei bwnnio pei curech i o a gordd. Mae'n siwr i chwi mai gweled dillad gwychion Sion Tomas ag eraill a droes ben y llangc, ond Duw 'styrrio mae hwnnw yn ddigon di-wreiddyn, er bod ei dad yn cynnyg iddo arian mawr iw sefydlu. Mi rois gynnyg ddoe ddiwaetha am *Fallwyd* i Ronw, ond fal y mynnodd d——l roi mhen'r Esgob, mae hi gwedi ei gadel ers dwy flynedd cyn marw'r person. Ond pei gwelai Dduw'n dda alw am berson etto, yn enwedig yn Esgobaeth Elwy, rwy'n meddwl y byddwn siwr o honi. I have not so great interest in Bangor,—dyn bawaidd drewllyd di-ddaioni. Felly gwneuthur, neu geisio gwneuthur, personiaid yw ngwaith neu nghrefft i 'r wythnos yma. 'Roedd yr Iarll mwyna'n fyw yma'r boreu heddyw; have not I done surprizing things to bring such great men to wait on my levee! Ond Duw'm helpio nid wyfi ond Llewelyn dlawd gwedi hynny, digon di ffrindiau ag heb ddyn o *sens* yn fy ngwasanaeth,—a terrible case. Pwnnio'r byd, a miloedd ar filoedd o bunau'n berwi o nghwmpas i, ag etto nid oes ond ychydig yn glynu wrth fy mysedd o eisiau medru celfyddyd cyfrwysdra a gwasgu'r gwan, etc. Ni fedrafi moni oll, na gwenheithio i'r cryf chwaith, mean spirited people can do both. I have a kind of a spirit that cannot bend, and now they call me here about ye offices the *proud hot Welshman*, oblegid er fy mod yn Llundain er dechreu Chwefror, nid eis i etto i ymddangos nag i ymostwng i un o wyr y Treasury, er cymmaint ydynt. Nid oes ryfedd ynteu fy mod yma cyhyd. Gadewch iddo. I will have it done in my own way, or it shall not be done at all; mi af i Ffraingc, mi af i Fflandrys, mi af i Gaerdroia, cyn y caffont y gair i ddywedyd fy mod i yn dwyllwr nag yn rhagrithiwr. This was attempted, and all the ill offices that could be done me. I was the greatest rogue in ye kingdom, not to be trusted with money, or with the king's effects. Was it not my business to clear these affairs up before I went to cringe to any of them? I dont want their favours, if I have but fair play I shall get off with money in my pocket, a draen yn eu cappiau. Dyna eu hymladd nhwy! Ond cadwed Duw fy *nghadpen* i, a rhaid cael help Dduw hefyd yn erbyn y cyfryw geiri nerthol. The Cymrodorion go on bravely, they sadly want Gronow. Nid oes yma ond fy mrawd a minneu yn eu cadw ar eu traed yn awr; neither of us having any leisure to assist much, but you'll be pleased with their printed constitutions which you shall see soon, and next to that the first number of their transactions. L. to W. contd.

You must make your cregyn Welsh names if they have none, there is no if in the case. You must give them names in Welsh. I'll send you a catalogue of ye English names of some sales here, which are all foolish whims, and it is an easy matter to invent new names, and I warrant you they will be as well received as Latin or Greek names. Tell them they are old Celtic names, that is enough. They'll sound as well as German or Indian names, and better. So you'll have a language which none of them understands, and they will be glad to learn of you. But take care you make use of none of your Popish names, crogen Vair, etc. Wawch! Dyma Ronwy ai wraig ai ddau fachgen yn dref, a glowafi'r munyd yma, ni welais i mono, ag mae'n debyg na welaf mono ddiwrnod neu ddau etto. Mi eis i Newgate y dydd arall i edrych am ddynan truan, ag a gefais glefyd y carchar mewn 5 neu 10 munud o amser, mi fum yn ysgothi (neu fal y dywaid y *Ceredigwyr* ysgarthu) er hynny hyd yrwan ag a gefais yr anwyd, sef y peswch, wrth noethi'r din mor fynych, a dyma fi ar fy nhraed 5 o'r boreu ddifiau o achos ffaelio aros yn y gwely gan beswch, o ffei hono! Mae Dug y Cas-newydd yn dywedyd mae fi sy ar yr iawn, ag felly ni wn i pa fodd y doir or afael dost. Pei ceid dros y peryglon hyn fe allai y gallai ddyn helpu brawd i amgenach pethau na rhain yma; ond nid eill dyn ai din yn y dwfr wneuthur fawr. Aie brychiaid afon Alaw ydych yn ei fwytta. Gwyn eich byd chwi, gwell a fyddai gennif fwytta *crothell* o Gymru na *gleisiad* o Loegr, h.y., glâs iâd, ac mae un a elwir Penllwyd ac un ieuangc *Penlas*. Hai, nid oes dim lle ychwaneg.

Eich brawd gwirionllyd, *Llewelyn.*

CAER GYBI, Brydnawn Dydd Gwener, sef y 23 o Fai, 1755.

Dear Brother,—F'aeth llythyr i mi yna yng ngwrthgefn hwn o'r eiddoch or 17eg, a sgrifenwyd ar frys cethin. Newydd da clywed fod eich petheuau yn yr argraphwasg. Ymhell y bwyf os gwn i ymhle y ganed nag y maged y personion yma, y pennaf o honynt, sef ein Mr. Ellis ni, sydd i fod fal hyn: The Rev. Mr. Thomas W. to R. CCXXXIV.

W. to R. contd. Ellis, Batchelor of Divinity, Senior Fellow of Jesus College, Oxon, and Lecturer of Holyhead, a native of Flintshire, ni wn i a rowch i, a corresponding member of the Society for Propagation of Christian Knowledge; Rev. Mr. Lewis Owen, Rector of Llanallgo, a native of Meirionydd Shire, ni chlywais i fod ganddo radd yn y byd. Ni wn i ddim oddiwrth Jones or Dumares; mi a welais ei dad yn Seismon Llanerchmedd, Niwbwrch, a Chaergybi, ni wn ymha un or tri lle y ganed. Fe wyr Wil Parry mae'n debyg. Gresyndod mawr na chawsai Oronwy Fallwyd. Gobeitho y gwnewch yn fawr am dano hyd na chaffo rent wrth ei fodd, yn rhodd fy anerch at y gwr bach. Mae arno lythyr i mi ers llawer o fisoedd mawr. Gofynwch iddo pa beth a wnaeth im Telyn,* nid hwyrach iddo ei gadael ar led ymyl, a bod plant Alis y biswail yn dryllio ei thanau. Dyma un o'n llestri ni yn myned y foru neu drennydd i Gaer Nerpwl, cyfleu odiaeth iw chael adref. Nid rhaid i chwi mor gofal, byddwch sicr o gael gwybod yn union deg os bydd marw yr un or personiaid yma o'm blaen i. Ni chais Ffortunatus ddyfod adref (er y geill os yn rhyfel fal y mae'n debygol y daw), rheitiach iddo o lawer *ffysto'r Ffrains*. Roedd gyd a mi neithiwr y cefnder Dic Jones; dangosais iddo fy nghregynach etc., ni thybiodd erioed fod y fath beth ar wyneb (neu yn y mor na'r ddaear). Hen ddyn cribgoch. The first list is right, by all means follow it. I don't know how to get them down, it will be a great additional expence to have 'em [down by land without a pretty large parcel were to come together. If you have a good boxful to come to this part of the world you would better send 'em by a wagon. How can I yspysu pa beth a wneir without the consent of the subscribers? Nis gŵyr neb yma par un ai, meini gwŷr, ynta meini gŵyr, neu yntau meini gwyr o'r cerrig yma a osododd yn hen deidiau ni gynt ar ei pennau rhyd y meusydd. Goronwy a ŵyr oreu, ond gan eu bod yn eu hunion sefyll, nid ynt yn gwyro. Par bryd y ceir y clawddiadau o Fahone? Mae'n rhywyr cael eu gweled, ac y mae'n rhywyr chwilio am lwdn ceffyl yn llog iw gipiaw rhwng traed, i fynd i olrhain cregyn, cloddiadau, llysiau, etc., o amgylch glennydd Môn dorrog ai mân draethau. Roedd y nhad yn iach o fewn y tridie aeth heibiaw. Pam na

* Y "Delyn Ledr," a MSS. lent to Goronwy by William Morris.

roddwch dippyn o hanes Meirian? Mae fy neugyw i yn rhwydd iachus, a theulu'r chwaer yr un modd. Annerchwch fi at y brâs, a byddwch wych. *Eich brawd trwmbluog, Gwilym Amhorys.* W. to R. contd.

CAER SANT GYBI, 2nd o Fehefin, Haf, 1755.

A glywch'i f'eneidiau!—chwedl y dyn ymedel y Siawnsler Wyn pan welai rywun yn myned heibiaw, ac yntau eisiau gorphwyso. Pa beth ydyw'r achos eich bôd bod y pen fal yr hwch yn haidd heb na siw na miw iw glywed oddiwrthych? Nid oes bosibl fod y Downsiend yna wedi mynd ar goreu oddiar y Llew gafael fawr, oni chlywais i ei fod o yn golchi mwyn pobl heb yn ddiolch iddynt, os drwg Pywel, can waeth hwn yna. Ai nid oes dim modd i gael y llaw yn drecha ar y cono maleisddrwg? Roeddwn heddyw ar fedr mynd i Bentrerianell i edrych y nhad ac i hel cregyn a ffosilod, etc., ond fe farw cymydoges, felly rhaid aros gartref iw chladdu. Roedd yr hen wr yn iach y dydd arall. Nyni a gawsom wrth ein hangen law odiaethol yma y dyddiau diweddaf, a dyma dês, ie, moeldes ar ei hol, yr hyn a bair im gardd lawenychu a'r blodau, etc., sydd ynddi guro eu dwylaw ynghyd. Codwch, da chwitheu, yn foreuach o un chwarter awr, a dodwch i mi dipyn o hanes Llewelyn a Goronwy, dau arwr hynod o'r ddinas yna. Nid wyf yn ammeu pe sgrifennai rywun stori oi holl helyntion au bucheddau, na byddai ddigon digrif. Wala hai! Dyma fi newydd ddarfod sgrifennu at y ddau wyr ardderchog rheini, sef ŷnt y Bennant, a'r Ellis yna, ac i atteb eu llythyrau mwynion hwynt. Mae un i yrru i mi lonaid croen ci cynddeiriog o gregyn, etc., ar llall ynteu yn diofyn gosod ei lyfr cwrel wrth fy nhraed i edrych a ydyw wedi ei wneuthur yn ei le, mae'n debyg. Ond yn ddistaw bach, ymrawd Rhisiart, nid yw eich Gwilym chwi ond lloercan o ddynan anesgydig, anghywraint, anghelfydd ddigon. "Dywedwch i mi ryw newydd," meddwch chwithau. Nid oes yma ddim newydd a dâl hatling; nid yw newydd yn y byd i chwi glywed mae fi o holl bobl y byd i gyd wyf *Eich caredicaf frawd, William Morris.* W. to R. CCXXXV.

P.S.—Pan weloch y brawd arall dywedwch iddo fy mod ymron torri fy nghalon am lythyr oddiwrthaw, ac nad allaf ddim dal allan yn hir heb un oddiyna oddi gan rai o honoch. Pa beth mae Gron yn ei wneuthur nad eill roddi pin ar bappur? Byddwch wychion.

HOLYHEAD, 12th June, 1755.

W. to R.
CCXXXVI.

Dear Brother,—Wawch! a dwbl *Wawch!* Dyma'r eiddoch o'r 7fed, a *Llyfr y Cymrodorion** wedi dyfod o'r diwedd im llaw, er tramawr ddiddanwch a chysur i'r periglor yma a minnau. Ni wnaethum i ddaioni yn y byd a dâl nodwydd er y boreu ddoe ond llygadrythu a dwys fyfyriaw arno, esgeuluso cregyn, blodau, a Chostwm Hows, a phob peth. Yn gôch y bo 'mhais, ond cywrain yr arfau, a digrif caniad y dewis, a hyfryd iw gweled y nifer sydd o honoch y cytrigiaid. Ewch ymlaen, a Duw gyd a chwi bod ac un; bydd ry'wyr bellach gweled Cowydd y Farn, ai frodyr undad yn dyfod allan wedi eu nodi. Bydded yspys i chwi mai Dydd Llun y daethym adref, wedi bod bum nos o hono Ym'hentrerianell yn chwiliaw am anrhyfeddodau, sef cregyn, dail, etc. Ni bum fawr well, ond etto, er hyn, mi gynhullais ryw faint at fy nghasgliaid. 'Roedd y nhad yn rhesymol iachus, achwyn ar y fors sydd yn o anoddefus ambell dro. Cerddasom ir Eglwys, roedd yno o ddeutu hanner dwsing a adwaenwn i yn yr hen amseroedd:—Wmffra o Ddulais ai wraig, Sion'ch William Owen, eill dau yn abl sionc, Twm Rolant, yn hen ddynan cul musgrell, a mab iddo yr un lun ac oedd yntau 30 neu 35 mlynedd i'r awron, felly byddanbw o dad i dad tra bo byd a glo a haearn ynddo; Gruffydd Dafydd, yntau yn hen gorph a chanddo wyrion a gwalch dreng ydyw. Rhaid ai fodloni, ac onite gwiliwch attoch. Gerwin o'r drafferth sydd arnoch, ond mae un peth rhagorawl och tu: chwi ellwch droi matterion y sidanwyr ar llieinwyr heibiaw pan fynnoch, a chael llonydd gan rheini. Dô, mi ge's linell neu ddwy oddiwrth Oronwy, ac mi ai hattebaf cyn y bo hir, nid oes un gair o sôn am y Delyn; yn ddistaw, mae arnaf ofn fod yr hen wrechyn honno y canodd iddi wedi gwneuthur iddo, heb yn ddiolch yn ei ddannedd, ei gwystlo hi ac eraill er mwyn bodloni yr widdon anynad; ni roddaf i byth

*The reference is to the "Constitutions of the Honourable Society of Cymmrodorion in London," 1755. The book, which is a quarto of 52 pages, contains an introduction in English and Welsh, the Constitutions or Rules of the Society, in English; Caniad y Cymmrodorion ar ol dewis brawd o'r Gymdeithas; general heads of subjects to be occasionally considered and treated of in the correspondence of the Society; an alphabetical list of the members, and an account of the British Charity School.

fenthyg i brydydd ond hynny. Ond na soniwch air wrtho er corn eich gwddwg, rhag iddo ganu duchan imi. Felly y mae yn abl costus cadw teulu yn y fan yna. Ai nid oes dim ciwradiaeth iw chael o gwmpas y Ddinas yna? Gresyn bod dŷn or fath yn llewygu. Da oedd gwaith ddilladu'r gwr modd y gallai ymddangos gar bron Ieirll ac Arglwyddi. Gresynach na bai yna Ieirll ac Arglwyddi Cymreig o ben bwygilydd, yno y gellid disgwyl daioni, nid yw rhai yna ond hanner pan. **W. to R. contd.**

Gwnewch chwi a fynnoch a'r Aldremon, mi roddais i lawer puntig allan drosto, ac au cefais yn ol bod y beil, er bod rhaid aros tipyn weithiau, mae yn achwyn yn gethin ar y Llew. Nid da bod yn rhy gwtta or gymwynas a allom, fe fu'r gwr yn llesol ir llall mewn llawer modd, ni wiw mo'r gwadu, os nacca, gwell nacca drwy foesgarwch a llariedd-dra. Nid adwaen i mo Ddic ab Samwel ab *Sion Evans y crydd*, o Dref Wyn, a ddaeth ai blant o Arfon mewn cewyll ddydd a fu. Hiliogaeth pa un sydd yn awr yn glychiaid (sef yn dwyn y gloch) drwy barthau dwyreiniawl Môn Ynys. Dynion dihafarch oedd y clychiaid gynt, o bai rai ydd ym yn deilliaw. Dynion (chwedl yr hen Owain William, or Nant Bychan, gerllaw Moelfre, am ei fab Ierwerth) a ymafaelai ynghroen bol y byd! Celwyddog oedd y porthmyn erioed hyd yn heddyw, ac yn wir felly y gwelaf i y rhan fwya o blant y byd yn ei marchnadoedd. Ond efo'r Gweddi Cyffredin ar Darluniadau* y gyrwch ir aelodau anghytrig ei llyfrau, pe baent ymma ni byddwn i hwy nag y bai arall yn llyncu llidiart yn eu hanfon. Ond pwy a dal y gost? Gadewch iddo, mi drinaf y dreth oreu gallaf rhag bod y ganwyll yn guddiedig dan lestr; rhaid i mi derfynnu. Duw gyd a chwi oll.

Eich caredigawl frawd, *Gwilym Gregynwr.*

* William Morris frequently refers to the set of plates issued by Richard Morris, for insertion in his edition of the Book of Common Prayer. These cuts sometimes occur in the 1752 edition of the Prayer Book, but they are usually found in the splendid edition issued at Cambridge in 1770. This edition has a frontispiece and an engraved title page bearing the following words: "Gwasanaeth Cyhoedd Eglwys Loegr, wedi ei addurno a LIV o Ddarluniadau Newydd Ystoriawl: A ddychymygwyd gan S. Wale; ac a Dorrwyd ar Efydd, gan Ravenet, Grignion, Scotin, Canot, Walker a Ryland. Llundain: A fwriadwyd gan Risiart Morys, LL.C.C. [Llywydd Cymdeithas y Cymmrodorion]. Ac iw cael gantho ef yn y lle a elwir y Navy Office, 1755."

LONDON, June 12, 1755.

L. to W. CCXXXVII. Dear Brother,—Just received yours of ye 7th from Pentre Erianell. Dedwydh ych i gael pleser o weled hen gydnabyddiaeth a gwlad lawn o bob difyrrwch ; digrif yw'r henwr o'r Brynddu fod gan ie'nged. Wele ond gwell yw llaeth o bob rhyw na chwrw llwyd gwan. Gwych oedd llamriaid, a chregyna gida Griff Dafydd! Bara cam (sic) a brithog hefyd mae'n debyg, ffâr wych, pei ceid hi! Ond dyma finne yn llyngcu mwg a niwl, a phob afiechyd, ag yn cael fy ngwasgu rhwng dannedd fy ngelynion, ag heb wybod pa bryd y ceir yn rhydd. Etto rhaid yw ymdrech, and obstinately resist. Gwych oedd ir buarth cerrig fynd yn berllan, a gwychach a fuasei ei berchenogi gan etifeddion y sawl ai gwnaeth. Ceiff y bardd ryw fywoliaeth yma tocc; ni welais i mo'r *transcript* hwnnw etto, a siawns y gwelaf byth na hwnnw na'r *original.* I was in Brown Willis's company a few days ago. I expected to have seen something extraordinary in him, ond Duw ystyrio, nid yw ond creaduryn digon diedrych, a digon diwybodaeth. He hath not so much as a notion of any old British authors. Lloercan *yslyfan* bendew tebyg i . . . . . . mi ddweda i chwi pwy, yr hen Forgan y Gôf gynt, ond bid y fynno mae gwedi addo rhoi anrheg i'r Cymmrodorion oi lyfrau, *The Cathedrals*—and advises them to apply to Jesus College for assistance to go on. I presume you have received the Constitutions, etc., ere now. If I had not been involved in troubles the queries would have been better, but they'll do to begin ; the next edition if I have any senses about me shall be better. I dont think it worth while to give you any account of my affairs here till I am at some certainty for I am like a llwdn dafad mewn drysi, cant o fieri a gafael yn fy ngwlân. Have made surprizing defences here, and God visibly helpd me by unsearchable ways. If this great opposition had not been made to me, I should have been no more known among them than Loli'r *Gw'ydd*, but now my name is as well known at ye Treasury and at ye Duke of Newcastle's Levy as the name of the Attorney General. "I dont know how this man came to be made boatman at Aberystwyth" (meddai un o'r secretaries wrth y Duke N. Castell y dydd arall), "Lewis Morris used to have the nomination of the officers in that country." I must give the Commissioner a rebuff about this affair.

Ag etto yn y cyfamser y chwiwgi yma yn fy erbyn i tan dîn, nawdd Duw rhag ffalsder Saeson. Gwas i Bowel a roesont yn *Boatman* yno. Rwyf wedi digio'n fy asgwrn wrthynt. Daccw fab Lord Lisburn yn sefyll yno i fod yn *fember* Parliament yrwan drwy *interest* y *Government*! Monstrous!—Y' dyn oedd y dydd arall yn gwneuthur iddynt warrio miloedd o bunnau ar y gyfraith gan daro gida Phowel a'r Jacobites. Plant yn y pistyll, fei gwyr Duw a dynion hefyd, and though the Lords of the Treasury know that Townsend is a rascal and a bite, yet they suffer him to make fools of them before their faces, ond beth yw hynny i mi ped fawn o'u bachau mewn rhyw seintwar a llonyddwch! No additional boy yet at Galltvadog though expected daily, next post very likely will bring an account of him. Mae pob peth yno, mawl i Dduw, yn ffynnu yn rhagorol. Gwae fi na bawn yn eu mysg, ac mewn llonyddwch, mae'n rhywyr bod, rwy gwedi blino yn ymdrech a'r byd croes yma; ond dyma fal y bydd yn dragywydd. Ped fuaswn i yn tyfu gan llawr fal mieren, yn lle ceisio bod yn dderwen, ni fuasai'r gwynt yn cael dim craff arnaf; ond o'r tu arall buasai'r anifeiliaid yn fy mathru tan eu traed—opposition and envy kick some people upstairs, but I dont know how it will be with me. Yn *llaw Dduw* mae rhannu. The wisest schemes is but a rational attempt at best, God only can see the movements, and knows how they will operate. A goeliech i, na neb arall yn ei synhwyrau, mae'r hen Gommissioner *βυχαν* a wnaeth wâs Powel yn *officer* yn Aberystwyth! Ond dyna fal y bu, er mwyn fy ngwrthnebu i. That shews I think a weak stroke of malice, and that I should thank God that greater things are not yet in his power—na soniwch am hyn. Mi fum unwaith ar fedr taflu'r lle hwnnw i fynu yn fy nigofaint, ond ni wn i etto: mi ai newidiaf os medraf am le gwell, fal na byddwyf dan law chwiwgi maleisus. Why should my father not sell ye wood in a lump when he is told that the money is wanted? Suppose there is twenty shillings lost in them what is that to the purpose? That is but poor æconomy to bring mustard after meat. If I ha'nt them when I want them, they'll be of no use. For God's sake stir in it. Your salt office bill is accepted. Here is no more time now to write. *Your affectionate brother trafferthus, L.M.*

L. to W. contd.

LONDON, June 14, 1755.

L. to W. CCXXXVIII.

Dear Brother,—I have nothing to say this post but that I have a son at Galltvadog, newly born and called by this time Richard. Your name shall be on the next; and chwedl William Sion o'r Ddreiniog, ni wn i pa enw i roi ar y lleill a ddaw gwedi hynny. This kind of notice of births is a rule among the highest class of mortals yclept princes. But they generally send ambassadors or people in great character to carry the news. I have none to send, not so much as a footboy, with me in this strange land, though I have idle people enough at and about Galltvadog which might have carried the news. So much for a son. A Cardiganshire correspondent wrote me word the other day, that his wife had brought him a new boy. Let critics examine how just the expression is. Gronow is here criticising and improving daily, and hope will get some certainty for bread soon. He wants pruning sadly, he hath been among positive people, and positiveness will not always do, though we are in the right. When it blows hard, an yielding branch will evade the storm. I have no news about my own troublesome affairs, it goes on with me but heavily, but must do at last. Patience and perseverance are the two best ingredients in this case. My affairs in Cardiganshire are, thank God, in a good prospect, farms, mines, etc. Time may come (if it please God) that I may have some quiet. Ned Hughes is of help to me now and then. I dont hear the cheese is got there, nor Peggy's cloaths. I write to my father this post, etc, *Your affectionate brother, L.M.*

Let me hear ye Welsh names of your shells when you have christend them. Bychod, hyrddod, teirw, ceirw, meirch, etc. Crychiaid, brychiaid, llygoden, pigoden, etc.

LONDON, 23 June, 1755.

L. to W. CCXXXIX.

Dear Brother,—Here is no time to write a half sheet letter. I received yours of ye 19th to-day, and one from Hugh Hughes, which I dont understand. He wants me to exchange some land at Rhoscolyn, and says he'll be in the country most of ye summer, and after mentioning some quillets to be exchanged, he says thus: "I wish Miss Peggy Morris was to visit her estate, perhaps she and I might settle the above exchange by joining both together, as so little now divides them, and would then be a pretty thing." Pray send me your explanation of ye above if you can, you may understand the Irish phrase better than I do. Just now heard from my wife. She is pretty well, thinks of getting another boy to be ycleped William. Is! I am a prophet, and have foreseen and foretold abundance of things. Gochelwch godi melin newydd, medda fi, nid pawb a dery wrth y cyfryw fenyw wirion ag sydd gennifi. Gwrda discybl Linden; there are many of them. Dyma fi newydd fynd yn rhydd o un llwyn o fieri, meddai Arglwydd Powys, a fu yma y boreu heddyw. Asswynaf nawdd Duw arno a'i deulu. Ai ie ni wyddech pa beth oedd *Seintwar*? Onid sanctuary ydyw? Seintwar yr adar yw'r llwyn coed. Ie, yn ddiammau, chwiwgwn lladron defaid ydyw plant Alis erioed. But I never felt their stings so much as I have this bout. Ie, mi wranta 'r un rhywogaeth yw merched modryb Catrin Williams o Fodavon o hil i hil, etc. Digrif y gregynog. There is no occasion to improve upon it except to make it as near a circle as possible, for it will contain more. Suppose an octagon, y cregin mawr yn y drôrs isa oi chwmpas, and then thin drawers an inch, and half inch thick towards ye top. The pyramid not to be very sharp at top, but a section, and a statue of a cregynwr a top of it. The drawers, which will be almost triangles, to have their points a little lower than the outside, or else they'll fall out in turning about ye machine. Mi fynna fi un o honynt i roi mwyn a cherrig, etc., os byddaf byw, ond beth a fydd y pen isa iddo, ai rhyw gist, ynte traed o'r post canol? They are a vast number of thin drawers that the virtuosos have here, and I have not seen many of them rightly sorted, but generally in confusion and disorder. O'r ffeinia yw pappir newydd Gwyddelig now and then. Direct your next and henceforth for me to be left with Mr. Richard Morris at ye Navy office, for I shall remove thereabouts soon. Ar frys etto. *Your affectionate brother*, L. to W. contd.

Llewelyn.

LONDON, July 4th, 1755.

Dear Brother,—I have yours of ye 28 ulto with the figure of your intended *cregynog*. I dont understand it at all without drawers, for your smallest cells are not to be above an inch square, which can contain but one shell, or two at the most, for if you put more they go out of sight; and your method will not contain the twentieth L. to W. CCXL.

part of ye number of shells as drawers exposed to ye light will. If you have some curious shells that are not to be fingerd, may not they be coverd with glass in drawers? One drawer with partitions will in my opinion contain more shells than half of one side of your top. However, as you and the engineer have considerd it more than I have, yours may answer better; but as soon as I have any heddwch and llonyddwch I will actually have a hexagonal one for fossils, shells, etc. Pa fodd roedd possibl imi wybod meddwl Colyn? Ai fi wyddai nad oedd ei wraig yn fyw? Was not he married and had several children? If his wife is dead, are the children so too? If any of them are alive was not his land settled on his children? If so, what settlement can he make on a wife and another brood? Heblaw hynny, dont you remember how the King of France married the heiress of Bretagne in order to swallow up that country?—a very apt comparison! I should be glad of your opinion upon this proposal of his, for the old proverb says "priodwch eich merch pan alloch, a'ch mab pan fynnoch." It is possible I might make satisfaction to ye other sister to give up her part of ye land provided everything else suited, and for a certain consideration perhaps I might give up the profits for my life, or to give him a sum of money in hand, and to wait for the whole till I went to another world. I have other children to think of, and must not go beyond my bounds. Gwych oedd y Benant yrru i chwi y fath gregyn; mawr na yrrai rywun i minnau hanner dwsing. Ni feddaf i grogen yn y byd, na chartref na thramor, oddigerth dwy neu dair o *fossil shells*. Mae pen Ieuan Brydydd Hir debygwn gwedi troi, sef ei 'mennydd; beth oedd anifail gwan tlawd oi fath ef yn ei geisio yn y Werddon—on his tour of Europe mi wranta! The poor lad is eaten up with vanity and pride, a kind of a canker or rust, and hath quite forgot from whence he came and what substance he hath for these tours. Benthygca arian gan bob dyn a pheidio a thalu byth, and running into all manner of vices. Perhaps that may get him a living as Christianity goes, who knows? Dyma Gronwy ymron cael curadiaeth, a rhywyr iddo i chael, ag oni bae fy mod i yma buasai'r bol yn wâg lawer tro. It is impossible to push Lord Powis about him any further till I have finishd my own affair with which he hath infinite trouble; pan wneler hynny i fynu fe fydd hawdd gwneuthur pob peth arall. It is not worth my while to mention my *mine* work of *Cwmervin* bach, just by Galltvadog, in which I have a good prospect, and I believe will be a great thing, and would have been before now if Ned Hughes had not liked to drink *cwrw llwyd* better than attending to see the mine opend. Providence threw it into my lap (i.e. the lease), unseekd for, and God hath visibly favourd me more than ordinary in all my proceedings hitherto, which is y[e] very reason that the devil and his children are so busy working against me. L. to W. contd.

The morning of y[e] day I moved to this lodging on Tower Hill, Lord Powis was with me at my lodging, and we appointed a place of meeting after his coming from the Treasury. He was obligd to stay there two hours to wait their pleasure; however, he did it with great patience, and I hope hath carried the point we wanted that day. As our adversaries have fortifyd themselves so well by bribery and corruption, we are obliged to fight our way inch by inch, ond ni wnawn eu *undermeinio* nhwy yn y man. We have now only one Tower unconquerd. Duw fo gida chwi a'r eiddoch; cofiwch am arian Richard Morris, mae yma eu heisiau. Doe y derbyniais arian am eich bil £14 10s. 1d. Ni fedraf gofio am ddim chwaneg iw 'sgrifennu y tro yma heblaw hyn, sef os gyrrwch i imi i Alltvadog gragen o bob rhywogaeth sy ganthoch, I mean foreign ones or rare British ones, mi yrraf finneu i chwithau bob minerals, etc., sydd gan inneu, y peth na welodd un *ffossilist* yn Lloegr eu cyffelyb, ond Pennant, i'r hwn y rhois i *drysorau* a dâl eu pwysau'n aur melyn.

Eich brawd digon trafferthus, Llewelyn.

Your single letters to me as usual may come to brother Richard at the Navy Office, but double ones when you have franks, may come to me at *Mr. Prestwood's, over against the Coffee House* on Great Tower Hill.

CAERGYBI, 7d o Orphenaf, 1755,
5 o'r gloch y bore.

F'anwyl Frawd Rhisiart,—Mi sgrifenais er's dyddiau byd attoch ryw brygowthen neu gilydd, a dyma fi etto yn mynd i fritho hanner llen o bappur, heb fawr achlysur yn y byd gyda dywedyd i chwi ein bod yma yn iach ac yn gorchymyn attoch bod ag un. Gwae fy nghadach mi sgrifenais at y mrawd arall i erchi iddo gymmorth ryw bechadur o ddyn, y bu farw *brawd Llwyd* or War Office yn ei W. to R. CCXLI.

W. to R. contd.

dd'lêd am lyfrau. Mi a wn os medr y gwna ei oreu dros y dyn tlawd. Perhaps he is not acquainted with Lloyd, I think you are, os felly, er mwyn Duw siaredwch ag 'e a dywedwch iddo mae eluseni mawr yw talu i'r dyn tlawd sydd ganddo wraig a phlant iw maentumiaw heb ddim ond ei gyflog as a foreman to a printer. Y wraig gan feddwed a hoedan beunoeth. Mi yrraf ei fil yna pan glywyf fod gobaith. Fe fu'r dynan truan yn dra gwasnaethgar i'r brawd pan ydoedd yn trin ei lyfrau o'r glennydd, ac y mae ettwa yn gwneuthur ei oreu glâs erddo, ag erwyf finnau. Mi a wn o'r goreu mai haws i'r goludog gaffael cymwynas yn Llundain na'r anghenus, ond gobeithio na ddysgasoch i mo'r gynneddf honno gan y mawrion. Rhowch eich pennau ynghyd, da chwithau. Mi dalaf fi'r arian, derbyniwch chwithau nhw, ontê? Mi debygwn wrth y papurau ein bod ni yn mynd i ymaflyd codwm o ddifri efo Sion Ffrainc. Hwi gyda Phrydain Fawr!!! Gwych o'r *proposals Seisnig yma* i'r Script. Prints, a gwchach fai gael gweled rhai o naddynt. Will a frank convey a number? If so, Mr. Meyrick's, as they are not to be bound, may come per post, yno cawn innau dorri fy mlys. I cant guess what *borders without prints* means. Pray explain it. A King's Messenger is in town going, as he says, to the Lord Lieutenant. I ba beth y gyrrasant y gwr drosodd? Oni fedrant fyw hebddo? Mae hi yn foregwaith hyfryd, felly rhaid cadw'r ddrec. Pa beth sydd yn dyfod o'r Penbardd? Duw a fyddo'n gwarchadw drosoch a byddwch wŷch. Cy'd a'ch bys o lythyr gynta galloch.

Eich brawd ungalon, *William Morris.*

L. to W. CCXLII.

LONDON, July 8, 1755.

Dear Brother,—I cannot help letting you know the joy of my heart, at a letter I receivd yesterday from Lord Powis, which gave me an account of Lady Powis's being deliverd of a son yesterday morning at five to the inexpressible satisfaction of that noble family. There were two girls before, and charming children they are. There are few couples in Britain so happy as Lord Powis and his Lady. He is one of the best of husbands, and she the most agreeable woman I ever set my eyes upon, and though not above 24 or 25, you hardly ever saw a woman more sedate or more humane. Had Milton seen her he would [have] made a finer picture of Eve than that admirable one which he hath given us.

Such a prudent, good family as this is a blessing to ye country they belong to. She loves the Welsh dearly. I happend to be with my Lord and her the evening before St. David's day, and asked her whether she had provided a leek. "O Lord" said she "I must get leeks for me and my children, I am greatly obligd to you for bringing me in mind of it, I never would have forgiven my self if I had neglected it." I entertain them often with the actions of ye Princes of Powys, and the ancient British poetry, etc., which highly delights her and diverts him. He hath perusd several things I have wrote on mines, etc., and in short I am as well respected by them both as if I was one of their own family or a near relation. I assure you this young Lord gives me the greatest pleasure I have felt this great while, for we expect great things from it. I have no leisure at present to write any more, though I could dwell upon this pleasing subject till to-morrow, I have heard from Galltvadog last post, all well, and his mother says that Dick makes a fine boy. Is not this something like O.P. and his wife? "I do assure you" says he (to my brother lately) "she is a very good woman." Who doubted it? But I assure you that *I am your affectionate brother*, *Llewelyn*. L. to W. contd.

LONDON, July 15th, 1755.

Dear Brother,—I have yours of ye 9th as to ye cregynog. It may be made big enough to hold your collection for a crown or eight shillings, it need not be ye size I mentiond, for that would hold half ye creation. Am *Golyn* I dont know what to say, I am informed a few days ago from Cardiganshire that my daughter thinks to cut for herself if she hath not done it already; felly boed rhwng y din a'r wialen. Or goreu oedd gael ymadel ag Ieuan Manafon* yn groen gyfa, anodd yw cael ymadael a bardd felly, *witness Gronwy*. But he hath just now got a curacy and a pretty one at North Holt, about ten miles from London towards Oxford. Ond pa fodd a fydd cael gwely i orwedd arno yno? Mae'n rhaid cymortha. It is a poet's fate to be distressd. Fe wnaeth gywydd yn y *Nennawr* y dydd arall (i.e., the Garret), that should be a good one, the proper element of a poet. My last told you *fod mab i'r Castell Coch* Ymhowys, sef Lord Viscount Ludlow, a llawenydd mawr sydd yno; Duw ai llwyddo L. to W. CCXLIII.

* Evan Evans, Ieuan Brydydd Hir, who was for a time curate of Manafon, in Montgomeryshire. ("Gwaith Ieuan Brydydd Hir," p. 107).

L. to W. contd.

i gyd, a most amiable family. Mae Gronwy yn llunio cywydd iddo, croeso i'r byd. A new subject I suppose; I gave him the *testyn* in writing. The more I advance in my affairs, new difficulties start, as if they had a mind I never should have an end. But they use Lord Powis as bad as they do me, so I suffer in good company, and I would not desire better. I shall hear to-day from Lord Powis how this last contrivance is like to turn out; surprizing people, made up of pride, ignorance and falsity. All well in Cardiganshire mines—Cwmervin will make a good thing. Gwae fi na bawn yn rhydd a rhein, i fynd i edrych ar ei ol, ag ar ol gwaith mwyn Llangynog. Y mae Arglwydd Powys yn ei gynnyg imi,—the great mine that produced twenty-six thousand pounds a year clear to ye late Duke of Powys. Ai tybied yr ydech i, na bo yno beth etto ar yr ôl? Oes, oes, ag amgenach lle i dreio lwcc na bod yn pigo ceiniogau a ffyrlingod dan bobl y dollfa a rhyw chwiwgwn o'r fath. Duw ro ini ryw beth o'n heiddo'n hunain yn lle bod yn ymostwng i greaduried penwagcach na ni'n hunain. Nid oes dim amser i sgrifennu chwaneg, ond gwilio am dippyn o arian oddiyna ped faent iw cael. *Eich brawd ffyddlon,* *L. M.*

LONDON, TOWERHILL, July 17, 1755.

L. to W. CCXLIV.

Dear Brother,—Dyma fi i'm diflino fy hun ar ol cerdded oddiyma i Dover Street mewn awr a chwarter, yn cymeryd pin i sgrifennu attoch i ddymuno arnoch ynghynta peth *baccio'r* cregynach yr ych ar fedr eu gyrru imi, ai rhoi mewn bocs a rhyw henwau arnynt, Ladin neu rywbeth, ai gyrru gynta galloch i Ddyfi neu Aberystwyth, oblegid mae imi obaith etto gael mynd adref ryw dro, ac ni wybod pa gan gynted, oni ddaw diawl etto yn drech na'r angylion da sydd yn fy amddiffyn. Rwy'n gobeitho gael o honof yn glir etto o'r Auditor's Imprest office. Dyna i hymladd hi drwy'r holl arfau! Mae Iarll Powys yn llawen iawn gael mab, Duw ai llwyddo. I'm just come from him, ac mae Gronwy yn gosod hên eiriau a sillafau mewn *ranks a files* i wneuthur cywydd croeso i Arglwydd Llwdlo i'r byd, and it is to be translated into Latin and I'll get it printed, etc. Er mwyn dyn ple mae'r arian, nid wyf yn gallu byw yma ar lai na phunt yn y dydd y rhan fynychaf; beth eill ddal, gan fod Cwmervin heb ddyfod iw llawn nerth hefyd? Trwy nerth Duw (a thano yntau Arglwydd Powys) ni orthrechwn ein holl elynion, ag os byddwn byw ni wnawn wastad ar bob aflwydd, ag a gawn Dduw a digon. Duw gida chwi medd *eich brawd ungalon*, *Llewelyn.* L. to W. contd.

P.S.—It is said here that we have actually beat ye French on the Ohio. Fy mhais arfau a gefais gan y Brenin neu rywun, a seliodd y llythyr hwn ag a fydd fy eglurnod o hyn allan. Sef *dau Lew elyn.*

LONDON, 18 July, 1755.

Anwyl Frawd,—The minute I receive a letter from you (for example that letter of ye 13th) I immediately sit down to answer it, provided I am at liberty, in order to teach you to do ye same by me, for I love dearly to know how things go in ye world while I am in it. Is! This *Bachgen y Castell Coch* hath made us all alive here, we are all spirit ag ni sai dim o'n blaenau ni. Did I think so of ye Trefri family, I had forgot it? I'm sure I thought far otherwise of them afterwards; ni bum i etto yn edrych y Gownsler Meirig mwya'r cwilydd. No, I have not seen Ellis yet nor his *corals*, ag nid wy'n chwennych y cyfryw gyfeillach, gwell gan i bobl ddifalch fal Arglwydd Powys. Cedwch 'ithe at eich arglwydd o Benrhos, oni wna dda, ni wna fe ddim drŵg. Dedwydd y chwi a'ch consuriwr gael chwilio afon Alaw, etc., an innocent charming diversion, free from the damnd villanous storms of fortune where dogs eat dogs; what will become of a poor lamb among them? Os da yr ymdrawn Ynghwmervin fe allai y bydd yno le i Sion *Gonsuriwr*, ond rhaid cael mynd adre ynghynta i roi pethau i gerdded. Ni chaf amser ychwaneg i draethu dim heddyw, ond fy mod gwedi gyrru gida gwas Syr Niclas Baily i nhad spectol of *five inches focus*, and if that is too young there is a couple of glasses along with it of four inches focus that will fit ye frame; but you or some *gwr ciwrus* must put them in, if they are wanted, ni thal pob amaeth aradr i wneuthur hynny. There are surprizing high winds here, blows the dust into my desk, eyes, etc. Duw gida chwi, newydd glowed o Alltfadog ag Esgair y Mwyn, pob peth o'r goreu, a chonsidrio'r drefn sydd. L. to W. CCXLV.

Your affectionate brawd, *Llewelyn.*

LONDON, July 21st, 1755.

Dear Brother,—Here yours of ye 16th lies before me. I'm tired with writing accounts, etc., newid gwaith sydd gystal a gorphwyso. I hope we can get poor Kendal's money, but query. Gwych yw'ch taith gyda'r Bennant, difyr dros ben, a minnau'n toddi fy mennydd yn L. to W. CCXLVI.

L. to W. contd.

hel arian i bobl ffolion i'w gwarrio etto, ac heb gael ond ychydig oi mwyniant fy hunan; nag ydwyf yn cael dim amser i folera etc., nag i ymgomio a dyn cywraint. I'm just moyderd. God hath sent away two of the dogs that barked at me in Ceredigion; one of them ye very worst in ye world; he died last week at a tenant's house of mine, (a public house) with ye d——l in his mouth,—a rare breed! Beth a dâl i chwi achwyn ar henaint a bod yn droedtrwm? Myfi a ddylai achwyn. You did right to get Mr. Ellis to sign Kendal's paper. I dont know how to write to Martin, a man I know nothing of his temper or ever corresponded with. I am surprizd at him; do you think he hath got ye money? What sort of letter should I write, let me know? What is his Christian name? We have had several brushes with the French in the West Indies and ye North, and perhaps before this reaches you war will be declared here. The D. Register of ye Admiralty said this morning that he is *drawing* ye declaration, and they say that the French Ambassador slipped off this morning; for to-morrow was expected to be the day. He left a manifesto behind him which they are now answering at Doctors Commons. There never was such a spirit for a war as there is here, all mad. God knows where it will end. Lord Anson says he wont leave the French a ship, Duw wnel hynny. I fancy we will not leave them one in *America*. The New England people are a surprizing powerful people. Out of ye town of Boston alone the Governor in about 48 hours got together 40,000 men that bore arms, and with their wallets on their shoulders, were ready to march at their own expense at ye close of the last war to drive the French into ye South Sea. They had in ye same short warning 50 ships and all manner of provision, etc., got aboard, but unhappily the news of peace arrived before they had orders to march, which was such a disappointment to them that they never recovered. Such a set of desperate fellows are enough to take any kingdom if they resolve upon it, and we are here so jealous of them that we are afraid of giving them too great a scope, and I am told we choose that the French should be in their neighbourhood, rather than they should set up for themselves. Just received letters from Galltvadog, etc., all well, and Cwmervin (nid maip) prospers. Ervin is ye name of ye river that runs cross ye vein, but I dont know what ye meaning of y[e] word is no more than Symlog, Rheidiol, Peithyll, Ystwyth, Leri, Wyre, Elerch; the names of other rivers in this neighbourbood, strange sounds! However, my chief delight now is in Cwmervin, but I am not certain but it is *Erfyn; Cleddau* or Cleddyf is ye name of a river, and so is *Gwain*, why not *Erfyn?* Consider this oblegid ni fynnwn mo lysenwi fy anwyl gwm. Mi ddywedais i chwi (mae'n debyg) fod Gronwy yn giwrad Northholt in Middlesex, yn ymyl y lle mae Owen Cornelius yn arddwr. Duw ai helpo, dynan trwstan, difeddwl ydyw; he hath no manner of œconomy no more than his wife; pob dydd trosto ei hun fal pob bardd arall. Mi ollyngais fy nhafod arno fo yn dda ddoe ddiwaethaf, ond ni choeliai y gwiw. Ni wyr o amcan pa fodd i rannu rhwng y bol a'r cefn, to be sure it is a great art which everybody ought to learn. Dyma hi'n nos tywyll, a minneu'n anesmwyth eisiau clywed oddiwrth Arglwydd Powys, ni chaf gysgu fawr heno, er bod fy llygaid ar gau. Gwae finneu, dyma ferched yn trystio ai traed wrth gerdded, mae'n rhywyr mynd i gysgu oddiar ei ffordd—nosdawch. Wele, pam na phacciwch chwithau'r cregin ar *cyrn amonis*, a'r holl ffosils? Ond ydyw mor ddifyr cyfrif cregin a chyfrif arian? Ond dyma fal y mae, mae'r rhan fwya o'r bobl mor ystyfnig na chymmerant mor cregin gwychion yn lle arian, ag felly rhaid cael arian i roi iddynt er mwyn heddwch a llonyddwch, a goreu pei cyntaf y ceir rhai o Fôn. *Eich ffyddlon frawd, Llewelyn.* L. to W. contd.

LONDON, July 29, 1755, Tuesday.

Dear Brother,—Full of hurry and doing little or nothing to ye purpose, born to be tossd about and spoke of as a proverb; full of patience and a great deal of preseverance; but too much patience is enough to drive a man mad. Patience is like stopping the current of a river which makes y[e] passions grow the stronger. I now speak of my own affairs, and the affairs of y[e] public seem to be just on y[e] same footing. The English passion is broke out at last against the French, and it seems we maul them to some purpose by taking their forts and ships in North America. Here is an account just come of a fort taken in y[e] Bay of Fundy, with about 500 men, who they say have been sent to Louisberg, (to help to starve it y[e] sooner.) Admiral Mostyn is stationd over against Louisburg, so that nothing can pass by the sea, and no victuals to be had by land, so that it L. to W. CCXLVII.

L. to W. contd.

must surrender soon and so all Cape Breton. Another fort at Chignetto is besiegd and must yield, if it is not already taken.

They say in the offices here that Boscawen and Mostyn will come home when they have demolishd them entirely, and only leave Holborn there to guard ye coast; and then I suppose next year we'll fall upon ye French at home, who will be helpd underhand by ye Spaniards fighting under French admirals. But the Spaniards will be at perfect peace with us as to trade. Thus it will be for certain, and you'll see if you live, as for my part I shall hardly live if they keep me in London for ye winter, which they are likely to do. All well in Cardiganshire, have heard from them yesterday, ond bod Ned Hughes yn feddw felldigedig, ni wna fo na lles iddo i hun na neb arall; a right son of *fyrth Hu. Pr.* Morris,—sucanwr pendeneu a hwyaden sychedig, blerwm bolerog a glafoeriwr chwydlyd, ffei ffei, Iorwerth, Iorwerth, yn meddwi yn lle agor *shaffts* yr hen *Roman rake*, lle mae digon o fwyn plwm ag arian. I cannot help being surprised at the odd tast of that man who understands things very well; that after I had given him orders to open an *ancient rake in ye mine* three months ago, and the command of any money wanted for that purpose, that he had not ye curiosity to do it yet, though I desired it. Perhaps there may be immense riches there. Who would not have looked into a chest where it is thought there is a hundred thousand pound? Wele, wele, gwell gan Iorwerth gwrw llwyd a lol mwynwyr meddw na'r cwbl i gyd. I can give you no account of my own affairs, having not seen Lord Powys this week, but shall see him to-morrow I suppose. They say ye Treasury will adjourn to-morrow. The militia here are exercising like mad, nothing but ye face of war to be seen. Everybody looks fierce but me. Oes dim arian oddiyna etto. *Eich brawd*

trafferthus dros ben, *Llewelyn.*

July, ye last day, 1755.

L. to W. CCXLVIII.

Dear Brother,—Gwae finneu dyma'r gaiaf tost yn dyfod, ag heb ddim gobaith iawn am gael mynd o'r mwg drewllyd yma. I have seen your joint letter to brother and self of ye 26th, with some account of your journal, a compleat journal would be very agreeable. Pwy ydyw Daniel Lysons yr adarwr? Aie rydech i yn wr mawr gida Threfri? Ai yno mae'r hên wr o Fodorgan yn byw? Oedd

Pennant yn sôn gair am danafi a'r rhoddion a gadd ef o grystalised ore, ie, mwyn crisialaidd gwyn. Wele, the intent of this letter is to bring you ye inclosed paper, which holds more news than any we have had this season, and it seems ye people in authority are not afraid of publishing their intentions. They were private at first. Dyma Ned Edwards wedi cael addewid gan ei *owners* am letter of mark man of 22 guns on one deck, ag yn mynd adref tocc tocc, i ymladd y Ffrancod. I buy some rum of him to carry home to Cwmervin, where you'll be welcome, some of y[e] best you ever tasted, and I buy some to make presents of to y[e] offices,—hynny yw, tynnu llaw hyd ben cian chwerw. My Lord Powys is so busy now about christening his son, that there is no seeing of him. If I dont hear from him or see him before Sunday I'll go to Finchley. Very busy and doing very little. *Your affectionate brother*, *Llewelyn*. L. to W. contd.

Mae gennych i Gwilym's heraldry neu rywbeth or fath, gyrrwch hanes imi pwy fu gantho erioed, neu pwy sy gantho'n awr yr un arfau ag sydd ar fy sêl i? I intend to turn ye dagger into a pick-axe, it is more honourable in my opinion. The Romans turned their swords into plowshares, a gwr heddychlon wyf inneu.

CAER GYBI, Awst 1af, 1755.

Anwyl frawd,—Nid mynych y bydd eich llythyrau cyhyd heb eu hatteb a hwn o'm blaen or 12d ulto. Chwi welsoch mae dringo gell-dydd, etc., y bum, ac na che's na'm côf na'm synwyr gan ryw weilch segurllyd er's pythewnos. Os mawr eich achwyn o'r blaen, can mwy a fydd bellach ar drafferthion, a hi'n myned yn rhyfel wellt rhyngom a Ffrainc. Duw yn ein cylch! Rwy'n hyderu eich bod wedi trechu y peswch brwnt hwnnw a neidiodd yn eich pen yn y fonwent honno, oblegid nid yw'r Llew yn son am dano. Ond pawb a wyr oddiwrth ei ddolur ei hun. Ai Cymrodawr ydoedd y marw? Aie rydych chwithau yn dechreu cynnull cregynach? Wala, digon da, peth digon difyr yw eu trin gartref. Ond difyrrach o lawer yw eu helcyd a'u cynull rhyd lan y môr, etc. There is something so innocent and amusing in it, a mixture of pleasure and a little dash of trouble, rhwydd debyg i'r diddanwch a fyddem yn ei gael pan oeddym blantos yn chwilio am deganau o gwmpas y Darren, Porth Fôr, Traeth yr Ora and nefol bleser ydoedd rheini, oni bai fod meibion y cawr yn ein lluchio a cherrig, ac ofn cael drwg am W. to R. CCXLIX.

W. to R. contd. wlychu traed, ac aros yn hwyr. Mae meibion cewri ymhob gwlad, a drwg a geir am wlychu traed ac aros yn hir oddicartref, fal y bu yma'n ddiweddar ddigon. Gwrda'r Gadwaladr am fod yn Gymro ac am roddi tlysau i chwi, ac am addaw ychwaneg, fe allai Ierwerth ap Iorwerth yntau gynull llawer peth, pe bai ddim ymadferth yn yr hurthgen, cymhellwch ô da chwithau. Gan fod y tri brawd wedi myned yn rhy hen i ymdreiglio 'rhyd y byd i olrhain allan ryfeddodau'r greadig'eth, rhaid yw ymegniaw am gael gan eraill ei cludo o bedwar ban bŷd, fal y gallom, (os ni chawn weled y gwledydd) gael canfod o leia eu cregyn au ffosilod, etc., pethau na wnant fawr ddaioni iw trigolion, ac yn fynych a gair am ei codi oddiar y maes. Rwyn gosod pawb om cydnabod ar waith dros y moroedd, bydd ambell un diwyd yn eu plith yn ddiameu. Digrif yw'r boblach yna efo chyfrifon y Llew. Ymha offis y maent rwan? Wfft ir gelynion sydd iddo, Duw a wnel iddo gael diben iawn ar ei fatterion, a llonyddwch o hynny allan, fe gadd ei ran o drwblaethau. Da iawn clywed fod Grono wedi cael lle i enill tamaid o fara, rhaid cael llymaid o ddiod hefyd iddo ei hun ac ir wraig *Ellin* rywiog oleu, y cebystr ir *sut* nad ellid byw heb lai o'r gwlŷch. Digon bychan esgobaeth lle bo'r wraig yn sychedig beunoeth. Mae fal yr erchwch ar Ioan y nai yrru imi gowydd Arglwydd Llwydlo, mae o wedi ei orphen er's talm byd mi a wranta. Nid oes yma ddiddanwch yn y byd ond a geir oddiyna, oddigerth ambell gragen neu lysieuyn. Y Delyn i ddyfod yna meddwch ir Nerpwl. Wala, wfft i hynny, o bai gwir y chwedl. Pam ir Aldromon ddigiaw am fod pawb yn ddigeiniog fal yntau? Ni ŵyr o druan ddim amgenach nad felly mae. Och fi, ha wr fab! Oes dim o'r gobaith ir Gendal dlawd gael dim or War Offis? Er mwyn Duw gwnewch oreu galloch, a chwi a gewch fendith ffynadwy am 'ch poen. Cewch Gywydd y Farn, Wil Wynn os gyr Ieuan o yma, gwell gan y bardd gwmnhiaeth na dim yn y byd. Er dim ar y fo, gyrrwch ir Bennant No. 1 o'ch gorchwyl, mae'n gaddaw bod yn aelod buddiol or Gymdeithas. He proposed sending you a collection of fossils, etc., anon. Pigion ll—dr, fe ddug nis gwn par faint o'm tlysau yngwydd fy llygaid. Gadewch iddo, fe gâ dalu'n hallt ryw ffordd neu gilydd. Mae hi'n dechreu mynd yn drafferth gyda ninnau—llymma West India Men yn dyfod efo ei siwgr a'u masnach iw pwyso, er mwyn llestair ir Gwyddyl allu gwerthu ei wâr cyn rhatted a gwyr Prydain Fawr, a mynd o hono yn rhy gyfoethawg, a gwingo yn erbyn ei feistr, mae o'n abl gwynafog eisioes. Mae Dermot yn gaddaw gyrru ei longau ai ddybacco yma hefyd, ni bu ymma yr un ermoed o rheini. **W. to R. contd.**

Roedd y nhad yn iach echdoe yn Llanerchmedd, meddai Huw Roberts or siop, a fu yn yfed rhan o beint efo ge'. Wrth son am beint, mi welais y dydd arall Beint Beddcelert,* a naw pintiaid a ennai hwnnw, sef oedd o *Biwter* ac yn hen ddihenydd. Fe fyddai'r hen botwyr gynt yn ei yfed ar yr un anadl, ond nid oes neb yn yr oes yma a wnaeth hynny. Mae aml ryngill yn mynd ac yn dyfod yn ol ac ymlaen drosodd y dyddiau yma, a phawb yn ddistaw. Daccw fy anwyl gyfaill y Capt. Weller yn ymadaw ar *Dorset Yatch* i fynd ar long o 70 o ynnau meddynt. Nid wyfi yn disgwyl moi gyffelyb ar ei ôl, hawddamor iddaw i ble bynnag yr elo. Fo ddywedir mai mab ir Amral Poklington a ga'r Iot. Rhaid rhoddi'r pin i lawr er difyrred iw dwndrio ar bapur. Duw a fyddo yn noddwr i chwi. *Eich brawd ungalon*, *William Morris.*

P.S.—Dyma lythyr (boreu dydd Sadwrn) oddiwrth y brawd Llewelyn yn llawn o newyddion a grwgnachau, pobl y byd yn ei grugo. Dim son am neb o honoch mwy na phe bae'ch wedi eich claddu bod y pen. Dymma arall oddiwrth Rhisiart Morris, o Fathafarn. Meddwl fod y nith Marged yn mynd iw phriodi—a strange girl; y wraig yno yn dechreu cynnyddu. Gwaed swllt! Dymma arall i wrth y Bennant, yr hwn sydd wedi gwneuthur iawn am bob camwri drwy anfon i mi un math ar ddeg o ffosilod tra gwerthfawr! Fal hyn y mae'r gwalch gwenhieithgar yn dechreu ei lythyr: "I reachd this place last Friday night, and now regret the necessity I was under of leaving you so soon, sincerely wishing that Fortune had not placed us so distant from each other. But since we can't have frequent personal comunication, I hope you'll not be remiss in the litterary way, and you may depend upon my endeavours to promote your laudable attempt for the promoting of natural knowledge." Ond ydyw'r gwr yn fwynaidd iawn?

* For a full account of this remarkable mug, the reader is referred to "Beddgelert, etc.," by D. E. Jenkins, pp. 37—39.

LONDON, August 2d, 1755.

L. to W.
CCL.

Dear Brother,—I have your Journal of ye 27th, which is very agreeable. Dau Lew-elyn sydd ar y sêl o achos bod dau Lewelyn Ynghalltvadog, na bond i grybwyll. Ni welais mo Gwnsler Meirig etto. I have other fish to fry, and his fish are nothing worth, so Ellis ye cwrel. Onid oes gan Ellis ddigon o fôr fwsogl a gafodd gan Mrs. Meirig o Fodorgan, a heliodd; chwiorydd Jack Evans iddi? Gwych eich bod yn tebygu ich brawd Lewis, mae'n dda gan hwnnw glywed. Kendal's affair I hope will be done, but you know there is nothing certain in this world among the actions of men *till it is done*. Man is such a queer unconstant animal, so volatile, so positive, so headstrong, so *pengaled* is better. Wele hai, mi ysgrifennaf ynte at Edward Martin, Esq., heddyw os gallaf. Mi wrantaf mai attochi y bydd oreu yrru'r llythyr iw roi o law Kendal iddo, or else he may conceal ye receiving it. Nage, nid balchder a laddodd Haddock. His hands were tyed down by y^e^ *Admiralty orders*, and to see an enemy's fleet passing by him, and he not daring to destroy them, would have drove any wise man mad. He attempted to engage them but not one of his captains would join him; and if they had, they would have been all broke by ye Admiralty. Digrif o'r doctor Lwyd, ai fwyn; mining is an art that a mere theorist will never learn. Gwych o'r *Society* yn y *Wyddfa*! Pwy sy'n byw yn Nant Rowlands, ped fae siawns i ddyn fynd i'r seler yno? A fydd Dan Lysons yn dyfod i Lundain? Ni wn i etto beth yw Llyn Eigiau. Aig in one sense is ye ocean, and is certainly a primitive Celtic word from whence the Greek *okeanos*; ebr rhyw fardd :—

Ni thai fy mhen am Wenno
Mwy na'r Aig ym min y ro,

i.e., the continual sound of ye sea on ye beach. From aig came *eigion*, but from whence came eigiau? Pa fodd y dewisir Humphrey Owen heb ei gennad? Ceisiwch gan y Mr. Ellis sgrifennu atto i ddywedyd iddo fod y Cymrodorion gwedi clywed ei glôd ag yn barod ei ddewis yn goresponding member os bydd da yn ei olwg. Mae'n dda gennif fod yr henwr yn dechreu adnabod *βιωσ* cyn cau ei lygad a marw a mynd i'r byd arall yn ffwl. Pan ddelo gan eich brawd Tew ddigon o fodd i fyw, fe dry i ben i sgrifennu Natural History of Anglesey and its antiquities.

"F'arglwydd" ebr Gronwy Ddu, etc. Gronwy's curacy is £40 a year and £10 towards a house, and some perquisites. If my affair was determined he would be sure of a living, but I cannot push things on so heartily as affairs are now circumstanced. Things are in a fair way of doing well, but that we move slow. Da ydyw clywed fod yr arian yn dyfod, goreu pei cyntaf. You frighten me when you say that Robert Jones's repairs will be a great drawback; I intended that to be but a small one, for he hath too great a bargain by half. *I am your affectionate brother*, *L.M.* L. to W. contd.

LONDON, August 20, 1755.

Dear Brother,—I had no letter from you last post, and have no more to say than that *y mrawd a minneu* intend to take a trip to Dover this week to stay a few days for our healths, and to look on ye French coast, but chiefly on ye fossils in Dover cliff, os rhydd Duw ini dywydd teg a rhwydd-deb. Ni choeliai na ddaw Wil Parry'r Mint, gida ni a Howel Lewis oi long yn Sheerness. Pobl o Fôn i gyd oll, neu ar gân, pobl lewion o Fôn fawr. Pam na yrrasech imi hanes y ddaulew yma, sef y ddau Lew elyn yn Gwilym's Heraldry? Chwi welwch fy mod i gwedi troi fy nghleddyf yn gwlltwr, nage yn *biccass*, ond mae'r cleddyf yno byth megys troed i'r biccass, ac felly os daw achos ymladd gellir tynnu'r cleddyf allan etto ac mi fyddaf ryfelwr cystal cynt, ond yn awr mwynwr diniwaid ydwyf i, a dau lew yn ei bais, sef llew ifangc a llew hen, neu henlew rhuadwy. Dyma Domas Salmon ye historian yn mynd i roi hanes y Cymmrodorion yn Stow's Survey of London sydd yn awr yn y *press*, ag ynte'n cael mynd yn honorary member am ei boen! Ond ymhle mae'r correspondence bellach ar rai o'r pyngciau yn y llyfr? Two letters is all that have been sent. I can write nothing here. I should be at home with my papers, but this leasure time hath produced something. I have compiled here a great part of a book on mines with a vast number of drafts of mines, etc. It surprizes the virtuosi here to see so much art in mineing. They thought it was only raising ore like digging of potatoes. But in this also I want to be with my papers. Felly nosdawch, mae nhad yn dywedyd ei fod yn ffaelio gweled trwy'r spectolau; a gafodd ef roi'r *four inch focus* i mewn? I intend to send him again a six or seven inch focus, fe allai mai mynd ieuangach, iangach mae ei lygaid ef. Duw gida chwi. *Eich brawd ffyddlonaf*, *L.M.* L. to W. CCLI.

CUSTOMHOUSE, HOLYHEAD, 23rd August, 1755.

W. to R.
CCLII.

Dear Brother,—Er na waeth gennych eich c——i na sgrifennu llythyr ambell dro i Gybi, etto er hyn mae'n debyg fod yn ddigon difyr ganddoch ddarllain rhyw wegni a ddêl-oddiyno. Fe fydd y brawd arall yn rhoddi i chwi hanes ein byd ni, for you reckon that we are out of your world. Chwi ydyw'r byd. Pa beth ydych chwi a'ch gwyr mawrion yn ei wneuther neu ar fedr wneuthur a Lewis o Ffrainc? Os oes coel ar y papurau, rydis yn ei drin yn anhrefnus, cymeryd ei longau yn nrws ei dŷ, na b'ond ei grybwyll! "Canlynwch eich dyrnod," chwedl Griff. Huws y Gof, wrth ei dri meib pan fyddynt yn paffio yn Llanerchmedd er's talm. Mae'r ddefod ganmoladwy honno o anafu eu gilydd mewn ffeiria' wedi ei dodi heibiaw er's dyddiau byd. Ceir gweled yn awr wyn o Lanfihang'l Tre'r Bardd, Penrhos Lligwy, a Llanfechell yn cyd bottio efo eu gilydd heb gymmaint a gair twn neu neswch draw, chwaethach torri cloliau a breichiau fal true Britons. Llymma lythyr y brawd Llew yn rhoddi gobaith ir Gendal dlawd gael y ceiniocach gan Mr. Lloyd or War Offis; fe dal Duw i chwi am gymeryd trugaredd ar y tlawd ar anghenus. Dyd, dyd! Dyma lafn o epystol oddiwrth fanwyl Bennant, a llawer o hanesion pwysfawr ynghylch cregyn a ffosilod, etc. Nid oes dim yn eisiau i ddwyn yr holl greadigaeth i oleuni yn y cwr yma ir byd, ond ein cael beunydd efo'n gilydd, y cebystr ir sut nid oes modd i hynny fod, gan ein bod wedi ein plannu mewn amrafael wledydd, however he says that he will lay aside all thoughts of going beyond sea next summer, and come and live for three weeks or a month with me at Holyhead i gael ymroi atti hi yn iawn. What signifies skimming on the surface? Rhaid mynd i berfeddion y ddaiar, ac i waelod y môr eigion cyn caffael pob peth at eu gilydd. Oes dim hanes am ffosilod y Canol-fôr neu'r Perfedd-fôr? Mi yrrais i'r Ellis'r dydd arall ryw ychydig o betha' godidog, ni che's ddim oi hanes ettwa. Rwyf ar fedr gwneuthur casgliad ir Cymrodorion ryw ddydd. Ceir gweled enwau Pennant a Gwilym mewn llythyrennau eurog yn eich tlysgron; ond oeddwn i yn lew allu lenwi'r papurau yma cyn llawned a gwagedd? Duw gyd a chwi.

Eich brawd ungalon, *William Morris.*

LONDON, August 26, 1755, Tuesday.

L. to Mrs. M. CCLIII.

My Dear,—I have receivd yours of ye 19th owning the receipt of ;40 from Henry Jenkins's wife, which I shall pay this day. The ill is very well, only the direction to me should have been on he same side of the paper as the bill was, and not upon the back of :. If she pays you more I will accept of your bill. Griffith riffiths wrote me word that he wanted not above thirty pounds to ay ye officers, for he hath duties in his hands, so I hope you had ıoney to pay him so much. I have wrote to Thomas Herbert ord that he might pay into your hands £150 which he wanted to uy corn with, and Edward Hughes tells me the corn was intended ɔ be put on board Henry Jenkins. But I find that Henry Jenkins ath taken a freight of some Mr. Edwards to go to Aberdovey, and intend to send some things by him. Since I received yours I eceivd two lines from Edward Hughes giving an account of our oor child's death, which gives me very great concern, especially as he whole weight is upon your self, and that it is not in my power ɔ administer you any comfort in your trouble. But God knows est what to do with us all, a little matter takes us away, when He hinks fit to call for us; and that poor child is happier than any of s who have had so many opportunity's to sin, and to break through he rules which the God of nature hath given us. Have patience hen, my dear, for either God will give you another in his room, or vill take us to Him to the same place with this innocent child, when Ie thinks proper to do it, as we must as certainly die, as we vere born. I pity you with all my heart and soul as you have ıot one real friend in the world to advise with, or to comfort you; I ıope to God to be with you before winter. In the mean time pray o God for fortitude to bear your troubles, and follow my directions s near as you can, and I dont doubt of everything coming very vell. We are to expect nothing in this world but rubs and misortunes daily, for God hath put us here to try us, and to see what ve can bear. I have already had my share of troubles, and more than ny share, and I hope to see the sunshine of quietness and happiness y and by. The account I have from Cardiganshire about my silly ınfortunate daughter gives me great uneasiness. She hath been

L. to Mrs. M. contd.

always stubborn and wrongheaded, and thought she had sm perfections which she had not, for, God help her, she never h common sense, therefore I dont wonder at any of her silly act Some kind of advise from a friend might have deterrd her fr this undiscreet scheme, but alas, she had not a friend in the wo that cared what became of her, and now she must take her chan as she publicly says she values neither father nor relations but w do as she pleases, as her mother did, and that it shall cost he father dear. These are expressions of people in Bedlam, and if sh and D.M. have made a fool of *you*, they will not find it so eas to make a fool of *me*. I hope for your own sake and fam you have spoke to her what I desired you in several of my la letters, and that in case of her refusing to hear you or despis your advise, you have orderd her to her sister, for your givi her shelter at my house will actually be construed by my enemie that their whole affair is my contrivance, an affidavit of which w make a fine piece of work of it. You know what kind of thin a woman is when her tail is ripe. She, like other animals, w jump at any animal that offers ; all reason and sense is then gone But it is not quite so with man in general, though it is wit some. Man will hearken to reason, but no reason can mak an impression on an infatuated woman whose blood is on fire A gentleman from Anglesey who hath a pretty estate of his own, besides a post in the revenue, hath made proposals to me about her, and is ready to settle his estate, etc. It is likely he may come to Galltvadog. If he doth come, make much of him, though by what I understand it may be to little purpose. His name is Hughes—such a man of sense and character would have been a credit to be allied with, and might have made that silly creature happy ; but it seems she chooses to be allied with dirt and rags and ignorance. You may tell Mr. Jones that I receivd his letter, and am obliged to him, and shall answer it soon. I beg of you, my dear, make your self easy, and thank God for His blessings, and that He hath favourd us with life and health to look after the rest of our poor family, whom He hath thought fit to leave us.

I am, your affectionate husband, L.M.

LONDON, August 27, 1755, Wednesday.

Dear Brother,—I write this against to-morrow to send you with : sad news of the defeat of our silly people in America; one uld have thought that the trick of an ambuscade was so old and le that no fool, no, not even a hare or a rabbit, but what knows it. t a hot-headed General hath less sense than any other animal, thing but conquest hath room in his head. The Duke of arlborough would not have been catched in such a net, nor any id man; ond gwr poeth oedd y *Bradog* a roes Wiliam, mab ors, i mewn, a phawb yn dwedyd mae rhedeg ei ben yn erbyn y red a wnae ef. Gobeitho y ceir gwell hanes o'r tair câd eraill. vyr llymion y Masachusets yw y rheini. Dyma air hyd y dref ddyw yn chwilboeth fod Bodysgawen gwedi cymeryd 6 eraill longau rhyfel y Ffrangcod, ai carrio i Halifax. We shall know ore of it to-morrow. Your letter to brother Richard I saw; mae'n igon i wneud y dwr i redeg o ddannedd dyn glowed son am pleser ydych i a Mr. Pen-y-nant yn ei gael, a minneu yn fy lladd hun yn gwneuthur dim yn y byd. Some spare hours (and a eat many of them I have had) I have employd in laying the undation of a book of mineing, from its first root through all branches. I have done a good deal, but before it can be lld perfect I should go to Cornwal and Darbyshire, and take aughts of some of their greatest mines. I have a great many afts already and drawn to proper scales. The thing is curious if was finishd, only it gives too much light if it is done and publishd uring my life, for it would deprive me of reaping the benefit of hat I may otherwise expect, in describing things too minutely r the benefit of others. Dyna fy swydd inneu. Londoners id not know there was any art in mineing, more than digging f potatoes. Oes, oes mae, celfyddyd ddofn iawn ydyw, and I now no man master of it. Ond mae'n fy mryd y bydd

Eich brawd, *Llewelyn.*

L. to W. CCLIV.

LONDON, September 1, 1755, Monday.

Dear Brother,—This makes you a letter in my debt; when I wrote ast I was extremely low, on account of Lord Powis's illness; on hose life depends my welfare, as much as my family depend n mine. His steward brought me a line from him this morning

L. to W. CCLV.

L. to W. contd.

that he is better and desires to see me to-morrow at Finchley (where he lives), and I have hired a chaise, and shall take my brother along with me there, for whom my lord hath a great regard I hope God will save his life to assist y[e] distressed; such good men are very uncommon, at least unknown to me. I dont know whether I gave you an account of my poor child's death. The chincough killd him at two months old. I am afraid my daughter Margaret is incurable—quite obstinate and silly. I have wrote to my wife that if Hughes came there, to use him handsomely. It is now seven months since I came here. You may ask me what I have done all this while? I dont know,—nothing worth talking of, and yet I dont know I have had an idle day. I have wrote a great deal in antiquity's: Notes upon Selden's, notes on Drayton's Polyolbion, notes on Burton's Antoninus' Itinerary, notes on Lambard's Historical Dictionary, notes on Sir Winston Churchill's Divi. Brit., notes on Cooke's Druids.* But what is all this for?—nothing at all. Wrote also a good deal on mines, all vanity, etc. The chiefest pleasure I have had was an opportunity of making microscopical observations, which I might never have lookd into, if I had not this leisure time. And I have also made some improvements (which hath not been seen before) in the structure of my microscope, having an opportunity here to get a thing done according to direction, and I insist upon it that my microscope exceeds everything of the kind ever yet publishd. It is plainer, more useful, more natural, and not a quarter of y[e] price of some of them. If I was once at home and in quiet I could make you a microscope that would serve as well as y[e] grandest made in London. This is the most amusing study in the world, and it is impossible to make any progress in natural philosophy without microscopes; it is amazing, it is beyond conception, and beyond description—a new world! The microscope for opaque objects being imperfect, checked my observations in y[e] country, so that I was quite tired . . . . till I had

*Lewis Morris's copy of "Drayton's Polyolbion," heavily scored with notes, was recently for sale in London. His copy of "Cooke's Druids" is in the Editor's possession. It is not clear to which of Selden's numerous works he refers, but the fifth book he mentions is "Divi Britannici; being a Remark upon the Lives of all the Kings of this Isle, etc.," a work written by the father of the first Duke of Marlborough.

an opportunity of setting about it here, which hath given me vast satisfaction, but I have not the objects here, as I can come at in ye country. Would not you wonder to see millions of animals larger than elephants? And is not ye wonder greater to see millions of animals of which a hundred of 'em would not make the thickness of ye hair of one's head, and all in as great or greater perfection of beauty, etc., than an elephant? Rhyfeddodau annhraethadwy! Dyma hi'n tywyllu, nosdawch! *Eich brawd ffwdanus,* *L.M.* L. to W. contd.

LONDON, September 4, 1755.

L. to W. CCLVI.

Dear Brother,—I received yours of ye 30th, and that you may have no manner of excuse for not writing, I whip this away in answer [to it], but my head is extream unfit to vent its thoughts to-day .... Staid last night at ye Cymmrodorion Society till two in the morning. Sad work! And I dont know that it servd any purpose [in] ye world, except meeting an ingenious friend or two, but very little in respect to ye promoting of ye Society, and we have few others I am sure that any thing can be expected from them. Gronow yno gwedi meddwi fal llo, a rhai eraill yn ymdaeru, etc. Mae'n rhaid cael gwell *ordor* na hyn, ag onide ffarwel Gymrodorion. Aie jasper ydyw'r asbestos? Ebr un or beirdd: "Maen jasper mae'n anyspys." Some critics may infer that the bard meant this very quarry, i.e., as much as to say, it was not publicly known that it was ye jasper. I am glad Pen-y-nant hath thoughts of publishing something on fossils. Wel, mi logais *chaise* ddydd Mawrth, ag a aethym a'm brawd gyda mi i Finchley i dy Arglwydd Powys, ag roeddwn yn disgwyl ei weled yn sâl yn ei wely. Ni ches i gyttrum pan eis i i'r ty, na welwn ef yn fy nghyfarfod dan wenu, ag yn fy llusgo gerfydd fy llaw i'r 'stafell lle cawsai godwm wrth ddringo i gyrraedd papir ar ben *escritore*; "ar fendi" ebr ef "bu agos imi a thorri fy ngwddw. Edrychwch yma, dyma'r clais; mi syrthiais o ben y fan accw ar fy mhen i lawr, ag fe neidiodd y *vertebrae* oi lle." "Duw gattwo'r mark," ebr finneu. It was a very narrow escape. Surprizing it is that there are so many people alive when death appears in such various shapes! Bid a fynno, rwy'n well fy nghalon ar ol gweled mwyn ei galon mor llawen. He will be in town to-day or to-morrow, and he'll call with me. The yatchs are gone for ye king; and Lord Anson, though in ye gout or rheumatism, went off yesterday. Actual orders to sink, burn, and

L. to W. contd.

destroy all French ships that will oppose their being brought into Sheerness till the king's pleasure is known how to dispose of them. Another attempt shall be made about Kendal soon. I am in a hurry in sending some things by a ship for Aberdovey [to] ye family. Duw wnel na chyffwrdd y Ffrancod a hwynt, yn . . . . rwy'n eu hofni yn dost, mae yno 32 gallons or rum gorau a brofais erioed, a brynnais gan Ned Edwards, etc. *Eich brawd ffyddlon, L.M.*

LONDON, September 8, 1755.

L. to W. CCLVII.

Dear Brother,—Mae'n gas gennif weled llythyr yn rhythu ei lygaid arnaf eisiau i atteb—so I have yours of ye 1st. The inclosed paper will tell you ye news, except that four of us went yesterday in chaises to see Gronwy, and by chance heard Dr. Nicol, his master (person y plwyf) preach. Mae Ifan yn siarad am Mr. Wynne fal y Cardinal am y Pab. One letter to ye Society from Mr. Pennant, another from a clergyman in Norfolk, a rich old fellow, means well, but of no great capacity, enquires about ye etymology of *Bangor*. You need be in no hurry in sending them any curiositys, shall send you a specimen when I have leisure. I have read over ye Cywydd y Farn of Mr. W. W., but it is far inferior to ye other—all in a cloud. There is in it a good strong line now and then, but too much art and too little nature. My bones are all sore after jerking yesterday. I cannot spare time to describe our elegant entertainment at y Persondy, six dishes of meat, etc., fruit in abundance, apricots, nectarines, green plumbs, pears, apples, eirin duon, plwmmws, figs, etc. He is very happily situated, ped fae ddim yn tyccio, ond nid eill dim ddal. Daeth Owen William hefyd a ffrwythydd coed ini yno, a rhai oddiwrth y Person. Dyna fyw! Fe ddaw'r Brenin yma tocc, a gobeitho y caf finneu fynd adref gwedi hynny, mi arhosais i yn ddigon da yna i edrych ar ol ei dref ef tra bu oddicartre. My wife writes me word that she hopes Peggy hath turnd her mind, and that she is to go these days to Mathafarn. Had good news last post from Cwm Ervin Vach. Chancellor Wynne had three or four Welsh manuscripts, which I used to read for him. Cannot you borrow them of R. O., Esq., and return them when he wants them or understands them? I think there is one of them due to me for this scheme. Had a letter to-day from my father, the last spectacle fits him pretty well—my head is to-day in a flurry, cannot sit and write. *I am, your affectionate brother, L.M.*

HOLYHEAD, 9th September, 1755, Boreu Ddyw Mawrth.

Dear Brother,—Ai ni thyccia dywedyd wrthych am atteb ebystyl eich brawd Gwil sydd yn hiraethu cymaint am glywed oddiwrthych? Chwi ellwch fwrw'r bai ar y rhyfel (os rhyfel ydyw) ac ar Sion Ffrainc, ond ni thâl hynny ffydownen rhwng deufrawd. Ag i gyfaddef y gwir ni wiw i chwi fwrw'n ol eich brawd William, dyma fal y bydd o'n dechreu ei lythyrau bob amser. Pwy debygach i a ddeuai im ty echdoe im hymofyn (a minnau gyda fy medel) ond y Pen Llywydd eu hun. Ni adawodd mo'i henw, a neb nid adwaena ef. Ni chawn i gydtrym nad dyma ringyll oddiwrthaw yn erchi i mi ddyfod iw letty. Wawch! hebai finnau, ai Mr Fychan or Gors ydoedd y gwr a fu yma gynau? A âf i atto! Af yn siwr ddiameu, i gael unwaith weled glân ei galon. O ran ni welswn i erioed Seneddwr o Gymro or blaen; yno cipio fy nghippan am cappan ag i ffordd a myfi, yno taro wrth y llywydd a chyfarch gwell iddo, a chwedi iddo ymofyn am y ddeufrawd, etc., dywedodd wrthyf ei fod y mynd ir Werddon, efo'g un Mr. Gwyn, o Daliarus, yn Sir Gaerfyrddin (Garnons or Rhywgoch yn mynd yn ei ol adref). Wrth gofiaw mi roisym wadd i hwnnw iw frecwast felly rhaid rhoddi ordors. Wala, wedi i mi gaffael gafael ar y Cadpen a siarad am welyau, etc., mynd yn llu ir lletty i swppera ac i yfed iechyd y brodyr, etc., byw'n rhwydd lawen tan ennyd o nos, yno ymadaw. Cyn y boreu fe aeth y llong ar llywydd ir fordaith a gwynt dogn croes o wranta. Roedd yatch y gwr ei hun i ddyfod yma iw gyfarfod, ond ni ddaeth etto.

W. to R. CCLVIII.

P.S.—Gwaed gwreinyn glas! Onid oedd gan y Siawnsler bersenoliaeth yn Sir Fon, ac nid y fo oedd person Llantrisant, etc., felly dyna dair rhodd gan *yr Esgob* tuag at foddloni ei ffrindiau. Ond y mae un gamp ar y gwr, na wna ddaioni i ddyn yn y byd ond i ryw weilch a fo ei greaduriaid yn eu mawrygu ag yn eu canmol, ffei arno. Nid oes dim siawns i ddynan cywrain dysgedig oni bydd o dwlsyn i dwlsyn. Gwaed crwst! Beth debygachi? Mi aethym i wneuthur gwair ac a anghofiais orphen hwn ai yrru ir offis wedi'r cwbl, y glaw a ddaeth arnom yn ddisymwth ai parodd, nid oes mor help. Cofiwch am Mr. Kendal a byddwch iach a llawen. Yr eiddoch mal or blaen.—*W.M.*

LONDON, September 10th, 1755. Yn bur foreu glas, pur oer.

L. to W. CCLIX. Dear Brother,—I promisd you in my last a specimen of a letter to ye President of ye Cymmrodorion Society on ye subjects they propose to examine, and I cannot do it better than in ye inclosed copy or an extract of a letter from my acquaintance, Mr. Henry Baker, to ye Royal Society, about his miscroscopical observations in which he hath exceeded all that Society of which he is a member. He is a great collector of fossils, shells, etc., in which I have assisted him by adding to his collection, a *pheth sydd fwy*, by explaining some of his subjects which he was unacquainted with before, particularly a piece of fossil gold, that weighd at least five guineas. Is it not strange that among all ye curious men that had seen his collection no body could tell him what *that* was? But so it was! Mankind are not so infinitely superior to one another in knowledge as you and I thought formerly—a close application and resolution, and tolerable natural parts, may perform wonders. Why? Because men in general are indolent, lazy, and mind nothing, but expect others to labour for them—so the world goes. Pocock is a particular friend of Baker, ag fe allai mae mwy yw'r twrw na'r taro gida phob un o honynt. The improvement I have now made in ye pocket miscroscope of Wilson never came into any of their thoughts, and you'll see it will be by and by universal. The costly apparatus of the double microscopes makes y~m~ intolerable, besides some inconveniences attending ye instrument of inverting objects and making concaves appear convex. Lauwenhoek made all his observations in open air by single lens, but in England most of our observations have been made in darkness, especially in opake subjects, which made me so backward in making any advances that way; never knowing till late what Lauwenhoek's method was. I have bespoke lens's and as soon as I have any peace and quietness, I shall fit you up a microscope in my own way, which shall do as well as any, or better. I have no time to write more this post, but that *I am your affectionate brother*, *L.M.*

LONDON, September 16, 1755.

L. to W. CCLX. Dear Brother,—Have nothing to write this post, but to send you the inclosed paper to show you how things are, and also to shew it Nel Edwards that her brother is on his voyage to Halifax.

I am, your affectionate brother, [*Lewis Morris.*]

LONDON, September 22, 1755.

Dear Brother,—Na ddaeth yma un llythyr oddiwrthych heddyw, ond etto chwi welwch eich brawd yn cadw'r arfer i fynu, rhag cael o honoch esgus i ddiogi. I am greatly confounded when I look on y[e] state of our public affairs, and we stare at one another like a parcel of fools. Mi ddywedais i chwi'n aml nad oedd dim pennau ar gyrph ein rheolwyr ni, ag yn wir nid oes. Duw a'i helpio, mae eisiau rhoi bwyd a diod iddynt (chwedl Sir Roger Mostyn), ni feddant iaith yn y byd. A Welsh tenant of his pretended to talk English to him, but he had neither Welsh nor English so he calld John Jones to give him meat and drink because the poor fellow (says he) hath no language in y[e] world. Ond etto, mae ganthynt ddigon o nerth a chastiau i ymryson a mi er nad allant ymhel a'r Ffrangcod, a dyma lle byddaf y goeliai dan y Nadolig. Gwae, gwae, a ymhelio a ffyliaid a chnafiaid! It is here all corruption and luxury,—a sinking people, unless a war or famine or plague brings them to their senses. I dd——l un da o honynt. The printed paper will tell you our foolish news. I have no more to say this post, but that I expect orders this post to begin on y[e] examination of my account. L. to W. CCLXI.

I am, your affectionate brother, L.M.

LONDON, September 25, 1755.

Dear Brother,—Yours of y[e] 20th I have, and am glad you are able to sip a little with Mr. Monachdy and Mr. Car. Lwyd. Pobl na wn i fawr oddiwrthynt. Aie rhaid bwyta ag yfed fal nhwythau? A fydd y Dr. Lwyd yn son dim am eich brawd Lewis? I suppose he thinks himself made of better stuff than pobl dlodion. Iorwerth is y[e] man you describe y[e] family to be, and I am told is intolerable to his men and servants,—never made a voyage here without being put in y[e] Commons for beating his men: the effect of bad examples in his youth and a bruitish nature. If it is a war, I believe he will have y[e] command of a twenty gun privateer, and as fit for it as any Indian of them all, a dexterous desperate fellow, half American, half Welsh mountaneer. I have a history of y[e] North American Indians now before me, a real picture of the old Britons when they strove with the Romans and Saxons for their country; all bravery, courage, honour, virtue, and people that L. to W. CCLXII.

L. to W. contd.

would conquer the world if they had a commander. But their Government is not monarchical, but is something that wants a name. Something like the United Provinces, but really *united.* Iorwerth is as like them as if he had been born there, stubborn and of an headstrong spirit. It is very odd of Hughes Colyn that he hath not spoken to you, instead of going on a quixot errand to a wild country. But as it happend I had given my wife a hint that such a man had made such a proposal, and if he came to use him well. I had also wrote to R. Morris, Mathafarn, where the girl now is, that an officer of Kinsale had made some proposals that he might divulge it, etc., but did not tell him who he was. Wele hai, dyma fal y mae! Mae hyn yn abl tebyg i'r hen stori ynghylch cadw ysgyfarnogod a'r tinau cochion. There was a vast deal of art in it. Ni wiw son am dy Sion Michael. All London in confusion exactly like y[e] animalcules in pepper water, on account of this ill-concerted rhyfel. Mi ddywedais lawer gwaith nad oedd dim pennau ar gyrph y bobl fawr yma, ond *i wneuthur* drwg. I'll send you a pamphlet next post if I can on that, which verifies my prediction. Nawdd Duw rhag *dyli* a chnafeidddra pobl! I am like a little, little fish carried away by y[e] stream of y[e] great river where porpusses, etc. wallow, ag nid oes dim help a welafi.

Eich brawd, *Llewelyn.*

CAER GYBI YM MON, September 28, 1755.

W. to R. CCLXIII.

Y Caredigawl Frawd,—Llymma fi yn taro atti hi i atteb eich tra chymeradwy lythyr or 13th inst. (pa beth ydyw hynny yn Gymraeg?), a sgrifenasoch, meddwch, drwy *ysbectol* (dyna air brwnt arall). Nid oedd raid ir hen Gymru gynt wrth wydrau, oni bai hynny, ba'sai well enw arnynt, byw'n dymherus ag ymattal oddiwrth wîn; a fyddan nhw felly yn Llundain? Rhaid ymwrthod a gormodedd, o achos da paham. Mae'n ddrwg gan fy nghalon i glywed fod y beswch mor dost wrthych a'ch gyrru bob yn awr i'r wlad, trafferthus a drud o'r gwaith hwnnw. Ar henaint y mae'r bai, y fo sydd yn hudo haflug o gymdeithion anynad iw ganlyn a phwy sydd bennach cyfaill iddo na Mr. Peswch? Ni wn i a ddaeth y Bennant adref o Shugborough, Stafford Sîr. Ce's lythyr oddiwrthaw oddiyno, ysgrifenasai y 21; roedd heb dderbyn eich un chwi debygwn i. Mae'n broliaw o focys yn llawn o dlysau a ddaethai o Sisli, wedi bod ar gyfrgoll 18 mis, containing fossils, shells, ores, corals, peri, fuci, vases, etc. Mae'n gadael ***rhan i mi.*** A pha beth pan gaffwyf ran gaddoch chwithau o gregyn Mahon ai ffosilod, a rhan hefyd o dlysau Pensylvania Cadwalad? Mae arnaf ofn y bydd raid imi adeiladu ***museum*** newydd, ond y cebystr ir sutt *Υμλη υ καιρ υρ αριαν?* Ie a rhan o deganau New Inglont hefyd i wrth y Cadpen Ierwerth. Er cariad ar dd—— na omeddwch gadw rhan i'ch brawd Gwilym wirion ffol o bob pethau gwerthfawr a gaffoch; chwi fyddwch siccr o gael y pwyth yn ol gan y Bennant a minnau. ***Ynghylch rhyfel,***—a ***letter of marque*** roedd yr aldremon yn sgrifennu, mi wrantaf. Duw a wnel i rywun fod yn well ar y gwaith. Aie tebyg i'r gwyr mawrion ydyw'r Llew, cadw ei holl gyfrinach iddo ei hun, mae Sionach yn gwybod y cyfan mae'n debyg. Mi gefais lythyr oddiwrth y Secretary Owen y dydd arall a chywydd diddan iawn o'r eiddo ***Goronwy***; mae'r ffargod hwnnw wedi fy esgeuluso i yn deg, ffei arni hi'r Delyn Ledr. Hi oedd mam y drwg. Peth echrydus ydoedd colli'r Delyn ***a'r Cyfaill.*** A wnaed cywydd i Arglwydd Llwydlo dywedwch? Can diolch am hanes y daith i Northol, er fy mod wedi cael rhan or stori gan ddeu wr eraill, etto nid oedd ei hanesion nhw hanner cystal, sef oedd y gwyr hynny y Llywelyn a'r Agrippa. Gresyndod mawr na fedra'r bardd lunio'r gwadn fal y bo'r troed, yno gallai fyw yn happus ddigon yn y fan honno tra b'ai yn aros i Bowys drugarhau wrtho. Aie 'e gadd Hwlyn long; gwnaed yn fawr o honaw ei hun, fe eill ddyfod yn amgenach dyn (os nad ydyw eisioes) na'i ddeu frawd penbylaidd or ynys hon. Yn nef mae enaid Morys,—dyn i bob dyn ydoedd Moi; gwae ni ei farw cyn gynted ag na ddaethai i Drysglwyn. Pam na wnant Siac ab y Doctor yn ben meddyg bellach? Pei gyrrech yma rai o'r gosodedigaethau nid hwyrach y medrwn werthu ambell un o honynt. Ni a gawsom ffordd yma wlybaniaeth mawr iawn ysywaeth, y rhan fwyaf or ydau allan. Duw a ddelo a thywydd sych, ac onite bydd trefn ddrwg ym Môn Ynys. A chadwodd y ddryghin finnau rhag hel na chregynach na môr blanhigion, etc., y rhyferthwy diweddaf, yr hyn oedd somedigaeth creulon im cregyn frodyr a minnau. Mi wrantaf na wnaeth Esgob Bangor ddim er y bardd bach, lle da yw disgwyl. Gwych a

W. to R. contd.

fydd clywed y newydd eich wedi myned y Llwyd yna am arian Kendal. Chwi gewch chwithau dâl am y darluniadau. Mi a ddylwn ofyn nawdd am grybwyll yr oferedd yma mor fynych, pe bawn heb wybod eich bod o dymer amuneddgar, ie, a maddeugar hefyd. Pa bryd y gwelsoch fy ffrind J. Ellis, F.R.S., rwyf yn arofyn er's dyddiau sgrifennu atto ynghylch ei lyfr Cwrel a ddaroedd iddo addaw ei yrru i mi; bydd cyfleu o'r ffeinia yn y box gyda'r darluniadau. Pa beth a fyddai gael tippyn o wraidd i wrth Agrippa hefyd? Rhaid sgrifenu at hwnnw yntau. Ni choelia i na bo lythyr neu ddau o'r eiddwyf gennych heb eu hatteb cyn cael hwn, felly trewch atti hi gynta galloch. Duw a fyddo'n gwarchad drosoch, a byddwch wych. *Eich brawd anwiw,*

Gwilym Amhorys.

LONDON, September 29, 1755.

L. to W. CCLXIV.

Dear Brawd,—Received yours of ye 24th owning ye receipt ot map of America. Oes, mae golwg gwych Ynghwm Ervin, ond daccw Ned Hughes wedi colli i le gida Chorbed, felly Ynghwmervin y mae yn awr. The chief intent of this to *carrio ffrancod*, ag i ddywedyd fod d——l gwedi mynd trwy'r bobl fawr yma i gyd, yn troi i gilydd allan. Fe gyll Duc y Castell Newydd y maes meddan' nhwy; fei bwrir ef *tros oed* i wneuthur gwasanaeth. Duw wnel imi gael mynd oddiyma, cyn iddynt yrru'r byd bendrosfwnwgl. Dyma'r cwbl am heno, ni cheir mor amser gan *gonsidrio* beth sy oreu i'r brawd Rhisiart wneuthur mewn rhyw droeadau sy'n'r offis yma. Mae yma le gwych os gellir ei gael. Duw gida chwi

Eich brawd, Llewelyn.

LONDON, October 3, 1755.

L. to W. CCLXV.

Dear Brawd,—I had no letters last post from any body, and write this to no other intent than to carry ye news paper, ond nid oes mwy o goel ar un o honynt nag ar din dyn bach—an out of ye way proverbial expression, but very proper, oblegid ..... grefft a wna rhain pan fo amheua gan ddyn. Dyma nhwy yn bendramwnwgl a'i gilydd, ag ni wybod pwy sy iâr na phwy sy geiliog; mae yma gant o chwedlau yn eu cylch, rhai'n dywedyd fod parti'r Duc William gwedi cyttuno ag ysgwyd llaw a pharti'r Tarw mawr. Ond mi glowais i frân yn dywedyd y bydd tra thebyg y bydd troeadau pan gyfarfyddo'r *Palmant*, ond na wyddai hi pa fodd bossibl iddynt drin y dreth, o achos ni feddant neb a digon o nerth gantho yn y Ty Isaf. Felly rydym yn bryssio yn erwin gael diwedd ar y materion yma o'r eiddofi, cyn y delo'r diwrnod hwnnw. Dyna fal y gwelais i fy meistred i erioed; Duw ro rad arnynt, yn gadel pob peth dan y dydd diwaethaf. I have often been sent to for affidavits when the time was so short that I have been obligd to sit up two nights and days successively, and to send them by a purpose messenger to London, for the post would not have reachd time enough. Dyna ddynionach braf am garrio materion pwysfawr ymlaen. Rwy'n ffyddlon gredu nad oes dan haul ddynion dylach yn ceisio trin materion mawrion. I know they are so, because I have been with them as a helping hand, planning answers to accusations, etc., and framing Bills of Information, etc. Ond y peth gwaetha sy'n perthyn iddynt yw eu cybydd-dod, ai drwg natur ffals. Calon Sais wrth Gymro. L. to W. contd.

Oni bai fod creifion y badell iw gael wrth ferwi gruel iddynt, i dd——l rual a gant gennifi yn eu byw. You see how long this letter hath run without any matter at all, but you will not have such long empty letters from me hereafter. Daccw'r warrant iw chael o'r Treasury heddyw a goeliai, i ddau wr i drin fy nghyfrifon. Pwy debygachi ond Sion Paynter o'r Penrhyn gynt ydyw un? Ond na [soniwch am] hyn, rhag i rywun sgrifennu at y rhain mae hen gydnabyddiaeth imi ydyw. Hynny a wnaeth nadel i Williams y Geirchen ag Will Parry Gwredog fod yn *examiners*. Ond ni wyddom ni etto pa fath ddyn yw'r llall, ond ei fod yn stiward i Iarll Darlington, un o Lords y Treasury. Os yw'r gwas fal y meistr ni wnawn o'r goreu ag ef. *Eich brawd pendeneu ddigon, Llewelyn.*

Wawch! wawch! wawch! gwedi cau'r llythyr ar fedr ei selio dyma lythyr oddiwrth Baynter yn dywedyd mae dyn o'r ffeinia yw Mr. Tydy, stiward Iarll Darlington, ag yn ei lythyr *ordors* imi o'r Treasury imi ddylifrio fy accounts iddynt, ag i Mr. Sharpe eu helpu os bydd raid. Felly dyna hyd yna gwedi dyfod wrth hir dynnu'n wysg tin, a bod yn bengaled. If they are other people's fools, pam na fyddant i minnau? Wawch etto, dyma eich llythyr o'r noswyl Fihangel. Ni wnaed dim cerdd i Arglwydd Llwdlo etto, mwya'r cwilydd. The man doth everything but what he ought to do. I

L. to W. contd.

wish you a good harvest. I have had mine in Cardiganshire, I wish it was so here. Remember me to Dr. Lloyd and tell him I have a mine of more value than his estate. You shall have a microscope, tewch a sôn.

L. to Mrs. M. CCLXVI.

LONDON, October 10, 1755.

My Dear,—I have yours of ye 3d and thank God that you're all well. It vexes me more than the value of ye hats that the whiffling fellow should deny that they were deliverd him. The hats and handkerchiefs and ribbons were in a bandbox (of ye same stuff with hat cases) which I had seald and tied with my own hands and directed to you, and it was with the two other boxes deliverd to his mate on board the ship by John Owen, and I afterwards sent John Owen with a bill of parcels of all ye things which I sent by others, or he deliverd to Henry Jenkins's own hands, so it is in vain for him to deny that they were deliverd aboard, let him look into the bill of parcels. If he hath sufferd the women passengers that he had to steal the box, he is answerable for it. They were two fine hats with neat silver laces, and three of ye best kind of silk handkerchiefs, with a parcel of knots, etc. Insist upon their finding them out, or I will play ye devil with him. John Owen writes this post to Griffith Griffiths also to speak to him. He says the band box with ye hatts was carried into the cabbin directly when he deliverd them and the cord that tyed them thrown overboard by accident. H. Jenkins, I am afraid, is what people say he is—a trifling, tricking fellow ; but I shall be upsides with him if he pretends to trick me. You should have told me how you like the rest of ye things. Dont talk of giving away to my daughters or any body else the coat, though it doth not fit you. There is no reason to throw thirty shillings away, they are not so easily got, and it seems you dont know who deserve to have presents made them, and that you want to prove your self their fool as long as you live. Did you ever see any body so silly as to give you such a pretty coat without good reasons ? I dont like my self that Evan Williams should be there if we can do without him, for it is an unnecessary load to keep a man and his horse, but I expected he would have come when he was wanted. But every one for himself. Baulking the poor boys about their fine hats, and you of your coat and handkerchiefs vexes me as much as it doth you, and I hope you will exert your self, and insist upon his delivery of ye hats, etc. For if he denies, then he must deny the bill of parcels that was deliverd him by John Owen. Insist upon seeing that bill, it was wrote by my own hand. Send the inclosed letter to William Jones directly, and dont lose a minute, for Townsend's people are upon playing tricks with him as they find he is a fool. Here is a bold attempt a making by Townsend to abolish the bargain I made with Evan Williams and the two Morgans, and to call them to an account. I presume Oliver is at ye bottom of it. I have no more time to write this post, but my love to you and blessing to ye children. The box I sent to Salop will be there next Tuesday senight, which is ye 21st of this month, I wish I had sent the other things also by land instead of trusting a rascal. *I am, your affectionate husband,* *L.M.*

L. to Mrs. M. contd.

P.S.—Send your measure of your coat next post without fail. My winter cough comes on, and is pretty severe, though I have got a convenient lodging enough for open air. I expect no good of Cwmervin till I come home, Edward Hughes is like a moyderd man.

LONDON, October 13, 1755.

L. to W. CCLXVII.

Dear Brother,—Just now Lord Powys's agent and John Paynter and self sitting together over a bowl of punch in my room. I received your letter of ye 8th at ye same time with other letters from Cardiganshire—all well there. Good ore at Cwmervin, but Ned Hughes say that the d——l sits cross-legd upon ye ore in ye Roman rake, and they cannot get ye water out. I suppose ye d——l keeps a cask of ale there and makes the people all drunk. What do you say to that? I shall tell Paynter about his brother. He has told me already that Tom hath not one single grain of sense, and never had any. It is impossible for dunces to make any thing either of war or peace, ni wiw son am y fath ysgrubliaid. Onid oedd Arglwydd Powys Lwyd a minneu yn bobl ryfeddol ei hymladd hi hyd yma, a chael Sion Paint y dyn clifria yn y deyrnas am y fath beth? Oeddem, oeddem. Gwych ydychi fod gennychi dai pobl onest i fynd iddynt. Nid oes gennifi nag yma na chartref dy ffrind i fynd iddo. I have no leisure to write any more, but that I am

Your affectionate brother, *L.M.*

October 14th.—Yr Arglwydd uchod newydd fynd oddiyma yn llawn yspryd.

O'M CELL YNG NGHAERGYBI, Nos Sadwrn,
y Deunawfed o Hydref, 1755.

W. to R.
CCLXVIII

F'anwyl Frawd,—Nis gwn i par sut i sgrifennu attoch, obleit ni wn i par un ai llawen ynteu prudd, iach ynteu claf, byw ynteu marw ydych; ni chlywais i air o son am danoch er pan g'es eich llythyr diweddaf. Do, mi glywais wrth gofiaw; soniawdd y *Tew* rywbeth ynghylch rhyw gynnwrf yn eich offis, ond i wenwyn sillaf byth gwedi er i mi daer erchi arno adael imi wybod os deuai haid i gŵch. Mi fyddaf yn cael oddiwrth y pendefig hwnnw lythyr agos bob post, a llawer o bolitics, a thippyn bâch weithiau o hanes ei faterion ei hun. Wfft, a dwbl wfft, ir fath bobl sydd ganddo iw trin. Gwae fi na chlyw'n ei fod wedi dyfod drwy'r afael yn bensych. Mae'n rhyfedd fod gelynion iddo ymhob man; yn rhôdd, pa beth yw'ch tŷb chwi o honaw? Ai tybied na bu'sai fodd iddo grêu llai o naddynt? Ai tybied nad yr Arglwydd Powys oedd yr achos iddo golli'r hen ffrindiau? Os felly y fo a ddylai sefyll wrth ei gefn. Rwyn cyfaddef nad wyf fi yn hanner deall mo'r pethau yna. Rwyn gobeithio i chwi drechu'r peswch, fal y gwnaethum innau, mi ai hymlidiais o iw grogi, er iddo roddi imi y codwm cynta drwy chwareu hagr; neitiaw a orug ar fy nghefn ryw noswaith, a chydiaw yng nghorn yngwddwgi yn ddidrugaredd, nid oes dim nawdd iw gaffael gan Mr. Peswch pan gaffo unwaith y llaw ucha. Yr ydwyf fi yn hollawl ymroi gadw gard rhag iddo fy nal i yn fy ngwendid mwyach. Genau brych! Mi welais yn y papyr newydd heddyw fod i chwi Gontroler newydd. Bid da y b'o. Er mwyn dyn a gawsoch chwi ddim uwch swydd na dim daioni? Roedd y Llew, mal y dywedais or blaen, yn dadwrdd rhywbeth ynghylch rhyw droadau oedd yna. Gan nad oes ar wyneb y ddaear neb yn gofalu mwy am eich llwyddiant na'ch brawd Gwilym, chwi ddylech chwithau adael iddo wybod y mymryn o'ch helynt. Diau mai fy ngorfoledd penna i ydyw clywed bod y nhad a chwithau'r ddeufrawd yn mwynhau iechyd. Mae'r Llyw yn edrych yn o henaidd, roeddwn yn meddwl bob amser mai sgrabwth o ddyn rhwydd ieuanc ydoedd, mae o'n bur ddifyr a difalch, gresyn ei fod mor ebolaidd. A fydd gennych fercheda ynghyfarfodydd y Cymrodorion dywedwch? Duw a helpo'r Gendal wirion, ni chlywai ddim son am ei fil ô. *Er mwyn dyn na anghofiwch mo'r trwstan*, chwi gewch chwithau dâl yn y drugaredd. Gwaed swllt! Y peth diweddaf a ddywedodd y Pen Llywydd wrthyf ydoedd ei fod yn deisyf ei garedigawl annerch attoch eich deuwedd. Fe archodd imi ddywedyd i chwi ei fod wedi derbyn llyfr y Cymrodorion oddi wrthych, ond 'roedd brŷs a ffwdan wedi llestair iddo sgrifennu i ddiolch i chwi, etc. Ni choelia fo byth fod cywydd eirian Mr. Wynne yn well nag un Gronwy, yr oedd y llall, medd ô, ar fai gynnyg canu ar yr un testyn, mae'n son am ddyfod ffordd yma yn ôl, os felly ceir amser i gystadlu'r ddau gywydd. Oes dim gobaith i Gronwy gael myned yn bersonyn? Chwi a addawsoch rywbeth i'ch brawd *y cregynydd*; a number of the Script. Cutts. Ag fe addawodd ynta yrru sampier iw frawd Mynglwyd, ond ni wnaeth. Wala, os coeliwch chwi'r gwir, mae gennyf lonaid *siwg* wedi eu piclio yn barod *i chwi* er's mis, yn disgwyl am gyfleu yw hanfon, a pheth sydd fwy, ni bu ond y dyd rhyngwy' a thorri chwilgorn yn'gwddwg wrth ei hel! Myned a wneuthwn i gregyna, efo Wil ab y Doctor, ag yspio gwrâdd o'r dail yng nghlin craig, a dringo attynt yn galonog heb gonsidrio'n mawr berygl i laprwth trwm om bath i fynd ir fath sibert; ond mawl i Dduw, mi ddeuais yn ddiangol o'r mawr berygl y bum ynddaw. Ni ddieddyf rhyw lygad brwnt sydd gennyf imi graffu gormod ar y papur yma, ac heblaw hynny dyma fi wedi dyfod i ben y tir. Duw gyda chwi bod ag un. **W. to R. contd.**

Y fi wyf, *Eich caredigawl frawd*, *y Cregynydd.*

P.S.—Mae fal yr annerchwch fi at y car Gwilym Parri o'r Tŵr Gwyn a'r ceryn gan Mr. Hugh Davies. Gwaed swllt! Pa beth a wnaethoch im llythyr ynghylch Pyrs Llwyd, a ddarfu i urddo'r gŵr? Ni welai ddim hanes am y pen llywydd yn dyfod yn ol mal y gaddawodd. Nis gwn i par un ai byw ai marw o'n Bennant, ni che's yr un llythyr oddiwrthaw er ys (mi a wna'n dda) dair wythnos neu fis! Mi yrrais iddo'r dydd arall foccys ac ynddaw oddeutu i drugain o riwiau cregyn a ffosilod, etc. Ni wybod beth a ddaethai o hono oni buasai iddo gael edrydd eich brawd Gwilym, poed buan y caffoch eich tlysau o Fahôn a Phensylvania fal y galloch gael y pleser o anrhegu'ch ffrindiau *yma* ac accw. Braith ei gôd a gynnull. Mae'n rhyw i chwi fod yn hael ac yn gymwynasgar. 21ain.—Wawch. Llyma lythyr i wrth Risiart Morys o Fathafarn a hanes newydd tanlli fod i'r Llew bwmp o ŵyr arall, bu agos i mi ei

W. to R. contd.

wneuthur yn hendaid. Gwreigdda Elen. Mae Marged hithau ddialedd o eisiau gwneuthur wyrion efo rhyw lymgi afluniaidd. Nid hwyrach mai felly bydd heb yn ddiolch i bawb—Adieu

Ειχ βραωδ μαλευντ,* W.

W. to R. CCLXIX

[*Fragment of a letter*]. October 18, 1755.

. . . a dedwydd. Gan na chawn weled mo'n gilydd ond odid tra bôm ar wyneb y ddaear front yma. Gadewch i ni yntau ymgyfeillachu drwy lythyrau fynycha gallom dan obaith ymgyfarfod llawen naill ai yma neu draw tu hwnt ir bedd. Mi sgrifenais at Mr. Ellis, F.R.S., i erchi iddo yrru y llyfr (ydoedd wedi ei anrhegu imi) attoch chwi, i ddyfod yn y boccys efo'r llyfrau y'ch i anfon yma ar darluniadau ynddynt. 'Sgrifenais hefyd at Owen Cornelius i erchi iddo yntau yrru imi rai hadau, etc., os medrai bigo i fynu ambell un a fai odidawg, ni chlywaf ddim son a ddarfu i'r ddeuwr hynod rheini gyflawni ai peidiaw. Byddai dda gennyf gael gwybod par bryd yr y'ch yn meddwl y bydd eich pethau chwi parod, fal y gallwyf edrych o'm hamgylch rhag bod eisiau rhyw bethau eraill. Ni phrisiwn frwynen er eich coethi fal hyn bob yn awr er maint eich trafferth, pei gwyddwn eich bod yn mwynhau eich iechyd, obleit annioddefus pob afiach. Ni wiw i chwi nag i minnau bellach ddisgwyl fawr hyfrydwch. Fe aeth y dyddiau diddan heibiaw, ac ni welwn monynt mwy, y rhai on blaenau sydd yn dwyn gyda hwynt ofalon, helbulon, a heintiau, cymdeithion digon anynad, on'te? Par sut sydd ar Feirian? Ni byddwch un amser yn rhoddi imi ddim o hanes y lodes. Mae fy neugyw i, moliant i Dduw, yn cael pigion iechyd ac yn yfed eu dysg yn dda iawn. Y bachgen yn trin teiriaith yn rhyfeddol, ar herlodes hithau yn abl hyddysg ar ddwy. Os gwêl Duw yn dda imi gael hoedl, etc., i roddi iddynt dippyn o ddysg, da fydd. Grâs rwyn hyderu a gânt. Par fyd s'yn dwyn Goronwy? Fe ollyngws yn angof ei hen ffrindiau, gresyn fod ei gof cynrhwg. Oes dim gobaith cael gweled ei gywyddau yn argraphedig? Mae Mr. Ellis ein bugail ni yn dywedyd y rhydd o i chwi bunt neu 30s. tuag at argraphu Cowydd y Farn, etc., with notes, rhag iddynt fod fal canwyll tan lestr. Gwae finnau na welwn dippyn o newydd da i Gendal Wyddel; nage Manaw wr o'r dynan wrth gofiaw. Roedd y nhad yn rhwydd iachus echdoe, son am ddyfod yma yr wythnos nesaf. Duw gyda chwi,

Eich caredigawl frawd, *William Morris.*

*Mal cynt.

LONDON, October 18, 1755.

Dear Brother,—Yours of y[e] 13th I have, nid oes fawr amser iw atteb gan drafferth. Take care you dont venture too often into dangers in that foolish boat in those rapid tides. It is not necessary, a elo i'r ffair heb neges a geiff neges i ddyfod adre. Brother Richard is pretty well, in hopes of advancement, which he shall certainly have if he lives. He is to be here to-morrow, in order to go and dine in y[e] open air in some village. Lord Powys here yesterday, very hearty, going to Suffolk and his family for a fortnight and then to come here and give my affairs y[e] finishing stroke. The examination goes on glibly. Sion Baintiwr yn ddyn rhyfedda fu erioed,—all pride and vanity and good sense, extraordinary parts, a heap of contradictions. Ned Hughes by last account yn mynd feddwach, feddwach, fal ei dad, yn ffaelio tynnu'r dwr o'r gwaith gan dynnu cwrw. My wife says she has given him up as incurable. An account last post of another grandson for me at Mathavarn. Hynach, hynach, beunydd, and you are not far behind, only you have not been so forward in propagating, and have not given your strength to women, as the Jewish writer expresses it. A great and hot battle (tongue battle) at y[e] Cockpit a few nights ago—ffaelio cyttuno pa fodd i wneuthur a Mr. Legge, Chancellor y Sieccer. God be with you; answer several of my last letters which you have laid (mislaid) by. L. to W. CCLXX

I am,

your affectionate brawd llwyd, Llewelyn.

If you write to Peggy tell her of Mr. Hughes's proposals and of his preferment, etc., and that I could give him no answer, being not willing to force her to anything she might not like, therefore she ought to behave on her side the same.

LONDON, 20th [October,] 1755.

Dear Brother,—Just now received yours of y[e] 16th, and as I am alone in my room, and shall be busy to-morrow, I sit down to *correspond* with you. What is that in our language, *cydatteb* or *cyfatteb* llythyrau mae'n debyg. Pam na throwch chwitheu'r Berson a Sion Chwilottwr allan i gael llonydd i sgrifennu. Wele, if I know anything of mankind I had rather trust this *pagan sperdunog* that tells his mind frankly than a thousand hypocritical christians that pretend sanctity and religion. This man owns a L. to W. CCLXXI

L. to W. contd.

God, therefore is not a Pagan; but he could never find but one God, and if his head or faith cannot comprehend those things, who can help him? He is the oddest mixture I ever met, a fund of knowledge and good sense, and yet the emptiest man alive, nay, he owns that fools have made a fool of him, and to my knowledge they have ruind him. Mae yma chwiwgwn o *Grisnogion*, ie, *crys nogion*, that attempted to ruin me too, but this Deist endeavours to save me and spares no pains to do it: oni haedde fe *Frontiniac!* Religion here makes no man honest, I dont know what it doth with you. Interest is ye only tye here that binds an honest man; mae'n ddiammeu gennif nad oes mwy o grefydd ymysg gwyr Eglwysig nag sydd yn uffern fagddu—all here that I know a set of reprobates and so in *Ceretica*, a thousand times worse than the laity. They have nothing but ye shapes of men. You mistake in ye terms in describing ye vein of copper; a vein of three or four yards and a yard diameter is no vein. Veins have no diameters nor lengths. If it is a spot of four yards long and a yard broad, it is a pipe or belly of ore, in Cardiganshire called also a horn. The vein may *be miles* long and the breadth of it is as it happens, sometimes more or less, from a quarter of an inch to four or five yards. So I suppose they have discoverd a spot of ore in ye vein of four yards long and a yard wide; perhaps the vein may bear ore for thirty, forty, or one hundred yards together, perhaps not ten yards till it comes to a twitch where there is no ore at all. But, by the by, I suppose I have seen about fifteen tun of this fine copper ore sent here to London the other day by Mr. Lewis Nannau, from Caernarvon, and if that is it, I will give them my word it is no copper ore at all, but a wild marchasite or pyrites fit for no use but to make copperas, i.e., green vitriol for dyers, and is not worth the freight to carry to any place. I have seen a bit with ye sailors, got on some freeholder's land in which was a little (but very little) copper, but ye great body was found, I think they said, on Mr. Knight's land. If you have any value for ye people that spend money there, you may undeceive them. Da clywed newydd fod arian ẏ coed yn dyfod. Lord Powys just gone to Suffolk for a week or two, finneu'n dywedyd yn dêg, etc., wrth yr examiners yma; they seem to be convinced of the reality of my case, which ye other rascals have a mind to conceal. Pwy wyr na ddaw hyn yn llês? Ni cheir dim yn y byd yma heb ymladd am dano. Beth yw *scoundrel* debygech i? Hys cŵn, y drel, a rhywogaeth y drel hwnnw yw'r *llym* yma o'r Gorllewin, o fileiniaid! Ar fedr amdwyo dyn a'i deulu i borthi eu pendro gythreulig—worse than dogs or serpents. Just heard from Cardiganshire, all well. Lewis wants a book, hath gone over his Primer, dyna philosophydd i chwi. Gwyn y gwêl y frân ei chyw. We expect an invasion here from France. Batteries orderd along shore, guardships in ye offing, against ye meeting of Parliament some say, i gael arian o boccedau'r bobl wirion, y genedl wirion. Duw gida chwi. *Eich brawd, Llewelyn.* L. to W. contd.

My eyes close, cannot hold out. 21st.—Just now I hear Farington's copper mine is near Drws y Nant. Query whether it is ye same as I heard of?

LONDON, October 24, 1755, dydd Gwener.

Dear Brother,—I have yours of nos duw Sul (diwaethaf mae'n debyg) and because I shall have no leisure to-morrow I answer it to-night. Tebyg i butain yw Sion Paynter, meddwch, ie'n wir, digon tebyg, oblegid mae gantho ddau buteindy yn ei eiddo i hun dybygwn, and to this day is as fond of a girl as ever he was. Ni welais i erioed ei ail o ddyn gwrthun, ond mae ef fal y dur er hynny. Self interest is ye great tye. The last part of my vouchers I deliverd to-day, ag rwy'n gobeithio y gwnant report gonest mewn ychydig ddyddiau. You did very well in destroying silly letters. I did ye same with vast numbers at Galltvadog when I set out for London in January last. Mae Iorwerth heb ymlid y fall etto o Gwmervin, mae o'n gwneuthur cymaint o ddwfr yno (hynny yw....) onid ydyw'r plwmp yn ffaelio ei dynnu. But I have a very good account from thence to-day that they have discoverd an ancient conduit there with signs in it which shews there hath been a very great work there. I dont expect any great matters till I get there my self. Your corraline book will be here in a few days; Ellis says you are ye most curious and learned man in ye kingdom. You had better leave off now while you are in your glory. Duw gida chwi medd *Eich brawd pendeneu*, *Llewelyn.* L. to W. CCLXXII

W. to R. CCLXXIII

BRON YR EIRA, GERLLAW CAER YR HEN GYBI SANT,
Tachwedd y 6ed, 1755.

Anwyl Frawd,—Rhag bod arnoch ormod o eisiau llythyr i dorri hiraeth am glywed oddiwrth eich Gwilym, dyma fi wedi cymeryd grafol im llaw i lunio un yn y modd goreu gallwyf. Ag fal hyn y dechreua: Daeth yr eiddoch o'r 28 ulto. yma, rhag ei flaen yn union deg, ac os wy' yma onid oedd yn dda iawn ei gael, a diolch yn fawr am tanaw. Chwi welwch wrth hyn ein bod yn fodlon yma i gymeryd un am ddau neu dri. Hyn a wiria'r hen ddiareb: "Da cael ûs gan ddrwg dalwr." Wfft, a dwbl wfft, i'r bagodas ar fanams, etc., ydych yn eu clandrio, mae rhain yma yn gan' gwaeth na'r anthropomorphites's, dendrophoree's, entrochis, glossopetra's, ichthyopetra's, pectunculites, stalactites buccardites, astroiles's, etc., a chanmil o ffosilods eraill a fyddaf fi beunydd yn ei dyludo, heb sôn un gair am y cregyn eu hunain, nid amgen y telinas, strombi, cochlea's, burgau's, nautilus's, poussepieds, echinis, solenes, globosee's, rhombi's, etc., ie, nag yngan sillaf am y llysiau ar blodau yma, nid amgen y staphylodendron's, hiphium', toxicodendron's heliotropiums, lithospermums, hippolapathums, echynomelocactus's, fritillarias, granadillas, androsemums, moldavica's, dorycniums, etc. Mi anafais i ddwyres o bigion dannedd wrth eu cnoi, ac er hynny yn ffaelio cael ganddynt fyned i lawr yn lanwaith. Pe busai yr enwog Ddoctor Sion Dai ap Rhys yn y byd i'w troi ir Gymraeg, fo wnaethai ryw ddaioni. Gwych y trinodd yr hen feddyg enwau'r mesurau Cymreig, fal y gallai'r dysgedigion eu deall a'u hamgyffred, ond ê? Ai ê mae gennych ryw scheme (h.y. yscaem) ar droed? Da iawn os *cewch* chwi ei dwyn i ben, ni wiw hyderu ar ddyn bydol. Duw a ran. Nid oes bost yn myned heibiaw, nag oes un na byddwyf yn derbyn ac yn sgrifennu llythyr at y Tew Mawr or Deau frŷ. Dyna bobl yn hollawl ymroi i gyfatebu yn iawn, 'rwyn deall fod *y gelynion* yn saethu ambell ergyd atto o hyd y bwa hên. Ond os y Tarw Mawr or Castell Newydd a geidw'r maes, drain yn ei capiau, ond beth os cwympir yr hen Darw? Da mrawd am addaw i mi ffosilod a chregyn gwell o lawer nag arian, ni chlawdd lladron trwodd i ladratta mo rhain. Sôn a wnewch chwi am ddilladu'r herlodes yna. Dyma Wilym yn bwydo pum nyn o bobl ag yn dilladu 3 onaddynt, talu cyflog i un arall, a hynny allan o lawer

Lai cyflog na chwi, ag mewn drudtach lle o lawer na Llundain, pe bai fatter yn y peth; ond rhyfedd hyn Rhisiart! Rhaid bod yn amuneddgar ynghylch materion y Gendal dlawd. Duw a roddo ynghalon y Lwyd dalu ir truan. Dyma ddau o llythyrau'r marw, mae un o honynt yn gaddaw taledigaeth, a fynnwch i ô yna? Mae'n dda gan fy nghalon eich bod wedi gallu cael cystal lle i Dwm Parri dlawd, gobeitho y bydd fachgen ufudd a gonest a Duw a dâl i chwithau, heblaw bod y cyfryw weithredoedd caredig yn dwyn eu *gwobr* gyd a hwynt. Inward satisfaction y geilw'r Sais y peth. Os yna y daw'r Delyn Ledr nid hwyrach y ceir ail afael ynddi, os nid ê, bwriais fy arian a llawer o amser yn ofer, ond y cebystr ir sut, mi gollais y bardd o'i phlegyd. Gresyn fod cymaint o wendidau yn perthyn i ddŷn—ydyw, ydyw, y mae'r pryf ynghynffon Marged, ac nid tad na thaid chwedl chwithau a eill i dynnu allan. Diolch yn fawr i chwi am ymweled ag Ellis y Cwrel, a diolch iddo yntau am y llyfr godidawg; mae'r Llew yn gofyn i mi par sut y caf ef yma, ond yn y box gyda llyfrau mrawd Rhisiart, etc., hebai finnau. Dyn ydyw Sion Ellis fal dyn arall, ac fe eill gam gymeryd ambell dro, fal y dangosais iddo, oblegid bu ei lyfr gyda myfi fis neu ddau; y Bennant ai dygasai imi oddi cartref yr hâ leni, ond mi a'i gyrrais yn ol. Mi af i yn feichiau dros Agrippa y daw drwy'r afael. Gwae ni, tra bai'r bardd gan bured, ond mae yno mi wranta wendidau ddogn. Ni chlywais i ddim oddiwrth y nhad er's ennyd. Pe bai amgen na da fe sgrifenai'r nith Marged Owain—a surprising girl that! Writes an excellent hand and very correct, without ever having had any education to signify anything. Ond mae eisiau gwr yno fyth. Rym yma oll yn rhwydd iachus, ac yn gorchymyn attoch. Duw yn eich cylch. *Eich brawd ungalon,*

Gwilym Rwyddfras.

W. to R. contd.

P.S.—Fe haeddai'r dyn ei grogi a grafodd y tri golch bren yna yn eich pais chwi, pam na wnewch iddo eu trwsiaw? Dyma'r llun iawn. Pa beth ydyw'r ddeulew accw sydd gan y Tew?.

HOLYHEAD, 30 November, 1755.

W. to R. CCLXXIV

Dear Brother,—Gwaed swllt! Mi gefais lythyr oddiwrth y Tewfrawd yn adrodd ei fod yn amcanu cychwyn tu a thre y foru nesaf, ac heb un gair ynghylch y matter mawr; arwydd ddrŵg yr wyf yn ofni, ac mewn stage coach hefyd, yn lle dychwelyd mewn

W. to R. contd.

chaise fal y deuad yna. Ar fy ngonestrwydd i nid iwch brawd Gwil hanner esmwyth o'r achos. Er cariad ar Dduw gyrrwch yma ychydigyn or hanes rhag ofn na chaf glywed oddiwrth y Brâs ni wybod pa'r brŷd. Mae encyd er pan sgrifennais yna atteb i'ch llythyr diweddaf ac mae bellach le i ddisgwyl llinell oddiwrthych. Nawdd Duw rhag y fath drychineb ac a ddygwyddodd i drigolion Lisbon, *siampl* ddychrynadwy i holl bechaduriaid y byd. Ai tybied na finia beth ar galonau'r anffyddloniaid yna, mae'r bobl yma ac ymhob man ysywaeth yn rhy ddrigionus o lawer, ond fe a ddywedir eu bod yna yn rhagori ymhell ar bawb yn y deyrnas, y mawrion yn dysgu ir gwerinos bob campau gwaharddedig. Dymma hi yn ddyw Llun ac heb inclin gair iwrth y Llew, nis gwn i pa peth i feddwl, mae arnaf ofn yn fy nghalon mae cael ei nacca' a gadd y Castell Côch, os felly ffarwel ir Esgair Fwyn. Gobeitho gael or Llew daledigaeth da pa wedd bynnag y bu wedi. Nid oes yma newydd yn y byd, pob peth yn bur farwaidd ar tywydd yn oer greulon. Pa beth a wneir am Almanac Ryland iw osod ar y barth partition. Rwy'n ffaelio'n glir lân gael cyfleu i yrru'r Siwgar Sampier, mae un o longau Dulun yn cychwyn tua diwedd y mis, nid hwyrach y cair ganddynt ei chludo, rhaid im fynd at fy misawl gyfrif ir dollfa. Duw gyd a chwi, *Eich carediccaf frawd*,

William Morris.

P.S.—Pawb yn iach, mawl i Dduw.

CAERGYBI Sanctaidd, 10d o Ragfyr, 1755, nos Fercher.

W. to R. CCLXXV

Anwyl frawd,—Bendith yr Arglwydd i chwi am eich llythyr o'r 6ed. Nad elwyf byth i geibiaw onid oedd well gennyf ei gael na phe rhoesai rywun i mi lonaid fy het o aur melyn, chwedl gwraig Domos Barma am eiddo'r gwr, ynghrog y bo'r ci onid oeddwn yn drâ anesmwyth. Gwendid digydwybod rwy'n cyfaddef. Nid oedd dim achos i anobeitho oblegyd fod Rhagluniaeth o blaid y Llew or dechreuad, oni bae hynny, f'ei llyncasid er's talm. Gwych yw clywed mai'r Castell Côch a biau'r maes mawr ym Mambri. Dyn drwyddo o Sion Baentiwr, ni allasid byth daro wrth ei fath pei chwiliasid holl ynys y cedyrn. Mae'n dda gan fy nghalon eich bod wedi cefnu matter y Gendal wirion. Fe dâl Duw i chwi dros y tlawd. I writ him by to-day's pacquet an account of your negotiation. Dyma ryw lymgi wedi dyfod ir dref a rydd attal ar fy ngwaith am heno. Dô, dô, 'e roddwy[d] attal a che's fy ngadw ar fy nhraed ni wybod par hyd i glybod tyngu a rhegi ac araith ddrwg. Da iawn os rhydd yr Ysgawen dippyn o gymorth i chwi i gael lift, ffei arno' yr Fostyn, ni bu erioed ddaioni o uchder a balchder—cynneddfau diawledig ŷnt, Duw a gadwo pawb rhagddynt. Da clywed bod Siac ab y Doctor wedi cael codiad, rwyf finnau ar y ffordd o wneuthur dyn oi frawd ieua, os Duw ai myn. Gwyn ei fyd a gai goppi o gatalogue y Bennant sef yr annerch iwch y Cymrodorion. Mae ô a minnau yn cyfattebu bob wythnos oddigerth siawns. Roedd y Penllywydd o fewn ychydig mewn rhyw *Hunt* neu helfa oedd gan ryw weilch Siacobeaidd yn Llangefni accw, rhyfedd ei fod yn cymeryd pleser o fôd ymhlith bagad o ddynion gweigion heb un gamp dda yn perthyn iddynt, your down right roaring country esquire, wfft iddo fo. Duw a gadwo'r Castell Goch a phob pendefig cymwynasgar, nid oes dim sydd well na bôd *fellow feeling* yn y peth. Llwydded yntau. Bydd falch cael llythyr oddiwrthych gynta galloch a hanes y byd ar amseroedd: roedd y Llew'n dda tra bu. Gwae finnau na fedrai yr Prif Fardd ymgadw rhag yfed gormodd. Gwendid creulon a gwae arall na chawn fy Nhelyn Ledr anwyl, mae arnai ofn yn fy ngalon na welaf moni byth bythoedd. Bydded i Dduw warchad drosoch a'ch cadw mewn iechyd yw taer ddymuned. *Eich caredigcaf frawd,* W. to R. contd.

William Morris.

P.S.—Pray is Mr. Ellis's Book of Corals with you, if so, is plate xxxvii in it? I writ to him to know which way I was to send him some shells which he wanted but have received no answer, ai byw'r gwr?

CAERGYBI, Nos Iau, 21st December, 1755.

W. to R. CCLXXVI

Fy Mrawd Anwyl,—Mi sgrifennais attoch y dydd arall linell neu ddwy yn atteb i'r eiddoch or 6d, ac yn ol eich addewid dyma arall ac ynddo newydd oddiwrth y ser fal y bai naill ai Tomos Diôns ai Sion Diôns yn galw eu halmanaccau. Can diolwch am tano heblaw talu, siersiwch o yn eich bil, the design is apropo' enough, suiting the times. Mi ges innau gwpl o bystolau oddiwrth y Llew er pan gadd ei gaban, neu'n hytrach ei ffau arno, mae'n rhywyr clybod par fodd y trinodd yr examiners. Ceir yr hanes os gwynfyd a gadd. Ond os adfyd gwenwyn lillig (linellig oeddwn i yn eu geisiaw

W. to R. contd.

ddywedyd). Gerwin pe basai haid o williaid yn ei orddiwes efo'i filoedd, nid rhyfeddod yn y byd a fasai ac ynte yn trafaelio tan hanner wedi 6 y noson gynta lle roedd mwya'r perygl. Gwaed y ditw lâs! Ai yna mae fy hen feistr? Wala, mae yna ddigon o fwstr mi a wranta. Ac mae'n edifar yr awron droi'r sipog neu'r gôb, ni wn i par un, fe fuasai fy hen batron i Mr. Salisbury yn ffrind iddo, ie, un da hefyd, ac nid gweddus sorri wrth y cyfryw am faw beth, a chodi sawdl yw erbyn. Ond er hyn i gyd os yw yna dodwch fy ngwasanaeth atto, a'm bod yn dymuno llwyddiant iddo, pa peth bynnag sydd ganddo yn llaw, os ar ei lês y digwydd. Ystori gau ydoedd honno ynghylch y Winchelsea, ni bu ddim or fath beth, sŵn y canans mawrion oeddid yn eu saethu yn Nulun ar Dydd Gwyl Tywysoges Gymru, a glybuwyd ym Môn ac Arfon the 30 ulto, and a smugler built upon the report. Dim gwybod par un ai rhyfel, etc., meddwch. Ond daccw fy anwyl ffrind i yr Cadpen Weller wedi ymadael ar Dorset yatch i fynd i ymladd a Sion Ffrainc yn yr *Assistance*, Man of War, ai steward yr hwn hefyd oedd glarc iddo. Dyn ieuanc o gymydog a char ir hogiau yma wedi mynd iw ganlyn, is to be lieutenant, colled anfeidrol i Wilym ar eu hol, Gresyn na basai'r nai Wil Owen ynta yn mynd yn lle bod gartref yn llamhurtiaw, bai'r fam debygwn. Gobeithio nad yw ein materion yn Lisbon cynrhwg ac oeddid yn ei dybiaw, ac y daw yr arianwyr yna attynt eu hunain cyn y bo hîr. Ochafi na wnant ryw beth ir llongau Ffreinig yna, eu condemnio iw crogi i gael ymadael ar chwiwgwn yna sydd yn bwyta pobl out of house and home fal y dywaid plant Alis. Mi ges innau ebystol Agrippa, dim gobaith gwraidd, etc. Ni chefais i linell oddiwrth Oronwy er's hanner blwyddyn, y cebystr ir Delyn Ledr honno, 'rydych yn cofiaw'r modd y canodd Dafydd ab Gwilym i'r Ceryn diffaeth, mae i mi fwy o achos o lawer. Colli yr trysor a roddaswn yn'ghadw ynddi, a cholli'r prif fardd ir fargen, ffei or sut! Fe gododd fy ngwallt yn ei union sefyll ar fy mhen pan ddarllennais yn llythyr y Bennant fal hyn "The specimens sent me by Dr. Lloyd were very fine, and will enable me to draw up a more accurate account than has yet been published, I did design it for the Cymrodorion, but your brother, the president, has so neglected me of late that I must lay it before another society." Gwaed swllt!

How came you to neglect so worthy, so ingenious a member, who would have been of credit to the society and his country? Blush if you can't recall him, what he means is the stone at Monachdy where the asbestos or salamanders wooll is found, it was reckoned a kind of marble, but he has made it out to be a jasper. Da Costa agrees with him in it; rhaid tewi am heno, rwyf wedi blino yn sgrifennu at y brawd Llew heno, a chwithau gydagê. Duw yn eich cylch a byddwch iâch. *Eich caredigawl frawd* W. to R. contd.

tra bo' ynddo ffun, *William Morris.*

Ben bore ddydd Llun.—Dyma lythyr a sgrifenodd y nhad ddoe ddiweddaf y pryd yr ydoedd iach. Ie, llythyr meddaf, drwy law Huw ab Sion Probert; mam Huw ydyw, Nan'ch Huw Gruffydd Dywyll, a brawd Huw Gruffydd ydoedd Twm Gruffydd Benwyn a fyddai'n gweiddi "llanciau drwg erioed oedd llanciau yn gadlas." Cadw y mae'r Huw yma dafarn barchedig ddigon, lle y gwelsoch William Sion Tomos yn taring gynt yn city Dulas. Chwi ryfeddwch fy mod mor yspys ar achau y bobyl fawrion yma, ond cofiwch y bum i yn hir yn astudiaw'r gelfyddyd fuddiol honno, ac nid oes pennach achudd oddiyma hyd yna.

CAER GYBI, Nôs Calan, 1755.

Anwyl Frawd,—Llyma i chwi linell neu ddwy cyn diwedd blwyddyn i ddymuno i chwi un newydd hapusol. Om rhan i nid oes imi achos yn y byd i achwyn ar yr hên, er bod miloedd oedd gwell na myfi wedi cael eu torri ymaith yn ddisymwth. Echrys o'r hanesion yn y papurau ynghylch y daiargrynfâu mawrion sydd wedi bod 'ymmhob cwr o'r byd fel pettai, Duw a'n gwaredo rhag digwydd i ninnau yr un ddrychineb. Mi fum yr wythnos ddiweddaf oddicartre yng n'hynhebrwng hen ffrind imi, sef Edmund Meyrick or Drefri, Esquire, brawd yr *hên wr* o Fodorgan, ac iddo ef y gadawodd ei stât ag agos ei holl gyfoeth meddir, ac ar ei ol eilmab y Gawnsler yna, sef yw hwnw Iemwnd Meyrig. Ir pant y rhed y dwfr. Mae'r wlad yma yn wlybyrog erchyll. Os gwnaeth hi yna cymain' o wlawiau ac a wnaeth ffordd hyn, nid oes bosibl na bo'r gwledydd isel yna tan ddwfr bod y fodfedd. Gwaed yr hŵch gôch, dyma'r Sampier wedi dyfod yn eu hol o'r Werddon, y tair llong bost wedi eu gyrru i'r Skerries, deg i un na bydd y llong wedi hwyliaw i Lundain cyn y cânt fyned i Ddulun. Os rhwydd-deb a W. to R. CCLXXVII

W. to R. contd.

a gânt chwi gewch glywed ar fyrder, os afrwydd-deb, ni bydd ond tewi a sôn a gadael iddynt tan y tro nesaf, mae'nt yn bigion eiddo! Dyma fy neu gyw i yn gwaeddi fal gryrod arnaf am gael fy nghwmni i chwareu un o'r ddeg ar hugain ar y cardiau am afalau, felly lle da ceisio llonyddwch. Nos dawch heno. Byddwch iâch a llawen. *Eich caredigawl frawd, William Morris.*

P.S.—Nawdd, rwyn deall mae anwir a glywais, nid oedd mor Pen Llywydd ymhlith yr helwyr gwallgofus rheini a soniais am danynt. Dymma Fegi Owen o Bentre'rianell yn dywedyd fod fy nhad yn rhwydd iachus, ond fod y tor llengig yn ei *drwblio* ar gyrsiau, dyna ei geiriau hi. Mae son bod hon yn myned iw phriodi a llongwr or fan yma, rhan o slwp ganddaw, etc.,—mae'r tadau ar mammau yn fodlon. Boreu Dydd Calan. Diwrnod teg! Darogan blwyddyn dda. Duw ai danfono ini bod ac un; you see how I endeavour by my chit chat to draw a letter out of you unwaith yn y pedwar amser. Dyma om blaen lythyrau ddogn os gwel pobyl eu digon at y mrawd Llewelyn, at y nhad a ddyleswn enwi ynghynta, at y mrawd Rhisiart, at Mr. Pennant, at Mr. Mosson or Dumares, at Gendal o'r Werddon, etc., felly mae'n rhywyr tewi bellach.

W. to R. CCLXXVIII

CUSTOMHOUSE, HOLYHEAD, 12 January, 1756.

Anwyl Frawd,—Rwyfi yn ei gweled hi yn encyd o amser er pan glywais oddiwrthych, ond mae'r amser (mae'n debygol) yn myned heibiaw yn llithriccach ffordd yna, lle mae digon ar ddigon o waith a mwstrio beunydd, pam waeth i chwi yna ddryghinoedd na thegwch? Nid felly yma, mae'r ardymyr gwlybrog, temhestlog, anrhugarog yma yn ddigon er magu'r coler du, a milcant o glwyfau a heintiau eraill, na wyddoch chwi gwyr Llundain ddim oddiwrthynt. Bellach am fy neges; dywedyd a orug y meistr Vickers yma wrthyf y boreu heddy, fod llong i ddyfod oddiyna yn o fuan a brâg ir fan ymma, ac os oedd gennyf ddim i ddyfod o'r ddinas fawr fod i mi rwan bigion cyfleu. Ni wn i, hebai finnau, mi ysgrifennaf at y mrawd Rhisiart, ond odid bydd rhyw lyfrau yn barod, os felly, fe sparria dwysgen o arian i ryw un, ond par sut yn rhôdd y byd iddo ddyfod i hyd ir llong? Nid rhaid iddo, ebr ynte, ond directio'r boccys attaf i, ai yrru at Mr. Simpson, corn factor at Beachey y ceir i hyd iddo. Felly y darfu'r ymgomiaw, a dyma i chwithau'r cyflawn hanes, amen. Ni chefais i ddim llythyr er's dyddiau byd oddiwrth y Glew o'r Deau, da chwithau rhoddwch dippyn o'r hanes pan gaffoch glywed. Ai tybied mai'r Downshend sydd yn trin y dreth yn yr Esgair o hyd, beth meddwch? Ai tybied na fedrach i gontreifio cael protecsiwnau ir mân lestri yma? One Martin, in the secretary's office at the Customhouse, gets a considerable deal of money from these parts by procuring them, for which he hath ten shillings each and they don't stand him in above five shillings (as I am told). I have had two from him lately and he is very thankful for the office. His money is paid the collector of Beaumaris, who can easily remit them. But the difficulty with ye would be how to come at the cash, I mean how to have it returned, as to receiving of it here I would take care of that, as most of the coasters in these parts have paid the ten shillings, they cant think it too much. But mind that Martin sends 'em down in letters post paid, which he can do at Custo' by a kind of hocus pocus. If I can serve you in this affair let me know. I propose myself no benefit but that. Pa beth sydd gennyf chwaneg i ddywedyd na'n bod ni i gyd yn iach ac yn gorchymun attoch, ac erchi ar Dduw warchad drosoch. W. to R. contd.

Eich caredigawl frawd, *William Morris.*

CUSTOMHOUSE, HOLYHEAD, 22nd January, 1756.

Dear Brother,—Ni chaf yn awr ond yn unig amser i ddywedyd i chwi fy mod wedi derbyn yr eiddoch, a'r catalogue of rarities, a barddoniaeth yr Hirfardd or Deau, ac atteb y Bardd Du o Northolt—*gweith cywrein!* Can mil o ddiolchiadau am bob peth, mi attebaf y llythyr o ben bwygilydd y foru neu drennydd. Dyma fal y mae: y munud yma y cefais linell neu ddwy oddiwrth fy ffrind y Dr. Lloyd, y jasper o'r Monachdy, a dyma eu sylwedd—"Sir, I sent to a friend at London to procure me a protection for the Speedwell Sloop (of Kemlyn) in the coasting trade, burthen twenty tons, John Williams master and two mariners besides, I have not received it, therefore think my letter is miscarried or that my friend is not in town. I beg the favour of you to send to procure the said protection as soon as possible in case the same is not issued out in the interim which I suppose may be known at the board. I am, etc." Yn awr os y chwi a fedr gael hwn allan o law, da fydd, ai yrru yma i'ch brawd Gwilym. ond par sut a fydd trin y W. to R. CCLXXIX

W. to R. contd.

dreth ynghylch y postage rhag iddo fod yn ddwbl ac yn *drebal?* Mae'n debyg os na fedrwch ei gael yn ffri nad rhaid i chwi ond ei ddirectio without being inclosed. Mae yn y cwrr yma ir byd ryw lymgwn a fydd yn 'sgyrnygu eu dannedd os digwydd im post bill i fod yn hogyn mawr, ie, weithiau yn taro allan 3 swllt neu 4. Roeddwn yn disgwyl rhyw feistr llong o Seville alw yma i brotestiaw yn erbyn y môr a'r gwyntoedd (the collector being abroad) ond ni welaf mono ettwa, felly attebaf y llythyr hyd lle gallwyf. Oni fyddaf yn gweddio drosoch bob dydd a nos a elo dros fy mhen i, nid hwyrach mai gwell trafferth na seibiant er lles enaid. Gwych o'r gistiad yna o ffosilod a yrrodd y Bennant i chwi! I have a letter of his dated 16th giving me an account of a box he hath made up for me, consisting of about sixty articles, fossils, shells, etc. Mi a wnaf fy ngoreu er gwneuthur cymmod rhyngo ef ar Llywydd Llwyd. Aie *mablyfr* yw'r gair goreu yn y byd am goppi? Nid hwyrach hynny, ond nid yw fy nwyglust i yn dygymod ac 'e yn iawn ettwa, nis gwn par sud a fydd. Gwyn eich byd chwi sydd yn cael ymgyfaillachu a phobl fwynion a f'ai'n caru brawdgarwch a phob cyneddfau da; ni welais i ddyn a'm llygaid er's llawer o amser a mymrun o ddiddanwch yn perthyn iddaw. Dô, mi ge's lythyr i wrth Oronwy a hanes trwscl ynghylch fy nhelyn. Ffei, ffei, ni wn i fod dim chwaneg or llyfrau i ddyfod. Rhwymwch rai'r hen Feurig fal y lleill; mi wna iddo dalu fal pobyl eraill. Mi glywais fod naill ai mab (neu frawd) ynghyfraith i Mr. Salisbury wedi cael Searchership Liverpool, ni wn ai gwir. Ymhlé mae ffosilod Mahone iw rhoddi yn y box gyda'r llyfrau yna? Ie, a rhai Harwich, a Dover cliffs, etc. Bydd Ellis falch o fod yn Gymrodor, mi wranta y taera mai Cymro ei daid o bella, felly bydd pob Gwyddyl. Mi yrraf i chwi gregyn ddigon os gwna rheini les. Yr wyf am yrru i Mr. Ellis yntau flychaid ar fyrder, dywedwch hynny wrthaw. Ni chlywais innau ddim oddiwrth y Llew er's llawer dydd, ai ni cheir byth ddiben ar ddrysni yr dyn hwnw? Os dyna'r modd y byddis yn dringo i ben pinacl anrhydedd a mawredd, nis gwn i pwy fyth a ymdrafferthа am y coegbeth hwnnw. Pan gaffoch dippyn oi hanes, gadewch glywed. Gobeitho nad gwir hanes Russia. Fe â'r Foscawen irm ôr ac yno yn iach gymorth ganddo. Nid yw hwn wedi'r cwbl ddim yn atteb iawn i'r eiddoch, rhaid rhoddi mending arno ryw dro. Gwaed crwst! Pa beth a wneir am ffrancod i yrru'r barddoniaith yn ôl? Mae hi yma yn hêsp. Pawb yma yn iach, mawl i'r Goruchaf; ni chlywsom ddim o Bentre'rianell ers wythnos neu fwy. Duw a fo yn ymddiffynnwr i chwi. *Eich caredigawl frawd,* W. to R. contd.

William Morris Gregynwr.

CAERGYBI, 4th February, 1756.

Anwyl Frawd,—I received your eulun llythyr of the 29th with the protection, which I forwarded to Dr. Lloyd, whom I acquainted that (as you could not attend the office yourself) the instrument cost ten shillings, yr hyn a yrraf i'r tad cyn gynted ac y delont im llaw. I hope there was not another taken out. Diolch am gael cadw'r barddoniaeth i spario'r tudded a fuoch cyn fwyned ai roddi imi. Yn wir ddiau ni bu yma ermoed y fath eisiau rheini, rhaid i hwnw fynd ynghylch llythyr neu ddau i Fathafarn y foru nesaf. Gwaed swllt! Mi debygwn wrth ddau o bystolau a ge's 'iwrth y Llew or 9d ar 15d ulto, fod yr Iuddew Brŷch wedi ei ymddangos yn ei liwiau priodawl, ni feddyliais i ôll y byddai bur a ffyddlon,—ni ddwg drain rawnwin. Er carriad ar Dduw dodwch dippyn o'r hanes, 'rwyf dra anesmwyth o herwydd y Llew, ag nis gwn i amcan am bai'r achos na pha herwydd. Na chanaf fi ddim Te Deum, am fod Sion Ffranc wedi ffyrnigo. Roeddwn yn disgwyl y b'ai heddy chwaneg or hanes ond i wenwyn damaid, ni choeliai y bydd y Cybiaid fawr well er rhyfel. *Er heddwch nac er rhyfel, gwenynen farw ni chasgl fêl,* roedd yr hen ddiareb. Gwenyn meirw ydym ninnau, a phe bai byw ynom, ni chaem ond ychydig iawn gan y gwenyn gormes mawrion yna. Rhan y gwâs o gig yr iar, mi wranta. Digrif yw'r hên Aldramon sydd yna 'rhŷd yr amser. Dêg i un na bo cyn llawened ar gôg ar y gainc, a ŵyr o ei hun pa beth y mae yn ei wneuthur neu yn ei geisiaw wneuthur? Mae'r wraig odiaethol honno sydd iddo, yn cael ei gw'nfyd yn ei absen. An exceeding good woman! on'te? Ie, o'r *ffeinia*, fydda i chwi yrru llythyr i'r Bennant, mae o wedi sgrifennu yn ddiweddar at y Llew ynghylch Natural History Sir Fôn; mae o'n tyngu i'r cyrs ac ir coed y dylae fo a minnau (chwedl y mochyn) daro atti hi W. to R. CCLXXX

W. to R. contd.

i sgrifennu un, nobody in the world better qualified, medd ! Wrth gofio, mae fal yr ymofynwch (os cewch eich côf) 'da'r Aldremon (yn ddistaw bâch), par fyd sydd ar fy hen gyfaill Mr. Wright o Leghorn ? I have some private reason for this enquiry. The young fellow whom I suppose is a lieutenant on board Captain Weller's, and who was his clerk and steward on board the *Dorset* yatch, is one John Henry of this place. You perhaps may remember his father, master of Peter's brig at Dulas in time of yore. Gwyddel oedd ei dad a briodws Gybi wraig. Ni welais etto mo gadpen newydd yr iot, Bonfoy ; adwaenoch chwi o? Ni chefais etto ddim o hanes y sampier, y tair llong bost yn awr yn Werddon ; ar gwynt dwyrain yma ai ceidw yno yn ddigon o hyd. Roeddym yn disgwyl y chwaer adref heno o Bentre' rianell, ond ni ddaeth. Roedd y nhad yn rhwydd iachus echdoe, roedd y protecsiwnau wedi eu derbyn. Wala hai ! Rhaid a myned i hel gwmon 'rhyd gerig a chreigiau'r môr i Mr. Ellis yna. "Let me know," meddai ef, "whether you still continue in the botanical way and what seeds you want." Dywedwch wrtho, os gwelwch, that I am as foolish as ever, ac eisiau pob hadau pur ddieithr arnaf. Garddoriaethu heddyw ddiweddaf fy ngoreu glas er gwaetha'r dwyreinwynt ysgyfigar. Fe dalai'r swydd ei gwasanaethu i chwi ddyfod oddiyna hyd yma i weled fy mharadwys-ardd i. Roedd gennyf y mis diweddaf oddeutu deugain math o lysiau a gwydd yn eu blodau, y peth nad oedd mi wranta mewn nemawr ardd o amgylch Llundain. Ni bu yma ddim rhew y leni a laddai'r planhigyn tyneraf allan. Rhaid imi sgrifennu fy hun at y gŵr ar fyrder. Gwych a f'asai gael tippyn o hadau yn y box. If you have not waited of him, you may tell him of the opportunity. I am conscious to myself that you will be tired with my chat ere you reach thus far. Felly Duw gyda chwi. My compliments to my brother Comptroller Gwil Parry. I am, dear brother,

Yours most affectionately, *William Morris.*

P.S.—Nid oes dim hanes am arian yn dyfod oddiwrth y Lwyd yna i'r Gendal dlawd accw, er maint y drafferth a gesoch yn eu cylch. Mae'r gair fod Miss Jones, Plas Gwyn, wedi priodi y cynghorwr Pantwn o Degeingl.

CUSTOMS, HOLYHEAD, 10th February, 1756.

Anwyl Frawd,—Mi sgrifenais attoch linell y dydd arall. Yr achos a bair im eich cyfarch yr awron yw hyn: I have been disapointed of an almanack for my office, must beg you'll send me a small London Almanack, I mean your copper plate sheet ones, obleit rheini fydd gennyf bob amser, Ryland yn y parlwr gartref; mi dalaf y chwecheiniogyn gyda'r chweigan i nhâd. Roedd y Doctor Lloyd yn gweled y protecsiwn yn ddrud am hynny, ond pam raid i chwi roddi eich llafur yn ofer, fe ddylae bawb dalu fal eu gilydd, onide fe fyddis yn achwyn chwedlau. Och y fi, dyma lythyr pruddaidd amhosibl oddiwrth y brawd or Deau; Duw a ddel ac ef allan o'i orthrymderau; rwyn ofni y basai well iddo beidio a syrthio allan a'r hen gydnabod. A fedrwch chwi roddi dim o'r hanes pa beth y maent yn ei wneuthur? Mae Mr. Mosson yma, ac yn gridwst yn erchyll am ronyn o lythyr oddiyna; fo ddangosws imi lythyr i wrth y Davies yna yn dywedyd eich bod yn sôn am sgrifennu. Gwelais arall oddiwrth Siac ab y Doctor yn dywedyd ei fod drwy eich cymorth chwi yn gobeithio cael dringo rîs uwch. Dyma finnau yn anfon efo'r llong bost nesaf ei frawd *Gwilym* iw wneuthur yn feddyg dan fy anwyl gyfaill, the Surgeon General. Os Duw a rydd iddo râs fe ddaw yn ddyn gwych. Byddwch chwithau gwych, da chwithau. Mr. Mosson desires his compliments. *Eich caredigawl frawd,* *William.* W. to R. CCLXXXI

P.S.—Onid oes ffrencyn, gyrrwch o mewn tudded caeth—tudded rhydd o ffrencyn, ond ê? Mae d——l ymhob migwrn ac asgwrn o'r Iuddew Brych medd y Llew, mi ddywedais i ddigon pe'i tycciasai; fe gadd wybod yr holl ddirgeloedd mae'n debyg, ac yr awron yn prifio'n gnâf pîg.

CAER GYBI, 2d. o Fawrth, 1756.

Anwyl frawd,—Ymhell y bwyf onid ydwyf yn dra anesmwyth am gael clywed oddiwrthych, mae arnaf ofn yn fy nghalon fod y peswch neu ryw beth wedi eich nychu, yr anrhas iddo, mae o yn ddigon tost wrthyfi, sydd yn cael yngwala o awel denau iachus, chwaethech y chwi sydd yn bwyta mwg a tharth mal y bwytae eidion du wair gwndwn. Y cebystr i'r llyfrau ar almanacau, ni waeth gennyfi pe baent yn y Bala am y cawn i glywed fod fy mrawd yn hawntus. Oes, oes, mae imi arall frawd nas gwn mwy o'i hanes nai gyflwr, W. to R. CCLXXXII

W. to R. contd.

nag y gwyr Brenin Ffrainc fy hanes innau. Ni chefais lythyr oddiwrtho er's cryn fis, a hwnnw yn un digon tywyll, mae gyda hwnw lencyn o nai i mi, ce's hanes ei fod yn afiach; Duw a ddelo a newyddion da oddiwrth bawb o honoch. E ddaw'r post i mewn y foru, pwy a wyr na ddaw haid i gwch, "Pan fo ingaf gan ddyn, ehenga' fydd gan Dduw," ac am hynny dodaf hwn heibiaw am heno. Roedd y nhâd yn rhwydd iachus ddoe, ac yr ym ni yma oll felly, mawl i'r Goruchaf Dduw.

Dranoeth.—Wala! Moliant ir Goruchaf am bob diddanwch; bydded iddo dalu i chwithau am eich caredigrwydd. Dyma eich llythyr wedi gwneuthur imi fwy o lês na phe'i rhoddasai rywun imi olud lawer. Gwendid erchyll y'w anobeitho, ni wnaf mo hynny ond hynny, debygai. Yn awr am eich ebystol bywhaus (nid oeddwn i ond lledfyw cyn ei gaffael). Digrif oedd i chwi ymweled ac Ellis pan ydoedd yn trin eu hadau. 'Rwyf yn rhwymedig i'r gwr am ei anrheg. Mi sgrifennais atto o fewn y pythewnos yma ac a yrais iddo gryn ddwy wns o bethau anrhyfedd mewn tudded at Shelvocke o'r Post Offis yna; ped fuasant yna yn gynt, cawsid mwy o hadau. Mi sgrifenaf y foru at Freuan o Lanychmedd i erchi arnaw beri'r clydwr ymofyn am y gofiwch hwnnw a'r llyfrau. Ni wiw taro atti hi i ddiolch i chwi am y peth yma a'r peth accw nês y delont i ben y daith. Chwi a wnaethoch o'r goreu beidio eu helcyd nhw 'rhyd y môr, rhag ofn y buasai Sion Ffrainc gaffael gafael arnaddynt. O chwiw leidr! Aie mae arno flys Plymwth ai oes? Fo gâ ei grogi ynghynt. Gwyrda Answn a Hawg am fyned yno i gadw gâl, Duw gyda nhw. Wfft i chwi am rhoddi cymaint o ddiawlaid yn y gistan efo'r Sgrythyr lân, ni wnaetha' Dwrc ddim yn rhagor. Na châdd y Weldon weddw ffarlling na dima byth o'r arian cloaths bill. Gwyn ei fyd na fedrach ei chynorthwyaw. Nid difalch a fydd fy mrawd Mosson gael clywed fod Jenkinson ar y ffordd i gael pensiwn. Wfft i'r Sharpe a'r West a'r Baynter—an excellent triumvirate; ni allasant byth daro wrth well offeryn, ac ni allasai'r Llew fyth daro wrth bennach cnâ na'r Paintiwr; roedd o yn broliaw gormodd o hono, a minnau ni fedrwn yn fy myw gredu y deuai ddaioni byth oddiwrth ymhel ai fâth, gwr mwyn, mwyn, hyd na chadd wybod pob dirgelwch, ac yno troi yn y cogwrn. Mae'n dda genyf glywed fod gobaith y daw'r Castell

Coch a phob peth i ben y tir, er gwaetha'r cwbl. Gwaed swllt! Ni thal stitched almanack ddim i myfi, rhaid iddo fod yn gyfan gwbl i gael ei hoeliaw ar y fagwyr wrth fy *mord* yn y dollfa ar ucha llawer o'i frodyr sydd yno er's llawer dydd. Mae arnaf beth cywilydd eich trwbliaw am ryw oferedd o'r fath, a chwithau cymaint eich ffwdan a'ch trafferthion. Hir iawn y buoch yn annerch y Bennant druan. Had a letter from him last Saturday, and at the same time another from Mr. Lysons, of Hémsted, in Gloucestershire; an ingenious gentleman, who was with us at Snowdon last summer. Cael hadau gwchion oddiwrth hwnnw yntau, a ffossilod ddigon i wrth Pennant. Ni chlybuwyd ermoed son am y fath gregyn yr wyf fi yn eu ddyfod o hyd iddynt beunydd yn y moroedd yma, ac nid oes ond y Bennant a minnau a ŵyr fymryn o'u hanes—a great variety of nondescripts. Aie siwrnai seithug a gadd yr Aldromon ap Rhisiart, trwstan erioed er pan wyfi yn ei gofiaw. Ffei arni yr Ysgawen na basai yn cyflawni, cadd a fynnodd mae'n debyg, ac yno anghofiwyd y peth a addawyd, nid oes fawr hyder ar blant dynion. Da chwitha', anerchwch finnau yn garedigawl at y Comptroler Parry; 'rwyf yn dra rhwymedig iddo am lawer cymwynas a wnaeth erwyf, Duw a dalo iddo, o ran deg a thrugain i un, y daw byth ar fy llaw i allu talu'r pwyth yn ôl. Cê's lythyr y dydd arall oddiwrth y Doctor Evans ô'r Nassau. Daccw fi newydd anfon ei frawd Wil o drosodd i'r Iwerddon i ddysgu myned yn surgeon general. Os Duw a rydd iddo ras ac iechyd, fe ddaw yn gefn dŷn. Wala, wala, mae'n rhaid imi bellach gadw noswyl er difyrred iw dadwrdd, felly Duw o'i fawr drugaredd a fyddo yn noddwr i chwi, ac i bawb o honom. Amen. *Eich caredigcaf a'ch rhwymediccaf frawd*

i'ch annerch, Gwilym Cybi.

W. to R. contd.

O.S.—Ie, bendith'ch tad (a'ch mam sydd yn y pridd) i chwi. Sgrifennwch gynta fyth y galloch a hanes Dewi a chant o bethau anadnabyddus i'r Cybiaid. Er mwyn dyn pa beth a wneir ir Lwyd yna or War Offis. Nid oes dim o hanes yr arian yn dyfod ir Gendal dlawd, pei tala fo nhw i chwi, mina ai talwn i'r tlawd gan Gendal. Ai tybied pei baech yn ei ddwyn ar gof by a penny post letter na wnai o rywbeth ac ynte wedi gaddaw? Pe basai gennyf dudded rhydd sgrifenaswn ymhell cyn hyn at y prifardd Goronwy. Par ddelw sydd arno? Adieu.—W.M.

GARTREF, 24dd o Fawrth, 1756.

W. to R.
CCLXXXIII

Anwyl Frawd,—I would have reply'd to yours of the 9th sooner (which came in company with one from Ceredigion ar yr un testyn), but that I waited for the arrival of the box which came to hand three days ago all safe, and I have begun to distribute the contents, and to begin. Here's old Bodorgan hath return'd his, aledging that the print is too small for his reading, mae'r hên wedi hurtiaw. I'll dispose of them as soon as possible, and of the Cymrodorion Constitutions. I had paid my father ten shillings for the protection and sixpence for the Almanack. Diolch yn fawr am y cregynach, etc., 'roedd gennyf 'run pethau a rhan fwya o honynt, ond ni feddwn i 'r un cythrael; ie diolch am yr ink, ni ddeuaf i ben i roddi diolchiadau am bob pêth. 'Roedd y ddau lythyr uchod yn cyttuno agos air yn air im mawr dristwch, nis gwn i pa beth i feddwl, na pheth i ddywedyd, ac nid oes gennyf fi iw wneuthur ond taer weddio ar i Dduw ddyfod ar gŵr ai dylwyth allan o'u cyfyngderau. Dyma arall oddiwrtho heddyw, a thrist iawn y cynhwysiaid. Gwaeth na dim oedd oeri o'r Castell; ni wn i a ga'ed golwg arno Ymhengwern Bowys, mae'n debyg fod yscêms hwnw yntau wedi eu gwyrdroi, yn wir os coeliwch fi rwy wedi llamhurtio. Mae'r Iddew Brych, debygwn i, wedi anfon at ei ffrins or cyrrau yma'r newydd, felly mae'r ewyllyswyr dâ a'r ewyllyswyr drŵg ddialedd am gael 'r hanes, a minneu'n tewi a sôn ac yn gadael iddynt a gwyneb llawen a chalon drom gennyf. Duw Goruchaf a'n diddano i gyd, mae'n debyg y bydd cyn i nemawr o ddyddiau fyned heibiaw i rywun fod mor drwyadl a dywedyd ir hen wr ein tad, rhaid a myned ffordd honno gynta gellir i roddi carreg ar y ffagl.

Am glad you are of opinion that there are friends and fair play to be had at Caerludd; na atto Duw chwedl amgen, pam waeth pa beth a fo yng Nghwm Erfin na chwm arall os y B—— a gaua ei law am tano? Mae'r bobl yn darogan mae'r Iuddew Brych sydd i feddiannu pob lle a phob peth Yngheredigion. Ond dyn a feddwl, Duw a ran; a bydded iddo wradwyddo bwriadau'r gelynion cartrefol a thramor, ni wybod pa rai waethaf o honynt. Aie gelyn brych or Gommisionwr Fychan? Os felly, fe gofia ond odid am tanom ninnau ffordd yma, ond ni âd rhagluniaeth i bob dyn drwg dichellgar gael mo'i ffordd ei hun, oni bae hynny ni byddai dim byw yn y byd hwn. Gwaed swllt! mae rhyw ffrind i mi wedi erchi arnaf yrru am ddau brint Hogarth at 12d, representing the English and French coast. If you can get them for me and send them down in a ffrank, minnau a dalaf yn onest i nhad am danynt, a chewch chwithau fendith am eich poen, un o'm meichiafon yw'r gwr. Mi welais yn y papurau farw o fy hen batron i Thomas Salisbury alias Brereton ; yn nef ma'i enaid, 'rwyn gobeithio. Mi glywais fod yr Aldremon yn y pen draw ir wlad y dydd arall; oni wnaethe fô burion Seneddwr iddynt y Lerpwliaid? Mi glywaf mai Mr. Chas. Pole oddiyna sydd i fod—mi adwaen y gwr, a dau frawd iddo, nid amgen, Col. Pole, ac Aldremon Pole o Lerpwl. W. to R. contd.

Fal hyn y dywaid y Benant y dydd arall: "I have heard from the President, who complains that he is hurried out of his life. I pity and forgive y llall frawd at yr hwn y sgrifennais er's talm ond heb gael atteb." Rhyfedd pei cawsed, ebr finneu wrthyf fi hun. My cabinet and garden fills daily, ond gwagedd yw'r llowndra ysywaeth. Ond am hynny yr un peth yw pob llawnder tan haul; beth meddwch? Mi heuais yr hadau a yrrasoch imi, *Lupins* oedd y pys rheini. Roedd y nhad yn achwyn y dydd arall yn gethin am lythyrau oddiwrth y brawd arall a chwithau ; mi yrrais atto am iddo beidio ac ymddigio o herwydd trafferthion ac helbulon ai para. Mae'n rhaid imi bellach dewi a son. Duw o'i fawr drugaredd a fyddo yn gwarchad drosoch bod ac un. Bydd da cael *llythyr* gynta gellir. Fe addawodd y llall un yr wythnos nesaf, rydwyf wedi mopiaw nas gwn beth i ddywedyd ; hyn a ddywedaf, fy mod i yn hyderu y gwna'r Goruchaf Dduw ein diddanu oll. Amen.

Eich caredigawl frawd, *William Morris.*

P.S.—Oes dim o'r fath beth a chael haner dwsing o ffraink gan yr hawddgar bendefig y Pen Llywydd? Mae eisiau sgrifennu at Oronwy. Dyma gywydd gwych iddo newydd i eni, y Bardd Côch a'i hymddûg. Chwi ai cewch os daw oddiwrthych dudded. Mewn difrif pwy a rôdd help llaw ir Ifans i sgrifennu'r pamphled Cymraeg? Mi a dyngaf fi am llaw ar lyfr, nad efô ei hun a wnaeth y peth nag yr un o'i gydwladwyr deheubarthaidd, ni waeth gennyf ped fai ei ddwy glust yn clywed er drycced ei dafawd. Wfft iddo

W. to R. contd.

fo am ymgegi. Dymma frawd y Brindled Jew yn y fangref yma yn ysgwyd ei gynffon arnaf. O genhedlaeth gwiberod! Nid un or Ceredigioniaid mo Rhos Goch, ai ê? Os ê ni ymddiriedwn iddo am gadw dirgeloedd. Adieu.—*W.M.*

W. to L. and R. CCLXXXIV

CAERGYBI, Ebrill y 1af, 1756.

Anwyl Frawd Hynaf,—Dyma fi yn eistedd i lawr i sgrifennu attoch, ac nis gwn i pa beth i ddywedyd gwedi. Mi gefais eich tri llythyr o'r Esgair, o Goventri, ac oddiyna, a diau mai erchyll eu cynhwysiad. Nid oes gennyfi ddim i wneuthur ond offrwm fy ngweddi drosoch ar i Dduw oi drugaredd ddyfod a chwi ir lan o'r dom yr ydych wedi soddi ynddo, a hynny yr wyf yn ei wneuthur o ddyfnder calon, a gobeitho y clywir fi. Duw yn unig a wyr pa beth sydd oreu ar ein lles, ai hawddfyd ai blinfyd; mae nghalon i yn tosturio dros y teulu. Gobeitho na sorrodd y Castell Côch; os do, nid rhyfedd, ac nid oes dim hyder ar bobl y byd yma—gwae'r sawl a feddyliodd fôd. Rwyf wedi cynnull yr ardreth gan y tenantiaid yma oddigerth rhyw 30s. sydd o arrears ar y ty bach yn Rhosgolyn. Daeth yma ddyn ddoe o Bentre'rianell a llythyr oddiwrth y nhad. Mae'r hen wr yn achwyn ei fod yn bur afiachus, nid eill fwyta dim bwyd hallt na dim caled, na bydd yn bwys garw ac yn llosgi ar ei galon; some excoriation or ulcer in the stomack, or perhaps an apostem; if the latter it will go hard with him; beth meddwch chwi? Nis gwn i beth oedd yn eich llythyrau oblegid maen't i gyd yn lludw. Da chwithau, sgrifennwch fynycha y galloch. Fo fu Twm, brawd yr Iuddew brych, yma'r dydd arall yn ei ffordd o Sir Abernoeth; mae'n debyg fod ganddo ddigon o newydd ir ficws ai ffrindiau. Ces lythyr dydd arall oddiwrth y crechwennwr o'r Duwmares; roedd yn mynd i'r Sir honno, mae'n debyg fod eisiau swydd tan yr Iuddew.

Y brawd arall. Mi yrrais heddyw deir punt i nhâd ar gownt y llyfrau, nid oes neb a ŵyr par bryd y ceir gwerthu'r 4 eraill. Roeddwn heb dderbyn arian y Brynddu,—roedd yr hen wr yn achwyn bod ei heisiau,—fo gostiodd carrio'r box 2/6 i Gaer; 15d. i Lanerchmedd; 6d. yma; cwbl 4/3. Ni wn i a dynwch i rhyw faint allan am garrio fy llyfr i, gwnewch a fynnoch. Nid oes yma ddim ond sôn am y Ffrancod: nhw allant ddyfod os mynnant, ni ddywaid neb ddim yn ei herbyn, pe bai bob man cyn wanned, ni byddai annodd iddynt eistedd i lawer ar dir sŷch. Gobeitho eich bod ffordd yna yn cymeryd mwy o ofal. Wala! wala! [waeth te]wi a sôn, Duw oi dramawr drugaredd a fyddo yn nodded i [ddyn ?] W. to L. and R. contd.

Eich brawd ungalon, William Morris.

P.S.—Ymhle y mae Prints Hogarth? Oes dim gobaith ir Gendal dlawd?

CAERGYBI, Ddyw Llun y Pasg, 19th April, 1756.

Anwyl Frawd Rhisiart,—Mae encyd er pan glywais fod y peswch yn dost wrthych a bod Meirian yn wan iawn, a dyma lythyr oddiwrth Ald. Prichard, o Fangor, yn dywedyd y canfu o chwi wythnos i ddydd Gwener diweddaf, a'r un hanes. Gwae fi na chlyw'n eich bod wedi dyfod drwy'r afael. Nid hwyrach y daw'r post heddyw a rhyw newydd oddiwrthych'i ar brawd arall. Poed dâ y bô a buan y delo. Nid oes yma ond myned ymlaen yn yr un wedd ac y bydded arfer. Rym ni i gyd, i Dduw bo'r diolch, yn iachus; roedd y nhad yntau yn rhwydd dda ar ei iechyd o fewn y tridie yma. Bum unwaith yn amcanu myned iw ymweled heddyw, ac yno ir sessiwn i fynd ar y grand jury fal ym rhybuddiwyd, ond rhwng cynnildeb, ychydig o orchwyl yn fy swydd, diogi a musgrellni wedi eu cymysgu ynghyd, mi ymrois i dario gartref, ac a erchais ar ffrind fy escusodi ag ni chlywais i fod yno ddim i wneuthur ond bolera. Mae un o'n dau ustus ni ddialedd eisiau dyfod yma i weled fy natural curiosities i, medd Mr. Hwlant, ac arno eisio fy hudo ir sessiwn, gwr cywraint o White. Rwy'n disgwyl y foru focsyn llawn o dlysau anianawl i wrth y Bennant, ac un arall cyn y bo hir. Dyma finnau beunydd yn olrhain allan bethau anrhyfeddol yn y cwr yma ir byd, er mawr syndod ir dysgedigion. Chwerthasech pe i'm gwelsech y dydd arall ar lygad distyll a ffon badl i'm llaw am mhab ai fasged ar ei fraich yn cludo'r prog, roedd y bobl yn meddwl mai clappio y bu'som, ac yn wir roedd lle i feddwl hynny a hitheu yr wythnos o flaen y Pasg. Ond mi ollyngais i yn angof mai at wr afiach yr wyf yn sgrifennu ac nid oes ond odid dim blâs ar wansens o'r fath yma. Ond gobeitho'r goreu a'ch bod chwi ar lodes well, well, bob dydd. Am y brawd arall nis gwn i beth i feddwl o honaw; disgwyl newydd da ac ofni newydd drwg—Duw yn unig a wyr pa beth a ddigwydd a pha beth sydd oreu ar ein lles, ai adfyd ai hawddfyd. Dyma eisia W. to R. CCLXXXV

W. to R. contd.

protectsiwn, ond os afiach ydych nid hwyrach na waeth gennych par un am ymhel ag 'e. Os felly nid rhaid i'ch[wi ond] rhoddi yr darn lythyr yma mewn tippyn o bappur ai yrru at M[r. M]artin at the secretary's office, Customhouse, ac fe ai cais i mi heb ddim chwaneg o ddyrecsiwn. Talaf y chweigain i nhâd, roedd y Dr. Llwyd yn gridwst yn dost. "Please to procure me with all speed a protection for two men belonging to the *Hopewel* of Beaumaris, burthen twenty tons, employ'd in the coal and coasting trade, John Thomas, master, and you'll oblige, Sir, your very humble servant, *William Morris.*

Ocra for brother quoth you? Ni wn i pa beth ydyw, par sut y byddynt yn ei arfer mewn cawl? Daccw fi wedi ei hau ym mharadwys ar chayan pepper gydage, i borthi'r bendro. Moliant ir Goruchaf am bob diddanwch. Dyma'r eiddoch or 13/15 wedi dyfod im gafael ai gyd trafaeliwr gyd ag e', a chan diolch i chwi am bob lein, ie, am bob gair o hono, bu agos imi ddywedyd am bob llythyren ynddo. Yn wir, yr ysprydoedd mau wedi soddi yn dra isel ond yn awr fal arian byw o flaen tegwch a sychder maent wedi cyfodi yn dda iawn, nid oes ond eisiau hanes da o'r Drysorfa ac yno nhw ant cuwch ar nenbren. Fe eill Duw ddyfod a hwnw, mae hi yn rhy hwyr i mi geisiaw atteb'ch llythyr heddyw, ac i chwilio am y cywydd, etc., rhaid aros tan y post nesa i gael llenwi bol y ffrencyn, ni bu im heiddo yr un er's llawer dydd or blaen. Wawch etto, dyma'r box iwrth y Bennant ac o ddeutu thirty o glawddiadau o Biedmont, a rhyfeddol iawn ydynt, ni thrawodd y dynan hwnnw ermoedd wrth fy math sef pennau ffwlcyn, mae o yn taeru yn fy nannedd i y bydd raid i mi roddi allan Natural History Ynys Fon, *Mona Illustrata* a fydd y gelwid o. Ond ê wyr Huw a Harri hefyd na fu erioed yn fy meddwl i gynnyg y fath beth, mae'r gwr yn gadael pob cymorth yn ei allu, a daccw fo wedi gosod pobl eraill ar fy nghefn i, Mr. Hwlant o Gonway. Gwaith y ddau y dydd arall pan oeddynt ynghyd ydoedd fy hyssio i ymlaen; pei cai'r Llew amser a llonydd, y fo a fedrai wneuthur y gwaith. Ni fedraf ddeall i ba beth y daw Dic ab y Doctor i Fôn, he is an idle boy, gresyn na bai ymwrdd Man of War, nid oes yma ddim swcr iddo, ac yn wir ni haeddai. I had agreed with a good master for him but he ran away from him at Dublin, and from two or three since—

have nothing to do with him, for he's a sad foolish boy; I wish he was settled, but I despair of ever seeing any good of him. I have put his younger brother in a way of becoming a credit to his family, and would have servd him if it had availd. Henry's ship is for sailing soon, I suppose he could not come up. Ie, ie, rhyw gadffwl or brawd Mosson, ond pwy eill help iddo fo? Drwg iawn yn ddiau yw bod yr hen Deyrn yn afiach. Duw Goruchaf ai cadwo. Da clywed fod y lodesig yn mendiaw. Bid iach y bo'ch bod ac un. *Eich carediccaf frawd,* *W.M.* W. to R. contd.

CAER GYBI, 21 Ebrill, 1756, Gwedi bod Nôs.

Anwyl Frawd Rhisiart,—Mi sgrifenais attoch ryw 'strodwm echdoe ac i geisiaw protectsiwn i *slwp* ŵyr i'r Hen Owen William, or Nant Bychan, a'i meistr yw mab Twm Edward Gôch 'ab Ellin'ch William Tomos Lewis y Gof, o Lanallgo, ai mât hi mab Owen Sion Owen bengrych o Foelfre, yr ownor ysef Dafydd Saer ap Sion Rolant Gloff o Bentre'r Garreg, ac aer Bodsilin yn y Llechwedd ucha yn Arfon a wasnaethodd ei brentisiad i William ap Huw Williams y Seinar ger llaw'r Forllwyd, ac sydd yr awron yn cadw ty boneddiga'dd ddigawn yn y Garreg Felen yn y borthladd hon. Hyn o hanes rhag ofn i'r Arglwyddi yna fod yn holi pwy o'r bobl ac o ble ir hanwyd hwynt. Mi addewais atteb eich llythyr ac felly gwnaf bod y gair, ac i ddechreu; yn wir mae gennyf fi bob amser ddigon o gwyn i chwi gan faint eich llafur a'ch lludded yn ymdrafferthu ar byd brwnt yma, heb gael amser prin i ymgroesio, na bo'nd i grybwyll! Ymhle y mae addewidion Bodysgawen? Fe gadd ei neges mae'n debyg, ac felly can ffarwel. Mi ryfygais wneuthur im my hun ddoe yr anrhydedd o sgrifennu at yr Aldremon Prisiart cyn ddiflased gwr ar Fosson am ei en, continually plaguing one with his insignificant errands. Mi welais Asheton, yr heir apparent, ryw dro—dynan diniwaid debygwn. Mi glywaf fod Alanson (ein pen Siri) yn erbyn y tenantiaid attournis i Smith, a bod yr Stewart Evans yn dilyn ei orchymun, felly fe fydd siawns i O.P. Gerwin dost o'r ffrigwd rhyngddo a'r Commissioner Davies a gerwinach bod y Long Acre yn dyfod arno am ddeg punt y Plasgoch. Gresyn na bai Ddick Evans Secundus ym mwrdd y Nassau efo Sionach; am affraid the boy will never do any good; I took a great deal of pains to have him fix'd W. to R. CCLXXXVI

W. to R. contd.

with a good master at sea to little purpose. Rwy'n gobeitho nad felly y bydd imi lwyddo wrth drin ei frawd ieua. I had a letter the other day from my worthy friend, Surgeon General Nichols, wherein he thanks me for some trifles I had sent him and particularly for Will Evans, who he believes will make proper use of his time and opportunities of learning. "'Tis a thousand pities (quoth he) he had not been better grounded in school learning; but I will find some method of helping him in that likewise." Gwrda'r corph! I knew the Surgeon General and the boy perfectly well, and that they were made for each other. Da bod y Wheldon yna yn gowir ac yn onest, mae o'n deilliaw o bobl rodresgar biniongar, ac os clywais yn dda nid bastardd monaw. On'd ydwyf i yn arofyn anfon yna lonaid cist o gregynach, etc., ond gwrandewch, pa beth a fyddwch nes oni ba'i fod gennych ryw un a wyr ragor 'rhwng cregyn malwod a chregyn westras? Ie, a llê boneddigaidd i'w llettyfa? Par fodd bynnag, myfi a yrraf i chwi ddogn ryw ddiwarnod; ond par sut y cewch hwynt? A fyddoch i foddlon i dalu am ei cludo rhyd y tir o Gaerlleon gawr?

I have heddyw ddiwaethaf a letter from Mr. Pennant, wherein he acquaints me that he hath received the Sicilian Prince's cargo of fossils and shells, a daccw fo yn gyrru imi ddau flychaid o honynt. Ni ddaeth erioed or naill wlad i'r llall mo'r fath dlysau. Gwae fi na allwn fyned i Degeingl. Gweled bod ac un, mae imi ddigon o wahadd. Ond pwy a dâl ir Pibydd? Bendith yr Arglwydd i chwi am feddwl am y Gendal wirion. Aie mae i'r prifardd bob math ar ddodrefn yn ei dy, ni wn i amcan oes iddo delyn ledr dan ei gronglwyd; beth meddwch? A waits arian hefyd, pan dalo pawb iw gilydd. "Good morrow, John, how d'ye," meddai rhyw hen gan ar y dôn a elwir the "Parson of the Parish." Dyna i chwi Gywydd y Bardd Coch. Gerwin o'r chwerthin a wneir am ei ben, mae'r hen ddyn wedi colli ei gellwair. Gwych a fyddai gweled nodau Goronwy ar y caniad yma; nag oes, nag oes dim eisiau mawr yn y Brynddu, ond etto er hyn ni welais i beil oddiyno ettwa, nhw a ddeuant yn y man. Ces lythyr y dydd arall i wrth ein hanwyl frawd ysêf, Owain Hwlant, ysgwier o Gonwy, yn diolch am y Gosodedigaethau ag yn deusyf arnaf drosglwyddo eu wasanaeth at y Gymdeithas, ac y mae yn erchi i mi dalu ei ffîs, sef yr hanner gini, mae'n debyg. Pan gaffwyf innau'r arian mi ai talaf i nhad ac felly ym mlaen. Mi dreiaf a gymer o un o'r llyfrau yma hefyd, ond gwaetha dim, nid hawdd cael arian o ddwylo yr boneddigion yma, ġwell deilio a masnachwr am filoedd na rhain am sylltau. Gwrda'r Brenin am wneuthur marchog o'm hen Gymydog Ellis Cunliffe,* bychan a wyddai Foster ei dad y byddai fab yn Syr pan oedd yn cadw siop y dydd a fu. **W. to R. contd.**

22nd.—Ces lythyr ddoe oddiwrth y Llew; 'rwyn deall fod yr Iuddew Brych ai gydwr wedi dodi barn; mae'n rhywyr clywed par sut a fydd, os nad yw allan o bob rheswm yn y byd, gwell i'r brawd smitio na dal allan, beth a dal gwingaw yn erbyn symbylau, nid hwyrach y gadawant iddo Ddyfi, nid lle iw daflu i fynnu mo hwnnw. Os Esgair yr Erfin a dry allan yn werth cantoedd pann fal y mae'n tybied, e wna'r ddau yn dda iawn, yr ofn mwya' sydd arnaf fi yr awron y blina Bowys yn ymgeintach ar bobl fawaidd accw o'r drysorfa, ac yr oera wrth y Llew, ac yno pwy a fydd ffrind a all ei gymorth? Neb ond Duw ei hun, ac yn wir nid yw ond gwagedd a ffolineb mawr hyderu ar neb arall. Ie, da chwithau, cedwch eich golwg ar yr afon yna, fal y galloch ganfod Iedw yn dyfod a thlysau Lloegr Newydd yn ei gaban, "rhan i mi," oedd y gair er's talm pan ddeuid i hyd i fottwm neu ystwmp. Gobeitho eich bod chwi a Meirian yn ymendiaw fwy fwy bob dydd. Rhaid im derfynu bellach i gael sgrifennu llinell at y brawd arall, Duw ai helpo, felly, byddwch iach a llawen. *Eich caredigawl frawd,*

Gwilym y Garddwr.

P.S.—Ni chaf mor amser yn fy myw i sgrifennu at y brawd arall heddyw, ac nid oes gennyf ddim iw ddywedyd ond a welwch i, anerchwch fi atto, mae wedi cael gwybod yr eithaf, mae'n debyg, bellach bydd rhywyr clywed.

HOLYHEAD, 26th June, 1756, Dydd Sadwrn.

Dear Brother Richard,—Mi sgrifenais yna wythnos i heddyw ac a yrrais ryw brygowthen. Nid oes gennyf fi i ddywedyd yr awron namyn fy mod yn lledfyw ac heb gaffael dim llythyr oddiyna er's dyddiau byd, a rheittiad yw eu teimlo er lles ir hegl ofidus yma. **W. to R. CCLXXXVII**

* Sir Ellis Cunliffe, son of Foster Cunliffe, a Liverpool merchant, was M.P. for Liverpool in 1755 and 1761. He was knighted in 1756 and created a baronet in 1759. He died in 1767. (Palmer, "History of the Thirteen Townships," etc., p. 173).

W. to R. contd.

Dyma fi yn gallu dyfod i lawr or glwyd, sef y llofft, lle bum yn gori un niwrnod ar ddeg heb symud oddiyno; mae'r esgair yn dipyn gwell, y briw yn dechreu tyfu yn dda iawn, ond er hynny yn dra gofidus! Mae'r chwaer yn helpio tippyn iw ymgeleddu. Dywedwch i'r Llew ddyfod o Ierwerth Geff yma ddechreu'r wythnos, a heddyw fe aeth yn ol tua Dulas mewn llong, a threnydd mae yn ei fryd fyned i Swydd Degeingl i geisio dillad; mae'r lleill wedi heneiddiaw, a chwedi aros yno ynghylch wythnos daw yn ei ol, oni ddaw hanes heddwch. Pe bai achos i sgrifennu atto yno, it might be directed to Cath. Lloyd, at Cornel y Cae Celyn in Whitford, to be left at the Post Office, Holywel. Mae'r dyn yn edrych fal rhyw anifail a fai wedi ei lygad tynnu, fe dyrr ei galon ar fyrder, mae'n debyg. Er cariad ar ddyn a oes dim newydd oddiwrth Fyng; ai cachgi ydyw yntau rhyfelwr pen sych mal ei dad? Gerwin y chwedlau sydd gan boblach yn ei gylch o, ai gwmni, nid oes bosibl na wyr y mawrion yna yr holl hanes. Am y gwerin nid wyfi yn ddeall y gwyr neb o rheini ddim o edrydd y llynges na pha beth sydd yn dyfod or Hen Flakeney efo'i Gaer. Aië prifio yn rhonwyn a wnaeth Siac ab y Doctor wedi yr holl drafferth a gawsoch efoge? Wala! wala! ni waeth tewi na siared mae rhyw ffolineb yn rhedeg yngwaed rhai pobl. Pa beth sydd yn dyfod or Bennant? Echdoe y derbyniais ei lyfr tra gwrthfawr, sef Lister's Conchyliology, er mawr leshad im archoll. Mi sgrifenaf at y gwr pan gaffwyf fy nghof am synwyr, ond prin y meddaf yr un or ddau yn awr gan ofid blin; os gwelwch gip o olwg arno mae fal yr anerchwch fi attaw. Ie, ac eisiau hanes yr Aldremon hefyd, mae rhan fwya o fonddics y wlad yn y gymdogaeth yma y dyddiau hyn yn dilyn priodas y Garreg Lwyd a Berw, ac ni choeliech i fyth fal y maent yn heidiaw o gwmpas Gwilym dlawd sydd yn ffaelio codi ar eu ddeudroed ol i wneuthur bow iddynt. Bu'r Arglwyddes Bwclai lawen ddigon yma ddoe yn pesgi ei golygon prydferth ar fy nghregin am ffosilod, etc., ac yn ceisio fy hudo i ddyfod ir Baronhill i weled ei phethau hithau. Virtuosa o'r wraig, a thyma un arall nis gad iddi, sef y Meistres Griffith ieuanc, or Garreg Lwyd, gwreigen fwyn gywraint ddigon. Roedd y nhad yn rhwydd iachus y dydd arall, ac yr ydym ni yma oll felly, mawl ir Goruchaf am ei drugareddau. Bydded iddo warchad drosoch bod ac un, ach cadw rhag pob drwg ag anffawd, felly y gweddia, ac felly y terfyna'r bystol yma. W. to R. contd.

Eich caredigawl frawd, Gwilym Dollgoes, neu Goes-dolly.

CAER GYBI, Dydd Sadwrn, Gorph 3dd, 1756.

Anwyl Frawd,—Wele yma yr eiddoch o'r 29, a diolch yn fawr am dano. Nag ydy', nag ydy' mor hegl yn cael mor cwarters mwy na phe bai goes yr Iuddew Brych, un o'r dynion casa dan haul. I have often thought that Providence might order this mischance to turn out for the good of my *limb*. Diau ei bod yn bygwth ffaelio ymhell o flaen y llall, a continual numbness o'r tu allan i'r forddwyd, the leg always too cold, chwydd ynghefn y troed y prydnhawn a gofid yn fynych o'r fawd hyd ochr y troed, a'r fawd agos heb ddim teimlad ynddi, and consequently a weakness in the foot, yr anhwylusdra yma, chwi allwch feddwl, a barai i friw mawr ar feinedd y grimmog fod yn un dychrynadwy ar y cyntaf. Ond i Dduw y b'or diolch, mae'r ofnad drosodd yn dda iawn, a phob peth yn dyfod ymlaen yn araf deg, the flux of humor a little abated. I have often experienced the efficacy of lint and brandy bâch (er fy mod yn gwawdio yn fy niweddaf), ac rwyf yn rhwymedig iddynt y tro yma, yn enwedig men's brandy. Nid oes dim ymgeledd iawn hebddo. Nid yw ond ffwl wrth tincture of myrrh. Dyna'r gwalch a fydd yn saethu pobl drwy eu calonau ac allan. Mi ai hadwen yn rhy dda. Ai tebyg wyf fi i'r Duc Cumberland? Mi glywais ddywedyd fod y Mrs. Wheldon yn fyw yn y pen draw i'r dref. Ni welais i moni er's llawer dydd: y hi'n glaf o'r fawdwst a minnau yn anafus or tu arall, ond hyn a wn i, that Barlow was an apothecary who fitted out Dr. Wheldon, who gave him a will and power, and he accounted fairly with the widow and paid the balance of the wages, and the son did what he could to find out the purser, etc., but in vain, so he returned the will and power, cloathes bill, etc., ac felly nid oes dim i ofni oddiyno nag o unlle. Mrs. Bayly of Deptford hath a power of Attorney to receive Mrs. Wheldon's pension, but she could do nought in the Cloath Bill affair, felly dyna'r ffordd yn rhydd os gellir cymwynas i'r druanes yma, da fydd, gadewch wybod par angenrheidiau sydd raid gaffael oddiyma. Wala! wfft, a chan dwbl wfft i'r Byng yna. Ni fedraf W. to L. CCLXXXVIII

W. to L. contd. fi gyffelybu mo Galision hîr ac yntau ond i ddau geiliog a fyddai yn dianc oddiar y pŷt, un ffordd yma a'r llall ffordd accw, rhwng traed pobl dan grôch weiddi, ni choelia i nad ceiliog y gelwyd y Ffreinsmon medd y papurau newydd. O ffei arnyn, chwedl gwraig Grono. Dyma lythyr oddiwrth Siac Owain, pawb yn iach yno, gadael tipyn o ddiddanwch! Roedd y nhad yn Llanerchmedd ddydd Mercher. Echdoe y daeth y Surveyor oddiyno, sef oi dy, gweiddi am eich hanes. Ierw yn cychwyn y dydd hwnw i Degeingl, dim ond hynny. Eich brawd ai goes yn merwino yn greulon dost. Duw gyda chwi eich deuwedd ac a'ch cadwo rhag pob drwg ac anffawd. Amen. *William Morris.*

Dyna i chwi ddarn arall o gowydd, nage o awdl, ac un neu ddau o byttiau. Oes yma ddifregwawd Taliesin (very incorrect) (ymddifregwawd medd llyfr arall). Ond y mae hen lyfr daroganau Bodhenlli, yr hwn a welais gyda chwi ymenthyg ddydd a fu, yn dywedyd yn niwedd y gerdd mae Jonas Athro y Fynyw, ai cant. Ac yn wir mae'r holl awdl o ben bwy gilydd yn sawrio yn dra chryf o Babyddiaeth yr oesoedd diweddar, ac mae ôl traed y mynach moel rhyd bob cwr o honi. Onid wyf fi yn camgymeryd mae'r copi ganddoch gartref rwyn credu. Par sut y gelwir y llong a'r meistr yr aeth Huwsiaid Cwyllog efo nhw? Mae Wil ab y Doctor yn myned ymlaen yn odiaeth yn nwylo fy anwyl gyfaill y Surgeon General, and he surprizes all the gentlemen of the Fac. Dyn trwyddo fal y doctor ei hun, socrell yr un lun ac yntau, un penddu ac nid gwinau fal Huwsiaid Cwyllog. Rhywogaeth Dol y Garreg yn eu nerth.

HOLYHEAD, 7th July, 1756.

W. to R. CCLXXXIX

A glywch i fy 'neidiau?—Dyma ddeubost neu dri wedi dyfod heb ddwyn dim llythyr oddiwrthych, ni wn i pa beth ai para, nid hwyrach fod rhywbeth ar droed, neu ar droad, yn y matterion dyrys yna. Gwych a fai gael diben arnaddynt, mae edau'r einioes yn mynd yn fyrrach bob dydd nau gilydd tra bobl yn dargysgu; ai nid oes dim modd i wthio swmbwl i din y llymdreiniawg yna? Y fo mae'n debyg yw tad y drwg. Gan na cha'r Gendal dlawd (am a welaf fi) ddim cyfiawnder gan Lwyd or Rhyfeldy, wedi ei holl addawiad. A ga fo wybod gennych a ddarfu ir Ffreins ddihenyddu ei frawd John Kendal, a sailor on board the *Defiance*, late came

Captain Andrews? It's presumed that a dead list is come into your office; mae'r dyn 'lawd yn bur anesmwyth eisiau gwybod. Perchen plant oedd Sion, ac ydyw os byw, a cholled a fydd am tano. Gadewch wybod per return of the post, a chwi a gewch dâl yn y drugaredd. Dim ond hynny, ond Duw a fyddo gyda chwi. W. to R. contd.

Eich caredigawl frawd, *William Morris.*

P.S.—Since I writ the above have a line from Ald. Prichard, writ at Coventry on his way to your City to manage some affairs of my friend Natus. Gerwin yr achwyn y mae'r Aldremon ei fod wedi ffaelio gweled y Caer Lewis when last in town, ond roedd o'n bwriadu y mynnai fo ei weled y tro yma er gwaetha'r Pab o Rufain. "Nid hwyrach iti gamgymeryd," ebr finnau, "oni threwi wrth ryw ddyn rhi-dwll mal ti dy hun." Os y chwi ai gwel o, mae fal y dywedwch wrtho gael ohonof ei lythyr, ac yr 'sgrifenaf atto yr post nesaf, os medraf gaffael ffrank yn unlle, ac yn rhodd. Annerchwch fi atto; diau ei fod yn cymeryd llawer o drafferth arno er mwyn y mab-ynghyfraith, llwyddiant i hwnnw yn erbyn y Gelyn Brych. Beth ganddoch chwi? Oni fum i ddoe wrth fy unffon yn y dollfa! Mawl i Dduw, mae'r hegl yn dyfod ym mlaen yn dda iawn. Byddwch iach! Dyma lonaid siwg o siamper wedi ei harlwy ar eich medr.—*W.M.*

HOLYHEAD, 19th July, 1756.

Dear Brother,—I have yours of the 3rd, etc., of the predt., ond ni attebwn monow yn fy myw, ac ni chaf ond yn unig amser i yrru i chwi y ddau bappir yma, ni yrrodd Barlow mo'r ap Robert yma ddim, dyna lythyr diweddaf y mab; os bydd raid cael y Probat nid rhaid ond dangos ei lythyr ei hun iddo. Ond os nis ceir mono nes sgrifennu atto (a phwy a wyr i ba le) ni fynnwn wneuthur clobyn o lythyr ir pwrpas. Ond yr achos y brys yma yw hyn: fy nhad ai gymydog, Mr. Ffoulk Jones, Pen Cerddor Cymru, a ddaeth im hymweled echdoe, a dyma nhwy yn myned adref heddy, fe ddaeth yr hen wr yma o Bentre'rianell heb dynny moi droed or wrthafl, ac y mae o, mawl ir Goruchaf, yn dra sionc yn ol ei oedran; mae gwroldeb yr hen Flakeney yn rhoddi yspryd newydd iddo, mae hwnw yn hŷn nag ê o 3 blwydd neu bedair. Da clywed fod gobaith ir Llew gael dyfod allan oddi dan y llengêl, poed buan y byddo hynny, mae yma lawer o gwyn iddaw. Dyma fi, mawl ir W. to R. CCXC

W. to R. contd.

Arglwydd, yn dechreu ymlwybran yn dda iawn, wedi bod yn yr Eglwys ddoe, heddyw yn e'ch fy ffrindiau yn dref yma gryn chwarter milltir o ffordd! Ni chaf m'om cof gan Ffoulkyn yn peraidd ganu fy ffidil i. O fwyned yr hen sidanen ar hen feillionen, etc. Aie fe ddaeth clawddiadau'r Arglwydd Esgob Bergen i Mr. Pennant, ê addawodd i mi ran o bob criglyn o naddynt, gyrrwch nhw iddo gynta galloch. Aie e ddaeth Iedw yntau yna, mae'r pethau gwrthfawr oeddych iw cael gydag efo? Mi drawaf atti hi i lenwi cist i chwi yn ddi ymattreg, y gorchwyl cynta fydd hwnw. Eisieu newydd oddiwrth Flakeney yn erwin dost, gobaith da meddynt. Yn ystwythach meddwch—byddaf, byddaf, obleit nid oes yma mo'm hanner na'm traian chwaith, pe bai iâch fy hegl mi redwn a chwi am y ddeu le. Pam na sgrifen yr Aldremon attaf? Gwych y Cymrodorion newydd yna. Mrs. Wheldon yn dymuno arnoch gymeryd tâl o ben yr arian am eich trafferth, nid oes gan Farlow ddim i ddywedyd wrthi nai heiddo. He paid (that is his father paid her) a large ballance, above forty pounds; rhaid atteb yr relyw or llythyr tro nesaf. Mae nhad yn anfon ei fendith i chwi eich deuwedd. Duw a fo gyda chwi, a byddwch iach.

Eich brawd hergloff, *William Morris.*

Dyma fi wedi rhoddi'r gwyr ar gefnau eu meirch ac yn rhywyr selio hwn cyn ir bost fyned i bant. Do, mi ge's lythyr y brawd echdoe, arall iwrth Ellis y Cwrel, arall iwrth Agrippa—4 yr un post!

L. to Mrs. M. CCXCI

[LONDON,] July 31, 1756.

My Dear,—I have yours of ye 24th, which gave me great pleasure to hear of your good health and the children. As for my letting you know anything about my affairs, it is impossible as yet, though I expect I can pretty soon, and God only knows how things stand. However, I would have you go on the same as you did, makeing all the improvements you can at Penbryn as if you were going to live there immediately, for that may happen. You may lime some small matter there, but not as if we were on a certainty. If Robert Lance pleases to send his son to Aberdovey for a week or a fortnight to attend the Custom House upon trial, that Griffiths and Mr. Morgans may see his capacity, I shall afterwards let them know whether I like him, or have any employment for him, and in the mean time give you his father the bit of paper that is in this letter, for him to answer, that I may see how he writes. When Jane's bill comes to my brother's hands I shall give him orders to pay Jones what money the corn comes to, but the master of the ship should attend my brother with the account. I know nothing at all of Paynter nor where he lives, and I cannot find that any of my acquaintance do. The ale is the finest you ever saw, the sea hath workd it so, that I never saw such in Cardiganshire; one pint of it is as strong as two of London beer, which is all the fault of it. I have orderd the other cask up if any vessel comes soon. I am surprizd at John Owen he doth not send me the franks as I desired, I was obligd to borrow this. God bless you and the children. *I am, your affectionate husband, L.M.*

L. to Mrs. M. contd.

CAER GYBI, Awst 12fed, 1756.

W. to R. CCXCII

F'anwyl Frawd Rhisiart,—Mae'n afraid imi draethu i chwi, na fagodd gwraig, ag ni chwythodd a bochau croen erioed neb tu hwnt i'ch brawd Gwilym am gyfattebu, am hynny ynteu, llymma fo yn eistedd i lawr o ddifrif calon i atteb yr eiddoch or 31 ult, ar 3ydd o'r presennol. Odiaeth yw clywed fod gobaith i'r weddw fusgrell yma gael yr eiddo cyfiawn. Da ydyw eich gwaith yn cynorthwyo'r cyfryw. Aie fe orphennodd y Bardd Ganniad Arglwydd Llwydlo—glo llwyd oeddyd yn ei gael yn y fan, ond e? Yntau oddiwrth y llyfon oeddid yn ei gymeryd yn y cwrt hwnw pan oedd y Cymru cneccys yn ymgyfreithiaw au gilydd, e wyr y Llew mae'n debyg. Wfft i'r mawrion rheini sydd yn ymgribo a'u gilydd yn lle meddwl am amddiffyn y deyrnas ai pherthynasau, gwaeth na chwiw ladron, ond ê? Os argrephir y Caniad fe ga Wilym, ond odid olwg maes arnaw, ond os ni wneir, yn iach ymenyn glan. Mae'r Llew yn sôn am ryw Gywydd o'r eiddo Grono i'r Bardd Coch ac i Wlad Fon, ni wn i ai "Mal Seion yw Mon i mi" mae yn ei feddwl ai peidio, os nid ê, pa beth a wnawn am ei weled? Yn pysgotta mae o. Gwastrawd y Bath meddwch o gwmpas Northolt. Fe fyddai fo yn derbyn ystym weithiau, ond nid oes yr arw hon (yr awr hon oeddwn yn ei geisiaw ddywedyd) neb a saif ar adwy galed; wrth hyn y gellir gweled yn eglur ddigon fod yr hyn y mae Mr. Ellis a'r offeiriadau yn ei ddywedyd yn rhy wir,—sef bod y byd yn myned waeth waeth beunydd. Rhad Duw ar waith y Daliarys os Cymru y mae yn ei foldiaw, ni welais

W. to R. contd.

un amser wr bonheddig or Deheudir mwy Cymreigiawl nag ydoedd, ond odid i fodloni'r Hen Geiliawg,* ac y bydd Seisnigaidd ddigon bellach, beth meddwch? Gwae finneu na bai yma hanner dwsing o bob rhywogaeth o'r cregyn a ddug Iorwerth o Siamaica; aligators, etc., sydd yn y botel, ond ê? Rhwydd-deb ir ddau Gwyllog pennau chwiban, nid felly mo Wil Duflun, Dôl y Garrog yn ei nerth o hwnnw. Fal hyn yr 'sgrifennodd fy anwyl gyfaill, y Surgeon General, attaf y dydd arall gyda chår iddo o New York oedd yn dyfod yna i geisiaw man o' war iw gludo adre: "Evans goes on extremely well, and I hope will do us all honour. I wish every good thing for Anglesey," etc. Gwrda'r hen wr bonheddig, hanner Cymro ydyw, ac o Gaerlleon y mae'n dyfod. Nid hwyrach fod coel ar y Dr. Cadwaladr, ni choeliai fod fawr ar y Doctor Sion. Rhwydd-deb hefyd i Iedw ap Rhisiart ab Iedw a buan y caffo herwlong dan ei droed i ymddial ar Ffrancod. Wawch, a dwbl wawch! Dyma fi newydd fod yn croesawu my brother virtuoso the Bishop of Ossory, sydd newydd ddyfod ir lan o'r llong bost, a rhaid o myned i ginhiewa efo'r Arglwydd yn y man, ac yna mae o i ddyfod yma i edrych dros fy ngholecsiwn, h.y., fy nghasgliad i o ffosilod a chregyn, etc., mal y gallo weled fal yr amlhaodd er pan fu yma ddiweddaf. Fo geir ganddo ddigon o sir, ond i wenwyn un ffosil a gair ganddo, fe addawodd yn deg imi ryfeddodau y tro or blaen, ond fo anghofiws. Yn awr af ymlaen: diolch am hanes yr Aldremon, anerchwch fi atto yn rhodd. Gwych a fai glywed ei fod wedi gwneuthur matter 'Natws yn draeth, poed felly y byddo. Gyrrwch yma un o'r petisiwnau mewn ffrenkyn, da chwithau. Aie yna y mae'r Prydydd Hir? Mae arnaf eisiau atteb ei lythyr a ges er's gwell na blwyddyn am a wn i. Par sud y llwybreiddir atto? Duw a gadwo'r gwr yma rhag bod yn ail i Syr Walter oddieithr mewn dysg a dawn. Wala! gwnaed 'Natws yntau baderau ir Blewmoniaid drwy nad elont yn Bapistiad bod y pengyrch. Gwell a fyddai iddo fo druan ddysgu gwneuthur hunan service na national service, ar yr ôl y bydd y rhai gan mwyaf a wnelo'r diweddaf. Taled yr Arglwydd i chwi dros Gendal, par un bynnag ai ffynnu a wna'ch gwaith ai peidiaw; ffei arno'r Lwyd na chywira ei air. Aie torri'ch

*D. Jones Gwynn, of Taliaris, in Carmarthenshire, married Ann, the only daughter of William Vaughan, of Corsygedol, on July 6, 1756.

gwynt a wnaethoch, ni thelwch i ynta ddim i redeg, nofiaw, nag i ymafael, ond dedwydd fod y llaw ddeheu yn ddiffawt i drin aden yr wydd, dedwydd i chwi ac i minnau. Mae'r *Hopewell* hono wedi myned tua Milfordd, a Will Owen ynddi, darpar ei frawd ynghyfraith o'r Sion Roberts hwnnw, half owner, na bo'nd i grybwyll! Pa beth ydych ar fedr wneuthur i'r Llychlyniaid yna? Ond gwell a fydda eu dal a rhoddi yng ngwarchae? Nid oes bosibl y dianc y Fing yna heb ei ddihenyddu, os felly, ffarwel gyd a ni. Hawdd ammor i'r Aberystwythion a ddychrynnodd Sion Ffrainc. Nid oes yma a roech i yn eich llygad o newydd; mae'n rhywyr i mi ddechreu rhoddi fy nhlysau mewn trefn erbyn y prydnhawn, rhag i'm Harglwydd Esgob fy nwrdiaw. Na feddyliwch i fy mod yn gollwng yn angof gist y Cymrodorion; o, nag ydwyf, nhw gant y cyfryw halsiad o gregyn, etc., na welwyd ermoed mo'u bath yn Llundain nag yn Llanrwst. Dyma fi yn arofyn paccio cistiaid arall i fynd im hanwyl gyfaill *il Princepe di Biscari* o Sisilia draw, a da yr haeddai yr Tywysog beth o bob peth a llawer o bob un. Annerchwch fi at y Llew; fe gai owdyl neu ddwy pe bai ffranc im perchen, ond nid oes; ond er hynny mi atebaf ei lythyr cyn pen nemawr o byst. Duw a fyddo yn goruchwiliaw droswch eich deuwedd. **W. to R. contd.**

Y fi yw'r trydydd brawd, *Gwilym Ogloff.*

August 17th, 1756.

Dear Brother,—Digon o waith a gefais i sgrifennu'r cywydd atteb i Huw Goch,† ond gan fod arnoch ei flys, dyna fo. Mae pethau godidog tua i ddiwedd, a dyna ffranc i chwi i yrru hen bobl‡ yn ei le ef. Fe ddygodd y Cywydd yna lawer o hen eiriau oddiar y Dictionary. A dyma fi ymmron cysgu uwch ben fy mhappir, newydd fwytta nghinio yn drwmbluog iawn, a hitheu'n glawio'n drwm dros ben; gwae'r gweiriau, a dedwydd y sawl sy ganddo wely i fynd arno i gysgu. Now my eyes are open, three times I attempted to write ye above line and three times failed, and the pen scratchd the paper, etc., so adieu. *Eich brawd, Llewelyn.* **L. to W.** CCXCIII

†This refers to the "Cywydd" written by Goronwy Owen to Hugh Hughes (y Bardd Coch). It is sometimes called "Molawd Mon," see "Barddoniaeth Goronwy Owen," Liverpool 1896, p. 104.

‡h.y. hen gywyddau.

L. to W.
CCXCIV

LONDON, August 28, 1756.

Anwyl Frawd,—I have yours of ye 20th, and am glad to find you in such spirits, and I thank you for ye piece of caniad i H.O.G.*—a most curious piece!—excessive dark and deep. There is an affected grandeur and a . . .rk of great knowledge in ye language through the whole. I can compare it to nothing but the language of Milton's "Paradise Lost." It is so far above ye common stile of other writers. There is an uncommon force in ye words of Cynddelw and in some other writers of that age. What caused it but ye spirit of war, of learning, of liberty, breathing forth in that critical time? *Canniad* is certainly ye root of *Caniadhau*, and you may find many roots that Dr. Davies knew nothing of. The cabinett I have making for Lord Powys is no more than *Drôrs y Sioppwrs* Sir Fon. It is three foot high, two foot long, and eighteen inch thick towards ye wall. . . . . iding on a frame of two foot, two drawers of three inches, one of two and half, four of a inch, ... of an inch and a half, without any partitions. The drawers running in grooves in ye sides. It costs four guineas. Dyna'r cwbl. The ores are to be all numbered with a small paper pasted on them, big enough to receive the figures of ye numbers in each drawer, thus 15. The drawers to be letterd on their fronts A. B. C. D., etc. Then if ye ore or other fossil be too small for to fix a paper on, the paper (or card boat) it is in is to be numberd. Some of ye virtuoso's have small deal boxes to hold their sands, etc., but I think *card boats* better. I have seen several great collections, but have never seen among them all any curious contrivance to keep their ores from confusion. When the ores, shells, etc., are markd and numberd, then a book is made for that cabinet, giving an account of ye matter under such a number. That is, I intend such a book for Lord Powys who hardly knows one of y^m, but I never met with one collector of fossils yet that had such a book, and but only a bit of paper, sent them with some small parcells and the rest without order or knowledge; and sometimes they did not know their own things. I met one time with a piece of fossil gold worth five or six guineas among ye raritys of a very curious man,

* Probably Hywel ap Owen Gwynedd, to whom Cynddelw wrote a poem.

which he had always taken for some mere mineral. There is also a chance of confounding drawer A and B together in this kind of distribution. You see by ye papers I suppose that Fortunatus's vessel is taken from him by ye Government of Leghorn. French power. Some hints in to-day's paper of a battle between Hawke and ye French; not confirmed. In a small battle we got ye better in America. Ned Edwards knows ye officer. He sails in a few days, broliwr a dwndriwr fal tonnau'r môr. Alderman Prichard is gone home. I would advise you to write to a friend in Liverpoole to enquire of Reese Jones, ye hosier that broke there lately, whether he hath your *Telyn Ledr*. Gronwy says he left it and all his books with that man to be sent after him, but did not owe him a penny, but I am sure he pawnd them, a needy man will lie confoundedly. Nid oes ond y celwydd yn ei ddal wrth ei gilydd, fal rhai eraill [adwaenaf fi] a chwitheu, yn barod eu hesgusion geuog i safio'r wyneb rhag c[ywilydd.] Nid yw hi ond siawns fawr i chwi byth weled eich llyfr, ond dyna'r . . . . i chwi gael ei hanes bid a fynno. O'm fy materion i yr un fa . . . . er pan sgrifennais ddiweddaf. Fe dyng y Castell Newydd na wyr ef ddim oddiwrth fy hel i o Ddyfi, ond mae gwaith pobl eraill oedd; but he dare not a . . . . refuse the Jacobites any thing they ask—an old mortal, without bottom [or] solidity. I know they'll carry their spight against me to ye utmost, and [he] hath neither courage nor honesty to stop them, but there will come a time soon that the scenes will be changd. Last Thursday the people of London shewd a spirit on Tower Hill, i.e. raised a devil which will not be easily laid. About a thousand people met, and there upon a high gibbett hang'd ye effigy of Admiral Byng, dressed in ye naval uniform, and his face painted to ye life—shot at him, etc., and at last burnt [him]. This was done against ye Lord Mayor's door, and shews ye nature of ye people; a small matter will drive them to extreams. Nid oes yma ffranc iw gael, ond mae digon yn Ngallt Vadog, ond bod eisiau synwyr yno iw gyrru, nid oes dim ysywaeth. Next Saturday I shall begin to put ye fossils in ye drawers, please God to give me leave, and it would be an . . . . thing to have some of your collection to adorn it. [*Lewis Morris.*]

L. to W. contd.

LONDON, September 6th, 1756.

L. to W. CCXCV Anwyl Frawd,—I have yours of ye 30 August, with darn o farwnad Ywein. Ardderchog oedd y . . . .r a gwych y canwyd iddo! A gwrda'r Bardd Coch; dyma'r peth goreu a ganodd ef erioed.* There is humor and sense in it, and a sharp sting not to be often met with in *Barddoniaeth y Dispyddaid.* "By gad, I'd rather be gon," is infinitely the best of ye three. Mend another line, "rhyw ddynion di-ddaioni" . . . . another r. Llawer Byng sy'n llywio'r byd. Llwyddiant i Farged Owain, rhaid i bob ceg gael bwyd. Colledion mawrion sy yma ar ydau. Hi wnaeth heddyw'r glaw trymaf ar ellai fod, ar ol wythnos o degwch. Those that were industrious have saved some. Pwy briododd Emrys Lewis pan allo fo ddal i ryfel i'r Brysgaw? Aie rhyfel Cybi hefyd? Gwyddelod a fyddai chwannog o ennill y fan yna, ai tybied nad Boadicea and her Irish auxiliaries will carry ye day; os chwi yn unig a ddiangodd, mae'n debyg fod maes gwedi bôd. Cedwch eich bysedd or . . . . affaith ag iach a fyddwch. As for ye cabinet, which you say is dear, I [think] it is ye cheapest of ye kind that hath been made here. My brother's acquaintance would not make it under five guineas; others askd six, seven, eight and even fifteen guineas! Ten guineas is very common to give for such, but that have double bottoms, etc. [I dont] take this to be dear; it is a pretty piece of furniture, and if I am ever master of my self, I'll have one made in ye country, which will [be] cheap there when made by my directions. If there are spare drawers they serve to keep papers, instruments, etc., [and are] more convenient than deep drawers where things are heapd. Rwy'n ofni am Ronwy ei fod yn cael ei droi allan oi offeiriadaeth, mi glowaf fod ei benaeth yn achwyn, medd'dod neu redeg mewn dyled i'r wlad neu ryw ddiawl. Dyna lle bydd o'n ymgrogi neu ryw ddiben drwg mae'n debyg, os bydd beirdd yn gwneuthur eu diwedd eu hunain. Na fyddant a goeliai, maent yn dlodion bob amser, felly nid oes dim chwithdod bod ar herwr. Da iawn os yw Edward yn gwadu'r cwrw, ond ni choeliai byth nes gweled—ni welais i feddwyn fawr erioed yn ymendio. Maent yn dywedyd yma fod yr hen wr yn mynd i newid

* This refers to the "Cywydd Galarnad am Ynys Minorca," written by the Bardd Coch, see "Dewisol Ganiadau," 1759, p. 79.

ei holl weision; na atto Duw chwedl amgen. Clowais heddyw hefyd o Alltvadog, ag mae pob peth yno fal o'r blaen, mae'r wraig yn dywedyd ei bod yn meddwl nad oes llai na gwerth can punt o farlis Ymhenbryn os ceir cynhaiaf da arno, dyna beth na bu yno erioed o'r blaen. Och na chawn fynd i fwytta ag yfed peth o hono. I have sorted all the fossils that I had here and put them in card [boats], and they make a noble shew. I have also some sea plants, corallines, which I have put in ye same kind of card-boats, and shall put a piece of glass over each, which will keep them down, and if I can contrive to fasten ye glass it will be better. But I have neither books nor .... to mind those things, and they shall be by way of Welsh raritys, and perhaps some kind of Welsh names given them, if I can coin any to ye purpose. Remember I have four different kind of boats which stow together very regular, I have not borrowd this from any body, though perhaps others have them.

L. to W. contd.

Cards are bought here (and you may buy them in Dublin) at 4½d. and 6d. a [pound] taking two pound together. I don't know what the fancy of that is. They are such as have some small blemishes, not fit to be put in ye packs. My first boat is a whole card. I draw four lines with a sharp point for ye margin, and then a sharp line from ye corners of lines to ye corners of ye card, then it will fold up to ye shape I want. The second kind is a card cut through the middle along the length, which will make two for long things. The third kind is made by cutting ye card athwart. The fourth kind is made by cutting ye third kind lengthways, which is small enough to [hold] ye smallest sample of ore or shells. Perhaps I tell you no news in all .... things, for necessity is ye mother of invention. Then the ores are .... with numberd papers, or if sands, etc., ye boat is numberd. A bit of ye Monachdy marble and wool would be welcome, and of ye white, black and gray Anglesey marble or other stones that have names. I have several kinds of spar .... most kinds of lead ores, some copper ores, I want some of ye Wicklow and .... Irish copper ores—and of ye Irish iron ore rich in silver. You may throw a handful of different kinds of sea plants, very small samples will do. I have not above a dozen kinds of sea plants, which I had thrown among some shells gatherd on ye beach at Aberdyfi. Here is Tuesday come and very busy, so

L. to W. contd.

have no time to add, but beg you would hasten ye fossils as soon as possible, and mention in a letter that they are for Lord Powys' cabinet, or else they will be claimd by ye Cymrodorion, who neither can, nor will, make any use of them. They shall have what is to spare, as I have now here what would fit up several cabinets all left to them. Direct ye box to Mr. Richard Morris of ye Navy Office, London, to be left at ye Inn till called for.

[*Lewis Morris.*]

LONDON, September 20, 1756.

L. to W. CCXCVI

Anwyl Frawd,—Yours of ye 14th I have with Cynddelw and Prydydd y Moch; roedd gan y *moch* well prydydd y dyddiau hynny nag a fu gan *ddynion* byth gwedi hynny; he is a sound solid writer. Well done Emrys a Deikyn, they are plagues sent for the people's sins. When you make a cabinet for shells or ores, if you make one as I would for myself, let it be about three and half foot high on a stand; let it be two foot six inches wide, and let there be a partition in ye middle up and down so that the length of ye drawers will be about fourteen inches, and one ring in ye middle to pull them out, for one hand holds ye candle or something else, and two rings are troublesome. Let it have also two folding doors; but if you have large shells, etc., you may make your large drawers quite to ye ground. Two large drawers will be unhandy and heavy, so short drawers are best, and your case will be stronger. This cabinet of Lord Powys looks very well but I find inconveniency in it. I used the same card boat with yours at first, but I found it very troublesome—they lay so close together that I could not take out one without disturbing all ye rest, but in my new method you may take anyone out between your finger and thumb, which will save peoples' pokeing their noses into your drawer; and if you have some curiosity that you would not have finger'd, you should have glasses over ye face of ye boat, which is easily fastend with a bit of wax. I have got glasses for several in this cabinet, I pay sixpence ye dozen for them: so much for the cabinet. Gresyn na ddoe'r pethau yma mewn amser; beth bynnag ydynt, os oes e . . . . caledion arnynt, they'll cut a great figure in a nobleman's house The Bishop of Pontopidan, Prince of Piscari, etc., are the collectors for this cabinet! Who would not be in their company?

. . . . Ffarwel i'r Delyn Ledr, mae'n debyg, oni chewch gan ryw un yn Nerpwl ei dal. . . . . oedd chwilcath hen, aie, now at Dover? Wele hai; mae'n barod i . . . . Holant neu rywle felly. [Nawdd] Duw rhag y tacclu dynion yr ydych, oes dim i'w gael am hynny ond y glod, a Huw'ch catto? Mi gefais inneu gynt ddigon o hynny, ond pei doe Bawl yr Apostol neu Archesgob Caergaint neu'r Pab o Rhufain attafi y rwan, ni thrwssiwn i goes un o honynt heb dâl am y mhoen, oblegid ni wnan nhwythau un gymwynas i minnau am ddim. Mi glywaf hefyd o Lanerch-y-medd [Mediolanum] fod y nhad yn well, ... medd R.P. wrth fy mrawd, rhyw *ysleccod* oedd arno. See Dr. Davies. . . . . *ysleccod* arnafinneu'r dyddiau ymma, bwytta ag yfed gormod a pheidio ysgwyd . . . . glo ai perai, violent reachings, etc. Peswch y fygydfa, etc. [An] account from home that I have got in my *bara lys* etc., and that people [die] there fast of a fever. I have nothing more to say this post but that I am *Your affectionate brother*, *Llewelyn*. L. to W. contd.

LONDON, September 25, 1756.

Dear Brother,—This tells you I had no letter from you last post. Bysedd pwy eill ddal meddwch 'ithe i sgrifennu drwy'r amser. Did I tell you that I had begun a translation of Tyssilio out of ye Welsh into the English? Ni welais i beth digrifach erioed, very much like the Eastern stile of ye Jewish prophets, etc.—odd repetitions and forms of speaking not used by modern polite tongues. A hundred to one that I shall ever finish it, for it is (with the notes) ye work of a year. Who knows but I shall go again to Wales Deheuberthig. Dyma'r Arglwydd gwedi sgrifennu attaf fod pob peth yn mynd ymlaen o'r goreu; and I find Smedley came to town a few days ago by ye direction *of D——l y Drysorfa*, dyn cethin, a elwir *Tingaled* alias *Hard din ge*, gwr poeth iawn yn erbyn ein pobl ni. Ond fal y mynnodd Duw, daccw fo'n (Smedley) mynd adre' ai fys yn ei gêg, ag yn dywedyd na wnaed ffwl o neb cymmaint ag efe. Fe gynnygiodd forty shillings y dunell o *dduty*, ond fe glywodd mae Arglwydd Powys ai cae, cynnygied a fynno, felly nos dawch. Townsend ynte'r dyn a fagwyd yn uffern, ag un o ieir y fall a orodd arno [yn y] tân—a gynnygiodd ddau cymmaint ag a dalai'r peth, ond fal y mynnodd d——l he was too light in the scales against Lord Powys though he had another member to L. to W. CCXCVII

L. to W. contd.

be partner with him (Vaughan of Crosswood), and it seems he could not give proper security. However, Smedley has been a complaining to a friend of his that no body has any chance with Lord Powys for that he insisted upon having it, and he could lead y^e^ *morthwyl* mawr as he pleasd. Pa fath wr ydyw'r Arglwydd hwnnw (meddai'r adroddwr wrth fy llattai i) sydd yn gyrru pob peth oi flaen? So thus stand affairs at present. Rwyf finneu'n gweithio ddydd a nos ar y cregin a'r mwyn, a gwaith caled ydyw; yn enwedig y boen o wneuthur y *card boats*. Ugain mewn ugain munud ydyw'r eithaf a allaf i wneuthur o honynt a gweithio fy ngorau hyd na bwy'n chwysu. The cabinet looks charmingly, and it is in far better order than any thing of the kind I ever saw among ye virtuosos. But now experience shews me that if I make one for my self, it must be four times as large as this, and drawers to ye ground, or rather two of ye do . . . . of this, for I have almost filld this with the few things I and my brother had. Lister's great book is also wanted, where was it printed? What will it cost, if to be had? The contents of this cabinet is as follows, and I suppose you have but a few things more to put in it. The drawers are letterd from ye top:—*a*, Aberdovey sea plants, with glasses over ye card boats; *b*, copper ores from different parts of ye world; *c*, sea shells from Aberdovey; *d*, seeds of trees, plants, etc., from Jamaica; *f*, *g*, *h*, *i*, shells from Jamaica and Portmahon; *e*, iron ores, ambers, ambergrease; *k*, empty; *l*, petrifactions and fossil shells from Sicily, Portmahon, Norway, Wales, England; *m*, several native sulphurs, productions of Mount Etna, and coals of different countrys; *n*, earths, boles, stones, sands, from different parts of ye world; *o*, lapis calam. or ores of zink, a great variety; *p*, lead ores: blue, of all ye various kinds; green; white, a great variety and transparent; *q*, various spars, several with ores mixt, of lead, copper, tin; chrystals, selenites, belemnites, talc, etc.; *r*, a few large fossil shells from Mahone, etc.; *s*, *t*, empty. *Dyna hanes y cabinet*. The shells, seeds and sea plants are to amuse ye Countess of Powys, the ores for ye edification of his Lordship. I am certain no cabinet in London can shew such a collection of lead ores, for that is my trade, and the spars are concomitants, being part of ye vein stone. Perhaps my next letter may bring you some account of my own affairs, which are not to my liking, till I see how things turn out. I am not well in health—want of exercise, henaint, anhunedd, give me great trouble, and it will be hard upon me if I dont get to ye mountains before the depth of winter. I send a *tudded* for another awdl os yw iw chael. *Eich brawd llwyd, L.M.* L. to W. contd.

CAER GYBI YM MON, Hydref 2d, 1756. W. to R. and L. CCXCVIII

Anwyl Frodyr,—Llyma i'r hynaf liaws o englynion ac awdlau o waith amryw ueirt godidawc ddigawn yn y hamseroet gynt amgen Kyndelw brydyd uawr; Llywarch brydyt y moch, etc., ny chaf nemmawr o amser y ysgriuennu yr awron y can drafferth ac aghymmendawd, uelly, ni waeth roti y swyt y uynu no pheidyaw. Wb! wb! Daccw yr karn lleidyr y can Sion Ffranc wedy dala uy anwyl gyuaillt y Cadpen Tomos Fwg, yr hwn a uuasai yn yr Afric a yr Americ yn olrhein kregyn a ffosilod, a phop math ar ryuetodeu i mi, a dyna bryuet hir o ynys y Garn (ys ef yw hono Guernsey yn yr ieith Saesonaec) wedy eu heil gymeryd. Dyfod yr yttoet y Domas o Siamaica a llwyth o siwgyr, etc., heblaw kregyn. Wala! wala! nyd oes onyd ceisyaw ymuodloni. Duw a uyto gyd a chwi, bytwch yach, mi yttwyf, *Eich caredigawl frawd, Gwilym.*

P.S.—*The James and John*, Henry Brown, Master, laden with sugar, etc., arrived here yesterday from Jamaica, met nothing at sea. Huw Jones, alias Huw'r Cwn, wedi marw heddyw; yr hen wraig o Ben'r Orsedd wedi ei chladdu echdoe, y slwp a'r cregyn yn barod agos i hwyliaw; dolur o'm pen o herwydd bod dryghin ar ddyfod; pobl y dref wedi mynd i gyd i Ffair Fathew Llanerch-medd; fy neugyw i yn darparu mynd i Bentrerianell i ymweled a deida, bydd yno gymaint o fwstr ac yn Byfleet. Dim sgadan phirfai yn y cyrrau yma. Haid fawr o ryw bysgod yn maeau Carnarvon; herring hogs medd rhai, bottle noses medd eraill, a sort of young whales medd y trydydd. Maent o 20 i 30 troedfedd o hyd, trwyn ysmwt, a llygaid yn ei yml. They've taken about a dozen of them. Pethau mawfaeth ydynt, mae dialedd o eisiau eu lluniau.

CAER GYBI, 4 October, 1756.

Anwyl Frawd y Llywydd Llwyd,—Dyma i chwi bwt o atteb ir eiddoch or 18 ult., ac fal hyn mae y matter yn sefyll: Chwi welsoch eisioes ddyfod o'ch llythyr im llaw i; oni bai hynny, ni buaswn yn W. to R. CCXCIX

W. to R. contd.

atteb mono, am hynny ynteu mi wn o'r goreu nad gweddus gwamalrhwydd i hynafgwr, ac na ddigymydd y fath saig a chylla gwr sydd wedi fal pettai swrffedu ar ddarllain a sgrifennu, o herwydd paham rhaid imi ddywedyd fy stori ar fyr o eiriau. Gwych gweled dan eich llaw eich hun eich bod yn bolliach, poed hir y bo'ch yn mwynhau'r fendith hono; os clywch fod Mr. Peswch yn curo yr drws na agorwch iddo am bris yn y byd, ac na roddwch gyfleu iddo eich dala y rhwng cynfasu lleithion, etc., o ran mae o bob amser ar ei fantais. Meddyg sydd yn eich cynghori. Dyma lythyr heddyw o'r Blymwth yn ceisio taeru fod y Will Williams hwnnw yn fyw, ond celwydd bod y gair mae'n debyg; par sut y deuai'r dyn yn fyw ac ynteu wedi ei fwrw i'r mor mewn amdo a phwysa wrtho, oddigerth i ryw forfil ei lyncu a chynesu ohono yn ei geudawd, ac felly adfywio a chael ei fwrw ar y lan mal Ionas gynt? Ond ni choeliodd Domas Prisiart y fawr mor stori hono erioed, esamiwch eich llyfrau i e'ch a fydd pobl yn dianc i foliau milod môr or main i wars. Pe bawn i fal chwi, mi yrrwn bapurau Mosson iddo fo, a thrined hwynt fal y mynno, oni chewch rywbeth oddiwrthynt, mi dybiwn wrtho ei fod yn meddwl bod yr arian wedi eu talu, neu bod rhyw esgeulusdra yn y peth. Da chwithau am helcyd yn y Cloaths Bill, mae pawb yn fodlon; a da y dylent fod, onde rwan? Om rhan inneu mi ges lawer o drafferth ermoed hyd yn heddyw yn trin materion pobyl eraill, ni welai i fawr neb a dâl y pwyth yn ol, ond am danom ni'n hunain mae rhywbeth megys dyled arnom gymmorth naill y llall; mae er hynny rai o honom yn fwy bydol nau gilydd, a rheini weithiau yn fwy ar yr ol na neb. Trefn ddrwg a fasai ar y Llew oni bai chwi yn ddiameu, ni wn i a gofia os digwydd cael cyfodiad, ond os ir gwrthwyneb nid oes ond maddeu iddo. Oni chaf 'inneu ddim rhan o deganau Sion ab y Doctor? Diau yr haeddwn rai pei gwyddai Sionach y cwbyl. Ar feinioes i mae'n rhywyr gennyf glywed rhywbeth ynghylch Goronwy drwstan offeiriad; gwae ni na bai'r wraig yn New York neu rhywle lle mae eisiau gwragedd i fanu. Nid oes bosibl nad oes wmbwrdd o gregyn am ddau bystol; gwyn ei fyd a fai ganddaw un gragen o bob math. Mae gennyf lawer o rai Siamaica, ond gwae fi am gynhulliad y Captain Ffoulkes, dyn cywrain o hwnnw a llygaid yn ei ben, a wêl bob rhyfeddodau ou amgylch, daccw nhw wedi ei ddwyn yn garcharor i Ffrainc. Mae'r slwp yma oedd i garrio'r cregyn i Gaerlleon yn aros am brotecsiwn, roedd rhyw Domos Jones yw anfon. Roedd y nhad yn Ffair Llanerchmedd dydd Sadwrn, felly mae o yn prifiaw well well ar ei iechyd; ni busai yno er's talm byd o'r blaen. Duw hefyd a gadwo Frenin Prwsia ai luoedd, onide can ffarwel. Newydd drwg o Oswego, mae'r Freins yn rhy drech i ni o hyd, bostiwn a fynnom. Mae hi ymma yn dywydd creulon. Ym'hle mae tês Mihangel? Duw Goruchaf a fyddo'n gwarchad drosoch; annerchwch fi at y Llew yna a byddwch eich deuwedd iach. *Eich caredigawl frawd,* W. to R. contd.

William Morris.

P.S.—Par ddelw sydd ar Feirian?

CUSTOM HOUSE, HOLYHEAD, October 7, 1756.

Fy Mrawd Rhisiart, Lywydd Mynglwyd,—Mi wna'n dda y byddwch yn diflasu ar fy llythyr i sydd yn dyfod attoch fal hyn pob post, ond pwy eill help pan fo'r esgyd yn gwasgu? Oni ddywedais i chwi naill ai ddoe neu echdoe, neu ychydig cyn hynny, fod yma ryw ddyn yn myned i Afon Gaer a box o gregyn, etc., ir Cymrodorion yn Llundain, Duw a'u cadwo, a bod yr hurthen wedi anfon at ei gefnder Tomos Dsiôns, a tide-waiter in London, that lives on Tower Hill, to procure him a *protection* for his sloop the *Hopewel* of Holyhead, Hugh Davies, Master, burthen thirty tons; two men besides himself, in the coal and coasting trade. Now what is to be done? The man cannot budge from hence without it, for no hands will go with him. Perhaps it may be in vain to inquire in the Admiralty Office if such protection be taken out, for the man doth not remember exactly what tonnage he mentioned, nor where he said his sloop belonged to, and how could he, indeed, when the man was on the point of marrying one of our Holyhead nymphs, in whose option it is to station the ship? But the *Hopewel*, Hugh Davies, Master, is still right. Perhaps you may be acquainted with your neighbour, Tom Jones, on Tower Hill. Mi adwaenwn inneu Sion y Gôf o Nefyn y Pysgod, if so, you can know of him if he hath taen out a protect. Otherwise you may procure one from the office. Fe dâl yr Huw Dafydd i minneu y chweigain. Er carriad ar ddyn na esgeuluswch mo'r matter pwysfawr yma un diwrnod, and your petitioner will ever pray. Dyna ddiwedd ar hynny. *Eich brawd anwiw ddigon,* *William Morris.* W. to R. CCC

W. to R. contd.

O.U.—Pa beth a glywaf? A gadd fy mrawd Rhisiart ryw ffawd yn ddiweddar? Codi cyflawg neu rywbeth o'r fath mae'n debyg. Fe fyddai arfer a gadael iw frawdyn wybod peth oi helyntion. Defod digon canmoladwy o honno, gresyn ei rhoddi i lawr, on'de? Duw gyd a chwi.

O.S., neu mendin.—Ddyw Llun dryghinog er echnos, torri tai a diwreiddio coedydd, ysgyttiaw llongau, disgwyl clywed fod digon a gormod o golledion, ar fôr yn enwedig. Dyma lythr i wrth y Bennant yn crefu am nawdd am fod yn dawedog. Gobeithio yr ymddwg y wreigyn etifedd iddaw Ynghaer Llion Gawr, lle yr erys hyd na ddêl ir gwellt. Rwyf wedi bod drwy'r boreu mewn oerfel a dryghin yn ceisio fforddio'r boblach i nadel i'r gwynt fyned a tho gwellt ac ysglattus i ffordd oddiar yr hên deiach accw. Roedd y gwynt mawr yn drêch na 5 o honom. Roedd y Bennant newydd gael llythyr oddiwrth Linnaeus yn dywedyd ei fod yn myned i roddi allan a new system with additions. Dyma gennyf ddwy gyhoeddiad o honynt eusioes, digon anhebyg iw gilydd. Ai fi eill *fforddio* prynu un arall er maint fy mlŷs? Dyma hanes aderyn dieithr, rhaid codi allan mewn arfau am ei groen. Byddwch wych!

YN LLUNDAIN GOCH, October 14, 1756, Dydd Iou.

L. to W. CCCI

Anwyl Frawd,—I have yours with an Awdl Marwnad to Cadwallon ap Madog ap Idnerth, who was *Priodawr* or *Gwledic* of ye country between Hafren a Gwy which was once part of ye Principality of Powys. It was a country (of all the marches of Wales) most plagued by ye Saxons, Normans, etc., and gave the owners opportunitys enough to fight, but we dont find in Caradoc's Chronicle much of this man's exploits, though it seems by Cynddelw's account he was a brave warrior. See whether Priodvawr Clodfawr be not *Priodawr*. His sons mentiond in this Marwnad were with Owein Gwynedd at Corwen when Henry II., King of England, came to Berwyn with the power of England, Normandy, Anjou, Gasgoign, Guien, Flanders and L. Britain, and where O. Gwynedd shewed great generalship, and defeated all the schemes of the Normans, and if that rascal Madog ap Mred. ap Bleddyn had joined ye Britains they might have demolishd the whole Norman army, ni feiddir dwedyd Saeson rhag iddynt ddigio, a'n galw ni r'un enw ag Owain Glyndwr. I never heard of

Gruffudd, son of Hywel ap Ywain Gwynedd; fe allai fod rhai or eppil etto yn brydyddion yn rhyw gyrrau o Gymru. Inclosed I send you the supposd form of your cabinet intended, and I suppose I am not far from hitting it. You see I would have eighteen drawers that are but an inch deep, which is for samples of sea plants and for sands, etc., the other thirty-six drawers of an inch and half will hold abundance of shells, ores, etc., and I dont know but you might bear more of ye inch ones. The two perpendicular partitions must be at least an inch and half thick of wood that will not *cast*,—sycamore or some hard foreign wood. The channels for ye bottoms of ye drawers to run in are to be cut with a *cŷn a thwcca*, as coopers cut their *corddynau*, and not with a saw; any kind of workman would make yours by your directions. The quantity of wood it will take is surprizing. You may contrive it without doors, for they are chargeable and troublesome, being so very wide as two and a half foot. As there are three columns of drawers, there may be three mortices in *c*, *d*, and *e*, in ye bottom board for three ledges to cross all the drawers to *f*, *g*, and *h*, where there may be three locks of ye same key to secure the ends of them, or some such contrivance. This shews I have very little to do; but I *have* though; for Camden's Wales is now on the table, and I daresay I have a fortnight's work to compare him with my dictionary, etc., and with my other solid affairs, [this] is enough to employ any one man. Ow am y corallines! chwedl Esau wrth ei dad, ai nid oes ganthoch ond un fendith; bendithiwch finneu hefyd. My triangular shell is a bivalve and very neat, the hinge in one of the angles very small. I never lookd closely into shells till now I had business to sort them for this cabinet; and it surprizd me that our Cambrian coast produces the very same shells as are dug in ye mountains of Sicily and many of those found in Jamaica, and now I am certain that upon diligent search we may .... many (aye a vast number) more in Wales, for I have very few of ye turbines kind. It surprizes me to see the Welsh shells look so well in ye cabinet, a great many of them being dead shells. My way of sorting them is thus: of large shells as big as a walnut, I have but one in a boat; of shells the size of periwinkles two or three; of smaller half a dozen or more; of

L. to W. contd.

L. to W. contd.

very small, perhaps forty. So that the use of this collection of shells is chiefly to shew the various kinds, not to pair them, as your great collectors do, who polish and varnish them, mine are as Nature made them. Is! is! Esgair y Mwyn was certainly cursd by ye Ystrad Fflur monks, but we shall take off the curse by and by, and it will be more blessed than ever. We have rallied our forces and will make a decisive conquest at last. Surely Mr. Lister hath some names, if it was but of ye classes and genus's, etc. Pray, what are those? Univalve, bivalve, multivalve, etc. What is ye name of a bivalve which has always one that is about half size of ye other? I have some from Aberdovey, and some of them from Mount Sicily, Cragen y Wefl. A Londoner of whom Gronwy had bought household stuff to a considerable value, went to him the other day for his money, and a writ in his pocket to take his body if he did not deliver him back the goods and a watch, etc. But Gronwy [like a] valiant Briton, on sight of him bristled up, and rattled him, and told him he had no business to trouble *him* or to come so far, that he was not to be used in that manner. But the man told him: "I have a writ in my pocket and an officer here to execute it, and if you dont deliver me my goods by fair means I shall make bold with your body and carry it to ye county gaol which is Newgate. Give me that watch first of all," says the tyrant. The ancient Britain's courage failing him, put his hands in his fob and took out ye watch and deliverd it, but first he took off a silk string that was to it, (value 2d.) and then put up the affront. The Briton insisted that he was of a good family and a very ancient nation, and it was not right to strip him of all, for he had no bed to lie on, and after abusing his tyranical creditor to some purpose, he got off clear for that time at the expense of the watch which he had never paid for, nor ever intended to pay for it, nor ever will pay for any thing if he can help it, for I believe he thinks all mankind obligd to find him all necessaries. Is not he poet for the nation of ye Britains? Mi sgrifennaf at fy nhad ar fyrder. Gadewch glowed hanes Cregyn Llanddwyn. Shell madness is like the itch, very catching. Wawch, dyma'r papir gwedi darfod, mae'n rhaid rhoi heibio.

Eich brawd ffyddlonaf, *Llewelyn.*

Brother Richard's promotion is not yet quite finishd, but it will be a fine thing, and I think cannot fail. Tom Davies (a clerk above him), mab Dafydd Owen a dorrodd fottymau Bawdfel, hath a place just now of about £500 a year, and hath a chance by and by for £1,500 a year! L. to W. contd.

CAERGYBI, 10d o Dachwedd, 1756.

'Mrawd Rhisiart unwaith etto!—Wawch! a threbal wawch! Ai yn *yswain* yr aethoch? Wala! wfft, a dwbwl wfft, i hynny! Ond wrth gofiaw, "It is what we must all come to at last" chwedl y porthwr pan ganfu'r Arglwydd mawr yn myned o amgylch yn ei bontificalibus's. "F' Arglwydd," ebyr Grono Ddu, "pa bryd y bydd hynny?" Pa bryd bynnag, Duw a'ch llwyddo ac a roddo ras, hir hoedl, ac iechyd i chwi fwynhau eich newydd swydd a'ch teitlau, etc. Gwyn ei fyd a gai unwaith glywed fod y Llew yntau wedi caffael rhyw fara iawn, a chwedi cael yn rhydd or canglwm yna y mae ynddo. O'm rhan fy hun nid anesmwyth fyddaf a'm pawl yn y llawr yn y fan hon, tra clywaf fod pawb o honych yn dringaw gorifynu i deml bri ac anrhydedd. Fe fai gwych gennyf weled dan eich llaw eich hunan ronyn o hanes a natur y lle newydd a ddaeth i'ch rhan. Ni bydd y Llew ond crybwyll. Nid oes fawr sud ar Wilym Cregynwr y dyddiau hyn, rhyw ysleccod arnaw. Dyma'r gauaf yn dechreu lledu ei esgill drosom ni yn y wlad, ar holl ddiddanwch yn dianc i'r dinasoedd mawrion. Y ni ai piau hi yr haf, ond fe aeth y diweddaf ym'ith yn ddiswttan, tra bum mi yn enill fy mhedolau. Gwae fi am fy anwyl gyfaill y Cadpen Foulkes; a ddarfu ir Ffreins ddihenyddu a dwyn fy nhlyseu gwerthfawr hefyd! A gwae ni am Ierwerth a ddaliasant y lladron duon! Oes gobaith iddo gael myned yn rhydd? Ni wn i a ddianc fy nghyfaill i Fortunatus oddiar y giwed felldigedig heb ei gymeryd. Gwych y canawdd Ieuan (ond ê?) i Frenin Prwsia,* mi faswn i yn tyngu mai Goronwy ai cant oni bae ddywedyd imi ir gwrthwyneb. Yn wir ddiau un gorchestol iawn yttyw, pwy na lithia feirdd i ganu fal hyn? Ai tybied y byddwch yn cymeryd amynedd i W. to R. CCCII

* Ieuan Brydydd Hir wrote an "Awdl i Frenin Prwssia," which is printed in "Gwaith y Parch. Evan Evans," p. 81, but the poem here referred to is probably "Awdl i Frenin Prwssia, yn ol dull yr hen Feirdd," which is not inserted in the printed collection of his poems. It may be seen in Addit. MS. 10314, p. 200, and in Peniarth MS. 122, f. 69.

W. to R. contd.

ddarllain y brygowthen a fyddai yn ei anfon at y Llew bob yn bost, os ê, ry'ch yn gweled par fodd y mae'r byd yn bod yn y gongl hon or byd. Ces lythyr gynneu oddiwrth Mosson yn dywedyd iddo gaffael llythyr mwyn oddiwrthych, hanes ugein punt i Jenkinson, am y llynedd. Ond y llynedd o boutu Gwyl Fihangel y darfu am ei gwr; nage, nage, wrth gofiaw, yr amser hwnnw y darfu am y llong. Fe aeth y dyn oedd yn crochwaeddi am brotection prentis i Lerpwl i dyngu, ac anghofiodd alw am y direcsiwn a roddasoch. Mi dawaf a son am heno. Duw gyda chwi.

Eich caredigawl frawd, *Gwilym.*

N.B.—Roedd y nhad yn rhwydd iachus ddoe. Mae'r chwaer Elin i'ch annerch, ac yn ddigawn balch glywed eich bod yn Yswain. Pray send me the etymology of the word.

HOLYHEAD, 24th November, 1756.

W. to R. CCCIII

Dear Brother,—Dyma fi yn rhoddi cais ar atteb eich llythyr diddan o'r 18 am yr hwn ydwyf dra diolchgar iwch. Gwae'r sawl na faddeua iw frawd, os buoch hwyrfrydig i atteb, gwnaeth hwn iawn am y cwbl. Mi yrrais yna lythyr ers dyddiau ich llwyddo ar yr achos hwnnw o fyned o honoch yn Yswain, ac nid bychan y glod a haeddech am fedru dringaw mor uchel heb neb i roddi help llaw. Aie yswain o'r Ddafis yntau, oes peth daioni yn perthyn iddo? Ni chlywais i fawr son am ei wrthiau. Mae'n dda gennyf yn fy nghalon fod y câr Parry wedi caffael cystal peth. Er dolwyn annerchwch fi atto: Nid oes dim a saif o'ch blaenau chwi eich driwedd yn yr offis yna, mae'n debyg mae Commissioners a fyddwch bod y pen cyn y bo hir—Commissioner Morris, Commissioner Davies, a Chommissioner Parry, ond ê? Wala! wala! Duw a ro'r gras i chwi bod ac un, heb hwnnw ni thal yr holl fyd ddraen crin. Llawer a weddiawdd yr hen bobl o Bentre' rianell am ras iw plant, ac fe ffynnodd ganddynt; er y bu rheini fal hogiau eraill yn ddigon diriaid, Duw ai gwyr. Da bod gobaith ir Weldyn weddw yma, hi a gadd fil am ei phensiwn o £14 1s. gross—felly roedd 10/6 at 6d per pound yn rhy fychan am wasnaethu'r Fosson yma, gwr abl diddaioni, ond rhaid imi gadw'r ddysgl yn wastad, o herwydd mai drwy ei ddwylo y mae fy nghyfrifon i yn myned fisawl a chwarterawl ir Comptroller General's offis yna. Oni bae hynny, ni byddai waeth gennyf mo'r llawer ymhle y byddai. Rwyn tybied y bydd yma yn y man, i actio yn lle yr Geirchan.

Par sud ddyn ydyw hwnw? Rwyfi wedi gellwng yn angof. Rhyfedd na bu'sai Iedwarth yn sgrifenu o'r Groyne. Nid oes ammeu na byddai ar goreu gan Natws gael bod yn amral neu yn gadpen o leiaf pei gwela'i yr Henŵr yn dda. Trefn ddrwg sydd ar Aldreman O.P. meddynt i mi; nid yr un fath a hynny y bydd pobl y'mynd yn ddedwydd yn ei henaint ai ê? Mi yrrais atteb ym mlaen llaw i'r cwestiwn ynghylch dynion a f'ai gymmwys, i allu commissioners o honynt, oes, oes yma ddigon. Ag oni bae fod yn rhaid i'r Llew wrth Siac Owain e wnaetha i chwi ecslant glark, llencyn rhywiog, cywraint, a fasai yn gwneuthur y peth a fynasech. Dyma Will ei frawd yntau, a lusty, likely, young fellow, writes a good hand, is tractable and ingenious. Cofiwch am y rhain. Dymma finnau yn darparu i chwi glerkyn o hyn i ben yr wyth mlynedd draw. Y cebystr iddo fo y Mr. Peswch am grugo y'mrodyr yn y modd yna. Onid oes digon o ddynionach yna na thalant iw codi oddiar y maes, pam na yrrwch i felldith i gowdal at y rheini? Ni waeth peidio na dianc rhagddo, fe ddeuai i hyd i chwi pe baech dan linyn y cyhydedd. Nid oes dim lwc ir corn carw môr, mi ddywedais i chwi par amlwc a fu'r llynedd, ac ar fy ngair gwir mi brynnais y leni gybynaid o honynt ac a delais am eu picliaw, oblegyd nid oes yma ddim or fath beth au cael am arian wedi. Mi brynais siwg a ddaliai'r cwbl oll ac ai rhoddais ynddi, mi roesym doppyn o gork ynddi, ac ai simentiais yn bur dda, ond tra bum i yn sal yr haf leni ae yn ffaelio edrych allan am gyfleu iw hanfon, nhwy a ysbwyliasant bod ac un, oblegyd erbyn myned i'w hedrych rhag ofn bod eisiau pickyl arnynt, ni thalant ddim yn y byd. Mi fum digawn anfodlonus o'r achos, ond beth a dalai cwynaw; ni wn i a dreiaf byth ond hynny ai peidiaw, nid oes wybod dan yr haf bellach. Mae gennyf bot i'r Fosgawen am warchad cyhyd a chystal ar y lladron ym Mrest. Bydded yntau yn ffrind cywir i chwi, nid un ar flaen tafod. Digrif y mae'r mawrion yna yn ymgymysgu, ffei or sud os bydd tynny dyddiau am ymgyfwrdd y Palment. Ni fynaf ymwrando ynghylch Testamentau, mae un or rhai drudion wedi ei werthu gan fy.nhad i Fodafon, ond ni chawsai ddim arian y dydd arall. Beth os clyw subscribers eu gwerthu am 10 swllt? Ie, da chwithau, cofiwch am Wilym pan gaffoch ffosilod. Daccw'r post ymron canu ei gorn, byddwch iach a Duw gyda chwi.

Eich caredigawl frawd, *Gwilym.*

W. to R. contd.

LONDON, or thereabouts, November 30th, 1756.

L. to W.
CCCIV

Dear Brother,—No letters from you last post, when I expected impatiently for the catalogue of the shells, etc., which came in ye box from Chester, perhaps next post may bring it. No alterations yet at Galltvadog, though the midwife hath continued there this month past. Paynter going on after the same wild manner, building and throwing down at Esgair y Mwyn even in the depth of winter. I hope he will play some of them a trick by and by. I cannot send you my system of ye two shelld fish till I have your catalogue, and even then it will be but a *cynnyg*. I have a person at work here to get me specimens of ye Materia Medica, about 180 articles, which will fill about two or three drawers of a cabinet, and will be very curious and useful. The earth and the rest of ye planets turn about incessantly and measure the time of our duration. Let us make much of it, not one of them will stand still to let us trifle and loyter, therefore you should never drop your pen but to eat and drink and sleep a little, and you (I suppose) no more than myself are fit for no other labour but writing. Cynnilo yw hyn gwedi mynd i din y cwd. I take nightly some pills of squills, etc., for ye cough, and some astmatic tincture day and night, which I fancy makes me cough easier, but I think these things affect my memory, or else ye cough. I never found it so bad as it is now, by fits. I have heard of a bishop that had so bad a memory that I used to wonder at it, he kept a memorandum book but forgot that he had one. I dont now wonder at all at it, for I am guilty of ye like blunders. You dont like the London poetry I sent you, and I am surprized at your want of tast. I have my ears saluted frequently in this solitary lodging of mine with a very agreeable sketch of it, which is impossible for me to forget, for it is as natural as if Eve sang lullaby to her sons Cain and Abel. Suppose a black sheep passd by ye nurse, would not Adam have laughd to hear her sing:

Bâ, bâ, black sheep have you any wool?
Is marry have I, three bags full,
A bag for my master, a bag for my dame,
And a bag for little Abel that lives in our *lane*.

You may talk of your Popes and your Drydens, etc., but none . . . . ever spoke more natural than these field poets. I have several more curious anecdotes of this kind, what I have collected, and it would have been the same trouble to me to collect shells and fossils if they had come in my way; but this happens to be my entertainment that fills up the vacant spaces of my present life. No, no, I would not have Pennant think that I have any tast to shells, ac onide fe allai y bydd yn meddwl fy mod gwedi tolli ei gwynos ef a ddaeth i'r felin yma. Mae'r stori hyd y dref fod y Brenin yn pallu siarad a'r Gweinidogion newydd, ond troi ei wyneb draw at *Anson* pan oedd Temple yn cusanu ei law ef. Fe allai eu bod gwedi gwenwyno meddwl yr hen wr, ag na bydd ond y dryswch yn eu mysg. Mi glywais wr mawr yn dywedyd, ai tybied yr ydych mae mynd allan y maent heb obaith dyfod yn ol pan ffaelio'r lleill a thrin y dreth? An odd contrivance! So they will be a bustling in and out till the French comes upon their backs while they are striving for places to cheat one another. The report is in town that we have lost Jamaica, and that Loudon is beat. Inclosed I think to send you news from Holyhead. I ask the news's pardon because I did not believe it till I saw it in print. I see here the French were confind prisoners on board y^e^ *Boyne*. Let us have a fuller account of that affair, and what they did with the French. Were they sent to Beaumares? I have met here by accident a curious thing in relation to ye Celtic affairs, a letter from M. Pezron to the Abott Nicaise, giving an account in ye year 1699 of his intended book the Origin of Nations. I can think of nothing else to fill this paper but that it is very cold, freezes hard, and I cannot get warm in bed, which makes me cough more. Oni ddywaid yr Sgrythur: "Pa fodd y geill un dwymno mewn gwely!" Duw gyda chwi a ninnau, dyna hi'n pallu sgrifennu chwaneg. *Eich brawd, Llewelyn.* L. to W. contd.

LONDON, December 17, 1756, Friday.

Dear Brother,—I have yours of ye 10th, a gwych oedd glywed fod pob peth yn rhesymol. Wele mi sgrifennais attoch fod gennif lodes newydd Yngalltvadog, which was a false alarm by a mistake of a joke in my wife's letter, but she was not brought to bed till ye 11th at night, but did not mend the matter at all for it is only a *fine* girl still. My friend, Evan Williams, (the *honest* Cardiganian) writes me word I have a *new* girl, and for ye curiosity of the thing, I send you the original, which was a postscript in another letter of L. to W. CCCV

L. to W. contd.

his. My Lord Powis often reads his letters to me, and they are certainly originals in their kind; my Lord was at my poor habitation yesterday, all is well hitherto. The materia medica are for my brother's cabinet, which is almost finishd; my Lord's cabinet is filld, and is to be sent to his house in a few days. Lady Powis can hardly refrain from coming here to see it before it comes. Gwych ydych i gael *bocsys* o ffossilod gan Bennant! Nid oes yma ddim o'r fath roddion. Yes, yes; Lord Temple was a Grenville. No, no; I have no amanuensis of any kind, not so much as a boy to go of errands, byw'n gynnil iawn, ag etto gwarrio mwy nag sy'n dyfod i mewn yn bresennol. If there are muscles as well as cockles that are poly ginglymis, how comes Woodward to put them on ye same distinction with ye astrea and concha anomiae? It was that which confounded me. What is ginglymis but gêngwlwm? Canclwm or ganglwms—will that do for a hinge? It is a kind of *cwlwm*. What shells are the *cynion?*—rhai mín deneuon mae'n debyg; onid oes cynion tewion hefyd? If the tellinae, chamaes, pholades and musculi are confounded by writers, how are they to be distinguished? All is a chaos, and nothing known by its own name. If you mean by ye shell I *mention* the . . . . . it is no muscle; the name trochi comes from *troi cynffon*. I take the Dwyran fossils to be more like a gryphites than a *malwen*. Wele hai, aie Mr. Blair owner of the Packets? Ond er lles i Vic. y bydd gwaith o'r fath honno, mi wranta mai ychydig a gewch i na minneu oddiwrth y fath bêth; . . . . oes dim iw ddisgwyl ond geiriau Gwyddelig teg . . . . . . gadw'r papir, a phallu ei roi yn ol, ni byddafi . . . . . . iddynt wneuthur rhyw les i'r fangre dlawd yna er cof am . . . . fwyttawyd ag a yfwyd gynt ynddi; ond cyn gollwng y papir o'ch llaw cymrwch goppi o hono yn ddistaw deg, oblegid bydd dda gennifi fe allai ei gael etto ryw dro os byw fyddaf. A very thin paper pind on the draught will direct you to draw the lines on it well enough, and be sure to add ye scale, and if you could draw it tolerable I had rather they should have a copy. I suppose the P.M. General carried ye fair draught with him to uffern fagddu. As the shell masters are so unconstant and wavering, how dare I to send you my method of sorting them? I must defer it to another time. They talk of more alterations still, and nothing goes down but a triennial Parliament and the Militia Bill, which I suppose will hardly include Wales. Onid oes ar y Saeson ofn i'r Hen Frutaniaid daro gyda Brutaniaid Llydaw? Mark the end of it! Nid oes yma un newydd a ellaf fi ddywedyd yn awr, ond mae amser i bob peth. Diog y mae'r geirlyfr yn mynd ymlaen o achos cregin a gweithiau mwyn, etc. Ni chlywai air am arian Dulun, a welir ceiniog fyth debygach i? A oes yna un tenant yn talu? Dim ond hynny heno, prysur y foru os byw ag iach. *Eich brawd pendrwm*, *Llewelyn*. L. to W. contd.

CAERGYBI, 22d December, 1756.

F'anwyl Frawd Rhisierdyn,—Bendith yr Arglwydd i chwi am anfon i mi ronyn o lythyr wrth raid; on'd oedd hyfryd gweled un hefyd iwrth y Llew, arall wrth y Bennant, ac arall iwrth Agrippa yn dyfod, *eill bedwar law yn llaw*, a minneu'n ofni eich bod chwi eich deuwedd wedi ir peswch neu'r Ffrancod eich dihenyddu. Pwy debygach i gadd wall arnaf y dydd arall? Nid y fall, nawdd Duw rhagddi, na'r cnawd ychwaith, er taered yw, nag hefyd y byd a'i ryodres a'i orwagedd, ond y cenau maleisgar gan y Mr. Peswch, byr oes iddo, a neidiawdd ar fy nghefn a mi yn cymeryd physygwr-iaeth i'm coes, ac am daliodd yn fy ngwendid a bu raid i mi heb yn ddiolch yn fy nannedd roddi iddo letty, a dyma lle taring, mae'n debyg, hyd na ddelo'r dydd yn hir ac yn deg iddo i ymdaith i bant. Felly y mae'r ceryn anynad wedi cael y llaw uchaf ar y tri brawd. Wala, dwbl wfft i'r bardd am eich digiaw, a daed oeddych wrthaw. Pa beth a ddaw o hono nys medraf ddirnad, nag or llyffethair honno o wraig sydd iddo efo'r mân blant. Mae Agrippa yn dywedyd ei fod yn awr yn drafferthus iawn ynghylch gwaith mawr maith anniben, sef tadogi pob gair yn yr iaith Gymraeg. Ai gwir hynny? Da os ceir arian y weddw yn Ionor. Fe fu'r Fosson yma ennyd, ond ni sonniawdd ddim am yr arian rheini, fe wyddai fy mod wedi lledfrochi wrtho o'u hachos, gwr drosto ei hun yw ef, a shaver, chwedl chwitha' am *Mr. Oats*. Diolch yn fawr am stori'r gwr 'nheddig hwnnw, mi fyddaf innau yn cael ambell 'bystol trist ddigawn iwrth yr Aldremon; mi yrrais'r dydd arall iddo werth 13s. o menyn melyn Môn—deg i un y gwelaf hatlin byth am tanaw. Mae'n dywedyd imi fod ei stad yn y wlad yma wedi ei rhoddi drosodd iw nai Jones Mollwyn i dalu cantoedd oedd hwnnw wedi W. to R. CCCVI

W. to R. contd.

mechnio drosto. Nis gwn i par sud y bydd byw oni cheiff bensiwn gan dref Nerpwl; nhw fyddant yn rhoddi rhywfaint i'r Aldramyn a fydd yn mynd yn dinbleth. Mi glywsom hanes Iedw o Fodedeyrn, Duw a roddo iddo ryddhad a hynny'n fuan hefyd. Mi glywais lawer iawn o son am eich almari chwi, ni waeth i honno er hwyed y bo'r Llew yn ei ffau, a chwithau cymmaint eich ffwdan beunoeth. Fy mendith i chwi am yr almanac, yn wir yr oeddwn yn dechreu grwnan am un, ond roedd arnaf gywilydd eich hudo am werth swllt bob blwyddyn, heblaw aneirif ddoniau eraill; rhaid s'fennu at Mr. Parry, athraw ysgol, i ymorol ar Maswn am dano. A fedr y nhad debygech chwi ymadel ar 50 Testamentau? Os ni fedr, fe gymer y Mr. Ellis a minnau arnom rannu rywffordd oddeutu 20 neu 30 o naddynt. Ond os medr o gael siecmyn i'r cwbl, chwi ellwch chwithau, os mynnwch, anfon yma gistiaid, a chwi a gewch arian gloywon am danynt. Dyna lle bydd dihareb gyfleu i anfon i Wilym wirion hailsiaid o gregyn Siamaica, few of each sort, e weddai fod yna yn dŷn at ddeng math a deugain nas meddaf monynt, ie, a rhan o ffosilod Mahon hefyd yn yr un rhyw gisten, a llawer peth gyda hynny a ellir eu stwffiaw i mewn rhwng y llyfrau i lestair iddynt rwbiaw gormodd wrth eu gilydd. Mi ofynaf ynghylch yr almanaccau, os caf gwsmeriaid cewch glywed ar fyr. Duw hefyd an tynno allan o'r siglen ac an gosod ar graig unwaith etto, rwy'n ofni ein bod yn dra drwg ein trefn. Mi glywaf i'r Arglwydd yna ymweled ar Llew—arwydd dda iawn. Mae'n rhywyr cael myned adref i edrych ar ol y ty ar ardd mi wranta. Nid oes na chragen na ffosil na seren fôr debyg i amynedd, Duw ai dodo ini. Dyma hi yn bryd myned ir glwyd, felly nos da'wch heno; bydded ir Goruchaf warchad droswch chwi a ninneu.

Mi wyf, eich carediccaf frawd, *Gwilym Amhorys.*

L. to W. CCCVII

LONDON, 28 December, 1756.

Dear Brother,—I have yours of ye 22d with awdlau, which in my next I'll give you my opinion of. So Peggy Owen has got a cripple I suppose. My brother will enquire about ye certificate. The postscript to it sure is no part of ye original, and was only intended as direction to draw it. Enquire and consider it, for it seems to be nonsense gwâg. Na fum ddim ar lawr yn glir gan beswch, ond yn isel iawn. I thought cregyn diluw and crogen hir lydan y Traeth coch were of ye chamae kind having a one-third hinge; they may be so too and called *cynion* ceimion. Da fyddai cael bil gynta gellir, i gael arian i fyw arnynt, the stocks are so excessive low at present, that it is a monstrous loss to sell out, about forty pounds less in y[e] hundred. I shall draw out a paragraph just now about Fortunatus Wright's son and send it to the printer of y[e] *Public Advertiser.* If you have extraordinary news at any time, they will be inserted gratis. Gwyliau Nadolig dylion iawn sydd yma, I am obliged to live low because of my cough, and yet I grow fatter for want of exercise. I am afraid my wife is ill of a fever, though they conceal the thing from me, ... not wrote yet. I have .... to write this post. *I am, your affectionate brother,* *L.M.* L. to W. contd.

LONDON, January 1 [1757].

L. to W. CCCVIII

Dear Brother,—I have yours of y[e] 25 December erbyn trennydd (i.e. tri nydd). I have a microscope for you, and discwyl yr wyf am ddyddiau gwell, ag yno gwell a fydd y microscope, and I can afford to send you a better apparatus, dyna'r gwir. You talk of making a great collection next summer, so do I, but query, oni fydd reidiach hel arian na chregyn, i gael o'r plant fwyd, etc. Dyna i chwi ffranc etto. Gwae fi mae'r ddannoedd yn gwneud im llaw suglo yn dost, a'r spectol yn gwasgu fy arleisiau; och fi! Daccw'r Baynter gwedi mynd o Esgair y Mwyn tridie cyn y Nadolig, dan esgus mynd at Arglwydd Powys i Oakley Park, ond mae'n debyg ei fod yn Llundain cyn hyn and I hope the country is bit in a great deal of money, which is oweing there. Daccw fi gwedi gyrru at Evan Wiliam onest i brynnu ynghylch gwerth £200 o goed sydd yn y gymdogaeth honno fal y caffo'r Arglwydd goed i weithio'r Esgair, but they are bought in Evan Williams's name for certain reasons. Mae Powell yn dywedyd y daw Lewis Morus yno unwaith etto, ac nad oes dim coel ar Baynter! Dyna droead mawr ar feddwl gwr. Gwych yw'r prydyddion yna o dad i dad; hil y derwyddon mi wranta. Ond daccw Ronwy ar fynd yn alldud; an unaccountable fellow! his story is too long to tell. His wife on the brink of delivery and not a rag provided for y[e] child. He without a penny in his pocket, his salary stop'd by y[e] Rector to pay his debts, sends to London a sawcy letter to borrow two guineas, being obligd by y[e] Rector's orders to distribute the surplice fees among

L. to W. contd.

the poor, which money amounting to about forty shillings he had spent every farthing. We know the Rector offer'd ye curacy to another person, who did not like it, but Gronwy will not believe but he is to stay there, and now talks of publishing his own works by subscription, which is a genteeler way of begging than what he has made use of hitherto, like a sturdy beggar abusing all about him. Ydyw, mae'r Gwarlydan yn sefyll hyd yn hyn, ond mi debygwn na fydd o'n hir. They talk of diminishing ye number of Commissioners on ye meeting of ye Parliament and I believe there will be abundance of alterations still. Mi wn y bydd yr Arglwydd Powys yn neidio o ddigofaint pan glywo gastiau'r Frysgo—ni bydd eisiau swmbwl. Aie, taro allan 3s. 10d. o 4s. 11d. felly chwi gewch lwfio 13d am lythyrau. Well done, a poor shitten fellow, but it is not worth while mentioning these low things. "Goddeu fân gammau" is an excellent Cardiganshire proverb. Pwy wyr pa beth a ellir wneuthur ar fyrder ym Môn, pan ddel i'n llawn bower? I wish you would send me as soon as possible the names and places and salaries of all the officers of ye Customs and Salt belonging to ye Port of Beaumares, and which are on ye establishment, which not. If James Morris is compos mentis, he would give you also a list of South Wales, if you tell him it is at my request. Mr. Nicolson once gave me a list, but it is in Cardiganshire, and my Lord Powys now wants it; I cannot come at it. I'll send you no more chargd letters to pick your pocket, and you may charge ye 3s. 10d. to me for I dare say they were most of them mine, but I'll try to have it out of ye skins of some of them. I suppose poor *Oats* will be obligd to go under instructions. I wish he had the sense to write a proper letter to Lord Powys which I am afraid he cannot. He should set forth the qualifications of his predecessor but I'll do it if he do's not. Can spare time to say no more this post. *Your affectionate brother*, *Llewelyn.*

O'M CELL, Nos Fawrth y Fatel a honno yttoedd y drydedd o Ionawr, yn y Flwyddyn 1757.

W. to R. and L. CCCIX

Ha Wŷr Frodyr,—Mi ddywedais wrth rai o honochi'r dydd arall fod y gelynion brychion am ddyfod i'n hymweled, a heddyw nhwy a fuont cystal au gair, ond gan na fedrwn ni yr Cymru nag ymladd, na rhoddi i lawr hanes ymladdfa yn iawn o Gymroaeg, dyma i chwi o Saesoneg gyflawn hanes o'r fuddigoliaeth a enillodd y Cybiaid y dydd heddyw dros y Dumaresyddion a'r Llanerch-meddyddion :—Tuesday, about 7 morn, I was calld up with the alarm that an army of about 400 or 500 men were marching through Llanynghenadl to attack this fortress, and I was desired to take up arms and to act as an officer of the cavalry to go and meet the enemy to give them battle. I declined the command as I had a small garrison of my own to defend, etc. About eight the drums beat to arms, and the two strong places secured where the attack was threatened to be made, viz., Llanfawr and Ynys Rug—at the latter place were some corn warehouses, or rather magazines of corn. The hours 9, 10 and 11 were taken up in forming two armies, one at each place. About 12, one of our scouts brought word that the enemy had advanced as far as Tywyn y Capel, whereby it was thought adviceable that there should be a junction of the armies, and then to march boldly to meet the enemy.* Ours had not marched further than Penllech Nest (Hold! there's one of our general officers coming to be dressd). Now at it again; when they discoverd the enemy opposite to Penrhyn Giriol. As they approached each other the enemy perceived that our army were well disciplined and armed with fire arms, swords, etc., they made a stand. When our troops found they were dismayed they broke upon them helter skelter, whereby they were put into confusion, and on the first onset the whole of their army were thrown into a pannick, so that they threw down their arms, bagage, and provisions,† and took to their heels, and our army pursued them sword in hand and hunted them down like rabbits. About 2 o'clock the prisoners began to come in: some scalpd, some marked with the signs of the cross on their heads and backs, but all damage done was behind, except a few that had the skins of their foreheads hanging down over their eyes. It is now about 7 o'clock, and the number of prisoners amounts to sixty wounded and taken. Captain Gambold distinguished himself, so did General Vickers and Colonel Lloyd, and the soldiery in general

W. to R. and L. contd.

* N.B.—A mineu yngysgod gwernen yn bwyta clun myharen. [W. M].

† They had broke open storehouses at the Bridge and carried away with them cheese, etc. [W. M.]

W. to R. and L. contd.

performed wonders; in short, this was as compleat victory as ever was gaind by Ffrederic of Brandenburg. The garrison of Ynys Rug in the absence of the army was comanded by the Surveyor and Oats. Guns had been brought on shore and planted, and all the ships in the harbour were put in a posture of defence, being in number ten or a dozen, many with guns, some without bottoms, others without masts, etc. It is agreed on all hands that the enemy were about 150 strong and ours about 100. Both armies on advancing kept shouting and huzzaing like the Indians—perhaps the old British way. The prisoners are secured in the King's warehouse for security, etc., except the wounded, who are put into torture by Holyday. I was offered the office of being surgeon, but I chose to decline it. Perhaps, gentlemen, you may blame me for refusing these honourable employments, but I'll assure you I had cogent reasons for so doing. You know well that a virtuoso is not a fit person to go a skirmishing with an enemy: perhaps in the height of the pursuit I might spy a shell or a fossil, which inevitably must have drawn away one's attention to his charge. Many things more I could urge in my own defence. I may be able tomorrow to give you some further anecdotes of this glorious victory, but now I will leave off by bidding you adieu.

Yr Hen Dydd Natalig.—Fe debygai ddyn fod y rhyfel drosodd, ni chlywais i heddy gymaint a thwrw un gŵn yn myned allan. By an exact list taken of the prisoners they amount to 65 or 66. They were yesterday suffered to march out of the prisons without dishonour, after promising upon the knee not to serve again, etc. Their General was sent, guarded with a party of armd light horse, to Brynddu, there to answer, etc. It is thought that the victory would not have been so decisive had not General Gambold introduced the Cardiganian exercise among our squadrons. You, Llew, know that art. Wawch! dyma ddau lythyrun oddiwrth bob brawd, ac un Grono hefyd. Diolch yn fawr am danynt, mi au hattebaf bod y sillaf foreu neu drenydd. Pen y chwarter heddyw, cyfrifon mawr i fyned ymaith y foru. Duw gyda chwi a byddwch wychion. *Eich brawd anwiw,* *Gwilym.*

P.S.—Ni wn i a ddeil hwn y Llew cyn cychwyn o'i ffau, os ni wna, gyrrwch iddo, da chwithau. The squadron of light horse hath returned. The General of the Mopiaid hath been bound over to appear at the Sessions, and hath given good security and the sufferers bound to prosecute. Evidence bound to prove . . . . . so the Convention is quite settled, but query whether the French policy mayn't prevail. Adieu.

W. to R. and L. contd.

CAER GYBI SANT, 6 Ionor, 1757.

W. to R. CCCX

Anwyl Frawd Rhisierdyn,—Mae yn eich cell laprwth o lythyr yn disgwyl cael ei atteb ryw drô pan gaffoch gyfleu, yr achos a bair imi yr awron eich cyfarch yn benodol heddy yw hyn: daccw ein nai Will Owen wedi bod yma yn gwneuthur ystyrgwyn am ryw le i fyned ar led. Mae'r gwr wedi diflasu yn hwylio efo ei frawd ynghyfraith mewn rhyw gragen gyda'r glennydd yma, ac y mae yn ymroi o fyned y gwanwyn yma naill ai ir *East Indies* neu i *Man of War*. I've endeavoured to perswade him to the latter, but he seems to be inclined to the former. However, he wants to know your oppinion, and whether you could get him any little *post on board an Indiaman*. He hath all the qualifications necessary (ac er nad yw ugain oed fe allai bassiaw am 4 neu bump ar hugain). He is tall and lusty, and as he served his time on board the Dublin yatch is a thorough bred sailor. He writes a good hand, understands the art of navigation, hath learnt arithmetic and geometry, though perhaps these affairs may have been a little neglected of late. He is made for the sea and the sea for him, would rather be a petty officer on board a ship than a commissioner on shore. Rhowch eich *pennau* ynghyd, da chwithau, a gadewch imi wybod pa beth a ddaw o honynt. Meddyliwch am y llanc a fu farw yn rhai o'ch llongau chwi. Os ca'r dynan tlawd yma o dad iddo geiniawg ar ei ol, dâ fydd. Ni chaf lonydd gan boblach i sgrifenu chwaneg y tro yma. Byddwch iạch. *Eich caredigawl frawd,*

William Morris.

HOLYHEAD, 10th January, 1757.

W. to R. CCCXI

Dear Brother Richard,—Inclos'd have sent you, or do send you, affidavits to procure a protection for three years, for Robert Jones, apprentice to Watkin Thomas of this place, which please do, as soon as you can conveniently. I hope brother Lewis will have received ere this comes to hand my letter of the 8th with a bill in't, ag onide ceisied ei gipan ai gapan a rheded i'r bank to order

W. to R. contd. payment to be stopt of No. St. 238 for £20, dated 22 September last. Duw gyda chwi eich deuwedd ac a ddel a newydd dâ oddiwrthych. *Ich brawd penrhydd, William Morris.*

P.S.—Dim almanac wedi dyfod etto, er maint or hiraeth am ei weled. Eisieu atteb ir llythyr hir hwnnw a yrrais attoch er's dyddiau bŷd.

TRE NEWYDD, February 4th, Friday, 1757.

L. to W. CCCXII Anwyl Frawt,—What should hinder you to write for three or four posts past? What but the cabinet? I hope it is nothing else, I should have been uneasy if I had not known *that* was in agitation. It is about a month's work I warrant it for a saerpren Cymreig. My brother Richard's cabinet is not yet come home though it has been above two months in hand, and my Lord Powys's was not above eight or nine days a makeing by two men—ond mae'n rhaid i saerpren o Gymro wneuthur pob peth yn rhy gryf o'r hanner, a churo hoel bedair gwaith yn lle dwy, a rhoi dwy hoel yn lle un, etc., a dyna waith Cymro, about which I always quarrel with my Cardiganshire folks. Wele (not well) my Lord's lease of ye mine is not yet finished, but is now on ye brink of it—y twymnad diwaethaf. I heard from him yesterday, all is well, he hath been lately very ill and confined to his bed. I am afraid the physicians will kill him at last; he has too great an opinion of them. It is to no purpose to tell you of ye unaccountable proceedings about Esgair y Mwyn, and Paynter's working ye mine and building houses there, and driving levels, sinking engine shafts, rioting, etc., for those things will be over by and by, and that honest *Iuddew* known there as well as in other places. The reason I write this is on account of W. Owen, about whose affair of ye East India Service, etc., I wrote to you some time ago and expected to hear your resolution about it, or rather his. Thus stands the matter. Here is an opening for him to prefer himself to be a captain, or an admiral by and by for aught I know. Admiral Boscawen is gone just now to Portsmouth to provide our Navy there (or naval power) against the spring, we having no proper persons there to look after that affair, dim ond rhyw hen wrageddos dylion. The Admiral's secretary is a particular friend of my brother's and has promised to speak to ye Admiral to get Wil Owen made a midshipman in the Admiral's own ship, which he can certainly do, and if W.O. was now here he would be enterd in pay directly. The Admiral's stay at Portsmouth may be perhaps a month or longer (I dont know how long) and the secretary has orderd my brother to send W.O. *after them* to Portsmouth if he comes while they are there. The Navy Office will grant a ticket for him to go safely there if he was safe here. But here lies the great difficulty—the money to fit him out, for he must have a suit of what they call *uniform* and a gold lace hat, before he is fit to appear on ye quarter deck. Now what is to be done? I presume (and not without reason) that his parents cannot fit him out. What then is to be done? If he is *thoroughly bent* on this affair, let them stretch all they can, and send him up directly. By answering for his character we can get him a twelvemonth's credit here for some cloaths and be besides of some little help to him. My brother John formerly would have iumpd at such an offer as this; but I have no more to say, as I know nothing of ye character of ye young fellow, whether he is solid and sober or no. Wele etto, we have receivd the Portmahon box which was about eight inches long and three inches broad, and containd nothing curious—a few clustiau Gwener, dannedd siarcod, a mân gregyn gwirion, and one little piece of net coral. Nid oes yma ddim yn y byd a dâl i son am dano, ond mi fynaswn i lawer o gregynach pei gallaswn i fynd allan. Ond daccw fy het i ar yr hoel heb fod ar fy mhen ers tair wythnos, o achos tywydd drwg a phobl ddrwg. Let me see what curious books have I pickd up lately? Flaherty's Ogygia, J. Major's History of Scotland, Euseb. Socrat. Sozomen, and Thodoret's Ecclesiastical History, Stillingfleet's Origines Brit., The Cologn Edition of Hum. Llwyd's History of Britain, Leland de Script Brit, Ph. Harvey's Defence of Brutus against Buchanan, George Owen Harry's Geneol. of James I. If you have not a Dr. Davies's Grammar and an H. Lloyd, I'll send them you, ond fe allai mai gwell ganthoch i lyfr cregyn. I was offerd one of Edward Llwyd's Lythophyl for a guinea but it is too much money. Ni chlywai i sôn am Linkius a llyfr mawr Lister. There are none in London, for I have all ye catalogues of any consequence. You never told me a syllable about Bodewryd MSS., it is impossible you should

L. to W. contd.

forget them. I have seen also in Llanddyfnan some few old MSS. Is not ye old gentleman dead? If Will Owen comes, he should not lose time, and it is to no purpose to fit him out with any new cloaths there for they'll be of no use here, except shirts—some money in his pocket will be the chief thing. Mr. Macpherson (y dyn mwyna erioed) is Admiral Bodysgawen's secretary and he being always with the Admiral is an extraordinary recomendation. I think I told you enough about John Roberts's smart money, it will be perhaps four or five guineas, but he must come *himself in person* to receive them, and if he comes, it will be easy then to get him an out pensioner. Beth a wneir am stwff i orphen y pappir? Arglwydd Powys yn dyfod i'm lletty y foru neu drennydd i gonsidrio materion, ond nid yw'r iâr nesa i'r ceiliog i wybod dirgelion or fath hyn. Taw ar y gwaith gweithwyr blychod. Nos dawch.

Eich brawt, *Llywelyn.*

LONDON, February 7, 1757.

L. to W. CCCXIII

Anwyl Vrawt,—I have yours of ye 30th December or January; os nad oes yna ffrencyn nid oes yma chwaith, owing to ye jolt head of our member, quite wrong set on. Hugh Jones was young enough to live twenty or thirty years, but I suppose he killd himself with kindness to others. I am sorry for the loss of him, an honest well-meaning man. I suppose he has left children. You surprize me when you say your cabinet is quite finishd and partly furnishd. Brother Richard says *his* will be finishd the latter end of this week. *That* must be a fine one indeed when it is finishd! The workman perswades him it is better work than can be made in London. Would *you* be so perswaded and baffled? Da cael hanes y Delyn Ledr. Yw O.P. yn cael ei ryddid? Colled fawr am Sion Welsh a theganau. Must not y[e] *indenture* of Prentis Watkin come up, before the protection can be got?—and it is not yet come; you have forgot *that* I suppose. Onid yw 3 phacc o gardiau am 6d. yn ddigon? Maent yn costio yma 9d. neu 12d. But these by y[e] pound are only y[e] blotted ones that are laid by, not fit for use to play with because of .... little spots on them. About three packs make a pound. I think I have computed I must have about twenty pound weight of them for my intended cabinet. I have had no letter this post from home which makes me very uneasy, for fear that things are not well there. [*Have had one since, all well*].* If it is thanks by thousands and millions that you have of Pennant for stars, I could add three or four cyphers to what he has given you. Here is no alteration since my last, only a report about town that Bing's sentence is referd to ye twelve judges. Do you mean Ray's Nomenclatura? I never heard of any other dictionary of his. Why should it be interleavd? Hath it not a margin for Welsh names? My head this week turns upon wheels, that is, I am inserting in my Bockler's book of machines, all ye curiositys that I have pickd out of Monsr. Gallon's Machines of ye Royal Academy of Paris, 1735, and of Belidore's Hydraulics, 1748, Ramelli's Machines, 1588, the best of them all, though first wrote; and some improvements of my own upon all these. It is plain there are but few men born for this kind of knowledge. Too many of these writers are mere theorists, others mere mechanics. Have not I closed this letter already with this stuff. *Your affectionate brother*, *L.M.* **L. to W. contd.**

After I had finishd this letter, I received a letter from ***Arglwydd Powys***, which says that all is well, and as soon as he is able to get out of doors he'll come and see me. Doth not this look like a paradox? Am I so lazy or indolent or great or whimsical that I cannot vouchsafe to wait on him?

CAER GYBI SANT, Nos Fercher, 9d o Chwefror, 1757.

F'anwyl Frawd Mynglwyd,—Fy mendith a'ch canlyno am y llythyr yma om blaen a chan croeso wrtho. Ychydig a wyddoch i ddaed gan Wilym, druan gwr, glybod oddiwrthych; gwir yw fod y Llew yn fy mhorthi ac ambell lythyrun yn abl mynych. Ac oni bai hynny ni ŵn i pa beth a ddaethai o honof y flwyddyn a aeth heibiaw. Fe ddigwyddawdd iddo fo a minneu gaffael gormod o amser i epystolaethu. I sent directions to Liverpool (where Watkin Thomas now is) concerning Robert Jones's indenture; I presume he'll send it you from thence. Am glad that Mrs. Wheldon's affair is in so good a way; mae hi'n gweddiaw yn ddigon dygn efo chwi, a hi a dâl hefyd i chwi yn onest am eich trafferth; she is sensible that you have ta'en abundance of trouble already, which no other friend of hers would or could have done. **W. to R. CCCX V**

* These words were inserted after the rest of the letter was written.

W. to R. contd.

Ac am hynny mawr yw ei rhwymedigaeth, a minneu hefyd er ei mwyn. I told William Williams's father how the affair stood in regard to the lad's wages, ac mae hwnnw yntau yn gweddio ei oreuglâs gyda chwi, ac yn gaddaw talu yntau. Roedd yma'r dydd arall yn derbyn yr hanes, a rhwng y cwrw oedd yn ei fol ar egni oedd yn ei roddi yn eich bendithiaw, roedd y dwfr yn llifo rhyd ei ruddiau! However, am sorry that you have so much trouble with these affairs, ond pa beth a wna poblach? If there were nobody (that understood these things) of a benevolent disposition fe ai'r cwbl ir gwellt; felly mae Rhagluniaeth wedi eich gosod chwi yn y fan yna i gymorth trueiniaid. John Roberts and Will Owen are at Chester Water, pan ddelont yn ol we must call a council of war to determine what can be done or attempted to be done the approaching campaign. Fe gostiodd i mi ddarn o arian i gysuro gwraig Rowland Jones am newydd drwg y prizes cyn y rhyfel. She'll have enow i gyd gwyno efo hi os y Ffreins a ga eu llongau a'u llwythau yn ol—chwareu plant yn y pistyll, ond ê? Mi glywais er's dyddiau hanes Hwlyn. Ond och! roeddwn yn meddwl fod Sior y Doctor o Ddofer yn gyfoethocach dyn na hyn yna! Pa beth a ddaeth or miloedd? Ai anhwsmonaethgar a fuwyd? Ffei or sud! Deg i un na wna naill ai'r Ffrancod ai'r siarcod lyngcu Sion ab y Doctor am fod mor gyndyn. Will a gadd holl nattur y Doctor, yn nefoedd iddo; llanc yw hwnnw na bu mo'i fath yn yr oesoedd yma. One of the most eminent of the profession told a friend of mine the other day that Will Evans was a surgeon born, or born a surgeon. Nid yw hi mor flwyddyn gyfan er pan yrrais ef drosodd at fy ffrind the Surgeon General, who hath thanked me for him, when at the same time he refused 150 or 200 guineas before a noble lord's relation. Os ca'r llanc iechyd (gras a ga ond ei geisiaw) ac o bydd yr hen wr byw ddwy flynedd neu dair, fe fydd Will yn gefndyn. Aie mae'r almari i fod yn wcha un yn y byd? *'N rhagori ar almari Will Morus.* F'eill hynny fod ond odid, ond pei bae'ch yma i weled yr olwg brydferth sydd ar hon oi mewn rwy'n tybied y gwanobeithech na bai bosibl myned tu hwnt iddi, am deganau destlus o bob math tan haul a lloer! Gwych yr ydych yn amcanu trin y dreth Wyl Ddewi, a gwych a fai eich gweled yn myned mewn *processiwn*, mae hi ynghylch pedair blynedd ar hugain er pan fum i yna yn rhythu fy llygaid (am boly) arnoch. Deg i un y deuaf yna y leni, mi wna yr hen wr fy meistr anfon am danaf. Wfft, a dwbl wfft, i Oronwy Gethin! Ni chefais linnell oddiwrthaw er's blwyddyn, y Delyn Ledr ai para, perhaps he is offended because I did not bear that injury with better grace; I have some hopes since I proposed *paying 5s. or 6s. for my own book.* Na roddaf fi fyth fenthyg dim i brydydd ond hynny. Hawdd amor i Ieuan Fardd Deheubarth, os paid yr hwch a myned drwy'r siop ganddo yntau. Ni chaf mo'r amser, oni bae hynny, ysgrifenwn at Ieuan i Rydychen oblegyd yr wyf ebystol yn ei ddyled er's llawer dydd, yn rhodd anerchwch fi atto yn garedigawl. Os *Testamentau* a ddaw yma bydd dda ei cael mewn amser, obleit roedd y Mr. Ellis ar fedr rhannu rhai o naddynt y Grawys yn rhodd ac yn rhad i blantos tlodion, etc.

Sgrifenu a orug y *Frisco* at y Commissiwners a dywedyd fod Oats yn anealldwrys. Nhwythau a roddasant orchymun iddo fyned naill ai i Nerpwl neu i Gaerlleon Gawr dan instructions dros ddeufis. Ac yn ddistaw mi glywais fod y Surveyor General a'r Frisco yn cydymgynghori am represento i'r Commissiwners that he was not capable of the duty, being too old, etc.,—but this under the rose. Mi glywais heddyw ei fod wedi dyfod o Gaer ir Duw-mares; os felly, mae rhywun wedi cael y goreu. Fight dog, etc., hynny yw: hw'i gyda'r ci, ha'i gyda'r geinach, ond ê? Mae'r Aldremon yn broliaw y tâl o i bob math ar ddyn 20 swllt yn y bunt, a pha beth a fynnont yn ychwaneg? Os tlawd a fydd gwedi, fe gâe ond odid ugeinpunt yn y flwyddyn o bensiwn gan Nerpwl. Mae'n debyg mae marw ai wddwg dano a wna Iedws, fal Tom Ffŵg, fy anwyl ffrind. Dyna lle gefais golled am gyfaill ac am dlysau, o waith y chwiw garn lladron gan y Ffreins; ac os gwir a ddywaid y papurau daccw nhw wedi dala a chario i Martinico, fy nghyfaill Captain Welch, yr hwn oedd i gasglu (ac mi wn ei fod wedi casglu) imi bob math ar deganau yn yr Afrig ar Americ, pwy a faddeua i williaid digydwybod or fath accw, ni faddeuwn i yn fy myw. Foulkes and Welch had brought me their last voyages each a great many curiosities uninstructed, but this voyage had given them both directions, etc. Wala! wala! ni waeth tewi na son; Duw a gadwo Fortunatus o'u bachau melldigedig. Nid oes

W. to R. contd.

bosibl na welir terfyn ar lywodraeth y Baynter accw, fe gadd rydau odiaethol yn ddiweddar, ond drwg y ceidw diafol ei wâs, medd yr hen ddiareb, a gwâs ffyddlon iddo o'r Iuddew Brych, Anglice, Brindled Jew. Wrth gofiaw, par ddelw sydd ar y Doctor Bifan? Aeth o yn ffrins ar soseieti fach ettwa? Rwyf finneu yn ymguro ar anwyd a Mr. Peswch, ond ni chadd o ddim crys gwlanen na chrys pais chwaith ond un ffustion gennyf fi. Oni fyddaf inneu yn cymeryd deigryn o bwyns brŵd yn o fynnych iw cadw draw, ond nid bob nos chwaith; oni ffâg pwyns y gofid, ie gout, wrth ei hir ymarfer medd y doctoriaids? Tost o'r gorchymun yna am weini tan naw o'r gloch nos, na bond i grybwyll! Mi fydd yna williad yn yr heolydd gefn nos fawr, beth pei trawant wrthych? Mi weithiwn inneu hyd naw neu ddeg bob nos pei cawn dâl da am fy mhoen, ond yr ym ni yma yn rhy bell oddiwrth y Twr Gwyn lle mae'r câr Will Parry yn bathu arian. Annerchwch fi at y gwiwddyn hwnnw, da chwithau. Wala hai! Ni chewch mor llonydd a welaf i, nid yn unig y Cymry druain sydd a'u golwg arnoch, ond pobl o deyrnasoedd eraill hefyd. Dyma lythyr oddiwrth y Gendal dlawd yn gridwst yn dost, ni chlywodd ei chwaer ynghyfraith nag yntau fymryn o hanes ei frawd, John Kendall, o'r *Defiance*, er mis Mawrth diweddaf; nid hwyrach mai ei ladd a wnaeth y Ffrancod pan giliodd Byng, beth meddwch? Chwi gawsoch lawer o drafferth efo'r Gendal yma eisioes, mae arnaf gryn gwilydd geisiaw gennych ymofyn ynghylch ei frawd. Daccw Mr. Ellis wedi sgrifennu at ei frawd, yr hwn sydd briod a chwaer Llwyd or War Office yna, i edrych a ga'r truan accw ei arian sydd ddyledus iddo. Ffei o'r dyn a fai waeth nai addo! Dymma'r chwaer wedi dyfod heddyw o Bentre'rianell, mae nhad yn o salaidd rhwng y peswch ar fors, ac nid rhyfedd gan hyned ydyw, a chynrhwg yr hin, hi wnaeth yma y gauaf gerwina wyf yn ei gofiaw, gwaeth na'r rhew mawr o lawer byd. Pwy a feiddia achwyn ar Fam Gymru? Dyma ni yn anfon llwythi llongau o ydau beunydd i Gaer, ac i Gonwy, ac i Nerpwl (ar tlodion gartref, medd rhai, yn ffaeliaw cael cibyned o yd am ei ceiniawg). Chwi glywsoch ddywedyd nad yw gweithredoedd y Senedd ar Proclamasiwns yn dyfod ddim pellach na phont Gaer, am hynny, nos dawch, fy mrawd Rhisiart, ir brawd arall y perthyn yr olysgrif. Duw gyda chwi. [*W.M.*]

LONDON, February 15, 1757.

Dear Brother,—I have yours of ye 3d, and another of an after date, a piece of ore. Just now am about filling up brother Richard's cabinet which came here a few days ago, a mere bite (i.e. the fellow that made it, and charges it ten guineas, I believe). Slight work, and ill set off. Dyna fal mae pobl yn trin y brawd. He believes them all honest till he smarts for it, and then wonders at them, and is very angry, and irreconciliable, but he that deals with all mankind as if they were rogues is never mistaken or uneasy. If he judged wrong he is easy. The cabinet is three feet by four feet and eighteen inches deep, consequently eighteen cubic feet, that is just twice as big as Lord Powys's, which cost but four guineas, frame and all, but this has no frame. Out of what was to spare in filling it, I have packd up for you as much as fills ye little box you sent here, but I suppose you have several of them before, but some of them I am sure you have not. Brother shall send them to ye waggon, for my situation will not admit of it. My largest specimens if reduceable will only fill a whole card boat. The ores I break to that size, and pack up y^e *duplicates* with their names on them ready for a friend. I make no use of cards that are smaller than half, for I find the smaller to be apt to overset with ye wind of one's sleeve, and besides, as I use labels of blue paper such as ye inclosed in every boat to shew what it contains, the small ones are too small for a label, and goods without knowing what they are, are of no value. The same sized label as the inclosed fits the whole card boat and the half card boat, so there will be some part of ye boat coverd by ye label. Your square boats are firmer and stand closer but not so easily handled or so soon made. I have not ye patience to wax them. Bu agos i'r peswch am lladd yr wythnos yma. I have been a coughing and vomiting most violently for about two days,—an overflowing of ye bile I suppose, and want of exercise—but am now somewhat better. Na chanfu'r Gowntes mor *almari* etto? Mae'r Arglwydd yn sâl etto, ag heb fynd allan oi dŷ, mwy na minneu. I'll send the list of ye materia medica in my next. So much for ye first letter. Is! is! Glossopetrae a elwir yn Mahone shark's teeth, so all sailors call y^m. Well I have enquired (or some for me) all over London, and I cannot find

L. to W.
CCCXV

L. to W. contd.

Linneus. Llwyd's book of fossils and had cuts in it, and sells often for thirty shillings, felly dyna ddarn o atteb i'r llall.

Wele gwedi'r cwbl, mi welaf, gamgymeryd o honof yn y cabinet yma, arfer a ddysg, nid cyfarwydd ond a ymofynno. One quarter of my intended drawers shall be but half-inch deep, or less if they can be made so; one half not exceeding an inch; the rest an inch and half, and two inches, and a few of three and four inches. Another consideration—give your opinion of it. Would it not be better to every two or three small drawers of half an inch, etc., to have a two or three inch drawer next to them to put the large shells etc., of ye same kind that they may be had together, as, suppose, a thin drawer for very small Buccinums, and a thicker next to it, and a third or so thicker still? Then begin a thin one again, etc. I find such an order wanted. Well, again, my brother Richard is so ill cut out for affairs of this kind that you could not believe he was a brother. If you were to see him sit down and read ye news or any trifling paper, when he sees me at ye same time busy in making boats, sorting, etc., just as if I were born only to make up cabinets for people; and when the materia medica, etc., were shewd him in ye drawers makeing a most charming appearance, would you not be surprized to hear an ingenious man say "what is this ugly piece of lapis calaminaris put here for? What made the fool of a druggist send me such things as allspice, cloves, long-pepper? We can get enough of them in any shop for a penny!" All that delights him is the drawers of blue lead ores, and chrystals, and talc, etc., because they shine and look pretty. But a true *ffosilwr*, would give room in his cabinet for a piece of a miner's . . . found in a mine 500 year old. What a different way of thinking we have! Let this then be once for all a caveat to you who you send any curiosity's to. One will thank you for them, another will say they look ugly, and are common everywhere. But brother R. has the least notion of any man living to make a collection of natural curiositys, for he'll never take the trouble of putting one of them in a drawer or a card board as long as he lives, and I am sorry that I foresee, that this pretty collection that I have taken so much pains with to sort in his cabinet, will fall into the hands of a broker (God knows how soon) and perhaps his family nothing the better for it. I was sorry to hear that my fine collection of ores, etc., that I made a present to W. Jones, F.R.S., were sold at a public sale of his goods on his death, but that was a trifle to this. This is all to-day. You shall hear when the box sets out. *Your brawt*, *Llewelyn*. L. to W. contd.

LLUNDAIN, February 18, 1757.

Anuil Vraut,—Yours of ye 14th lies before me. I sent you last post ye druggist's list of ye materia medica sent here, and by Monday's waggon comes a small box of about ye bigness of your head, of some of ye things that were to spare after ye filling my brother Richard's cabinet. No, it is not above half full; now I see more than ever the fault of having too few thin drawers, half inch and threequarters of an inch. I am afraid there are but few things in this box that you had not already, except about a dozen gingerbread nuts which filld up a space instead of paper. There is also the Cologn Edition of Humphrey Llwyd's Commentariolum, and a fair copy of Davies' Grammar, and Alanus de Ins. Notes on Merlin's Prophecies. I had nothing else curious by me, nor room if I had. The mechanic wheels are out of my head for a while, by reason of a letter receivd this day from Cardiganshire that David Morgan is dead and hath left me a mare, saddle and bridle in his will, and to my daughter Margaret £200, but I suppose there will be some difficulty to come at them. On the other side I have some money there in danger. Such are the troubles of this life. I am heartily glad that one of poor Dick Evans' children doth well, I wish it was in my power to promote his good. This I write to-night against to-morrow night, perhaps I may have no leisure to write any more before I seal it. L. to W. CCCXVI.

Your affectionate brother, *L. M.*

The box is directed to Mr. Thomas Bryan, merchant at Llanerchymedd, to ye care of Mr. Goodwin, grocer, in Chester,—so look out. I have just finishd a draught of my intended cabinet, let me have your thoughts upon it and some improvements if you can think of any; the inclosed paper will give you an account of it.

LONDON, February 25, 1757.

L. to W. CCCXVII.

Braut Uiliam,—Dyma'r eiddoch o'r 21ain yn cael ei atteb y munud yma gyda'r nos, yn lled ddiog, besychlyd, ar fygydfa ymron fy ninistrio. Ni fedrwn lai er hynny nag edrych dros bob erthygl o hono yn ofalus, a chynnyg atteb i bob un o honynt, ond mae rhyw sŵn gwirion yn fy nglustiau ymron fy rhwystro:

"Mary, what makes your ducks to die?
I gave them wheat, I gave them rye."

You shall know the meaning of it another time. Enquire no more at present. You complain of not having curiositys, and you have the best shop in the kingdom to go to. I thought it was but just now you had hazarded Lister's great book by sea, and comes to you again. The study of shells, fossils, and plants is vastly natural to youth, and I suppose to people that are grown children ye second time, and that is the reason I am catchd with it now. About forty I minded little but drinking. No such thing as Linnaeus now to be had in London, I believe, unless it be some foreign bookseller, Vaillant or such. I see an advertisement to-day that Dr. Hill intends an English translation of Linnaeus's Genera and Species Plantarum. I have sent you a sketch of the disposition of my drawers. I will have none in one another, and it is as natural and as little trouble to have them two and a half inch as if two or three, and I would have them less than two and a half inch if it was possible to make them. Glew iawn y canodd y Bardd Coch, ni adawswn i mo'r llawer o le iddo, peth mawr yw cael gosod allan ynghyntaf. I have made some of your square card boats, but I don't think I should be able to make a dozen of them in a whole night, a gresyn eu bod yn edrych mor foelion, for they take much less room than the Chinese ones, but the others neater. The little box is gone towards Llanerchymedd since Monday, I suppose; it was deliverd at ye Inn (Blossoms Inn) a Saturday; ond mwy'r twrw na'r taro, nid oes yno ddim a dâl am ei garrio, ond nid oedd yma ddim gwell. Yesterday Lord Powys wrote me word that he believd his lease would be signd yesterday at ye Treasury, and God knows how it will affect me. It is said that Mr. Pitt and ye prevailing Party have made a motion yesterday in ye House about Bing, and that they will take his part in order to bring the weakness, etc., of ye late Ministry to light. Ffei o'r peswch a'r llysnafedd sydd ar fy nghylla (cwll calon) rwy' agos a threngi. Great preparations making againt St. David's Day, but I shall have no share of it. Dyma fi yn cysgu o drymder uwch ben y pappir ac yn ffaelio sgrifennu dim chwaneg. L. to W. contd.

Eich brawd ffyddlon, *L.M.*

Dyma'r llygaid gwedi agor etto, a daccw George Evans, Stiwart Mathafarn, gwedi foddi i hun yn feddw ; nage, fal hyn :

Yn feddw f'aeth iw foddi,
O Bentre Aberdyfi,
Gan yrru i'r môr yn wâg i siol,
A llon'd i fol o frandi.

And so in a freak he fell off his horse and was drownd in an instant. We have been framing a letter here to Mr. Kynaston to have him succeeded as agent by R. Morris o Fathavarn, and I have some hopes it will do. We shall know in a few days.

Saturday 26th.—Just now have a letter from Lord Powis that the lease was signd a Thursday and passes ye seal (Great Seal) to-day.

LONDON, March 2, 1757.

Dear Brother,—Dyma fi gefn y nos newydd fwytta afalau a llaeth im swpper rhag y fygydfa, a rhag llawer peth gyda hynny, a gynneu fach y daeth y brawd Rhisiart a'ch llythyr yma o'r 25 February, gwedi bob ddoe yn llenwi ei fol yngwledd y Cymru, ai lygaid yn wêr heddyw. Cof pob diwaethaf, ni welodd o erioed wledd fwy. Minneu yma heb weled Cymro a'm llygaid na phrin Sais chwaith, a phei gwelwn, pesychu wnawn i. Mi ollyngais dros bwys y cwyr o waed Dduwsul, ond nid nes i mendio. I hear my mare is come home from D. Morgan's brother, and that is a sign I think that he'll do pursuant to the rest of the will. The money that was in danger (and great danger) is safe once more, but perhaps may run into danger again ; for my money is so often in danger that they are hardly ever safe. I dont understand yet ye use of blychau *sedar*. If the subjects are large won't they stand by themselves without mixing with others, but experience teacheth. Gwir a ddywedwch achos uchder y cabined. I dont like it my self ; that is brother's cabinet that is six foot high, for though the drawers are easily drawn they are not so convenient as those the L. to W. CCCXVIII.

L. to W. contd.

eye can see y[e] bottoms of, before they are taken out. Therefore it is likely mine shall not be so high in drawers, but that part, about a foot or so, shall be pigeon holes for papers; and hidden money drawers back, oblegid fe allai y bydd rhai miloedd iw cuddio yno os y byd a eiff ymlaen yn iawn. I wish I had the 130 drawers, and I should not be long contriving some use for them; some for mathematical instruments and philosophical apparatus's, some for ancient Roman coins, some for mechanical tools, some for curious copper plate cuts, maps, etc. This is a new contrivance. I have heaps of things already collected that [have] to be put in order, and a man may as well be without (even) money if he doth not know where they are. Dyna i chwi siryf arall yn lle O.P.—Peswch, peswch, peswch ydyw diwedd pob rheswm, felly nos dawch medd.

Eich brawd, *Llewelyn.*

Ni wn i fydd dim iw ddywedyd y foru.

LONDON, March 9, 1757, Mercher.

L. to W. CCCXIX.

Dear Brother,—Just now receivd yours and having read it, and dined, and afterwards drank tea, and talked nonsense, etc., as usual, I sat down to answer it before I take my scale and compass in hand to compleat my collections of machines, or the little time I apply daily on my Critical and Historical Dictionary of Proper Names. So thus I begin. Robert Prisiart, gwr merch Nan, is a great fool if he troubles his head about these people. They offerd it me formerly, but wanted a good deal of money for it, so if he has a right and a possession, what business has his conscience to trouble itself about it? If any thing is proposed as from him to these people they'll be sawcy and probably dip him into a lawsuit, especially as they will think it worth something if he stirs. Therefore if he is in his senses let them make their claim, and then let him send them a full state of y[e] case how the right is in him. I hope he is not turnd childish. Gochelwch fod yn rhy hyf i wlychu'ch traed a'ch dwylo yn plannu coed, etc. That is a labour fit for a robust gardener, nid yw llinyn yr einioes ond brau. Aie *salutiferous cough*, peswch iachus? Gwae fi na bae hwn ar y Dr. Nicols neu ryw ddoctor, a minneu heb ddim peswch iachus tra bwy byw. Ni chefais i gysgu hun ar fy nghefn, nag ar un o'm ystlysau ers rhai misoedd. Ai iachus yw gorwedd ar fol yn wastad? Ag er hynny, fe ddaw ymbell hynt o hono a wna imi chwysu fal pei tynnid fi trwy afon; dro arall gloesio, a gorfod yfed dwfr twymyn i helpu i'r llysnafedd ddyfod i fynu. Ond etto ped fawn gartref i gael y fwyd ar ddiod a chwenychwn, mi ai gorchfygwn. Ni cheir yma ddim bwdran llygadog, na diod fain chwibsur, na dŵr ffynon redegog yn rhedeg at godiad haul, nag uwd ag ymenyn o dan yr ordd, na llymru a llaeth gafr unlliw, na llaeth enwyn sur a phytatws, na brithylliaid afon Melynddwr, na sil y gro, na chant o ddanteithion gida hynny a gaid yno. Dedwydd ydych chwi gael coed ieuaingc heb eu gofyn, gan wragedd *ynddigions*, pei cawn i rai er talu am danyn mi ddiolchwn hefyd. Pei cawn inneu adref etto yn iach ddiberygl, mi heliwn ryw ychydig o goediach o Sir Drefaldwyn, etc., oblegid mae gennif le rwan yw plannu. Os rhydd Duw gennad mi symudaf i Benbryn glanmai. All this is spoke as if my affairs were quite determind here, but they are not; and when they are you shall hear. My mare, etc., given by D. Morgan is come home, and I believe the rest of ye legacy's will not be disputed. Bing is now past recovery, and several deserve shooting as well as he. Gwraig Powel Nanteos, sef merch Mr. Owens, Ynys y Maengwyn, gwedi marw ar enedigaeth plentyn, o hil ddrwg ddigon, roedd yno ormod o'r rhywogaeth ddrwg o'r blaen. The husband was in London plotting of mischief. Dr. Nicols's salutary cough will hardly give me leave to write any further, unless I steal an interval now and then. Nothing new to say, and there is nothing new under the sun. One word more about ye cabinet. You'll put your coins in wooden boxes. Though I have not a drawer full of them, I'll put mine in a drawer by themselves and paste a thick paper on the bottom of it, with holes in it little more than their size, then they will not run together and mix. I dont know yet but I may have wooden boxes for *môr gyllill* and such bodies if they are easier made than pastboard ones, ond nid yw hyn ond cyfri'r cywion cyn eu deor. I should be glad to have the catalogue of your cabinet, the contents of each drawer, when you have put them in order. It would help me, and tell me what I want. "Want" says he, I want everything almost, all my choice things are given away, and lost and scatterd by these skirmishes of ye enemy. I dont know that I have any thing of consequence; or

L. to W. contd.

L. to W. contd.

that will fill twenty drawers out of y[e] hundred that I intend to have. My head is giddy, and breast sore with coughing. I can drink no London malt liquor, nor punch, and but very little wine. Just a little to give my spirits a motion. So I am very fit for study, and one would think that a whole year I have spent here in writing and reading might have produced something good, but it really has not anything to boast of, for I had but very few tools (books); and what can a workman do without his tools? I have not hardly anything to shew for all the year's work. *L.M.*

W. to R. CCCXX.

CAER GYBI YM MON, Mawrth 9d, 1757.

Fy Anwyl Frawd Rhisiart,—Wele gan dderbyn derbyniais eich ebystol. Can diolch am tano, ac am bob erthygl ynddo. Ni wn i a ddaw'r Power of Attorney yn hwn, dim stamps y ffordd hyn. Ni yrraf fi ond hynny ynghylch matterion mal rhai'r Gendal, oni bydd rhyw ddynan tlawd gonest, diwyd, cwrtais, diniwed yn crefu yn daer daer arnaf. Pwy a fedrai nacca'r cyfryw? Nid ymrawd Rhisiart mi dyngaf am llaw ar lyfr. Cewch swllt yn y drugaredd, chwi ai ca'ech oddi-yma pei medrwn ai estyn i chwi. Nid oes dim hanes am Will Owen yn dyfod adre, mae'r gwynt byth yw erbyn. Your kind intention perhaps will come to nothing. Da clywed eich bod wedi dyfeisiaw ffordd i Iedw i gael ei ryddid, poed felly y bo. You see the Alderman hath drawn his neck out of the collar. It would be shocking cruel to curo dyn ac ynta ar lawr, fal y byddant gynt yn ffeiriau Llanerchmedd. That martial spirit is quite laid, nid felly ymhob man, gobeitho. Y peth debygwn i a fydd gwaetha ar les Doctor Dofer, colli cwsmeriaeth y siop, megys treftadaeth, enw da, etc., ond os ceir miloedd ar y weilgi, bydd cystal a gwell ond odid; gwell aderyn mewn llaw, etc. Llencyn o'r mwyna oedd Sior, and I wish him success. Wfft i'r modd y mae Fortunatws yn cael ei libindiaw gan y Maltese—a set of sad scoundrels, ond ê? He hath too great a spirit for a low station. Och na bai gan ein Harglwydd Frenin 50 o'i fath yn gadpeniaid ar ei longau rhyfel! Rwy'n llwyr gredu na byddai chwaith hir yn dinistrio llynghesau Ffrainc. Pam na ddywaid rhywun hynny wrtho? Ie, ie, anrhydedd ddigon oedd caffael ymlochlach a Llyw Powys, ac yfed oi wirawd ugeinmlwydd oed, yn wir ddiau roedd 'y nghalon i yn llammu gan lawenydd weled y newydd oi fod yn eiddo'r Esgair. Nid oes bosibl na bydd bellach ddiwedd ar deyrnasiad yr Iuddew Brych, ac ar ddalfa'r Llew. Pa beth a ddaeth o stiwardiaeth Mathafarn, dywedwch? Ni choeliafi na bo'r bara wedi codi cymaint yma, sef Bara Gwyddel, ac yna gerwin o leied y dorth 6d., ac amled y cegau sy'n gofyn gan Wilym wirion. Gresyn na basai'r Palment yn llestair i'r bobl yna ddistiliaw dros saith mlynedd yn lle seith mis. Os byw fyddir, bydd da cael gweddill yr almari odidawc yna o dlysau'r India, etc. Mae arnaf ofn na chaf fawr o hanes plant Dewi. Par un ai canu ai peidiaw a wnaeth Goronwy y leni? Mae'n rhaid cadw noswyl heno, Duw yn unig a wyr par sut a fydd yma y foru, par un ai iach ai claf. Gobeitho yr goreu ac ofni'r gwaetha. Duw a fyddo gyda chwi eich deuwedd y ddeu frawd. **W. to R. contd.**

Myfi yw William y Trydydd.

P.S. 10fed.—Ha wyr frodyr! Ymlawenhewch gyd a myfi, oblegyd mi orchfygais modryb Acsus dros byth, gobeitho. Amen. Llyma stamps; dacw'r Fadws hwnnw yn yr Iwerddon. Byddwch iach bod ac un.

[CAERGYBI], Mawrth, 1757.

Dear Brother,—Inclos'd with this you'll find a Power of Attorney and certificate for the purpose therein mentiond. When the wages, etc., is receivd, please to deduct out of it what may be *sufficient* for your trouble, o ddechreu hyd ddiwedd, oblegyd nid oes dim rhwymedigaeth ir dyn ond y gwrthwyneb. A gwir a ddywaid yr hen ddihareb, fod gweithiaw'n rhâd yn waeth na rhodiaw, oddigerth lle bo eluseni yn y peth. Ni chofiais i ddywedyd i chwi'r dydd arall fy mod wedi gwerthu (wrth siawns chwedl Wil Bened y ffidler, o Lan Eilian y Ceimiad) un o'r Testamentau am ddeuddeg swllt i Mr. Bwclai, Person Mechell, yr hwn oedd un or subscribwyr. Gobeitho na chlyw o fod y nhad wedi gollwng am lai. Ai i nhad y rhoddaf y 12 swllt? Ond wrth gofiaw etto, ni siersais i ddim am eu carriaw i lawr ettwa. Mae tippyn bâch, bâch, lleiaf a fu erioed o asgen yr acsus arnaf, yn ddigon er cymysgu'r mennydd, felly ni wiw ymhel ar pin. Ni chlywais i ddim oddiwrth y Llew er's deubost neu dri; gobeitho mai darparu y mae i ymadaw a'ch Dinas fyglyd, a ffoi ir gelldydd cyn ir fygydfa ei ddihenyddu. Duw'r diddanwch a fyddo gyda chwi. Byddwch iâch. *Eich brawd anwiw ddigon, Gwilym Cybi.* **W. to R. CCCXXI.**

LONDON, March 12, 1757, Saturday.

L. to R. CCCXXII.

Dear Brother,—I have yours of ye 7th and am heartily sorry you have met with one of ye worse companions I ever met with. I thought so when I had the ague; but I have since got ye cholic by wetting my feet, and had it but twice, and for a few hours, but extremely racking, so these two *terrible ones* now guard me against wetting my feet. *Moment* a fydd poblach Sir Aberteifi yn ei gymryd rhag y wrâch. Da i chwi os ewch i gan deneued a Mr. Ellis, os gedy hi chwi yno. Gwedi i'r Dr. Evans stwffio yn fy mol i loned cŵd o'r powdwr coch mewn amryw ffurfiau, bolus, pills, infusions, electarys, etc., rhoi dyrnaid o hono mewn pottel o rum a wnaeth y lles goreu imi, and that in a great measure takes off the bitterness which to me at last was intolerable, and is still. My brother will answer about Kendal, etc. Mae Huw Price yn deitwaiter tlawd yma, ai wraig (merch y Cichle) newydd farw; nid oes dim iw ddisgwyl gantho os oes ar eich tenantes eisiau. Dyma'r peswch, *chwaer nage brawd yr acsys*, agos a nadel imi sgrifennu at yr acsys ond pan fynno fo. A spring ague as I am told by a very sensible old woman, is a very salutiferous thing, ond Duw a Mair am cadwo i rhagddi. I am something feverish every night if I eat any thing that doth not please, *peswch*, or even if I dine upon any thing of hard digestion, felly chwi welwch fod y *machine* allan o drefn yn erchyll. Os cuddiaf y cregyn rhag lladron, ond dyna fi gwedi dwedyd wrthoch chwi ple byddant I have had above £8000 in money in ye house at ye same time, where the meanest shepherd might have come at them, but such is ye honesty of Cardiganshire in that respect, and their ignorance, that I never was robbd of any. Our thieves are not numerous, but we have some. But I would not advise any man to keep his money in known drawers, for it may be a temptation. It is not yet determind *when* I am to go homewards—my motions are very slow. No more to-night. *Your affectionate brother*, *L.M.*

There is a bouncing lye in all ye papers, a pretended account from Holyhead of thieves on Bodedern Heath, it seems intended to lessen the credit of the late accounts from Holyhead, but query.

LONDON, March 15th, 1757.

Dear Brother,—By the inclosed you'll see that Pen Sibolen hath like y[e] man in y[e] *Spectator*, sent your letter to me, and I suppose mine and my wife's to you, which were to come here. If you have not forwarded them, lose no time, for I am uneasy, lest he might have sent them to some other place. Did you ever see a goose hideing her eggs when she is dry or hungry after long sitting? She picks up straws and throws them behind her, even when she has gone ten yards from her eggs. Most people in the world (that is the chief part of them) are like this goose, they attempt to do something, but they dont know what. I have nothing more to say by this post, but that I have seen yours to brother and that I congratulate you on your conquering the *wrach*. Nid gorchest vawr yw trechu gwrâch, a honno'n afiach hefyd. Nid oes yma nag awen nag amser iw orphen. *Eich brawd ffyddlon*, *L.M.* L. to W. CCCXXIII.

LONDON, March 19, 1757, Saturday.

Dear Brother,—I must answer yours of ye 14th in some manner, though I am loth to put pen to paper. I never heard till now of petition Cybi. Caled farw Bwclai, ond fe gyfyd rhyw Fwclai arall. Na cheiff Gronwy un bersonoliaeth am a wn i, oblegid ei ffolineb. Aie chwi sy'n profeidio Mrs. M. a hadau? Pa beth a gewch i ganthynt hwy? I agree to y[e] blychau coed when I have need for blychau at all. I rejoice with you for your recovery of y[e] *Telyn Ledr*; croeso iddi! I have drawn up some sort of an answer to y[e] Bodedern Heath thieves, and I suppose you'll hear of it. Wawch! Dyma'r Bennant gwedi galw ddoe gida'r brother Rhisiart yn gwaeddi am gael gweled ei gabined, canys fe ddywedodd Gwilim wrtho fod yno un gwych, etc. Gorfod arno ynteu ei wadu, ai fod heb ei orphen, ag onide fe ladratasai'r Benant y pethau goreu oddiyno pei gwelsai mai oi ystor ef y cawsid hwy gan mwyaf; canys mae'r papirau (labels) yn dangos mai o Norway, Sicily, etc., y daethant. Felly ni cha'r Benant moi gweled dros un flwyddyn etto, nes y ceffir ychwaneg o bethau, fal y caffo'r naill ymguddio ynghysgod y llall. Ni fu ddaioni erioed o fostio pastai. I am glad you have sent some skirts of y[e] ague, a sad companion, and a surprizing one, to move so periodical. Is not the motion of y[e] sun L. to W. CCCXXIV.

L. to W. contd.

at its power on ye fluids the cause of that regular return? Certainly it is. But I cannot find the cause of my cough, for it appears in all manner of shapes, sometimes of indigestion, sometimes of obstruction, of perspiration, sometimes of a flow of humors, sometimes of a dryness in ye vessels. But is it not more likely that it is occasiond by a defect in ye machine to perform its offices, and is a concomitant of old age beyond the power of physic or knowledge of the physician? Henaint ni ddaw ei hunan! I have got Sir John Prise's Defence of British History translated into English, and also Humphrey Llwyd's [De] Mona [Druidum] by a noted translator here, but he knew so little of ye sense that I am obligd to take a vast pains to brings it to its self. It is surprizing how a good scholar and a poet could commit such egregious blunders, as to take *Circius* and *Aquilo* for two Generals of ye Scots and Picts, when any old woman might have known they were *south* and *north*; i.e. the situation of the countries of those people. But enough of this, for among five thousand people you'll scarce find two men of clear heads, as *Selyf ab Dafydd* said. Nothing yet determind about my return home, all dark and mysterious. All my family well in Cardiganshire last post. Hopes yours are so.

Your affectionate brother, *L.M.*

W. to L. and R. CCCXXV.

CAERGYBI, y Dydd diweddaf o Fawrth, [1757].

Fy Mrodyr,—Daccw dri neu bedwar o byst wedi myned heibiaw heb ddwyn cymaint ac un llythyr oddiyna; a pha beth ydyw yr achos nis gwyddis yma. Trafferthion 'rwyn gobeithio ai para, os felly, bodlon yw Gwilym, obleit nid oes dim yw gaffael yna, ie, nag yma chwaith, heb ymdrafferthu, ai oes? Diammeu fod llawer o bobl 'nheddigions yn cael ei gwala yn ddidrafferth, ar boen fwya ar y rheini yw gwariaw yr hyn a gasglasai eu tadau au mammau drwy ymdrafferthu. Ond nid nhw mo bawb. Wel, beth sydd gennyf yw ddywedyd yn hyn o bappurun? Dim yn y byd ond bod yr ardymmyr yn gethin, h.y., y tymhor yn ddryghinog ynial, yn gymaint nad wyf yn clywed ar fy nghalon weinyddu tippyn yn fy mharadwys, chwythu gwynt Gogledd—orllewin ysgithrog, ie, ac ysgythrawg hefyd, mal prin y meidr dyn aros yn ei union sefyll. Daccw'r haul yn tewynnu, rhaid ei rhoddi hi ar do unwaith etto, o herwydd fod llawer o waith ar yr ol, a hi a fydd yn ddyddiau C'lanmai ar fyr. I met the other day with a small but curious concha veneria with the fish alive in't—a nondescript differing widely from all other shell fish I ever saw. Letter from Southall ger llaw Northall advice that the Penbardd is resolved not to make any more cowyddau; nid oedd yn cael mor ymenyn i roddi ar ei fara oddiwrthynt. Colled am ganu da. Here's a war lately broke out betwixt two great men, viz., Pen Siri Sir Fôn, a'r Frysgaw. Cyfreithio ag ymwirio, dyma Frysgo wedi sêsio ar lwyth o benwag llongdy, a'r llall wedi ei roddi yntau yn y Crown Offis. Cewch yr hanes ryw dro, nid hwyrach yr ymgrŷg rhai o honynt pei caent ddigon o râff. Rhaid mynd i dacclu bawd y dyn sydd wedi mortiffeio, felly byddwch iach, a Duw gyda chwi. W. to L. and R. contd.

Eich caredigawl frawd, *William Morris.*

LONDON, April 8, 1757, Friday night.

Dear Browdyn,—I begin this to-night, lest to-morrow may deceive me, for one day cannot answer for another, nor doth a great man that is to-day in ye Ministry know where he'll be to-morrow. Here is another total change in ye Administration, y Duc W. a ddoedoedd wrth ei dad nad ellai ei gydwybod ef ei adel yn nwylo ei elynion. But however it is, out they are most of them, and there is nothing certain under the sun. Pan gynta y cenais gywydd i'r wrach, ni chawn i gyttrym nad dyma hi'n neidio o Gybi yma, a bu agos iddi am gwenwyno i, ag mae rhyw *farr* ar draws fy nwyfron, ag nid 'r un fath a'r beswch sydd yn awr. Nid yr un yw peswch y wrach a'r pesychau eraill. Dwedwch wrth y Coch mae gwell iddo beidio a chanu iddi rhag ei ffyrnicced. Ffei bottes bawneidr, *snakeroot*, etc. Dr. Allen was a negro if he meant your cabinet was worth no more than twenty-two guineas. It is more likely worth above a hundred. A good collection of that kind is inestimable, and few people have tolerable collections. Gwyddel bod y fodfedd yw *Allen*, na rowch fawr goel ar Wyddel gwyllt; "cythrel o *kil Gwyddel* gwyllt," ebr y bardd, so according to him they were beyond a *cythrel*. I take all the care I can with this machine of mine, and yet some accident happens to it that I dont expect. Who would have expected y *wrach?* Ond dyna geir am L. to W. CCCXXVI.

L. to W. contd. ganu heb achos, cymryd ci'n erbyn ei glustiau. Aie Cymrodorion yw Gwilymod? Diau mae ie, a dedwydd ych chwi gael y fath gymdeithas pei gwelech.

O dedwydd, dedwydd, dedwydd,
Pei gwelei i fod yn ddedwydd;
Y Dyn sy nghysgod mynydd Twr,
A dyna'r Gwr sy ddedwydd.

As for rowling in money, and plenty, and plagues and great men and cheats, and grimaces and lies, and tricking and breaches of promises and contrivances, etc., there is an impossibility that *dedwyddwch* should ever follow a man there or bodlondeb either. Wele, of all the mothers and fathers in ye world I dont believe you can pick out a pair so simple as poor Wil Owen has. Wonder the lad that has seen a little of ye world should not have had more sense. Here Admiral Boscawen is in town, and the midshipman's place applyd for and granted. He one of ye last set of Lords of ye Admiralty, and continues in ye new change. The recomendation from his own secretary, a man in great friendship with my brother. I am positive he would soon have been made a lieutenant and very probably a captain if he had any spirit to drive through the world. Such a step to preferment is uncommon. Good Gods! And so he is to be a negro like Mwcc mawr and people of that class, to carry coals to ye old woman of Holyhead, and to have a mammy's *didy* now and then! Well done woman! Mae mrawd Rhisiart gan iached ar glain ond bod corn ar fys ei droed—mae rhyw *ddolyr* a thristwch ar bawb. Mae arnaf ofn mae priodas vach Sir Aberteifi fu yn Leghorn. Mae gennifinne ryw ffassiwn ar Ginseng, but query which ye right, or what it is good for. Ieuan Fardd has his warrant in his pocket to be Chaplain of a Man of War, and a very fit fellow for it. If I have leisure I'll send you his last ode; Duw wnel na bo. Ni waeth gennifi beth a ddelo o Fechell nag un Saint arall. Thus your letter is answerd. Now for new stuff. I am here much in ye same trim as the 22nd of March last year, the day I came to London. I have been writing something ever since, in search of what they call *bodlondeb*, and in defending my head against the strokes of rascals and villains that would have demolishd me, to save themselves from the popular clamor of some people that had common sense and saw that they had used me ill; but I thank God they are all now out of power but one, and God with his little finger may thrust him out of y[e] way too. My wife is moving to Penbryn as fast as she can, ag fe fydd yno nyth clyd dda iawn, pei cawn fynd yno i'w osod mewn trefn, oni welsoch i nyth y dryw? Pa beth am dd—l uffern aeth a'r Iuddew Brych yn ei gorpholaeth o Esgair y Mwyn. A messenger from London arrived in *that neighbourhood* y[e] 26th March; and 27th, early before the man came, Paynter took horses and slipt away to Salop, and some think to London. I suppose his pride and folly reachd y[e] ears of y[e] Treasury, and that they sent a man to supersede him, after he had drawn Arglwydd Powis into a scrape, and all the country besides. Felly rhyngwyfi a chwitheu, nis gwn i pa fodd y mae'r matter yn sefyll, mwy nag y gwyddoch chwitheu. But I believe in my heart he has drawn Arglwydd Powis into a scrape, for I have reasons to think so. The demands of y[e] country is some hundreds of pounds, and one rascal there (no matter) is about £500 or £600 deep in the mud. The London messenger, after looking about him, and seeing Paynter had given him y[e] slip, went back to London, and a change happens in y[e] Ministry at that very crisis. No body can pretend to determine how it will turn out. Most of it is a mystery to me, though I make shrewd guesses how it happend and what will be y[e] event. It is surprizing what confusions money will make. Is it any wonder that the d——l should sit crosslegd in *ogo maen Cymrwd* to guard the *treasures* there? You talk of news from Northall. If I beent much mistaken Gronwy has overreachd that poor O.W. by borrowing money as he has every body else that he has had to do with, and it would be a deed of charity to guard the poor fellow against going too deep. L. to W. contd.

I never yet met with a piece of contradiction as that fellow is. The low blood is prevalent, and they may say what they will against innate principles, this man is an example beyond everything. Would any thing but a tinker (un yn tincian pedyll hyd y strŷd) have behaved as he has done to his best friends? Eurych is too good a name for him. "Tincer ai can wrth fol tancer cul," D.G. I hope your *Telyn Ledr* is come home. Ieuan Brydydd hir has copied a vast deal of Llyfr Coch Hergest, his MS. when bound will

L. to W. contd.

be a quarto of three inches thick. Dyma hi'n hwyr, a'r coesau'n oeri a'r peswch yn cryfhau, nos dawch.

Saturday morning.—A charming fine day, summer all over. Coughd and ymgomio a'r *wrâch* last night, raveing in the spirit, etc., depend much on the syrup of lemons against them all. I thought much of Dr. Allen last night. Grown immensly rich and *then* turnd virtuoso, doth not that shew him a man of sense? And then undervalue people's almari's, and say they are worth twenty-two guineas, to see if he can buy a collection ready made for a trifle! *You'll see* that he is not a man of great knowledge though he is rich. Riches and knowledge are hardly ever concomitants (Solomon excepted) and perhaps *his* knowledge consisted much in buying collections of proverbs and of plants of Hen Gyrus o Ial, etc. But to what purpose are all these reveries? They are only ye sediments of ye peswch and ye wrach to fill up a sheet which you sadly wanted. Wawch! daccw hen ewythr yn Sir Aberteifi gwedi gwneuthur ei lythyr cymmun, a chwedi gadel i Sion fy mab i a reversion of a tenement in Cors Fochno, (a kind of an island there near ye way as you come from Dyfi to Borth), after the lives of two old persons, but they may live too long. It is about £12 or £18 a year, I have forgot which. I am just now packing up the several articles in each drawer by its self of my brother's almari, to be removed to his own lodgings, having been with me since it came from ye maker, but is extreamly ill done. The bottoms being of unseasond wood, and in thin drawers, the sides being very weak, have all warpd; that is, they are grown narrower, and the sides being naild to them are obligd to give way and bend upwards, because the length of ye side cannot shorten, so that they are all archd upwards, and the whole strength of a man can hardly draw them out of their channels. This is a thing learnt from others misfortunes. If your bottoms were not dry they'll be the same. So much for this important affair.

The common news in ye papers need not be touchd upon. The City of London shewing such esteem to ye discarded Ministry, some refusing to be employd in high offices, etc., would not a stander-by think the nation mad to quarrel in this time of danger? Who can send fighting orders? Who cannot see they are a ruind people—now sending out troops to foreign parts, at the same time they have foreign troops to defend them from invasions? Lladd amreliaid because they could not conquer with an inferior force! Advancing a man to y[e] management of y[e] kingdom because he sailed round about other kingdoms, and saw the people and fish, and stole a ship from one of y[e] nations by accident and when he came home lost his money *ar gardiau a disiau!* Ai tybied nad gwaed plant Llywarch Hen a'r cyffelyb sy'n codi yn eu herbyn y dyddiau hyn, cadwed Duw'r ychydig weddillion sydd yn y mynydd, a Duw wnel i minneu gael diangc yno, oblegid nid da calon Sais wrth Gymro, chwedl yr hen ddyn. A geir dim arian o Ddulun byth? Dyma'r almari yn galw am danaf, a'r pappir ar ddarfod, felly byddwch iach a bodlon. L. to W. contd.

Eich brawd ungnawd yn ymgnoi, *Llewelyn.*

CAER GYBI, Ddywllun y Pasg, [11th April, 1757].

Ha W9r Frodyr,—Mae deubost neu dri wedi myned heibiaw ir Werddon draw heb ddyfod a cyhyd a bys o lythyr oddiyna, ond er hyn i gyd rwyf yn o lawen glywed o Deifis fod y gwalch boneddigaidd ganddo fo Painter wedi troi ei gefn o'r Esgair lle'i bu yn teyrnasu nis gwn par hyd. Mae Mr. Ellis yn ein dysgu nad oes dim anffawd yn digwydd i ni ond a fo er lles ini ryw dro neu gilydd. Ergo Painter playing the rogue was a kind action of his. Myfyriwch ar y pethau hyn, ac a wiw coelio yr offeiriad ai peidiaw. Fe allai mai er ein lles bod y gynffon y darfu ir Iuddew wneuthur yr hyn a wnaeth. O'm rhan fy hun nis gwn i pa beth a ddaethai o honof oni bai fo—y fo Sion y gwr drwg oedd yr achlysur i mi gaffael pethau gwell nog elïon o'r ddau, pan yttoedd fy nghrimawg archolledig ddwywaith yr un tymhor. A pheth oedd y rheini debygach i? Beth oeddynt meddwch? Llythyrau o Lundain bob yn awr am cadwodd yn fyw. Oni bai hynny torraswn fy nghalon yn fy nghystudd. Oni bai'r bradwr ni chawswn basai llythyr unwaith mewn chwarter blwyddyn oddiwrthych fy 'neidiau. Dywedwch ir meddygon yna beth sydd oreu ar les tor crimmog. Dyma Watkin, nage Wadcyn—*Watcun*—wedi dyfod adref, a chwedi dyfod i hyd i'r dentuwr yn ei gist gartref. A dyno fo i chwi, mae son yn ei waelod am ryw ddiwti, mae'r dyn yn gobeitho nad rhaid iddo fo mor talu mono. Da chwithau, mrawd Rhisiart, W. to L. and R. CCCXXVII.

W. to L. and R. contd.

na anghofiwch mor neges. Nid drwg cael swyddau or fath yma a chael tal am waith ai e? Roedd y nhad yn iachus dda iawn ddiwedd yr wythnos pan ddaeth Marged Owain oddiyno. Ac rym ni yma, mawl i Dduw, i gyd yn *iach ddianaf.* Byddwch chwithau felly eich deuwedd ar hyn a berthyn i chwi.

Eich brawd ungalon, *William Morris.*

P.S.—Dim llythyr heddyw ond un oddiwrth fy meistr, sef Thomas Pennant, Esq., Fellow of the Royal Society at Upsal, in Swedland, etc.

LLONGDDIN, April 26th, 1757, Tuesday.

L. to W. CCCXXVIII.

Anwyl Vraut,—Here lay before me three letters of yours, stareing me in ye face for an answer. April 7th gives an account of Surveyor General gone to Dovey; I don't care, but am glad he doth not draw yn yr un iau a'r chwilcathod. Mi wranta i Oats ai wên ffalsla, os ca' fe le iw drwyn. April 13th says rhowch risg iddi; na rôf, hi fodlonodd ar saig arall, ac hi ddaw, medd hi, at y Bardd Coch. Ysbigod rychog I suppose I call your wentel trap. I have very fine ones from Dovey. A ddoeth yr Iuddew Brych i Gybi ai peidio i fynd i'r Werddon? Rhai a ddywaid mai do, ond ni wn i pwy i goelio. Duw wnel mai do.

Gwae hefyd y sawl a roddo fenthyg MS. i Brydydd, a phle y tybygechi y mae MS. *Transcript* y Ll. K. Hergest, ond yn fy llaw i fy hunan (ie fy hunan), ac nid o'm bodd yr a fe allan o honi tra bo fy llygaid yn agored. I suppose you'll want to have some account of it. This is all I can afford now, even in a fit of ye hyp, having just received £20 by ye help of ye Earl of Westmoreland, and having £20 more on credit of ye Captain: drank with my brother one night till his heart opend and he* gave him ye book (three vols. quarto), a quarter of a year's writing. Next day he ownd the gift and corroborated it, but in a few days after came to beg them again for God's sake, but they were gone out of town *to me eighty miles*, who was writing a dictionary; so there was no coming at them, and here they are indeed! I have just made an index to them, and they are to be bound in one volume, which will be near three inches thick. The index contains 141 articles, some very ancient. It is a surprise to me that a drunken idle fellow had

*This probably refers to Ieuan Brydydd Hir.

such patience and such weakness to give it away. There are several of ye odes that you have in Llyfr Gwern Eigron, some of Rhisierdyn, Sefnyn, Casnodyn, Llygad Gwr, Dd Benfras, Cynddelw, Llewelyn Vardd, H. O. G., P. M., Ein. Wann., D. Ll. Mew, G. Meil., O. Cyfeiliog, y Br. Vadog, Gr. ab Mred. ap Dd., Gwynfardd Brech., Tysilio, a great deal of Ll. hen, Taliesin, Gr. Vn. ap Gr. ap Dd., Gr. ap Dd. ap Tudur, Iorwerth ap y Cyrriog, Gr. ap yr Ynad Coch, ach Cyrriog a Chattwn, and these are all ye authors.† That fatherd on Tysilio St. is a poem of Eira Mynydd. I have not had time to read them through, but those of Llyw. Hen that Mr. E. Ll. hath transcribed, Tit. 7, differ greatly. He gave too great a scope to his fancy, and I daresay Ieuan Fardd hath copied pretty correct, and was a far better judge of a dark passage than Mr. Llwyd, as being an excellent poet. In short you are to trust to none of Mr. Llwyd's quotations.

You say that vinegar, sugar candy and oil is ye medicine with you for sore throats. Juice of lemons is better, and flower of brimstone added is best. I have none of ye four requisites belonging to my garden, so no hopes. My aspect east under a southern hill. My soil not above six inches deep before you come to a shaley rock, and no water that can come into ye upper part of it, it shelves to the east. Mae'r Benant a mrawd yn ciniawa ynghyd heddyw, ag yn brolio oi cabinets—but my brother's is spoiled, being made of new wood, and must be all alter'd. Unless you can get something better than his *duplicates* it is hardly worth going so far as *Downing* for them, ond ni chlywai air o sôn oes yno ddim MSS. Pawb at ei bwrpas, fe ddywaid rhywun yr un peth am y rheini. Yours of ye 20th says fod ymgno, etc. Am ba beth y mynnant grogi *Bess Manwel?* Ai lladrata o dylodi a wnaeth? Dwyn bytatws neu rywbeth, mae'n debyg. Duw gattwo Mr. Bwcclai, ni chlywai inneu ddim sôn am Natws: nid yw e ddim yn segur, os byw. Mae'r Llywydd Llwyd yn dywedyd sgrifennu o honof attoch, and sent a protection and some other paper lately, hopes you have received them. Ai hen ddynan cwla y galwch i Ddeiniel

†The MS. he quotes here is probably "Panton MS.," 15, which is stated to have been transcribed "in the year 1757 by me Evan Evans then of Merton College." In spite of his statement in the letter, Lewis Morris must have returned the MS. to its rightful owner.

L. to W. contd. y Gof? Younger than yourself, I believe. Pa beth a ddaw o hono fi ynteu sydd yn mynd fal Llywarch Hen nad allaf ddarymred. Daccw Ddafydd neu Ddewi Fardd o Drefriw yn addo hela imi enwau holl gangennau afon Gonwy. Gwych a fyddai cael enwau holl gangennau afonydd Môn. Nid oes yma air o wybodaeth pa bryd y ceir mynd adref (sef dibennu'r matterion dyrys yma), oblegid ni wiw mynd adref cyn hynny. My critical Dictionary calls me and I must close this—aie tynnu'n wysg i din y marthin? Nid oes gennifi ddim a dal iw sgrifennu at fy nhad, ag onide?

Eich brawd ffyddlonaf, *Llewelyn,*

CAER LONGDDIN, May 3, 1757.

L. to W. CCCXXIX Anwyl Vraut,—I have yours of y[e] 27th April open before me which requires this answer. Wawch! dyma newydd a ddaeth i'r ty cyn imi orphen y gair. *Answer* a gewch i yn niwedd y llythyr hwn pan gaffwyf chwaneg o ysbysrwydd. Well done *Oats*. I'll answer for him that he'll manage the people of *Bonover*. My brother has got his son a post in a Man-of-War; but I don't know the least obligation in the world there was for it, unless imprudence of one side. Well done Aldremon P. Bawddyn yw hwnnw na fedro na dywedyd na gwneuthur. I cannot get a Linnaeus for any money. Brother can give you y[e] best account of y *Benant*. Gwych fydd cael *Cywydd y Wrach*. I hear y[e] bellman—so must close. The news is, and all the bells ring, etc., that the King of Prussia .... [letter torn] ....

CAER LUNDEIN, May 6th, 1757.

L. to W. CCCXXX. Anwyl Vraut,—Heddyw erbyn y foru, dyma gynnyg ar atteb eich llythyrennau o'r 2ed o'r mis. Aie spigod gefnog? Oes, mae rhagor rhwng rhych a chefn, ond ni bu erioed gefn heb rych, ni cheisiais ond barn Llywarch Hen, ac mae ei gan Calan Gauaf ef yn agored om blaen y munyd yma. In y[e] orthography of Llyfr Coch Hergest:

Kalan gaeaf llum godeith,
Aradyr yn rych, ych yggneith,
or Kant odit Kedymeith.

Wele oni welwch mae rhych yw llwybr yr aradr? Paynter is in London sure enough, and pushes his long nose no doubt into Lord Powys's ears. We shall see y[e] event one time or other.

Diolch i chwi am hanes Penbryn; fe allai'n wir y gwna cysgodion beth lles, ond ni wn i pa bryd y ceir mynd yno i blannu. L. to W. contd.

Mwynach prydydd na Thaliesin a ganodd i'r Brwyn
Ynghysgod y rheini cawn feinir yn fwyn.

Na welodd Penant ddim ond y *drawers*, ag mae'n cyfadde mae un gwych yw'r almari. Nid oes ryfedd i chwi fod yn glaf ag yn ffaelio cysgu, a chwitheu yn eich lladd eich hun yn palu'r ardd heb fod yn rhaid; ychydig o balu sydd o'r goreu i gael chwant i fwyd, ond nid da rhy o ddim. Dewi Fardd o Drefriw a yrrodd Gywydd i'r Cymmrodorion, dan obaith cael *subscriptions* i ryw lyfr cân o waith Huw Morus, Edward Morus, etc., a minneu ai rhois ar waith i hela afonydd, a nentydd a chornaint! Nag oes modd yn y byd i nadel Loli bwtler dderbyn cyflog i fab, trwy na wneir rhyw gyttundeb ag ef ymlaenllaw am roi rhyw ran i'r wraig os rhoir help iddo. Digon digrif fydde i chwi gael y Surveyor General o'ch tylwyth Ynghybi. James Morgan, Comptroller of Aberdovey, writes me word that the Surveyor General has been there and inspected the accounts of y[e] new collector but said he would not meddle with the account of y[e] collector that had been superseded, because he had been superseded, and that he gave them strict new rules, all new molded! I have an account from my wife that she is removed to *Penbryn Paradwys Gymru*, and that she likes it better than ever. John Owen is not well, but recovering; supposed to have had the measles or some such iruptions. I have recoverd my £30 and interest of that rascal Catteral, and for his attempts have put another upon him. Here died lately Lord Powys's two daughters, there is only the boy alive, but the Lady I believe is big. Ni ddwedai ddim am y gwr nes gweled ei waelod. I am afraid he is but a weak brother; ond etto er hyn nid oes le i syrthio allan ag ef, ond gadel iddo ddyfod atto i hun. I have done an undiscreet thing—mi delais drosto am goed £188, ag mi debygwn nad ydyw'r arian yn bur barod gantho, felly mae ef yn ddieithr dros dro mae'n debyg, ond arnafi roedd y bai, onidte? Gadewch iddo, mae'n rhaid ymrwbio trwy'r tew a'r teneu, hyd nad eir o'r byd yma i fyd a fo gwell, a hynny fydd gobeitho, oblegid nid oes yma ond yr anhunedd a'r aflwyddiant yn cyfarfod dyn beunydd,—mwy o'r chwerw nag or melus. Ond etto

L. to W. contd.

mae peth melus ond ei gymryd yn bwyllig; a dyna fal y dysgais i gan Lywarch Hen yn y Gorwynnion:

Gorwynn blaen perth, hywerth—Gorwydd
Ys da pwyll gyda nerth,
Gwnelid anghelfydd Annerth.

I have nothing more to say this post that is of any consequence for you to know at present. *Eich ffyddlon frawd,* *Llewelyn.*

Wawch! Here is Ned Edwards just come to town, having grown as fat as a hog in y[e] French prison; and his owners are for giving him an armd ship of 18 or 20 guns. He says he has lost near £200 by being taken, but I dont believe him, for his owners insured for him £150 unknown to him. His owners say that they got him out of prison, but brother Richard is sure that they had no hand in it, but that brother himself got him exchangd for a French captain.

LLONGDDIN, May 13, 1757.

L. to W. CCCXXXI.

Y Braut Gwil,—Yours of ye 7th I received, ac ol bodiau'r wrach arno. I am glad ye chwilcath fawr is agreeable, and that she digests Oats and herbs and fossils, etc. Nid oes niwaid ei bod yn ymdrech a'r Bonoveriaid. A ydych chwi yn cofio'r englyn gynt i hen wrâch? Eich crach ar eich croen ai dygodd im côf. Fe fydd y wrach arferol a gadel crach ar groen wrth ymadel a phobl. Nicholson, the General Surveyor took an affidavit of an old woman that she heard another old woman say that an old woman (Gwenn, the smugler) had run goods, and it was poetizd thus:

Hen wrach a chrach ar ei chroen, a dyngodd
A dangos yn ddiboen,
Ddwe'yd o afiach wrach grachgroen
Fod gwrach a chrach ar ei chroen.

Diolch am chwedlau Gogerddan; but they are fumes, etc. Griffiths, my old clerk, is clerk to a great brickmaker, at £50 a year. Nid oes yma ffranc pei rhoid gini am dano. Daccw Sion Owain yn yr *kyp* dros y pen a'r clustiau, lowness of spirits, disappointments, etc., and want of resolution and strength to support himself under difficultys, but custom and practice will make things easyer. Put a woman that is startled at a mouse in a room full of mice for one day, and she can bear the sight of a mouse the next day. To mend the matter my Treasury enemies caused him to be servd with an Exchequer writ y[e] beginning of this month, at y[e] suit of y[e] Attorney General by information, and this hath frightend him and my simple family there out of their wits. I had notice of it beforehand and orderd him out of y[e] way, but he was so *hyp'd* that he could not move an inch or did not think my information was of any consequence. You see what low shifts my enemies are put to to seek out for matter of information against me, for this is intended for that purpose; ond ebr yr hen ddihareb "ni *thwyllwyd* a rybyddiwyd"; felly minneu wnaf y goreu o'r gwaethaf. Dyma newid etto meddant hwy ar y Llywodraeth Deyrnasol. *Pwll a choes a chastell** yn cyduno. Dont you remember the old (and almost infallible) remedy for y[e] ague formerly used at Pentre Erianell? Bleeding y[e] very moment the fit is found to come on, seldom faild to throw it off for good and all. There is a report in town of Jamaica's being blockd up by sixteen French Men-of-War, and they fear it will be lost. Ned Edwards's owners are in treaty for a ship of 800 or 900 tun for him, to carry forty or fifty guns, an East Indiaman, provided the story about Jamaica be not true; one of them has fifteen or twenty thousand a year there in real estate. If *Ned* had y[e] luck to have a head fit for preferment he might have been made a great man. He has given Admiral Boscawen an account he took when in prison of the French privateers and their stations, etc., which will be of great service. Several hours thrown away in reading O'Flaherty's History of Ireland; gelyn brych i Dysilio, and he knows not why, unless he suspected Galfrid had told more lies that he. However, this also helps on y[e] Brittish Dictionary to which I still want a name. Brother does a little every morning towards setting up the things in y[e] almari. It is now in his room near y[e] Navy Office for public view. I packd them after I had once sorted them in cards, because of carrying them there, and now they are to be put up in the same cards again, about a thousand articles I suppose. His almari costs £15, which is twice the value of it. [*L. Morris.*]

L. to W. contd.

* In June, 1757, a Coalition Ministry was formed. The Duke of Newcastle went to the Treasury, Legge became Chancellor of the Exchequer, and Pitt Secretary of State.

LLONGDDIN, Mai 21ain, 1757.

L. to W. CCCXXXII. Anuil Vraut,—Dyma'r eiddoch o'r 14eg o'm blaen, a difyr oedd ei weled, a chlywed neu weled fod y wrach gwedi cael codwm arall. Is, is; the same wages and usage on board a tender as a great ship of war! Nag oedd cywydd pêr gan Drefriw, digon diflas, ond fe allasai Sion Peri gynt ddywedyd enw afon Ddulas a Mynydd Trysglwyn. Mi drwsiais beth ar gywydd Robert Llwyd o'r Garth drwy ddymuniad Mr. Vaughan, ond fe allai na chadd Huw ond y cyntaf yn noeth heb ddim i guddio ei noethni. Mae Dewi o Drefriw yn sôn am fardd 20 oed yn Arfon. Ie'n wirionedd, Paradwys y Deheu, neu Baradwys Ceredigion, yw Penbryn y Barcud; pwy nad ae i baradwys pei cae? My wife begins now to be pleasd with it and to despise Galltvadog. The victory obtaind by ye King of Prussia ye beginning of this month makes great noise here. It is said, there is an express come this evening from the King of Prussia to our King with a fuller account than we had in last night's *Gazette*. I have just bought Moreri's Great Dictionary in four volumes folio of men and places, to see what he had done on that head. He is but a laborious collector, and hath neither etymologys nor any thing curious, but abounds with blunders about our British affairs. He says Taliessin and Myrddin Emrys were great friends and great philosophers, but there was above a hundred years difference between their times. My *Celtic Empire* will be a hundred degrees beyond it. His book is all French which is some inconveniency to me for I have almost forgot the little French I had. His plan is general for all ye world, but mine only the Celtic Empire and of that only those names that are of some tolerable account. [A portion of the letter has been cut off at this point]. I have a notion Lord Powis hath been trickd about Esgair y Mwyn, and that this new Ministry just come in and the Duc Castell Newydd will fall out with him. Mae'n debyg ei fod gwedi ymrafaelio a hwynt eusus, drwy fod yn rhy gybyddaidd. Query whether Iuddew hath not led him into a scrape, ni waeth fyth. My next will give you a better account, pedfae fatter i chwi pwy a enillai na phwy a gollai. Jack Owen is gone to Aberystwyth for his health. He is almost eat up with the hyp, etc. Here is never a frank for love or money. I have open'd a door into'r Drysorfa, a kind of a private access, by which I shall discover the intentions of men. I wish I had seen it sooner, but this was only a work of Providence, and could not be sooner. *Your affectionate brother,* L. to W. contd.

Llewelyn.

LONDON, June 1, 1757.

Dear Brother,—Yours of ye 24th ulto. I have this day and am glad you are well. Here it is fourteen months since I am in this strange country among infidels, etc. Dedwydd ych chwi gael gweled tad a chyfaill cywir a phlant iw meithrin, fal y bo cymwys. Wele hai ni chewch chwithe un llythyr ond hynny a gyst wyth geiniog, yr un fath y bydda'i yn plygu pob llythyr siengel. Here is a bill of three skins of parchment filed against me and John Owen. It is with a view to take off his evidence from being on my side, but for all this I shall fight them through all ye weapons. John Owen is much recoverd, it was at first ye hyp, and afterwards Dr. James's Fever Powder that threw him down—gwr gwych i fod yn ddoctor! Ie, hiroes i Lyw Prwssia i guro'r gelynion. Moreri is very useful, though a poor performance. The book is not called the Celtic Empire *alone*, but the *Celtic Empire described*, or some thing to that purpose. Pam na rowch chwithe enw arno, ai rhaid imi geisio plentyn, a throi 'n dad bedydd hefyd? Profi mae Selden yn y *Mare Clausum* neu'r *môr gwarchaedig*, mai i Ynys Prydain y perthyn pob môr sydd oi hamgylch hyd at diroedd pobl eraill sydd ar y lann, and this from even *Galfrid*, *Nennius*, and old British traditions. It is a pity he had not seen the Triades, which shews that King Arthur had three admirals, (probably red, white, and blue). I have drawn up a representation to ye Postmaster General about ye taking 8d. for letters that have postcripts, and you shall have an answer soon. I have also employd all this morning till dinner in makeing an addition to Cywydd yr Ardd, which my brother is to carry to-night to ye Cymrodorion, upon reading of which it will be proposed to have ye Bard chose a corresponding member, and I daresay it will be so, which will enliven his *Awen* very much. I will send you the addition to-morrow night if something doth not intervene. Na laddwyd mo Ffortun, he is born to greater things. I am glad you are come to ye scheme to have glasses on your card boats, for you'll find them L. to W. CCCXXXIII.

L. to W. contd. for many reasons convenient; it will not be easy for spectators to steal little things, and it makes ye cards steady. By ye time I wrote this, I have yours of ye 20th. Nid oes gennifi flas yn y byd i lwfio am godi gwaliau sguboriau a theiau o fesur punt, pan fe allai mai 5s. a fydd y gost i'gyd. Onid yw'r Gobed Sion yn tyrru cantoedd o bunnau yno, ag yn cael y tir yn yr hen rent, a phobl eraill yn codi eu tiroedd i ddwbl rhent y dyddiau yma? Beth a ddigwydd os pallaf i lwfio punt am godi gwal; rhoi'r tir i fynu fe allai, ac yno daw rhyw un ag a rydd £20 yn y flwyddyn am dano. Mi wranta fod rhai ai rhydd, felly gwell i'r Gobed daclu'r wal ar ei gost ei hun, y peth eill ef wneuthur am ychydig o sylltau i barhau dros ei oes. Nid dyddiau yw rhain i iro tin hwch dew a bloneg. Benben etto bo'r Bonoveriaid, hys. Gwiriach yw hanes Gorthrech yr Awstriaid nag y dywaid y Ffrancod. Are not most of ye officers pent up in Prague, and cannot send a letter home? Ni ddymunai Ffredrig chware ddigrifach na dal y cathod i gyd mewn trap, brechtan o fel gantho gael y fath chware. Fe wna iddynt fwytta eu hên sgidiau, oni ddont iw rwyd ef. I have gone through a very curious book of ye lives of our British Saints, where were among them, Cadog, Illtud, Padrig, Dewi, Dyfrig, Deinioel, Samson, Cybi, Pedrog, Dunod, etc., which I have inserted with additions and critics in my Celtic Empire Described, and am now going through Leland's Script. Brit. — the most industrious, curious man (that ever wrote) of ye English nation. But he was acquainted with Sir John Pryse and Humphrey Lloyd who helpd him much. Nennius is a most valuable piece of antient history, and I am sure (almost sure) it never yet hath been understood by any modern, not even Mr. R. Vaughan, the great antiquarian, for I have found things in it by comparing it with Llywarch Hen's works that no modern ever thought of; and Gale's Notes on Nennius are such as an antiquary ought to be ashamed of.

It is the greatest treasure next to Tysilio and the Triades, that we have extant of our British affairs. I wish I had the Hengwrt copy, for Gale hath not dealt honestly in ye publication, having left out a whole chapter or chapters because he could not give them credit, and perhaps there is nothing in him but what may be defended. The wonders of Anglesey I happend to copy out of y^e

Hengwrt MS. which Gale hath ommitted with several other things, which was a roguish way of dealing with an ancient author—calon y Sais wrth Gymro. I have bought two folio volumes of Historians chiefly for ye sake of Nennius that was among them, they could not be separated, and the rest are but trāsh to him—Gildas, Eddius, Asser, Higden, Malmsbury's Glaston, History of Ramsey, History of Ely, Wallingford, Fordon, Alcwin. Twenty authors in all, not unuseful, but most harp on ye same string, and are eccho's of ye few ancients. Terfyn ar hwn nos Fercher; y bore dranoeth such a great defluction on my lungs that I have hardly my senses, a salt rheum, but about noon turnd a looseness and something better. *Eich brawd, Llewelyn.*

L. to W. contd.

CAER YR HEN GYBI SANT, Mehefin 2d, 1757.

W. to R. CCCXXXIV.

Anwyl Frawd Rhisiart,—Chwi ganfuoch lawer llythyr or eiddof fi er Gwyl Alphage hyd yr awrhon, ac ambell un o honynt yn dyfod at y Llywydd ei hun rhag eu blaenau; ond byth er hyn ni chadd hwnnw mo'r odfa i 'sfennu llinellig ond yn unig cyfrifon yr hen wr yna; Duw a'i cadwo. Pa beth a all fod yr achos i dri phost fyned heibiaw heb un llythyren oddi dan bawen y Llew? Ond odid mae ysglyfaethu y mae, os felly lle dâ disgwyl, a pha beth a ddaw o Wilym druan edn os bydd pob creadur yn ei esgeuluso? Gadewch iddo; dyma nhad heb fy ngwrthod ettwa, fe ddaeth i'm hymweled nos Sadwrn y Sulgwyn, a dyma ni yn ymgomiaw er hyd yr 'wan. Mae'r iechyd, y clywed, ar gweled ganddaw yn bur salw. Hi wnaeth ddwyreinwynt y dyddiau diwaetha a gogleddwynt ffyrnig; hynny a barodd ir fors fod yn ddrwg o fath, ar golwg yntau yn ddolurus, er hynny fe fedr ar droau ddarllain print brâs heb ysbectol, yr hyn sydd ryfedd. Nis gwn i a ddarfu imi atteb eich llythyr mal yr ydoedd yn haeddu, felly rhaid edrych drosto o ben-bwygilydd rhag ofn fy mod wedi gadael ambell falc. Mi soniais am Ddeintur Watkyn a'm bod wedi talu'r gini i nhad, etc. Fe fydd tad Will Williams o'r St. Alban's, yn galw efo mi bob siwrnai i ofyn par sut yr ydych. "Symol," meddai inneu. "Oes dim newydd o Lundain?" "nag oes," a dyna yr holl ysgwrs rhôm, mi fanegais iddo'r hanes er's dyddiau byd byd. Nid yw Mrs. Wheldon yn ynghenyd gair oi phen un amser, gwan obeitho, debygwn. Annigrif yr ymrysonion yna ymhlith y mowrwyr, ffei o'r sud. Ai

W. to R. contd.

tybied y daw Pwll a Choes* i chwareu bys yn y bastai eilwaith? Ni wyddwn i fod gan Boba Williams, Bodafon, yr un wŷr heblaw offeiriad Llanfihangl Tre'r Bardd, ysef yw hwnnw, Rhisiart, fab Rhisiart William dew, o siawns, e weddai, y digwyddodd hanfod hwn yna. Pa beth sydd yn dyfod o Iedw; a gadd o long newydd fawr? Daccw ei chwaer yn dechreu codi, wedi bod yn hir yn orweiddiawg. Oni chlywais i ei fod o wedi pesgi yngwarchau? Arwydd dda iawn o honno, ond ê? Pwy oedd yn achwyn ar Sion Ffreinig nad ydoedd yn bwydo mo'r Brutaniaid? Aie mae'r mawrion nhwythau yn Ffrainc yn colli eu coau, ni waeth fyth, goreu'r cwbl. Gwych a fa'sai cael cistiaid o Destamentau rhyngom, mae nhad yn tybio mai chwarter cant a wna ei waith o, ar chwarter arall i Mr. Ellis a minnau. Deg i un na chawsid ambell degan anianol a naccâ fynd i'r almari dau, mae yna aml gragen a chan mil o bethau sydd yn eisiau yma. Pwy yw Will Middleton? A berthyn ddim ir hen gorph o'r enw hwnnw? Par sut a fu rhyngoch i ar Bennant? Ymofynion moelion o rhain, meddwch chwitheu, ond dywedwch a fynnoch, ni ddeuwn i byth ben i gael defnydd i lenwi hyn o bapuryn oni bae i mi gymeryd i mewn beth priddach a siwrwd yn llanw. Dyma fi wedi bod ymhell bell yn y plwyf yn gwledda efo nhad, a daccw fo wedi myned iw wely yn sâl gan y lenngig, a mineu yn s'fennu at ymrawd Rhisiart, fal y gwelwch a chil eich llygad pan ddarllenoch. Agos yn ddig wrth bob peth Cymreig meddwch, a hynny o achos brilyn o brydydd; wala, wfft i hynny! Cymodwch, cymodwch! Fe allai y daw'r bardd atto ei hun ettwa a[c a] gân i chwi gerdd a beru hyd ddiwedd byd. Gresyndod mawr na fasai wedi ei wneuthur o well defnydd, yn enwedig y rhan honno a blanwyd oddimewn iddo o'r tu asw, sef y galon fach, nid hwyrach mai ar yr ymennydd y mae'r bai, ple bynnag, bai anfeidrawl sy'n rhywle. Ni chlywais byth na siw na miw ynghylch stiwardiaeth Mathafarn, ni chadd y Tàl† moni mae'n debyg er mwyned llythyr Kynastwn. Nid wyf yn hanner leicco Llyw Powys; chware'r ffon ddwybig, rwyn ofni; beth meddwch? Rwy'n ofni ei fod yn gostwng ei glust at yr Iuddew Brych, os felly nid oes iw ddisgwyl ond b—weidd-dra, ie yn wir

* i.e., Pitt and Legge (Lord Stowell).

† Richard Morris of Mathafarn, son-in-law to Lewis Morris.

matter tywyll ydyw. Fal hyn yr aethym dros eich llythyr o benbwygilydd felly rhaid bellach ymorol am destyn o'r eiddof fy hun. O ie, a gawsoch cyn wyched gwlaw yr wythnos hon ag a gawsom ni y Monwysiaid; roedd llawer oi eisiau, a Duw a'i gyrrodd ini yn dymhoraidd, mawl iw Enw Bendigaid. Daccw Domos Owen, fab Owen Sion Tomos o'r Nant Mawr gynt, wedi marw yn amherod o gyfoeth, nid oedd ganddo na phlentyn nag etifedd ond o ddeutu hanner cant o neiod a nithod a phawb yn disgwyl ei goreu glas. 'Roedd Surveyor Kybi yn un o naddynt, ni chlywai fod fawr wedi syrthio iw ran—roedd yno ddigon o le. Fe ffaeliodd gan Wilym druan orphen yr ebystol hon cyn ir bost fynd i bant, felly rhaid ai adael dan drennydd heb yn ddiolch ir ewyllys, a chan ei bod hi yn dŷn at ddeg or gloch mi ai rhoddaf heibiaw am heno. W. to R. contd.

Nos drannoeth.—Ar ol cael diwrnod teg i weithio ac i rodiaw efo'r tad einym, dyma fi yn eistedd i lawr i roddi gronyn o ystyn yn yr ebystol hon, a pha beth iw ddywedyd nis gwn. Mi glywais gynneu fod y wraig o Fathafarn wedi dyfod echdoe dros Borth Aethwy, nage chwaith, Porth Ddaethwy ydyw, ynghwmwd Tin (neu Din) Daethwy, nis gwyr yn awr ymhle yr yttoedd y Din,—ie myned yr oedd y wreigdda honno ai gwâs oi blaen tua Phentre Rhianell, yr oeddym yn ei disgwyl yma heno ond ni ddaeth, ac ni ddaw bellach. Mae fal y gofynnwch ir etymologist yna a ydwyf yn fy lle ynghylch Porthddaethwy, ai nad ydwyf. Mr. Rowlands's conjecture of Porth-aeth-hwy will not bear water—beth meddwch? Dyma fi newydd dderbyn a cargo of fossils from Dwyran. Ni adwaenoch i un Sion y chwilottwr. Here are some curios, concha anomia's, coraloid bodies, entrochus's, rhai cregyn, etc., all found in Cwmwd Menai ym Môn. You must have Linnaeus's Systema Naturae cyn y bo'ch virtuoso iawn. B'ai ryfedd gennych weled erchylled yr wyf yn trin y Lladin. Mae llawer er pan fu Owain Parry'r crupl yn ceisio ei guro im pen, ond yr oedd y fan honno yn rhy galed neu yn rhy feddal (nis gwn i par un) i dderbyn fawr o addysg yr enwog athraw hwnnw. Daccw Loli Huws o Ligwy, a Harri, fab Twm Prisiart Gawr, o lan mor Dulas, y ddeunolff penna yn yr ysgol, yn ymherod o gyfoeth! Erbyn hynny, nid angenrheidiawl bod yn ddysgedig, ai ê? Dyma hi yn ddeg heno ettwa felly rhaid rhoddi'r papurun heibiaw unwaith mwy cyn ei orphen. Mae fy ngobaith y

W. to R. contd.

cawn newydd da oddiyna y foru nesaf ynghylch y Llew or Dean. Tri meib William Sion Owain or Fagwyr gynt, fab Sion Owain Tomos y saer cerrig, o ymyl Pen y Coed, oedd aerod Domos Owain, left them about a thousand pound each in land. Torri'r braich, torri trybedd yr ysgwydd, torri tri or senna, torri'r forddwyd, etc., meddai yr hen Sion Owen Thomas. Chwaer i Domas Owain yttoedd gwraig William or Fagwyr. Chwi fuoch yn danfon gwirod yno'r dyddiau gynt, ond do? Mae fal y dywedwch, par sud y mae rh'om ar Ffrancod accw? Nid oes dim coel ar y papurau newydd. Dyma fi yn rhannog o ddau o honynt, ac nid wyf yn cael fawr am fy arian namyn celwydd noeth, na bo'nd i grybwyll. Dranoeth wedi hynny dyma'n awr bedwar post wedi myned heibiaw ac heb ddim llythyr oddiwrth y Llew! Gobeithio ei fod yn drafferthus yn dibennu ei fatterion; dim ond hynny. Mae'r tad einym yn anfon i fendith i chwi bod ac un, ac yn erchi i chwi sgrifennu gynta galloch; y mae hefyd i'ch annerch f'eneidiau.

Eich caredigawl frawd, *Gwilym.*

LONDON, June 18, 1757.

L. to Mrs. M. CCCXXXV.

My Dear,—I have yours of the 10th and I thank God that you are pretty well. I hope the small pox will use you as well as the neighbours, God's will be done. I did not forget the boys about caps, but I thought hats more suitable for them, and it doth not signify what they have to throw about in school in dirt over head and ears. If I live they shall have caps again. If the boxes will ever come, they are come home by this time, but I am sadly afraid about them. John Owen is to come up directly, and it is probable I shall get him into some business here, for there is very great uncertainty now of doing any thing in the country, and as the world is among the great men here turnd topsy-turvy, my affairs among the rest undergoes the same fate, and till they are settled it is impossible for my affairs to be settled. Therefore I have wrote to him to tell Mr. Pryse to bring you his bill for his lodging and that you would pay it, and if he owes any thing else pay it, and dont let him lose time, but with his best suit of cloaths on and a pair of bags with his best shirts, let him ride David Morgan's mare to Shrewsbury, and take a place in the stage coach from thence to London. If you have no body to send with him to fetch

L. to Mrs. M. contd.

the mare, I have told him to leave her in grass at Shrewsbury, and to get Mr. Jones, Rhosgoch, to get a carrier to call for her and pay for her grass. She wont do at all for me here as things are now. You need not tell John Owen to be in hast, for I fancy he'll lose no time for his own sake, but the sooner the better he comes; and the neighbours need not know where he goes, that they may not have business to talk. Give him three guineas to bear his expences up, which will be sufficient, for though he tells me he has very little left, but is mostly gone for cloaths and drugs, I cannot believe it is so, for I can see no way it could go. However, take no notice of this to him. He is a very thoughtless lad, and it belongs to the family, or many of them. I have not seen Griff. Griffiths yet and I dont know how it is between Pryse and I as to accounts. You may ask Mr. Pryse by the by whether there is any account between him and I; and if he allows there is and that he owes me money (which I suppose is the case) you may ask him whether he'll allow that bill as part. But if he will not allow of such a thing, pay him his bill. There is also money due to John Parry for John Owen about two years ago. You should pay that also, for I cannot find by any of the bills here that he has been paid. But perhaps that would be better left in account, as he owes me rent for the house and I owe him for y[e] warehouse. I cannot give up that warehouse as yet, till I see how things turn out. Enquire of John Owen if he himself has paid John Parry that bill, it was about forty or fifty shillings. If he has not paid it, tell him it must stand in account between me and John Parry. How doth Charles Lloyd go on? If I can get some genteel place for John Owen perhaps his old cloaths will be of no service to him and not worth the bringing up, but in some kind of place they may be of service. I have therefore bid him leave all his cloaths with you, and that you may send a box with some of them up if he should have occasion for them after he is settled in some business. I have desired Jack Jones to push Cwmervin on, if he thinks any thing can be got out of it, and if he can get proper hands, I will give you orders to subsist them through his hands. I hope your next will bring an account that you and the children are well. I am very uneasy about the small pox, I thought both the boys had it. If your tooth is hollow you

L. to Mrs. M. contd. had better get it drawn, and I suppose that is the case. The tooth ache was like to drive me mad, and I had two teeth drawn in one day. I have nothing to say that I care to tell you in a letter, for as a letter of mine of consequence miscarryd lately, another may as well miscarry. *I am, my dear, your affectionate husband, L.M.*

LONDON, June 18th, 1757.

L. to W. CCCXXXVI. Anwyl Vraut,—I have yours of ye 9th and also of ye 13th, and that they may be put up with their predecessors I have here taken pen in hand to answer every word in them. Dedwydd ych chwi gael gosod ein tad ar farch, mi chwenychwn inneu hynny. Mae natur pobl Llanallgo a'r Fferi gynt yn fy merch Elin,* ddyfod gyn belled o ffordd i weled ei gwlad heb ddim negeseuau. The ancient Gauls were also noted for that kind of fondness for relations, etc., and so the Northern Pictish Britains with their clans. Ond nid oes fawr o hynny yn y Deheudir, they are another nation of people. Rhywogaeth estronol. I have sent for John Owen up, and will get him some post to get a livelyhood here. I hope his mother cannot hinder him. Nid oes yma un cyngor ynghylch Eglwys Vigel,† ag om rhan i ni fyddai waeth gennifi ferddyn cappel i gael o'r plant le i chware, na chael gwasanaeth cylch unwaith mewn tair wythnos a hwnnw'n bader buan, di bregeth, di grefydd, etc. Fe dderfydd y dreth Eglwys gwedi hynny mi debygwn, ond bid a fynno gan nad oes neb ond chwi eich hunan yn y plwyf sy waeth ganddo pa un ai bod ty i Vigel a'i peidio, mi debygwn i na fyddai wiw sgrifennu at yr esgob yn ei chylch. Nid ydynt ond disgwyl gan yr Eglwysydd syrthio au pennau ynddynt i gyd, ag yno fe gae'r personiaid lai o

* On his mother's side Lewis Morris was descended from William Thomas of the Ferry House, near Conway, and also from the Lewises of Ty'nllan, Llanallgo.

† William Morris had property at Llanfigel see (p. 91). Many years afterwards an Anglesey poet, Robert Hughes of Neuadd y Blawd, wrote two poems descriptive of the ruinous state of the Church there, from which it would appear that it was never restored:

Fy nau lygad i pan welsant
Ddull annhirion dy 'senau noethion
    Synu wnaethant,
Gynt a fuost fel rhyw seren,
Fe droes y chwedl, 'nawr mae'r deml
    Fel rhyw domen.

Lewis Morris also wrote a poem to Wig-Llanfigel (see *Diddanwch Teuluaidd*, 1763, p. 191).

drafferth yn gweddio ag yn ymdrafferthu. Religion in this country is quite out of taste, it is such an old fashiond thing. I am positive if Mahomet had any dareing fellows to preach him here, he would gain ground immediately, or any merry religion like that. And if Sadlers Wells and the play houses could be brought in as branches of a new religion it would have abundance of converts and would take extremely well. My defluxion on y[e] lungs thickend all at once, and I have now as great trouble in dissolving it, etc., as I had then to stop it,—dyna ddangosiad palliant y corph. Gwych o'ch tywydd gwresog chwi, we have had as yet but three warm days. Aie clerc Elin yw'r Gobed? Ni chlywais i fod mo'r gwr gwedi marw, ond hwnnw fyddai'r clerc? Da y gwnaethai'r ffolog yrru'r bachgen at ei ewythr, fe wnaethai les iddo. He faild to have the first ship, but is resolved to have another Indiaman at any rate. Ni chafwyd un atteb etto o'r llythyrdy, mae'n rhaid ysgrifennu at y Secretary; a ydynt yn codi'r geiniog fyth ag etto? Wfft ich siwrnai i Sir Fflint! mi a glywais wragedd gwedi passio amser planta yn dywedyd yr ant bellach i gymeryd i pleser, ag i weled ffrindiau na welsant ers deuddeg mlynedd. Mae'r gair yn dref fod Ffredrig gwedi cymryd Prague, a'u lladd fal llygod, ond beth 'yw hynny i mi? Yesterday Lord Stowell (Mr. Legge o'r blaen) took his place, First Lord of y[e] Admiralty, all the rest I believe except Boscawen to be out. Daccw hwnnw yn mynd i'r Bay of Biscay, a Macpherson gidage. Dyna lle buase'r ffwlcyn gan W. Owen rwan ped fuase ras. Ag mae Sion hefyd yn dywedyd fod ei dad ai fam yn anesmwytho 'blegid nad yw'n enill bara. They have had no great trouble with him yet, nor are likely to have. There is no work (raising of ore) going on yet at Esgair y Mwyn; Paynter is there and I hope he'll bite them all, he certainly will. It is to no purpose to tell you the history of that affair. I am fighting them now in Equity and have the same Council as was against the King in the great trial. Must not I change sides as well as others? A glowsoch i hanes General Brown? Gwyddyl oedd ef yngwasanaeth Brenin Prwssia ag fe aeth i Gwrt y Frenhines Hungari i edrych am Mr. Keith yr Ambassador oedd yno, ag fal yr oeddynt ill dau yn siarad ynghyd, heibio daeth yr Ymerodres Frenhines. "Och im calon," ebr Brown, "os gwelais i erioed venyw mor brydferth a

L. to W. contd.

L. to W. contd. hon . . . ." ; a'r llall a chwarddodd, ar ymerodres a ddaliodd sylw arnynt, a thranoeth hi a yrrodd am Keith ond mi ddylaswn ddoedyd mae un or dynion sythaf, propraf, a glanaf, a mwyaf ei wrhydri oedd Brown ag a safodd erioed (nage a . . . . erioed) rhwng amhiniog a phastwn. "Pwy oedd y gwr oedd gida chwi ddoe" ebr hi, "pan oeddwn i yn mynd heibio, ag am ba beth roeddych yn ymgomio? Yno Keith a wyrodd ei ben gan wylder, ag nid attebodd ddim. Yn y man, ebr ef, "Captain yw ef yn llu y Brenin Prwssia, a ffrind imi, a dywedyd yr oedd na welodd ef erioed neb gyn laned a Brenhines Hungari nag mor gariadus o'r olwg arni." . . . . "Yna" eb y Frenhines "nid oedd arno ddim eisiau ehondra" (assurance), ag felly darfu'r ymgomio. Tranoeth neu dradwy dyma gymissiwn Lieutenant General yn dyfod i law Mr. Brown, ag ni wyddai na'r ci na'r gath o ble daeth ef, ag o hynny allan meddan nhwy fe fu'n dad i holl blant y Frenhines, ag aeth i ymladd trosti hi ai phlant, a Brenin Prwssia ai saethodd yn ei goes a bwled canan, meddan nhwy, ag ef a fu farw er mawr golled i'r wraig a'r plant. This story is said to be got out of his own mouth. Ond ydwyf yn ddigon diwaith pan sgrifennwn y fath strodwm? Nag ydwyf! The Dictionary goes on apace, and I dont know that I have spent an hour idly this month past except in bed, always writing or reading, and generally antiquity in search of matter for my collection. But the matter for this letter is at an end, and I can spin it out no longer between laziness and dulness, etc. I am told Jemmy Morris is married here, and gives an odd account of the people of Beaumaris. Here is one Thomas Hughes of Caernarvonshire going or gone there, that says he'll outdo them all, creadur y Vrisco debygwn. He has been with my brother a-bragging. Dyma ni newydd gael y llyfrau a fenthycciasom i Gronwy gelwyddog, mi a feddyliais a maint ei ystumiau ai esgusion na ddaethent byth adref. He sent along with the books a MS. of his to be returnd, which is a translation of his own out of ye Greek into Welsh, one of Lucian's dialogues. The subject is lying, lying stories and spirits, and I believe he sent it as a defence for telling lyes in some cases. It wont bear publication ; it is too stiff, being too literal a translation, and the Greek hard and unconcocted names retaind, enough to break a man's teeth; such as Tychiades, Philocles, Arignotus, etc., whereas they should have been Gwrnerth, Llywelyn, Cynddelw, etc. I have taken the story in hand and wrote it over and new molded it, with new storys, where some things would not bear in a Christian country, and it really makes a very merry tale, and would bear publication, if people were so inclined. We shall return him his own MS. back. I wonder how the poor devil of an *offeiriad* goes on now. I dont hear anything of his being to be turnd out, I suppose they dont drink as much as they did, poverty hinders them, and the alehouse will not give them credit. Nawdd Duw rhag y fath ddyn! a surprizing composition! What poet ever flew higher? What beggar, tinker, or sowgelder ever groped more in the dirt? A tomturd man is a gentleman to him. The juice of tobbacco in two streams runs out of his mouth. He drinks gin or beer till he cannot see his way home and has not half the sense of an ass, rowls in ye mire like a pig, runs through the streets with a pot in his hand to look out for beer; looks wild like a mountain cat, and yet when he is sober his good angel returns and he writes verses sweeter than honey and stronger than wine. How is this to be solved? His body is borrowd or descended from the dregs of mankind and his spirit from among the celestial choir, what a stinking dirty habitation it must have. What doth ye Bardd Coch say to ye addition to Cywydd yr Ardd? Is it too ludicrous? I know it fits the taste of blundering Welshmen better than the first part which is a better thing. Duw a helpo pobl ddylion! Llyfr gwych, meddan nhwy, yw Llyfr y Viccar, ie myn dyn meddwn inneu, llyfr braf yn iawn yw hwnnw. Was not the world also so—more geese than swans? Dont cry when I tell you that among the numerous meeting of A. Br.* [rhai a ddarllen Ancient Brutes] at ye Cymrodorion room, when that cywydd was read, one, and one only, said he thought that cywydd was an allegory, and so all with one voice desired it might be read over again, and explaind in English. Would not the English laugh at the idiots if they knew this? The wisest thing they ever did is to admit no strangers among them. And for all this I cannot help thinking but that the Welsh were always so, and that the ignorance of y^e

L. to W. contd.

* Ancient Britons.

L. to W. contd.

multitude in general, and the great regard they paid their poets, as poetry seemd inaccessible to them, was owing to their ignorance, and gave these few poets spirits and a thirst after fame. You remember how Davydd Manwel a Sion Pr. Prys and Sion Rhydderch* were admired in their times, very bright men! and wonderful for their dulness. Can you imagine there were their better in those days? No certainly, or else we should have heard of him. Is not the body of ye nation the same now as it was then? No doubt full as dull. The Lord have mercy upon us, what a stupid stock we are. I know what it is owing to, but I won't tell you now for I am obligd to finish my letter.

Your affectionate brother, *Llewelyn Ddu.*

L. to W. CCCXXXVII.

LONDON, June 30th, 1757.

Dear Brother,—Yours of Dydd Gwyl Ifan I received, ag i borthi'r bendro ar cricc sy'n fy ysgwydd mi ai hattebaf er nad oes blas yn y byd i sgrifennu ben borau. Daccw Ned Edwards (pendew fyth) gwedi bod yma neithiwr a'r brawd gidag ef dan agos i hanner nos, mae'n dywedyd y daw yna i geisio 20 neu 40 o ddwylo i fynd ar ei long, mae'n siccr y ca fe un, er ei dwyllo am y gyntaf. The only commendable great thing in him is that he refuses to accept of a ship unless it be of good force, from thirty to thirty-six guns. Garw y ddŷled ydyw, Duw ai helpio! But all sailors almost are so. It was a silly thing in the officers of ye post office to send the letter down, it was not intended in that light, but no answer is yet come, so that my brother will call with Shelvock by word of mouth if there be such an order, or about bills if not on separate paper. What is it to any body what I write on my paper? All single letters

* *Dafydd Manuel*, a native of Trefeglwys, Montgomeryshire. He wrote many carols and ballads, and his compositions are often found in eighteenth century Manuscripts. He was buried at Trefeglwys on May 16th, 1726. (See *Mont. Worthies* by *Richard Williams*).

Sion Prichard Prys, who is frequently mentioned in these Letters, was a native of Llangadwaladr in Anglesey. He published a book of religious poetry in the year 1721, which bears the title *Difyrrwch Crefyddol*. He was the father of Owen Jones, gardener to the Earl of Tilney, and one of William Morris's correspondents.

Sion Rhydderch, was a native of Cardiganshire. He was in business as a printer at Shrewsbury from 1715 to 1728, and brought out the first English-Welsh Dictionary in 1725. He died at Cemmaes, Montgomeryshire in November, 1735.

should pay but the same, the other is nonsense in its' self. You shall know the event soon. The ministry was not settled yesterday, all at a stop at the Treasury. There is no work going on yet at Esgair y Mwyn; mae d—l dwbl wedi mynd dros y lle ar bobl hefyd. I know nothing of Siamas Morus but what I told you. T. Hughes is a prodigal empty fellow, no matter what side he is of. L. to W. contd.

Nid codi celwyddau mae *Lucian*, ond dangos i'r byd lowned o gelwyddau ag ofergoelion, dewiniaeth, hen chwedlau ynghylch ysprydion, etc., a most excellent piece, and runs prettily in the Cambrian language and the stile of the old writers of chwedlau, such as Iarlles y Ffynon, y Llong Voel, Doethion Rhufain, etc., but did not run well at all in y^c^ stile of ye Greek writers as Gronwy had translated it; and he has since ownd it. Gwych o'ch mefus a'ch cucumeriaid! a'ch *anomias* a Sion Dwyran, nid oes imi ddim lwcc yn y cyfryw bethau. Ni wn i etto pa hyd y bydd raid tarrio yma.

A pham waeth i wr maeth main
Bridd na'i gilydd ar gelain.

Wele ni waeth gennifi beth a ddygo Sion Ffrainc, am y gadawo fe lonydd i hen wraig sydd heb fod o du'n y byd. Wele etto nid Celtic Dictionary mono. The title is *Celtic Remains* or the *Celtic Empire* described in ye English tongue, being a etc., etc., in two parts, etc. Gwych a fydd clywed yn iawn oddiwrth Farthin o'r Post Offis, mae'n ddrwg gennif dros Gendal dlawd. I read in the paper this morning that there is a coaliton of ye partys that strived for governing; and so all are to be in, and no body to thwart them in ye House of Commons hereafter. Gwaethwaeth fyth, mi wranta bydd *Coes* a *Phwll* fal y lleill, a r llwynog yn dwyn gwydd. Gwiliwch lwytho Cywydd yr Ardd a gormod o bethau; digon yw digon o ffigys. Here is great plenty of excellent garden productions, cabbages, colly flowers, carrots, beans, pease, cucumers, siles, lettuce, excellent white and red heart cherries, etc., but the bread exceeding dear and I suppose scarce, for ye price is almost double to what it was this time 12 months—other things moderate. Mutton and lamb 4½d. and 5d. per lb; beef 4d. and 4½d. per lb.; veal 4½d. and 5d.; mackrel 4d. a piece; lobsters, good middling size, 4d. to 6d.; salt butter 5½d. and 6d. a lb., fresh from 7d. to 10d.; milk, very good, 1½d. a wine quart or less; good Cheshire cheese 3½d. and 4d. per lb.; Gloucester do. 3d. and 4d. Excellent

L. to W. contd.

small beer, Saturday's brewing, near 4d. a gallon, Tuesday worse; rum 7s. 6d. to 8s. a gallon; brandy 10s.; wine, port and mount and Lisbon 6s. a gallon even by a single bottle. But I suppose it will rise upon this new license act. Syder very bad, made of turnips, etc., in London 6d. a quart; ale worse than small beer, beer or porter, mere poyson, 3d. a quart; gin raised in price but still too cheap,—most of the distillers have given up all hopes of going on with their business any more. Loaf sugar, good enough for tea, is 8d. a lb.; Bohea tea from 5s. to 6s.; green from 8s. to 10s., very good; coals 40s. a chalder; candles 7d.; soap 8d. These are the most common necessarys. Milford Haven is going to be made a place for men of war, with docks and yards. I believe my book gave the hint. Perhaps I may now publish my large draught of that place. I'll shew it some great ones by and by. What stuff shall I have to finish this, nothing unless it be a word or two of the translation of Lucian's dialogue, the pain in my shoulder makes me unfit for anything else. The dialogue is between Gronwy and Llewelyn. Gronwy tells Llewelyn what company he met at the House of Rhydderch ab Ednyfed o'r Fynachlog, about apparitions, charms, spells, etc., etc. Rhydderch himself being as great a lyer as any of the rest. Charms and spells were in great vogue among the Greeks, as they are at this day in Wales. About ye middle of their discourse "Rhof a Duw" ebr Rhydderch, "mi ddywedaf i chwi un peth arall a ddigwyddodd imi fy hun, nid y peth a glywais, ag f'allai Gronwy pan glowech y gorfydd iti ei goelio, gan wiried yw'r chwedl. Pan oeddwn i yn byw yn Ynysoedd yr *Heledd* (Hebrides) yn y Gogledd yn hogyn o langc, lle gyrrasai fy nhad fi i gael dysgeidiaeth, fe ddaeth arnaf flys fynd i Ynysoedd *Erch* (Orcades) mewn llong, ag oddiyno i Lychlyn i glywed y rhyfeddod honno, sef y morforwynion yn canu, ag iw gweled yn cribo eu gwallt a chrib aur, ag mi a'i gwelais ag a'i clywais hefyd, ag a fum yn siarad ag un o honynt, a hi a ddywedodd imi ddewiniaeth gan gerdded hyd y mor ag adrodd saith air, a phe bai achos mi fedrwn ddywedyd i chwi'r geiriau. Ond tra roeddwn ar y dwr fe ddigwyddodd fod gida ni yn y llong wr o Degeingl, un o'r beirdd sanctaidd rhyfeddol o ddoethineb, ag yn gwybod holl ddysg y morforwynion, y tylwyth teg a'r Aiphtiaid, ag fe ddywedid ei fod gwedi byw dair blynedd yn Ogof Maengymrwd, a thair blynedd hefyd dan y ddaiar yn Ogof Llanddulas yn dysgu celfyddyd dewiniaith a thrin y ser a'r planedau gan y Dr. Dafydd Ddu o Hiraddug. L. to W. contd.

"Y Gwyddyl Gorr oedd hwnnw mi dynga," ebr Cynfelyn Goch, "fy hen feistr a'm hathraw i wyti yn ei feddwl, gwr santaidd dysgedig gwedi ei eillio, ag yn gwisgo dillad lliain, ag yn siarad Gwyddeleg a Lladin yn ddilediaith gan rhiccled ai bader. Dyn byr llydan, a thrwyn ysmwt gwefldew, go eiddil ei goesau." "Ie, ar fy nghydwybod yr un un fyth," ebr yntau, "Gwyddel Gorr oedd ei enw ef ond nis gwyddwn i ar y cyntaf pwy oedd ef. Eithr pan welais ef yn gwneuthur llawer o wyrthiau, yn cerdded hyd frig y tonnau, ag yn marchogaeth ar gefn llamhidyddion, ag yn ymgomio a'r môr forwynion ar rheini yn ei berchi ag yn ysgwyd eu cynffonau arno, yno mi ddeallais mai rhyw wr santaidd ydoedd, ag o dippyn i dippyn wrth fy addfwynder mi ymlithrais iw gymdeithas ef, a chwedi ymgynefino a'n gilydd fe ymddiriedai imi ei holl gyfrinach. O'r diwedd ni aethom i'r lan i Lychlyn, ag fe'm cyngorodd i adael fy holl weision yn nhre Laswig (Leswick) a myned fy hun gydag ef law law i rodio'r mynyddoedd a'r diffaethwch i edrych am yr hen ddewines sef Angharad Goch, y Gringroen Wrach o Fynydd y Rhew, i gael peth o ddoethineb honno, ag felly buom yn trafaelio ag ni bu arnom ddim diffyg gwenidogion, canys pan aem i'n lletty y Gwyddyl Gorr a gymerai'r ysgublawr neu droed gordd, ag a droe gadachau yn ei gylch, ag a ddywedai ryw wers ag a wnae iddo gerdded ag ymddangos i bawb arall megys dyn, a hwnnw a aai ag a nolai ddwfr, ag a drwssiai fwyd ag a arlwyai ag a wnai bob gwaith ag a weinyddai ini yn bur hylaw, ag yno gwedi cael digon oi wasanaeth, fe ddywedai wers arall ag ai troe'n ysgublawr neu fe droe y troed gordd yn droed gordd cystal cynt, etc." Then he proceeds to tell how he hid himself, and overheard the spell of three words, and how he tryd one day, being alone, to turn y^e^ *troed gordd* into a man and orderd him to fetch water, which he did, but as Rhydderch had not ye other spell to turn him into a troed gordd, he carried so much water that he was like to drown him, etc. This specimen will show you that it is an excellent ridicule on such lying stories and conjurations, etc. My shoulder pains me I can write no more now.

L. to W. contd.

If Vic. had not done amiss, why a charge against him? and how could there be a charge against him, if the Surveyor of ye Post Office orders him? You may tell him that some Members of Parliament will examine into it, if it cannot be found out otherwise.

Your affectionate brother, Llewelyn.

L. to W. CCCXXXVIII.

LONDON, July 9th, 1757.

Anwyl Vraut,—I have yours of ye 2nd and it is a pity to suffer such weather as this to pass without writing. I think I never suffer any of your letters to stand here above one post without some kind of answer. If Gronwy's bookseller has the money in his hands, he may possibly publish something, otherwise he'll drink ye money before the book is printed. Dyna fâr! A'i dyn yw fo? Mae'n ddrwg gennif fyned o dd—l a Joset, mi wranta daw ei waeth yn ei le. Mae'n dra thebyg mae'r Brysgaw a ddaw o achos pechodau'r Ynys. Gwrda'r Veurig am vamhaetha, mae pob creadur yn dda i rywbeth. Wawch dyma chwi'n dywedyd yn y P.S. mae'r 11eg yw'r diwrnod cychwyn i Degengl, felly dyma ergyd i'r gwellt, ag mae'n rhaid i hwn aros hyd na ddeloch adref. [*L.M.*]

W. to L. and R. CCCXXXIX.

GARTREF, Nos Sul, 24 o Fis Gorphena, 1757.

Y Brawdyr,—Dyma lle rwyf er neithiwr wedi bod yn fawr fy lludded yn ymdeithiaw drwy bedair o siroedd Cymru, mewn myllni ddigon. Ni bum ond un diwarnod o bythewnos o amser heb fod ar farch yn trafaeliaw yn galed in search of natural curiosities, weithiau ar fy neudroed ymron fy lladd fy hun yn dringaw gelldydd a chreigiau, rhai o naddynt na bu'sai nemor ddyn rhyd-ddynt o'r blaen. Ni wn i a gawsoch i gerpyn o lythyr a sgrifenais o'r Ddwning neu'r Dwning.* Mi addewais yn hwnnw *a Journal*, ond ni cheir mor ofa heno, a daccw y foru i fod yn wylmabsant Cybi—new stile. Ni choeliach i fyth y nifer o ffosilod, etc., a gynhullais y daith hon, ie ar ariant a weriais i hefyd. Par fodd bynnag mi allaf yn awr orwedd yn fy ngwely, mae fy enw, etc. Gerwinol o falched oedd y bobl ar hyd y ffordd ymhob man lle rhodiais, o byddai ganddynt ddim tegan yn y byd a fai gymeradwy gan y Gwilym. Daccw fi wedi gadael gyda fy anwyl Bennant gryn bwn ceffyl i ddyfod ar hyd y mor, heblaw a gludodd Wil y Newri yn y portmanteau. Dyma hi'n Ddywllun ac heb ddim llythyr o unlle

* Downing, the seat of Thomas Pennant.

a'r dref yn llawn o wylmabsant. Marged Owain newydd ddyfod o dy ein tad ac ynteu yn rhesymol iachus. Mi glywaf fod Sion ar y ffordd i Lundein y dydd arall. Ni chaf amser i ddywedyd dim chwaneg yn awr, ond Duw gyda chwi bod ac un, dywedwch chwitheu Amen. *Eich caredigawl frawd*, *William Morris.* W. to L. and R. contd.

Olsgrif. Nid hwyrach mai llythyr dwbl fydd o'r achos, fe aeth y bost ymaith echdoe (heddyw yw dyw Mercher) cyn caffael fy llythyr, yr archlod iddo, dyma heddyw heb gymaint ac un llythyr o unlle yn y byd. Ow fy 'neidiau, ai colli'ch cellwair a wnaethoch? Mi glywaf eich bod chwi y brawd Rhisiart yn sgrifennu at boblach y ffordd hyn, tyst llythyr at Mosson wedi ei seinio Richard Mosson 'r dydd arall, dyna lle'r ydoedd ffwdan pan ydoedd y gwr yn gollwng yn angof ei enw ei hun, wfft i hynny! Ymhle mae proposals Grono bellach? Och ni, mae arnaf ofn na welwn mwy mo 'Natus wirion. Colled anfeidrol yw dylwyth, gwae finneu ei golli. Wale, wale, dyna ddyn heb ond ychydig oi fath ar ei ol. Gonest a didwyll ydoedd, nefoedd iddo. Cosin Ned Edwards writ to his sister of the 21st to send her boy up, but no mention is made whether he hath got a ship or what time the boy should come up and where he is to be met with. Sion Sais comes up with him. He should name some house where the boys might be received with directions to take them in. She desires a line from him on these heads. Rhaid im derfynnu heb yn ddiolch imi.

Eich brawd mal cynt, *W.M.*

LONDON, August 2nd, 1757.

Anwyl Vraut,—I have yours before me of ye 24th July, and am glad you have reachd home after your pilgrimage to Gwenvrewi Santes, etc. To what purpose would it have been to write to you at Holyhead when you were at Holywell? By the inclosed, you'll see I began to write to you ye 9th of last month, but threw it aside. I hope your next will give an account two sheets long of the curiositys you have met with, MSS., coins, etc. John Owen is come here, I suppose he'll write to you. I think his brother William might do well to go with Ned Edwards, but what signifys thinking or advising. Grono's proposals are in the press, you'll have some next post. I am afraid indeed poor 'Natus is gone, for there are but broken accounts here from the Leghorn people that L. to W. CCCXL.

L. to W. contd.

would perswade us he is alive. My brother Richard will write to you I suppose about the sea-boys to be sent up. In looking over a set of coins that happend to fall into my brother's hands and sorting them and takeing an account of them, I find that the coins you had of *Sion Dwyran* are very curious and uncommon, being really of ye age they appear to be, for the dye that stampd them was ordered to be broke, etc. I had never studyd coins so much as I have done these, ag mi lithiais y brawd i edrych arnynt, er na wyddai yn y byd pa beth oeddynt o'r blaen. Here are also in the same collection a parcel of modern medals of Lewis 14th, King William, Queen Anne, George I., George II., some Popes. His Emperors are of ye middle copper. If you meet with any coins or medals of ye Romans, whether Emperors or others, whether common or no, pick them up, for there is nothing that corroborates history like them. My collection in the country is but very poor, mostly of ye small copper. There are no English books that give thorough instructions about medals, so I am obligd to study them out of the French and Latin with hard labour, but great pleasure, because they illustrate our ancient British History. I can think of no more to say this post. *I am, your affectionate brother, L.M.*

END OF VOL. I.

F. Fo

Lightning Source UK Ltd.
Milton Keynes UK
UKHW020616250420
362256UK00008B/125

9 780341 872986